EVERYBODY'S GUIDE TO
NATURE CURE

A comprehensive and popularly written book
describing the self-treatment of common ailments
through Natural Healing methods.

By the same author

BETTER SIGHT WITHOUT GLASSES
COMMONSENSE VEGETARIANISM

EVERYBODY'S GUIDE TO NATURE CURE

by

Harry Benjamin N.D.

THORSONS PUBLISHERS LIMITED
Wellingborough, Northamptonshire

First Edition 1936
Thirteenth Impression 1958
Second Edition 1961
Sixth Impression 1977
First Trade Paperback Edition 1981

ISBN 0 7225 0703 8

Printed in Great Britain by
Nene Litho, Earls Barton, Northamptonshire,
and bound by Weatherby Woolnough,
Wellingborough, Northamptonshire.

DEDICATED TO

STANLEY LIEF, N.D., D.O., D.C.

FOUNDER OF "HEALTH FOR ALL"

*who did more to forward the work of Nature Cure
in Great Britain than any other man.*

CONTENTS

PART I—NATURE CURE IN THEORY AND OUTLINE

PART II—DISEASES AND THEIR NATURAL TREATMENT

CONTENTS

PART III—APPENDICES

PREFACE TO FOURTEENTH EDITION

NOW that another large edition of this book is required, it is opportune to review the situation since the first edition was published twenty-five years ago.

During the quarter of a century in question Nature Cure methods have not changed one iota, and the measures outlined in this book when it was first published are still as effective as ever in the treatment of disease of all kinds. But what a difference we find when the orthodox medical scene is viewed. New methods of treatment follow one another in bewildering array, yet the sum total of disease is not one whit less than it was before. Indeed, it continues to mount steadily, as witness the data supplied by what is called the National "Health" Service. Since this scheme was first put into effect, in 1948, the total spent each year on drugs alone has increased so much that patients are exhorted by those in medical and governmental authority to think less about the medicine bottle and more about common-sense health measures in the treatment of their ailments! Yet, by every publicity avenue, *i.e.* press, radio and TV, the public is regaled almost daily with the new marvels of medical science, with its latest "wonder drugs", sera, and the like. It is not surprising, therefore, that the public still believes that drugs can cure disease, and that only along that path can health be restored to the sick.

It is often only after years of disillusionment at the hands of orthodox medicine that people come to realise the truth that the drug way is *not* the way to health. But it is a hard and bitter lesson for most to learn, and they are fortunate whose steps are then led in the direction of Nature Cure, and, perchance, to the acquisition of a copy of this book. It has led many thousands the world over to the better health which they sought in vain at orthodox medical hands when they were the victims of a wide variety of diseases, often regarded as incurable by the best medical authorities.

An important point that should be noted in regard to many of the newer methods of treatment that are in vogue nowadays in orthodox medical circles is the dangerous side-effects or after-effects which they produce. In a book entitled *Diseases of Medical Progress*, the author, an American Doctor, indicates the trend towards the development of a wide range of new diseases which have been brought into being by the very types of medical treatment that are so much exploited in publicity value through the press and over radio and TV. The antibiotic drugs alone, such as penicillin, streptomycin, etc.,* have a wide range of harmful side-effects to their "credit", which are causing increasing concern to the more thoughtful members of the medical profession, but very little of this information gets into the press. It is reserved for the medical journals which contain regularly, in almost every issue, accounts of the harm that such drugs are doing to patients under medical treatment. Deaths from the use of antibiotic drugs are by no means rare, either, and so the trend towards physical bankruptcy goes on apace under orthodox medical guidance. The effect of such methods on the mental health of the community should also be considered. It is just as bad as, if not worse than, the deleterious effect on physical health and well-being.

All this makes a sorry picture, and so it is a matter of the greatest urgency that the truths which Nature Cure is seeking to inculcate into the minds of diseased and suffering humanity should have an increasingly wide appeal. It is in this respect that this book has played, and we hope will continue to play, an important part. That is why the author is glad to see that a further large edition is needed to satisfy the demand all over the world for its explanation of the Nature Cure view of disease causation and cure.

The truth will always be the same—today or a thousand years hence—and the truths which Nature Cure has to reveal are, and always must be, identical in content, no matter what new discoveries are made in regard to man and the universe of which he is a part. That more skill will be attained in treatment by practitioners is to be expected, of course, but the basic principles of Nature Cure cannot alter. If, therefore, further editions of this book are needed, even one hundred years hence, there is no reason to suppose that anything need be altered of the text, except for possible minor changes here and there. It is with these thoughts, therefore, that the author commends this latest edition of his book to new readers throughout the world. May they derive as much help from it as the many thousands who have already benefited from its contents. In gratitude, it is to be hoped that they will pass on the good news to others who have not yet come in touch with the basic truths about disease causation and cure that are contained in the following pages. This information can be a boon and a blessing to countless people suffering at present under the well-meaning but misguided efforts of the medical profession.

HARRY BENJAMIN.

* The term *antibiotic* means *anti-life*, in the sense of destroying germs. That is, indeed, all that this type of drug can do. It destroys the germ, but leaves the basic causes of disease quite untouched, so that further and more serious disease is bound to arise later in the body of the person so treated.

INTRODUCTION

THAT there is a very great necessity for a popularly written book on Natural Healing—or Nature Cure, as it is called—in this disease ridden world of ours has been only too obvious to the writer for several years. The present volume may be taken, therefore, as his attempt to meet this long-felt need.

For everyone who knows anything about Nature Cure, and has realised through personal experience what its methods of treatment can do for suffering humanity, there are tens of thousands still completely ignorant as to its very existence in the world of healing, and who continue to rely implicitly on orthodox medicine, even though in many instances they have had ample evidence of its inability to help them in their own particular cases.

In the course of his daily experience as a Naturopath—or practitioner of Nature Cure—the writer is being brought continually into contact with scores of people, drawn from every rank of society, who have passed from doctor to doctor, specialist to specialist, hospital to hospital, in the vain hope of being cured of the diseases from which they had been suffering, only to find these same diseases becoming *worse*, not *better*, at medical hands. Indeed, in many instances, they had at last been given up as " incurable," doomed to a life of chronic invalidism, because of the inability of orthodox medicine to do anything for them.

Imagine, then, the joy of these same people on coming into contact with the methods of treatment embodied in the science of Natural Healing—or Nature Cure—and finding themselves being freed at long last from the disabilities which had dragged them down for so many years and were threatening the remainder of their lives with ruin and disaster!

Naturopathy, by its methods, has done for thousands upon thousands of sufferers from disease, in this and many other countries, what Medical Science, despite its inestimable advantages, could never do for them : *and that is cure them*! They have been really cured, not just patched up and tinkered with, so that they might drag their weary bodies about for a few more years, a burden to themselves and everyone else around them, before being finally cast aside as hopeless —" incurable "!

Naturopathy has given to these thousands of sufferers the possibility of new life; and, with that new hope, new enthusiasm to face the world and its problems again. It has turned them from the mere wreckage of humanity they were fast becoming into vital men and women!

Contrast these new methods of healing, with their reliance upon the sovereign healing power of Nature, and the employment of only the simplest, most natural means, with those of orthodox medicine, with its continual drugging and dosing, its nightmares of operations, its inoculations of poisonous and loathsome cultures and bacilli, its gland therapy, and the like.

Think of the former, with its regard and reverence for the wonderful powers latent within the body of man, and of the latter with its overweening pride in its own prowess and skill, its total disregard for the essential " sacredness " of the human body. The body is, to the orthodox medical mind, all too often regarded as being a mere mechanical contrivance, a machine to be tinkered with and handled as such.

But enough for the moment ! The complete indictment of the philosophy and practice of orthodox medicine must be left for a later stage in this book. It cannot be dealt with in an Introduction.

It may interest the reader to know that the falseness of the popularly accepted views as to the nature of disease as put forward by the medical profession to-day, and the futility of orthodox medical methods of treatment, were brought home forcibly to the writer himself in the first place through his own personal experiences at the hands of Medical Science. But, as with so many more, not until he had had his eyes opened by coming into contact with Nature Cure, and seeing what *its* methods could do for him in his own particular case, did this realisation come to pass. Until then, like practically everyone else, he had believed implicitly in the skill and wisdom of medical orthodoxy, and its power to " cure " disease. Until it was nearly too late, indeed !

His case was in the best medical hands for many years, but, despite all their aid and skill, he found himself growing steadily worse and worse, until in time his particular disability was regarded as hopeless. " Poor chap! Nothing more can be done for him," they said; and he was left, without any hope of recovery, doomed for the rest of his life.

Medical Science—the universally accepted healing agency of mankind —was powerless to offer him any further help.

In this stage of hopelessness and despair the writer was brought, by what he still regards as nothing short of a miracle, into touch with Natural Healing. Immediately his whole outlook changed. From despair and hopelessness his spirit rose once more to a realisation of the possibilities and joys of existence. He began to improve almost immediately under natural treatment, until in a year he was well on the road to recovery, having escaped what to him would have been the greatest of all blows, the loss of his sight.

It is surely no exaggeration to say that, because of diseases from which they are suffering which grow steadily worse year by year under orthodox medical treatment, there are millions of persons in the world to-day who find themselves in a very similar position to that unfortunately occupied by the writer not many years ago—that is, who feel themselves placed under a slow sentence of death because of the inability of orthodox medicine to do anything for them (except perhaps palliate their condition for the moment), despite all the facilities and opportunities for increased knowledge and technical skill the medical profession possesses.

It is for persons such as these, persons totally unaware of the existence of methods of healing other than those practised by the medical profession generally, and which, if given the opportunity, can place these same condemned ones on the road to renewed health once more, that this present volume is primarily intended, to let them know what Nature Cure is, what its methods are, and how it can help them back to health.

Not only, however, does this book contain within its pages a message of genuine hope for suffering humanity, such as has never been held out to the sufferer from disease, but it embodies a philosophy of life which, if the reader is ready to accept it, will mark the ending of his present more or less haphazard mode of existence, and the inauguration of a new era, a new chapter, in his life, spiritually and mentally, as well as physically.

The writer is fully aware that before the general public can be expected to understand the possibilities and value of Nature Cure as put forward in this book, and accept, and act upon, its principles, they must first be made to realise fully the inadequacies and blunders of present-day accepted standards of healing. They must be made to realise in what way orthodox medicine is wrong, and how its methods of treatment not only *cannot cure disease,* but inevitably tend to make its appearance in our midst far more widespread than it otherwise would be. That, in fact, in their efforts to alleviate the ills of suffering mankind the members of the medical profession tend to *increase,* not to overcome disease.

All this the public must know. For it is only when their old prejudices and beliefs in these matters (which are nothing more than stumbling-blocks in the path to the truth) have been broken down that they will be ready for this new gospel of healing, that of Nature Cure—when they have delivered themselves once and for all out of the hands of the forces of custom, tradition, ignorance, and habit.

The writer fully realises that his first task must be to make possible for his readers this emancipation from the thraldom of the accepted dogmas and doctrines of orthodox medication, which is so vitally necessary if they are fully to grasp the significance of Natural Healing. And if in so doing he is compelled to denounce Medical Science, if he has to challenge the great hold over the public mind—based upon ignorant acceptance and blind faith—enjoyed by the practitioners of orthodox medicine, the writer would like it always to be borne in mind that it is not the medical profession as such that he is attacking, but their views as to the nature and correct treatment of disease.

As a matter of fact, the writer has nothing but the utmost respect and admiration for the honesty of purpose, self-sacrifice, and genuine good faith which actuate the members of the medical profession in their work, either as individuals or as a body. The tragedy is that such valuable lives should be devoted to a cause so essentially well-meaning, but, alas, so utterly mistaken in its direction.

For the point it is essential to grasp is that the philosophy of disease, which is the basis upon which the whole fabric of modern medicine is erected, is *fundamentally wrong.* So that no matter how genuine the purpose, or how praiseworthy the efforts of those who practise its methods of treatment, or how *apparently* successful these same efforts may appear to be, the inevitable result must be an *adding to*—*NOT* a subtracting from—the colossal annual disease-bill of humanity. So long as the accredited leaders of the medical profession continue to misunderstand the true, essential nature of disease, as they now do, so must the whole medical world be doomed to further and yet further futility and error in its efforts to cope with it, despite all the power, prestige, and years of accumulated skill and knowledge it possesses.

Once the reader has grasped this fundamental " wrongness " of orthodox medicine, then the vital need for the adoption of the philosophy of healing which it is the object of the present book to put forward will become at once apparent to him. He will know then *why it is* that the way must be made for a newer and truer conception of disease and a more enlightened technique of healing—one which by its results is daily proving its right to be regarded as the *true healing mechanism of mankind*. He will be ready to accept in full conscious understanding that philosophy of Natural Healing which is summed up under the general heading of " Nature Cure," with all that it means in promise of renewed health and a fuller life to the suffering millions of our disease-ridden humanity.

OVERCOMING SEASONAL FOOD SHORTAGES

IT is possible that certain readers may experience difficulty in obtaining adequate supplies of fruit and other commodities usually deemed essential parts of a properly balanced dietary, and so the following suggestions are given. They will help readers to make the best of seasonal food restrictions in regard to the various dietetic treatments advised. In some cases it will be possible to obtain suitable fresh fruits at certain times of the year but not at others, and the same applies to salad-stuff also. It is therefore incumbent upon readers to make any alterations they think necessary (with the aid of the following suggestions), as circumstances arise which call for any departure from the dietary instructions given.

If fasting patients find orange juice difficult to secure, they can use apple juice instead (obtainable in bottles at all Health Food Stores), or carrot or swede juice may be used, which can be made by grating the raw vegetables and squeezing out the juice through butter-muslin. As regards fruit breakfasts, if fresh fruit is not available at any time, soaked dried fruit, sweetened with a little honey or Barbados sugar, may be used instead, or a breakfast may be made of grated carrot mixed with Bemax, a few raisins or sultanas, or currants and milk. Alternatively, any raw salad-stuff desired may take the place of fresh fruit for breakfast. Sultanas may be used instead of raisins, but always wash them well before using, as they may be sulphur-dried. Prunes or stewing figs may be used as an alternative to dates.

If salad-stuff is scarce, a very attractive salad may be made by using raw cabbage, savoy, sprouts, carrot, turnip, etc. These ingredients should be finely grated or shredded. Soya beans may be purchased—already cooked—at Health Food Stores, in various flavourings, according to the ingredients used, and they are a nutritious and valuable alternative to eggs and cheese.

Steam quickly all vegetables, if possible, or cook in a casserole. Always steam or bake potatoes in their skins and eat the skins. Always use honey, black treacle, or Barbados sugar for sweetening. When cooking vegetables are scarce, use the varieties you *can* secure in place of any others which are not available.

Special Note re *All-Fruit Diet*—If fruit is scarce, salads and cooked vegetables may be substituted for the *All-Fruit Diet* where indicated in the *Treatment Section*.

PART I

NATURE CURE IN THEORY AND OUTLINE

CHAPTER I

WHAT IS " NATURE CURE "?

THE FAILURE OF ORTHODOX MEDICAL SCIENCE

ONE has only to pay a flying visit to any hospital or busy doctor's waiting-room, or watch the stream of cars continually rolling up to the various doors in Harley Street—or read the proprietary medicine advertisements in the newspapers!—to realise that the world's disease problem is *still* waiting to be solved at medical hands. Indeed, it appears to be growing more and more insoluble every day.

Why? Because Medical Science looks to externals for the cause of disease, instead of to factors at work *within* the body of the individual concerned, and—as the following pages will make abundantly clear—bases its theory and practice largely upon a conception as to what disease is, and how it should be dealt with, which is entirely false and misleading. Consequently, despite its skill and honesty of purpose, the medical profession continues to add error to error, and pile up enormity upon enormity, in attempting to " cure " disease by means of the administration of poisonous drugs and vaccines, and the very drastic employment of the surgeon's knife, thus *adding* to the disease bill of the nation, rather than subtracting from it.

Although called a " science," orthodox medicine has never been able to formulate any scientific rules or principles governing the appearance of disease in the human body, and of how it might be overcome. It has always proceeded by the method known as "trial and error," with disease exerting a wider and ever-firmer grip all the time. What is considered the " fashionable " form of treatment in one decade is superseded in the next by a different form, and the " blood-letting and leeching " which were the chief therapeutic agencies in the time of Bob Sawyer (of *Pickwick Papers* fame) are sneered at by a later generation of medicos who pin their faith to deadly and dangerous drugs and the " surgeon's knife " as

1

" healing " agencies, whilst from a still later generation it is the serum and vaccine which command the fullest allegiance.

The fact that the medical profession has always been so ready to throw over one form of treatment for another (whilst at the same time retaining a sort of " hotch-potch " or jumble of them all)—the process is going on with ever-greater rapidity before our eyes these days, what with ray therapy, gland therapy, chemotherapy, and the like—must surely convince the more thoughtful among us that not only are its methods not so efficacious as it would like us to believe (else why be always trying new ones?), but that at bottom Medical Science has *no fundamental views and principles* governing its actions in the field of disease. The only thing which supplies in some measure a more or less definite basis for the promulgation of a medical theory of disease and cure is the " germ theory."

For whatever conflicting views and theories it may incorporate within itself and whatever divergent methods of treatment, disease has always appeared to the medical mind as something inimical to the human body, which has to be fought against and overcome. So that when Pasteur elaborated his celebrated germ theory of disease about a century ago (as a result of a complete misunderstanding of the findings of another French savant, Professor Béchamp, whose work Pasteur plagiarised), the medical world accepted it, with some reluctance at first, but later wholeheartedly in the full belief that here at last was the conclusive solution to the vexed problem of disease, the solution they had long been waiting for. At last the dread cause of disease was fully established. It was germs! Disease was due to germ infection ! All one had to do was kill the germs, and the disease would disappear !

But after nearly a hundred years of adherence to the germ theory, and despite literally astonishing feats in bacteriological science, disease exerts as firm a hold upon humanity as heretofore. The germs appear to thrive better than their victims!

Alas for the germ theory ! With all its plausibleness it is wrong, as more enlightened minds in the world of healing had realised long ago. The cause of disease has to be sought much deeper within the organism than in its fortuitous invasion by germs.

Mr. J. Ellis Barker, the eminent health authority, is getting very near to the truth—a truth, be it noted, known for many years to the founders and pioneers to whose work the erection of the philosophy of Nature Cure is due—when he says : " Very likely the whole fundamental conception which is fashionable at present, that the micro-organism ' creates ' the disease, on which the huge building of modern bacteriology has been erected, is utterly and preposterously wrong ; for it may be that, in absolute opposition to this conception, the disease creates the micro-organism."

Pasteur, because of the superficial plausibility of his germ theory, has set the whole medical fraternity on a wild-goose chase which is leading them nearer and nearer to the brink of futility in the effective understanding and treatment of disease. And, blinded by its theories, orthodox Medical Science is failing more and more completely to fulfil its function as the one effective healing mechanism to which mankind can turn with certainty for help in its efforts to extricate itself from the clutches of the fell dragon Disease.

But Medical Science still holds public sway, and has society's complete sanction for what it does, because the vast majority of people are still completely unaware of the underlying futility of orthodox medical methods of treatment. On the surface these methods *appear* to be doing something, the cutting and slashing and dosing and doping *appear* to achieve results ; so that even the medical profession itself is hoodwinked into genuinely believing that it is actually overcoming disease . . . until the yearly disease statistics are looked at !

The mass of mankind has the most touching and implicit belief in the " wonder-working " powers of " the Doctor " ; the word of the " Great Medical Authority " is accepted without cavil or question by all in matters relating to disease ; the medical profession is universally revered for its great and unselfish work in " ridding " the world of suffering and ill-health, simply because the public knows nothing about what is *really* happening when it places itself so completely into medical hands. Besides, if medical theory and practice *were* known to be wrong, the world would feel itself to be utterly lost. For who else would there be to turn to to help humanity in its continual struggles with disease, if one could no longer rely on the doctor ?

It is the object of the present volume to make the reasons for the failure of orthodox Medical Science, and the inefficacy of its methods of treatment, abundantly clear to all capable of serious thought. And to show, moreover, that the only hope of salvation for the suffering humanity of to-day lies in an understanding and acceptance of the completely divergent philosophy and methods of treatment of another and " unorthodox " school of healing—that of Nature Cure.

What is " Nature Cure " ?—The methods of disease treatment which constitute what is now termed the unorthodox practice of Nature Cure have, ironically, very much in common with the gospel of disease and cure expounded by Hippocrates, the Father of Medicine, about 400 B.C., and practised throughout the centuries by other enlightened physicians. Even during the past century, when the medical profession has drifted further and further from the course of true healing in its vain quest for germ-killing drugs, there have always been men dissatisfied with such methods, and who have looked to simpler, more natural means whereby disease may be overcome than through drugging and surgery. And the remarkable remedial results that can be obtained by such simple measures as abstinence from food, proper exercise, the judicious employment of hot and cold water, the exposure of the body to the revivifying effects of sun, air, etc., has led certain men to rediscover a technique of healing along purely natural lines, such as these, which would be capable of really overcoming disease, and thus liberate the healing art once and for all from the questionable practices associated with orthodox medication.

The remarkable successes that attended the efforts of these " natural healers " soon led them to realise that in their simple treatment lay a possibility of cure undreamed of by the medical profession, with its inordinate belief in the omnipotence of the drug and the surgeon's knife as therapeutic agents ; and the whole conception of disease—its causes and cure—came to be seen in a new light. These men realised that disease owes its origin in the human body more to wrong habits of living than to anything else ; and the remarkable curative value of their simple treatment lay just in the fact that it allowed the body to cleanse and purify itself internally, and thus throw off the impurities and waste matter which years of wrong living had accumulated therein, and which were interfering with proper functioning.

That disease was in essence something which arose in the system as a result of the accumulation of toxins and impurities generated therein through years of wrong habits of living, and that the only real basis of cure lay in these same habits being rectified, and the body thus allowed an opportunity to cleanse itself and put itself right again internally—a procedure it was quite capable of carrying

4

out, if only allowed to do so—was the gospel of disease and cure these pioneers of Natural Healing began to preach far and wide as a result of their remarkable curative experiences in the treatment of disease.

Of course this understanding of the nature, cause, and treatment of disease was intuitive and vague to begin with in the minds of the men who brought the science of Natural Healing back into the light of day ; it took many years to reach the clarity and understanding of first principles embodied in the later teachings of Nature Cure; but the seemingly miraculous cures affected by the simple, natural measures they employed proved beyond all doubt the rightness of this understanding of what disease is, and the real process of cure possessed by these first pioneers of the modern art of Natural Healing, half-formed and indefinite though it might have been as measured by present-day naturopathic standards.

Thanks to the efforts of these pioneers of Natural Healing, that simplest, most natural of all healing mechanisms, *the fast*, has been rediscovered (a natural and instinctive expedient resorted to by all living creatures when unwell, but foresaken by man since his dominance by the " medical mind "). And with fasting restored to its rightful place as the principal agent in the technique of healing, it was only natural that the need for careful dieting and proper attention to food and eating should be recognised and given their true signifi-cance in the scheme of natural treatment—a significance not afforded them in orthodox medical philosophy.

The first to restore these natural methods of treating disease were Vincenz Priessnitz and Johannes Schroth, who set up cure establish-ments in Germany and Austria respectively in the early middle of the last century. And the remarkable triumphs achieved by these two " unorthodox " practitioners of Natural Healing—whose fame spread far and wide, carried by grateful patients, and who numbered amongst their patrons noblemen, scientists, political leaders, and many others of the highest rank and note in European society, who had failed to secure relief for their ills under orthodox medical treatment—definitely marked the beginning of this new phase in the art of healing : healing by natural means.

The fact that many people regarded as " incurable " by orthodox medical standards were brought back to a condition of health never deemed possible, by the simple treatment of the practitioners of this new school of Natural Healing, made it obvious that not only were these methods more effective than those practised by the medical profession, but that the methods of orthodox medicine, in addition to being unnatural, actually *hindered* and *retarded* the healing process, instead of helping it, and were based on a complete misunderstanding as to what disease was and how it should be treated.

Men like Sebastian Kneipp, Arnold Rikli, Lehmann, Kuhne, and Just, all added their share to the new science of Natural Healing, and so, as the outcome of nearly a century of patient labour in the *effective* treatment of disease, has been evolved that philosophy of disease—its causes, nature and treatment—which to-day bears the title of " Nature Cure "; a philosophy completely antithetical *in every way* to the popularly accepted one of the day. And let it be fully understood that not by spiritual methods, such as faith-healing, or auto-suggestion, or Christian Science (with its denial of the exist-ence of disease in the human body), are the results of Nature Cure obtained—although the mental and emotional factors at work in the causation of diseased conditions are never overlooked—but by a thoroughly scientific understanding of *what disease is, the actual factors at work in its causation, and the application of methods of treatment which make for its effective removal from the system* (these methods being of the simplest, most natural character).

Nature Cure has had a remarkably rapid development since its inception many years ago, and its great home to-day is America. There, through the great work of such leaders of Naturopathy as Dr. Jackson, Dr. Trall, Dr. Kellogg, Dr. Lindlahr, and Dr. Tilden (to mention only a few), it has settled itself largely in public favour, despite the hostility of orthodox medical circles. Trall, Kellogg, Lindlahr, and Tilden were all orthodox medical practitioners, to begin with, but seeing the futility and uselessness of the methods they were called upon to employ daily in their work of healing the sick, they instinctively turned to methods more humane and natural in their character and effect.

Dr. Lindlahr studied the basis of Natural Treatment in Germany, and on his return to America, in addition to founding the largest Natural Cure institution in that country, gave to Nature Cure the scientific basis it needed, in two great books on the subject. Dr. Tilden, through his work in the realm of dietetics, has helped to revolutionise completely the subject of diet (in conjunction with such dietetic pioneers as Otto Carque, Arnold Ehret, Dr. Dewey, and Alfred McCann), making the part played by wrong feeding in the causation of disease clear and established beyond all doubt. (Clear and established beyond all doubt to all but the hide-bound orthodox medical intellect, that is ! For in addition to overlooking completely the wonderful curative value of that most instinctive and natural of all therapeutic agencies, the *fast*, the medical profession pays almost no attention to the diet factor when attempting to find the causes of disease.)

In this country Naturopathy has spread very rapidly during the past forty years or so, and, with the late Mr. Stanley Lief as its chief exponent and his magazine, *Health for All*, to give its philosophy utterance, is gaining more and more adherents every day. The soundness of its doctrines and methods of treatment can only be judged by results, and these are overwhelmingly in its favour.

The medical profession as a whole, however, refuses to pay any attention whatsoever to Nature Cure, except to class its practitioners as " quacks," and, overlooking completely naturopathic achievements in the world of healing, goes along the same old way, blinded by its own dogmas and pet theories, seeking more feverishly than ever for new means whereby to exterminate the obnoxious germs which it *still* supposes to be the main cause of all our ills.

CHAPTER II

THE FUNDAMENTAL PRINCIPLES OF NATURE CURE

NATURE CURE, then, is a philosophy of disease and healing built up and elaborated as a result of many years of patient investigation and research into the nature and cause of disease, by pioneers dissatisfied with orthodox views upon these matters, which realises that disease is something quite other than it is supposed to be according to orthodox medical teaching, and which resorts to nothing but the simplest, most natural, and instinctive measures to bring about its results.

It is based upon a conception which realises that disease is something which arises in the system solely as a result of the body's attempts to rid itself of obstacles to its proper functioning, these obstacles originating in the first place from factors at work *within* the body of the individual concerned, and not from factors *outside*, as Medical Science would have us believe. Thus, instead of disease being looked upon as something inimical to the organism, and having to be fought against, as in the popular view, it is recognised as being in reality nothing else than the body's attempts—blind and unconscious though they may be—at *self-cleansing* and *self-healing*. Disease is regarded, therefore, as being something *directly* connected with the life and habits of the individual concerned—as the direct outcome of these same ways and habits of living, in fact, and not as something apart from, or foreign to, them.

Further, the power to cure disease is taken to reside *always and only* within the body of the patient himself, and will manifest itself as soon as the wrong habits of living and harmful practices which have hampered its activity in the past and obscured its presence have been rectified, as a result of naturopathic treatment and guidance.

Going further still, it is fully accepted by the Nature Cure philosophy that orthodox medical treatment, with its drugging and surgical operations, not only cannot cure disease, but succeeds merely in turning simple diseases into far more serious ones.

The Three Fundamental Principles.—The three fundamental principles enumerated in the following pages, upon which the whole of the philosophy and practice of Nature Cure is built (and which will be

8

developed more fully in the succeeding chapters), will make all this abundantly clear to the reader, however startling and strange it may all sound to begin with. It must be fully understood that these three fundamental principles of Nature Cure are not the outcome of mere *theorising* into the nature and treatment of disease, but are the logical deductions and conclusions arrived at from nearly a century of *effective* naturopathic treatment of disease, in Germany, America, and in this country, and tested and proved over and over again by the results obtained.

(1) The first and *most* fundamental principle of Nature Cure is that *all forms of disease* are due to the *same cause*, namely, the accumulation in the system of waste materials and bodily refuse, which has been steadily piling up in the body of the individual concerned through years of wrong habits of living, the chief of these being wrong feeding, improper care of the body, and habits tending to set up enervation and nervous exhaustion, such as worry, overwork, excesses and abuses of all kinds, etc., etc.

From this first principle of Naturopathy it follows that the only way in which disease *can be cured* is by the introduction of methods which will enable the system to throw off these toxic accumulations which are daily clogging the wheels of the human machine ; and to that sole end all natural treatment is directed. (It must be pointed out for the readers' guidance that during the vital processes which are going on continuously in our bodies, waste products are always forming ; but in the healthy individual they are immediately removed from the system through the medium of the organs of elimination, which are the kidneys, bowels, lungs, and skin. But if, as is the case with most people, the waste products accumulate at a rate in excess of the capacity of the above-mentioned organs to deal with them, then commences the clogging process which is the fundamental cause of all future ill-health.)

(2) The second principle of Nature Cure is that the body is always striving for the ultimate good of the individual, no matter how ill-treated it may be ; and that all *acute diseases*—such as fevers (scarlet fever, measles, diphtheria, typhoid, etc., etc.), colds, diarrhœas, skin eruptions of all kinds, inflammations, etc., etc.—are nothing more than self-initiated attempts on the part of the body to throw off the accumulations of waste material (some of them hereditary) which are interfering with its proper functioning ; and that all *chronic*

9

diseases—such as valvular disease of the heart, diabetes, kidney disease, rheumatism, bronchitis, etc., etc.—are really the results of the *continued suppression* of these same acute diseases (or self-initiated attempts at body-cleansing) by orthodox medical methods of treatment. (These methods include the administration of poisonous drugs, vaccines, narcotics, gland extracts, and X-ray therapy ; and the removal of affected parts by means of surgical operations.)

From the Nature-Cure standpoint, therefore, when a doctor " cures " a patient of an acute disease through the agency of drugs, sera, anti-toxins, etc., or through the medium of the " surgeon's knife," what he *really* does is to force the toxins (waste products), which the body is endeavouring to throw off, farther back into the system ; and it is the concentration of these toxins (plus the drugs, etc., administered by the doctor) in the vital organs and other structures which form the basis of future chronic disease. Obviously, the form which chronic disease will take in any given individual—whether it be rheumatism, Bright's disease, asthma, diabetes, etc.—will depend upon his bodily constitution and hereditary tendencies ; but *the main fact to be noted* is that, according to Nature Cure, *all* chronic disease originates in the first place through the suppression, by wrong medical methods of treatment, of acute diseases.

(3) The third principle of Nature Cure is that the body contains within itself the power to bring about a return to that condition of normal well-being known as health, providing the right methods are employed to enable it to do so. That is to say, the power to *cure* disease lies not in the hands of the doctor or specialist, but *within the body itself*. Within *this* will be found the source of that healing power which Nature is ever ready to bestow on all who are willing to accept her laws and live in accordance with them.

It is only when people realise that there is no magic in the " surgeon's knife " or medicine (patent or otherwise) and are ready to accept the truth of the above statement—which is literally " that the only ones capable of curing them are themselves "—that we can hope for a diminution in the appalling and ever-growing amount of disease present in all civilised countries at the present time.

The Methods of Nature Cure.—It is upon the three principles just enumerated that the practice of Nature Cure is built, and it is by employing methods which *aid* the body in its attempts to regain its normal condition, instead of hindering and thwarting it, that such remarkable results are being achieved by practitioners of Natural Healing throughout the leading countries of the world to-day. These methods are all directed to the one end, *i.e.*, the purification and regeneration of the bodily mechanism to allow the healing power latent within the body of the individual under treatment an opportunity to assert itself and bring about a restoration of normal functioning. And the chief measures whereby this is achieved—all of which will be dealt with in fuller detail in a later chapter—are as follows :

(1) *Fasting*, because fasting is Nature's most potent healing agency. Through the medium of the fast, waste products and impurities, which have sown the seeds of disease in the human body, can be removed in the simplest, easiest, and most natural way.

(2) *Scientific dieting*, because wrong feeding is the most potent factor in the causation of disease (far more so than any other) ; and through proper dieting, and proper dieting *alone*, can the further accumulation of toxic and waste matter in the system be prevented, the blood purified, and all bodily structures allowed to work at their highest level of efficiency.

(3) *Hydrotherapy*, because (in addition to the tonic and cleansing effect upon the system of judiciously applied hot and cold water) through hydrotherapy, or water treatment, effete bowel matter can be removed from the system in the simplest manner possible, without having to resort to the use of any of the harmful and deleterious drugs and purges of orthodox medication ; whilst in the form of *wet packs*, hydrotherapy offers a remarkably simple natural expedient for abating fevers and reducing pain and inflammation. (Again without any harmful after-effects, which can NOT be said of the anti-pyretic drugs used for the same purpose by the medical profession.)

(4) *General body-building and hygienic measures*, because only through proper exercise, deep breathing, effective care of the skin, use of sunlight, fresh air, etc., can the healing process taking place within the body of the individual undergoing natural treatment be given the fullest possible expression.

(5) *Psychotherapy*, because the mental factor plays a part—to a greater or lesser extent—in all diseased conditions, and properly applied mental therapy is therefore as necessary a factor in all natural

treatment, which would be in the highest degree effective, as any of the measures indicated above.

By these simple, natural measures, then—aided by such subsidiary healing agents as spinal manipulation, massage, artificial sunlight, etc.—does the practitioner of Natural Healing seek to deliver our modern humanity from disease ; and it is surely no exaggeration to say that, thanks to his efforts, tens of thousands of people the world over, who thought themselves doomed to a lifetime of chronic invalidism, have been given the possibility of new life and health once more—a possibility denied them by orthodox medical methods of treatment.

Nature Cure, based upon a conception of disease and cure which is nothing but the outcome of common-sense principles applied to the phenomena of health and disease, is waging a war against disease which cannot fail to be successful in the long run, however much it may be held back and hindered at the moment by public ignorance and high-handed medical action ; and it is to help on the arrival of *that* day, by bringing the knowledge of its existence in the world of healing within the range of an ever-increasing circle of intelligent and self-responsible men and women, that the present volume has been written. Let us hope, for the sake of the suffering millions of our present-day humanity, that the day will not be too long distant !

CHAPTER III

NATURE CURE VERSUS MEDICAL SCIENCE

THAT Fallacious Germ Theory !—By ignoring the part played by the individual *himself* in the setting up of disease within his own body, and throwing all the emphasis on to purely extraneous factors, such as germs, our medical scientists have succeeded in giving the word GERM a significance and dread power ludicrously out of all proportion to the part these organisms actually play in the life-processes of the individual human being.

It is time the public realised what germs *really* are, and the part they really *do* play, if any, in the setting up and development of disease.

One would imagine, from the way the medical profession speak, that one tiny germ or bacillus (countless thousands of which could scarcely cover the head of a pin) has only to enter the body of a " healthy " individual for that individual to be stricken with some fell disease or other. Perhaps typhoid! Perhaps tuberculosis! And modern man goes around terrified out of his life because of the existence of these tiny creatures which he endows with such malevolent properties, and which he believes are always threatening him, and which only the most powerful microscope can reveal to his shuddering gaze.

What nonsense it all is! Our bodies are *always* full of germs; they play a most important part in the working of the body, especially in the destructive processes. For constructive and destructive processes are always going on within the body, night and day, asleep or awake, whether we know it or not.

When any living matter dies, it immediately begins to disintegrate into the simple chemical elements of which it is composed ; and it is in breaking down dead organic matter into its elemental constituents that bacteria are always employed by Nature.

We all know that a dead animal left lying about unburied will soon begin to rot ; and it is precisely in this rotting process—which is simply the reduction of the once living organic matter back into the elements of which it is composed—that germs are active. They are just as much a part of natural phenomena as anything else in Nature, and are brought into existence to do their allotted task by

13

that omnipresent Power which, for ever invisible, rules the workings of the universe.

All living mattter must die and be reduced to dust again, and bacteria are the appointed agents! They are the agents of disintegration!

Now, the germs which help in the breakdown of dead organic matter—whether it be of dead bodies or of cell waste and other effete matter thrown off by the living organism—are not very different in kind from the germs hysterically *supposed* by Medical Science to be the main cause of disease in the human body; and it is simply because they so lamentably misunderstand the work these tiny creatures do that the medical world attaches so much significance to germ action inside the body, when seeking for the solution of the problem of disease.

Germs take part in *all* disease phenomena because these are processes requiring the breaking down or disintegration of accumulated refuse and toxic matter within the body, which the system is endeavouring to throw off. But to assume, as our medical scientists do, that merely because germs are present and active in all disease phenomena, they are therefore the *cause* of these same diseases, is just as wrong as it would be to assume that because germs are present and active in the decomposition processes connected with all dead organic matter, they are the *cause* of the death of the organic matter in question. The analogy is absolutely just and fair! And equally ridiculous!

But no one would say that because the decaying body of a dead dog is full of bacteria, the bacteria are the cause of the dog's death ; we know that they are there as a part of the natural disintegrative process taking place as a *result* of the death of the dog. AND SO IT IS WITH GERMS AND DISEASE. Germs are part of the *results* of disease, *not* its cause.

Germs are present in disease *not* as causes, but as superficial helpers brought there by Nature to *rid the body of disease*. They are the " scavengers " employed by Mother Nature to break up and " bring to a head " the accumulated internal filth of years of unhygienic and unwholesome living, which are clogging the tissues of the body and preventing proper functioning.

It is the elimination of this accumulation of internal filth and waste material which is required if the treatment of disease is to be effective, *not* tinkering with germs. *They* will automatically disappear when the bodily filth and refuse have been disposed of, upon exactly the same analogy as that of flies and household filth, instead of bodily filth. *Naturopathic practice proves this beyond doubt every day*! (Treatment which is directed merely towards the end of killing germs is treatment that can never be really effective, because it ignores the *real* causes of disease).

Thus, although germs are the very bugbear of orthodox Medical Science, they are of little account to Naturopathy, because the Naturopath realises that they are part of the *effects* of *disease,* and *not* its cause, and will disappear when the real cause has been disposed of. *But that does not mean to say that disease may not be contracted through germ contact.*

Germs may be the *apparent* causes of disease in certain instances, and people may " catch " diseases from each other, but only because they have within their systems the soil for the propagation of these diseases in the shape of accumulated toxins and bodily refuse. No ONE WHO IS CLEAN AND HEALTHY INSIDE CAN BE AFFECTED BY GERMS OR BECOME THE VICTIM OF GERM INFECTION.

When people understand *this*, they will be freed at last from the dread germ-bogy which Medical Science has created for them out of its imperfect and superficial knowledge of the real action and effect of germs within the body ! It is the outcome of medical inability to distinguish between the real causes of disease and its superficial effects and manifestations.

In face of the question, " What proof have you actually that the germ theory of disease is wrong ? " it may be said that even in the case of acute infectious diseases—where the germ theory *seems* to explain the facts most fully—it can be demonstrated quite conclusively that people in ordinary health contain within their bodies the same germs that are claimed to be the cause of those same infectious diseases in others. This proves quite clearly that there must be some pre-disposing factor present in the body before an attack of any acute disease is possible. Given this predisposing factor, the germs become active; without it, they are harmless. This predisposing factor *is in every case a lowered vitality and a body clogged with waste materials and impurities.*

Members of the medical profession have themselves refuted the theory upon which practically the whole of present-day medicine is based.

In an address on " The Falsity of the Germ Theory, and its Evil Results," given by M. Beddow-Bayly, M.D., at the annual meeting of the Anti-Vaccination League in 1928, Dr. Beddow-Bayly said : " I am prepared to maintain quite definitely that in *no single instance* has it been proved that an organism or germ is the primal cause of a disease. Secondly, that in no single instance has any serum been produced which can be shown to be successful in either preventing or curing disease. I would go further, and say that I have abundant evidence that the use of sera has resulted in incalculable harm and even death in man ; that the discovery, manufacture, and testing of these sera are responsible for untold suffering among our younger brethren, the animals ; and that the obsession of the minds of the medical fraternity by the clumsy and illogical germ theory has greatly retarded the progress of Medical Science by obscuring the solution of the real causes of disease."

During the course of the same address, Dr. Beddow-Bayly quoted numerous extracts from records of investigations made by medical investigators and research workers, all showing the *untenability of the germ theory*, of which the following is a fair example :

" Dr. Hamer, late Medical Officer of Health for the County of London, in his report for 1915, dealing with the investigations of Dr. Houston, the Water Examiner to the Metropolitan Water Boards, finds that the evidence supports the theory ' that it is typhoid fever which leads to the development of the bacillus,' and not *vice versa*, and ' that the bacillus should be looked upon as effect, rather than cause.' "

Perhaps the most striking illustration of all, given by Dr. Bayly in support of his contention as to the unsoundness of the germ theory, is the following :

" The celebrated Professor Pettenkofer, to show his disbelief in the then recently mooted germ theory, swallowed a test-tubeful of cholera germs—supposed to be sufficient to kill a whole regiment of soldiers !—before a classful of gaping students. Nothing happened ! As Pettenkofer maintained, in support of his amazing act, ' Germs are of no account in cholera. The important thing is the disposition of the individual.' "

These quotations and illustrations, from authoritative medical sources themselves, regarding the instability of the germ theory can be multiplied *ad lib.*, if one has a mind to. But why go farther? Surely the reader has here sufficient proof of the inadequacies of that theory of disease upon which the whole fabric of modern medication is built?

To seek for the cause of disease in merely extraneous factors, such as germs and other outside agents, is to turn one's mind, once and for all, away from the possibility of an understanding of the true nature and cause of disease. THAT IS WHAT THE WHOLE MEDICAL WORLD IS DOING TO-DAY. With what result? The state of our hospitals and the general health of the nation are ample witness !

The Unity of Disease.—The reader will now be fully ready for the acceptance of the cardinal principle of Nature Cure, which is, that although, thanks to the pedantry and misconceptions of the leaders of orthodox Medical Science, the names of diseases are legion, in reality *their basic and fundamental causes are the same in every case*, viz., a body clogged with waste materials and impurities ; and that no matter *what* the particular disease in question might be *called*, apart from shock, or direct injury, or mechanical interference with the blood and nerve supply, its causes can always be found in disturbance of function due to three main factors :

(1) Wrong feeding ;

(2) Improper care of the body ;

(3) Habits of living tending to set up enervation and nervous exhaustion, such as worry, fear, overwork, excesses of all kinds, sexual abuse, temperamental and environmental difficulties, etc.

It is these three main factors, coupled with hereditary and predisposing influences, such as physique, personal peculiarities, and the like (and aided by previous medical interference with drug and knife), which decide exactly what form disease will take in any given individual—whether it will be rheumatism or sciatica, kidney trouble or diabetes, bronchitis or eczema, typhoid or pneumonia, cataract or deafness. So that what one has always to remember is that no matter what any disease may be described as in medical terminology, in essence " disease " is the same in every case, because the underlying causes which determine the condition in the first place are identical, although the superficial symptoms and manifestations appear in so many different guises.

17

Nature Cure and Medical Science.—It is because they understand this fundamental oneness and unity of all disease that practitioners of Nature Cure are enabled to secure such seemingly miraculous results in the treatment of disease. For, instead of being appalled by the apparent intricacy, vastness, and hopeless complexity of the spectacle of disease opened up to the mind by a study of pathology along orthodox medical lines, and spending his time in vainly endeavouring to grasp the significance of those merely superficial and extraneous manifestations of disease, which, through a total lack of understanding of the matter, the medical profession *calls* disease—a thousand different diseases according to a thousand different symptoms—the Naturopath gets straightway down to the root of the trouble (the actual fundamental causes of which are the same in every case), and by rectifying these is thus enabled to effect a *permanent* cure. Whereas his medical confrère aimlessly flutters about the surface of the matter, attempting to patch up or get rid of symptoms, which are really the superficial effects of disease and not the real trouble at all !

The Naturopath deals with fundamental, unchanging causes, and pays very little heed to symptoms, except as they may guide him in locating the actual seat of the trouble (which is always deep within the system) ; the medical practitioner deals merely with the symptoms themselves, looks to externals for causes, and remains blissfully unconscious as to the very existence of the real underlying factors involved. The result is, that under orthodox medical methods of treatment not only is such a thing as *real cure* impossible in any given case, because of the neglect of the chief factors concerned, but the underlying disease-condition is yet further intensified and aggravated by this tampering with symptoms. For not only does Medical Science mistake symptoms for diseases, but these self-same superficial symptoms and manifestations—which the Naturopath uses only as guides to locating disease, and which he leaves quietly alone because he realises that they are *not harmful in themselves*, but really Nature's attempts at self-healing and self-cleansing—are suppressively treated with drugs and surgery, and irreparable harm is thus done to the system by this " thwarting " of the body's natural attempts at healing itself.

Disease a Self-healing Process.—What the medical profession calls a " cure " is merely the suppression of superficial symptoms, to cause further and more serious trouble later on ! What the medical profession never understands is, that in every case disease itself, with all its varied multiplicity of expression, is merely NATURE'S ATTEMPT AT SELF-HEALING, and must never be thwarted, fought against, checked, or suppressed, but helped (as it were) out of the system by an understanding of the real causes at work and by active or passive collaboration, as the case may be.

" The Nation's Fighters against Disease "—that is the proud title of the medical profession, and in it is expressed all their failure to understand the real essential nature of disease !

Disease is *not* inimical to the system, something to be fought against ; but it is a self-healing crisis brought about by factors, already described, which the system finds a hindrance and impediment to proper functioning !

Disease, in short, is the result of man's own follies and mistakes which Nature is doing her best to rectify for him !

In effect, therefore—and if the reader can follow this clearly, he or she will be for ever emancipated from the universal besetting fear of disease—*disease is nothing more or less than Nature's blind attempt at cure.* It is the system's attempt to deal as effectively as it can under given conditions with factors which, through man's ignorance, folly, and self-indulgence, are causing impediment of function !

Two Completely Divergent Philosophies !— All too often the great surgeon or physician, and even the general practitioner, vainly imagine that " he " *can cure disease* by suppressing symptoms and thwarting Nature's work. The practitioner of natural methods of treatment, knowing full well his own feebleness within the mighty, all-embracing powers and forces of Nature, bows his head with humility, and says, " Not I, but Nature cures. All I can do is help Nature to do her work by all the means within my power." Herein lie the failure of orthodox medicine and the triumph of natural methods of treatment.

One is based upon a philosophy which looks upon disease as something which " happens " to man quite by ill-luck, accident, or chance ; something which enters the body from without—germs or microbes—and has to be fought against and defeated. The other is based upon a philosophy which realises that all disease emanates from within the body, is self-generated as a result of individual mistakes and errors of living, and is Nature's blind attempt at self-healing. *Two completely antithetical and contradictory philosophies of disease* !

The one exonerates man from all blame with regard to all the ills that befall him, allowing him to pity himself as a much-injured martyr, always at the mercy of a wayward and malign Providence, never knowing when he may be attacked by some awful microbe or prowling germ, and by means of outside agents attempts to " cure " him ; and the other states definitely and conclusively that man's ills are in every case the outcome of his own mistakes and misdeeds— " as a man sows, so shall he also reap "—and that only by rectifying these same mistakes will his troubles be finally overcome and a definite cure effected.

The medical profession claims that *it can cure disases* by means of drugs, surgery, inoculations, etc. ; Nature Cure says that *man must cure himself of disease*, but with the aid of help and advice from those qualified by training and experience to give it !

" The Fruits " of the Old Philosophy of Disease !—" Every tree is known by his own fruit," said Christ to His disciples. Let the men and women of to-day see for themselves the " fruits " of orthodox medical philosophy ! They, are there before our eyes !

New diseases, such as neurasthenia and pernicious anæmia, arising every few years ; an appalling advancement in chronic diseases, such as cancer, rheumatism, diabetes, kidney disease, asthma, bronchitis, heart disease, etc., etc., every year ; devastating plagues of 'flu ; nervous disorders triumphantly ascending ; indigestion, constipation, colds, coughs, catarrh, and such-like " home "ailments more prevalent than ever before—is it not time for the new to supersede the old ?

Away with the effete and worn-out philosophy which sees no connection between man's food follies and maltreatment of his body and bodily functions and the diseases he suffers from ; which attempts to " fight " disease, yet cringes before it in fear and hopeless inconfidence ! Let us inaugurate a new era in world history !—an era in which man will accept the full responsibility for the diseases from which he suffers as being the results of his *own follies and mistakes* (either knowing or unknowing), and *not* iniquities and tortures devised for and thrust upon him by a malign Providence !

CHAPTER IV

WHAT MEDICAL TREATMENT DOES

PAUSING here for a moment, the writer hopes that the reader
will not mistake the last chapter's attack on the utterly worthless
and useless philosophy of Medical Science for an attack upon the
medical profession itself, either as individuals or as a body. This
is the last impression the writer wishes to convey. For his part, he
has nothing but admiration and respect for this self-sacrificing, hard-
working, well-meaning, and truly courageous body of workers for the
welfare of society. But it is surely the greatest tragedy of modern
times that men such as these, actuated by the best and highest motives
—motives for the alleviation of the sufferings of mankind—should,
by virtue of the methods they employ, be directly instrumental in
*actually causing disease to be far more widespread and prevalent
than it otherwise need be*, simply because the whole of their practice
is based upon and upholds a philosophy of disease which is so
completely and irrevocably false, so completely " unaware " of the
true facts of the matter !

What Medical Treatment Actually Does.—By the administration
of drugs, vaccines, sera, anti-toxins, etc., and the extremely free use
of surgery, the medical profession seeks to rid mankind of " disease,"
simply because it can never understand that " disease " is a natural
attempt on the part of the body to protect and free itself from the
harmful effects of poisons generated and accumulated in the system
as a result of wrong living, dietetic and otherwise.

These methods, instead of allowing the toxins and poisons in
question to be *really ejected from the system*—eliminated, that is—
as Nature intends, and as the methods of Naturopathy allow, succeed
only in forcing these same toxins and poisons farther back into the
system, where—plus the drugs, vaccines, sera, etc., administered by
the doctor—they collect around the deeper structures, or find lodgment within the vital organs, to form the basis for far more serious
troubles later on.

Thus, apart from the fact that it allows man to shirk the responsibility for the diseases from which he suffers, by telling him that
they are the result of chance, accident, or ill-luck—there is always the

21

weather to fall back on as an excuse, if no luckless germ can be cited as the culprit !—and so leading him to look upon disease as something which just " happens " to him without any reference to his past habits and present ways of living, orthodox medicine, by suppressing the outward manifestations and symptoms of disease and seemingly effecting a " cure," ACTUALLY AIDS MATERIALLY IN THE INCREASE OF DISEASE—the very thing it is out to prevent !—in the following two ways :

(1) By lulling its victims into a false state of security by leading them to believe that the diseases they have been suffering from are *really cured*, whereas they have merely been forced beneath the surface ; and

(2) By turning what would otherwise be simple *acute diseases* (Nature's direct attempts to cleanse the body of toxins and impurities), such as colds, diarrhœas, skin eruptions, boils, inflammations, and fevers, into *chronic diseases* (something far more stubborn and persistent than acute diseases, and, correspondingly harder to eradicate from the system once they take hold), such as rheumatism, bronchitis, asthma, diabetes, kidney disease, heart disease, etc., etc. Obviously chronic disease does not follow *immediately* upon the suppression of an acute disease ; it is the *continued* suppression of acute diseases which leads to the ultimate development of chronic disease within the system.

Where people have got *really well* under medical treatment, with no after effects of any kind, that has been *in spite of,* and *not because of,* the treatment! Because the system has had enough vitality and recuperative power successfully to withstand the action of drugs and medical agents upon it!

A Menace, NOT a Blessing.—Now, I am quite aware of the impossibility of expecting the vast majority of people—accustomed as they have been all their lives to regard the medical profession as the one safe refuge always there to be turned to in times of illness and suffering; as the fitting recipients of the admiration and respect accorded them by society; as the worthy inheritors and upholders of the traditional prestige and dignity due to them by virtue of their high calling—I am quite aware of the impossibility of expecting people such as these, overawed by the " majesty " of medicine as they are, to straightway accept the truth of the iconoclastic statements here being made.

I can hear them saying incredulously to themselves, " What, the medical profession the cause of more disease than would otherwise be the case if there were no doctors ! Actually *causing* disease, *not curing it* ! Am I reading aright ? Does this man mean to say that through the methods they employ (the results of hundreds of years of patient scientific investigation and research, and tried and tested again and again), doctors not only cannot *cure* disease, but actually turn what would otherwise be simple diseases into far more serious ones ? Impossible ! Ridiculous ! Why, if what he says is true, the medical profession is *a menace to society, not a blessing* ! "

Yes, it does sound impossible and ridiculous, I know, but it is none the less true for all that ! The medical profession, thanks to its hidebound and obsolete attitude to disease, *is* a menace—quite unwittingly of course—and not a blessing to society ! And the sooner people begin to realise this no doubt startling fact, the better !

No one who has not tried can understand the almost utter hopelessness of attempting to convey these simple truths to the conventional-minded people of to-day, steeped as they are in implicit belief as to the wonder-working powers of " the doctor "; accepting everything he says with childish faith and obedience, as coming from one who surely knows all there is to know about disease, its causes and cure ; absolutely convinced as to the efficacy and healing value of the vari-coloured medicines they trustingly carry home with them after a visit to the surgery ; speaking with bated breath of " great specialists " and miraculous eleventh-hour operations performed at a moment's notice which have saved the lives of near and dear ones ; fully satisfied that the ills they suffer from are nothing whatever to do with their habits of living or the food they eat, but are due to nasty pernicious little germs, sent by a perverse Providence to harass them, or " the weather "!—no one, I repeat, who has not tried can understand the hopelessness of trying to convince people such as these (and they make up fully ninety-nine per cent. of the population of all civilised countries) that medical practice—based as it is upon a completely erroneous philosophy of disease—despite all its skill, knowledge, position, prestige, power, authority, and so-called " achievements " in alleviating the sufferings of humanity, *is really and truly a menace*—and a most insidious menace, be it noted—to the health and welfare of society, by actually *intensifying* disease instead of overcoming it !

What People do not Know.—If people knew the true effects of orthodox medical treatment upon the bodies of those who so willingly accept it and undergo it, the wholesale extirpation of tonsils and appendices which takes place to-day, the attempts to remove pain by the use of nerve-deadening drugs, the " curing " of constipation by the administration of purges and laxatives of ever-greater strength, the use of such terribly injurious mineral agents as mercury and arsenic for the " curing " of venereal and other diseases, and such-like enormities which have constituted the stock-in-trade of the medical profession in recent years, would no more have been tolerated than would the methods of the witch-doctors of old, with their paraphernalia of sorcery and black magic!

To remove enlarged tonsils and adenoids is *not* to get rid of the underlying cause of the trouble ; to relieve a headache by prescribing aspirin is *not* to remove the cause of the headache ; to " cure " constipation by advising the use of purges and laxatives is *not* to get rid of the cause of constipation, but to make it more stubborn and deep-rooted than ever—yet these are the methods Medical Science has employed to " rid humanity of its ills "!   No wonder these same ills persist in growing more serious daily before our eyes!   These are the methods which, one and all, have led inevitably to the increase of disease, because of their infantile tampering with symptoms, without paying any attention whatsoever to the real fundamental causes involved.

The pity is that people do *not* know these things, and so, orthodox medical treatment is allowed to do what it does, unchecked and unchallenged, with results that are telling more and more each year upon the health and vital life of the community.

The whole point is this : when one understands the unity of disease, one realises at once that if a disease is wrongly treated or suppressed in one organ or part of the body, it will only crop up again in another *and more serious form* in another organ or part later on.   Members of the *medical profession do not understand this*, hence the havoc wrought by them in their treatment !   To the Naturopath, all diseases in the same organism are related, from measles or whooping cough at the age of two, to catarrh at fourteen, and rheumatism at forty. But to the medical practitioner there is no connection at all.   These things just " happen " to the individual during his lifetime as isolated facts or instances of disease.   To suggest to him that there *is* a connection, and a most *definite* one, a connection of cause and effect all the time (a connection of wrong treatment plus wrong living in a gradually more devitalised organism), would be beyond his comprehension. But so it is. *And that is the whole crux of the matter.*

For instance, the doctor sees nothing incongruous in treating a patient for acute bronchitis or 'flu, say, and seeing that patient develop pneumonia and die from it whilst under the treatment. To the Naturopath it is at once clear that it is the doctor's suppressive treatment which has forced the less serious disease into the graver and fatal one ; it is WRONG TREATMENT which has brought about this unfortunate result, pure and simple. But not so to the doctor. To him it was just that the patient was unfortunate enough to develop pneumonia, whilst being in a low state vitally and unable to fight off the pneumonia " germ "—and that is all !

And so it is with every kind of disease. How many people have been treated regularly by the doctor for simple chest complaints every winter, only to develop asthma or chronic bronchitis in later life? How many have been treated for nerve trouble for years, only to end up nervous wrecks, or, worse, the inmates of asylums ? How many children have had tonsils or adenoids removed, only to become affected in later life with a disease such as tuberculosis, asthma, chronic middle-ear disease, deafness, etc., for no apparent reason at all? *These are all results of wrong treatment*, of suppressive medical treatment which removes symptoms and superficial causes, only to pave the way for more serious and lasting trouble later on in life, by its complete neglect of *real underlying causes*, which are thus left to go on unchecked and unhindered to undermine the after-life of the unsuspecting sufferer.

Let the reader look at his own past medical history, and into that of his relatives and friends, and see if he cannot trace many instances of a similar nature to those quoted above. They are legion. The trouble is that people just accept these things as a matter of course, and see no relation whatever between their increasing impairment of health and the doctor or doctors whom they so trustingly obey in matters relating to disease.

Why, the writer himself has seen people who have been under the SAME doctor for *ten or twenty years,* and have been just as far from health at the end of that period as when they first went to him—have been worse in fact ! What can be said for methods of treatment which keep patients coming for the relief of one ill or another practically all their lives, only to find themselves more in the doctor's hands at the end of the time than ever ? They start with indigestion, say ; the doctor's medicine, in " curing " this, gives them constipation or affects their heart. Then they are given something for the constipation or the heart trouble, and so on, and so on. More drugs and more drugs are poured into a system becoming more and more enervated and devitalised. Disease after disease then follows in turn —'flu, colds, rheumatism, lumbago, chest complaints, neurasthenia, heart disease or kidney disease perhaps, high blood-pressure, etc., etc.—all of which are set down to the weather, or germs, or what not, but never to the *real* cause : THE DOCTOR'S TREATMENT OVER MANY YEARS WITH DRUGS AND OTHER SUPPRESSIVE MEASURES, COUPLED WITH THE PATIENT'S OWN UNHYGIENIC HABITS OF LIVING AND UNWISE FOOD HABITS !

And so it goes on in instance after instance to the millionth degree ! Is there any wonder, then, that chronic disease is on the increase in all civilised countries, when methods such as these of treating disease are the vogue ? And is it any wonder that to the Naturopath the doctor who—all in good faith, and from the best motives—is instrumental in administering such treatment is *himself* sowing the seeds of future disease more surely than any other member of the community ? And think of the weight of authority the medical profession possesses, and the crowds of unfortunate supplicants who come daily to them for help in the crowded cities and towns of civilisation ! Surely it is enough to make the mind pause and wonder if " the doctor " is not some divinely inspired instrument of affliction sent by a long-suffering Deity to wipe out our present civilisation altogether, under the guise of restoring it to health and fitness !

And remember—the doctor always holds the trump card : *he can sign death certificates* ! Where the Naturopath—should he be so extremely unfortunate as to have a patient die on his hands under treatment—might have to take his stand in the dock on a charge of *manslaughter*, the doctor is exonerated from all blame whatosever, no matter what the results of his treatment might be ! *His certificate covers all*, no matter how negligent he might be ! The Naturopath must *never* lose a case ; to the medical practitioner the matter is not of such consequence. . . . Which gives much food for reflection to the thoughtful reader !

The writer can quite understand that, even with what has just been said, many readers will still find it difficult to grasp the full significance of the harm caused to the sufferer from disease by the usual medical methods of procedure in vogue throughout the civilised world to-day (and, please, let it be fully understood that the doctor who is instrumental in applying them is *himself completely unaware* of the harm he is causing), so that perhaps the illustrations given in the following chapter of *what actually does happen* when an individual is treated first by orthodox medical methods and then by natural methods of treatment will help to clear up this most vital point.

SPECIAL NOTE.—The point about the action of drugs is most important, and is perhaps needful of a little elaboration so far as the average reader is concerned. Drugs affect the body, and have a definite effect upon disease-conditions, *but not in the way the medical profession believes*. To the medical mind generally the body is a sort of *passive agent* where disease is concerned; it is assumed that the body is " attacked " by disease, and that drugs act directly upon the disease and dispel it. The part played by the body *itself* in the matter is largely disregarded. *It is not assumed to play any appreciable part at all.* It is here that the whole trouble with drugs—and other medical agents—arises.

For, far from the body being a passive agent where disease is concerned, it is a most active participator in the matter all the time ; indeed, as already pointed out, all disease arises in the first place through the body's attempt to get rid of, or deal with as best it can, toxic deposits which are an impediment to its normal functioning. Hence, when drugs or other medicinal agents are employed in the treatment of disease, it is *the body* they act against all the time, by opposing its self-cleansing work, and *not* the disease, and the more they do so, the more efficacious they appear to be !

No drug is readily tolerated by the system; the chemical and vegetable elements of which drugs are composed are entirely foreign to it ; and so, when drugs are administered during the course of medical treatment, the body has to relinquish its self-cleansing work to deal with the drug, and it is in this way that the purely superficial effects of drugs upon disease are secured. For IT SIMPLY MEANS THAT

27

2*

DURING THE DRUG TREATMENT OF DISEASE THE ACTIVITY OF THE BODY (WHICH WAS DIRECTED TOWARDS THE CLEANSING OF THE SYSTEM OF TOXINS AND IMPURITIES) IS SUSPENDED IN ORDER TO DEAL WITH THE DRUGS INTRODUCED, and in this way the disease—which, as already pointed out, is nothing more than a natural attempt at body-cleansing —is stopped. (Providing the drugs are strong enough in their effect, of course.) The doctor says the patient is " cured "; the Naturopath says the patient is *not* cured, the disease has simply been *suppressed* (pushed beneath the surface), because it means that the toxic matter is *still left in the system* after drug treatment, plus the drugs employed.

It follows as a natural corollary to all this that the more deadly the drug, the more quickly will it make its presence felt—that is to say, the more quickly will it interfere with the body in its self-cleansing work ; and so, the more highly will it be prized in medical treatment for this very reason. For it will mean that such drugs have the effect of suppressing disease far more quickly and " effectively " than others.

CHAPTER V

THE DIFFERENCE BETWEEN MEDICAL AND
NATURAL TREATMENT

T HE three examples given in this chapter of the difference between medical and natural treatment have been carefully chosen with a view to making this fundamental divergence as clear as possible to the reader. That the one is based upon a conception of disease which is entirely superficial and erroneous, and that its methods of treatment *must* lead to the intensification of trouble within the system of the sufferer from disease, whilst the other is the outcome of sane and logical reasoning, and its methods of treatment the only ones capable of really effectively *curing disease*, will be made obvious to all.

Example 1

The case of Mr. X—one familiar to us all.

Mr. X has a cold. He goes to the doctor, is told he "probably caught it from someone," is given aspirin or codeine to reduce the temperature, and in a day or so is better—"cured", as he fondly imagines. And so far as both he and the doctor are concerned, that is the end of the matter.

But that is *not* the end of the matter—not by a long way. Neither the doctor nor Mr. X *has the slightest idea* that the cold in question was the result of Mr. X's system being surcharged with an accumulation of waste matter directly attributable to wrong feeding habits, and that it was a natural attempt at body-cleansing made possible by a sudden lowering of his vitality. (Whether its appearance was finally due to spontaneous generation or germ contact does not matter in the least.)

The result is that these self-same impurities and toxins, instead of being allowed to eliminate themselves harmlessly through the medium of the mucous membranes of the nose, throat, eyes, etc., as Nature intended (for this is what the extremely uncomfortable and seemingly never-ending pouring stream of mucus usually called a " cold " *actually is—a natural eliminative process!*), these waste and effete materials which the body is doing its best to get rid of are thrust back again into the tissues by the action of the drugs administered by the doctor, to cause the yet further intensification of more deep-seated trouble elsewhere within the system by this thwarting of Nature's eliminative efforts. In the case of Mr. X it is the rheumatism from which he suffers (and which is *itself* the outcome of continued suppression of many similar attempts at self-healing carried out over a period of many years, but which of course he attributes to " the weather ") that will quite unaccountably suddenly become worse.

What, then, does this " curing " of Mr. X's more or less harmless cold amount to? It has been *stopped* by the suppressive action of drugs. But what has happened to the pouring stream of mucus which would *still* be flowing from the body if the cold had *not* been " cured," *i.e.*, checked ?

The medical mind never worries about this ! Its calm serenity is *never* disturbed by thoughts such as these ! Neither the doctor nor Mr. X stops to reflect as to what has happened to this seemingly unceasing flow of matter—as to where it has gone ! They are both satisfied so long as it is for the present no longer visible !

They neither of them can be brought to see that this continuously flowing stream of impurities discharged from the body during the process of a cold is far better *outside* the system than *in* ; that a " cold " is the simplest and safest method Nature has of ridding an already overclogged organism of the toxins and waste materials which are daily being added to it through the criminally unwise feeding habits of to-day.

So Mr. X's cold has been " cured." Medical Science and orthodox medical practice have gained another triumph. But at what cost? *That*, only the future will show !

. . . . . .

Now let us look at the other side of the matter. We have seen what the suppressive treatment of Medical Science does ; let us see what Naturopathy can do.

Mr. X, having by chance read a copy of *Health for All*—he picked it up at a railway bookstall out of curiosity—consults a Naturopath the next time he has a cold. He is immediately informed that his cold is nothing more than a natural attempt on the part of his body to rid itself of some of the accumulated toxins and waste matter with which it is being continually encumbered as a result of his unwise feeding habits. (He eats, like practically everyone else, far too much starchy, protein, sugary, and fatty foods, and practically no fresh fruit or raw green vegetables.)

He says he believes he "caught the cold from somebody," but is made to understand that unless the refuse in question was present in his system, no germ could become active there. Also that it is a *good* thing for him, and *not* a bad thing; as the more rubbish (mucus) he is able to throw off during the progress of the cold, the better will it be with regard to his future health. (Providing, of course, that he does not continue his present unwise feeding habits and methods of living.)

He begins to see that he could never have possibly "caught" a cold if his system had been *perfectly clean inside*, and realises the truth of the statement that his cold is a natural "healing crisis"—a natural cleansing process instituted by his body through the opportunity afforded by a sudden lowering of his powers of resistance (either as a result of a sudden chill, overwork, over-eating, sexual excess, excesses of other kinds, etc., etc.).

He sees that his cold is *not* due to accident or chance, but is a natural effect set in operation as the logical result of various predisposing causes; and is thus made aware, for the first time in his life, of the existence of the law of *cause and effect*—which is in essence, "as a man sows, so shall he also reap."

Mr. X has learnt, moreover, that he must accept the onus of his own illnesses, *not* blame them on to chance or extraneous happenings not directly connected with his daily life; and by assuming the responsibility for his own actions—past as well as present—is brought face to face with yet another of the basic laws of life and well-being: the law of *self-control*. For it is by self-control only that one can hope to live *really healthily* in this self-indulgent world of ours! (*Self-indulgence!* *That* is at the bottom of nine-tenths of the ills of to-day, whether it be with regard to food, sex, or anything else; and until one has learnt *self-control*, how *can* one hope for the establishment of a proper mode of living? It is upon this that the future health of the individual depends!)

Mr. X leaves the consulting-room of the Naturopath a by no means sadder but a certainly much wiser man than when he entered it a short hour previously, having in his possession NOT a bottle of medicine or a box of pills (containing drugs of which neither he nor the medical profession knows the effects upon the system, except that they are instrumental in removing the superficial symptoms of disease), but instructions for a short fruit fast, hot Epsom-salts baths, a general diet-sheet, exercises, etc. These have all been given him with a view not only to ridding him of his cold—this, these various measures will soon accomplish, by *promoting* and *increasing* elimination, (*promoting* and *increasing* elimination, mark you, NOT preventing, checking, or suppressing it, as is invariably done by orthodox medical methods)—but of overcoming his chronic rheumatism, too ! The latter, he now sees, is the accumulative result of many years of wrong living, coupled with allopathic ignorance in the treatment of disease, the acid impurities his body would have liked to throw off having been forced continuously farther and farther back into the system, until they have finally lodged themselves around the bony structures and joints of the knees, legs, arms, hands, etc.

Perhaps the reader *now* begins to understand the difference between medical and natural treatment ?

Example 2

Another common instance. One of the many "triumphs" of modern surgery !

Mrs. Y has appendicitis, is carried off at once to the hospital, operated upon immediately, her appendix removed, and after a few weeks of hospital treatment is discharged as " cured "—to all intents and purposes " a completely healthy individual," minus, of course, her appendix, which, however, she has been led to believe served no useful purpose in the body, and which she is therefore better off without !

It all sounds beautifully simple and straightforward, doesn't it, dear reader ? First of all we have Mrs. Y, a normal, " healthy " individual, carrying around with her an appendix given her by Nature (out of spite probably), which may at any time, for some quite unknown reason (according to orthodox medical doctrine, that is), become a centre of infection and disease within the body. One day, quite without any previous warning, she suddenly discovers that she has a violent pain in her right side, calls in the doctor, is told she has appendicitis (why, the doctor cannot say, except that perhaps it may be due to a " germ "), is operated upon, the offending appendix is triumphantly removed, and in a few weeks we have Mrs. Y about again in far better health than before (according to medical reasoning, that is), because she no longer possesses within her person that pernicious plague-spot of probable infection, the vermiform appendix!

Mrs. Y's appendicitis is not related *in any way* to Mrs. Y's former history, to the fact that for years and years she has been *constipated*, and has been in the habit of taking all kinds of salts, aperients, purges, etc.—any and every thing, in fact, that she sees advertised in the papers as a " cure " for constipation—that for some months before her attack she had been unable to obtain a movement of the bowels for days at a stretch, even with the free use of the constipation " cures " she relied on so completely to carry out the impeded work of Nature. *These factors are all ignored by doctor and surgeon alike !*

So that, when Mrs. Y returns home after her month or so in hospital—a normal, " healthy " individual, forsooth !—she has *still* to face her chronic and stubborn constipation, minus, however, her appendix, which, be it noted, far from being a useless appendage left in the body by a thoughtless and perverse Nature to cause trouble and annoyance, is a most useful little organ, playing a very important part in the work of the large intestine, and by its oily secretion helping to prevent and allay the very condition from which Mrs. Y is suffer- ing, *i.e.*, her constipation ! (Which must now of a certainty become worse, by the way.)

Now perhaps the reader can begin to see what this example of the wonders worked by modern surgery really amounts to !

The appendix is *not* a useless part of our anatomy ; appendicitis is *not* a disease liable to attack any and every one without rhyme or reason (nor is it due to swallowing grape pips!) ; the body is *not* better off without an appendix than with one. These are all utterly futile and ridiculous medical assertions put forward to hide their ignorance by men who have no conception whatsoever as to the workings of the *living* human organism, but who, nevertheless, never hesitate to maul and cut it about at the slightest provocation !

Appendicitis *never* appears except in the wake of chronic bowel trouble, and is really inflammation of the appendix with resultant fever due to the accumulation of toxins and effete waste matter in the colon (large intestine) and cæcum, which the system is piling up there every day through the medium of the food eaten, and which (owing to the constipated condition of the individual concerned) it is unable to evacuate.

Appendicitis and chronic constipation thus go hand in hand ; but is Medical Science aware of this most elementary fact ?   Not at all ! It just goes blithely on, allowing its victims to have their appendices removed, assuring them they will be all the better without them, and generally leaving the said luckless ones to struggle harder than ever before with a chronic and stubborn constipation which must inevitably grow worse as the years elapse, because no attempt is made to rectify the feeding habits and general manner of living of the individual concerned, *which are really at the root of the trouble* !

The case of Mrs. Y shows clearly that modern surgery is just as suppressive and harmful in its effects upon the future health of the individual as any of the other methods employed in orthodox medical practice, because it removes the *superficial symptoms of disease*, only to allow the real cause of the trouble to continue unchecked and become more deep-rooted than before, whilst the trusting patient fondly imagines that his or her sufferings are now over once and for all.

. . . .

Now, in the full light of our knowledge as to the true effects upon the health of the community of the " blessings " of surgery (think of the thousands having tonsils and appendices removed every day!), let us turn to the other side of the picture, and see what would have happened to Mrs. Y if she had known enough about these matters to call in a Naturopath instead of an orthodox medical man to her illness.

Would he advise an immediate operation ? Oh dear no !— incredible as it may seem !

In the first place, instead of not having the vaguest notion of the real cause of the trouble, but putting it down to an infection by germs (much the safest way of disguising one's complete ignorance in the matter, and resorted to freely by all the medical fraternity, who must keep up an air of omniscient knowledge at all costs, as necessary to the dignity and prestige of their profession !), the Naturopath would have known at once the real cause of the attack—Mrs. Y's many years of constipation and bowel trouble. She would have been put on a *complete fast*, and her pain relieved by the application of hot and cold packs to the affected area.

After a day or two of this treatment her condition would have so improved that the enema could be used with good effect, and the clogging contents of her bowel removed, and in a week or so from that time—still being kept on water and fruit juices only—*her appendicitis would have completely disappeared* !

Note the difference between the two methods of treatment, dear reader !

Mrs. Y would have been left with her appendix intact, her bowel thoroughly cleansed *and ready to work properly after its enforced rest*, her appetite keen and healthy ; so that, being put on a sensible diet, she would have been well on the way towards renewed health and vigour—her constipation overcome—and she could have looked forward to a future which gave every promise of happiness and mature, virile old age ! Instead of which, she has now no appendix, is more constipated than before, continues with her old habits of living, which must inevitably lead to further and yet further trouble (not having the least idea that they are harmful), and so is left to face a future which gathers black and gloomy in front of her, because of her impaired health and lowered vitality !

Example 3

Yet a further illustration of what medical treatment CAN, *and* DOES DO, *daily, by* SUPPRESSING *the superficial symptoms of disease.*

Jimmie Z, a young boy, has rheumatic fever ; the doctor is called in, and with the free use of salicylates the fever is reduced in time, and young Jimmie pronounced as " cured." Unfortunately, it is discovered that his heart is now affected, but, as the doctor informs his mother, this practically always happens in cases of rheumatic fever, the fever usually affecting the heart of the patient.

So little Jimmie Z is left to face the future as best he can with a permanently weakened constitution, due, as the medical profession assert, entirely to the ravages of the fever, something it is quite outside their power to prevent.

Something it is quite outside their power to prevent ! Yes, I can hear the family doctor muttering to himself as he bends over little Jimmie's bed, listening with his stethoscope to the now faulty beating of the young boy's heart, " Poor lad ! Poor lad ! Most unfortunate !

Still, it is only to be expected! Rheumatic fever always leaves its victims like this!"

But little does this same well-intentioned, good-natured, hard-working family doctor suspect that it is actually *his treatment* which has brought about Jimmie's heart trouble, and *not* the fever ! That it was the action of the salicylates he employed *in such large quantities* to reduce the fever and neutralise the uric-acid effusions in the joints—the characteristic feature of rheumatic fever—which, by their deleterious effect upon the heart's action, have succeeded in permanently injuring it! Further, that the neutralised product of the chemical interaction between the alkaline salicylates and the uric-acid emanations in the joints, by being brought into the circulation and carried around by the blood-stream, have—

(1) By finding lodgment in the heart-structures and setting up irritation there, intensified yet more the harmful effects of the direct action of the salicylates upon that now injured organ ; and

(2) By being carried to the kidneys in order to be ejected finally from the system, likewise found lodgment and set up irritation there, to sow the seeds for future kidney disease (nephritis)—a very common sequel, be it noted, not only to rheumatic fever, but to many other fevers treated upon similar suppressive lines !

The reader, unless he or she is conversant in some degree with these matters, will here look up with horrified eyes, and exclaim " But is this *really* so? Does chronic heart trouble follow in the wake of rheumatic fever solely because of the treatment employed, and *not* from the actual effects of the fever itself ? "

The answer is " Yes ! Chronic heart trouble follows in practically every case where rheumatic fever is suppressively treated in the orthodox medical manner, and *never* if natural methods are resorted to ! "

Also please note, dear reader, that not only with regard to rheumatic fever are there harmful after-effects observed (due entirely, as the medical profession quite sincerely believes, to the direct action of the fever itself, but in reality to the methods of treatment employed), but with practically every other kind of fever treated in the orthodox manner.

Why ? Because a fever, being an " acute " disease, is an example of a natural healing crisis generated by the body—with germs as the superficial agents—to rid itself of some of the toxins and impurities with which it is being daily encumbered owing to the wrong habits of living of the individual concerned. So that when the superficial manifestations and symptoms of the disease are suppressed by the efforts of the medical profession, and the patient is *apparently* cured, what it means is that more serious and lasting trouble will develop later on, owing to the toxins and impurities in question—which the body was endeavouring to throw off through the medium of the fever—being forced farther back into the system, plus the drugs, vaccines, sera, antitoxins, etc., administered by the doctor. The results of this apparently successful " curing " of fevers by orthodox means will thus make itself apparent in later life by the seemingly unaccountable appearance of such diseases as chest complaints (asthma bronchitis, consumption, etc.), ear trouble (otorrhœa), heart trouble (valvular disease), kidney trouble (nephritis), and a hundred and one other ailments and diseases. (For no apparent reason whatsoever, according to ordinary standards of reasoning ; but for most sound and valid reasons from the Nature-Cure point of view !)

This, then, is what suppressive treatment *can* and *does* do daily, not only with regard to rheumatic fever, but, as I have said, with other fevers, such as scarlet fever, diphtheria, measles, smallpox, pneumonia, etc., etc. *Let the reader think this well over for himself* !

A most important point to realise in connection with the orthodox treatment of fevers is that the *feeding which takes place during the time the fever is in progress* (with a view to " keeping up the strength of the patient " !) causes as much harm as, if not more than, the actual treatment itself !

．　　　．　　　．　　　．　　　．　　　．

The origin of those mysterious after-effects and complications which so persistently follow in the wake of the " apparently " successful medical treatment of acute diseases, and which are so puzzling to the minds of the medical profession, has now been revealed to the reader. *It is the direct result of the treatment itself* !

Now let us see what would have happened to Jimmy Z under natural treatment.

Instead of deleterious and injurious drugs being employed to reduce the fever and get rid of the uric-acid effusions in the joints, the

Naturopath—knowing full well that the fever was entirely the result of the excessive amount of protein food (meat, fish, cheese, eggs, etc.) Jimmy has been made to eat daily for years past by his fond parents, to say nothing of equally large quantities of bread, potatoes, sweet things, etc., who thereby believed that their little boy would grow up strong and healthy (meat gives strength, doesn't it ?)—would have *fasted the boy*, used the *enema twice daily* to cleanse the bowels, and, with the aid of hot and cold *packs* applied when necessary (all of these measures to *increase* elimination, and allow the toxins in question to be thrown off by the system, please note, *not* suppress or diminish it), Jimmie's attack of rheumatic fever would have completely disappeared in a fortnight or so, leaving his heart as sound as ever, and his general health much better than before, owing to the thorough cleansing his system would have received during the course of the treatment.

Surely there is no need to draw further comparisons between these two methods of approaching and treating disease ? These three examples could be multiplied into three hundred if one wished; but surely they speak eloquently enough for themselves ? The destructive effects of medical theory and practice upon the life and health of society are here made manifest to all !

Not until our medical scientists realise the fundamental unity of all disease, not until they realise that tinkering with symptoms is not the same as ridding the body of the underlying causes of disease, not until they realise *what* these fundamental underlying causes *actually are* and alter their methods accordingly, can society hope to be delivered from the menace to life and health which orthodox medical treatment actually is at the present day—a menace the more insidious because coming from a quarter the least expected of all.

CHAPTER VI

HOW NATURE CURES

AFTER what the reader has now learned, he will see that it is to Nature Cure, or the methods employed in the natural treatment of disease, that the sufferer from disease must turn, if he wishes for normal health and proper functioning to be restored to him in this world of false medical values and ignorant acceptance of medical standards.

Unlike Medical Science, Nature Cure has *not* the sanction of society for its efforts to relieve man of the vast burden of disease and suffering which he is at present bearing upon his, alas ! weary shoulders ; but, none the less, it is making its presence felt more and more surely day by day, throughout every walk of life and every branch of society, by the seemingly miraculous results it is achieving in the cure of disease.

For, after all, *it is results that tell in the long run,* not popular acceptance or official approval ; and by its results must Nature Cure inevitably be given its rightful place in the estimation of all clear-thinking men and women ! Of the mass of mankind little can be expected as yet ; they are too overwhelmed by popular opinion— whether the result of custom or tradition, or manufactured for their consumption by the Press—to be able to formulate definite opinions and points of view for themselves.

How many people in this country, to say nothing of Germany, Switzerland and America, have been rescued by Natural Treatment from the doom of chronic invalidism to which they have been sentenced as a result of years of reliance upon the methods of orthodox medicine ? How many men and women have been given a new lease of life as a result of having their whole outlook changed— mental as well as physical—by coming into contact with the epoch-making truths and revolutionising methods summed up under the heading of " Nature Cure " ?

Let these people be a living testimony to the efficacy and value of these new methods of healing ! The philosophy and practice of Nature Cure have a contribution to make to the life and health of humanity which is as yet little realised by mankind as a whole.

The Healing Power of Nature.—The essence of Nature Cure, and the various methods of treatment which spring from it, is the realisation and fundamental acceptance on the part of those practising it of the fact that *within himself* every individual possesses the power to *cure himself* of any disease from which he may be suffering, providing:

(1).—The right means to bring this about are employed ;

(2).—The vitality of the individual concerned has not sunk so low as to render recuperation impossible.

In the last analysis, therefore, not only is it the physician with his many drugs or the surgeon with his array of knives who cannot cure disease, but the Naturopath also ! This can only be accomplished by the natural healing powers latent within the body. *These alone* are capable of bringing about that return to normal functioning which is synonymous with health. NOT MAN, BUT NATURE CURES !

Surely it is a wonderful thing to realise that within ourselves are contained powers and forces capable of putting a disorganised (or diseased) organism to rights, as soon as the said organism is allowed to return to a mode of living which provides these same forces with an opportunity to operate? *And it is the sole function and purpose of all naturopathic practice and treatment to bring this about !*

The Naturopath does not, like his medical confrére, grandiloquently claim that *he* can cure disease, but, by elaborating a system of treatment which will allow the sufferer from disease (in each individual case) to return to a mode of living which will afford the natural healing forces within him an opportunity to operate, he leaves it to that healing power of Nature which he knows exists in all creatures, human or otherwise, to do the work which it alone can accomplish.

Although the healing power in question cannot be seen or weighed or measured, there is, nevertheless, no doubt as to its existence ; for it is the same power within us which is responsible for the carrying on of all the multifarious activities of our bodies. It is the same power which, year in and year out, in the deepest unconsciousness of sleep and the greatest height of activity, controls the functioning of every organ or part of the human organism without our conscious knowledge, or even our realisation sometimes.

That power within us, which makes the heart to beat, the blood to flow, the eye to see, the ear to hear, the hair to grow, lungs to breathe, the brain to function, will, if given a suitable opportunity, renew diseased tissue in an organ or part of the body which is functioning wrongly, cleanse the cells, purify the blood, give new vitality to a degenerate digestive system, and, in short, make life worth living once again to the sufferer from disease who has the sense to realise the fact and the determination to carry out the necessary measures.

New Schools of Healing.—It is this realisation of the healing power latent within the body which has led to the formation in recent years of various schools of " faith healing " and " mind healing," such as the Christian Scientists and Auto-Suggestionists. But whether it be faith healing or mind healing, spiritual exhortation or hypnotic suggestion, none of these methods can effect a really permanent cure in any given case—except in a few isolated instances—because of their complete neglect of all physical factors.

By calling upon this healing power which they know exists within the body—call it what they will—by prayer, power of the mind, will, suggestion, release of hidden complexes, etc., etc., each and every one of these new schools of healing attempts to effect cures of disease, without, however, in any way altering the physical condition of the sufferer.

It may be possible to restore mental confidence and balance to a self-conscious and neurotic individual by suggestion or analysis, and even hearing and vision may be brought back to normal sometimes by the application of these new methods of approaching disease ; but how can any sane person really expect to overcome such a condition as a gastric ulcer or diabetes by the methods of Christian Science or faith healing ? *It is the body that must receive attention in these cases as well as the mind or spirit.*

Of course, the mental attitude plays a great part in the effective treatment of all diseases, and by psycho-therapy a great deal can be done to overcome nervous disorders and diseases of a *functional* nature; but what is required is a thorough understanding of *all* the various factors—both mental and physical—involved in any given disease-condition, and the giving to each of these factors its proper significance and place in the scheme of treatment. (Rheumatism can no more be overcome by suggestion or hypnosis than can a neurotic condition be removed by advising a fruit fast and hot Epsom-salts baths !)

Reliance upon the healing power of Christ, or upon the power of the mind over matter, or upon meditation, will not overcome disease ; only the complete rectification of *all* the various controlling factors—physical and mental—which have made the appearance of the disease in the body possible will bring about normality.

Auxiliary Aids to Natural Healing.—Once the essential significance of the healing power of Nature in the treatment of disease has been assigned to her, all the various measures employed in Natural Treatment fall immediately into their proper place as auxiliary helpers and aids.

Fasting, dieting, osteopathy, chiropractic, massage, radiant light and heat, electrical treatment, water treatment, etc., etc., all play their part and have their value (in greater or lesser degree), *but only in so far as they allow the natural forces within the body a fuller opportunity to manifest themselves than would otherwise be possible.* To claim for any one of them that *it*, and it *alone*, can " cure " disease (as is done in many instances by misguided individuals carried away by a misconception as to the value of the special treatment in question) is as ridiculous an assumption as any of those made by orthodox Medical Science, and is a negation of the basis upon which all *Natural Treatment* rests—the sovereign power of Nature herself as the *one* healer of disease.

Osteopathy cannot cure disease ; chiropractic cannot cure disease ; massage or artificial sunlight cannot cure disease ; even fasting and dieting—the two greatest factors in the scheme of natural treatment—cannot be really said to *cure* disease ; yet each and all of them have their rightful position in Naturopathic practice, as subsidiary helpers of the omnipotent healing power of the natural forces latent within the body of each and every individual.

Nature is the only healer ! Upon this concept Naturopathy stands, and will one day achieve its rightful place as the true and only healing science.

How Nature Heals.—Having led the reader thus step by step to the realisation that, primarily and ultimately, no matter what the auxiliary methods of treatment employed may be, all Natural Cure *must and always will* depend upon the setting free within the individual sufferer of the healing powers and forces which he possesses by virtue of the fact that he is a living being, we can now turn our attention to the manner in which these same forces operate within the organism if given an opportunity to manifest themselves.

It has already been demonstrated that the essence of all disease is the accumulation in the system of waste matter and impurities due to wrong habits of living (especially dietetic), and that their *elimination* from the body is what Nature is striving for all the time ; so that it will surely not be regarded as strange, therefore, when it is said that it is *through detoxication* (through the increase of the powers of elimination of any given individual) that these same healing powers, latent within all of us, can be given a free hand to function and fulfil their self-appointed task.

To introduce what we Naturopaths call a " detoxicating régime " is to increase the individual powers of elimination ; is to throw open wide the portals of the organism, as it were, to the healer within ; is to allow the accumulated waste matters of years to be swept from clogged and infected tissues, and thus pave the way for that process of regeneration and rebuilding of muscle, nerves, blood, and vital organs which only Nature herself—the creator of all—can accomplish.

As I have already said, it is no secret as to where this cleansing and healing power resides, that is going to accomplish the work of regenerating the system of the sufferer from disease. It does not have to be evoked by spells or charmed into existence. It is there already within us at work all the time. *It is the self-same power responsible for the daily upkeep of the body.* Only in everyday life all its activities are taken up in " keeping things going " as best it can under the burden imposed upon it through the wrong feeding habits and general unhygienic ways of living of the sufferer from disease (as well as through the drugs he is taking !), and the work of self-cleansing has to be left in abeyance (except in the case of *acute disease*, when, for some reason or other, the body is enabled to make a really determined effort at self-cleansing in spite of all obstacles) ; in a general way it is only when the body's powers of elimination are enhanced, that this process of self-cleansing can be put into operation by the healer within.

Through the introduction of natural treatment in the form of fasting (that is, cessation from food) and/or scientific dieting, conjoined with measures for the increasing of skin and bowel action, exercise, deep breathing, etc., this same power within us, which is for ever looking after the body's welfare to the uttermost of its ability, but is always overworked (in the vast majority of cases), is *at last* given an opportunity to turn its attention to the work of reconstruction and repair. It is at last free to cleanse and renovate bodily mechanisms in which all the cylinders (so to speak) are choked up or sooted, *i.e.*, clogged with impurities and bodily refuse generated in the system through unhygienic ways of living, but which heretofore it has been unable to deal with. *It is at last free to rid the body of disease,* because at last it is being *helped* in its work, not hindered !

That is all there is to it ; there is no mystery attached to the matter at all (except in so far as it is part of the eternal mystery of life, which will ever remain a mystery, never to be solved even after death). Just as when, after one cuts a finger, it heals *of its own accord* if the right conditions are permitted, so, when a gastric ulcer is present or a lung is diseased, if the right methods are adopted, will the ulcer be reabsorbed and the injured stomach-lining repaired or new lung-tissue built, as the case may be, by the eternal healer Nature. Nature, the eternal and only healer, who is for ever ready to do her work of cleansing and healing, but who, thanks to his reliance upon the drugs and paraphernalia of orthodox medicine, man rarely calls on for aid, with such dire results to life and health.

CHAPTER VII

THE METHODS OF NATURE CURE : FASTING

HAVING explained to the reader in the preceding chapters exactly what Nature Cure is, what its methods of treatment are, and how it differs from the commonly accepted philosophy and practice of orthodox Medical Science, it now remains to give an account of the principal measures employed in the natural treatment of disease, and to show how these measures achieve the end they set out to accomplish—namely, the restoration of the individual sufferer from disease back to vitality and health once more.

The principal therapeutic measures of Naturopathy have already been touched on briefly in the preceding pages, but unless the reader is fully conversant with the part each of them performs in the curative process as a whole, and can see exactly how it does its work, there is a danger of its value being misunderstood, and of it being misapplied and misdirected by the sufferer from disease, who, although anxious to avail himself of Natural Treatment, sets out without a proper grasp of the matter to attempt his own self-cure along natural lines.

The present volume being intended as a complete and comprehensive guide to Nature Cure and Natural Healing, it is the author's desire to make it as practical and helpful as possible ; to that end the present chapter on fasting and the succeeding one on diet have received a great deal of attention at his hands. For he feels that only when the value of fasting and proper dieting has been *thoroughly* understood by the reader can the said reader be in a position to undertake successfully any self-treatment along the lines indicated in Part II of this book (which deals with diseases and their home treatment by natural means).

Fasting.—As the writer has gone to great pains to point out, the basis of all natural treatment is, and always must be, the release of the healing powers resident within the body of the individual sufferer from disease, to enable these same healing powers the fullest opportunity to operate within the organism, and thus bring about that restoration of normal functioning which is known as health.

Now, of the various measures employed in the course of natural treatment, some effect this release of natural healing power far more than others, and are, as a consequence, far more valuable as natural curative agents. Of these natural curative agents, by far the most important is *fasting*.

That fasting is not employed as a therapeutic agency in orthodox medical circles is evidence of how far the medical profession has allowed itself to become oblivious to the simplest facts relating to *natural* processes of cure in its attempts to overcome disease. For they would only have to look to the manner in which the members of the animal and bird kingdoms recover from disease or accident without any external aid whatsoever to see these natural processes in full operation before their eyes everywhere around them.

But the medical mind is so full of *theories* about disease, and of how it may be artificially overcome, that it never thinks of looking to see how living creatures—other than man—behave and react when confronted by the phenomenon of disease within their midst. If it did, it would learn far more that would be of value, both to itself and its patients, than any amount of laboratory research or examinations of the bodies of dead persons.

It is to the living that we must look for guidance in understanding the laws which govern life and health, and the fact that much of medical information about these vital matters is derived from the study of anatomical specimens—corpses—or from the action of germ cultures under the microscope accounts for much of present-day medical incompetence to deal with disease when face to face with it in the living organism.

In the animal world or bird world, disease as disease is very rare ; but accident or injury from conflict is of very common occurrence. One has to look to the domestic animals—those brought up under artificial conditions and fed so unnaturally—if one wishes to see disease amongst the lower orders. But whether it be in the recovery from injury or accident or the overcoming of disease, all living creatures—excepting man—display a most definite and marked uniformity of action which can only be understood when it is realised that it is the direct action of the instinct of self-preservation which is thus being allowed to come into full play for the purpose of bringing the animal or bird organism back to abundant vigour and strength once more.

The first thing one notices about all animals or birds when unwell—perhaps insects and fishes for that matter, but one cannot be sure—is that they immediately cease from taking food. *They stop eating at once.* (Anyone who possesses a pet dog or cat can verify this statement for himself the next time the said animal falls ill.) They will not take food, no matter how much they may be pressed or cajoled. They will eat nothing perhaps for a week or longer—they may sip a drop of water now and then—until the disease or malaise has run its course, and the natural "prompter" within them (the instinct of self-preservation) tells them they may now begin eating.

Fasting, then, we may see, is a natural expedient resorted to by all living creatures when unwell. It is a natural reaction to disease or malaise of any kind by which the living organism seeks to set itself in proper equilibrium again. Why, then, has man refused to take advantage of it ? Because, as man has grown more and more "civilised," his natural reactions (or instincts) have become more and more overlaid with a veneer of artificial reasoning and logic ; so that, instead of giving heed to the natural promptings from *within*, he has turned more and more to *outside agencies*—to those who can appeal to his credulity, to those in authority—for guidance in the treatment of his body when confronted with the phenomenon of disease.

This is not to say that clear thought and sound reasoning are to be discouraged, but the thought-processes of the average human being are far from clear or sound. He is at once a prey to superstition and custom, to habit and tradition ; to all the forces, in fact, which exert the wrong influence over his mind and reasoning faculties. And by giving heed to these and denying the existence of the instinctive and natural guides within, modern man does more harm to himself— not only in matters relating to health and disease, but in all the general affairs of life also—than the world at large could possibly believe or imagine.

The Physiological Processes of Fasting.—Having established the fact, then, that fasting is the most instinctive of all healing mechanisms (as exemplified in the reactions of the lower orders towards disease), let us now see exactly what takes place within the body when a fast is instituted. We shall see at once why fasting is such an invaluable natural curative agent.

During health the body is concerned primarily with the carrying on of its various functions and activities and in trying to keep these at the highest possible level of efficiency. To carry on this work effectively, it needs food. Food is therefore of absolute prime importance to life and health; and it is through the assimilation of the nutrient elements of the food we eat that the body is enabled to carry on its work.

But thanks to civilised man's ignorance as to what real food should be and what foods and what quantities of such foods should constitute his daily dietary, instead of the body deriving the maximum of benefit from the food eaten, it is at a constant disadvantage all the time. It has, first, to use up constantly some of its own invaluable materials to replace those wantonly withheld from it through the thoughtless cooking and refining habits of to-day (materials which Nature abundantly supplies for its use, and which it constantly needs for its provision if it is to function at all properly) ; and secondly, the demineralised and devitalised products which form the bulk of modern man's food are fed to it in such overwhelming quantities that the body is literally at its wit's end to know what to do with them.

Instead of a normal daily supply of the simple, unspoilt natural foods proper to it, the body receives a vast bulk of denatured and devitalised food products, which the people of to-day, thanks to their complete ignorance concerning the proper nature of food (an ignorance shared to the full by the medical profession in general also), force upon it day after day through the medium of their four " good, square " daily meals. What is the result ?

Forced to deal with this constant daily stream of excessive food materials thrust upon it by a food-ignorant owner (food materials denuded almost completely of the natural mineral elements and vital properties all proper food should contain, and without which real health is impossible), the body finds its work of keeping the efficiency of the organism at the highest possible level impeded more and more seriously each succeeding year of the individual's life. But not only is bodily efficiency thus continually impeded and impaired ; the over-plus of food materials, which the body is unable to use up or throw off, remains behind in the system to form the basis of that most puzzling of all phenomena to the orthodox medical and lay mind alike : DISEASE.

The physical basis of all disease in the human system (or animal system for that matter) is *wrong feeding* ; so that the value of fasting as a curative agent must surely begin to be apparent to the reader now ?

By not eating—or fasting—the body is given an opportunity for *self-cleansing* which the daily ingestion of a regular quantity of food renders impossible. Whilst eating is in progress—no matter how small the quantity taken daily—the body is forced to deal with it, and the positive process of *assimilation* is still the dominant process of the organism. But when food is withheld, as during the process of fasting, then assimilation stops, and the reverse or negative process of *elimination* takes its place.

The dominant physiological process in the living organism may be, therefore, either the positive one of *assimilation* or the negative one of *elimination*, but both cannot proceed to any extent side by side. (There is always a certain amount of elimination taking place daily through the usual organs of elimination, the lungs, skin, bowels, and kidneys, but that is only a subsidiary process to the main assimilative process as a whole.)

For real elimination to set in, there must be complete cessation from food. Having no food to deal with, the body is then free, at long last, to deal with the accumulations of toxic materials present within it—accumulations brought there in the first place through wrong feeding habits, and accentuated by such factors as overwork, nerve exhaustion, worry, excesses of all kinds, etc., *and which the philosophy of Nature Cure recognises as the physical basis of all disease*. Without this basic residue of toxic matter supplied to the system through the agency of wrong feeding, disease as we know it to-day would be impossible !

Thus, generally speaking, no matter what the disease, fasting is the surest medium for its elimination from the system, by virtue of the fact that through the fasting process all the body's available energy can be turned to the work of self-cleansing. For a really *clean* body, internally, means a *healthy* body ; and fasting is the body-cleanser supreme.

But to claim that fasting is a " cure-all," to assert that *all* disease—no matter of what nature or what duration—can immediately be overcome by the institution of a fast, would be foolish. Obviously the age of the sufferer, the nature of the complaint (whether acute or chronic), and various other considerations will all have to be taken into account. But this much is certain : the paramount healing value and efficacy of fasting in the treatment of disease has only to be tried for it to become manifest to all !—to even the meanest intelligence !

When will the day arrive when fasting will be given its rightful place as the foremost of all healing agencies ? When will the day arrive when people will turn to the fast as the quickest and surest path from disease to health ? Only when the world has become emancipated from the errors and blunders of orthodox medication, and turns once more to Nature for guidance in the overcoming of disease !

The Procedure of Fasting.—The age of the sufferer, the nature of the complaint, its duration, etc., are all factors which have to be considered before a fast should be set in progress, and before deciding of what duration it should be. That is why skilled naturopathic advice and attention should *always* be sought (where possible) before this most efficacious of all natural healing agencies is undertaken by the individual sufferer from disease.

Depending upon the condition of the patient, a fast may be carried on for two, three, five, ten, fifteen, twenty, or even thirty or forty days. But any fast over a week in length is by far the best carried out in a properly organised Nature Cure institution, where every convenience and aid can be guaranteed to the faster. Usually the longer the fast, the better the results ; but whether a short or long fast is undertaken, the procedure is exactly the same.

The fast may be conducted on water only, or else the patient is given fruit juices—usually orange juice—at two-hourly intervals during the day. (If the patient is unable to take orange juice, vegetable juices are given instead.) These vegetable or fruit juices are in no sense food, and serve not only to cleanse the alimentary canal (or digestive tract), but to supply the system with some of the invaluable mineral salts invariably lacking in the body of the sufferer from disease.

As soon as the fast is begun, the body begins its self-cleansing activity. The tongue begins to fur (get coated), the temperature of the body visibly lowers (as a result of the absence of food to keep up the normal body temperature), and a general sense of weakness sets in. This weakness or debility when fasting is far more marked in some cases than in others, and is in direct proportion to the stamina and vitality of the faster. With some it is more apparent at the *beginning* of the fast than later on ; but more generally it continues to make its presence felt more and more as the fast proceeds.

The prevalent idea about fasting is that one immediately begins to *starve* oneself. But fasting and starving are quite different things.

Fasts can be so prolonged that in time the faster *does* begin really to starve himself, but there is a well-marked line where fasting leaves off and starving begins.

Whilst there is surplus nutriment in the tissues to be absorbed, the body lives on it during the process of the fast. Obviously, the *living* process is not the same as when real food is eaten; but nevertheless there is quite a definite activity going on within the body, during the process of which excess acids and other surpluses are absorbed and toxins released and eliminated. *Fasting restores physiological balance.*

Starving implies *living upon one's own vital tissues,* by virtue of which the body is brought to a level of emanciation such as to render further life impossible. But a properly conducted fast—of even forty or fifty days duration—runs no risk of this taking place. It is only the confusion in foolish minds which looks upon fasting and starving as the same thing.

The deaths which are *supposed* to occur from starvation—those cases which we read about of people starving to death on derelict boats or on desert islands—these are the results of *fear* rather than actual starvation. People have got accustomed to the belief that if one goes without food for even a day then one is surely beginning to starve to death. So that when they are forced to do without food for several days, even though there is no actual danger of starvation setting in and killing them, they believe they *are* starving to death, and it is the fear thus generated in their minds which brings about the result in question. They die not from not eating, but from the fear of the consequences of not eating.

Having swept away this stumbling block in the path of fasting, this fear of what will happen if one does not eat food—a fear subscribed to by the medical profession also—we may now go on with our description of the fasting process.

Toxins and waste matter which have been slowly accumulating in the tissues for years are now brought into circulation by the self-cleansing activity of the body, and thence, through the medium of the usual organs of elimination, the skin, lungs, bowels and kidneys, finally ejected from the system. It follows from this that, during the fasting process, the kidneys (and also the heart, through which the blood, now heavily laden with toxins, continuously passes) will

51

have an additional strain placed upon them ; so that with sufferers from kidney and heart troubles, this is an additional reason why skilled naturopathic advice should be sought before a fast is undertaken.

The urine will become thick with waste matter and body poisons being thrown off during the fasting process, and the bowels will also have their share of waste material to deal with. But during a fast the usual peristaltic process which makes bowel action possible is suspended ; so that, if auto-intoxication is to be avoided, *i.e.*, if one is not to a certain extent to *reabsorb* one's own poisons back again into the system, it is imperative that the bowels should be cleansed daily whilst fasting with the warm-water enema. This is a very simple procedure, but if neglected, much of the value of the fast will have been wasted. *Auto-intoxication is the greatest danger to guard against when fasting* ; but if the enema is used as stated, the danger is easily avoided.

In fasting for chronic diseases—such as rheumatism, diabetes, heart disease, etc.—the procedure is relatively simple. The patient may be up and about all the time, making use of the sun for sunbaths, having walks, other treatment in the shape of baths, massage, manipulative treatment, etc., all to aid the fasting process. But with those suffering from serious acute diseases—such as fevers—the procedure is not the same, obviously. Here the patient is confined to bed all the time the fever is running its course, whilst, at the jurisdiction of the attendant Naturopath, hot or cold packs are applied to relieve congestion and fever. In these cases also the enema has to be used twice a day at least during the first stages of the fast.

When one is conducting a fast oneself, there are symptoms which sometimes occur which may cause alarm, but that is only because their origin and nature are not understood. For instance, palpitation sometimes sets in, and the patient believes that his heart is becoming seriously affected. But the palpitation is only due, usually, to the increased work the heart is called upon to do whilst fasting is taking place, and soon passes off without any untoward effects.

Then there is sometimes a slight rise in temperature—slight fever ; this, again, is a sign that the cleansing process is proceeding as per schedule and that the waste matter is being burnt up in the tissues. Also, as mentioned already, the tongue becomes very coated indeed, and some are led to infer from this that the fast is injuring them instead of helping them. Again a mistake ! The tongue furs more and more as the cleansing work going on inside the system proceeds, and, indeed, it is the tongue which gives the first indication that the fast has succeeded and that it is time to stop the fasting process.

When the tongue begins to *clear*, that is the time to begin thinking about stopping the fast. For a really clear tongue is evidence that the body is at last really clean *inside*. IF THE FAST IS CONTINUED AFTER THE TONGUE HAS CLEARED, THEN THE DANGER OF ACTUAL STARVATION SETTING IN ARISES.

It is only in protracted fasts that there is this waiting for the tongue to clear for the fast to be brought to a close. In the fasts of a week or ten days the tongue is rarely clear when the fast is broken.

There is a common idea prevalent that during a fast one would become so hungry that to continue it for more than a day or two would be impossible. But this is only another of the errors disseminated by those who have no practical experience of fasting and who wish to throw doubts upon its healing value.

For the first day or two there may be appetite present, but once the system becomes adapted to the new conditions, *i.e.*, the conditions of fasting, the appetite disappears altogether, and does not return until the fast has gone on sufficiently long for the tongue to clear. When the tongue has cleared—especially in those cases which are being fasted for fevers—appetite then begins to return. And it is time to cease fasting and begin eating again.

In a fast of a week or ten days or so, appetite will not have returned when the fast is first broken ; but as soon as food begins to be eaten, a really sound, healthy appetite will make itself apparent. This is because, while elimination is going on, the body has no thoughts of food—indeed, food is repugnant to it ; but as soon as food is taken again and the assimilative process set in operation, then the body shows its readiness to welcome food in no uncertain manner. (By this the writer does not mean that an enormous appetite will make itself manifest, so that the faster would feel that he must keep on eating all day to make up for the food he has missed. This is another common fallacy. No ; what is meant is, that a really clean, *healthy* appetite will develop, in contradistinction to the old appetite, which always had to be stimulated by the sight or thought of food before it developed.)

This matter of the complete repugnance for food during fasting is only realised by those who have had actual experience of a fast or have learnt something about fasting from books, and it is very significant. It shows that the body is NOT starving during a fast, otherwise there would be an *insistent demand for food* all the time from within. If the body really wanted to be fed, it would let its owner know in no uncertain fashion !

When a fast is being broken, great care must be taken not to *overeat*. Overeating after fasting is the greatest danger to be avoided, and here again skilled naturopathic advice and attention are indispensable. It depends upon how long the fast has been carried on as to how it should be broken ; but generally a sweet fruit (such as grapes) or milk are the foods chosen. Indeed, after a prolonged fast, the " Milk Cure," as it is called, is of inestimable value in building up the system anew in almost every type of disease.

Gradually, and only gradually, can the faster return to a full diet again after completing a fast of some duration. And then, having been placed upon a properly balanced dietary all the good of the fast can be maintained, and the system built up to a higher and higher level of efficiency and strength all the time. But if wrong and indiscriminate feeding is restorted to after a fast, then practically all the value of the fast will be lost.

One hears sometimes of people who, having undertaken a fast, have died during its progress, or else have had to have medical aid summoned to " rescue " them from its deleterious effects. In all these cases it is ignorance—on the part of someone or other—which is to blame. Investigations of such cases invariably show that the patient was in *too low a state vitally* for a protracted fast to be carried out, but did so without proper advice or supervision ; or else, having been forced to call in medical advice through the pressure of well-meaning but misguided friends or relatives, the unfortunate faster has been put immediately on to a " nourishing" diet by the medical man in question. Knowing nothing about the principles of fasting, these " nourishing " diets prescribed by medical men upset all the work of the fast, the body is unable to deal with the food given it—usually something like beef-tea or some meat extract, of strong stimulating power, but useless for breaking the fast on—and trouble results. This, of course, is laid at the door of the fast, but it is the dietetic treatment *after* the fast—the food on which the fast has been forcibly broken—that has set up the trouble.

The writer himself

The writer himself has read of a case of an individual who, quite misguidedly, set out on a prolonged fast to cure himself of some dread disease, without proper guidance in the matter. After thirty days his condition was so serious that medical attention was deemed necessary. The doctor who was called ordered at once a certain well-known meat extract to be given the patient ! Imagine what that means to one who has not eaten for thirty days, to be suddenly forced to eat highly " nourishing " food of this nature ! Of course he died ; and no wonder ! And the blame was all laid on the fasting, and never, of course, on the disastrous feeding method employed.

There is proof on proof to be had of the unexampled healing value of fasting in the treatment of disease, and many books have been written dealing expressly with the subject. To these the reader must be referred if he or she wishes for more detailed information on this most important of subjects. It is beyond the writer's province to deal with it more fully in the confines of the present book.

CHAPTER VIII

THE METHODS OF NATURE CURE (*continued*):

DIET

FROM what has already been said in the present book, the reader will have come to the conclusion by now that proper dieting is *the* essential factor in health production, and that, conversely, wrong feeding is the main attributive cause of disease. But as to what constitutes proper dieting as distinguishable from wrong dieting, there, I doubt not, will be considerable cloudiness of thought in many readers' minds.

Accordingly, although the writer has dealt fully with the subject of diet in its relation to health and disease in his book, *Your Diet—in Health and Disease,* the diet factor is of so vast an importance, it plays such a paramount part in the effective control and treatment of disease, that a brief introductory survey of its most salient features is absolutely necessary for the reader's sake, if he is to follow intelligently the actual subject-matter of the present chapter, which is the dietetic treatment of disease along Nature-Cure lines.

We eat in order that we may live, and for that purpose food is taken into the body ; but some people seem to have lost sight of this sole purpose of food, and instead of looking upon eating as a necessary function, to be performed with the same object as breathing and sleeping, it has come to be regarded as a means of gratifying our desires for the nice things of life (not of satisfying our hunger), and the chief criterion of its value is not that it should contain the elements most necessary for the health of our bodies, but that it should please our palates and our senses generally.

Having removed food and eating from their proper sphere, then, is it any wonder that, in most civilised countries to-day, there is a tendency to make articles of diet as artificial and pleasing to the eye as possible, without any reference to their ultimate health-value ?

This has led to the refining and demineralising of bread, sugar, and cereals (such as rice, barley, etc.), and to the preserving and potting of meat, fish, fruit, etc. Commodities such as jams, cakes, chocolates, etc., are in normal times eaten to the neglect of natural foods such as fresh fruits, salads, green vegetables, and nuts ; and where green vegetables *are* used as an article of diet they are invariably boiled, thus denuding them of their valuable salts and health-giving properties.

To those who have never thought about these matters, the artificial and refined foods we see everywhere seem to be quite all right ; and as everybody eats them and seems to thrive on them, why worry about them ? Food is food, anyway !

On the surface this sounds all right, especially as orthodox medical authorities tell us to *eat what we like.* But during the past twenty or thirty years (thanks to the work of the pioneers of Nature Cure) it is becoming more and more evident to enlightened people that the artificial and concentrated dietary of the civilised portion of this globe is *itself* in great measure responsible for the vast array of present-day diseases so vaguely attributed to germs by the same medical authorities who so glibly tell us to eat what our fancy dictates.

Orthodox Food Fallacies.—The whole trouble lies here : in their study of the diet question in its relation to life and health, the medical profession have *completely* overlooked the part played by the mineral salts contained in all natural unspoiled foods. To them, it has just been a matter of supplying the body with proteins, starches, sugars and fats, and that is all. They have reasoned that proteins are needed for body building, sugars and starches for energising purposes, and fats for warmth. That the body should need the continued supply of the mineral salts contained in all natural unspoilt foods, for *cleansing* and *purifying* purposes, has never occurred to those medical authorities who have expressly made a study of the food question.

Hence have arisen all the food anomalies of the present day. Our medical advisers see nothing wrong in a world refining and demineral-ising its foods or boiling or cooking them (all of them processes which ruthlessly remove these essential mineral elements from our food); and they also see no reason at all why the said demineralised and devitalised foods should not be consumed in any quantity or in any combination to suit the whim of the individual concerned. That ill-health follows such practices is not connected *in any way* by our leading medical authorities with the practices themselves.

Thus have arisen the criminally unwise and foolish feeding habits of to-day—habits responsible for more than ninety-five per cent. of the disease one sees on all sides around us, in young and old alike. *Their root basis lies in this medical inability to distinguish between what is good for the body and what is not !*

In addition to overlooking entirely the basic value and necessity for a liberal supply of organic mineral salts in the daily food of civilisation, and paving the way for all the food follies of to-day, the medical mind has been led yet farther astray by its preoccupation with what is known as " the calorie theory " of food. This theory, claiming, as it does, that food values can be measured in relationship to the amount of " energy " the said food is supposed to be capable of supplying to the human body, is as far from the real truth as it is possible for any theory about anything to be ; and it has been exposed in its entirety in the writer's book on diet already referred to. *Energy is something vital and fundamental to the organism. It cannot be obtained from food. But we express our energy through the food we eat.*

By ignoring the *cleansing* and *purifying* qualities of food, and looking entirely to its supposed energising or nutritive qualities as a guide to its worth in the economy of bodily welfare, the whole diet question has been turned topsy-turvy ; and thus misunderstood and misapplied, it has been presented to the present-day world by its medical advisers (whose word is taken as law in these matters) *as the final truth.* With what effect? Foods of unexcelled purifying and healing qualities, such as fruits and raw vegetables—but of low calorific value—are seldom considered as staple articles in the daily bill of fare, whilst meat and bread and similar rich foods have been given pride of place. This has led to gross overeating in the latter class of foods, with corresponding undereating in the former class of foods; and thus has been perpetrated a feeding system out of all harmony with the laws and edicts of Nature. And the result is—DISEASE.

The body, forced to deal day after day with excessive quantities of demineralised and devitalised foodstuffs, and deprived at the same time of its due share of the vital mineral elements all food worthy of the name should contain, finds its work more and more seriously impeded as time goes on, until, swamped under an accumulation of highly toxic materials brought there via the medium of the food eaten, it succumbs to the extent of having to retaliate upon its food-ignorant owner in the form of self-initiated *cleansing bouts* in order to save itself as best it can from this ever-higher-piling mass of waste toxic material deposited in its tissues through unsound feeding habits. *In other words, disease, in one or more of its manifold forms, occurs.*

The reader is by now sufficiently conversant with the philosophy of Nature Cure to understand the relationship between the periodic self-cleansing bouts referred to above and disease. In effect, these self-cleansing operations ARE disease ; for, as has already been explained, disease is nothing more than the manifestation within the body of a move towards self-cleansing, which, being misunderstood by the medical profession, is wrongly taken to be the result of germ action from without or other external cause.

Diet in Natural Treatment.—Having given the reader this necessarily brief summary of the theoretical aspect of the diet question, and shown how vitally the diet factor is linked up with the correlated problems of health and disease, we can now turn to the main subject in hand, which is the use made of the *true* science of dietetics in the natural treatment of disease.

All natural unspoilt food—that is, all food as it comes direct from the earth, plant, tree, or animal—contains the essential elements necessary for health ; and unless *all* these elements contained in natural unspoilt foods are taken into the human body through the medium of the food eaten, and the diet kept within definite limits, the result is—as we have seen—ultimate disease.

Now, as has already been explained, thanks to medical misunderstandings of this most elementary fact, the food of to-day is allowed to be robbed of most of the mineral content proper to it, through the modern habit of refining foods, and boiling and cooking them, and the demineralised residue eaten in vastly excessive quantities, without the public at large being in the least aware of what is being done to its health as a consequence. Is it any wonder, then, that *proper dieting* should form an essential part of a treatment which would restore the lost health to the food-ignorant public of to-day, which wrong feeding has filched from it ?

The elaboration of the *true*—as distinct from the false or orthodox—science of dietetics has been the work of the pioneers of the Nature-Cure movement, and, next to fasting, is the greatest curative weapon

59

3*

they possess in their fight against the ignorance which causes disease. Not everyone can enter a properly equipped institution and undergo fasting treatment ; but what a protracted fast can do quickly, sound dietetic treatment will accomplish if not so quickly, yet just as surely.

By a judicious combination of short fasts, fruit fasts, restricted diets, etc., the individual who comes under natural treatment, and who, far various reasons, cannot afford to undergo a protracted fasting cure, can be assured of as good results in the end, even if the time taken to effect a cure is longer. But in either case, whether the long fasting method has been used or the less stringent dietetic method, sound, sensible dieting MUST form an essential of the patient's *future* life, for only in this way can the possibility of further diseases be avoided.

What is the good of being cured of a disease by Nature-Cure methods if one is going back to the old ways of living and eating which have been the cause of the disease in question ? Surely such a procedure would be the height of folly. Yet many a person who has been restored to health by natural treatment, after having been given up as incurable by the medical profession, has done this very thing. With what result ? Either the same disease has returned in time or *another* disease has arisen in the system to take its place !

One cannot fly in the face of Nature's laws with impunity, and once these laws have been explained and applied in the patient's life— as in natural treatment—with real curative results, there is no excuse for backsliding. No, the individual who has been rescued from the ranks of the chronically diseased by the methods of Nature Cure must be content for ever after to live in accordance with natural laws and edicts ; and the first of these natural laws and edicts is, that his future diet should be one from which his body can derive *all* the elements necessary for its proper sustenance and active functioning, and in the quantities and proportions commensurate with his age and occupation.

Practical Dietetics.—Thus it will be seen that not only is sound dietetic treatment essential to the overcoming of disease—either in conjunction with or in place of fasting treatment—but the individual under natural treatment must be prepared to live in accordance with the dictates of sound sensible dietetics *for ever afterwards*, if he wishes to maintain his future health at the proper level of efficiency.

The necessity, then, for some practical understanding of this vitally important subject of diet must be manifest to every reader (irrespective of whether he wishes to overcome disease or prevent its appearance in the system) ; and the following summary of natural dietetic treatment cannot afford to be ignored by anyone who has his health and future welfare at heart.

(The following survey of the various dietetic treatments used in the course of natural treatment will give the reader not only a clear idea of what natural dietetic treatment *actually* is and how it works, but will place him in a position effectively to link up the knowledge thus gained with the actual directions for practical dietetic treatment given in Part II of the book.)

The All-Fruit Diet.—The necessity for a proper supply of the essential mineral salts in our daily food has been already made clear to the reader, and fresh fruits are one of the classes of food which contains these essentials to life and health in greatest abundance. That their cleansing and body-purifying properties are neglected by the medical profession in the treatment of disease is one of the tragedies of our age.

The victim of disease is always lacking in these mineral elements essential to health and sound vitality, and when he comes under natural treatment, an exclusively fresh-fruit diet is often prescribed, with a view to both cleansing his system of toxic matter and supplying to it at the same time some of the essential food minerals it so sadly needs. When first taken into the system, fruits are acid in reaction, and this fact has thrown many people into confusion as regards their health-giving value. The weak fruit acids are quickly broken down in the system, however, and valuable *alkaline* mineral salts are left behind in the tissues. It is this residue of organic alkaline mineral matter, left behind in the tissues after its oxidation, that gives fruit its great value as a curative and body-cleansing agent.

Some patients who for some reason cannot take fruit are given raw and steamed vegetables instead, which serve exactly the same purpose in the curative process.

The Restricted Diet.—This diet, which is composed of fruits and salads mainly, serves the same end as the all-fruit diet, and by introducing a variety into the dietary is preferable at times.

Fresh fruits and raw salad vegetables—as also the root vegetables—abound in food minerals such as calcium, potassium, sodium, iron, silicon, etc., all of which play a vital part in the work of the body, and if absent from our food vitally impair proper functioning. The present-day habit of looking upon fruits and salads as mere adjuncts to the daily dietary instead of basic portions of it, and of peeling, boiling, and cooking fruits and vegetables in preference to eating them raw, is one of the biggest crimes against health our age is guilty of. The placing of these victims of an artificially impoverished dietary upon an exclusive fruit and salad diet when they first come under natural treatment is the quickest and best way of supplying to their depleted system the essential food minerals so badly needed.

The Fruit and Milk Diet.—Milk is the one food which is complete in itself—that is to say, it contains all the elements the body needs for full sustenance and cleansing purposes, and as such it is highly prized in natural treatment. But *not boiled*—always raw and un-pasteurised. (It may be slightly heated in cold weather.)

When a patient has been on a fast or on the all-fruit diet, the next step is often to place him on the fruit and milk diet. This carries on the internal cleansing work the fasting and all-fruit diet has set in operation, but at the same time the body is provided with vitality and nerve and muscle-building elements also (these latter coming from the milk). Thus the fruit and milk diet is a kind of half-way house between the direct cleansing action of the fast, all-fruit diet, and restricted diet, and a definite full dietary designed to build up the patient's system afterwards.

The Full Milk Diet.—The value of milk has already been pointed out to the reader, and often, after a protracted fast, what is called the " full milk diet " is prescribed. For this, the patient is fed on raw unboiled milk only, in gradually increasing quantities, until he is sometimes taking as much as six quarts a day. The full milk diet should only be carried out under expert guidance, and its results are often little short of amazing. (At Champneys, the Tring Natural-Cure Resort, the long fast followed by the full milk diet is used with the greatest effect, and, solely by means of these two natural thera-peutic and dietetic agents, diseases as diverse as pernicious anæmia, diabetes, arthritis, Bright's disease, and neurasthenia have been cured.)

A Properly Balanced Dietary.—By means of long fasts, short fasts, the all-fruit diet, the restricted diet, the fruit and milk diet, the full milk diet, and variations and combinations of these, the patients who come under natural treatment are placed on the road to health once more. *Then* is the time for a properly balanced dietary to be given them, a dietary to which they must adhere from then on, if they wish to move steadily healthwards and not revert to their former level of bodily inefficiency.

From what has already been said in the present chapter, the reader should have little difficulty in following the logic and reasoning employed by the Naturopath in drawing up such a daily dietary for his patients, the main underlying points of which are as follows :—

For its sustenance and repair, the body requires a certain amount of protein, starchy, sugary, and fatty food elements to be supplied to it daily through the medium of the food we eat. Unfortunately for us, all these foods leave behind them in the system acid by-products, as a result of their metabolism in the tissues. This means to say that if one lives almost exclusively from these four food groups —as is the case with the average individual of to-day, with his white bread, white sugar, boiled potatoes and meat dietary—the system becomes overloaded with acid waste matter in time, and thus the way is paved for that over-acidity of the blood and tissues which is the first and basic cause of disease.

For the body to function properly, the blood and body secretions must all be alkaline ; by living on the conventional dietary of to-day this alkalinity is very soon spoilt, and, as has already been pointed out, the way paved for disease. Thus the first task of the Naturopath, when outlining a diet for the patient, is to restore the *lost alkalinity* to the blood and system generally which wrong feeding habits have destroyed. He does this by arranging a scheme of diet in which at least seventy-five per cent. of the foods eaten are definitely alkaline in reaction in the system, and only about twenty-five per cent. acid forming. That is why fruits and vegetables—especially *raw* fruits and vegetables—form the bulk of his diet. These foods are the only definitely alkaline foods in Nature.

This, then, is the real secret of all Nature-Cure dietetics, as opposed to any other forms of dieting in vogue to-day ; and explains why naturopathic results in the treatment of disease are so eminently satisfactory. Under such a scheme of dieting, the body is given all the food elements it needs for its sustenance, from the four main food groups, but the foods are so balanced with fruits and vegetables that their inherent acid-forming propensities are checked all the time by the alkalinity of the fruit and vegetable portions of the meal, and that final alkalinity of the system is achieved without which real health is impossible.

The Naturopath goes yet farther with his knowledge of the food question in arranging a suitable scheme of dietary for his patients. Even though we only select twenty-five per cent. of acid-forming foods for our dietary from the four main food groups, we have still to be careful of the choice of such foods made, for the following reason. Some foods are more acid-forming than others from the same food group; therefore it is to our advantage to select those foods for our dietary from these groups which give our system the maximum amount of the food element in question—whether protein, starch, sugar, or fat—with the formation of the least amount of acid waste matter as a result of its ingestion by the body.

Thus, a food such as meat, in addition to its extreme liability to putrefaction in the intestines and its consequent high toxicity, is very acid-forming in comparison with the amount of protein material supplied to the system as a result of its ingestion, and is not considered a good food from the Naturopath's point of view for this reason. It is therefore kept down to the very lowest limits in arranging a properly balanced dietary, and in many cases excluded altogether, where indicated—not from vegetarian or " humanitarian " motives, as the reader can now see, but for purely common-sense and scientific reasons.

Again, other foods, such as sugar, bread, and cereals, for instance, are very acid-forming if eaten in the refined state as white bread, white sugar, polished rice, etc., as are also potatoes if eaten in the conventional manner, by being peeled before cooking. But these foods are all far less acid-forming in character if eaten in the natural state as natural brown sugar, as wholemeal bread, as natural brown rice, etc., or, as in the case of potatoes, if baked or cooked in their skins. In addition, and what is equally important, such foods when eaten in their natural state retain all the valuable food minerals and other vital properties endowed them by Nature, which are sadly lacking from these same foods when eaten in the refined or cooked state.

Thus, from his knowledge of the real science of dietetics and the *practical* application of such knowledge to the foods we eat, the Naturopath is enabled to elaborate for his patients a comprehensively arranged and thoroughly well balanced dietary capable of supplying the body with all the elements it needs, in the best possible manner.

As before stated, the groundwork of such a dietary is made up of the natural foods of proved alkaline reaction, the *fruits and vegetables*. Cooked vegetables, where included, are expected to be steamed or conservatively cooked, to retain their health-giving properties, never peeled and boiled. Instead of refined and demineralised foods, such as white sugar, white bread, refined cereals, etc., only *natural whole products* are permitted ; and, as far as possible, dried fruits and honey are made to take the place of sugar, as the sugar they contain is of the best quality as judged from health standards. Butter, cream, and olive oil are the three forms of natural fats most favoured by the Naturopath ; and where protein foods are concerned, there the dairy products, eggs, cheese, and milk, are used to the fullest advantage, to the very great exclusion of flesh foods (for reasons already stated). Nuts are also highly favoured by the Naturopath as a natural form of protein food much to be preferred in many respects to animal protein.

With eggs, cheese, milk, and nuts for his main proteins, with wholemeal bread for his main starch, with dried fruits and honey for his sugars, with butter, cream, and olive oil for his fats, the Naturopath then sets about arranging his diet for his patients, in combination with fruits and vegetables, knowing that in this way he is giving their bodies *all* the food elements they need, preserving all that is best in natural food for their sustenance, whilst at the same time reducing toxicity to a minimum. (Specimens of such a scheme of dietary, properly combined and arranged, will be found in the Appendix in Part III of this book, and should be followed out by every reader, irrespective of whether he or she is in need of health advice or not, as nothing but good can accrue from the adoption of such a scheme of natural feeding.)

Such things as cakes, pastry, jams, puddings, pies, etc., are *not* included in such a scheme of dietary, for obvious reasons. Neither are condiments, sauces, etc.; or in a general way beverages such as tea and coffee. Tea and coffee are stimulants, and as such have harmful effects upon the system, in the same way as, but to a lesser degree than, alcohol. But there is no reason why a cup of weak China tea, without sugar, should not be taken in the afternoon by those who want to, providing no food is taken with it. Tea first thing in the morning, or with meals, is strictly taboo. Drinking with meals, even of water, is not permitted under naturopathic dietetic treatment, as this dilutes and weakens the digestive juices. (For what and when to drink, the reader is referred to the Appendix, where he will find full information on this most important point.)

. . . .

This, then, is the little-known science of natural dietetics as applied in the natural treatment of disease by Naturopaths the world over ; and by its aid practitioners of Natural Therapeutics are achieving the most amazing results in the curative treatment of diseases as diverse as rheumatism, diabetes, heart disease, neurasthenia, kidney disease, asthma, etc., etc., to say nothing of the " common ailments " (so called), such as catarrh, indigestion, constipation, etc. Many of the cases thus treated, and restored to health, had been previously given up as *incurable* by the leading lights of orthodox medication.

These cures—miraculous as they may seem—have simply been effected by a sound understanding of the principles of proper dieting, combined with suitable fasting and other eliminative treatment, and the application of other natural aids to health, to be dealt with in the following chapter. Obviously—with regard to diet—each individual case must be treated on its own merits to a certain extent, for what may be good for one patient may not be quite so good for another ; but, generally speaking, the dietetic rules and formulas given in the present chapter give the reader a comprehensive idea of what modern dietetics is, and how it is applied.

Then, again, every Naturopath has his own little pet ideas about dieting which he seeks to use in his own practice, but the *underlying principles* adhered to by all are as given herein.

Before concluding this chapter on natural dietetics, there is one little point that needs touching on. That is the question of *vitamins*. Many readers will no doubt be surprised that no reference to vitamins has been made in the review of natural dietetic theory given in the present chapter. The " vitamin " is the most-talked-of factor in modern dietetics, as far as orthodox dietitians, the Press, and public are concerned, but it has little place in the scheme of natural dietetics as outlined in this book. The pursuit of the " vitamin " has served to throw more people off the track where correct dieting is concerned than any other factor.

When we realise that it is *alkalinity* we need, if we wish to preserve or regain health, then the part played by the natural organic alkaline mineral salts found in all natural unspoilt food will be at once apparent to all. That is why these organic food minerals are always stressed so much in natural dietetics. Vitamins, in so far as they play a part in building up health, can only do so *in conjunction with* the aforesaid organic mineral salts, *and have no actual curative value of their own.*

Vitamins are the *living* elements in all natural unspoilt foods, and if one is living on a dietary rich in natural foods, such as those always advised for patients in naturopathic practice, the said patient can be sure he is obtaining all the vitamins necessary to life and health, and, what is more important still, all the organic mineral salts the body requires for its efficient functioning.

For a fuller exposition of the diet question in its relation to health and disease the reader is again referred to the writer's book, *Your Diet—in Health and Disease*, published at 10s. 6d. net (11s. 3d. by post) by the HEALTH FOR ALL PUBLISHING CO.

．　　．　　．　　．　　．　　．

SPECIAL NOTE *re* " HEALING CRISES."—In many cases where natural dietetic and other treatment has been instituted, the patient is often alarmed to find all sorts of unwelcome visitations appearing, such as heavy colds, eruptions of boils, diarrhœa, skin eruptions, etc. These are often taken to show that the treatment is tending to make the patient *worse* ; but this is not at all the case. These sudden colds, eruptions, etc., which put in an appearance when natural treatment is begun, are what in naturopathic circles are called " healing crises." They are a manifestation of Nature's healing and cleansing work, and are a sign that the treatment is being effective in getting down to the root of the trouble and dislodging toxic matter from deep-seated structures and organs and bringing it to the surface of the body for final elimination from the system. Such " healing crises " are the very best evidence that the treatment is doing good ! (See also Appendix : " Complications which may Arise during Treatment.")

CHAPTER IX

OTHER FORMS OF NATURAL TREATMENT

Hydrotherapy—General Hygiene—Psychotherapy—Spinal manipulation
Osteopathy and Chiropractic—Electrical treatment—Radiant heat—Massage
—Artificial sunlight—Other treatments.

THE two main features of Natural Treatment—features which give
it at once its essential distinction from orthodox medicine or any
other school or branch of healing—are its reliance upon *fasting* and
scientific dietary as its basic therapeutic agents, and its refusal to
employ any method of auxiliary treatment which is not in every
sense of the word natural.

Thus many forms of electrical treatment and even herbalism are
taboo to the real authentic Naturopath, as these seek to stimulate the
system into activity along lines which are not always entirely in
accordance with natural laws and usages. But other measures there
are which the Naturopath adopts in his work to supplement the direct
cleansing and healing action of fasting and proper dietetics, and these
form the subject-matter of the present chapter.

Hydrotherapy.—The medical profession has become so wedded to
the drug habit that it spurns to use even water—either internally or
externally—in anything like the proper proportions its undoubted
therapeutic qualities demand. But the Naturopath makes the fullest
use of the cleansing and healing qualities of hot and cold water.

For cleansing the bowels during fasting or during the early part
of natural treatment in cases where sluggish bowel action is present,
the warm-water enema is invaluable. There is a prejudice against
the use of this harmless mechanism in many quarters (particularly the
medical), but it is based entirely on ignorance. Where purges and
laxatives, by lashing the inactive bowels into activity, perform their
work with the worst results to the patient's after-health, the enema
does its work with ease and precision and without any undue after-
effects whatever.

The enema is not intended to be used *continuously* by patients
undergoing natural treatment, but only during the beginning of the

treatment—until, in fact, the bowels have been set working properly for themselves as a result of the treatment instituted.

Constipation is one of the easiest of diseases to overcome by natural treatment, but who has been cured of this common complaint as a result of taking purges ? The condition inevitably becomes worse as a result of these practices.

The enema is the only form of water treatment that is applied *internally* by the Naturopath ; but as an *external* healing and cleansing agent, water is used in a variety of ways.

The hot bath, the cold bath, the warm bath, the hot Epsom-salts bath, the sitz-bath (either hot or cold), are all forms of water treatment which are used in conjunction with the other forms of natural treatment with the best results, and are applied to the case in hand solely in conformity with the nature of the complaint and the condition of the patient.

For instance, the morning cold sitz-bath is one of the finest tonic agencies it is possible to employ in revitalising a depleted system, but some people would find it too rigorous a measure for them. The Naturopath has to use his discretion in applying it, therefore, in cases under treatment.

Then, the hot Epsom-salts bath is a very fine cleansing agent, but people with weak hearts are not prone to get the best results from its use, because it is too enervating in its immediate effects for them. Here again discretion in treatment is necessary.

One of the greatest uses of water in natural treatment is in the form of *wet packs*. Cold packs are made by wringing out some linen or similar material in cold water, wrapping it round the area or part of the body to be dealt with, and covering with some warm flannelling. The cold application, covered as it by a warm material, has the effect of drawing out the inflammation, pain, and swelling in a manner little short of miraculous. (Most especially is the wet pack used in abating fevers.) When one considers what deleterious and harmful drugs the medical profession employs for the achieving of the same purpose, it makes one wonder if the medical mind, in its slavish adherence to drugs, is not becoming thereby completely unable to use common sense in its work at all, despite the undoubted real talent it possesses. (The truth is, however, these natural methods being simple, they are deemed unworthy of medical attention ; they are contemptuously assigned to the class known as " old-wives' treatments," and their obvious merits ignored in favour of complicated and dubious drugs and vaccines which satisfy the modern medical craving for something which mystifies and at the same time overawes the ever-credulous public mind, and does homage to the magic and mystery of " SCIENCE "!)

General Hygiene.—The same motive which turns medical attention away from the use of hydrotherapeutic measures in the treatment of disease, in favour of drugs and vaccines, is responsible for the small store set by the medical fraternity upon the value of fresh air, sunlight, exercise, and bodily hygiene, in the curative treatment of disease. Yes, the medical profession TALKS about the value of these things to their patients, but that is all. By their manner and actions they let it be implicitly understood that the real curative agents are the drugs they employ or the operations they perform. General hygiene ? That is merely by the way.

To the Naturopath, however, the use of fresh air, sunlight, exercise, and such-like measures forms an essential part of his treatment. What is the good of giving a man who suffers from chronic bronchitis (for instance) drugs, and doing nothing more ? Yet that is what the medical profession does ! Besides being told *what to eat*—the most important essential of all—he needs to be told how to breathe deeply and properly, how to get the maximum of benefit from the air and sunshine so liberally provided for our use by Nature, to ventilate his bedroom properly, to wear sensible clothing which allows his skin to breathe (not effectively clog up his pores) ; and so on. *That* is general hygienic treatment, and all natural treatment worthy of the name makes use of it.

In addition to not really knowing what to eat, the people of to-day have not the faintest idea of how to dress correctly, what footwear to wear, what rest they need, what exercise to take—in short, civilisation has rendered them completely unable to take care of themselves in a sensible, hygienic, and healthy manner.

Look at the clothing men wear, for instance ! (The modern woman is not so bad ; but her mother and grandmother ! !) Modern man has not the slightest idea how to dress for health. He wears underwear which effectively prevents his skin from breathing—in which practice he is aided and abetted by his medical adviser, who tells him " always to wear wool next the skin "!—he wears ridiculous hats which interfere with the growth and health of the hair, boots or shoes which prevent proper action of the feet and correct walking, collars which prevent him from breathing comfortably, and so on and so on. Added to this, he is constantly inhaling the smoke from tobacco into his lungs instead of the air he so much needs, the modern motoring habit renders him less and less capable of using his body for proper exercise, he stays up late at night when he ought to be obtaining the sleep and rest his body needs, he gets up late in the morning in consequence—when the demand of his natural urges and instincts is for early rising—the atmosphere he breathes in office or shop is debilitating ; and what does he do to put matters right ? Nothing !

When he is unwell—and who would not be, living in this fashion in conjunction with the endless food crimes he is daily perpetrating ?—modern man visits the doctor, who tells him his illness is due to " the weather " or to " a germ," gives him some medicine, and *leaves it at that* !

Let not the *female* reader imagine that it is only modern man who is wrong in his ways of living. Modern woman, although better than modern man in some ways, is far worse in others. Between them they offer a sorry spectacle to the gods who gaze down upon our planet in search of signs for *real* men and women to whom to hand on the torch of future divinity !

General hygiene, then, forms an essential part of Nature-Cure treatment, and by means of physical exercises, deep-breathing exercises, sun-bathing, rules for general living, etc., etc., the patient under natural treatment is led back to a more natural mode of existence—a mode of existence essential if real health is to be regained and subsequently maintained.

Psychotherapy.—Some people would maintain that psychotherapy should be placed first in the list of natural treatments, as the mind is the prime causative factor in all disease and the most potent factor in its removal from the human system. But the mental and physical are so intertwined that it is impossible to say exactly what cause is mental and what effect physical and *vice versa*.

There is no doubt, however, that the mental factor plays a part in *all* disease—to a greater or lesser degree—and so psychotherapy forms an essential part of all treatment which would be in the highest degree effective.

What does the writer here mean by psychotherapy? NOT psycho-analysis, or faith healing, or spiritual healing of any kind, but just the trained use of mental suggestion and plain commonsense psychology applied to the worries and problems of the patient's life.

Worry is one of the most potent factors in the undermining of the system, and if a patient has been brought low by worry, combined with wrong feeding and unhygienic living, surely this side of the matter must receive attention from the Naturopath also? (The medical recipe for worry is—don't worry! Which, although well meant, is, to say the least, worth very little.)

Then there is the neurasthenic and neurotic patient. In some of these cases psycho-analysis and other intensive forms of applied psychological treatment are not only helpful, but absolutely necessary. But not every Naturopath—indeed, very few—use these specialised forms of psychological treatment in their work. Special cases expressly demanding such a form of treatment have to be sent to the competent people capable of carrying it out. But *every* Naturopath worthy of the name uses applied psychology and common-sense suggestion in dealing with his patients. Only in this way can he achieve the fullest success in his work.

Properly applied suggestion—as the recent interest in *auto-suggestion* has shown—is a most effective healing agent. But unless it *is* properly applied, a great deal of its healing force is lost to the patient. The reason why *auto-suggestion* and psychotherapeutic agents of a similar nature have not achieved the success expected of them and claimed for them in certain quarters is because the physical side of the case has been *entirely neglected* during such treatment, and all attention focussed on the mental.

In natural treatment the physical and the mental *both* receive their due share of attention, with the best results to the case in hand.

Spinal Manipulation: Osteopathy and Chiropractic.—Spinal manipulation—both osteopathic and chiropractic—is used to a great extent in Nature-Cure work. Although osteopathy and chiropractic exist as separate healing mechanisms in the world of healing, and have their ardent advocates, who see in them the sole and only road to cure, osteopathy and chiropractic *alone* will achieve no lasting results in the effective treatment of disease. Combined with other forms of natural treatment, however, they are very efficacious indeed in bringing about the quickest possible return to health of the patient under natural treatment.

Osteopathy and chiropractic are rival forms of spinal manipulation, their birthplace being America, and each has its own theory of disease and cure by means of manipulation of the spine. They both assert that disease originates in the system in the first place as a result of the interference with blood and nerve supply through lesions in the spinal column, and that by correct manipulation of the spinal vertebræ these lesions may be removed and health restored to the patient under treatment. Their points of difference are simply in the significance they attach to the origin of the spinal lesions in question and the methods of manipulation they adopt to remove them. Most Naturopaths—although disagreeing fundamentally with osteopaths and chiropractors as to the origin and nature of disease—use *both* these methods in their work, with the most beneficial results.

Regarded as philosophies set forth to give a comprehensive understanding of the cause, nature, and treatment of disease, both osteopathy and chiropractic must be deemed inadequate from the Nature-Cure point of view; but this does not alter their undoubted healing value when used in conjunction with other forms of natural treatment, such as fasting, dieting, etc. There is a tendency for some people to regard every osteopath or chiropractor as a " Nature-Cure " man, simply because he does not use orthodox methods of treating his patients, but uses what is called " drugless healing." But this view is essentially wrong. Nature-Cure practitioners use both osteopathy and chiropractic, but every osteopath and chiropractor is not therefore a Nature-Cure practitioner ; any more than a masseuse is a Nature-Cure practitioner because massage is used in natural treatment. (It is important for the reader to remember this, as it will save a lot of confusion of thought on the matter. Many people who wish to undertake Nature-Cure treatment have gone in ignorance to an osteopath who was *not* a Nature-Cure man, and did not receive, in consequence, all the benefits from treatment that they would have received if they had visited an *authentic* Naturopath in the first place.)

The theory of disease and cure put forward by the founders of osteopathy and chiropractic may sound rather fantastic at first sight, but there is a great deal in it, and the successes being achieved by osteopaths and chiropractors in the treatment of all forms of disease must make these theories and views worthy of serious attention. The whole point lies here :

In common with the various other shibboleths of orthodox medicine, the brain is viewed entirely wrongly in its function by the medical mind. The brain is to them the source of all *nervous* activity, but in reality this is not the case. It is to the *autonomic* or *sympathetic nervous system* (so called), and *not* to the cerebro-spinal system of nerves (that directly under the control of the brain), that we have to turn for the source of motive force in nerve activity. *This* fundamental truth the founders of osteopathy and chiropractic have realised —either consciously or unconsciously—and founded their respective systems of treatment upon it.

The nerves from the sympathetic nervous system supply nerve force to all the important structures of the body, such as the heart, lungs, liver, stomach, ears, eyes, etc., and join up with the cerebro-spinal system of nerves by means of definite nerve connections. *These nerve connections are capable of being directly controlled by means of manipulation at the points where the various cerebro-spinal nerves make their exit from the spinal column.* Thus, by judicious spinal manipulative treatment, the action of the heart, lungs, stomach, liver, eyes, ears, and other important organs and structures of the body can be *directly* affected by the manipulator. So that the value of spinal manipulation is obvious. By his manipulative work the osteopath or chiropractor can quicken up and improve nerve and blood supply to affected organs and parts, and generally reorganise the action of the various body structures and organs, without in the least having to deal with these same organs and structures themselves. He exerts his control at the spine, by means of his manipulative activities, and the nerves of the body do the rest.

The above must not be taken by the reader as a complete exposition of the osteopathic or chiropractic theory—it is not. The whole atmosphere is very much clouded by talk of subluxations, contractions, the removal of spinal inhibitions, etc.; but the foregoing will serve to show that there *is* a relationship, and a *most definite relationship*, between manipulation of the spine and the health of the body. And that is all the writer is bent on showing in the present instance.

A great deal of mystery attaches to osteopathic and chiropractic treatment these days—a mystery which many osteopaths and chiropractors sedulously foster in their patients' minds, it must be admitted. But in reality the whole thing is very simple, as indeed most good things are.

Electrical Treatment.—During the past twenty years there has been quite a craze for electrical forms of treating disease—a craze in which the medical profession has been very much to the fore. But treatments of this nature are—in most cases—just as " unnatural " as are the other methods of orthodox medication.

Electrical treatments of the " high-frequency " sort do nothing but *stimulate* the system into enforced activity. This is entirely wrong from the therapeutic point of view, as enforced action of the various structures of the body through electrical stimulation leads only in the end to further depletion of nerve force, which defeats the end for which the treatment was instituted in the first place. Thus often under electrical treatment a fair amount of progress may *seem* to be made to begin with, but it is never maintained ; in most cases it is lost in the end.

Quite a number of Naturopaths employ electrical treatments of some sort or other in their work, but these are generally of a different nature from those employed by the orthodox medical man, who combines with his drugging the modern craze for " electro-therapeutics." (How impressive are these monuments of the electrician's art ! And how duly impressed are the patients by what they conceive to be one more sign of the onward march of victorious Medical Science !)

No, the electrical apparatus used in Nature-Cure treatment is of a different nature from that. The *electro-magnetic blanket*, for instance, is very much used. It is a very useful means of inducing *elimination*, and, in conjunction with fasting, dieting, manipulation, etc., performs very satisfactory work in cleansing the body of deleterious waste matter which has been interfering with proper systemic functioning.

Radiant Heat, employed for the purpose of breaking down muscular contractions, etc., is very useful too, and, in conjunction with manipulative and massage treatment, does some very good work in the field of practical naturo-therapeutics. Then, again, the curative and tonic effect of *artificial sunlight* is very great, but this form of electrical treatment is being dealt with on its own.

There is a tendency for many patients to put more faith in the action of an electrical machine or an apparatus of a similar nature than in the basic methods of Nature-Cure treatment such as fasting and dieting, especially so if they see some marvellous-looking piece of mechanism, and are made to believe that its curative effects are in proportion to its looks and size. (Alas, the human mind is very credulous and easily taken in !) And so, for purely " psychological " reasons, many a person has been given some showy form of electrical treatment, *not* because the practitioner thought it would be of any help, but merely to satisfy the patient's craving for something to be *really* done for him, the said patient not being able to see that dieting, exercise, general hygiene, and similar forms of treatment were really doing the healing work.

Generally speaking, the less part that electrical treatment and apparatus play in the treatment of the Naturopath, the better. Natural means are always the best, and give the best results, even if they do not impress so much by merely outside appearances.

Massage.—Quite a fair amount of use is made in Nature-Cure treatment of massage ; and this form of treatment is so well known to all that there is little need to go into its nature in this chapter on the various auxiliary measures employed in the natural treatment of disease.

Sufficient to say that massage is a helpful means of forcing toxic matter out of the superficial areas of the body, and getting it carried round by the blood-stream prior to being finally eliminated from the system via the kidneys. Before any kind of waste matter in the body can be thrown off, it *must* be brought into active circulation in the blood-stream. This, massage does, and is in consequence a useful adjunct to the Naturopath in his work.

The medical profession also uses massage, but there, in its hands much of its efficacy is wasted, owing to the suppressive forms of treatment used at the same time.

Artificial Sunlight.—Artificial sunlight is one form of electrical treatment which can be fully accepted as being in direct line with natural methods of healing. The artificial sunlight lamp is used to take the place of real sunshine, whose therapeutic value is inestimable, but whose presence in a country like England is so variable and uncertain as to render it of little direct use in therapeutic work.

Strange to say, many people who would disdain to make use of natural sunshine as a therapeutic agency look upon the artificial variety as being something truly miraculous. The medical world, for instance, has tried to use artificial sunlight treatment in its work to a great extent recently, only to declare, sorrowfully and with due and impressive solemnity, that it is *not a cure for disease* !

But who said that artificial sunlight is a cure for disease ? No one would say that ordinary sunshine is a cure for disease, so why should the artificial variety be a " cure-all "? The fact remains, however, that natural sunshine and artificial sunshine are *both* of extreme value in therapeutic work as *auxiliary* healing agents. Used in conjunction with fasting, dieting, manipulation, etc., they form a very useful and helpful healing mechanism. But alone ? How can we expect them to perform miracles ? Only the medical mind looks for miracles in the healing art. Real health has to be *earned* by the patient ; it cannot be given back to him for nothing, merely through swallowing drugs, or sitting before a machine or artificial sunshine lamp. When will the world understand this ?

Real sunshine is always to be preferred to the artificial variety ; but it is very hard to make use of it adequately when needed. That is why the sunlight lamp has become so useful in Nature-Cure work.

Other Treatments.—New treatments of one kind or another are always springing up these days, and the Naturopath must always be on his guard to see that they are not in conflict with the principles of sound Naturopathy before employing them in his work. People are always craving for something new, and the feeling in many quarters is to pander to this craving. But it is a craving that should be severely *dis*couraged, rather than *en*couraged.

The fundamentals of Natural Treatment are plain before our eyes. They are fasting, dieting, general hygiene, psychotherapy, manipulation, etc. By their aid, thousands of sufferers from disease are being restored to health daily. Why look for other forms of treatment, then ?

The natural curative process *cannot* be speeded up ; one cannot be *rushed* from disease into robust health. And any new treatment which is brought forward as something which will speed up this natural curative process must be examined with great caution before being made use of in natural therapeutic work. The medical mind, by its very outlook, is a ready prey to any new " miracle-working " treatment that may arise at any time, with results that are fore-doomed to failure, simply because these treatments one and all follow along lines which run *counter* to Nature.

X-ray therapy, gland therapy, vaccine treatments, radium treat-ment, are only a few of the new treatments the medical world has run after in its frantic search for a " cure-all " for disease, but without avail ; and the result will always be the same, no matter what the treatment is, until the medical fraternity learns to look at disease from a totally different angle—from the angle of Natural Therapeutics.

New treatments are not needed in Nature-Cure work, because the old ones are performing their function fully. It is only in circles like the medical, where the old forms of treatment are failing more and more completely to do the work claimed for and expected of them, that new forms of treatment are eagerly sought for. In this lies the completest indictment of orthodox Medical Science that can be obtained. Does it not *show* that the old forms of treatment are useless ? Else why look for new ones to take their place ?

Some people, even with a Nature-Cure leaning, look to *herbalism* as something which can with benefit be incorporated into natural therapeutic work. But this is a very moot point. The line that divides drugs from herbs is sometimes very thin indeed. It is true that herbalism is, in many ways, to be preferred to orthodox medicine, but that does not allow it to rank with Nature-Cure treatment. The genuine Naturopath does *not* make use of herbalism in his work. He keeps to the purely natural measures enumerated in this and the two preceding chapters.

At the present moment there is a form of treatment being used by some Naturopaths known as bio-chemic treatment. It consists of giving to the patient certain *tissue salts* in homœopathic quantities to increase the action of the fasting, dieting, and other forms of natural treatment employed in the case. As a general rule, however, the use of even these slight additional aids to healing is not desirable. The patient must be made to understand that it is the *natural forces within himself which do the work of healing*, not external aids and appurtenances which come out of a bottle or capsule.

CHAPTER X

THE NATURAL ROAD TO HEALTH

THE natural road that leads to health lies now open to the reader. Will he traverse it ? It is the road every sufferer from disease must pass along if he wishes to achieve the goal of his desires. Medical treatment has been shown to be worthless as a curative medium ; Nature-Cure treatment, and Nature-Cure treatment alone, will bring back the health the sufferer from disease is lacking.

It may strike many people as strange that Nature Cure, considering its overwhelming merits as a curative medium as compared with what orthodox Medical Science can offer, should so far have received so little attention from orthodox medical quarters—should, indeed, have met with antagonism and opposition from those whose expressed desire it is to serve the community as best they can in relieving it of its ills and sufferings. The average person would think that our leading medical authorities would be the first to welcome any form of treatment which offered a solution to the complex problem of disease, no matter how much out of line with orthodox views it might be. But, unfortunately, this is not the case at all.

In a recent little book Professor Soddy, the eminent scientist, says: " Hardly any step in knowledge or advance in thought, however commonplace to-day, has ever been made without those deeming themselves authorities in the matter being hostile and opposed to it when first made." And with none is this more so than with our medical scientists where new methods of healing are concerned !

The Reason for Orthodox Opposition to Nature Cure.—Ever jealous of guarding their position and authority, and ever afraid of having it undermined, no one is more opposed to methods of treating disease which are in the least degree " unorthodox " than these leaders of medical thought and opinion. New methods and treatments are judged NOT (as sensible and thoughtful people would think they should be) on their merits as curative agents—on their ability to cure, that is—but on whether they conform with *accepted* medical dogmas and theories ! Thus nothing which is in the slightest degree out of harmony with accepted medical teaching is allowed to be used in orthodox medical practice. And thus inevitably does the orthodox medical world cut itself off from any opportunity of getting its obsolete views and theories about disease into a true perspective with reality.

The line of divergence between orthodoxy and Nature Cure is so marked that the one cannot be taken up without the other being relinquished. One cannot practise orthodox medicine and Nature Cure *at one and the same time*. Herein lies the reason for medical antagonism not only to Nature Cure, but to all methods of treating disease which threaten the groundwork of accepted conventions about disease.

Is the general medical practitioner to give up all he knows and has struggled for, and start afresh with a new technique of healing which will take him years to acquire ? Are the great medical authorities—with their Harley Street consulting-rooms and knighthoods and honours as distinguished medical savants—to admit their ignorance about disease and cure, to throw all this away and start afresh at the beginning, with a new theory of disease and new methods of cure ? These are questions which strike deep into the very depths of human nature, and are the real—though unadmitted and un-acknowledged—reasons for medical reluctance to accept fairly and without prejudice newer and other methods of treating disease than those they make use of themselves.

No, it is not to be wondered at that these same great medical authorities—not to mention the general medical practitioner—look with disfavour at any new healing mechanism which threatens the foundations upon which their fortune, position, and security rest. Nature Cure is met with all the opposition and misrepresentation with which any new theory or invention—no matter in what realm of thought or activity—is met by those whose livelihood or prestige is threatened by its general acceptance and introduction into the social life of the community.

It is not here hinted that it is *solely* the monetary and personal motive which prevents Nature Cure securing its rightful hearing from those in medical authority—and there can be no doubt that, were it once accepted generally, the need for trained medical advisers, specialists, hospital staffs, etc., would tend to diminish rapidly to the vanishing-point, instead of the reverse as at present—but, nevertheless, it is a dominant and powerful *unconscious* mental factor which enters into all medical considerations of the subject, and, no matter what reasons the medical world *itself* might give, must never be lost sight of in seeking for the true reason for medical opposition to Nature Cure and allied methods of treating disease.

The World Fifty Years Hence ?—So Medical Science continues to look for the cure of disease along the lines it persists in believing to be the right ones, and, despite all that can be shown to the contrary, it will accept nothing which comes from sources *outside* its own closed circle. The spectacle thus opened up of a world still dominated by orthodox medical rule in, say, fifty years' time, is, to say the least, far from comforting. Imagine what a world it will be !

Every child will have its tonsils and appendix removed at birth, no doubt, to prevent these *unnecessary* organs becoming the centres of possible future infection ! Each and every unfortunate infant will have doubtless not less than thirty or forty different vaccines and sera injected into it, to prevent it contracting any of the " usual " complaints of infancy or early childhood ! Everyone who has the slightest suspicion of visual deficiency (from age two and upwards) will be immediately forced to wear glasses for the remainder of his or her unfortunate existence—much to the benefit of the optician and oculist of the day, who will no doubt wax fat and endow hospitals and clinics for the immediate fitting of all infants as soon as born with suitable spectacles to *prevent* future eye trouble ! New and ever more complicated diseases will be springing up to baffle the already overworked minds of the medical practitioners of the day—and no wonder ! The " common " ailments, such as colds, catarrh, indigestion, constipation, etc., will be taken as a matter of course—everyone will have them ! Cancer, rheumatism, Bright's disease, diabetes, heart disease, etc., will have been creeping up year by year to at length have reached colossal figures ! The yearly consumption of worthless medicinal drugs and patent medicines will have likewise reached figures of due proportion ! Surgical operations will have attained such a pitch of perfection and such a vogue that it will be hard to meet anyone who has not left some part of his anatomy behind on some hospital operating-table or other—only to discover after it was too late that his general health is, after all, worse, *not* better, as he had been led to believe it would be by his medical adviser ! The general style of living and eating of to-day, not having been censured in any way, will have grown worse and steadily worse, so that people with good teeth or healthy bodies will have grown so scarce as to be almost impossible to find ! . . . And so on and so on to an infinity of pathological horrors ! !

What a world it will be ! And how are we going to escape from it, or give our children the opportunity to escape from it ? *There is only one way.* Each and every intelligent individual must accept and put into practice in his own life, and in the lives of those dependent upon him, the laws and principles of common-sense healing and healthy living set forth under the heading of " Nature Cure " in the present book. THERE IS NO OTHER ALTERNATIVE ! If the world as a whole—either through ignorance or indolence—refuses to rescue itself from the disease-increasing despotism of orthodox medication, then each and every individual possessed of enough initial understanding, courage, and determination, and assured of the proper guidance, must do so for himself. It is expressly for this one purpose —to enable each individual so inclined to rescue himself from the fate that besets all the members of the human family who pay homage to medical suzerainty and authority—that this present volume is intended. Will it accomplish its purpose ? That is for every reader to decide in his or her own individual case !

A True Story.—Frequently in *Health for All* there is a prize given for a true story, a story written by a reader who has been cured by natural means of some disease or other which orthodox forms of treatment have been powerless to overcome. These stories are, without exception, monuments of *living* praise to the teachings and doctrines of that philosophy of Nature Cure it has been the object of the writer to put before his readers in the present volume ; and they range from such titles as " How I Overcame Chronic Constipation " and " How I Defeated Diabetes " to " How I Overcame Consumption " and " How Natural Treatment Cured Me of a Paralytic Stroke." There is nothing so convincing as personal testimony ; it *says* far more than anything else can. And it has struck the writer that he can conclude the present chapter—and incidentally the first portion of the present book—in no better way than by giving one of these true stories for the reader's benefit. It will show him, in a way nothing else will, what Natural Treatment *can* and *does do daily* in the effective treatment of disease.

In one of the early issues of *Health for All* there appeared a story entitled " From Operating-table to Star's Dressing-room," written by a young lady named Dorothy May—a name which, we are told, cloaks the personality of a well-known young actress—which is in my opinion one of the best that has appeared in that enterprising health publication, both for style of writing and for the material it contains. It runs as follows:—

" I freely used what was destined to be almost the only wholly healthy part of my body left to me—my lungs—when I announced my arrival into this world of suffering twenty-six years ago as an apparently healthy infant of eight pounds.

" I now look back with horror upon my childhood, and remember most of my birthdays as milestones upon a road of bodily discomfort. I am told that at the tender age of one month I was carried past a child who had whooping-cough, and that I immediately contracted this ailment. Coughs, colds and rashes followed in rotation, and soon, nourished upon three meat meals a day, with all the accumulated lunacy of the North-Country ' high tea,' I was never off the doctor's doorstep.

" My parents had a standing order with a chemist for a lotion with which to cool ' heat-spots ' (forsooth !), and I passed steadily and expensively through the old-fashioned influenza, mumps, growing-pains, tonsilitis, running eczema, discharging ear, measles, a splendid six-months' bout of anæmia with delirium to garnish, a broken arm and finger, yearly gland trouble and sore throat, with a set-piece in the shape of scarlet fever at the age of fourteen ! Strangely enough, after a six-weeks' isolation in a fever hospital, without any medicine, I re-entered a rather jolly world with a clean bill of health, which lasted for four years, in which I grew tall and fat.

" Leaving school, my parents forbade me to entertain any thoughts of the stage career upon which I had set my hopes, and apprenticed me to a firm of drapers. The incredibly long hours, and the hard work in the winter, so sharpened my appetite that I overtaxed my digestion, and, with very irregular meal-times, I became acutely miserable with indigestion. It soon became impossible for me to eat orthodox food, and my health broke down, necessitating my leaving my employment.

" Then followed a period of domestic duties in my home, upon a diet of lightly boiled fish, white bread and butter, and sponge cake, until boredom drove me once again into the labour market. This time

I went as nurse-secretary to a dental surgeon and receptionist to a physician and surgeon. For a year and a half I worked ten hours daily, with only an hour off for the increasingly painful ordeal of eating my meals. The last three months saw me living on soda and milk, and I reluctantly had to resign from my interesting work. Once more my feet crossed the same doctor's doorstep upon which I had stamped in my youth, and for a year I tried to resume a full meat diet—with four bottles a week of bismuth and pepsin, and cascara compound mixed with liquid petroleum. I was by now the picture of the typical civilised ' Miss ' of the age, tall, pallid, with unconvincing spots of rouge on thin cheeks, emaciated and listless, and so weary that when, after falling back to my milk-and-soda diet, my doctor told me that if I had a serious illness I could not possibly live, I was not very disturbed and wondered what it would be like to die. Then a surgical examination, and the pronouncement of the presence of a gastric ulcer and the necessity for an operation, which I declined —without thanks !

" I dragged on, existing on soda and milk, being sick every evening, until something happened which changed the whole course of my life, bodily, mentally, and financially.

" In a very cold January spell I was taken so ill with bronchitis that I was allowed to be without milk, as it made me cough so hard that I broke a blood-vessel in my nose, and I was given as many oranges as I craved to quench my terrible thirst. For four weeks I was in bed in an equable temperature, during which time an old school-friend who had married a food reformer came to see me, bringing grapes, a jar of honey from her own bees, and a copy of *Health for All*.

" The first intimation to my long-suffering family of my new régime was my scornful refusal of oyster soup, and the plea for two dozen oranges a day. They refused, and I did a hunger-strike, until hoarse quotations lifted bodily from *Health for All* brought a veritable orange grove into my sick-room.

" When I arose from my bed I attacked shredded cabbage and pulverised carrot with more determination than enjoyment, and Granose biscuits made my first solid meal for months a pleasure, instead of a torture. To progress to raw vegetable salads of beet, turnip, carrot, and cabbage was very slow work, but I ate nothing else but these and Granose biscuits until I began to find them delicious, and added raisins, soaked chopped prune—all this whilst drinking much orange juice and hot water for supper, and assisting my once chronic constipation with a handful of dates well chewed on retiring.

" Week by week I enlarged my diet—not without set-backs—afire with exploration and full of new hope and strength, adding, gradually, St. Ivel lactic cheese, eggs lightly boiled, and grated apple for supper. If Adam felt as I did when I ate my first rosy pippin for six years, there were no regrets in his heart as he turned his back on the Garden of Eden and the flaming barrier !

" Then I began to breakfast on raisins, cold brown bread toast and butter. I added conservatively cooked vegetables to my ' big meal ' of spring salad at one p.m., and had Granose biscuits and a ripe banana for tea at five p.m., and drank my beloved orange juice and honey on retiring. At no time did I eat and drink together. On this diet I continued for eight months, and at the approach of autumn I gradually added all manner of savoury dishes.

" Going ' all out,' I undertook two fasts at six-months' intervals— one of three days on water, and the other of six days on orange juice and water, not forgetting the daily internal bath. My constipation was now cured, and I omitted the dates. I substituted raw fruit for supper and breakfast, and gained in health and strength and began to look rosy and fit.

" I bobbed my hair, which I had never been able to do before, owing to constant sore throats, and started to study intensively. I won an important elocution competition without any strain. Owing to my improved health I was enabled to take up residence in London, and became a student at the Royal Academy of Dramatic Art . . . . I continued my new diet, my exercises, and my studies at the Academy for one and a half years, finally embarking on my theatrical career, faced with the difficulties of obtaining a food-reform diet on tour.

" These I surmounted by a careful study of food values, a fresh fruit supper and breakfast, a salad, vegetable and cheese luncheon, and an egg dish before the show, and a refusal to use any drug or medicine for any symptom of ill-health. At the time of writing I am fully recovered from the last elimination of all—a plague of boils (nine !), which healed swiftly without any remedy other than clay-packs.

" I have been playing a leading part in a strenuous farcical comedy since March, travelling every Sunday, faced with unhygienic working conditions, giving sometimes twelve performances a week and out-stripping all my beer-shifting, meat-masticating, bun-stuffing colleagues at the fall of the curtain. Briefly : from operating table to star dressing-room in four years—due solely to fruit, vegetables, salads, fresh air, determination, and *Health for All.*"

The Natural Road to Health.—The foregoing is only one of many thousands of cases in which Nature Cure and Natural Treatment have been successful in rescuing one more luckless-seeming individual from the ever-increasing ranks of the chronically diseased, and giving back to them real health and sound vitality once more. And what a tale they tell—life-histories such as these, of medical incompetence and bungling when faced with the fact of disease in the human body ! Medical methods and medical philosophy are condemning hundreds of thousands of unfortunate human beings to the scrap-heap of chronic invalidism every year ; Nature Cure and Natural Treatment could save at least ninety-five per cent. of these luckless ones from the fate that awaits them at medical hands ! What a pity that, through sheer ignorance of its existence in the world of healing, only one here and there is enabled to escape the fate that overwhelms the many !

The natural road that leads to health lies open to all who wish to traverse it. It is not an easy road ; it is a road beset with rigorous self-control, and demanding perseverance and determination from all those who would travel along it. But sound health and vigorous manhood and womanhood are the glittering prizes that await the traveller at the end of the journey—surely the greatest prizes life has to offer ! The philosophy and practice of Nature Cure and Natural Healing bring them within the reach of every sufferer from disease.

INTRODUCTION TO PART II.

THE object of the present book is to bring Nature Cure and Natural Healing before as wide a public as possible, and to show what natural methods of treatment can do for the unfortunate sufferer from disease. Not everyone is in a position to undertake a protracted course of treatment at a Natural-Cure resort, nor can many afford to undergo a course of treatment at the hands of a duly qualified Naturopath—of whom, by the way, there are not so many as yet in this country. Accordingly, it seems to the author that he can serve the interests of his readers best by outlining in the present section the natural treatment required for the overcoming of most of the diseases and ailments common to civilised man to-day, and in a manner in which these treatments can be applied without any untoward difficulty in the patient's own home, and without interfering unduly with his ordinary daily routine.

Such a scheme of home treatment he elaborated in his book, *Your Diet—in Health and Disease*, but there the treatments were given just briefly and without detail ; in the present instance the author intends to go into the question in a far more detailed manner. In this way he hopes to make it possible for every reader so inclined to undertake immediately the self-treatment of any disease from which he may be suffering, without having to seek the services of a Naturopath, and in an intelligible, simple, straightforward manner.

Obviously, really serious diseases are best treated by a qualified Natural-Cure practitioner ; and where such treatment is deemed necessary, it will be mentioned in the treatment for that particular complaint when being outlined. Then again, long fasts are not capable of being carried out by oneself at home for a number of reasons, so that he who wishes to avail himself of the great curative benefits of the long-fasting method will have to undergo this form of treatment in a Natural-Cure home, under the eye of an experienced practitioner.

But for the generality of diseases, and for all ordinary purposes, the treatments to be outlined in the present section of the book will be ample, and capable of bringing about the most gratifying results. Obviously, where disease is of long standing, results will be slower than in cases of comparatively recent origin ; but all in all every reader will be given the chance to place himself or herself on the road to sound health again, providing the treatment described for the particular disease from which they may be suffering is carried out thoroughly and perseveringly. Thus will they be able to test for themselves in the only real way possible the results to be secured from natural treatment.

Naturally, such forms of subsidiary treatment as spinal manipulation, electrical and sun-ray treatment, etc., are outside the scope of a self-treatment scheme. They cannot be applied at home ; they need to be given personally by the Naturopath himself. But they are not absolutely necessary. They are useful adjuncts to natural treatment, but do not form an indispensable part of it. The reader will get on quite well without them if he sets out with determination to carry out the detailed advice *re* treatment given in the section dealing with his own special complaint.

Where short fasts, restricted diets, fruit diets, etc., are mentioned in the scheme of treatment, these will be found described fully in the Appendix at the end of the book. In the Appendix will also be found details of frictions, baths, exercises, etc., all of which are necessary to natural treatment, and are given with a view to making the book as comprehensive and full as possible. By their aid the reader should experience no difficulty whatsoever in putting the various treatments into direct operation with the minimum of effort and possible misunderstanding.

In the Appendix will also be found specimen weekly diet-charts for adults and children, which are intended as guides to the setting up of a proper scheme of diet, not only for the sufferer from disease, but for everyone who reads this book. For sound, sensible dietetics is the indispensable basis for all healthy living.

The author has not followed the old practice of dealing with the diseases in their alphabetical order, but has grouped them in relationship to one another, thus : *Diseases of the Skin, Diseases of the Glands, Diseases af the Digestive System*, etc. He considers this plan far better, as it makes the sufferer from the particular disease in question view his disease as part of an organic whole, and not as an isolated disease, on its own, as it were. As a matter of fact, *all* disease—no matter what—is part of an organic whole (as the reader should now know after having read the first part of the present book). It is a sign and result of derangement of bodily function due to certain definite causative factors operating *within* the organism, such as wrong feeding, nerve enervation, etc., and the treatment for any one disease along natural lines is not very different from that for any other disease, for this very reason. The underlying causes of disease being the same in all cases, their treatment must, to a very large extent, be the same also.

The medical practitioner pays a great deal of attention to diagnosis, for until he has diagnosed accurately the particular disease his patient is suffering from, he cannot prescribe the necessary treatment. For every disease is treated differently from every other in orthodox medical circles, and unless the disease in question is definitely known, the treatment cannot be applied properly. To the Naturopath, however, all disease is one ; it is a sign of systemic disturbance of function due to certain definite causes, all of which are known to him. Consequently correct diagnosis, although useful, is not such a paramount necessity with him as with his medical confrère. His treatment is the same at bottom in all cases : *the cleansing of the system of toxic accumulations which are interfering with and preventing normal functioning, and the regeneration of the bodily mechanism as a whole.* Local treatment, as such, receives only a small share in his work, although a very useful share.

All naturopathic treatment may be described as *systemic* rather than local ; all medical treatment may be described as *local* rather than systemic. That is why the former is successful where the latter is not. For whereas local symptoms will disappear when the under-lying systemic causes have been dealt with and removed, local treatment applied to local symptoms merely suppresses these symptoms without removing the fundamental underlying systemic causes.

The need for correct diagnosis is almost a craze with the medical profession therefore, although we have seen that even when a disease *is* correctly diagnosed by them it is never treated properly ; but even with the greatly increased means at their disposal for the discovery and classification of disease, medical diagnosis is very often sadly at fault. A certain celebrated Chicago medical clinic recently proudly boasted that *fifty per cent.* of their diagnoses were correct*—a record,

* Proved by autopsies—that is, *by examination of the patient's body after death!* (What matters if the patient dies, so long as the diagnosis is correct?)

they said. In their opinion, the ordinary general practitioner was only right in *ten to twelve per cent.* of his diagnoses ! !

It may interest the reader to know that, although the Naturopath has not the need for knowing and placing in exact medical terminology every ache and pain of his patient as has his medical confrère, yet naturopathic methods of diagnosis are far more satisfactory than those employed by the medical profession. Examination of the spine, and particularly examination of the iris of the eye (iri-diagnosis), give the most informative results regarding the internal condition of the patient—results which Medical Science, despite the elaborate methods it employs, can never quite achieve.

Having given the reader this little discursion into the realms of diagnosis and symptomatology, with a view to showing him that no matter what terminology a disease may bear in medical language its treatment along Nature-Cure lines is very much the same as that for every other, we can begin now with the actual treatments themselves. But before doing so, the reader is again reminded that all the actual practical details as to fasts, diets, baths, exercises, etc., will be found in the Appendix at the end of the book. Having read the treatment for his particular disease, let him turn to the Appendix and he will there find full details for its carrying out.

SPECIAL NOTE.—*In many of the treatments reference will be made to the all-fruit diet. It cannot be too strongly impressed upon the reader that the reaction of fruit juices and fruit in the system is* ALKALINE *and not acid. Fruit enters the stomach acid, but reaches the tissues alkaline; on the other hand, bread, meat, etc., although not acid when entering the stomach, form strong acids in the system. They are the acid formers which set up disease;* NOT *fruits. Fruits are the body cleansers. It is most necessary to keep this distinction well in mind.*

As the author's experience has not been so comprehensive as to make him acquainted with all the symptoms of the various diseases dealt with in the following pages, he wishes to acknowledge his indebtedness to the book " How to Keep Well," by A. F. Currier, M.D. (published by Messrs. Werner Laurie, Ltd.), for the medical description of certain of the diseases dealt with. No attempt has been made to make use of the suggestions re treatment offered by Dr. Currier, as these are along orthodox lines and quite contrary to the Nature-Cure philosophy and practice.

PART II

DISEASES AND THEIR NATURAL TREATMENT

SECTION I

AILMENTS OF CHILDREN

STOMACH AND BOWEL DISORDERS : Acute indigestion—Chronic indigestion—Colic—Colitis—Constipation—Diarrhœa—Infective diarrhœa—Dysentery—Vomiting—Worms. DISEASES OF THE HEART, LUNGS, THROAT, ETC. : Bronchitis—The common cold—Croup (membranous)—Croup (spasmodic or false)—Enlarged tonsils and adenoids—Heart disease—Mumps—Pleurisy—Pneumonia—Whooping-cough. CHILDHOOD FEVERS : Chicken-pox—Diphtheria—German measles—Measles—Meningitis—Rheumatic fever—Scarlet fever. INFANTILE DEFICIENCY DISEASES : Rickets—Scurvy. INFANTILE SKIN DISEASES : Eczema—Ringworm. NERVOUS DISEASES OF CHILDHOOD : Convulsions—Infantile paralysis—Meningitis—Polio—St. Vitus' dance. PARASITIC DISEASES OF CHILDHOOD : Thread-worms. Also Bed-wetting—Teething.

O F all forms of disease, those of infancy and early childhood are most due to *wrong feeding*. It is the criminally unwise feeding habits of our age which are at the bottom of the vast amount of infant disease of to-day ; and until parents learn this, there can be little hope of rescue for their children from the so-called " children's ailments."

From before birth the child of civilisation is fed wrongly ; for we must remember that even in the womb the child depends for its nutriment upon what the mother supplies to it, and the modern mother seems to take a special delight in eating those foods which deprive her growing unborn child of the invaluable mineral elements it needs for proper bone and body building, and in making its entry into the world as potentially unhealthy as possible.

It is all a question of ignorance : of ignorance on the part of the mother as to what foods she needs for her own health, as well as for the health of her child ; and ignorance on the part of the medical profession in ascribing to outside causes, such as " germs " and " the weather," diseases which originate entirely from within the infant organism as a result of wrong feeding.

The mother who lives on the refined foods of to-day, and ignores the invaluable part to be played in the daily dietary by fresh fruits and raw salad vegetables, is making the path in life of her children very hard indeed—a path strewn with the " usual " children's ailments (usual only because of the abysmal ignorance of most mothers regarding the diet question). For most *unusual* would they be if mothers knew how to feed themselves and their children.

The medical profession has at last learned that rickets is a deficiency disease. But when will it learn that infantile paralysis, whooping-cough, measles, and all the other diseases of childhood—yes, even defective teeth—are merely the result of a grossly deficient (whilst at the same time grossly excessive) infant dietary ? Deficient in organic mineral salts, that is, but vastly over-excessive in the shape of refined sugar, refined starchy foods, proteins, and fats.

The mother who would bring healthy children into the world must get her diet right. The mother who would rear those same children healthily, and avoid the usual crop of children's ailments, must feed them properly. In the Appendix will be found full weekly diets for both children and adults. Let all mothers who read this book take this paragraph to heart and act accordingly. (For those who wish for a detailed account of the diet question in its relation to infant and adult disease, the reader is referred to the author's book, *Your Diet— in Health and Disease*, already mentioned.)

All babies should be breast fed ; but if this is not possible, they should be given either cow's milk or goat's milk (diluted) instead. Prepared baby-foods are absolutely worthless for building a high grade of health. Babies who have to be fed on either cow's milk or goat's milk should also receive plenty of orange juice during the day to make up for any mineral deficiency in the pre-natal diet.

The old medical idea that the baby should be fed every two hours during the day (with night-feeding if the child should wake) has received its death-blow at the hands of such pioneers of infant welfare as Dr. Truby King ; but it still lurks here and there in medical manuals for the bringing up of children. Babies should be fed at four-hourly intervals during the day, *and not at all at night*. This overfeeding in the earliest months of life is *the* greatest predisposing factor concerned in the setting up of ailments of early childhood, such as indigestion, constipation, diarrhœa, etc. (In the Appendix at the end of the book mothers will find a scale of tables for the feeding of babies along Nature-Cure lines, and also a scheme of natural feeding for children up to the age of five, with a fuller scheme of dietary for those from the age of five upwards.)

If any proof is needed to show how thoroughly the medical mind fails to understand the diet question and its relation to disease both in young and old, it is furnished by the following specimen daily dietary for a child of *between two and three* which was published in a medical book on health.* It has been elaborated by a highly esteemed American doctor.

Breakfast.—(1) A small portion of beefsteak, with oatmeal or other cereal porridge, and plenty of milk. (2) A soft-boiled egg, bread and butter, and a glass of milk.

Second meal.—(1) A glass of milk with bread and butter or with a soda or other biscuit. (2) Bread and milk. (3) Chicken broth.

Dinner.—Roasted fowl, mutton, or beef cut fine ; mashed roast potato with butter or dish-gravy over it ; bread and butter. As dessert, tapioca or rice or sago pudding, junket (or fruit).

Supper.—(1) Bread and butter. (2) Milk with soda or other biscuit, or with bread and butter.

It would be interesting for the reader just to compare this " ideal " diet for a child of *two* or *three* with the child diet-chart for those of the same age given in the Appendix herewith. Where is that daily abundance of fresh fruits and fresh raw vegetables so needful to the infant system ? Not thought of at all—just ignored ! Merely a belated reference to rice pudding, *or* junket, *or* fruit as a dessert after a meat breakfast and dinner ! But *plenty* of refined starches, fats, and animal proteins ! Oh yes ! there the whole fallacy of medical dietetics is exposed in a nutshell ; the kind of dietetics which is universal to-day, *and which is the main causative factor in all disease*. Wrong feeding *par excellence* ! (Let a child of two be brought up on such a dietary, and it will be well in the running for every childhood complaint from enlarged tonsils to St. Vitus' dance !)

.   .   .   .   .   .

We come now to the actual treatments for children's ailments ; but before beginning, the following special note must be carefully borne in mind by all those administering the treatments :

* *How to Keep Well*, by A. F. Currier, M.D. (published by Messrs. Werner Laurie, Ltd.).

SPECIAL NOTE.—*For babies or very young children, parents must, of course, use their discretion and modify the treatment given throughout the whole of this section where necessary.*

(1) STOMACH AND BOWEL DISORDERS

Acute Indigestion.—This is usually marked by vomiting, pain, and fever. When undigested food has remained so long in the stomach as to have caused inflammation, chronic indigestion follows the acute attack. The cause of the trouble is improper feeding (overloading of the stomach, the fermentation and decomposition of food, etc.).

*Treatment.—The child should be fasted for a day or so (it may be given hot water to drink, and orange juice), and the bowels should be cleansed once or twice with a small warm-water enema. If this is done, the symptoms will soon disappear, and the child should then be placed on the *all-fruit diet* for a further day or two, and then on to the *diet-chart* given in the Appendix.

Chronic Indigestion.—Vomiting is the most common symptom. The tongue is coated, the breath bad, the sleep disturbed, the temper irritable. The child fails to gain weight and becomes unnaturally pale. The bowels may be alternately relaxed and constipated. The cause, as stated above, is improper feeding, generally the giving of too much food, and the wrong kind.

*Treatment.—A day on orange juice, with plenty of hot water in between, followed by from one to three or four days on the *all-fruit diet* (according to the needs of the case), and with the use of the enema nightly, will soon help to rectify matters. If the child is then placed on a sensible dietary such as given in the Appendix, the trouble should soon be eradicated from the child's system for good.

Colic.—The feet are cold and pain occurs in paroxysms marked by a loud, violent cry with drawing up of the legs. The cry of hunger is more continuous and there is no evidence of pain. In colic the paroxysms are relieved by the expulsion of gas. Colic usually results from the distension of the bowels by gas (or wind). It is most common between the second and sixth month. The cause is *faulty feeding on the part of the mother,* this affecting the quality of the milk, or else is due to overfeeding of the infant—or more often, both.

---

* Where the patient is a very young child, treatment must, of course, be modified accordingly.

Treatment.—To nurse the baby whilst it has colic is useless and only causes more harm. The baby should be given a little fairly hot water to sip, and a small warm-water enema should be given to cleanse the bowel. *This latter is most effective.* Feeding should not be resumed until all signs of the colic have disappeared. (The mother might find that the application of heat to the abdomen—say a hot towel—would help materially in recovery.)

The mother should, in addition, look very carefully to her own diet, and regulate it according to the dietary for adults given in the Appendix. She should also avoid overfeeding of the child in future. Four-hourly feeds and no night-feeding should be the rule. Sometimes the milk of the mother is affected from a psychological cause, *i.e.,* bad temper, worry, great excitement, etc., and a baby should never be fed when the mother is in such a state.

Colitis.—See *Infective Diarrhœa,* page 98.

Constipation.—Constipation is one of the most troublesome disorders of childhood. The local trouble is frequently the only symptom, but in many cases there are colic, disturbed sleep, and irritability. Improper diet and irregular habits are the chief causes of this condition.

Treatment.—This will depend upon the age of the child—whether a very small baby or a child, say, of four or five. In the case of a young baby being breast fed, the constipation is usually the result of wrong feeding *on the part of the mother,* and it is *this* which needs correcting. But even so, the baby can be kept on water and orange juice for, say, a day, and a small enema of warm water given. The enema can be resorted to every second or third day for the next week or so (if necessary), until things begin to normalise themselves. A further day on water and orange juice may be required in some cases. *Never give laxatives.* Where the baby is artificially fed, the cause is wrong feeding, obviously, and this should be rectified in accordance with the rules given in the Appendix *re* child feeding. Treatment should otherwise be as above.

For the child of two, three, four, and upwards, one to three or four days on the *all-fruit diet* and the adoption of the *child menus* given in the Appendix should soon help to right matters. ON NO ACCOUNT SHOULD PURGATIVES BE GIVEN. A small warm-water enema should be given nightly whilst on the all-fruit diet, and the child should be encouraged to take plenty of exercise. (A little olive oil, given preferably with the salad meal, will help.)

Diarrhœa.—Simple diarrhœa is rarely severe, and passes away with the removal of the cause. It is usually the result of digestive disturbances (wrong feeding or the swallowing of a foreign body), and a day on orange juice, with the use of the enema, will soon put matters right. Correct dieting will prevent further occurrences of the trouble.

Infective Diarrhœa (also Colitis).—This is usually known as *summer diarrhœa*, and is the most common form seen in children. It presents two types. In the first the onset is gradual, and looseness of the bowels is the first symptom. There may be five to ten movements a day. Thin and frequently green, they soon contain mucus. More or less fever is present. The case may run a mild course, or become progressively worse and turn into *inflammatory diarrhœa (entero-colitis)*.

In the second type the onset is sudden and is marked by vomiting, fever, and numerous loose green movements. At first the movements may be large and watery and contain blood, but later they become green or brown and contain mucus. Vomiting is sometimes persistent. The number of movements is not always a guide to the seriousness of the condition, for some of the worst cases have a high temperature and but few movements. *The cause in all cases is wrong feeding*, especially the giving of large quantities of protein food in hot weather (meat, fish, etc.).

Treatment.—The treatment for this more serious type of diarrhœa is to keep the child in bed, cleanse the bowels night and morning with the warm-water enema, and give nothing but water and orange juice for a few days (*no milk or anything else*). As soon as the severity of the condition has been checked, and no more diarrhœa is present, the *all-fruit diet* may be adopted, and after a few days on this, the child can pass on to the regular *diet for children* given in the Appendix. If the condition is very serious, and the parent feels alarmed and does not feel capable of carrying out the treatment himself, a Naturopath should be called in, but in all cases, no matter how serious they may seem, the above simple home treatment will be found to be quite effective if applied properly.

Dysentery.—In young children dysentery is a severe form of inflammatory diarrhœa, in which the disease is located chiefly in the large bowel. It is most common in hot climates in late summer and is characterised by frequent, small, painful movements, consisting wholly or in part of mucus and blood. Straining and pain are present after the movements, a symptom known as *tenesmus*. The cause is wrong feeding of children, especially the giving of excessive quantities of meat and similar protein foods in climates and under conditions where the said food is very liable to putrefy quickly within the intestines.

Treatment.—The treatment is the same as for *infective diarrhœa*, although the child may have to be kept on orange juice, and subsequently on the *all-fruit diet*, longer than for the less serious complaint. (Fresh fruits and salads *must* form the major portion of the child's future dietary; flesh foods should be avoided in future as far as possible.)

Vomiting.—Vomiting is not a disease, but a symptom of numerous diseases of childhood. It may result from acute indigestion, chronic indigestion, temporary overloading of the stomach, nervous diseases, and reflex irritation. It also occurs in the first stages of scarlet fever and other acute fevers.

Treatment.—The treatment for vomiting must of course depend upon the actual cause of the trouble in each individual case. If the parent cannot discover this, the child should be kept in bed, given nothing but hot water to drink (no food), and the warm-water enema used to cleanse the bowels. If this does not put matters right, then the services of a Naturopath should be secured.

Worms.—See Sub-section (7), *Parasitic Diseases of Childhood*, page 122.

(2) Diseases of the Heart, Lungs, Throat, etc.

Bronchitis.—Next to indigestion and diarrhœa, "cold on the chest" is the commonest acute disease of childhood. It may be mild, with little or no fever ; in severe forms the temperature may rise to 102 degrees Fahr. The cough may be loose, with free secretion of mucus, or it may be short, dry, and teasing in character. It may become so paroxysmal as to suggest whooping-cough. The usual duration is between one and two weeks. Its cause, as usual, is *wrong feeding of children*, especially the giving of excessive quantities of starchy foods in the daily dietary in the shape of refined cereals, white bread, boiled and mashed potatoes, puddings, pies, cakes, etc., to say nothing of sugary foods in the shape of white sugar, jams, sweets, etc.

The impurities which arise in the system as a result of the daily excessive ingestion of foods of this nature invariably collect in the mucous membrane of the upper part of the body (especially in the bronchial tubes, throat, nose and ear passages), giving rise to bronchitis, catarrh, colds, enlarged tonsils, adenoids, etc.

Treatment.—The treatment for bronchitis is to keep the child on *orange juice and water only* for three days or so, that is until the more serious symptoms have disappeared; then the *all-fruit diet* should be adopted for a further few days. When the child is fully convalescent, the *dietary for children* given in the Appendix should be adopted and adhered to rigorously from then on. Starchy and sugary foods must be carefully restricted in future, and the sweet habit broken. The warm-water enema should be used nightly during the first few days of the treatment, and if the cough is troublesome cold packs (as described in the Appendix) should be applied to the chest two or three times during the day, and one at night. Hot Epsom-salts baths are useful for children of more advanced age when convalescing from bronchitis, and the regular daily performances of breathing exercises should be encouraged. (A set of such exercises will be found in the Appendix.)

The Common Cold.—The symptoms which characterise the " common " cold are so universally known that their description here is hardly necessary. The sneezing, the running from nose and eyes, the heightened temperature denoting fever, are within the experience of everyone. Why? Because the cold is Nature's simplest form of " healing crisis "—it is the form Nature uses most for the work of eliminating *rubbish* (systemic refuse due to wrong feeding) from the human system. All that has been said about the eating of excessive quantities of starchy and sugary food in the case of bronchitis applies with equal force to the common cold, both in children and adults. And if parents wish to see their children rid of colds, it is the child's dietary which must be attended to.

Treatment.—Proper dieting, and proper dieting *alone*, can prevent the appearance of colds in the child. When a cold is already present, the child should be put on orange juice for a day, then on to the *all-fruit diet* for a further day or two. If this is done, and the enema used on one or two nights to cleanse the bowels (and a hot Epsom-salts bath given), the cold will soon be got rid of. It then remains for the parents to place the child on a sensible dietary for colds to become a rarer and ever rarer occurrence in that particular child's life.

A point worth remembering with regard to both bronchitis and colds is, that *over-clothing* is a most definite factor in the production of these complaints in children, in conjunction with over-feeding. To clothe a child in a large number of garments is bad for that child's health, as by this the skin is not allowed to function properly and natural elimination is prevented, thus making it more than ever likely that colds, bronchitis, etc., will appear. The wearing of woollen under-garments is especially bad for young children. They should wear, *not* wool next the skin, but a porous cotton or linen material such as " Aertex."

To adopt one of the usual suppressive measures for treating a cold, such as aspirin, codeine, etc., is only paving the way for future trouble of a more serious nature.

Croup (Membranous).—Membranous croup is an inflammation of the larynx marked by the formation of a false membrane. As the larynx is in the narrowest part of the throat, the disease is very dangerous because it obstructs the breathing. In most of the cases the cause is diphtheritic in origin. The progress is slow as compared with false croup, but is relentless and continuous. The voice is hoarse, and at length is completely lost. Without proper treatment the disease is one of the most fatal in childhood, the child dying eventually from strangulation.

Treatment.—The medical treatment for membranous croup consists of anti-toxin treatment and intubation, often with the most disastrous results. The only sound logical treatment is that as given for *Diphtheria* in the treatment for childhood fevers farther on in the present section (page 109).

Croup (Spasmodic or False).—False croup is rare before the sixth month and after the fifth year of childhood, but it *may occur* at any time. The symptoms to the inexperienced are alarming. The child may have been perfectly well, or there may have been slight hoarseness or cold in the head. He suddenly wakes in the night with a loud, metallic cough. Breathing is difficult, the child often struggles for breath, being terrified at its own condition. The voice is hoarse but not lost. There is little or no fever. After a few hours the attack subsides, and on the following morning the child seems well. The

101

next night a milder attack occurs, and still another on the third night. In some cases the cough persists all day and ultimately turns into bronchitis. The cause, although heredity is sometimes claimed as a cause, is indigestion, brought on by wrong feeding.

Treatment.—Proper feeding and the avoidance of indigestion and constipation would make this childhood complaint impossible of occurrence. Where present, treatment should consist in keeping the child on orange juice and water for a day or two, then via the *all-fruit diet* on to the regular *child's menus* given in the Appendix. The enema should be used nightly for a few days. A cold pack applied to the throat at night will be very efficacious. (See Appendix for details as to how the pack should be made and applied.)

Enlarged Tonsils and Adenoids.—Enlarged tonsils and adenoids are perhaps the two commonest troubles of children to-day. Their surgical removal, although such an apparently simple and sound measure, is responsible for more ill-health in after-life than the world could ever imagine. The tonsils are lymphatic glands situated at the entrance to the throat, and their function is to cleanse the head and upper part of the body of toxic matter and systemic impurities. Given the way the average child is brought up and fed, what wonder then that these lymphatic glands should become enlarged—swollen with toxic matter and unable to function properly—at a very early age in the child-life ?

Enlarged tonsils are a sure sign that the child in question is suffering from a toxic condition of the system due to wrong feeding and unhygienic living ; and adenoids are due to a similar cause. To remove them surgically from the system is, then, hardly the right way of getting rid of the cause of the trouble, is it ? It is getting rid of the *effect*, and not of the cause at all ! Further, it is allowing the said cause or causes to operate with even greater force than ever within the organism, because the infant system will be working at a permanently impaired level of efficiency, once these bulwarks of defence in the upper part of the body—the tonsils—have been removed (under the specious and vain medical pretext that they are " useless " organs in the human anatomy, and that the child is far better off without these " centres of possible future infection " !).

When the medical profession does not understand the use of any particular organ or part of the human anatomy, it immediately says it is useless—meaning by this that it does not know its use, therefore Nature does not either. (Which, to say the least, is rather presumptuous !) Accordingly, if such organs can be removed from the system without unduly affecting its working, the public are at once led to believe that they will be infinitely better off without the said organs than with them. Not only *led to believe*, but *bullied and forced to believe*. Hence the present-day orgy of operations for the removal of tonsils, adenoids, appendices, etc.; which, from the surgeon's point of view—both financially and technically—is a very good thing indeed, but from the health point of view of the patient is a very bad thing.

The trouble is that many parents, being led to believe that their children will be far better off without their tonsils or appendices than with them, *really do think* they see a change for the better in the child's health after they have allowed the operation to take place. But this improvement, if improvement there be, is only temporary and transient. It is purchased solely at the expense of the future well-being of the child. One cannot function fully on an organism deprived of one of its parts—as any motorist will know with reference to his engine—and more especially will this be so if the bad habits which were at the bottom of the trouble in the first place are allowed to continue unchecked, as they invariably are.

The symptoms usually connected with enlarged and septic tonsils and adenoids are a tendency to be always catching colds, under-development—sometimes both physically and mentally—and a habit of breathing through the mouth rather than through the nose. The doctor says that if the offending tonsils and adenoids are removed, all these various disabilities will automatically clear up. This *sometimes* does happen ; the child appears to be far better in health in every way after the operation. But this appearance of improved health is only temporary and specious. Really, the organism suffers far more than is gained. *The surgical removal of tonsils and adenoids paves the way for all the more serious diseases of childhood*, from middle-ear disease and mastoiditis to asthma and meningitis.*

Treatment.—For parents to allow their children to have tonsils and adenoids removed by surgical operation is not only wrong, *but*

* For the further elaboration of this point, see remarks re *enlarged tonsils and adenoids* in Section 8, Diseases of the Ears, Nose, Mouth and Throat, p. 241.

unnecessary. Unless the trouble is of very long standing, *all* enlargements of tonsils and adenoidal growths can be got rid of in time by natural means. Even very septic tonsils can be set right by treatment along natural lines; only in this case personal naturopathic treatment will be desirable—treatment, that is, at the hands of a duly qualified Naturopath. Self-treatment is hardly likely to be completely effective here. But all ordinary cases of tonsil and adenoid trouble can be treated in the home as follows :

The child should be placed on the *all-fruit diet* for from five days to a week, and then the *diet for children* given in the Appendix should be adopted. (Further short periods on the *all-fruit diet* should be undertaken from time to time if necessary in certain cases, say for two or three days at a time at periods of from three weeks to a month.*) The bowels should be cleansed nightly with the warm-water enema for the first few days of the treatment, and longer if necessary ; and cold packs (as described in the Appendix) should be applied nightly to the throat of the child. The throat should be gargled night and morning with warm water and a little lemon juice. Fresh air and outdoor exercise are two essentials to successful treatment for tonsil and adenoid trouble, and care must be taken to see that the bedroom is well ventilated. The child should also be encouraged to breathe properly, and the exercises on breathing, in the Appendix, are invaluable in this connection.

The above treatment, although simple, has been effective in many thousands of cases of tonsil and adenoid trouble, but parents must not be disappointed if all signs of the disability do not disappear immediately. Some cases take much longer time to right themselves than others. In really stubborn cases, manipulative treatment at the hands of a Naturopath or Osteopath will be necessary. (See also Section 8, *Diseases of the Ears, Nose, Mouth and Throat*, page 228.)

Heart Disease.—Heart disease in children is almost invariably the result of wrong treatment of some former child-ailment or ailments. Usually it is an after-effect of the suppressive medical treatment of some fever, such as scarlet fever or rheumatic fever. Many cases of heart disease in children appear to right themselves in the course of

---

* In fairly serious cases the period on fruit should be followed by a week on *fruit and milk*, before beginning on the full diet. Begin with a cup of fresh cold milk to each fruit meal the first day, and increase up to about two pints daily.

time, as Nature does her best to compensate for faulty heart action where the very young are concerned, and often the heart lesion, where present, gives no trouble at all for the same reason. But where definite damage to the heart-lining has taken place as a result of faulty drug treatment of previous disease, proper treatment is needed.

Treatment.—To administer " tonics " in cases of heart disease, as the medical profession does, is only to make matters worse in the long run. The proper treatment for heart disease in children is mainly *dietetic,* although a great deal of good can be done by suitable manipulative treatment at the hands of a good Naturopath or Osteopath. The child should be placed on the *dietary for children* given in the Appendix, with an occasional day or two every now and then on the *all-fruit diet* ; and in order to build up its stamina and vitality to the highest level, it should be encouraged to take as much outdoor and general exercise of a gentle nature—*as is compatible with its condition.* (The breathing and other exercises given in the Appendix will be very useful in this connection if performed without undue effort or strain.) *Remember, parents, then* : proper diet, well-regulated exercise of a gentle nature, manipulative treatment (where procurable), and NO DRUGS, and there is no reason why most children should not grow out of heart disease in time.

Mumps.—Mumps is characterised by painful swelling of the parotid gland, which may spread to all the other salivary glands, and usually occurs in either the autumn or the spring. The swelling is triangular in shape, the upper angle being in front of the ear, another at the side of the jaw, and the third behind the ear. One or both sides may be involved, the one usually preceding the other by a few days. In swellings of the glands of the neck, the enlargement does not extend so high upon the face. In mumps, the lobe of the ear is lifted outwards. Usually the saliva is diminished, and the mouth is dry and parched. The disease continues for about a week on each side. An occasional and very peculiar complication is inflammation of the breasts and ovaries in girls and of the testes in boys. The cause of the trouble is dietetic.

Treatment.—The treatment for mumps is to *fast* the patient for the first few days, giving orange juice and water. The warm-water enema should be used daily during this time, and hot and cold fomentations applied to the affected areas. The fomentations should

105

be applied every two hours during the day for about ten minutes, and should consist of two or three hot applications, followed by a cold one. When the child can swallow food comfortably and the swelling has gone down, the *all-fruit diet* should be adopted for a day or two, and the regular *diet for children* given in the Appendix can then be gradually introduced.

Pleurisy.—Pleurisy is not uncommon in young children, but it is always secondary to pneumonia (and is a result of the wrong treatment of the latter). It is accompanied with fluid in the chest much more commonly than in adults, and the fluid is apt to be purulent. According to the medical theory, pleurisy in children requires immediate surgical treatment, unless the fluid can be absorbed by some other means. But this is only adding insult to injury in the child system, as it were. For if the pneumonia had been treated properly in the first place—itself the result of the wrong medical treatment of some former and less serious disease, please note—pleurisy would never have arisen. Thus does orthodox medicine force one disease into another, and still further into another, in its efforts to cope with disease by the use of drugs and the surgeon's knife.

Treatment.—If a child has developed pleurisy after pneumonia, it is, as has already been said, entirely due to wrong treatment. (More often than not, it is the crass feeding which goes on whilst the child is totally unable to take, or wishful of taking, any food during pneumonia, which leads to the formation of the pleuritic condition afterwards.) *The feeding of children during fevers is just as much a factor in the production of the after-effects and complications which so often arise as is drug treatment itself.*

The parent who has sense should call in a Naturopath as soon as possible if his child develops pleurisy ; for natural treatment is the only thing which will right the condition properly. Here, again, it is fasting treatment which is indicated, followed (at convalescence) by the *all-fruit diet*, and proper dieting afterwards. Packs to the chest and the use of the enema are both essential to the success of the treatment. Manipulative treatment is an asset.

Pneumonia.—There are two varieties of pneumonia, *broncho-pneumonia* and *lobar pneumonia*. The first is the common form seen in children under two years ; the second is rare before the third year, but is the common type after the fourth. Lobar pneumonia is far less fatal in children than in adults. It usually pursues a short and sharp course, terminating generally within a week.

Broncho-pneumonia pursues a course varying from ten to twenty days or longer. It terminates gradually, and not suddenly like lobar pneumonia. The onset may be abrupt, but is often gradual. In ordinary cases the symptoms are quite characteristic. There is a fever (usually about 102 degrees Fahr.) and persistent cough with evidence of pain. The breathing is known as expiratory—that is, the expiration is prolonged and exaggerated, and accompanied by a slight sound, often by a slight moan. When the child is quiet, this expiratory moan may be absent, but it appears when he is disturbed. The nostrils dilate with each breath. The child is commonly more patient and less irritable than in the digestive diseases, and rarely cries loudly. There is thirst, but the appetite is completely lost.

Treatment.—Pneumonia in children often arises as the result of the suppressive medical treatment of other diseases of a less serious nature, such as measles, whooping-cough, etc. That is to say, *its cause is wrong medical treatment.* It is a further complication of less serious diseases only because these same diseases have been treated wrongly in the first place. No wonder the medical profession says that measles is a serious disease—far more serious than most people are wont to imagine ! It is, if treated along orthodox medical lines, for many of the children thus treated develop broncho-pneumonia as an after-effect. But this would never happen if the children had been treated properly in the first place.

The treatment for broncho-pneumonia or lobar pneumonia in children is *Fasting.* All Fevers need fasting treatment for their *real cure*—cure, that is, without complications and serious after-effects, such as attend the efforts of the medical profession. A fever is a natural attempt on the part of the body to rid itself of toxic matter ; it is NOT the result of germ infection. That theory is mere medical ignorance due to wrong thinking and wrong training.

The treatment of all Fevers—pneumonia included—should be in qualified naturopathic hands. This, however, is not always easy to obtain, and any parent of strong enough determination and will-power can carry it through successfully for himself in the case of his own child. The child should be fasted for several days, until the fever abates in fact and temperature remains steady at normal.

It may have orange juice during this period and as much water as it likes to drink, *but nothing else*. (*No milk !*) Packs to the chest several times a day will be very beneficial and a pack to the throat at night will help greatly. The enema should be used daily to cleanse the bowels. (How to apply the cold pack is explained in the Appendix.)

If the above simple treatment is carried out, the fever will soon begin to disappear ; and when definite convalescence commences, the child can be placed on the *all-fruit diet* for a few days, and then the regular *diet for children* given in the Appendix should be adopted. A perfect and complete cure will result if these instructions are carried out, with no fear of after-effects or complications. What a difference from drug treatment! (See also Section 13, page 418.)*

Whooping-cough.—Whooping-cough is a contagious disease with catarrh of the mucous membranes and a peculiar paroxysmal cough. It is most common in the spring and autumn in children between the ages of four and twelve. It begins with a catarrhal stage, during which the symptoms are those of a cold, and develops into the spasmodic stage, which lasts for several weeks. The disease usually runs the following course : it increases for about two weeks, remains stationary for a further two weeks or so, and then gradually subsides. The paroxysms vary from eight or ten to forty or fifty daily. Vomiting is frequent, and occasionally every paroxysm is a struggle for breath. In some cases an enormous quantity of mucus is secreted ; in others the quantity is small. Sometimes the whoop may be heard but a few times during the course of the disease. The cause of the complaint is the feeding—and more especially the *overfeeding*—of children with refined and demineralised foods, together with the absence of a sufficient quantity of fresh fruits and salad vegetables in the child dietary, thus leading to the formation of excessive quantities of catarrh and mucus in the infant system, which the disease is a

---

* The treatment of pneumonia by the use of antibiotic drugs only serves to get rid of the superficial germ effect, leaving the underlying causes completely untouched. Thus, although the patient may appear to be cured quite rapidly, a recurrence of the trouble may be expected in the near or distant future, and of a more severe nature. Also, the respiratory tissues are affected adversely by antibiotic treatment, and the lungs tend to lose their elasticity, thus paving the way for *emphysema* to develop in many cases. In the author's view, the antibiotic treatment of chest diseases has a great deal to do with the subsequent development of lung cancer. Smoking is only a secondary factor.

natural attempt to throw off. Wrong medical treatment of former disease has also much to do with its development.

Treatment.—If wrongly treated, whooping-cough may hang about for months, and often leads to serious complications. The correct treatment is *to fast the child*, using the warm-water enema daily to cleanse the bowels, and to apply cold packs to the throat and upper chest as necessary. (See Appendix for details of these.) During the fasting period the child may be given orange juice and water to drink. (Never give children anything but these drinks when fasting. *Milk should never be given* ; it is not a drink, but a food.) When the more serious symptoms have begun to clear up, the child may be put on to the *all-fruit diet* for a few days, and then on to the regular *child dietary* given in the Appendix. (Epsom-salts baths will be useful in this complaint during and after the initial fasting period.) The adoption of the breathing exercises given in the Appendix is recommended when the convalescent stage has been reached, and the child should be encouraged to spend as much time as possible out of doors. *Manipulative treatment, where procurable, is strongly recommended.*

(3) CHILDHOOD FEVERS

Chicken-pox.—Chicken-pox is characterised by slight fever and the eruption of small vesicles. Each vesicle rests on normal or slightly reddened skin, and looks as though a drop of hot water had raised a round blister. The vesicles slowly dry and form scabs, which fall off. They come in successive crops, so that some are drying whilst some are beginning to form, thus differing from smallpox, in which the vesicles are all found in the same period of development. The rash appears over the whole body, particularly the back and shoulders. The period of incubation is fourteen to sixteen days. The cause, as with all other childhood fevers, is persistent wrong feeding of children leading to a natural healing crisis (Nature's attempt to rid the young body of toxic matter).

Treatment.—The treatment for chicken-pox is the same as that for *Measles* (given farther on in the present section, page 112), only in this case there is no need for special protection for the eyes. Care must be taken to see that the child does not scratch the vesicles, which it will be very prone to do, as these are very irritating. (See also Section 13, page 411.)

Diphtheria.—It is impossible to depict diphtheria by any single description, for few diseases show such extremities of mildness and malignancy. The following symptoms are those most commonly seen :

The onset is mild and often uncertain ; there may be slight fever and soreness of the throat, with prostration and weakness. Upon one tonsil, rarely upon both, a membrane appears and increases in size. It may be thick or thin, and of a grey or brownish colour, surrounded by a zone of red inflammation.

The membrane may not extend beyond the tonsil, or it may involve the whole of the back of the throat and soft palate. It may extend upward into the nose or downward into the larynx. It is possible to have diphtheria without the false membrane being present, the tissues being red and swollen and the bacilli being present. The glands of the neck are usually enlarged, and, when the nose is involved, they increase rapidly in size.

The child is prostrated, rapidly becomes anæmic and sallow, and, unless proper treatment is instituted, may die either from steadily increasing prostration or from rapid weakening of the heart. In favourable cases the symptoms gradually subside and the membranes slowly disappear. Duration ranges from a few days to two or three weeks. (The disease looks like tonsilitis very often in the early stages.)

The cause of diphtheria according to medical views is, of course, " germ infection." But the reader can rest assured that no child can " catch " diphtheria who has not the basis for its propagation in its system, in the shape of morbid and toxic matter brought there through the medium of wrong feeding and unhygienic living, with *habitual constipation* as a very pertinent predisposing cause. For if this were not the case, there would be hundreds of thousands of cases of diphtheria every year in both children and adults, instead of only a comparatively few thousand, as now; for the diphtheria bacillus is present in the throats of large numbers of children and adults without being in the least virulent.

Treatment.—Although the use of anti-toxin for the treatment of diphtheria is *sometimes* apparently successful, it fails in just as many cases as it succeeds in, its injection often leading to death. But its administration is *wrong practice*. The injection of any serum into the human organism—especially the child organism—is wrong, and in many cases fraught with great danger. Many a child (not to mention grown-up) has died from the administration of a dose (or doses) of some serum or other, whilst grieving parents and relatives have been led to believe (by those responsible) that it was the fever, and *not* the serum, which caused the death. It is just a matter of error developing out of error. Germs are *not* the cause of fevers, therefore anti-toxins and sera designed to get rid of the germs can *not* be a cure. They *appear* to get rid of the disease, in certain cases, but if the reader really understands what has been said in these pages about suppressive medical treatment and how it works, he will have no difficulty in realising that anti-toxin treatment for diphtheria (or any other fever) only succeeds in a " cure "—where it *does* succeed—by stopping *helpful* germ activity, and forcing the toxins and impurities which the system was endeavouring to throw off, through the medium of the fever, farther back into the system, to form the basis for more serious trouble in later life. *The germs are destroyed by the treatment, but the toxic matter they were actively engaged in getting rid of is left behind.*

The *real treatment* for diphtheria, as with all other fevers, is *fasting*. Give *only orange juice or water* for the time the fever lasts, and then only in small quantities. NO MILK AT ALL IS TO BE GIVEN.

The disease is so often like tonsillitis in its early stages that many parents go on feeding the child when they should not, and so only tend to complicate matters. The warm-water enema should be used regularly twice a day during the fasting period ; *this is most essential*, as effete bowel waste has much to do with the causation of the trouble in the first place. To avoid the swallowing of the secretions constantly forming in the mouth during the fever, the child should be placed on its side and not allowed to lie on its back. (Some absorbent cotton may be arranged in the mouth to absorb much of this matter, and can be renewed several times a day as required.) Cold packs at two-hourly intervals to the throat will help ; as will also packs to the whole trunk. (See Appendix for details as to how the packs should be applied.)

If the above advice is carried out, the fever will run its course without any trouble, and, most important of all, *there will be no fear of complications or serious after-effects* ; and the child can then be brought via the *all-fruit diet* on to the proper *diet for children* given in the Appendix. *Personal naturopathic attention is most advisable where procurable in all cases of diphtheria.* (See also Section 13, page 411.)

German Measles.—German measles is a distinct disease, and not a mild form of either measles or scarlet fever. In many cases there are no symptoms until the rash appears ; in others there is mild fever and nausea. There is no cold in the head and little or no cough. The rash consists of spots larger than those of scarlet fever, but smaller than those of measles. In many cases where the spots are coarser than usual, german measles is very difficult to distinguish from measles. The spots come out rapidly over the whole body and last from two to five days, followed by very little desquamation (peeling).

Treatment.—For the cause and treatment of german measles, the reader is referred to *Measles*, following.

Measles.—Measles is a contagious disease, more common in warm than in cold weather, which begins with feverishness, cold in the head, running of the eyes, and dry cough, followed on the fourth day by a rash which appears first on the sides of the face and the neck and slowly spreads all over the body, appearing last on the hands. The rash continues for about five days, when it fades away and is followed by a bran-like peeling, which is usually completed within a week. The rash consists of small rounded spots with reddened skin between. In some locations the spots run together. There is considerable swelling of the face, and the spots are blotchy, so that the appearance of the child is considerably changed. In malignant cases the spots are much darker and form what is known as " black measles." The fever is not, as a rule, as high as in scarlet fever. The child is frequently drowsy and stupid, but occasionally very restless. The bowels are loose frequently, a troublesome diarrhœa being not uncommon. The cough is hard and metallic and constitutes one of the most troublesome symptoms. The cause of the disease is the same as that for all the others of childhood : *wrong feeding plus unhygienic living*.

Treatment.—There is no doubt that measles is a natural healing crisis instituted to rid the infant organism of the toxins and deleterious end-products resulting from the assimilation of the vast excesses of starchy and sugary food (in particular) that young children are given in the civilised world to-day. (Think of the bread, potatoes, sugar, sweets, biscuits, cakes, puddings, and pies, children are given to eat!—food the child system does NOT want, but which foolishly-indulgent parents insist upon forcing on it, in the belief that such things are *good* for the child !) In a sense measles is a very good thing for children therefore, provided the case is treated properly and the child is fed in a sensible manner thereafter, that is ; but treated in the orthodox fashion, even if no complications ensue—as they very often do—nothing is gained, because the whole ridiculous process of child cramming goes on after the recovery just as before, so that toxic matter is piled up as fast as ever in the child system to take the place of that thrown off during the fever.

The natural treatment for measles is the same as that for any other fever—*fasting*. The child should be fasted, being given only orange juice and water to drink, and the bowels washed out night and morning with the warm-water enema. As light has a detrimental effect upon the eyes during measles, because of the weakened condition of the external eye tissues, the child should have its eyes shaded or else be in a dim light. The room should be well ventilated, however. As soon as the tongue clears and temperature is normal, the child can be placed on the *all-fruit diet*, and thence, as convalescence continues, on to the *full child dietary* given in the Appendix. If the cough is troublesome during the first part of the fever, cold packs to the chest may be applied (see Appendix for details ; see also Section 13, page 418.)

Meningitis.—See under Sub-section *Nervous Diseases of Childhood*, page 120.

Pneumonia.—See under Sub-section *Diseases of the Heart, Lungs, Throat, etc.*, page 106.

Rheumatic Fever.—It was formerly supposed that rheumatism was rare in children ; this error resulted from the fact that the symptoms varied so much that it was often overlooked. But now it is realised that all " growing pains " are rheumatic in origin ; so that parents should view such symptoms with concern, and not indifference, as in the past, as neglect may lead to an attack of what is known as inflammatory rheumatism or *rheumatic fever*. The symptoms of rheumatic fever are fever, pain and swelling in the joints (accompanied by

113

redness), profuse sweating and sore throat. Rheumatic fever is usually confined to children and adolescents; rheumatism in adults invariably takes the chronic form. The cause, as with all other forms of rheumatism in young or old alike, is the continuous over-consumption of strongly acid-forming foods in the daily dietary. The daily ingestion of meat two, three, and even four times a day, as well as excessive quantities of demineralised starches, sugars, and fats, as is very often the case in England and other large meat-eating countries (to say nothing of fish, cheese, eggs, milk, etc.), inevitably leads to the flooding of the system with highly acid impurities, which, the body being unable to throw off, collect round the joints and other inner structures to form the basis of all the so-called *uric-acid diseases*, such as rheumatism, neuritis, sciatica, etc.

Treatment.—No disease is so prone to leave disastrous after-effects behind it if treated along orthodox lines. The commonest of these after-effects is heart disease ; and it is such a commonplace occurrence that it has come to be regarded as almost inevitable. If the disease is treated properly, however, no complications or after-effects whatsoever need be feared. The treatment to adopt is as follows :

The child should be *fasted* until all swelling and fever have disappeared ; it may be given orange juice and water to drink (NO MILK !), and the bowels should be cleansed night and morning with the warm-water enema. To relieve the swelling and pain in the joints, hot and cold compresses may be applied several times daily, also cold packs to the whole trunk ; a cold pack to the throat is helpful also. (See Appendix for details of how the packs are applied.) When the tongue has cleared and temperature is steady at normal, the *all-fruit diet* can be adopted, and as convalescence progresses, the regular *diet for children* given in the Appendix can be gradually introduced. *Naturopathic attention is very desirable in all cases of rheumatic fever, where procurable.* The Epsom-salts bath is very beneficial during convalescence. (See also Section 13, page 419.)

Scarlet Fever.—Scarlet fever is a contagious disease, typical cases of which begin with strawberry tongue, vomiting, and fever ; within twenty-four hours a rash appears on the neck and rapidly spreads over the body, continuing for about six days, when it terminates in desquamation, or peeling, which lasts for three weeks or longer. The rash consists of minute points of bright scarlet colour, grouped on a slightly reddened skin. They run together in places, forming bright scarlet patches. Peeling begins at first in fine scales, which soon become larger, and in some cases the skin peels off in long strips. The fever is usually high. Sore throat is an early symptom, and if membranous may indicate diphtheria. The cause, although scarlet fever may be readily " caught " by a child, is the same old one of wrong feeding plus unhygienic living.

Treatment.—Scarlet fever is one of Nature's most volcanic " healing crises " ; through its medium vast amounts of toxic matter stored up in the child system for years are allowed to be thrown off via the skin. *Fasting*, with the administration of orange juice and water enough to quench the thirst, is the treatment required ; the warm-water enema should be used twice daily to cleanse the bowels, and cold packs to the body and throat will be beneficial. (See Appendix for details.) When the fever has run its course and temperature is steady at normal and the tongue has cleared—the sign always to be looked for when a fast is to be broken—the *all-fruit diet* can be adopted, and, as convalescence continues, the full *diet for children* given in the Appendix can be gradually instituted. The hot Epsom-salts bath, two or three times a week, will be very valuable during the peeling period, and plenty of tepid bathing should be encouraged during this time also.

Treated in the above manner, scarlet fever leaves its possessor in far better health than before, with a system almost free from toxins ; but treated in the orthodox way, no disease is more apt to leave such serious and varied after-effects and complications behind it. Chronic middle-ear disease, heart disease, and kidney disease are only a few of the results of the suppressive medical treatment of scarlet fever. (See also Section 13, page 419.)

(4) INFANTILE DEFICIENCY DISEASES

Rickets.—The medical profession has long recognised that rickets is the result of imperfect nutrition—or, in other words, of wrong feeding of infants. Would to God that they would apply the same reasoning to other diseases of childhood! Whilst the most important symptoms of the disease are found in the bones, it is not alone a bone disease ; the muscles, nerves, and organs are also seriously affected. The most common early symptoms are sweating of the head, restlessness at night, constipation, delayed and defective dentition (teething), and beading of the ribs. The last of these

symptoms appears as a row of small prominences extending in a
curved line up and down each side of the chest where the bone and
cartilage of the ribs join. Later, deformities appear, because of the
softening of the bones. The head is large and square ; the chest in
extreme cases shows two furrows, one running up and down, the other
round the body ; and the child is chicken or pigeon-breasted. The
spine is usually curved. The legs are either knock-kneed or bowed,
and in extreme cases they are otherwise deformed. The bones of the
arm may also be bent. An early and important symptom is swelling
of the ankle and wrist-joint. Catarrh is usually present.

Treatment.—If properly treated the rachitic child can grow out of
its unfortunate condition to an almost unbelievable degree. Proper
diet along the lines given in the Appendix, fresh air, sun and air
baths (or failing this, artificial sunlight treatment), will soon rescue
it from its parlous state, and sets its little feet on the path to sound
health. Rickets is a marvellous object-lesson of what can happen to
the human system when it is not given the proper elements needed
for building sound bone and healthy tissue ; yet, in spite of all that
rickets (and scurvy) can show in this connection, the medical profession persistently refuses to take the object-lesson to heart and
connect other diseases of childhood with imperfect nutrition and
unsound diet.

Scurvy.—Scurvy is another deficiency disease of children. It is
often mistaken for rheumatism, rickets, or paralysis. It is marked
by pain on motion, swelling of the extremities, bleeding or spongy
gums, and frequently by paralysis of one or more limbs, and black
and blue spots on the body. An insufficiency of *fresh food* in the
dietary is one of the causes of the disease.

Treatment.—Scurvy is a disease likely to attack the children of the
rich just as well as of the poor, because it arises in the system not
from an *insufficient diet* quantitatively, but from a diet lacking in the
organic mineral salts so essential to health and real vitality. Children
brought up on proprietary or patent foods, or on condensed milk,
are the most prone to the disease, as these foods are almost, if not
altogether, deficient in the life-giving organic minerals found so
abundantly in fresh milk, fresh fruits, vegetables, etc. Where the
disease is present, the child should be fed along the lines outlined in

the Appendix of the present book, with additional quantities of orange juice and fresh vegetable juices between meals ; and, with fresh air and sunshine, he will make a very speedy recovery from the trouble.

(5) INFANTILE SKIN DISEASES

Eczema.—This is a very common skin disease of children—especially eczema of the scalp—and is a constitutional disease brought on by wrong feeding plus (very often) previous suppressive drug treatment. (Eczema in a very young child may be the result of hereditary taints in the blood. It is a sign of defective health in the parents.) We must remember that the skin is one of the main channels through which bodily impurities are eliminated from the system, and the eczema of children is only another example of a natural healing crisis, similar in kind to that of scarlet or any other fever. The symptoms may be just a redness of the skin, or there may be a scaly formation or pustules. Extreme irritation is felt.

Treatment.—When it is remembered that eczema is the result of systemic toxæmia (or clogging of the body with toxins and impurities), the uselessness of attempting to deal with the condition by means of salves or ointments must be at once apparent. These medicinal agents only serve to *suppress* the disease and make it chronic ; they can never cure. Indeed, they may be even dangerous to life, for by forcing the eczema below the surface, they pave the way for some of the most dangerous diseases of childhood—diseases which may very easily lead to the death of the sufferer—such as infantile paralysis, consumption, etc.

The real treatment for eczema lies in *improving* elimination, by cleansing and purifying the infant system ; and for this purpose proper diet, sun and air bathing, Epsom-salts baths, the use of the enema, etc., are the measures required. A few days on the *all-fruit diet* to begin with, followed by the correct *dietary for children* given in the Appendix, together with the daily use of the enema, will soon begin the work of systemic cleansing ; and sun and air-bathing will be of immeasurable value. England being such a " poor " country where sunlight is concerned, the artificial sunlight apparatus will be found to be a very efficient substitute if the real thing is not procurable. Epsom-salts baths two or three times weekly will be most beneficial.

As regards local treatment, the affected parts should be bathed twice daily with hot water and Epsom salts ($\frac{1}{4}$ lb. to a bowlful), and a little olive oil applied. Scratching should be prevented as far as possible. *Use no dusting or drying powders, or ointments of any kind.* Further short periods on the *all-fruit diet* may be required at intervals in certain cases. (See also Section 2, page 125, for further information *re* skin diseases.)

Ringworm.—This disease belongs to the parasitic group of skin diseases, and minute parasites are found infesting the cuticle. It is shown in a yellowish discoloration of the skin and a peculiar circular area over which the disease extends. There is usually a slight itching of the skin, and scaly patches form. It may attack either the body or the scalp. The cause of ringworm is the lowered vitality and general unhealthiness of the sufferer. That is to say, the disease only attacks those whose health is poor, as a result of wrong feeding and unhygienic living generally.

Treatment.—The use of suppressive lotions or ointments for the treatment of ringworm is just as useless as their employment for the *successful* treatment of eczema, although the after-effects in this case will not be nearly so bad as with the more serious disease. As regards proper treatment, much that has been said concerning the treatment of eczema applies here. Proper diet, fresh air and sunshine, artificial sunlight treatment, the use of the enema, and the Epsom-salts bath, will all help to build up the child system and thus pave the way for the eradication of the trouble. As a preliminary to instituting the treatment, the child should be thoroughly washed all over with yellow soap and water. As to purely local treatment, nothing is so efficacious as artificial sunlight treatment.

SPECIAL NOTE.—*For all other skin diseases of childhood the reader is referred to the Section on Skin Diseases for Adults (Section 2, page 125), modifying the treatment as needed according to the age of the child.*

(6) NERVOUS DISEASES OF CHILDHOOD

Convulsions.—The symptoms of convulsions are too well known to require description here. In young children they are usually the result of digestive disturbance, and are not immediately serious. They may, however, be the result of epilepsy, brain disease, kidney disease, or the first stage of some infectious fever. They often occur in the children of the insane, the imbecile, and the hysterical, and also in those who have had a syphilitic or alcoholic family history.

Treatment.—For convulsions the most effective treatment is the warm bath. The child should be placed in a fairly hot bath (*not a really hot bath*), and kept there for several minutes. Afterwards, when its condition has quietened, the bowel should be emptied by means of the warm-water enema, and it should receive nothing in the way of food for at least twenty-four hours. It may have warm water only. The diet afterwards should be along the lines indicated in the Appendix. If the convulsion is the result of epilepsy or other definite organic trouble, the services of a Naturopath should be sought. (See also Section 5, page 177.)

Infantile Paralysis.—The children who suffer from this disease are in every case children who have been persistently *wrongly fed*. The medical idea of a germ being the cause of the trouble is just as wide of the mark as the claiming of a germ origin for diseases such as scarlet fever and diphtheria. The disease, once active in any child, can be transmitted to others, but only if these others are " ripe " for it—if they have the right soil in their system in the shape of systemic refuse for the germ to breed in, that is. The symptoms of the complaint are paralysis of the muscles of the extremities. Arms and legs may be involved, one arm, one leg, both legs, or only one muscle or group of muscles. There may be no symptoms until the paralysis appears, or there may be the usual chill, fever, convulsions, etc., which usher in other infectious fevers.

The cause of the disease is loss of tone and power of the nerve centres in the spinal cord dealing with the co-ordination and activity of the muscles of the arms and legs, brought on by systematic wrong feeding of children, the organic mineral salts so essential to proper functioning, and always so abundantly present in all natural uncooked foods, being absent from the child dietary. Pigeons and other creatures—mice, rats, guinea-pigs, etc.—when fed exclusively on a demineralised dietary as white bread or polished rice, exhibit all the symptoms of infantile paralysis after a few weeks of such a diet. Given wholemeal bread or unpolished rice thereafter, they make a rapid and complete recovery !

Treatment.—Whilst the fever lasts, fasting is the only treatment. The child should be given as much orange juice and water as it wants, and nothing else whatsoever. As soon as the febrile condition has subsided and the tongue has cleared, the *all-fruit diet* can be adopted, and, as convalescence increases, the full *diet for children* given in the Appendix can be gradually introduced. The warm-water enema should be used daily during the fasting period, and spinal manipulation at the hands of a competent Osteopath or Naturopath will hasten recovery greatly. *Massage to the affected limbs is especially good.* After recovery, the child should be encouraged to be out in the open air as much as possible, and fresh fruits and raw salad vegetables *must* be the main and staple items in the child dietary, together with fresh milk, wholemeal bread, and other un-refined and untampered food products, in order to make up for the great mineral deficiency in the child system due to previous wrong feeding. White bread, white sugar, refined cereals, and especially confectionery, jams, and other sugary products, must be rigorously excluded.

Meningitis.—Cerebro-spinal meningitis is an acute disease or fever attacking the inner lining of the spinal cord and brain tissue. It is perhaps the most serious of all the acute diseases of childhood, and is the outcome of wrong treatment of previous childhood and infantile disease along orthodox lines, in most cases. The attack usually begins with convulsions, violent headache, and high fever. The pain extends into the back of the neck and down the spine, the head is drawn backward, the back is rigid, the abdomen is normal or retracted, and constipation is obstinate. There is frequently delirium, which may be active, but there is often stupor and finally unconsciousness. In some cases spots appear upon the face and body, which have given the disease the name of " spotted fever." The cause, as already indicated, is wrong feeding plus the suppressive medical treatment of previous infantile and childhood disease, although a blow or fall may sometimes be the superficial initiating cause.

Treatment.—If left in orthodox medical hands, the treatment for meningitis is very unlikely to lead to anything in the slightest nature resembling a real cure. Most often the child dies under the treatment, or, if it recovers, the recovery is attended with all kinds of subsidiary ailments, such as deafness, blindness, partial paralysis, etc. The real treatment for meningitis, as for all other fevers, no matter which, is *fasting* ; but cases of meningitis should always be left to a competent Naturopath to handle *where at all possible*. Fasting, the use of the cold pack, the warm-water enema, etc., will all help to bring about the ultimate recovery of the child suffering from meningitis ; and being placed thereafter on to a sensible dietary, it will be in far better health after the disease than it was before—something which can *not* be said for the unfortunate patients treated along orthodox lines.* (See also Section 13, page 418.)

Polio (Poliomyelitis).—This is another name for *Infantile Paralysis*. (See treatment for this condition elsewhere in this section.) Present-day immunisation programmes for the prevention of polio may appear to give some degree of immunity, but many children are adversely affected by the injections, some far more seriously than others. Deaths also are sometimes reported from polio immunisation treatment. The Nature Cure viewpoint is that real immunity to polio or any other type of disease can be secured only through *right living, i.e.* through living on strict Nature Cure lines. This confers on the body a *natural* immunity to disease, which is far more potent and positive in effect than any type of artificial immunity conferred by dubious medical methods such as immunisation referred to.

St. Vitus' Dance (Chorea).—This disease consists of involuntary and irregular movements of many muscles or groups of muscles of the body. They are not under the control of the will, and are usually made worse by efforts to control them. They are rarely present during sleep, and are increased by excitement, fatigue, or embarrassment. They commonly begin in the muscles of the hands or face, so that children thus afflicted are often punished for dropping things or making grimaces. The mental condition as a rule undergoes change. Recurrent attacks are sometimes foreseen by the mother by the irritability of the child and a change in its disposition. The tongue is often thick and the speech indistinct. The disease runs a variable course. St. Vitus' dance is often closely associated with rheumatism in children, and, as with the latter, its cause is dietetic in origin ; although overwork at school and general nervous excitement may help on its occurrence in certain cases.

Treatment.—The usual medical treatment for St. Vitus' dance is to give the child arsenic in the form of *Fowler's solution*. This is

---

*Treatment with M & B or antibiotics is apparently far more successful than previous drug treatment, but it is just as *suppressive* in its after-effects.

undoubtedly the worst possible thing to do. It is loading the infant system with a most poisonous and harmful drug, and can lead to no ultimate good whatsoever. The real treatment for the complaint is as follows :

The child should be taken away from school at once and kept quietly at home. All reference to the condition of the child should be studiously avoided, and anything tending to heighten the nervous condition should be carefully prevented. Two or three days on the *all-fruit diet*, followed by the full *diet for children* given in the Appendix, is all the dietetic treatment needed in the less serious cases. Severe cases should be kept on *fruit only* for a week or longer if necessary, and rested in bed. The enema should be used nightly for the first few days of the treatment, and hot Epsom-salts baths once or twice a week will be extremely beneficial in all cases. A few days on fruit and milk, after the fruit diet, and before beginning the full diet, would be an advantage in many cases. For this the child has up to two pints of fresh unboiled milk daily with the fruit meals.

Rest, quietness and proper diet will bring the complaint to a close in the shortest possible time, but in the more serious cases a course of spinal manipulation would be very helpful. The child should be out in the open air so far as its condition permits, and anything conducive to increasing nervous strain, such as excessive reading, the learning of the piano, violin, etc., should be avoided for some considerable time after the disease has been cured. No DRUGS WHATSOEVER SHOULD BE GIVEN.

(7) PARASITIC DISEASES OF CHILDHOOD

Thread-worms.—The thread-worm is a small round white worm found in the large intestine and in the lower portion of the small intestine. The rectum or lower end of the large intestine is the spot most favoured by the parasite. The eggs are taken into the body by food or water, and there hatch out. There is no difficulty in detecting either the worms or the eggs, and the symptom which is ever present and prominent is intense itching, which is more troublesome at night when the child is warm in bed, and often prevents proper sleep. Other symptoms are irritability and fretfulness, burning pain, restlessness, disturbance of the functions of the bowels and bladder, loss of appetite, and anæmia. In sensitive children it is not unusual for convulsions and nervous twitching similar to St. Vitus' dance to be caused by the parasites.

Treatment.—Although it is true that the eggs of the thread-worm are taken quite accidentally into the body of the child through the medium of food or water, and there hatch out, they could never breed in the intestines if they did not find there a suitable medium for their propagation. This medium is an intestinal tract clogged with effete matter and systemic refuse due to *wrong feeding* of the child. Thus, although the taking of the eggs into the child system is accidental, the *real cause* of the persistence of thread-worms there is the same for all the other diseases of childhood—namely, wrong feeding.

Orthodox medical treatment for thread-worms is concerned exclusively with the extermination of the parasites and their eggs by means of often dangerous chemical agents, and no attention whatsoever is paid to the *underlying cause* of the propagation of the parasite, which, as we have already pointed out, is a toxic condition of the infant intestinal tract. It is this latter which needs primary attention, and not so much the worms and eggs. These will automatically disappear when the food they live and breed on—the systemic refuse and waste matter in the intestine and rectum—has been got rid of. Once this point is seen, everything else is relatively simple. The child should be kept on the *exclusively fresh-fruit diet* for up to a week, and then the *diet for children* given in the Appendix should be adopted, except that fatty foods, such as butter, cream, oil, etc., should be left out of the dietary for the time being, and meat and fish excluded also. In short, fruits, vegetables, milk and wholemeal bread should almost exclusively form the dietary until the parasites have completely disappeared. In some cases the all-fruit diet may have to be reverted to for a further few days at intervals, and in obstinate cases a short fast may have to be instituted. During the all-fruit or fasting period the bowel should be cleansed nightly with the warm-water enema, in the water of which may be infused a pinch of tobacco or a teaspoonful of oil of turpentine. No drugs or medicinal agents *of any kind* should be used. The eating of sugary foods, such as jams, marmalade, white sugar, confectionery, etc., must be strictly forbidden. Only extreme rigidness with the dietary will pave the way for the complete eradication of the trouble once and for all.

.   .   .   .   .   .

The subject of children's ailments cannot be left without reference to *bed-wetting* and *teething*, which are accordingly being dealt with in the following special note :

Bed-wetting.—Bed-wetting in children of fairly advanced age is usually due to mental strain, induced by over-stimulation of the brain through excessive school work, incitement by parents to learn too much, etc., etc. In these cases what is therefore required is plenty of rest and quiet, and freedom from all undue mental activity and nervous excitement. As regards physical treatment, a few days on the *all-fruit diet*, with the use of the warm-water enema to cleanse the bowels, will be helpful, with the *child menus* given in the Appendix to follow. A daily cold sitz-bath will help to tone up the bladder; or, failing this, the parts in the region of the bladder should receive a daily sponging with cold water, or even twice daily. The child should be out in the fresh air as much as possible, and outdoor games should be encouraged in preference to indoor.

Teething.—Practically every ailment which besets the child in the first two years of its life is set down to " teething." The term is a most convenient one, and usually satisfies both doctor and parent alike ; but the fact is that if a child is brought up properly as regards food and general hygiene, it will cut its teeth *without any undue trouble at all*. What is really caused by wrong feeding and wrong care of children is set down to a purely natural phenomenon which, in the ordinary way, should give the child no signs of its taking place at all, beyond a slight soreness of the gums, perhaps.

DISEASES OF THE SKIN (AND SCALP)

Abscesses—Acne—Alopecia—Baldness—Boils — Carbuncles — Dandruff—Dermatitis — Eczema — Erysipelas — Erythema — Ichthyosis — Impetigo — Lupus — Nettle-rash (Urticaria)— Psoriasis — Ringworm — Seborrhœa — Shingles—Sycosis.

THE skin, covering the whole of the body as it does, is a most marvellous and intricate piece of bodily mechanism designed by Nature for many purposes, the chief of which being the protection of the inner organism, the regulation of body temperature, and the elimination of cell-waste and systemic refuse. It must be pointed out that the skin is not a thing apart, as it were ; it is part of, and bound up intimately with, *the whole organism*, and for its healthy and efficient functioning depends entirely upon the way the rest of the organism *as a whole* is acting.

When we realise that the skin is directly connected with, and very intimately bound up with, the working of the rest of the organism, we can begin to understand something of the origination of skin diseases. We see that these diseases, far from being chance affairs, having nothing whatever to do with the body as a whole, are directly connected with it, and are indeed the outcome of its malfunctioning. Through the skin large quantities of toxic matter can be easily eliminated—owing to the enormous skin surface—and it is in this way that most of the skin diseases we are acquainted with originate. They are merely attempts on the part of Nature to throw off systemic poisons and bodily refuse which cannot be eliminated in any other convenient way.

For instance, one of the greatest causes of skin diseases is constipation. If the bowels are not acting properly, systemic refuse is not eliminated as quickly as it might be, the blood becomes surcharged with toxic matter, and the skin is used for the purpose of getting rid of the excess product. Especially is this so if the skin—either through unhygienic habits of living or other causes—is itself in a devitalised condition, such a state of affairs leading more quickly than any other to the setting up of that form of vicarious elimination known as " diseases of the skin."

Then, again, the skin is often utilised for the purpose of eliminating drugs—especially those of metallic origin—which have been stored up in the system as a result of former medical treatment of diseases of various kinds. Many cases of skin disease, especially *dermatitis*, originate in this way.

So that all in all, we can see that the skin is the great gateway through which Nature seeks to throw off the waste materials and poisons collected in the system through many causes—wrong feeding, unhygienic living, previous drug treatment, etc., etc. Thus do skin diseases originate, and to get rid of them what we have to do is to *help on* the eliminative process already set in operation by Nature, through the medium of the disease, and so literally *help the disease right out of the system !* That, in brief, is the secret underlying all *natural* treatment for skin diseases.

To the medical profession skin diseases are just things that happen to the individual without any reference to his internal condition and mode of living generally ; and that is precisely why these diseases, when treated in orthodox fashion, never respond properly to treatment. The disease is treated purely from the local point of view, and not from the systemic. To attempt to cure a skin disease such as acne, for instance (which is entirely the result of wrong feeding plus chronic constipation), by the application of external ointments and salves is the height of folly and ignorance. The disease can only be overcome by a thorough course of systemic cleansing, in which proper dieting plays a most important part. Yet that is how the medical profession goes on. No wonder skin diseases continue to baffle it, despite all the elaborate and painstaking efforts it makes to cure them !

If treated properly, diseases of the skin disappear, leaving the sufferer in far better general health than before, because of the great lessening of the total amount of toxic matter present in his system, and because of the rejuvenation of the bodily mechanism as a whole, resulting from the treatment ; but treated along orthodox medical lines, the disease, if it disappear at all as a result of the treatment, does so only because the toxins and impurities which the system was trying to throw off through the medium of the disease have been thrust back into the blood-stream again, to cause further trouble later on.

In short, the orthodox treatment for skin diseases by means of ointments, salves, etc., does not allow the toxic matter at the root of the trouble to be *eliminated*, as a real cure demands ; it merely *suppresses* the disease, that is all. And if the reader can see this clearly, then the fundamental difference between the natural treatment for skin diseases (about to be described) and that usually given by the medical profession for the same diseases will be recognised in all its full significant relationship to the future life and health of the individual sufferer. (The same remarks regarding suppressive treatment already applied to the ointments and salves prescribed by the medical fraternity for skin diseases can also be applied in full to such medical methods as X-ray treatment, radium therapy, and all other intensive forms of light treatment—other than artificial sunlight—used in the orthodox treatment of skin diseases. *They all suppress the disease; they never cure!*)

Having unburdened ourselves of the foregoing preliminary remarks, we can now go on to the outlining of the natural treatment for those forms of skin disease most prevalent in our midst to-day, at the same time assuring the sufferer that by such treatment not only can his disease be *really* cured (in the great majority of cases), but his whole general health can be reorganised.

Abscesses.—See Section 14, page 424.

Acne.—There are half a dozen or more varieties of this form of skin disease, all of them concerned with the sebaceous glands, or glands connected with the hair follicles (not the sweat glands). There is one form of acne in which there is an oily or greasy condition of the scalp, which extends also to the forehead and face; another in which there is dandruff and loss of hair, with crusts and scales on the nose and cheeks; another in which there are hard and horny masses on the face (this being the form in which it occurs in the aged). Then there is a form which comes on the face of children, in which there are usually a few lumps containing a kind of cheesy material; whilst the wens and tumours on the face and scalp of grown people also belong to the acne class of skin disease. The most common form of acne is that known as "blackheads," in which the nose, face, and forehead are covered with black points or spots. Whatever the form acne takes in any individual case, the cause is always *wrong feeding habits plus chronic constipation*, the waste matter the bowels should have thrown off being left behind in the system and vicariously eliminated as best the system can through the medium of the sebaceous glands, *as acne*.

Treatment.—To try to get rid of acne by the administration of salves or ointments is useless. The treatment is mainly dietetic, although local measures—about to be described—can also be used with good effect. To begin with, the sufferer should go on to the *all-fruit diet* given in the Appendix for from five to seven or ten days, according to the severity of the condition. Then the *regular weekly diet* given in the Appendix should be adopted. Further shorter periods on the all-fruit diet (of, say, three days' duration) will be necessary in most cases, at monthly intervals, until the skin condition has quite normalised itself. The warm-water enema should be used nightly to cleanse the bowels for the first week of the treatment, and the general rules for the eradication of constipation (given in Section 9, page 272) should be put into effect. Hot Epsom-salts baths two or three times a week will be extremely helpful in all cases of acne.

As regards purely local treatment, hot fomentations should be applied to open up the pores, and waste matter squeezed out. Then rinse with cold water. Exposure of the whole body to sun and air—sun and air baths—is also a very good thing ; whilst the morning dry friction and cold sponge, as well as the breathing and physical exercises given in the Appendix, should not be omitted from the treatment. Strict attention to the future dietary is essential to recovery ; and sugary, starchy, protein and fatty foods must all have a very watchful eye kept on them. *Very little* meat should be eaten ; no sugar ; no strong tea or coffee ; no condiments, pickles, sauces, etc. Fresh air and outdoor exercise are two factors in the treatment which must never be overlooked.

Alopecia.—Alopecia is a condition in which the hair falls out in patches, and it may occur at any period of life from infancy to old age. It is due to an affection of the hair follicles and of the sebaceous glands, but its actual cause may be very hard to locate in each individual case. *Defective nutrition*—due to the continual eating of demineralised and devitalised foods over a period of many years—may be the cause in many cases, whilst poor general health and/or prolonged emotional and mental disturbances may be the cause in others. Again, infectious fevers treated along orthodox lines sometimes result in alopecia, and a general toxæmic condition due to many and varied causes may often lead to the development of the trouble.

Treatment.—In all cases of alopecia the general health-level of the sufferer must be improved and the skin condition toned up. These are the first essentials to recovery. A few days on the *all-fruit diet*, followed by the *full weekly diet* given in the Appendix (with the use of the enema nightly for the first few days), would be the best way to begin the treatment. Further short periods on all-fruit should be taken from time to time. The hot Epsom-salts bath once or twice a week is most advisable ; and the morning friction and sponge, as well as the breathing and physical exercises given in the Appendix, must be gone through daily.

As regards local treatment, the whole scalp should be thoroughly massaged each night for five minutes, with the finger-tips, and in the morning the scalp should receive a good brushing with a stiff bristle brush ; and in order to let the sun and air get to the scalp as much as possible, no hat should be worn, where practicable. For the purposes of the daily scalp massage, the finger-tips can be dipped into a little olive oil or some dilute lemon juice, whichever proves the more beneficial. Placing the head under hot and cold water alternately, for a few minutes daily, is also most helpful ; as well as the application of hot towels to the scalp, followed by a rinsing with cold water.

Fresh air and outdoor exercise should be encouraged as much as possible ; whilst in cases where emotional or mental factors are connected with the setting up of the trouble, change of scene and rest are of great value. (See also treatment for *Baldness*, following.)

Baldness.—The causes of baldness, as of partial baldness (or *alopecia*), are many and varied, and cannot always be successfully named in any particular case. Poor health, an enervated or over-worked system, the constant wearing of a hat, the persistent use of hair-creams or hair oil—all these play their part in bringing on baldness. *Defective nutrition*—due to the eating of demineralised or refined foods over a period of many years—and the resultant impoverishment of the hair follicles and glands is one of the chief predisposing causes towards the condition. It must be mentioned here that the chief element the hair follicles need is *silica*. This is found in all natural unspoilt foods, such as fruits, vegetables, whole-grain cereals, etc., but *not* in white bread, cooked vegetables, and the other usual adjuncts of a demineralised dietary.

Treatment.—All that has just been said with regard to alopecia applies with equal force to the treatment for baldness. A few days on *all-fruit* (with the use of the enema nightly), followed by the adoption of the *full weekly diet* given in the Appendix, is the best way to begin the treatment. Where present, constipation should be overcome by following out the rules for its eradication given in Section 9, page 275. The improvement of skin action by the daily friction and sitz-bath or cold sponge is most essential, and all the other measures given in the treatment for alopecia must be given full attention, and should be carried out religiously by the sufferer from baldness. Going without a hat (as recommended in the treatment for alopecia), so as to allow full play to the healing and tonic effects of wind and sun, is a most helpful measure indeed. *Patent hair restorers, hair tonics, etc.*, should never be used, and electrical treatment for the hair—other than violet ray—is also not recommended. (This latter is often beneficial in conjunction with natural treatment.)

Boils.—A boil (or furuncle) is a painful inflammatory swelling of the skin which develops around a hair follicle. There may be a single one, or several may develop in the same area or different areas at or about the same time, or they may come in successive crops. The swelling is not necessarily limited to one hair follicle, and as many follicles as may be included in the inflammation, so many openings will there be when the boil is ripe and discharges. The cause of boils is a toxic blood-stream due to wrong dietetic habits and wrong living generally (*especially* the eating of excessive quantities of demineralised starchy and sugary foods), and their presence is a sure sign that that particular individual's system needs a thorough internal cleansing. They usually make their appearance when the sufferer is in a " run-down " or more than usually devitalised condition.

Treatment.—The treatment for boils is as follows : Have from five to seven or ten days on the *all-ruit diet* given in the Appendix (or else a fast for three to five days on orange juice), followed by the adoption of the *general weekly diet* also given in the Appendix Further short periods on all-fruit may be needed from time to time, or further occasional short fasts, according to the general health-level and bodily condition of the patient. The warm-water enema should be used nightly for the first few days of the treatment, and constipation (where habitual) overcome by the adoption of the rules outlined in the treatment for that condition in Section 9, page 275. A hot Epsom-salts bath should be taken twice or three times a week until the boil or boils have gone, and once weekly thereafter. The morning dry friction and sitz-bath or cold sponge outlined in the Appendix should be undertaken regularly, as also the exercises therein given, both breathing and physical. The bodily condition should be further toned up by plenty of fresh air and outdoor exercise, and the future dietary must be carefully watched. Starchy and sugary foods—especially cakes, pastries, sweets, chocolates, white sugar, white bread, etc.—are the chief dietetic offenders. All condiments must be strictly avoided, as also sauces, pickles, etc.

As regards purely local treatment, bathing with hot fomentations is the best thing. Vaccine treatment for boils, as practised by the medical profession to-day, *must* lead to the definite impairment of the future health of the patient, because of its *suppressive* action ; even though such treatment is *apparently* successful in certain cases for the time being, it should be strictly avoided.

Carbuncles.—Boils and carbuncles are very similar things, really, and it is hard to distinguish one from the other sometimes. Their main differences are : (1) a carbuncle is an inflammation which is more deep-seated than a boil ; (2) it covers more surface ; (3) it does not always present a swelling so much elevated above the surface of the body as a boil ; and (4) it may be accompanied by an intense redness which sometimes is suggestive of erysipelas. When a carbuncle discharges it does so from many openings and is accompanied by much sloughing of the skin. Its constitutional effects are very profound and prostrating, and sometimes may lead to fatal results, but only in the case of those of very poor vitality.

Like boils, carbuncles are a sign of a very toxic blood-stream due to wrong feeding and wrong living generally, and usually put in their appearance when the unfortunate sufferer is in an unusually low state vitally, through overwork, over-excess, etc., etc. Diabetics and those suffering from kidney disease and tuberculosis often have them as part of the development of the disease.

Treaiment.—The treatment for carbuncles is very much on the same lines as that for boils, only in this case more rigorous treatment is needed. If personal naturopathic treatment cannot be obtained, the best course to pursue is as follows : A fast for from four to seven days should be undertaken, on orange juice and water (or vegetable juices), after which the *restricted diet* given in the Appendix should be adopted for a further seven to ten or fourteen days. This diet may be then discontinued, and the *full weekly diet* begun, if the carbuncle shows satisfactory signs of clearing up. This full weekly diet should be adhered to as strictly as possible from then on. The patient should rest in bed during the first part of the treatment, or he should rest as much as he possibly can ; and the warm-water enema should be used nightly to cleanse the bowels. If the patient is habitually constipated, the rules for the overcoming of constipation, and the future use of the enema, should be carefully studied in Section 9, page 276. Hot Epsom-salts baths, two or three times a week, will be very helpful, and the morning dry friction and sitz-bath or cold sponge should be begun as soon as the patient is well enough. The breathing and other exercises given in the Appendix should then be adopted regularly too. All enervating habits or practices must be discontinued. Clean living—both dietetic and otherwise —must be the rule henceforward.

As regards local treatment, the best thing is the application of hot fomentations several times during the day. Spinal manipulation, where procurable, will be most beneficial in conjunction with the foregoing treatment.

Dandruff.—In dandruff there is a constant fall of little white or yellow scales from the scalp or face, particularly from the former. It increases whenever the hair is brushed or rubbed. It may also appear as lumps or crusts on the scalp. There is an oily kind of dandruff, too, which is the most annoying of all. Each and every form is, however, the direct result of a toxic condition of the system brought on mainly by wrong feeding and constipation, and its treatment is therefore largely constitutional. The application of hair washes and similar preparations is just a waste of time if a permanent cure is desired.

Treatment.—As a matter of fact acne and dandruff are very closely related as to cause and cure ; they are both attempts at vicarious elimination of toxins from the system through the medium of the skin and their treatment is almost identical. The reader suffering from dandruff should therefore put into operation the treatment given for *acne* in the preceding pages of the present section, although in this case there is no need to apply the hot fomentations to the affected areas. Instead, for local treatment, the hair should be washed once every week with hot water and good plain soap—such as castile—and the scalp massaged for five minutes every night with the finger-tips. (The finger-tips may be dipped in a little dilute lemon juice beforehand.) Exposure of the head to the rays of the sun is a good thing, and generally an attempt should be made to keep the bodily health at the highest possible level.

Dermatitis.—Dermatitis really means inflammation of the skin, both external and internal. It may occur as a result of plant poisoning—such as that which occurs from contact with poison ivy ; it may result from a burn ; it may be due to intestinal toxaemia; and it also may be due to the elimination of drugs from the system through the medium of the skin. In short, its appearance may be due to causes both many and varied, and treatment must also vary accordingly.

Treatment.—It is obvious from what has just been said that no two cases of dermatitis can be treated exactly alike. If the trouble is constitutional, however—that is, if it arises from *internal causes* (or previous drug treatment)—from five to seven or ten days on the *all-fruit diet,* or a short fast for from three to five days on orange juice, is the best way to start the treatment, followed by the adoption of the *weekly diet-sheet* outlined in the Appendix.

If the case is severe, there should be a fast for from three to five or seven days, followed by a week to a fortnight on the *restricted diet* given in the Appendix, before beginning the full diet, with further fasts and periods of restricted dieting at intervals thereafter, as required. The warm-water enema should be used nightly to cleanse the bowels during the first week or so of the treatment, and after as necessary, and hot Epsom-salts baths should be taken three times weekly. The affected areas may also be bathed twice daily in hot water and Epsom salts ($\frac{1}{4}$ lb. to a bowlful).* *Use no medicinal agents of any kind.*

* After Epsom-salts bathing a little olive oil may be applied.

Where the trouble is due to external causes, such as a burn or burns, see treatment for burns in Appendix B, First Aid Section, page 468.

Eczema.—Eczema is the most common and one of the most troublesome diseases which affect the skin. It is *essentially* a constitutional disease—the result of a toxic condition of the system —and covers a wide variety of forms, the majority of eczemas being of a chronic variety. The symptom which is most frequent is either burning or itching, and this is often severe enough almost to drive the sufferer distracted. It is usually worse at night when the heat of the body is retained by the bed-clothes. Scratching only makes the trouble worse. In some cases there is a watery discharge, and in others the skin becomes hard, and cracks. Sometimes there are papules or pimples. In short, the condition may be of the most varied external nature, but the underlying cause is *always* the same, i.e. a toxic condition of the system due to wrong feeding and wrong living generally. (Suppressive drug treatment of former disease is also a most potent subsidiary causative factor in many cases.)

Treatment.—Of all forms of skin disease, eczema is the most intractable to orthodox treatment, because not until the trouble has been *tackled at its source* can any hope of real cure be possible. To resort to the use of salves or ointments is worse than useless. Indeed, eczema treated in such a fashion often leads to serious trouble in other directions ; for the toxins thus forced back again into the system, as a result of the suppressive treatment employed, find lodgment in the vital organs and inner structures, and may be the basis for such diseases as tuberculosis, heart disease, kidney disease, etc., etc. The correct treatment for eczema is as follows :

Depending on the severity and duration of the trouble, a fast for from four to seven days on orange juice and water should be undertaken, followed by seven to ten or fourteen days on the *restricted diet* given in the Appendix. Then the *full weekly diet* given therein can be adopted. In many cases further short fasts and periods on the restricted diet will be necessary, at, say, two-monthly intervals, for some time to come, before the condition can be fully cleared up. (This will all depend upon the progress being made in the meantime, of course.) The warm-water enema should be used nightly to cleanse the bowels during the fast, and after if necessary ; and if constipation is habitual, the rules for its eradication should be observed, as given in Section 9, page 275.

The hot Epsom-salts bath is often exceptionally useful in dealing with eczema, and *three* full baths should be taken weekly until the trouble begins radically to subside, when the number of baths may be lessened to two weekly, and thence finally to one. The affected areas should also be bathed night and morning in hot water containing Epsom salts ($\frac{1}{4}$ lb. of salts to a bowlful of hot water).* Exposure of *the whole body* to sun and air is extremely good, and if this is not possible, a course of artificial sunlight treatment can be fully recommended, in conjunction with the treatment outlined above. The health of the skin (and body) should be maintained at its highest level by means of the daily dry friction and sitz-bath or sponge, and by the carrying out of the breathing and physical exercises given in the Appendix. Fresh air and outdoor exercise are also essential factors to be considered. The future diet must be strictly in accordance with the diet-sheet given in the Appendix, and tea and coffee, alcoholic beverages, and all condiments and highly flavoured dishes avoided. (By the term " condiments " is also here meant salt.) Sugar should be strictly avoided also, and likewise white-flour products, denatured cereals such as polished rice, pearled barley, etc., and all tinned and potted foods. ONLY EAT PURE, WHOLESOME FOODS. (Really stubborn cases of eczema may need a protracted fast or series of fasts, under naturopathic guidance, to effect a cure.) See also special note on " Clay Packs " at end of this section, page 140.

Erysipelas.—Erysipelas may begin on any portion of the skin surface, but the face is the usual part attacked. It is an affection of the lymphatic vessels, and it is the inflammation of these vessels which gives the disease its characteristic redness and inflammation. Occasionally the skin of the joints is the part affected, and it may set in anywhere as the result of a scratch or wound. It may be said right away that no one whose body is really clean within can have erysipelas; it only arises as the result of a highly toxic condition of the body. Treatment is therefore in every case constitutional rather than local.

Treatment.—The treatment for erysipelas should be as follows : The patient should be kept on water and orange juice or vegetable

* After Epsom-salts bathing a little olive oil may be applied.

juices for as long as the fever lasts, which may be for from three days to a week or longer. Then the *all-fruit diet* can be adopted for a further few days, and finally the *full weekly diet* given in the Appendix can be gradually introduced as convalescence progresses. The warm-water enema should be used nightly for the first week of the treatment, and longer if necessary ; and the affected area should have cold packs applied to it at frequent intervals during the day. (See Appendix for details of packs.) The hot Epsom-salts bath is extremely valuable in these cases, and, if possible, the patient should have one *every* day during the first part of the treatment, the number being gradually reduced per week thereafter. When full convalescence is reached, the morning dry friction and sponge should be adopted as a regular measure, together with the daily performance of the breathing and other exercises given in the Appendix. *Future strict attention to diet is essential.*

Erythema.—Erythema is merely a reddening or flushing of the skin, and may be due to many causes : working in a hot atmosphere, excessive drinking, digestive disturbances, etc. Where the trouble is constitutional—due to digestive disturbances, etc.—see treatment for Indigestion in Section 9, page 297. Where the cause of the trouble is vocational or due to alcoholic excesses, the course to be taken must be obvious if a cure is desired.

Ichthyosis.—This is a rather rare disease in which there is a scaly formation on the skin surface something like that of the scales of a fish or snake. Vocation sometimes plays a part in giving rise to its appearance, but really it is a constitutional disease similar in many ways to eczema.

Treatment.—This is a very difficult disease to treat successfully, but the treatment given for eczema should be carried out to the full. The Epsom-salts bath and sunlight treatment are very valuable assets to natural treatment.

Impetigo.—This is essentially a disease of childhood, although it not infrequently occurs in adults. It is met with most often in schools or institutions devoted exclusively to the care of children and is *constitutional* in origin, being due to the *malnutrition* brought on by persistent wrong feeding and unhygienic habits of living. It appears in the form of vesicles or blisters mainly on the face, neck, and hands, which later form into scabs and fall off. The disease is easily passed on to others by contact, but only if these same others are in a similar state of toxicity and impaired vitality.

Treatment.—As it is only those who are suffering from *mal-nutrition* who develop impetigo, the treatment required for its cure is *essentially constitutional*, consisting of proper diet, correct hygiene, fresh air, etc. For a child suffering from the disease, from four to seven days on *all-fruit* is the best way to start the treatment, whilst for an adult a short fast for from three to five days on orange juice and water would be best. The future dietary should be along the lines laid down in the Appendix, and great care must be taken to see that fresh fruits, raw salads, fresh milk, and wholemeal bread occupy the most important places therein. (Further short periods on all-fruit, or further short fasts, at monthly intervals, may be needed in certain cases). The warm-water enema should be used nightly for the first week of the treatment, and longer if necessary; and if constipation is habitual, the rules for its eradication given in Section 9, page 275, should be put into operation.

The hot Epsom-salts bath three times weekly is a most helpful measure (the number of baths can be diminished as the trouble disappears); and the affected areas should be bathed twice daily in hot water containing Epsom-salts ($\frac{1}{4}$lb. of salts to a bowlful of hot water). Sun and air baths can be strongly recommended, and the daily dry friction and sponge and the breathing and other excercises given in the Appendix must not be omitted from the treatment.

Lupus.—This is a skin disease of tubercular origin, and is essentially constitutional in character—that is to say, it only attacks those whose bodily condition is poor as a result of wrong living and wrong feeding generally. More often it is on the face than elsewhere, beginning on the bridge of the nose and extending symmetrically to either side of the face. Occasionally the lobe of of the ear is affected. It begins as a red spot, and as it spreads becomes scaly, but with a well-defined margin. It is a very disfiguring and annoying disease, and it is well worth the sufferer doing all he can to get rid of it. Orthodox forms of treatment are just a waste of time.

Treatment.—The sufferer from lupus should place himself under the care of a competent Naturopath at once, as personal treatment is most essential. Strict diet, fresh air, and all measures for building up the tone of the body are required. Sun and air baths, artificial sunlight treatment, and spinal manipulation are all indicated for this trouble. The Epsom-salts bath is also very useful. (Obviously the longer the disease has been in existence, the more difficult will it be to eradicate.)

Nettle-rash (Urticaria).—This skin disease is also called *hives*, and consists of an eruption of hard, slightly raised blotches or wheals, white, pink, or bright red in colour, with a white spot in the centre. There may be large numbers of them all over the body, either singly or in groups, ranging in size from a pea to a half-crown. The disease is most trying to the sufferer, because of the intolerable itching and pricking, and is aggravated by scratching. *The cause of the trouble is essentially dietetic.*

Treatment.—Five to seven or ten days on the *all-fruit diet* (or a fast for from three to five days) is the best way to begin the treatment, and this should then be followed by the adoption of the *full weekly diet-sheet* given in the Appendix. (Future strict adherence to this weekly dietary is absolutely essential if the trouble is not to return again at other times.) Two or three days on the *all-fruit diet*, every now and then, will also be a good thing to still further cleanse the system of toxic matter.

The warm-water enema should be used nightly whilst on the *all-fruit diet*, and later if necessary, and the hot Epsom-salts bath should be taken three times a week for the time being, reducing to two weekly as the disease disappears. A dry friction and sponge should be taken daily, and the breathing and other exercises given in the Appendix gone through regularly. Strong tea, coffee, alcohol and all condiments and highly spiced or flavoured dishes should be avoided in future ; also sugar, all white-flour products, and *unripe* or very acid fruits.

Psoriasis.—This is one of the most stubborn forms of skin disease, and, like eczema, is constitutional. No amount of external treatment in the form of ointments and salves will be of any *permanent* use. The disease appears on the elbows, in front of the lower limbs, the scalp, and the sides of the body, and sometimes on the back of the hands and feet, and face. In appearance it consists of round red patches of skin covered with shiny scales or crusts, which bleed profusely if more than the outer crust is peeled off. There is also a great deal of itching.

Treatment.—The natural treatment for psoriasis is identical with that for eczema, the causes being the same in either case, although psoriasis carries with it a suggestion of hereditary taints which eczema usually does not. The sufferer from psoriasis should therefore carry out in every detail the treatment given for eczema in the preceding pages of the present section. (See also special note on " Clay Packs " at the end of this section, page 140.)

Ringworm.—See treatment for *Ringworm* in the section on *Children's Ailments*, page 118.

Seborrhœa.—This is a disease of the sebaceous or oil glands which are distributed all over the skin surface to provide lubricating materials to the hair follicles. For cause and treatment, the sufferer is referred to *acne*, in the present section, with which seborrhœa is very closely related.

Shingles.—This is a disease of nervous origin, and is most often the result of intestinal toxæmia, especially through the eating of excessive quantities of flesh foods. There is fever for three or four days, followed by pain, which may subside after the eruption appears. This last is in the form of groups of vesicles or blisters, as large as a pea or bean, with as many as twenty in a group sometimes. The blisters come in crops over a period of weeks, and there is much inflammation and swelling of the surrounding parts. The vesicles eventually discharge. The eruption may be on any part of the body, but is most usually seen on the abdomen, face, chest, and arms.

Treatment.—The treatment for shingles is as follows : The patient should be kept on orange juice and water only for from four to seven days, according to the severity of the attack. The bowels should be cleansed night and morning during this period with the warm-water enema, and less and less frequently thereafter. As the more active symptoms of the trouble begin to disappear, the *all-fruit diet* can be adopted for a few days, and then the *full weekly diet* given in the Appendix can be gradually introduced. The hot Epsom-salts bath is extremely valuable in this disorder, and the patient should have one every other day, if possible, whilst the trouble is well advanced, and less frequently thereafter. The affected parts can also be bathed daily with hot water and Epsom salts ($\frac{1}{4}$ lb. to a bowlful).

When convalescent, the dietary must be very strictly watched, and the morning dry friction, cold sponge, breathing exercises, etc., given in the Appendix, should be undertaken regularly. Artificial sunlight treatment is a very valuable aid to recovery.

Sycosis.—This is a disease connected with the hair follicles, and is commonly known as *barber's rash*, or eczema of the beard. It consists of inflammation and swelling of the hair follicles, and is very painful and troublesome. Although the superficial cause of the disease may be external, it is essentially a disease of constitutional origin, and the treatment given in the present section for *Eczema* (page 134) will be found the most efficacious way of dealing with the condition. External treatment by means of salves, ointments, etc., will never effect a real cure. The full Epsom-salts bath, Epsom-salts applications, and sun and air bathing (as advised for the treatment of eczema) are most useful indeed. Artificial sunlight treatment is recommended as a desirable adjunct to the treatment here advised.

SPECIAL NOTE RE " CLAY PACKS."—The use of *clay packs* in the treatment of skin diseases has been found very valuable by many Naturopaths—of course in conjunction with a proper scheme of dietetic and other natural treatment. The writer has therefore thought it incumbent upon him to mention them here.

The packs are made by mixing the clay with a little water, and applying to the areas affected. After the clay has dried, it is removed and a fresh pack put on.

Clay packs are *eliminative* in their action, not suppressive, as salves, ointments, etc., are. They *absorb and remove* the toxins present in the diseased skin areas ; the toxins are *not* forced back into the blood-stream, as in orthodox treatment for skin diseases.

Clay for clay packs can be obtained through any Health Food Store. Clay packs are best suited for skin diseases of the eczema and psoriasis type.

DISEASES OF THE JOINTS AND
RHEUMATIC AFFECTIONS

Ankle-joint disease—Disease of the shoulder, elbow, and wrist-joints—Fibrositis—Gout—Hip-joint disease—Housemaid's knee (Bursitis)—Knee-joint disease : white swelling—Lateral curvature of the spine—Lumbago—Muscular Rheumatism (Fibrositis)—Pott's disease—Rheumatism—Rheumatoid arthritis—Slipped disc—Synovitis.

IN this section diseases of the joints will be dealt with, the most important being those of tubercular and rheumatic origin. (*Lumbago* and *muscular rheumatism*, although affections of the muscles and not of the joints, are also included in this section, as they are of rheumatic origin.)

There is no disease so prevalent to-day as rheumatism, and the inability of the medical profession to deal with it successfully lies simply and solely in the fact that they attribute its cause to everything but the right one, which is, most definitely and conclusively, *wrong feeding habits.*

At a medical conference at Bath in 1928, Sir W. Farquhar Buzzard, Physician to King George V., said that " They—the medical profession—*did not know the cause of rheumatism,* a disease which was costing the nation £20,000,000 every year through loss of work, sick pay, etc." Yet, do doctors refrain from treating the disease on that score ? Do they tell their patients that they are just as ignorant of the cause of the disease as the patient himself ? Oh no ; the said trusting patient is told to have his teeth out, or his tonsils removed, or prevailed upon to undergo an expensive course of inoculation or electrical treatment—all to no avail, as might have been expected in the first place. For if the cause of a disease is not known, how can it be treated successfully ?

In naturopathic circles, rheumatism is by no means the mysterious disease it appears to be to the medical profession. It is recognised as being purely and simply a disease of dietetic origin, and the most remarkable and gratifying results have been obtained in its treatment by Nature-Cure practitioners the world over. (The same remarks apply to rheumatoid arthritis too, although in a lesser degree, as arthritis is a far more serious condition to deal with than simple rheumatism, and results are not obtained so quickly.) When the medical profession ceases to look to germs as the cause of disease, and casts its eyes upon the food men take into their bodies instead, and studies its action on the system carefully, it will perhaps begin to see the cause of not only rheumatism and arthritis, but of all the other dread diseases which beset our present-day humanity !

The foods modern man is most addicted to—meat, white bread, sugar, refined cereals, etc.—all leave a large residue of acid toxic waste in the system, which is ineffectually neutralised as a result of the absence of sufficient quantities of alkaline mineral salts in the food eaten (through obsolete cooking and modern food-refining methods). The result is a continual piling up of these acid impurities in the system, first in the mucous membrane, where they are expelled in the form of catarrh, and secondly around the joints and bony structures, where they form the basis of what we now call rheumatism. (The retention of these toxic substances in the vital organs and body structures is the starting-point for *all disease*, as already pointed out to the reader.)

Everyone has heard of the connection between uric acid (the name popularly given to these acid waste materials) and rheumatism. (Even the medical profession has !) Yet how very, very few indeed are they who can trace the formation of uric acid in the system back to its true source (which is, daily and persistent errors in diet continued over a period of many years) ?

Which only shows how blind the world can be as regards the relationship existing between its own food follies and the diseases which are their direct outcome !

The reason why rheumatism and arthritis affect the bony structure of the body is quite simple to understand, once the underlying facts of the matter are made clear. These large quantities of acid waste matter which are steadily piling up in the unwise food-eater's system have to be put away somewhere (if the body cannot throw them off), and they have a very great affinity for bony structure, because the organic lime which is the most prominent constituent of bony material is an alkaline substance, and, as such, attracts these acids to it, for their mutual neutralisation. The effect is to be seen in the rheumatic conditions so well known to all of us—those inflammatory acid conditions which affect all the joints of the body, making the joints swell and perform their natural action with less and less thoroughness as time goes on, until we arrive at the stage when arthritis appears (which is the complete or semi-complete calcification and deformity of the joints of the body as a result of the erosive action of these acid impurities on the body's bony structure).

The chain of cause and effect resulting in rheumatism and arthritis having now been made plain to the reader (" the weather " is not the guilty party !), we can now turn to tubercular affections of the joints and say a few words about these before beginning on the actual treatments themselves. Tuberculosis is essentially a *calcium deficiency disease* (see the remarks *re Consumption* farther on in the book, in the section on *Diseases of the Heart, Lungs, etc.*, page 322, for fuller details as to what this means) ; and the fact that the bony structure of the body—which contains a great deal of organic lime (or calcium)—is sometimes affected by diseases of a tubercular origin should be easy to account for from this one thing alone.

The child who is suffering from calcium deficiency—as a result of a defective diet—cannot have such a good bony structure as a child who is adequately supplied with calcium for bone building. The result is that when such a child injures a bone (usually a joint) as the outcome of a knock or fall, there is quite a possibility that tubercular bacilli will become active there, because of the child's generally impaired state of health combined with defective bone formation. Thus it is not the injury itself—as such—which is the predisposing factor towards the appearance of tubercular affections of the joints, as is popularly supposed, but the underlying lack of tone of the whole organism, due to faulty nutrition. *Tubercular affections of the joints can only arise in a system depleted of organic lime and deficient in vitality—both conditions the direct outcome of defective nutrition.*

Having, it is hoped, paved the way somewhat for a clearer understanding of the matter—both with regard to rheumatic and tubercular affections—we can now proceed with the actual treatments.

Ankle-joint Disease.—This is tuberculosis of the ankle-joint, and is characterised by puffiness of the ankle and a slight limp. The child walks upon the toes, when walking is necessary, and there is pain and muscular spasm. Occasionally the joints in the arch of the foot are involved. The cause of the trouble, as already explained in the introduction to this section, is *defective nutrition,* although injury of some kind or other may appear to be the pre. disposing factor in the case.

Treatment.—The treatment for conditions of this nature should always be in the hands of an experienced Naturopath. Home treatment can never be completely successful, although a great deal can be done to improve the condition. The first essential is correct diet—the child must be fed on a fresh fruit, raw salad, fresh milk, and wholemeal bread diet similar to that given in the Appendix (foods rich in organic calcium and other valuable mineral salts), and skilled manipulative treatment to the affected joint, together with artificial sunlight treatment, are the next requisites. The tone of the whole body must be improved by proper hygiene, such as the adoption of the daily dry friction and sponge given in the Appendix, together with the daily performance of the breathing exercises given therein ; and (where possible) sun and air baths can both be fully recommended as being of the highest value. The full Epsom-salts bath and the Epsom-salts foot-bath are both very useful too. (For the foot-bath, about ½ lb. to 1 lb. of Epsom salts should be dissolved in a foot-bath of hot water, and the foot bathed therein night and morning.) The full Epsom-salts bath should be taken two or three times weekly. Up to a week on the *all-fruit diet*, to begin the treatment, with a period on fruit and milk to follow, would be very good indeed (together with the use of the enema to ensure proper bowel action) ; but, as already stated, the treatment should be placed in naturopathic hands, if at all possible. *Rest* of the affected joint is a very important factor in recovery. (For the fruit and milk diet, from two to three pints of fresh *unboiled* milk are taken daily with the three fruit meals.)

Suppressive medical or surgical treatment should be avoided at all costs. Operations cannot effect a real cure, and may cause the formation of a permanent disability for life with wasting of the tissues of the surrounding parts. *Natural treatment can only be in the highest degree effective if the case is taken in hand at once, and not after it has been in medical hands for a prolonged period.*

Disease of the Shoulder, Elbow, and Wrist-joints.—The joints of the upper part of the body are rarely affected with chronic disease as compared with those of the lower. This is probably due to the fact that the circulation of the blood in these joints is very active, and also to the fact that they have no heavy body-weight to support and are less exposed to injury. Tubercular disease in these joints invariably develops as a result of injury, and swelling, pain, and tenderness are the first symptoms observed. This is followed by wasting of the muscles, of both the arm and forearm. The trouble has always defective nutrition as its under-lying cause, and for treatment the reader is referred to the treat-ment for *Ankle-joint Disease*, above.

Fibrositis.—See *Muscular Rheumatism*, page 148.

Gout.—Gout is popularly supposed to be a rich man's disease, but it is just as much in evidence amongst the poor. It is essen-tially a disease of *wrong living*—whether of "high" or "low" does not really matter. In addition to faulty diet, the gouty individual stands convicted of a tendency to drink far too much intoxicating liquor, to take far too little exercise, and generally to undermine his constitution in various ways. The disease consists in a great excess of urates and uric acid in the blood and tissues—impurities collected there as a result of the above-cited bad habits—and shows marked preference for the joints of the feet in particular. In many cases chalky deposits (lime salts) appear in the joints, and also in the skin of the ear and other parts of the body.

The disease usually begins between the ages of thirty and forty and any special bout of over-indulgence or overwork may pre-cipitate an attack, which is very painful indeed. In an attack the big-toe joints are always the first affected, thus sharply character-ising the disease from ordinary rheumatism, to which it is very closely related. Heredity is sometimes given as a predisposing cause, but without many years of wrong living on his own account, the sufferer from gout would have little cause to blame his ancestors for his trouble.

Treatment.—For an acute attack of gout there is nothing to equal the fast in its curative effects. The sufferer should under-take a fast of from four to seven days (as directed in the Appendix), on orange juice and water, and the warm-water enema should be used nightly to cleanse the bowels. The feet should be bathed in Epsom-salts foot-baths twice daily ($\frac{1}{2}$ lb. to 1 lb. of salts to a foot-bath of hot water), and full Epsom-salts baths should be taken three or four times during the week if possible (being reduced to two weekly later). Cold packs at night to the affected joints will also be beneficial. As the attack subsides, the *all-fruit diet* may be adopted for a few days, and then the *full weekly diet* given in the Appendix can be gradually begun. This diet should be adhered to as closely as possible from then on. All intoxicating liquors should be avoided in future, and enervating habits dropped. The daily dry friction and sponge given in the Appendix should be carried out daily as soon as convalescence is reached, as also the breathing and other exercises given therein. Fresh air and outdoor exercise are essential. If constipation is habitual, the rules for its eradication given in Section 9, page 275, should be faithfully followed out. Spinal manipulation will be very helpful in all cases of gout.

For the treatment of *chronic gout*, see treatment for *Rheumatism* farther on in the present section, page 149.

Hip-joint Disease.—As usual in all tubercular affections of the joints, injury is the predisposing cause cited, but without a general underlying state of malnutrition due to defective diet the trouble could not develop. One of the first noticeable symptoms is a limp or stiffness early in the morning, which wears off later on in the day. As time proceeds the limp tends to develop greatly, together with eversion of the leg and foot, pain in the great toe and knee, and spasm of the muscles controlling the hip-joint. There is sure to be atrophy following the development of the above symptoms, and sometimes an abscess forms in the joint. There are also inflammation and pain of a severe nature. Medical methods by opening the joint to drain abscesses, and generally interfering with the joint structure, always result in the affected leg being shortened. The real treatment should be in the hands of a competent Naturopath along the lines already indicated for *Ankle-joint Disease.*

Housemaid's Knee (Bursitis).—This condition, popularly known as "housemaid's knee," is technically known as *bursitis,* and is really inflammation of a bursa, which is a sac or cushion containing fluid, in this case that placed between the knee-bone and its skin covering. An injury to this bursa, or constant scrubbing—necessitating the knees being on the ground frequently —may lead to its inflammation, and may cause great pain and discomfort, through the amount of fluid in the bursa greatly increasing in quantity.

Treatment.—Although the predisposing causes generally given are those cited above, without a system full of toxic material, bursitis could never develop. The real underlying causative condition is therefore *systemic toxaemia* due to wrong feeding and wrong living generally. For the treatment for bursitis, the reader is referred to that for *Synovitis* later on in the present section, these conditions being very similar in nature and identical in treatment from the Nature-Cure point of view.

Knee-joint Disease: White Swelling.—Tubercular disease at the knee begins in two ways. If it is the large capsule about the joint which is attacked at the outset, the first thing usually noticed is swelling, which has come on gradually without pain. There is no redness, but, on the contrary, the joint has a white, smooth appearance. There will be only slight pain and limp following fatigue. If, on the other hand, the disease begins either in the lower end of the thigh bone or the upper end of the leg bone, the symptoms are entirely different. Pain is usually present quite early, and there is a pronounced limp, which is most marked after rest. Motion is greatly restricted, and generally the leg is slightly bent back and is impossible to straighten. There is also wasting of the muscles of the surrounding parts. For treatment, which should always be in competent naturopathic hands, see the treat-ment given for *Ankle-joint Disease* in the present section, page 148.

Lateral Curvature of the Spine.—The cause of this con-dition is a weakened spinal structure due to malnutrition in early infancy and youth. The deformity is slow in its development, but insidious and progressive, unless checked early by proper treat-ment. The main curve in this deformity is in the middle region or the spine, with its convexity to the right, and with a compensatory or second curve to the left, in the lower region; but occasionally the curves are reversed. In addition to the spine itself, the ribs, shoulder, and hip on the side of the convexity are all affected, leading to general malformation. There is no pain or tenderness, as in *Pott's Disease*, which is tuberculosis of the spine, but muscular weakness is generally present, and the patient tires easily. The longer the condition is allowed to continue without proper treatment, the less possibility is there of correcting it, as the whole spinal structure becomes less and less flexible as time goes on.

Treatment.—In the natural treatment for curvature of the spine, nothing is so effective as spinal manipulation and properly regu-lated exercise. Correct diet is also essential. but in this trouble gives place to manipulation and exercise as the measures of first importance. The case should be placed in the hands of a competent Naturopath as soon as the trouble is detected (never wait till the condition develops), but an ordinary Osteopath would do almost as well if no Naturopath is near by. The exercises given in the Appendix—both breathing and physical—will be found most helpful, as also the morning dry friction and sponge.

Lumbago.—Lumbago is a disease of rheumatic origin which affects the muscles of the lower part of the back—that part known as the lumbar region : hence its name. It is a very painful disease, coming on in periodic attacks which get worse as the patient grows older—under orthodox medical treatment, that is ! For such treatment, omitting altogether, as it does, the diet factor, overlooks the real source of the trouble and the only possible avenue along which curative treatment can be directed.

Treatment.—As regards the effective treatment for his case, the sufferer from lumbago is directed to the treatment for *Rheumatism* given farther on in the present section, page 149. In addition to such general treatment, in all cases of lumbago, *spinal manipulation* is in the highest degree beneficial. Cold packs, to the painful area, are also very useful. (For details as to how the cold pack is made and applied, see the Appendix.)

Muscular Rheumatism (Fibrositis).—Although in rheumatic affections it is more often the joints which are affected, the muscles of the body are also sometimes subject to the disease. The sufferer from muscular rheumatism will find all he wants to know regarding the treatment for his complaint from a study of the treatment given in this section for *Rheumatism of the Joints*, page 149. The same treatment is equally efficacious in both types of the disease, as their underlying cause is exactly the same, although the superficial symptoms and manifestations are some-what different.

(It is manual workers such as bus drivers, mechanics, etc., who do a fair amount of hard muscular work in one position, without sufficient walking and other exercise to help throw off the acid waste products thus formed as a result of their activities, who are most prone to the muscular type of rheumatism.)

Pott's Disease.—This disease, named after a distinguished surgeon of a century and a half ago, is really tuberculosis of the spine. The spinal vertebrae are attacked as a result of a fall or injury, but, as already pointed out in the sections on *Tuberculosis of the Ankle-joint, Hip,* etc., page 143, without a predisposing *underlying* factor in the shape of defective nutrition, the disease could never develop. It is a serious malady, and requires the most careful attention at the hands of a competent natural practitioner.

All that has been said with regard to the treatment for other tuberculous affections in this section applies equally to the treatment for Pott's disease. And if the disease is taken in the early stages, there is every possibility of good results being secured. The longer the delay in securing adequate natural treatment, or the more the case has been tampered with by orthodox medical practitioners, the less likelihood is there of securing beneficial results from the treatment.

Rheumatism.—Rheumatism is a disease of such widespread range and "popularity" that a detailing of its symptoms is hardly required here. In the *acute* form, rheumatism is found oftenest among children and young people, but in the chronic form—that most commonly seen—it is confined to adults generally. Either the joints or the muscles may be attacked by the disease, but the muscular variety is far less common than that affecting the joints. All that has already been said about rheumatism (and arthritis) in the opening remarks to the present section should be carefully studied by the sufferer from rheumatism, because once he realises that the basis of the trouble is *wrong feeding* and *wrong living* generally, he will have gone a long way toward a satisfactory solution of his health problem.

Medical Science does nothing to help the sufferer in his quest for a cure; it merely succeeds in throwing him right off the scent and delivers him up a ready prey to any pill-monger or proprietary medicine vendor (or electrical massage "specialist") who can promise him a "cure", which, by the very nature of things, can never materialise. It is safe to say that more money is spent every year by the public on so-called "cures" for rheumatism—both orthodox and quack—*without avail,* than on any other one disease. If only these same people could be made to realise that their cure lies in their own hands, through the medium of the food they choose to put into their mouths, what a difference their would be!

Treatment.—As rheumatism is such a common disease, and as there are so many stages of the complaint—ranging from just slight affection of the joints to the most crippling and agonising manifestations of the trouble—it would serve readers best, I imagine, if I give examples of the treatment for, say, three stages of the complaint, instead of contenting myself with just dealing with it in one broad survey. This will give every reader who is suffering from rheumatism, and who is anxious to start right away and prove for himself what natural treatment can do for him, the best possible working basis for treatment. He can gauge his own treatment by a study of the treatments here given in relation to the severity (or othewise) of his own case.

Case 1.—This is a mild case of rheumatism, in a young man of twenty-six. He has been living all his life on the usual kinds of food, eating plenty of white bread, boiled potatoes, meat, bacon, eggs, fish, tinned foods, jams, etc., etc., washed down with large quantities of strong tea and coffee, dosed with a plentiful supply of denatured white sugar. His doctor (who confesses to being a sufferer from the disease himself !) has done nothing at all to alleviate his trouble, except to give him various bottles of medicine, and to talk vaguely about having his tonsils removed, as being the possible " likely " seat of the trouble ! He comes under natural treatment—having been advised to by a friend—and he is treated as follows :

He is placed on an *exclusively fresh fruit diet* for a week (as detailed in the Appendix), and then on to the *full weekly diet* (also described in full in the Appendix). He is told that further short periods on *all-fruit*—say two or three days—may be required at monthly intervals during the next few months, according to the progress he is making. (It is a curious thing, but the sufferer from rheumatism is generally warned off fruit by his medical adviser, as it is supposed to *increase* acidity. It does just the reverse! It is bread, meat, sugar, etc., which are the acid-formers.)

The patient is made to use the warm-water enema nightly to cleanse the bowels during his week on all-fruit, and to undertake every morning the dry friction and sitz-bath and exercises (detailed in full in the Appendix). The hot Epsom-salts bath—which is *invaluable* to the sufferer from rheumatism—he is told to take twice weekly for the next three months, and once weekly thereafter, and to have as much fresh air and outdoor exercise every

150

day as he can manage. Smoking he is told to cut down to the very minimum, as being in no way a healthy practice; and with regard to tea and coffee drinking, he is made to realise that these beverages are harmful in their after-effects upon the system (slight to begin with, but cumulative with time), and is made to give up coffee altogether, and to reduce his once very pronounced tea-drinking to two cups of weak China tea, without sugar, every day, taken in the afternoon.

As regards diet in general, he is told to read a good book on diet, to make himself thoroughly conversant with the details of this most important subject, and is made to realise that only *pure foods* —foods, that is, which have *not* been processed or refined, or had the life boiled out of them—are the foods for him to eat in the future. Fruits and salads, instead of being eaten as a luxury or novelty, as in the past, he is made to understand must be the major portion of his future daily dietary; whilst bread—to be eaten only once a day, not at every meal, as formerly—must be *one hundred per cent wholemeal* and nothing else. He is told to avoid all fried foods, all highly flavoured dishes, all seasonings, sauces, pickles, etc., and to have everything of the plainest and simplest nature.

It seems rather a wrench to the patient at first, but, having sense enough to realise what an asset real health will be to him, he perseveres, and in six months is a different person altogether, with a degree of health he never dreamed possible in such a short space of time.

Case 2.—This is the case of a woman, aged forty-five, who has had rheumatism for many years now, but is only troubled with it rather seriously at times. At other times she gets along without much trouble generally. Having undergone all manner of medical and spa treatment, and having had a perfectly good set of teeth out (on medical advice) with no avail, she decides to give Nature Cure a chance to show what *it* can do.

She is told to have a *short fast* for three or four days on orange juice and water (as described in the Appendix) to begin the treatment, and is then placed on the *restricted diet* (also given in the Appendix) for a further fourteen days. After this short fast and period on the restricted diet, she is then allowed to commence on the *full weekly diet*, and told she must adhere to this as closely as possible from then on. As she is chronically constipated—

constipation being a very common predisposing factor in the setting up of rheumatism, in conjunction with wrong feeding— she is told to use the warm-water enema nightly for the time being, and to resort to the principles for the overcoming of this condition as outlined in the section dealing with *Constipation and its Cure* (Section 9, page 275). Hot Epsom-salts baths are prescribed *three* times weekly, and she is told to make a regular habit of the morning dry friction and sponge, and to do the breathing and other exercises given in the Appendix in conjunction with them. In addition, the need for a certain amount of regular daily outdoor exercise, such as walking, and regular habits of living generally— such as regular meals, early hours, etc., etc.—are impressed upon her, as all these play a big part in regulating the health, or otherwise, of the system.

As regards her future diet, she is told the same as the young man in Case 1, and is, in addition, warned against the drinking of alcoholic liquors, in which she sometimes indulges.

She does as she is told, but as her case is rather a chronic one, her progress is not so rapid to begin with as Case 1, but, although slow, is nevertheless sure. She has a further *short fast* and period on the *restricted diet* three months after she commenced treatment —to help on the cleansing process—and increases her progress greatly by so doing. Her weight, which was far above normal when she began treatment, is now down to average, and her general health is far better than it has been these twenty years or more. In fact, she feels a new woman, thanks to natural treatment, which has revolutionised not only her health but her whole life too.

Case 3.—This is a case of an elderly man aged sixty-three, who is almost crippled with rheumatism. He comes to Nature Cure in despair, having spent a small fortune on his case, with no results whatsover. As he is fairly advanced in years, and not very strong, a drastic scheme of fasting treatment—which he really needs, and which would be given him if he were younger—cannot be put into operation in his case. He has to carry on as follows :

He is made to fast for a day, and is then put on to an *all-fruit diet* for a further three days, after which he is placed on the *full weekly diet* given in the Appendix. This diet he is told to adhere to rigidly from then on, with a day's fast and period on the all-fruit diet—say two or three days—every month or so. He is made to use the enema nightly to cleanse the bowels for the first week of the treatment, and uses it every *other* night thereafter, until constipation—which was habitual with him—is overcome (the simple rules for its eradication, given in the section on the cure of *Constipation*, page 275, having been explained to him). Epsom-salts baths are prescribed two or three times weekly, at a temperature not too hot for him to stand them, and he is given the morning dry friction and sponge and breathing exercises to perform daily. A course of *spinal manipulation* is also prescribed for him, together with a course of *artificial sunlight treatment*, as well as treatment in the form of general massage and manipulation of the joints, to aid in the work of loosening them up, as they are in a very crippled condition.

After six months of this treatment his condition shows great signs of improvement, although he is still far from completely well; but with perseverance he feels sure he will go forward to better and better health, the success achieved by the treatment thus far having given him this confidence.

SPECIAL NOTE.—All sufferers from severe rheumatism should read the following section on *Rheumatoid Arthritis*, as it is really impossible to say exactly where severe rheumatism leaves off and arthritis begins, in many cases.

FURTHER NOTE.—Where the rheumatic sufferer has swelling and pain in the joints, he should bathe the affected parts *twice daily* in hot water containing Epsom salts ($\frac{1}{4}$ lb. of salts to a bowl-ful of hot water; $\frac{1}{2}$ lb. of salts to a foot-bath of hot water, etc.), after which some olive oil should be applied.

Rheumatoid Arthritis.—When rheumatism has progressed so far in the system that the joints have become fixed and distorted and incapable of much movement, *rheumatoid arthritis* has appeared. (Arthritis may also be produced by the suppression, i.e. *wrong* medical treatment, of previous disease of many kinds, in conjunction with a rheumatic tendency.) All that has been said in the previous section on *Rheumatism* should be read carefully by the sufferer from arthritis, and taken to heart; and although, by the very nature of the case, such quick and definite results as those which follow the treatment for simple rheumatism cannot be expected, natural treatment holds out for the sufferer from arthritis the only hope of cure—or even partial cure—that exists for him in the world to-day. Orthodox medical treatment, by means of injections or otherwise, is worse than useless where real cure is concerned.

Treatment.—Unless taken in hand promptly and thoroughly, arthritis is a very difficult condition to deal with, and the sufferer should place himself *at once* under competent naturopathic advice where at all possible. For those who cannot avail themselves of personal treatment, the following résumé of natural treatment is given as a guide to self-treatment :

Fairly simple cases of arthritis can undertake the treatment given in the previous section on *Rheumatism* for Case 2, with good results. But in addition to all the various measures advised there, they should bear in mind to try to get some movement into the affected joints by moving them about gently for a few minutes several times a day. This attempting to move the affected joints by gentle manipulation daily is essential to real progress, as it prevents further stiffening, and gives the treatment a better chance to operate. If the patient cannot move the affected joints for himself, someone should be got to do it for him. Where possible, spinal manipulation and general manipulative treatment should be sought, in conjunction with the general treatment here outlined.

For more serious cases of arthritis a fast of from a week to two or three weeks will be needed to get the treatment into full operation. This is best conducted in a Natural-Cure home, of course, and in any case should not be attempted by the sufferer without proper guidance or advice. After the fast, the *restricted diet* given in the Appendix should be adopted for a few days, and then the *full weekly diet* can be begun. A further fast or series of fasts may be required from the patient, according to the severity of the condition, the progress being made, etc., and in every case the diet given in the Appendix should be returned to and adhered to rigidly thereafter. *Only in this way can a real cure be effected, if cure be possible in any given case.* The sufferer from arthritis, more so than any other, can afford no longer to tamper with his diet if a cure (or even a partial cure) is wished for.

Constipation, which is almost an invariable accompaniment of arthritis, must be dealt with according to the rules for the use of the enema, etc., given in the section dealing with the cure of *Constipation* (Section 9, page 275), and the morning dry friction and sponge, together with the breathing exercises given in the

Appendix, must not be left out of the treatment. The hot Epsom-salts bath is an indispensable feature of all treatment for arthritis, and the sufferer should have three at least every week ; whilst if spinal manipulation and general naturopathic treatment are not possible, the daily gentle self-manipulation of the affected joints already referred to in this section should not be omitted from the régime of treatment. With perseverance and patience a cure in many cases is possible ; whilst in others if a complete cure is not effected, at least a great improvement should reward the efforts of the sufferer.

SPECIAL NOTE.—To all sufferers from arthritis and severe rheumatism, the need for a sufficient daily supply of organic alkaline salts in the dietary must be obvious from what has been said in the opening pages of this section as to the causes of the trouble. Although the dietetic treatment here advised will give this to them, they can always do with more, so to speak. Accordingly, a very good thing for all such sufferers is to drink *plenty* of carrot and tomato juice, and the liquor from simmered green vegetables, as these juices and liquors are very rich in desirable alkaline properties.

FURTHER NOTE re FASTING.—Where heart trouble complicates rheumatism or arthritis, care should be taken not to undertake too long a fast or period on all-fruit at any one time. It is better to carry on for shorter periods and at frequent intervals—as for the treatment for Case 3 in the section on *Rheumatism*, for instance.

Slipped Disc.—This is a term in common use nowadays, and it indicates a condition in which the interior portion of a vertebral disc—the soft tissue which separates one vertebra from the next—protrudes out of alignment with the rest of that portion of the spine. It is a very painful condition, and under orthodox medical treatment it is often a very difficult one to cure; it is, in fact, sometimes incurable. Under Nature Cure methods, however, the condition is usually readily curable, the main method of treatment being osteopathic manipulation of the affected portion of the spine.

Synovitis.—The membrane which forms the lining of all the joints of the body is known as the synovial membrane, because it secretes a peculiar fluid called *synovia*. When this membrane becomes inflamed, through any cause whatever, the resultant condition is called synovitis. Of all the joints likely to be affected the knee-joint is the one most prone to synovitis, and the condition is often called " water on the knee." Synovitis may result from injury, but most frequently it follows in the wake of diseases such as influenza, pneumonia, typhoid, and other infectious diseases as a result of wrong, i.e. *suppressive*, medical treatment. In any case the sufferer from synovitis can take it for granted that unless his system had been in a highly toxic condition, the trouble *could never have developed*. It is this underlying toxæmia—due to wrong feeding, general wrong living, and previous suppressive medical treatment—which has made the appearance of synovitis possible in his system.

Treatment.—The treatment for synovitis is primarily a detoxicating régime, with only secondary attention to the actual place of affection. The sufferer should begin with a *fast* for from three to five or seven days, or with from five to seven, ten, or fourteen days on the *all-fruit diet* (according to the severity or otherwise of the condition), and then go on to the *full weekly diet* given in the Appendix. The warm-water enema should be used nightly to cleanse the bowels ; and if constipation is habitual, the rules for its eradication given in Section 9, page 275, should be carefully studied and put into operation. The affected leg should be rested whilst the inflammation is severe, and cold packs (as described in the Appendix) should be applied frequently during the day, and one kept on all night. The hot Epsom-salts bath will be extremely beneficial, and should be taken three times a week if possible, the patient being carried to the bath and placed in it if necessary. Gentle massage of the surrounding parts is useful.

If the above treatment is carried out faithfully, the trouble should soon begin to disappear, but the patient should guard against trying to use the affected leg too quickly. It is always wise to rest it for a day more rather than a day less. As convalescence continues, the morning dry friction and sponge or sitz-bath should be taken, together with the physical exercises given in the Appendix. The diet factor must never be overlooked when once the condition has been overcome, as this is the only way to prevent further trouble of the same kind recurring. Painting with iodine or other similar suppressive treatment is absolutely WRONG.

DISEASES OF THE BLOOD AND BLOOD-VESSELS
(ALSO CIRCULATORY DISORDERS)

Anæmia—Aneurysm—Apoplexy (Paralytic stroke)—Arterio-sclerosis—Blood poisoning—Chilblains—High blood-pressure—Leucæmia—Low blood-pressure—Nose bleeding—Pernicious anæmia—Phlebitis—Poor circulation—Raynaud's disease—Thrombosis—Varicose veins.

DISEASES of the blood and blood-vessels are very common indeed in these days, and are steadily on the increase despite all medical efforts to deal with them effectively. Drug treatment for complaints such as anæmia, high blood-pressure, etc., has been lamentably unsuccessful, and must continue to remain so, because the underlying causative factors at work in the development of these diseases are left entirely untouched by such treatment.

To the medical mind the *real* causes underlying such diseases as anæmia, high and low blood-pressure, arterio-sclerosis, etc., are mysteries really, and will continue to remain mysteries just so long as the diet factor is left out of account in medical reasoning into the causes of these—as well as all other—diseases. That there is a very close relationship existing between wrong feeding on the one hand and an impoverished blood-stream or hardened and defective arteries and veins on the other is obvious to the Naturopath from the very nature of things, but far from obvious to his medical confrère, suffering as he is from a very bad " germ complex."

Just let the reader consider : Here we have the blood coursing continuously without ceasing for one instant, through the arteries and veins of the body, either bringing nutriment to the cells in its forward surge from the heart, or carrying waste material away in its backward flow. Can it not be seen at once that if a person has a system whose tissues are continuously clogged with waste matter, as a result of wrong feeding habits and wrong living generally, there will be an ever-growing tendency for the blood-stream *itself* to become in time permanently laden with an over-accumulation of toxic material and systemic refuse and its work to be impeded, and for the arteries and veins it continuously passes through to become more and more silted up with a layer of this same toxic material and systemic waste as the years advance ?

Here we have, in a nutshell, the reason for circulatory disorders such as poor circulation and chilblains on the one hand, and diseases of the blood-vessels such as arterio-sclerosis, high blood-pressure, varicose veins, etc., on the other. Nothing could be simpler to understand. (The cause of anæmia and pernicious anæmia is not quite the same. These diseases are due to debility of the system generally, with resultant impoverishment of the blood-making organs, as a result of faulty diet and wrong habits of living.)

We notice that people generally develop high blood-pressure, arterio-sclerosis, circulatory disorders, and the like, about *middle life*. The reason why such diseases appear then, and not sooner, should be quite obvious to the reader now, from what has just been said. The arteries have been steadily accumulating around their walls a mass of toxic waste left behind in ever-increasing quantity every year by an increasingly toxic blood-stream, and by middle life the effects of this process have begun to be *really* experienced and names such as high blood-pressure, arterio-sclerosis, etc., applied to these effects. That is all ! What have germs or drug treatment or inoculations to do with either the cause or cure of such diseases ? Just nothing ! Only a *thorough cleansing of the system* to enable the blood and arteries and veins to *detoxify* themselves and build themselves up anew can ensure a cure in such cases.

Once the reader has thoroughly grasped the foregoing, the details of treatment now to follow will be appreciated in their proper significance.

Anæmia.—Anæmia really means deficiency of blood, but an anæmic person is generally taken to mean one whose blood is defective in *quality* as well as *quantity*. There is a deficiency of hæmoglobin in the blood, in the anæmic person, a substance without which no one could live. Hæmoglobin contains organic iron in its composition, and the presence of this organic iron is absolutely essential to health and life, as it takes up the oxygen brought into the system when breathing, and carries it in combination with itself to the multifarious cells of the organism for their sustenance.

Hæmoglobin is the red colouring matter of the blood, so that a person deficient in this substance will have a much paler blood-stream than one in good health ; but the anæmic person is not only pale and bloodless—as one can well imagine—he is also without appetite, energyless, and of poor nutrition too, because his impoverished blood-stream is not supplying the vital organs and body structures with their proper amount of nutritional material, and so the whole organism—both physical and mental— is affected. But, as a matter of fact, the anæmia *itself*, in the first place, is only the outcome of a general debility of the whole system (due to faulty diet, general wrong living, previous suppressive treatment of disease, etc.), so it is a case of a vicious circle all the time—a debilitated system leading to an impoverished blood supply, and an impoverished blood supply leading to yet further weakening of the system, because of the inability of supplying all the nutritional requirements of the various vital organs and structures.

Thus anæmia is not a disease at all really, it is a *condition*—a condition of bloodlessness or impoverishment of blood through systemic causes—and manifests itself as a factor in many diseases, rather than as a disease on its own ; and so to attempt to treat just the anæmia *alone* is poor policy therefore. It is the person *as a whole* who must be treated, as it is the whole organism which is at fault, and which, through wrong functioning, has led to the anæmic condition in question. To say, " Ah, this person has anæmia. That means he is deficient in iron. What he needs is iron to cure him ! " is just nonsense. Yet that, in the main, is the attitude of the medical profession to the disease (or condition, as I would rather have it called). No wonder it cannot cure it !

Anæmia, of all things, needs *constitutional* treatment if a real cure is desired. To depend upon iron tonics or iron injections is just a waste of time. No anæmic person has ever been cured in that way. It is not just iron that is needed, but the regeneration of the whole system. By the way, the iron given in medical treatment is quite useless, as it is inorganic iron, *not* organic iron. The organic iron the body needs can only be obtained *from food*— from such substances as green and root vegetables (if uncooked), from fruits, whole-grain cereals, and dried fruits—not from the chemist's laboratory or the drug store.

Treatment.—If what has been said above—as well as in the

opening pages of this section—has been understood by the reader, the treatment for anæmia about to be outlined should speak for itself. It aims at the regeneration of the whole system rather than at supplying a badly working organism with inorganic iron which it does not know in the least what to do with, and which ultimately only makes matters worse.

The anæmic person should carry on as follows: Have from four to seven days on the *exclusive fresh fruit diet* outlined in the Appendix, followed by a further two to four weeks on the *fruit and milk diet* (also outlined therein). Those who find the fruit and milk diet agreeing well with them will obviously stay on it longer than others—we must remember that all constitutions differ—but in any case the *full weekly diet* given in the Appendix should afterwards be adopted and adhered to as closely as possible. Further periods on all-fruit followed by fruit and milk may be required in some cases, but this must be left to the reader's own discretion to decide, depending upon the progress being made in the meantime.

The warm-water enema should be used nightly to cleanse the bowels during the first few days of the treatment, and afterwards if necessary; whilst those who are habitually constipated should carry out the advice given for its eradication in Section 9 (page 275). The daily dry friction and sponge or sitz-bath should be undertaken by every sufferer from anæmia, as also the breathing and other exercises given in the Appendix (these are most essential); and as much time as possible should be spent in the open air. Gentle outdoor exercise, such as walking, is needful—a good walk every day is an excellent thing—and where possible sun and air bathing should be indulged in. A weekly hot Epsom-salts bath is very good too.

All habits of living tending to set up enervation of the system, such as overwork, excesses of all kinds, needless worry, wrong thinking, etc., must be eliminated as far as lies within the power of the sufferer.

Upon such a régime as the above, anæmia will disappear in the most obstinate cases in time. *On no account should iron " tonics," tonic wines, etc., be taken. They are just a waste of money and time.*

Aneurysm.—An aneurysm is a dilated or expanded portion of an artery, forming a tumour with a wall of varying thickness. It may have one or more openings or communications with the arterial tube ; it may form a connection with an adjacent vein ; or it may gradually fill up and become solid, in which case Nature effects a spontaneous cure. This latter condition, however, is very rare, unfortunately. It is usually the arteries of the brain or lungs which are most often affected, or those leading directly from the heart. The disease is one of middle life, and is the direct outcome of wrong living and wrong feeding generally, although injury may be the superficial starting cause. Heavy drinkers are most prone to the condition, and it also follows in the wake of metallic-drug treatment for diseases of syphilitic origin, and from metallic poisoning, such as lead poisoning, etc.

Treatment.—It must be said at the outset that the treatment for aneurysm must always be left to a Naturopath, for such cases need most skilled attention. Nor can a definite cure be expected in most cases ; in many all that can be hoped for is a diminution of the seriousness of the condition as a result of manipulative treatment, ray therapy, correct diet, strict abstention from alcoholic liquor, avoidance of strain, etc. The patient should lead as quiet a life as his calling will permit. For those who cannot put themselves under naturopathic treatment, a few days' *fruit diet*, followed by the *full weekly diet* given in the Appendix, will be the best way of starting treatment, with, say, two or three days on *all-fruit* every month to follow. The enema should be used nightly to cleanse the bowels during the first few days of the treatment, and afterwards if necessary.

Apoplexy (Paralytic Stroke).—This disease, called *apoplexy* or *cerebral haemorrhage* in medical language, is generally known as paralysis, or paralytic stroke. It is a most serious condition, and although those in early life may sometimes be victims, it is in late middle life that it is most commonly seen. Recovery is complete in some cases—even under orthodox medical treatment ; but if the condition were treated strictly along natural lines, the percentage of complete recoveries would go up by leaps and bounds.

The initial cause of apoplexy is the rupture of a blood-vessel in the brain as a result of excessively high blood-pressure following on many years of wrong feeding habits and general wrong living ; but the superficial causative factor is most often intense excitement, strain, or some unusually heavy work calling for unwonted exertion.

Sometimes there is nothing tangible in the way of symptoms to warn the victim that a stroke is near, but more often the warning signs are most definite. Pain in the head, dizziness, thickened speech, dullness of intellect (accompanied by very high blood-pressure), are the usual warning signals given by Nature that trouble is brewing.

When a stroke definitely occurs, there is intense headache, usually vomiting accompanied by profuse perspiration, and then unconsciousness accompanied by loud snoring ; but there are all sorts of degrees and gradations of strokes which it would be outside our scope to classify.

The stroke may lead to death, or, more generally, it leads to paralysis of one side of the body, as a result of the blood pressing upon certain nerve centres in the brain area. As convalescence continues, this gradually decreases in intensity, until in some cases the complete recovery of power in the affected limbs is brought about ; but in many there is permanent loss of power in one or more limbs, together with a definite loss of intellectual ability and power of expression.

Treatment.—The natural treatment for apoplexy will, if carried out properly, result in a complete cure in very many cases ; but of course the previous medical history of the case and the severity of the stroke will all have to be taken into account.

The first requisite is *fasting*. The patient should be completely fasted for the first few days, being given only water, if such can be taken, and afterwards orange juice as well as water. The fast should be continued for several days—until, indeed, the severity of the stroke has passed off, and something in the way of more solid nourishment can be taken. Even then it should only be *fresh fruit* that is given, *nothing else*. It is a very great mistake to start feeding the sufferer from a stroke with so-called " nourishing " food, such as chicken-broth, beef-tea, milk, etc. ; this only tends to hinder recover, and makes a complete cure difficult.

A most important factor during treatment is proper cleansing of the bowels. The bowels should be cleansed twice daily with the warm-water enema for the first two or three days, and thence nightly until the bowels begin to function of their own accord. Nothing should be done to disturb the patient. Cold compresses to the head may be helpful in certain cases in relieving pain.

If the above treatment is carried out—that is, complete fasting until the severe symptoms have disappeared (with the use of the enema), followed by the exclusive fruit diet when more solid food can be taken with comfort—most sufferers from a stroke will soon be well on the up grade. Then a gentle massage of the affected limbs will be most beneficial, together with manipulative treatment, if such can be procured. The diet can be extended to include milk (fresh and unboiled), and as convalescence increases, the fruit and milk diet can be gradually followed by the adoption of the *weekly dietary* given in the Appendix. Never be in a hurry to " feed-up " the patient ; rather keep the diet as low as possible, with fruits and salads as the main features. NO DRUGS WHATEVER SHOULD BE TAKEN.

When able to get about again, the patient may begin taking Epsom-salts baths twice weekly, whilst the breathing and other exercises given in the Appendix should be carried out daily, together with the daily friction and sponge. Regular habits of living should be encouraged from then onwards, and the consumption of alcoholic liquor should be stopped completely in those cases where it was habitual. Smoking should also be discontinued.

Fresh air and outdoor exercise (as far as is possible), correct diet along the lines outlined above, and clean wholesome living will prevent further strokes occurring. All undue nervous excitement, needless worry, and excessive strain must be guarded against.

The treatment for *High Blood-pressure*, given in the present section, should be studied carefully by all those who have had apoplexy.

Arterio-sclerosis.—Arterio-sclerosis means hardening of the arteries, and is intimately connected with high blood-pressure, as the excessively hardened condition of the arterial walls present in arterio-sclerosis means that the blood will have to *force* its way through the restricted arterial channel open to it, thus increasing pressure. It is the external walls of the arteries which harden in arterio-sclerosis, and the inner walls soften. These degenerative changes take place *solely* as a result of improper care of the body and bodily functions, due to wrong feeding, lack of exercise, excesses of all kinds, etc. ; and the fact that arterio-sclerosis is to be met with very frequently these days in those who have not yet reached their forties is a definite indictment of modern habits of living—habits of living in which the daily purgative, the patent medicine, and the medicinal drug all play such an important part.

Arterio-sclerosis means getting old before your time !

Treatment.—When the arteries of the body have lost their elasticity, it means that all the bodily organs and structures will suffer in consequence. It must be obvious, therefore, that treatment for arterio-sclerosis *must* be constitutional. It is only by building up the tone of the *whole* system that the condition can be eradicated in time.

As already stated, arterio-sclerosis and high blood-pressure are intimately connected, and treatment which will cure the former will cure the latter, and *vice versa*. The sufferer from arterio-sclerosis is therefore referred to the treatment for *High Blood-pressure* given in the present section for guidance in his case. He can be assured that by following it out he will not only renew the tissue-tone of his whole system and vastly increase his general health, but he will add many useful years to his life also.

Blood Poisoning.—From the medical standpoint, blood poisoning implies that infectious bacteria or germs have entered the blood-stream and caused unpleasant or serious symptoms which are referred to as poisoning. Blood poisoning may be of various levels or grades—slight, more serious, and very serious ; and it may be said here and now that in every case of blood poisoning the root cause is a highly toxic blood-stream due to faulty feeding and wrong living, and NOT germ infection at all.

If a person has a blood-stream which is full of toxic matter, and has a scratch or cut or bruise which lets the dirt in, it is not the dirt which is responsible for the blood poisoning which sometimes follows (as is generally believed), but the toxicity of the blood itself which is at fault. The dirt which enters the system through the medium of the cut or bruise acts as a *focus of infection* by forming a nucleus around which toxic matter being carried by the blood-stream may congregate ; and it is this congregation of toxic matter around the nucleus supplied by the dirt (or whatever else may have been introduced) which leads to the condition known as blood poisoning. It will be seen from this that the severity of the condition will always depend upon the general health and state of the blood of the victim, and *not* upon external conditions or phenomena ; and this explains at once why some people are more liable to blood poisoning than others, and why some cases are much more serious than others. It is the individual state of health and quality of blood which is the deciding factor *every time*. To make it a question of " germs " and infection from outside sources is to miss the whole point in blood poisoning.

Treatment.—It is obvious that every case of blood poisoning will require slightly different handling from every other, depending upon the general health of the patient, the location of the trouble, etc. ; but the following rules *re* treatment will serve as a general guide to those who cannot obtain the necessary first-hand regimen from a qualified Naturopath.

A fast for from three to seven or more days, on orange juice and water, is the first requisite, the duration of the fasting period depending in every case upon the severity of the attack. The patient should either keep to bed if the condition demands it, or else rest quietly at home, during this time.

During the fasting period, and afterwards if necessary, the bowels should be cleansed nightly with the warm-water enema or douche, and a full Epsom-salts bath should be taken every day if possible. (If a full Epsom-salts bath is not possible, the affected area should be bathed several times daily in hot water containing Epsom salts—about ½ lb. of salts to a foot-bath of water or a table-spoonful of salts to a cupful of water.) This bathing of the affected area with hot water containing Epsom salts several times daily is a good thing even if the full Epsom-salts bath is being taken.

Under the above treatment the symptoms will soon begin to diminish, and then the *all-fruit diet* can be adopted for a few days, and as convalescence increases the *full weekly dietary* given in the Appendix can be commenced. The bathing can be decreased as the trouble lessens, of course, and the enema discontinued

The friction sponge or sitz-bath and exercises given in the Appendix should then be begun as a regular measure for building up the tone of the system and regular habits of living established. Outdoor exercise should be encouraged as far as possible.

The above simple treatment will be sufficient to cure any ordinary case of blood poisoning, if carried out efficiently, without any of the danger of complications setting in which is attendant upon orthodox medical treatment. In the cleansing of the blood-stream lies the cure, *not* in the use of suppressive drugs and medicinal antiseptics.

Chilblains.—Chilblains are superficially due to defective circulation or exposure to cold, and appear in winter on the extremities of the body, such as the hands, feet, ears, etc., where the circulation is poorest. But it is not only defective circulation or exposure to cold which is to blame, however, in the formation of chilblains; there is also an underlying toxic condition of the blood—due to wrong feeding and general wrong living—which has to be considered all the time. Owing to the coldness of the extremities in certain people in winter, the blood gets impeded in its circulation through these parts, and toxic waste collects in the small capillaries near the skin surface; it is *from this cause* that chilblains occur.

The theory held in orthodox medical circles—and to some extent in Nature-Cure circles too—to the effect that chilblains are in some way the outcome of a deficiency of calcium in the blood is, to the writer's mind, completely unsound, and capable of very simple disproof. For example, many people who come under Natural-Cure treatment for the first time develop chilblains where nothing of the kind was experienced before such treatment was begun. How can the calcium-deficiency theory justify itself in these cases? Frankly, it cannot. For such people are now getting *more organic calcium*—through the agency of the natural food eaten—than before; yet they never knew what chilblains were until natural treatment was started

No, the truth is that chilblains developed in these cases as a result of the temporary swamping of the blood with toxic matter, following on the eliminative effects of the treatment, and to the collection of some of this toxic waste in the extremities because of the abscence of stimulating foods and drinks from the dietary.

166

Calcium deficiency has nothing to do with the matter at all in these cases.

Treatment.—Where chilblains are the outcome of Natural-Cure treatment, as mentioned above, they need not be worried about ; they will gradually disappear in time as the toxic matter responsible for their occurrence is cleared out of the system through continuence with natural treatment. But still, the local measures for their alleviation given below can be carried out with the most beneficial effect. It is those whose chilblains are the outcome of a heavily toxin-laden and imperfectly heated system—through faulty dietetic habits, lack of exercise, insufficient clothing, etc.—who need to put the full treatment here outlined into operation.

The best way to begin is with a short fast for three or four days, or with from four to seven days on the *all-fruit diet* given in the Appendix. Then the *full weekly dietary* given therein can be begun. Further short fasts or periods on all-fruit may be required in certain cases, depending upon the severity of the case. The warm-water enema should be used nightly to cleanse the bowels during the first few days of the treatment ; and where constipation is habitual, the rules for its eradication given in Section 9, page 275, should be put into operation forthwith. A hot Epsom-salts bath as detailed in the Appendix should be taken twice or even three times weekly to begin with, and less frequently as the chilblains disappear.

The condition of the skin must be attended to, and the daily dry friction and sponge or sitz-bath given in the Appendix should be carried out regularly, as also the physical and other exercises given therein. A fair amount of walking or other outdoor exercise should be taken daily, and care should be exercised in the selection of clothing to be worn. This should neither be too thin nor too thick or heavy. (Underclothing should always be light and porous, never of the heavy woollen kind.) The chilblain sufferer is also advised not to sit too near a fire when at work, or at home (especially a gas fire), and to avoid extremes of temperature as far as possible. (It is best to take the chill off any cold water before using it for washing purposes, especially in a very cold spell.)

As regards local treatment, the best thing is to bathe the parts affected two or even three times daily in hot water containing

Epsom-salts ($\frac{1}{4}$ lb. of salts to a bowlful of hot water ; $\frac{1}{2}$-lb. of salts to a foot-bath of water).* Another good thing is to place two bowls or foot-baths side by side, the one containing hot water and the other cold, and to plunge the hands or feet—as the case may be—first into the hot water and then into the cold. This should be done several times at each sitting, and two or three times daily in all.

Getting the hands or feet into a good glow by exercising them for several minutes when cold is also a very good thing, both as a preventive as well as a cure for chilblains.

High Blood-pressure.—High blood-pressure is one of the " new " diseases the past fifty years have produced, and is the direct outcome of modern ways of living. As already intimated in the opening pages of this section, wrong feeding, excessive drinking and smoking, and wrong habits of living generally, are its direct precursors ; and it makes its appearance in middle life as the outcome of a gradual silting up of the arteries with a steady accumulation of toxic matter brought there during the passage of the years by a heavily toxin-laden blood-stream.

The more the arteries are clogged with toxic waste, the harder will have to be the force exerted by the heart in its efforts to pump the blood through the arterial channels in its passage round the body, and in this way arises the modern phenomenon *high blood-pressure*. As mentioned in the section on arterio-sclerosis, high blood-pressure and arterio-sclerosis are intimately connected, as the predisposing causes of the one are the same as for the other ; and both are direct signs of a life spent in ill accord with Nature's rules as regard sensible living.

The symptoms of high blood-pressure are pain or noises in the head, irritability of temper, dizziness, failing mental power and powers of concentration, shortness of breath, disordered digestion, various heart symptoms, and many others denoting a condition in which the normal functions of the organism are disturbed by interference with proper heart and blood action following upon the resistance set up by hardened and inelastic arteries. (Of course, some cases of high blood-pressure will have more serious symptoms than others, depending entirely upon the general condition of the patient and the force of the pressure exerted in the arteries.) * Then rub in some olive oil or vaseline.

Treatment.—From what has just been said, it must be obvious to every reader that any treatment other than *constitutional* cannot but fail to effect a real cure in any case of high blood-pressure or arterio-sclerosis. Drug or injection treatment may seem to alleviate the condition temporarily, but more often than not it only succeeds in making matters worse finally. The only real cure for high blood-pressure or arterio-sclerosis is natural treatment along the following lines :

A fast for from four to seven days or seven to fourteen days on the *exclusive fresh fruit diet* should be the way to begin the treatment, depending upon the condition of the individual patient and his ability to stand a more or less protracted period of " self-cleansing." The warm-water enema should be used nightly to cleanse the bowels for the first week of the treatment, and longer if necessary ; and if constipation is habitual, the rules for its eradication given in Section 9, page 275, should be put into operation.

After the fast or period on all-fruit the *regular weekly diet* given in the Appendix should be adopted, and adhered to strictly thereafter. Smoking, drinking, and the eating of rich clogging foods must be avoided in future if the condition is to be finally eradicated, and condiments, sauces, pickles, etc., likewise. Coffee should be rigorously cut out from the daily dietary, and tea should be *very weak*, and no sugar taken. (The eating of white sugar or white-sugar products, such as jams, confectionery, etc., is a very big factor in the setting up of high blood-pressure and arterio-sclerosis, to say nothing of white flour and white-flour products too.)

A further short fast or two, at intervals, or occasional further monthly periods on all-fruit (two or three days, say), may be needed in some cases, depending upon the progress being made, and must be left to the patient's own discretion to decide.

The daily dry friction and sponge or sitz-bath and the breathing and other exercises given in the Appendix, should all be put into operation daily, and outdoor exercise should be encouraged as far as possible. The hot Epsom-salts bath twice weekly is a very good thing indeed in cases of the kind we are here considering, and should be taken wherever possible.

If the above rules *re* treatment are carried out conscientiously, there is no reason at all why most sufferers from high blood-pressure or arterio-sclerosis should not be cured in time, but obviously some cases will need more prolonged treatment than others. Spinal manipulation can be strongly recommended in all cases where it can be conveniently procured. No DRUGS OF ANY KIND SHOULD BE TAKEN.

Leucæmia.—Leucæmia is a disease in which the white cells of the blood are much increased in numbers, and is directly connected with a completely disorganised lymphatic system and greatly enlarged spleen. It is a very serious disease, constitutional in character, and requires expert naturopathic treatment in an institution for any real hope of cure to be possible. Home treatment is no good at all.

Low Blood-pressure.—Low blood-pressure is a condition in which the heart's action in forcing the blood through the arteries is weak, and is a direct outcome of a weakened and devitalised system. Like anæmia, it is not a disease, but a condition ; and the treatment for *Anaemia* given in this section can be followed by those suffering from low blood-pressure with the possibility of the very best results.

Nose Bleeding.—Although not a disease, nose bleeding can be very disagreeable in many cases, and a word or two about it will not come amiss in this section. As a matter of fact, bleeding from the nose is often a very good thing, albeit uncomfortable, as it is one of Nature's ways of relieving pressure and congestion in the head. (Those who suffer from nose bleeding will not have to worry about the possibility of having a paralytic stroke.)

As regards treatment, see Appendix B, *First Aid Section* Nothing should be done forcibly to stop the bleeding, such as placing wads of cotton-wool up the nose, etc. If the dietetic rules and rules for healthy living given in this book are carried out, the frequency of the attacks will gradually diminish, until their occurrence will be very rare indeed.

Pernicious Anæmia.—Pernicious anæmia, although of directly constitutional origin, like ordinary anæmia, is a far more serious condition indeed. With this complaint the symptoms of ordinary anæmia are very greatly intensified, and more often than not some definite organic disease or other is directly connected with the trouble. Treatment for pernicious anæmia, if left in orthodox medical hands, is useless, so far as a real cure is concerned. Iron compounds, liver extract and vitamin B12 have all been used from time to time as a means of increasing the tone and red cell-count of the blood. But such treatments never get down to the root cause of the trouble, which is directly constitutional in character.

The sufferer from pernicious anæmia who would be *really cured* should enter a Natural-Cure institution at once. A *protracted fast* followed by the *full milk diet* has been the means of bringing to health again many sufferers from the complaint who were given up as hopeless by the medical profession. In the treatment of pernicious anæmia along the above lines, "Champneys," the Tring Natural-Cure Resort, has a very fine record indeed.

Phlebitis.—Phlebitis means inflammation of a vein or veins, and although the disease may occur in any part of the body, it is the large veins of the leg which are usually involved. It is most often associated with injury to a vein—especially varicose veins— and is a condition which demands careful and prompt attention. (*Personal naturopathic advice should always be sought where possible.*)

Pain, inflammation, and swelling are the usual signs of the trouble, with the affected veins tender, swollen, knotted, and hard. If the trouble is not treated properly right away, the whole limb becomes affected, and becomes hard and glossy and enlarged. (Injection treatment for varicose veins sometimes results in phlebitis—a most definite warning of the foolishness of such practices.)

Treatment.—The underlying cause of phlebitis is, of course, a highly toxic blood-stream, and the treatment is essentially the same as given for *blood-poisoning* in this present section. Only the complete cleansing of the blood and tissues can lead to the effective and early cessation of the trouble. The patient should stay in bed, and fast for from three to five, seven, or more days, according to the severity of the condition. The warm-water enema should be used to cleanse the bowels nightly during this period, and after if necessary. The affected limb should be raised above the general level of the rest of the body whilst lying in bed, by placing pillows under it, and hot and cold fomentations can be applied several times daily. (Wring out a towel in hot water, place it over the affected area for, say, three minutes, then apply another for the same length of time, and finish off with a cold one.) *Great care* in handling the affected limb is necessary to avoid thrombosis or other serious complications occurring during this stage.

When the more serious symptoms have disappeared, the full Epsom-salts bath and the Epsom-salts foot-bath can both be used with good advantage ($\frac{1}{2}$ lb. of salts for the foot-bath) ; but these should not be attempted until the patient can be sure the affected limb can be trusted to stand the strain of sitting up or moving about.

Once the inflammation shows definite signs of subsiding, the dietetic treatment should be a few days on the *all-fruit diet*, to follow the fast, and then the gradual adoption of the *full weekly diet* given in the Appendix.

(At this stage the sufferer from phlebitis should turn to the treatment for *Varicose Veins* outlined in this section, page 175, and carry it out as thoroughly and carefully as he can. That is the only way to build up the tone of the veins and the bodily health generally.)

Poor Circulation.—Defective circulation may be due to three main causes :

(1) It may be the outcome of a heavily toxin-clogged condition of the blood and blood-vessels ; or

(2) It may be due to a debilitated condition of the system generally ; or

(3) It may be due to heart trouble, either alone or coupled with disease of some other vital organ.

With regard to Group (1), the people so affected will often be stout or heavily built people, and their poor circulation is entirely due to the fact that the superficial blood-vessels of the body are so clogged with waste matter that an adequate supply of fresh blood cannot reach them properly, and so the external surfaces of the body are left in a permanently " half-active " condition, with resultant feeling of coldness, numbness of extremities, etc. In these cases the eating of excessive quantities of demineralised, starchy, sugary, protein, and fatty foods, the drinking of much tea and coffee and other stimulative beverages, over-clothing of the body (thereby preventing effective skin action), and lack of exercise are the chief factors at work in setting up the trouble.

In Group (2) a debilitated condition of the system due to prolonged previous disease, nervous exhaustion, excesses of all kinds, etc., coupled with *defective nutrition* due to malassimilation of food, is the cause of the deficiency of circulation in question. (Excessively thin people with poor circulation come under this group.)

With regard to Group (3) here it is inability of the heart to pump an adequate supply of blood through the system which is the direct cause of the deficiency of circulation, with wrong feeding and general wrong living—to say nothing of previous drug treatment—as the agents responsible for the setting up of the condition in the first place.

Treatment.—According to which group the patient comes under, so the treatment for poor circulation will necessarily be different. Those coming under Group (1) will find the treatment for *high blood-pressure* given in the present section not only the quickest and surest means of getting rid of their defective circulation, but of building up their whole general health as well. Those under Group (2) can carry out the treatment for *low blood-pressure* with equal assurance of good results accruing in due time both as regards their circulatory trouble and health generally. Those in Group (3) should turn to the treatment for heart trouble given in the section on *Diseases of the Heart, Lungs, etc.* (Section 10, page 301), or for that for the special organ such as the kidneys, lungs, etc., which may be responsible in their particular case.

All sufferers from poor circulation should see to it that they do not wear *too many clothes*, as this makes their condition really worse by preventing proper skin action ; underwear should always be light and porous, never of the heavy woollen variety. If any extra heavy clothing is needed at any time, it should be *outside garments*, not the *inner garments*, which should be considered for this. A fair amount of outdoor exercise should be taken daily by all desirous of getting the best out of the treatment. Walking is the best form of exercise of all, irrespective of age.

Raynaud's Disease.—This is a disease in which there are functional changes in the blood-vessels of the fingers and toes generally, although other parts may be affected too. The blood-vessels become contracted, and there is pallor and apparent deadness of the skin. This condition is sometimes followed by

173

EVERYBODY'S GUIDE TO NATURE CURE

dilation, and then there is a purple or red colour to the skin. In some cases the disease is accompanied by dizziness, disturbances of vision, fainting, etc. It is a condition very similar in many ways to frost-bite, and is nervous in origin, the vaso-motor nerves being those affected. The underlying cause of the trouble is constitutional, however, and wrong feeding and faulty living may be regarded as the chief factors involved, plus suppressive drug treatment of previous disease, and nerve trouble due to worry, emotional or mental disturbances, etc.

Treatment.—The treatment for Raynaud's disease should be in the hands of a Naturopath if at all possible, diet, manipulation, ray therapy, and massage being especially beneficial. As regards home treatment, the best plan is to follow the treatment given in the present section for *High Blood-pressure* (page 169) and *Arteriosclerosis* (page 164). In addition to the Epsom-salts bath twice weekly, the affected areas can be bathed twice daily—night and morning—in hot water containing Epsom salts (in the proportion of one tablespoonful of salts to a cupful of hot water). Sun and air bathing are both good for this complaint, and—as already stated—manipulative treatment, massage, and ray therapy are especially useful.

Thrombosis.—This is a condition in which a blood-clot forms in a blood-vessel after injury. It is a condition which may have serious consequences if not attended to right away, and a Naturopath should be called in wherever possible. If this is impracticable, treatment should be along the lines given for *Phlebitis* in this section (page 171). *Rest is essential.*

Varicose Veins.—Varicose veins are veins which have become enlarged, dilated, or thickened. They may appear on any part of the body, but are seen most often on the legs. The veins of the legs are the largest in the body, and have the burden of carrying the used blood from the lower extremities back towards the heart ; if circulation is sluggish—as a result of constipation, wrong feeding, lack of exercise, etc.—a varicose condition of these veins often results. A vocation which demands many hours of standing daily often acts as a predisposing factor (but is in no sense a primary cause), as do also the wearing of tight clothing, garters, etc., etc.

The condition is a very painful one in many cases, and it cannot be said that much hope of cure is held out to the sufferer by orthodox medical methods of treatment. To-day, medical treatment consists of either operation or injection treatment. Results are far from satisfactory, for in neither of these attempts at " cure " are basic causes dealt with. Operation merely removes one affected vein, to pave the way for others to become affected. Injection treatment has, to the writer's personal knowledge, led to many serious complications in persons who have allowed themselves to undergo such treatment. One case developed blood poisoning, another phlebitis, and a third developed serious ear trouble—all as a result of injection treatment !

Treatment.—The only treatment for varicose veins which can really be successful must be one that aims at the removal of causes, *not effects*. Treatment must be constitutional in the highest degree. A fast for four to seven days, or from seven to fourteen days on the *all-fruit diet*, is the best way of beginning the treatment. The warm-water enema should be used nightly during this period, and if constipation is habitual—as it usually is in cases of varicose veins—the rules for its eradication given in Section 9, page 275, should be put into operation.

After the fast or period on all-fruit, the *full weekly diet* given in the Appendix should be adopted, and adhered to as strictly as possible. The diet should be plain and simple—fresh fruits and salads predominating—and all condiments, alcoholic liquors, coffee, strong tea, etc., should be avoided in future ; as also white-flour products, such as pastries, rich cakes, etc., and white sugar, and white-sugar products, such as jams, confectionery, etc.

Further periods on all-fruit—two or three days at monthly intervals—or a further short fast or two may be required in some cases, depending upon the progress being made, of course.

The hot Epsom-salts bath is very valuable, and should be taken twice weekly ; whilst the hot and cold sitz-bath (as described in the Appendix) will be found most beneficial, and should be taken every night of the week, if possible, excepting those nights on which an Epsom-salts bath is being taken. The dry friction and sponge or sitz-bath and the breathing and other exercises given in the Appendix should be gone through daily, and fresh air and outdoor exercise should take their due part in the treatment. *All health-building measures are good.* (After any hot bathing the affected parts should be well rinsed with cold water.)

As regards purely local treatment, the cold pack is most useful and should be applied nightly before retiring, and removed in the morning. (See the Appendix for details of application of the pack.) Spraying of the affected parts with cold water is also good. Another very good thing is to rest the legs wherever possible by reclining on a couch with the legs at a higher level than the remainder of the body. *Place cushions under the legs for this*, or sit on one chair with the feet placed on a chair facing. This should be done between working hours for half an hour at a time if at all possible, and in the evenings for a longer period.

Manipulative treatment at the hands of a good Naturopath or Osteopath is also very good in all cases of varicose veins.

Obviously some cases will take longer than others to show results, but perseverance with the treatment will bring its due reward.

SPECIAL NOTE RE VARICOSE ULCERS.—The treatment for *varicose ulcers* is the same as for *varicose veins*, except that a fast of from four to seven days should be taken to begin with, followed by fourteen days on the *restricted diet* given in the Appendix, after which the *full weekly diet* given therein can be begun. Further fasts followed by periods on the restricted diet will no doubt be needed at two- or three-monthly intervals in most cases.

Besides the local treatment advised for varicose veins, the ulcer can be bathed several times a day in hot water containing Epsom salts ($\frac{1}{4}$ lb. of salts to a bowlful of hot water).

Another thing which has proved very beneficial indeed in many cases is the use of *clay packs*. (For further information concerning *clay packs* see note at the end of Section 2 on *Skin Diseases*.)

Poultices made with "Slippery Elm Food" are also most valuable.

DISEASES OF THE
NERVES AND NERVOUS SYSTEM

Bell's palsy (Facial paralysis)—Disseminated sclerosis—Epilepsy—Insomnia —Locomotor ataxia—Migraine—Multiple sclerosis—Neuralgia—Neurasthenia —Nervous breakdown—Nervous debility ; Nervous exhaustion—Neuritis— Progressive muscular atrophy—Sciatica—Stammering and stuttering—Tic douloureux—Writer's cramp.

THE nervous system consists of two parts : (1) the *cerebro-spinal* system of nerves, which is under the direct control of the brain, and is responsible for all voluntary movement and action, such as walking, touching, speaking, etc. ; and (2) the *autonomic* or *involuntary* system of nerves, which acts without conscious thought or interference, and controls the working of the heart, stomach, and vital functions generally.

Both these systems are intimately connected with each other, and together motivate the whole body by means of what we call *nerve force*. What nerve force—the power of actuating nerve action—really is, no one can be quite sure of. Its origin is shrouded in mystery, that self-same mystery which enshrouds LIFE itself. But this we do know : nerve force is something at once fundamental and vital ; something connected directly with, if not actually emanating from, the very *life essence* of our being, and directly proportional to it. That is why some people always seem to have a larger amount of nerve force (or energy) at their disposal than others ; it simply means that they are endowed by Nature with a larger share of inherent vitality or *vital power* than others, as part of their birthright, and so have more nerve force (energy) with which to express it than others less well endowed.

To say that energy is something we get through the food we eat—as the medical profession declares—is to give a purely materialistic conception to the term and to misunderstand completely the whole question. If it were just a matter of food (of stoking up with fuel), the people who ate most would have the most energy ; but we all know that those who eat most are the most sluggish in habits, thought, and action. No, nerve force— energy—is something which we cannot create for ourselves ; it is something vital and dynamic which is created for us. That does not mean to say that we do not require food for our sustenance and for the building up and repair of tissue, but simply that we cannot *create* energy with it.

Whether or no we have been blessed by Nature with a capacity for engendering more nerve force (or energy) at a time than others, that which we *do* possess is ours to use or squander daily as we think fit. But once used up (or squandered), the only way we can replenish it is by *rest* and *sleep*. *In no other way can nerve force be restored to us.* That is, indeed, the real reason for sleep. Everything we do requires the expenditure of nerve force (energy), and so it is something always in need of replenishing; and only during rest and sleep can a new store be furnished us, from out the ever-mysterious sources of our being. Thus replenished, we can go forward with zest and vigour with the carrying out of the activities and tasks which go to make up our day-to-day existence. In other words, nerve force is the electric current which makes it possible for our bodies to work; it is something which is always being used up, and has to be re-charged daily from Nature's "re-charging dynamos" and this re-charging process only takes place during sleep and rest.

Over and above the nominal amount of nerve force which we use up daily, and which is replenished by sleep, we each of us have a reserve store—some more, some less—which we can call upon in emergency. Now, those people who fritter away or use up nerve force needlessly or excessively (through causes to be mentioned hereafter), and do not give Nature a chance adequately to replenish their store, keep on calling upon their reserves more and more, until, in time, there is no more available reserve to call on. It is then that what we call a "nervous breakdown" arises. It simply means that we have bankrupted ourselves temporarily of our supply of nervous energy, and can go no farther.

All nerve diseases and disorders do not necessarily imply a complete breakdown of nerve force; nevertheless, nerve exhaustion is always present in a more or less pronounced degree, and it is because the medical profession seeks to restore the lack of nerve power by means of what they call nerve "tonics," and nerve "stimulants," and nerve "foods," of chemical origin, instead of seeking to rectify the conditions responsible for the setting up of the trouble in the first place, that diseases of nervous origin show such little sign of disappearing from our midst. Indeed, of all classes of disease which are on the "up grade" of recent years, those of nervous origin are most to the front, thanks to medical inability to deal with the matter in a sane and practical manner.

Now, after these few preliminary and necessary remarks concerning the question, what are the *actual causes* responsible for the setting up of diseases of nervous origin ? It can be doubted by no one who has studied the matter carefully that *modern living*, with its artificiality, its late hours, its hurry, noise, many distractions and pleasures, is the chief criminal in the case, because of the tremendous using up of nerve force that ensues. Diseases such as neurasthenia, for instance, were quite unknown in the days before the "Machine Age." Such diseases are part of the price modern man pays for twentieth-century "efficiency" and "progress," with its motors, tubes, telephones, wireless, aeroplanes, bustle, scurry, and noise generally.

Another factor of prime importance in the setting up of nervous disorders, however, is *wrong diet*. The changes introduced into the dietary of the civilised individual of to-day in the shape of refined, tinned, processed, and preserved foods all have a very bad effect indeed upon the health of the system in general, and upon the nerves in particular. Foods "denatured" in this way are deprived to a very great extent of their invaluable mineral salts and vitamins, and it is for lack of these that nerve starvation occurs and nervous disorders grow, in a great many cases. Especially so if the unfortunate victim is also trying to live up to present-day "high-pressure" standards.

Modern artificial ways of living, modern errors in diet—those are the two great physical factors to be considered in trying to understand the real basic causes of diseases of the nervous system, and the reason for their remarkable increase during the past fifty years or so. But the nerves play a twofold part in the life of the body ; they are the link between two worlds—the physical and the mental. Diseases of the nervous system can therefore originate in either mental or physical causes, or both. We must never lose sight of this fact in thinking of or dealing with nervous disorders of any kind.

Worry, overwork, fear, anxiety, destructive emotions or thoughts of every kind, all tend to use up nerve force unduly, and to react adversely upon the nervous system and reduce its capacity for effective work. Prolonged over a period years and combined with the two physical factors already named, and we have here the true cause and starting-ground for ninety-nine per cent. of the nervous disease so common to-day.

When over-indulgence in sex, self-abuse, excessive drinking, smoking, and "high living" in general come to complicate the foregoing, then the passage of the individual towards the more serious nerve disorders and nervous breakdowns, which form such a feature of present-day living, is very rapid indeed.

As regards the treatment of conditions such as those we are here dealing with, Medical Science merely makes matters worse instead of better by virtue of the drugs it employs to "tone up" or "stimulate" a flagging nervous system or to deaden pain. Once the real underlying causes of nervous diseases are under-stood, the uselessness of attempting to build up a disorganised nervous system by means of highly dangerous medicinal drugs must be obvious to all capable of serious thought. It is only by a complete regeneration of the system, and the cessation of all habits and ways of living and thinking which have led to the setting up of the trouble in the first place, that a cure is possible. In no other way. Least of all through the agency of drugs.

Medical scientists have discovered that certain drugs affect the nervous system in certain different ways, some stimulating it into enforced activity (and so called nerve " stimulants " and " tonics "), others paralysing or benumbing excessive nerve action (and so being called " sedatives," and " anodynes," or " pain-killers "). But the use of all such drugs is reprehensible in the highest degree. They stimulate or excite nerve action temporarily, only to depress it the more later on (in compliance with a definite law of Nature overlooked or ignored by our medical scientists) ; or if they suppress or benumb nerve action, it is only at the cost of per-manently damaging the whole nervous mechanism of the indivi-dual under treatment.

Drugs, such as arsenic and phosphorus, for instance, are very commonly prescribed in nerve disorders as "stimulants" and "tonics" by the medical profession, as also are bromides for

" sedative " purposes. All of these are highly dangerous chemical elements to introduce into any human system, and although they *may appear* to palliate matters temporarily, and may even *seem* to be beneficial, their real effect is far from that expected by either the patient or his medical adviser. Examination of the iris of the eye—as in iridiagnosis—reveals at once the destructive effects upon the system of the introduction of drugs such as those we have mentioned. Arsenic is a dangerous poison at all times, and although the smallness of the dosage administered in medical treatment minimises its effect somewhat, this does not alter the characteristics of the drug or its accumulative ill-effect upon nervous structure and nerve tissue generally (especially upon the spinal cord). Phosphorus, although so essential to life in general and nervous tissue in particular, can only be dealt with and used by the human system *if introduced through the medium of food, and in no other way. Organic* phosphorus is what the body needs ; not inorganic or chemical phosphorus. And organic phosphorus can only be found in natural unspoilt foods, especially the whole-grain cereals, such as whole wheat, whole rye, etc., which go to make up *real hundred per cent. whole-grain products.* White bread and white-flour products are lamentably lacking in organic phosphorus.

Instead of telling his nerve patients to obtain the phosphorus they need from natural sources, the medical practitioner gives them phosphorus direct from the laboratory and thinks it just as good ! What an error ! What ignorance of the body's needs is here displayed ! Inorganic or chemical phosphorus is a poison.

The same is true with regard to the use of bromides. These are most destructive in their effect upon the brain and nervous tissue ; yet medical science thinks nothing of using them—indeed, thinks them highly valuable simply because they tend to disguise or temporarily diminish the effects of nerve disorders by paralysing nerve reactions and stupefying the unfortunate sufferer. When it is said that bromides are directly harmful to health we are here saying nothing that is not strictly true ! *Let the reader think this well over.* So much, then, for nerve " tonics," " stimulants," etc. ! (It may be mentioned here, in passing, that the most terrible nervous and mental diseases, such as locomotor ataxy, general paralysis of the insane, etc., are the *direct outcome* of the use of mercury, arsenic, and such-like drugs in large doses in the treatment of venereal disease.)

Having dealt with the so-called nerve " tonic," etc., which is no tonic at all but a most insidious menace to life and health, we can turn our attention for a moment to the use of narcotic drugs and pain-killers in medical practice. Pain is a nerve symptom, and is one of Nature's signs that all is not well within the organism, and that something needs putting right. Merely to deaden the pain by temporarily suspending nerve action by means of drugs is not the way to set matters right. We have to get rid of the *cause* of the pain, not just the pain itself. Surely every reader can see that just killing or deadening pain is not the same as getting rid of the cause of the pain ? Yet the medical profession does not seem to be able to !

Aspirin is one of the most widely used of all drugs for the deadening of pain. It does this at the expense of the general health of the whole organism. Nothing is said on this point, though, either by those who advertise it or advise it. Aspirin, phenacetin, and all drugs of a similar nature have a most deleterious cumulative effect upon the heart (and kidneys too), and they merely succeed in deadening or killing pain by virtue of the fact that they have a numbing effect upon the nerve centres in the brain, from which source all feeling of pain originates, although the actual sensation may be felt in any part of the body. Morphia and other narcotic drugs are just as harmful in their after-effects as these former, or even worse in some ways, so all in all the use of medicinal drugs in the treatment of nerve diseases or disorders can truly be said to lead to a worse condition than the actual disease itself. The patient may appear to become *temporarily* better, but more serious trouble of some kind or other is *bound to develop* later. *The drug way is not the way to health ; it is the way to further disease.* (The same remarks apply to all patent nerve " tonics " and nerve " foods." None of them can bring *health* to a diseased system.)

Having shown the reader what the causes of disease of the nervous system are, and what effect the use of medicinal drugs has in such cases, we can now turn to the treatments for such diseases Natural Cure provides. That many thousands of nerve sufferers who had been previously given up as incurable by orthodox Medical Science have been restored to health thereby will be readily appreciated by the intelligent reader, as it is *fundamental causes* which Natural Cure deals with and removes, not superficial effects or such things.

Bell's Palsy (Facial Paralysis).—Facial paralysis is the commonest form of paralysis experienced by human beings. It means that the muscles of one or both sides of the face are unable to move because the nerves controlling their activity are out of action. (All muscular activity depends upon nerve activity primarily.) Facial paralysis may be slight or it may be serious, depending upon the underlying cause, but in any case Natural Treatment is helpful.

Treatment.—For facial paralysis the best treatment is undoubtedly manipulation and ray therapy. Manipulation of the spine increases nerve activity like nothing else does, and unless the nerves controlling the muscles of the face are completely incapable of further action, then much can be obtained from this form of treatment. Ray therapy is also most helpful in conjunction with the foregoing, and, of course, proper diet and massage. Indeed, the latter has much to its credit in the overcoming of facial paralysis, quite apart from any other treatment. Electrical usage of the high-frequency kind is not recommended. Treatment should always be in the hands of a competent Naturopath, but in any case the rules *re* diet and general health-building given in the Appendix should be carried out.

Disseminated Sclerosis.—See *Multiple Sclerosis.*

Epilepsy.—There are two kinds of epilepsy known as *petit mal* and *grand mal* respectively, the former being far less serious than the latter. Epilepsy is a most serious and alarming nervous disease because of the tremendous nervous upheaval that takes place during an attack. The whole nervous system becomes convulsed at such times, and nothing can be done to prevent the attack once it has given warning of its coming, by well-marked signs which are known as the " aura " of an attack. Medical treatment for epilepsy is, to say the least, ineffective. Dosing the patient with bromides or luminal not only never cures the condition, but it definitely makes matters worse as time goes on, turning slight forms of epilepsy into more serious and chronic manifestations of the disease.

It can be said here and now that Natural Cure holds out the one *real hope* for the epileptic ; but even so, only in some cases is a complete cure possible. Sufferers from epilepsy of the *grand mal* type can, at best, but hope for the alleviation of their condition under natural treatment, as definite disease of some portion of the brain-tissue is usually at the root of their trouble ; but in *petit mal* the chances of a complete cure are much more hopeful, as this condition arises less from definite disease of the grey matter of the brain than from periodic toxic disturbance of brain function, due to a highly toxic blood-stream.

Digestive disturbances or intestinal toxæmia (plus a highly strung nervous condition) are very often the cause of *petit mal*— the less serious form of epilepsy ; but *grand mal* is usually the outcome of hereditary influences, serious shock or injury to the brain or nervous system, or suppressive medical treatment of previous acute disease, such as meningitis, typhoid, etc.

Treatment.—Although a very difficult disease to get results with, there is much more hope for the sufferer from epilepsy who follows out natural treatment than for one who continues all his life dosing himself with poisonous drugs under medical advice and supervision. Correct diet, in cleansing the blood-stream, does much to get down to the seat of the trouble, which lies right here in the majority of cases ; and even where the epilepsy is definitely the result of disease of the brain-tissue, such treatment will help considerably to lessen the severity and frequency of attacks.

The procedure to adopt is as follows : Begin with a fast for four or five days, as directed in the Appendix. Break the fast as directed therein, and then the *restricted diet* also outlined in the Appendix should be adopted for from seven to fourteen days. This *restricted diet* may be then discontinued, and the *full weekly diet* begun. The diet should be adhered to as strictly as possible. Meat should be deleted as far as may be from the future diet of the epileptic, whilst white bread, sugar, rich cakes, pastries, heavy puddings, pies, and all stodgy foods should be studiously avoided. No tea or coffee should be taken, and no condiments, sauces, seasonings, etc. *The diet should be as light as possible.* (Take no milk puddings either, or mushy foods of this nature.) Fresh fruits and salads—Nature's cleansing foods—should form the major portion of the future daily dietary, supplemented by whole-meal bread, eggs, cheese, milk, etc.

During the fast, and after if necessary, the bowels should be cleansed nightly with the warm-water enema or gravity douche ; and if constipation is habitual, the rules for its eradication given in Section 9 (page 275) should be put into operation forthwith.

The daily dry friction and sitz-bath or sponge, outlined in the Appendix, should be undertaken regularly in conjunction with the breathing and other exercises also given therein. Such measures, by toning up and strengthening the system, are in the highest degree valuable. The full Epsom-salts bath, twice weekly, is also to be recommended. A very good thing is the application of alternate hot and cold compresses to the base of the brain (at the back of the head). The patient sits with his feet in a bowl of hot water, and first a hot towel and then a cold one is applied to the base of the brain, then a further hot towel and a further cold one, etc. Each towel should be kept on for two or three minutes, and the whole process can be repeated two or three (or more) times daily, at intervals, according to the severity (or otherwise) of the case. The number of hot and cold applications may be anything from two of each to four or five of each, at each performance of the treatment, for the same reasons.

Spinal manipulation, where procurable, is highly recommended in all cases of epilepsy. It is very valuable indeed.

Drinking, smoking, sexual excess, and " high-living " of any kind are much to be deprecated in the case of the epileptic. They will all hinder his recovery and retard progress. Quietness and abstemious living are the main lines of conduct for the epileptic who would get the best out of the treatment here devised for him. Above all things, excessive excitement should be avoided.

Depending upon the duration of the condition, the severity of the fits when present, age, etc., the treatment here given should be supplemented by further short fasts and periods on the *restricted diet*, at two- or three-monthly intervals, say. The progress being made in the meantime should be the guide as to the need for this.

SPECIAL NOTE RE DRUGS.—As many sufferers from epilepsy have taken strong drugs for many years, it would be unwise in these cases to leave them off entirely all at once. The dosage should be cut in half to begin with, then gradually reduced further and further, until it can be left off altogether, as possible.

Insomnia.—Insomnia has been included under the heading of nervous diseases, although as a matter of fact it is not a disease at all, but a condition of sleeplessness. Those suffering from insomnia may often find it difficult to place their finger on the seat of the trouble, but physical disease of some sort or mental stress or strain are its chief causes. In passing, it may be stated that indigestion and constipation are often the cause of insomnia, on the physical side; whilst worry, overwork, prolonged excitement, and such-like conditions are its chief causes on the mental and emotional side.

To resort to the use of drugs for inducing sleep in those suffering from insomnia is worse than useless, as not only does it not get rid of the cause of the trouble, but it steadily lowers the tone of the whole organism by virtue of the deleterious and under-mining effects of narcotic drugs upon the system. The only cure lies in the discovery of the cause of the trouble—mental or physical, or both—and the taking of steps for its eradication or removal.

Treatment.—Treatment for insomnia should be in the hands of a Naturopath where at all possible, and manipulative treatment is especially good for this condition. (The writer has known cases where people have been unable to sleep for days on end, but have had a really good night's rest after only one manipulative treatment.) A few days on the *all-fruit diet*, with the use of the enema nightly, followed by the *full weekly diet* given in the Appendix, is a good way to begin treatment in cases of insomnia, such treatment helping to cleanse the blood-stream and relieve possible digestive or intestinal disturbance. The daily dry friction and sponge, and the breathing and other exercises given in the Appendix, should also be gone through daily as a means of further toning up the system. A fairly long walk every day is something which every sufferer from insomnia should undertake, if at all possible, as the more gentle exercise of this nature they have, the better. A warm bath before going to bed at night is also very good indeed for the sufferer from insomnia, as this helps to relax the mind and body generally. The temperature of the bath should be about 98 degrees Fahr., or body heat.

Eating of a late meal often predisposes towards sleeplessness, so the sufferer from insomnia should take care to eat his last meal at least three or four hours before going to bed. When in bed, it does not do to think too much about sleep or the inability to sleep, but the patient should lie in as relaxed a position as possible, and just think of whatever comes into his head.

It is surprising how often sleep will suddenly come if this is done.

Correct diet, the building up of the system along the lines indicated herein, and the relaxation of mind and body are the necessary stepping-stones towards the eradication of insomnia. But, of course, if the seat of the trouble is neurosis or prolonged worry or mental depression, etc., there will be need for the attention of a skilled psycho-therapist in cases of an obstinate nature. However, even in these cases, the rules for treatment here given will be immensely valuable.

Where the cause of the trouble is definite physical disease, such as anæmia, kidney trouble, etc., etc., the treatment for that disease (given in the appropriate section) should be followed out by the sufferer from insomnia, as well as taking into account the general advice given above. Where the trouble is due to environmental causes, home troubles, etc., a change of scene is often all that is required.

SPECIAL NOTE RE DRUGS.—Where drugs have been taken over a long period to induce sleep, they should not be left off all at once, but *gradually*.

Locomotor Ataxia.—This is a condition in which there is progressive deterioration of the spinal nerves which are instrumental in directing the locomotion of the body, as in walking. Often there is connected with the condition great pain in other nerves or organs of the body, together with wasting of muscles or nerves, double vision, inability to control the working of the bladder and rectum, etc., etc.

The disease is a most serious one, and although Medical Science attributes it to the after-effects of venereal disease, there is no

187

doubt at all that it is the deadly drugs used in the *medical treatment* of venereal disease—drugs such as mercury and arsenic—which are the real cause of the progressive nerve paralysis resulting in *locomotor ataxia*, and *not* the original disease at all. When the world wakes up the fact that fasting is the only sure and definite cure for venereal disease, and that drug treatment by metallic drugs is just suppressive in the highest degree, it will begin to understand something of the genesis of those terrible conditions such as *locomotor ataxia, general paralysis of the insane*, and the like, which follow in the wake of medical treatment for syphilis. It is safe to say that the terrible after-effects usually ascribed to syphilis under the heading of *Secondary* and *Tertiary Syphilis*, and of which the world goes in such horror, are not the result of the disease at all, but of the medical treatment instituted as a supposed " cure " for it. Mercury and arsenic are the most deadly enemies to nerve tissue that there are ; locomotor ataxia is only one of the diseases which follow in the wake of the use of large quantities of these drugs over prolonged periods in the ortho-dox treatment for syphilis.

Treatment.—Although locomotor ataxia is such a serious disease there is at least hope of the sufferer arresting its spread, and perhaps even improving his condition, if natural methods of treatment are carried out. The medical way of giving more drugs to relieve the effects of previous drug treatment is just heaping insult upon injury, and does nothing but make matters worse. The sufferer from locomotor ataxia should place himself under a Naturopath as soon as he can.

It does not do to hold out too much hope in diseases of this nature—some cases will have progressed too far for anything to be done at all for them ; but manipulative treatment, eliminative baths, fasting, and diet have done good work in many cases that have come under natural treatment, whilst the *milk cure* has some excellent results to its credit in the treatment of conditions such as that we are dealing with here.

If the sufferer from locomotor ataxia cannot procure the ser-vices of a competent Naturopath, he can do much for himself by undertaking a series of short fasts, followed by the *full milk diet* given in the Appendix (a fast for from four to seven days followed by three to four weeks on the milk diet, then a month on the *full weekly diet* given in the Appendix, then a further fast and period on milk and so on). The regular weekly diet should always be returned to thereafter, and the other measures (also given in the Appendix) for toning up and generally improving the system adopted. The weekly or bi-weekly hot Epsom-salts bath is a very good thing too, and of course the enema should be used nightly during the first part of the treatment and afterwards whenever necessary. NO DRUGS OF ANY KIND MUST BE TAKEN IN FUTURE.

Migraine.—This is a form of nervous or neuralgic headache which is very troublesome. It is paroxysmal in character, occurring at intervals of weeks or months, each attack incapacitating the sufferer for several days in some cases. To attempt to treat the condition by means of drugs or " pain-killers " is not to get down to the root of the trouble at all, *which is—in every case—constitutional.* That is why the sufferer from migraine usually goes on year after year under medical treatment with no apparent possibility of cure for his condition. This continual treating of symptoms merely renders the trouble more and more difficult to eradicate as time goes on. As usual, medical practice and medical attitude to disease in general are to blame.

Treatment.—In seeking for a cure for migraine one must first look to primary causes. The condition may be due to chronic constipation and indigestion, to liver trouble, to nervous debility, or some such disturbance of physical functioning. It is only when the real underlying cause is discovered and eradicated that the sufferer from migraine can hope for a cessation of his periodic attacks of this troublesome complaint.

If a Naturopath cannot be consulted, the first steps to take in the treatment of migraine are a thorough cleansing of the system and the adoption of vitality-building measures, which will make for a complete toning up and revitalisation of the whole organism. A week on the *all-fruit diet*, or a *short fast* for four or five days, followed by the *weekly dietary* given in the Appendix, is the best way to start the treatment. Further short fasts or periods on the all-fruit diet will be needed at intervals of a month or two, in certain cases, according to the progress made. The warm-water enema should be used nightly during the first few days of the treatment, and later if necessary; and if constipation is habitual, the principles for its eradication given in Section 9 (page 275) should be put into operation.

The friction and sitz-bath or sponge should form a regular feature of the daily routine once the treatment is begun, as also the physical and other exercises given in the Appendix. The hot Epsom-salts bath once or twice a week is also a very good thing in cases of migraine. A walk of a few miles every day is to be recommended to all capable of undertaking it. Spinal manipulation is *most beneficial* in all cases of migraine, when carried out in conjunction with a scheme of natural treatment such as given here.

When an attack is impending, the sufferer should go to bed and fast for a day or two on warm water only. The enema should be used nightly during that period, and cold compresses can be applied to the head, changing them at frequent intervals. If this is done, the attacks will lose much of their severity and, as the treatment continues, will become gradually less and less troublesome until they fade away altogether. *On no account should any drugs or " pain-killers " be used.*

The strictest care with the diet is essential if a real cure is desired, and all highly seasoned dishes, condiments, pickles, sauces, white sugar, strong tea or coffee, rich cakes, pastry, heavy and stodgy foods and alcohol should be avoided.

Multiple Sclerosis.—This condition is characterised by trembling or tremor every time an action is performed, and also by slow, indistinct speech. Another marked feature is rapid oscillation of the eyeballs from side to side. There are other complications which may occur as the disease develops, the cause of the condition being atrophy of nerve tissues in the spinal cord or brain. It may be brought on by the orthodox treatment for syphilis (see the remarks on *Locomotor Ataxia* in the present section), by metallic poisoning of an occupational nature, by very prolonged and excessive nerve strain, by injury, by suppressive treatment of former acute diseases, etc., etc.

Treatment.—As regards treatment, Medical Science has little to offer the sufferer from multiple sclerosis beyond drug treatment. Such treatment, involving as it does the use of the very drugs which cause the condition in some cases (mercury or arsenic, for instance), can lead to no good results whatsoever. Natural methods of treatment offer the only hope of improvement or alleviation of his condition to the sufferer from the disease in question. A complete cure is almost impossible, as in most cases the injury to nerve tissue has gone so far as to impair permanently the working of the organism. However, many cases can keep the diseases in check and even make progress if natural methods are adopted.

Spinal manipulation is very helpful in all cases of multiple sclerosis, together with fasting, eliminative baths, light treatment, and corrective dieting ; and if the sufferer cannot obtain personal naturopathic treatment, he or she should follow out the advice *re* self-treatment given in the section dealing with *Locomotor Ataxia* (page 187).

Neuralgia.—This term is usually applied to pain in the nerves of the face, and is a most troublesome condition. To attempt to deal with it by means of " pain-killers " or such-like temporarily ameliorative measures is not of the slightest good, as such treatment ignores altogether the underlying causes involved in the condition. Neuralgia is really a neuritic condition due to excess acidity of the blood and body fluids. In origin it is directly allied to rheumatism and other uric acid diseases, and the outstanding underlying causes of its development are *wrong feeding* and *lowered vitality* due to overwork, nerve strain, etc.

Treatment.—The sufferer from neuralgia is referred to the section on *Rheumatism and Allied Ailments* (Section 3, page 150) for an understanding of the part played by wrong diet in the development of " uric-acid " diseases, of which, as just said, neuralgia is one. As regards treatment, that given in the following pages for *neuritis* will be found to give the most beneficial and lasting results to the sufferer from neuralgia, if carried out with patience and perseverance.

Neurasthenia.—Neurasthenia is *the* disease of the age. It is the direct outcome of modern ways of living and thinking, and the sufferer from this condition is referred to the introductory remarks made at the beginning of this section for an understanding of how the disease has arisen in twentieth-century civilisation. *Wrong feeding, wrong living,* and *wrong thinking* can be taken as its three chief predisposing causes.

Neurasthenia is essentially a condition in which the whole nervous system has lost tone and become exhausted, and to treat the disease by means of drugs and " tonics " is to leave the underlying causes of the condition quite untouched and to tinker about with the merely superficial aspects of the trouble. The writer has had something to say in the introductory remarks to the present section regarding the use of so-called *nerve tonics* and *nerve foods* in the treatment of neurasthenia and other nervous disorders. Not only is such treatment quite useless so far as real cure is concerned, it is often definitely harmful.

It is true that, in addition to dispensing drugs, members of the medical profession prescribe rest, change of scene, etc., for their patients suffering from neurasthenia who can afford to take advantage of the advice given ; and such advice is to the good, so far as it goes. The patient is also exhorted " not to worry." This dictum, although very well meant no doubt, is most difficult to carry out in actual practice by the neurasthenic, as his whole nervous system is so undermined that worry is the foremost and most impregnable inhabitant of his mental stronghold. All neurasthenics worry, because worry is a certain sign and development of lowered vitality and deficient nerve tone. It can never be exorcised by telling people " not to worry." The whole system must be built up first, and wrong habits and ways of living rectified, before the nerves will be in such a position as to make it possible to overcome the worry habit, which is so sapping in its effects upon the mind and body of the neurasthenic. This habit will gradually disappear if the neurasthenic will take himself in hand and build up his system aright ; by no other means can it be eradicated.

Treatment.—As regards treatment for neurasthenia, it is obvious that unless the patient is taken completely in hand, and his whole scheme of living changed, there can be no hope of a lasting cure of his condition. Patched up he may be by the prescribing of " nerve tonics " and " nerve food s in conjunction with rest, change of scene, etc., but cured he will never be. The trouble will be bound to recur in later life if the former habits and ways of living and thinking, which were the real cause of the development of the trouble in the first place, are returned to after the period of medical-recuperative treatment. To anyone who can think for himself this must be obvious.

Treatment at a Natural-Cure establishment is far the best for the sufferer from neurasthenia who can afford it, as such treatment combines all that is best in medical usage—with regard to change of air, rest, etc.—with the best that Natural Cure can offer. Sunbathing, ray therapy, manipulative treatment, and such-like measures, combined with fasting, strict dieting, eliminative baths and other forms of natural treatment, have resulted in complete cures in a large number of cases of neurasthenia, many of them cases which responded not at all to orthodox methods of treatment.

For those who cannot undertake institutional treatment, the following scheme of home treatment is devised : Begin by having from four to seven days on the *all-fruit diet*, as given in the Appendix. This should then be followed by a period on the exclusive *fruit and milk diet*, also given in the Appendix. The fruit and milk diet should be adhered to for from ten days to a fortnight ; but if it is agreeing particularly well, it can be continued with every benefit for a month or longer (in which case the quantity of milk taken can be increased up to as much as six or more pints daily). Afterwards *the full weekly diet* given in the Appendix should be adopted, and adhered to as strictly as possible from then on. (A mainly fruit and salad diet is *essential* to the neurasthenic.)

During the first few days of the treatment the enema or douche should be used nightly to cleanse the bowels. It should always be resorted to thereafter whenever constipation is present. If constipation is habitual, the principles for its eradication given in Section 9 (page 275) should be put into operation forthwith.

Further short periods on the all-fruit diet followed by the fruit and milk diet may be required in some cases at intervals of a month or two. The patient must decide about this for himself, according to the progress being made.

As regards vitality-building measures, the morning dry friction and sponge or sitz-bath are invaluable ; as also are the breathing and other exercises given in the Appendix. A hot Epsom-salts bath once or twice weekly can also be recommended to the sufferer from neurasthenia ; whilst the need for fresh air and gentle outdoor exercise must never be overlooked. Walking is by far the best form of outdoor exercise for the neurasthenic to take.

The neurasthenic needs *plenty of rest*, and an attempt should be made to *relax mind and body completely* when reposing. A few days' *complete rest in bed* is an excellent way of beginning the treatment in many cases, with a day or half-day in bed every week thereafter for some time to come.

Early to bed and early to rise are two dicta which apply with especial force to the sufferer from neurasthenia ; and late hours and late rising should be finally abolished when once natural treatment is begun. Proper personal hygiene is essential to health, so that scrupulousness with regard to one's habits should be observed by all undertaking treatment. Well-ventilated bedrooms are a necessity too. All highly flavoured dishes, pastries, heavy puddings, pies, and similar rich or stodgy foods which over-tax digestion should be studiously avoided, and white bread, sugar, refined cereals, condiments, tea, coffee, and alcohol entirely cut out. (No milk puddings, broths, beef-tea, or such-like invalid's fare, either !) Smoking should be entirely stopped, where habitual. TAKE NO MEDICINES WHATSOEVER, OR PATENT FOODS.

The pursuance of the above rules of eating and living will help the neurasthenic back to health again if carried out with patience and perseverance ; but it stands to reason that ways of thinking and feeling which have helped to produce the trouble in the first place must be guarded against from the moment the treatment is begun. The mental attitude must be altered radically from one of negativity to one of positivity. The " self-pity " habit must be destroyed. Instead of " I shall never get well," it must be " I am going to get well ; I *am* getting well."

Self-suggestion—of the *right* kind—is of immense value in the treatment of neurasthenia, and so, to help the neurasthenic to attain the right mental attitude, the following little scheme of self-suggestion is proposed. It should be undertaken as soon as treatment is commenced, and its beneficial effects will soon make themselves apparent to the neurasthenic sufferer. Repeat, with great concentration, the following phrase six times, each night before retiring : " I *am* getting better ; my nerves are *stronger*, and soon I shall be *quite* well," emphasising the italicised words ; and each morning on rising the sufferer should repeat, just as earnestly, this phrase : " Now for my *rejuvenating* treatment which is doing me so much good ! "

The practice of self-suggestion may seem very foolish to many, but it cannot be emphasised too strongly that, in all cases where nerve weakness is a factor, self-suggestion along the lines proposed is of the utmost value.

It will help the sufferer from neurasthenia greatly, too, if he can make himself realise *quite definitely* that his worry habit, depression, and introspection arise simply as a result of the defective state of his nerves, and that as the treatment is persevered with, *so must all these conditions automatically disappear. As the nerves improve in health, so must worry and depression fade from the mental consciousness.* It will pay the neurasthenic well to dwell on this often. Obviously his habit of worrying and harassing himself with doubts and fears will try to assert itself throughout the initial stages of the treatment, however much he may endeavour to control this morbid mental tendency ; but he should try to make himself thoroughly realise that they are the outcome of a defective nervous condition, and that by building up his system in the manner here described he is doing the best and surest thing to banish them for ever.

There is a lot of talk these days about the mental cause of nervous disease and the great need for psychological treatment ; but if the neurasthenic will bear in mind what has here been said, he can go forward to sound health again without having to spend any time or thought on treatment of this kind. In *abnormal* cases (of severe neurosis, morbid depression, melancholia, etc.) such treatment is highly desirable, and even necessary ; but in the usual run of neurasthenic cases it is not. The regimen here given will amply suffice. A clean diet, a clean body, and sensible living—these are the physical bases on which to build up health in the neurasthenic. Combine these with control of mental and emotional habits and tendencies which pull down the tone of the system, and with helpful self-suggestion, then neurasthenia will soon be a thing of the past, instead of a thing very much of the present, as now.

Nervous Breakdown.—The cause of what is called a " nervous breakdown " has already been made clear in the introductory remarks to the present section, and the only two methods of successful treatment are obviously REST and CORRECT DIET. A complete rest in bed for from a week to a month or longer—according to the severity of the case—will be necessary to begin the treatment, with a fast of from four to seven days and the use of the enema nightly ; after which the treatment for *Neurasthenia* given in the preceding pages should be begun, and the remarks *re general living after recovery* taken seriously to heart.

Nervous Debility ; Nervous Exhaustion.—The cause or causes of these two conditions will be made clear by a study of the introductory remarks to the present section. As regards treatment, this should be as for *neurasthenia* given in the preceding pages.

Neuritis.—This is a condition in which a nerve or series of nerves have become inflamed and nerve tissue destroyed, as a result of the blood and body fluids being in an excessively acid condition. All the body fluids should be *alkaline* in their reaction, but when the dietary is such that acid waste matter forms continuously in the tissues over a period of years, then a condition known as "acidosis" arises. Neuritis is merely one of the many forms which acidosis takes. In this case it means that the nerves are bathed continuously in an acid instead of an alkaline medium, and so become corroded and inflamed. The chief cause of this condition of acidosis, as explained in the section on *Rheumatism and Allied Complaints* (Section 3, page 150), is *wrong feeding*, although wrong habits of living, overwork, etc., play their part in lowering the tone of the nervous system and helping on the advance of the trouble.

Treatment.—Drug treatment for neuritis is just useless. It is true that the pain arising out of the condition is often unbearable, and "pain-killers" of the aspirin type are resorted to often in desperation, just to relieve the pain ; but this is not the way to get rid of the trouble effectively. The pain is relieved for the time being, at the cost of the health of other parts of the body—the heart and kidneys especially—but the neuritis still remains. Only *constitutional* treatment along Natural-Cure lines can effect a real cure.

The sufferer from neuritis is invited to read what has already been said about the relationship between wrong feeding and disease in Section 3, dealing with *Rheumatism and Allied Ailments* (page 150). He will see that it is the white bread, white sugar, boiled potatoes, refined cereals, meat, fish, tinned goods, tea, coffee, condiments, and other articles of food which habitually go to make up his daily dietary which are at the root of the trouble. Foods such as these flood the tissues continuously with acid impurities ; and continued over a period, *acidosis*—in some form or other—*must* occur. Whether it be catarrh or rheumatism, neuritis or bronchitis, depends entirely upon the make-up of the individual—upon his constitutional characteristics, that is. It is only by the adoption of a rational dietary, a dietary whose reaction in the system is essentially *alkaline*, that this condition of acidosis, of which neuritis is only one manifestation, can be overcome. Of such an alkaline diet, fresh fruits and salads are the chief ingredients. (There is a belief in medical circles that acid fruits are the cause of acidity in the system. This is quite wrong. The white-bread-white-sugar-meat diet causes the formation of acids in the system ; acid fruits are cleansing, and their systemic reaction is *alkaline*.)

The sufferer from neuritis, having imbibed the foregoing, should turn to the treatment for *Rheumatism* as given in Section 3, and carry it out according to the severity (or otherwise) of his case. The more closely he can follow it out, the sooner will he be freed from his pain and troubles. On no account should drugs be taken to deaden pain. The hot bath, the Epsom-salts bath, and the cold pack will do this for him. In addition to two or three—or even four—hot Epsom-salts baths weekly, the sufferer from neuritis should apply a cold pack to the affected area every night before retiring and remove it in the morning. (Cold packs are explained in the Appendix.) Also the affected parts should be bathed several times daily in hot water containing Epsom salts (a tablespoonful of salts to a cupful of hot water ; ¼ lb. of salts to a small bowlful of hot water). Where pain is severe, as in neuralgia, hot and cold compresses are very good. You wring out a towel in hot water, apply it to the painful area, leave on for, say, three minutes, then remove and apply a second hot towel. Use three hot towels in the fashion mentioned—one after another, of course—and then finish off with a cold towel. The hot and cold compresses can be applied several times daily as required, and always in the order named, viz. three hot applications and one cold one to finish.

Spinal manipulation, where procurable, is very useful as an adjunct to the treatment here advised.

Progressive Muscular Atrophy.—This is a condition in which there is wasting of the voluntary muscles—that is, those muscles which are under the direct control of the will, such as those controlling movement, etc. Muscles or groups of muscles are attacked consecutively, and the disease is often known by the appropriate name of " wasting palsy." There is strong reason to believe that heredity plays a big part in the propagation of this disease, but even so a devitalised condition of the whole system—and nervous system especially—is indicated as a first cause of the development of the disease, in which wrong feeding, wrong habits of living, suppressive medical treatment of previous acute disease, etc., etc., all play their part.

Treatment.—As regards treatment, all that can be offered to the sufferer from progressive muscular atrophy is that his condition may be prevented from progressing still further under natural treatment. Improvement other than this is hard to promise. Yet even the arrest of the trouble is surely something worth while ? More so as medical treatment has nothing at all to offer in the way of real help to the sufferer, whose condition is thus allowed to get steadily worse and worse through the taking of drugs.

The treatment given for *Locomotor Ataxia* in the present section (page 187) can be carried out with advantage by the sufferer from progressive muscular atrophy, whilst massage is also a very helpful additional measure indeed, and can be strongly recommended. Electrical treatment and ray therapy are also useful if carried out in conjunction with proper diet.

Sciatica.—Sciatica is merely a neuritic condition of the sciatic nerve (the large nerve which runs down the leg). It is the direct outcome of excess acidity of the blood and tissues, plus a rundown condition of the system generally, and is another of the many forms of " acidosis." The sufferer from sciatica is advised to turn to the treatment for *Neuritis* given in the preceding pages of the present section for the treatment for his complaint. Complete rest in bed for a few days is essential in many cases as a start. If the trouble is acute, it is best to begin with a fast of from four to seven days, following with the *restricted diet* given in the Appendix for a further seven to fourteen days. For sciatica, the cold sitz-bath in the morning and the hot and cold sitz-bath at night (as described in the Appendix) will be most beneficial indeed.

Stammering and Stuttering.—Stammering and stuttering are both conditions which may be, and often are, of psychological or nervous origin. There are definite physical signs of interference with the vocal organs in some cases, but in most cases the condition is purely functional. Treatment from a psychotherapist has resulted in many complete cures of stammering and stuttering, without any physical treatment being needed at all. Hypnotic treatment has also been successful in many cases too. The sufferer is advised to obtain naturopathic advice with regard to finding which treatment is best for his particular case.

Tic Douloureux.—See *Neuralgia* (page 191).

Writer's Cramp.—This is a form of paralysis of the muscles used to control the movement of the hand in writing. Writer's cramp may result from psychological inhibitions—as has been proved in some cases ; it also may arise from systemic poisoning from metallic drugs such as mercury and lead. Its cause in the majority of cases, however, is over-use of the muscles in question, combined with a lowered state of the system generally, due to unhygienic living, wrong feeding, etc. Injury to a portion of the brain-tissue may bring it on in some cases.

Treatment.—As regards treatment, some cases of writer's cramp are definitely incurable. But natural treatment should be undertaken in all cases, combined with manipulation, massage, ray therapy, etc. In some cases psychological treatment—alone—has resulted in some remarkable cures.

DISEASES OF THE
GLANDS AND GLANDULAR SYSTEM

Addison's disease—Bubonic plague—Diseases of the salivary glands—Diseases of the sweat glands—Enlarged glands of the neck—Exophthalmic goitre (Graves' disease)—Goitre—Hodgkin's disease—Myxœdema—Diseases of the prostate gland—The spleen and its diseases.

IN addition to the vital organs, such as the heart, the liver, the kidneys, etc., the body contains a large number of glands, or systems of glands, which carry on special functions of their own that are of extreme importance to the health of the organism as a whole. For instance, the lymphatic glands and lymphatic vessels, with the spleen at their head, carry out the vital work of "detoxifying" (i.e. removing toxins from) the blood and tissues; the salivary glands manufacture the saliva used in the mastication of food; the sweat glands help to throw off bodily waste matter in the form of sweat, etc., etc. (It is worthy of note that our medical scientists misunderstand *completely* the work and value of the lymphatic glands, and remove them on the slightest provocation. The craze for the removal of tonsils—which are lymphatic glands—is a marked example of this.) It is obvious, therefore, that disease in one or more of these glands or systems of glands may have the most marked effects upon the health of the individual, and indeed, in some cases, the ill-effects consequent upon their faulty functioning is as great as—if not greater than—that caused by disease in the seemingly more important vital organs themselves.

In addition to the lymphatic glands, the sweat glands, etc., there are also the now-famous " ductless glands," of which the thyroid is the best known. These glands, although quite small in size, play a most important part in the working of the organism, and defective functioning of one of them is quite sufficient to throw the individual sufferer into the most profound state of mental and physical ill-health. Medical Science, in realising the importance to health of the ductless glands, has over-reached itself, as usual, in attempting to devise a system of therapy known as " Gland Therapy " (or Organo-therapy), which purports to cure disease by means of sera made from the ductless glands of animals. " Gland Therapy," however, is proving just as ineffective as a panacea for human ills as any of the other fetishes of Medical Science, and is already falling into disrepute, its place being taken by still newer forms of present-day medical witchcraft.

"Thyroid extract," however, and thyroid tablets of various kinds are still very much to the fore in present-day medical usage, both as a "cure" for certain forms of thyroid disease and also as a "weight-reducer" (thyroid secretion having a very pronounced effect upon the metabolism of food). Needless to say, the use of extracts such as these for the purposes mentioned are much to be deprecated, where the best interests of the individual's future health are concerned. Thyroid troubles cannot be cured simply by introducing into the system of the patient thyroid secretion extracted from the glands of animals ; it is only systemic and constitutional treatment along approved natural lines that can accomplish this. Similarly, the tendency to corpulence of over-fed people cannot be checked in a satisfactory manner by telling them to go on eating in just the same way as before, but to take thyroid tablets two or three times a day. Such methods are in the highest degree pernicious. Not only do they pander to the self-indulgence of the patient, but the effect of tablets such as these upon the general health of the individual is very harmful indeed, as many a patient has found out to his cost. The heart especially is affected by thyroid tablets, yet the medical profession goes on prescribing them to its patients as an antidote to obesity, simply because it is an "easy" form of slimming, much to be preferred by slack-minded people to the more arduous task of proper dieting.

As with all other disease, disease of a gland or system of glands is only the outcome of errors of living on the part of the individual concerned, especially dietetic errors ; but the more serious forms of gland trouble may owe a great deal of their origin to suppressive medical treatment of former disease, whether by knife or drug, or both. The only real cure for such conditions lies *not* in further drugging or operations or in inoculation with gland extracts taken from the bodies of animals, but in the adoption of systemic cleansing and general health-restoring measures, of which fasting and dieting are the two foremost. Such treatment, properly administered, has succeeded in curing gland diseases of all kinds and of all degrees, many of the cases having been given up previously as "incurable" by the orthodox medical world.

Addison's Disease.—This is a disease of the *suprarenal capsules*, two small glands situated one upon each kidney. They are ductless glands, and as such are of extreme importance to the health of the individual, manufacturing a secretion known as adrenalin, which, when passed into the blood, has a great deal to do with the effective carrying on of all the multifarious activities of the body, such as breathing, digestion, excretion, etc. When these glands are diseased, all these various functions are affected to a greater or lesser degree, and the patient becomes very weak indeed. The skin also takes on a brownish or bronzed cast. Unless checked in time, the disease terminates fatally.

Treatment.—The sufferer from Addison's disease can point to a past history of ill-health of many years' duration ; and previous suppressive medical treatment by drug and knife, coupled with un-hygienic and unwholesome habits of living, are the root cause of the trouble. The only rational treatment lies in the adoption—*at an early stage*—of a very strict Natural-Cure régime at a Natural-Cure institution or else under the guidance of a Naturopath. Fasting, ray therapy, manipulation, etc., will all be required in these cases.

Bubonic Plague.—This is hardly the book in which to suggest treatment for the dreaded bubonic plague of the East, but I cannot resist a few words about the matter in this section on diseases of the glandular system. Bubonic plague is an affection of the lymphatic glands of the most virulent kind. We all know about the plague being caught from germs incubated in the intestines of bugs and fleas, and of millions dying in the East every year from it ; but that is hardly true, at least not from the Nature-Cure standpoint. The germ of bubonic plague may be bred in the intestines of fleas and bugs, but it is only those people whose lives are so unsanitary and unhealthy that their whole constitution is undermined who can develop the disease. Not everybody will catch the plague if exposed to it, although very many will because of the chronically impaired state of health of the races living in " plague " areas, through extremes of tempera-ture, wrong feeding, and unhealthy living generally. Once caught, however, the real cure for the plague lies not in injection or drug treatment—these having proved themselves worthless enough already —but in FASTING. If bubonic plague can be cured at all, it is only by fasting and the strictest adherence to other Natural-Cure methods of treatment for fevers, of which " the plague " is one, albeit the most virulent. The only way *the plague* can be wiped out is through *preventive* measures, in which sanitary living and wholesome feeding play the foremost part. Until these much-needed reforms take place in the over-crowded cities of the East, the plague will never be eradicated.

Diseases of the Salivary Glands.—The salivary glands are sometimes the seat of disease, the commonest being mumps. (See treatment for *Mumps* in the section on *Children's Ailments*, page 105.) There may also be stones or tumours present in these glands, in which case treatment should be in the hands of a Naturopath. The cause of the condition in all such cases is *constitutional* in character, although local irritation to the mouth, excessive eating of starchy foods, or the excessive chewing of sweets, etc., may be predisposing factors. Orthodox medical treatment of disease, by means of mercury and other mineral drugs, also sometimes affects the salivary glands.

Diseases of the Sweat Glands.—When the sweat glands, which are distributed all over the skin surface, become affected by disease, the skin may become either too moist or too dry. In either case the cause of the trouble is *constitutional*, and is generally connected with diseases of other organs or parts of the body. If no definite organic or other disease is present, however, a scheme of health-building treatment along the following lines should soon begin to normalise matters.

Begin with a few days on all-fruit followed by the *full weekly diet* given in the Appendix, with further short periods on all-fruit at monthly intervals as required. The dry friction and sponge, and breathing and other exercises given in the Appendix, should be gone through regularly each day, and Epsom-salts baths should be taken two or three times weekly.

If constipation is habitual, the rules for its eradication given in Section 9 (page 275) should be put into operation forthwith. In any case, the warm-water enema should be used nightly for the first few days of the treatment. Exposure of the body to the sun and air (by sun-bathing) is very good indeed, as also is sea-bathing. Fresh air and outdoor exercise are essential. The minimum of underclothing should be worn, to enable the skin to have as much air as possible. " Aertex " underwear is very good, as also is " Lahmann " underwear. Strict attention to the future diet is essential. (*Excessive sweating is often connected with kidney trouble.*)

Enlarged Glands of the Neck.—The glands situated on both sides of the neck are part of the lymphatic system of glands, whose work is to " detoxify " the blood and tissues. When excessive quantities of white bread, white-flour products, sugar, denatured cereals, meat, boiled potatoes, etc., are habitually eaten, a large amount of excess toxic matter forms continually in the system, and these lymphatic glands become overworked as a consequence, in their efforts to get rid of this surplus waste material. It is for this reason that disease (or enlargement) of the tonsils and glands of the neck so frequently occur. (The tonsils are also part of the lymphatic system.) Medical treatment usually consists in the removal of the glands, or other equally suppressive treatment; but this does not get rid of the root cause of the trouble—which is, in every case, a highly toxic blood-stream—and it also lowers the future tone of the system as a whole, by removing these essential guardians of the health of the head, throat, and body generally (which the lymphatic glands really are). It is only by building up the tone of the *whole* system, and adopting a rational and cleansing diet, that enlarged lymphatic glands—whether in the neck or elsewhere—can be reduced in a natural manner and their proper working efficiency restored.

Treatment.—A state of generally lowered vitality—as well as a condition of systemic toxicity due to overfeeding and wrong feeding —is always a definite factor in the appearance of enlargements of the glands of the neck; and treatment *must be constitutional* rather than local, if a cure is desired. *The whole system must be treated,* not just the neck. For the effective treatment for enlarged neck glands the reader is referred to that for *enlarged tonsils* given in the section on *Diseases of the Ears, Nose, Throat, etc.* (Section 8 page, 242.) The two treatments are identical.

Exophthalmic Goitre (Graves' Disease).—This is a disease of the thyroid gland, the best known of the "ductless" glands mentioned in the introduction to this section. In exophthalmic goitre there is protrusion of the eyeballs (hence its name), very rapid heart action, trembling of the muscles in various parts of the body, together with sensations of extreme heat and cold, the passing of excessive quantities of urine, etc. All this is due to faulty (or excessive) functioning of the thyroid gland, although the gland itself may not be enlarged as in simple goitre.

To understand the origin of diseases of the thyroid gland, such as exophthalmic goitre, one must first realise what part this gland plays in the functioning of the body as a whole. It seems that, in addition to contributing to the effective functioning of the heart and blood-vessels generally, by its secretions (in which secretions organic iodine plays an important part), the thyroid gland has also a great deal to do with the metabolism of food in the system, and *especially* with the destruction of toxic matter generated in the intestines as a result of the putrefaction therein of animal protein material. (Animal protein foods are meat, fish, eggs, cheese, and milk.) It must be obvious, therefore, that when excessive quantities of these foods are habitually eaten and the intestinal tract is continually clogged with their waste residue owing to a constipated condition of the intestines, the thyroid gland will be greatly overworked. Where this overworking is still further complicated by debilitating habits of living, coupled with excessive emotionalism, then the thyroid gland often becomes diseased. There seems to be as great a link between the thyroid gland and the mental-emotional nature of the individual as with the physical ; and its function is often disturbed greatly by strong emotions, whether of fear, worry, or such-like, as well as strong sexual emotions.

The reader will be ready to see now that disease or malfunction of the thyroid gland can only arise out of the abuse of the body generally, whether through wrong feeding, over-emotionalism, wrong living generally, or all three. What, then, can be done—as a means of cure for diseases such as exophthalmic goitre and goitre—by the surgical removal of the gland in question, by X-ray treatment, or by dosing with iodine, etc. ? Do any of these " curative " measures get down to the root causes at work in the matter ? Not in the slightest. Yet these are the methods Medical Science employs to combat thyroid-gland diseases, with all the wealth of brains and material at its command ! No wonder thyroid troubles continue to grow daily in the countries where medical treatment such as this is the rule !

The medical profession has discovered, by the rather unfortunate method of trial and error (unfortunate, that is, for the unlucky patients who have had the operation tried out on them), that the complete removal of the thyroid gland is a most harmful procedure indeed, consequently only part of the gland is removed nowadays. When will the medical fraternity learn that this also is harmful in the highest degree to the future health of the patient, leading as it does to serious emotional and mental disturbance, as well as to disturbance of function in vital organs of the body such as the heart, the kidneys, the liver, etc. ? (X-ray treatment likewise !) In any case, how *can* the removal of an organ be a cure for the disease of that organ ? One might as well cut off one's head to cure a headache !

The administration of thyroid extract can also never be regarded as *curative* treatment, in the real sense of the word. Such treatment is only palliative at best, and in many cases only complicates matters. And as for the administration of iodine as a means of curing thyroid troubles, nothing could be more hopeless than that ! The medical profession knows that *organic* iodine is secreted by the thyroid gland as part of its function (see remarks on *Goitre* with regard to the question of iodine deficiency), and so it proceeds to dose its thyroid victims suffering from iodine deficiency with *inorganic* iodine obtained from the laboratory, in the vain hope that such treatment will help to overcome the disease. Never was there greater nonsense. The writer himself has come across unfortunate thyroid sufferers who have been made to take so many drops of inorganic iodine daily, as a means of " curing their trouble," and one and all have found the most distressing symptoms arise as a result of the treatment. Indigestion and constipation invariably follow the taking of continuous doses of inorganic iodine, whilst the vital organs, such as the heart, the kidneys, and the liver, are affected to a marked degree. And this is called *curative treatment* ! Nothing could show more clearly the ignorance of the medical profession, when it comes to a real understanding of disease and how it should be treated, than the present-day medical treatment for thyroid-gland troubles.

Treatment.—The only real and sane cure for thyroid troubles— whether exophthalmic goitre, simple goitre, or otherwise—lies in a thorough cleansing of the system, the adoption of a future rational system of diet, and quiet and rest. Only in this way can a faultily functioning thyroid gland be restored to health and full activity. Not by cutting it out can this be done ! With regard to exophthalmic goitre, treatment at a Natural-Cure home or under the personal supervision of a Naturopath is best ; but if this is not possible, the patient should carry on as follows :

A short fast for three or four days, as directed in the Appendix, is the best way to start the treatment. If the patient can stay in bed during this time, it will be so much the better. In any case, as much complete rest as possible is desirable during the first part of the treatment. After the fast, the *restricted diet* also given in the Appendix should be carried on with for from seven to ten or fourteen days, and then the *full weekly diet* can be adopted. In some cases it will be advisable to repeat the fast and period on the restricted diet in, say, six weeks to two months after the completion of the first period, with perhaps a further fast and period of restricted dieting say three months after that. Each patient must decide for himself in this matter, according to the progress being made.

During the first week of the treatment the warm-water enema should be used nightly to cleanse the bowels, and afterwards if necessary. If constipation is stubborn and of long standing, then the rules for its eradication given in Section 9 (page 275) should be put into operation forthwith. The daily dry friction and sitz-bath or sponge are essential features of the treatment, and the breathing and other exercises given in the Appendix should be gone through regularly daily, as soon as the patient feels able to. The hot Epsom-salts bath should also be taken twice weekly for the first three months following the commencement of the treatment, and once weekly thereafter. (If a hot bath affects the heart at all, the bath should be taken not too hot, but just comfortably so.) Cold packs to the throat will also be beneficial (see Appendix for details).

The need for plenty of rest has already been emphasised, and a day in bed every week for the first two months of the treatment will be most helpful in the more serious cases, as well as the initial few days to begin the treatment. The less serious cases will obviously need less rest, but even so they should rest as much as they can at the commencement of the treatment and for the following few weeks. As they find their symptoms subsiding, so they can take more and more exercise.

The diet factor is of extreme importance, and the eating of high protein foods, such as meat, fish, etc., should be reduced to a minimum (or, better still, they should be cut out of the dietary altogether, and egg or cheese or nuts substituted) ; whilst white bread, white-flour products, sugar, boiled potatoes, stodgy puddings and pies, strong tea and coffee, alcoholic liquors and all condiments, etc., should be entirely given up.

Operative treatment should not be tolerated, neither should injection, X-ray, or other medical treatment be undergone. Although progress may be slow, natural methods, and natural methods alone, can effect a *real cure*. Once recovered, the patient must see to it that all habits and ways of living and thinking which undermine the normal health-level of the organism are given up in favour of a simple, rational scheme of living. Early hours, no excesses, etc. *Manipulative treatment, where procurable, is strongly recommended.*

Goitre.—All that has just been said about *exophthalmic goitre* should be read by the sufferer from goitre ; because, although the symptoms and actual physical disturbances of function may not be quite the same, yet the fundamental underlying causes of both conditions are similar to a very great degree, as regards wrong feeding, wrong habits of living, tendency to excessive emotionalism, etc. In the case of goitre, there is enlargement of the gland, to cause quite a large swelling in the front of the neck, which gives the disease its peculiar characteristic. The swelling can be of great size in some cases ; in exophthalmic goitre there is often very little swelling at all.

It has already been pointed out—in the remarks on *Exophthalmic Goitre*—that the thyroid gland makes use of organic iodine in its secretion ; and a dietary deficient in organic iodine is a predisposing factor towards the appearance of goitre in certain cases, especially if other physical and emotional disturbances are present. The natives of regions far removed from the sea often suffer with goitre ; in many of these cases it is simply due to the continued absence of organic iodine from their habitual food. People living near the sea rarely contract goitre, because all sea-food is rich in organic iodine. Let not the reader imagine, though, from this, that fish and other sea-food are essential to the dietary to avoid goitre, or that people who eat plenty of fish are necessarily immune from the disease ; on the contrary. Organic iodine is present in practically all foods which come from the earth as well as from the sea, and are eaten in their *raw* state ; such earth-foods being fruits, vegetables, and the whole-grain cereals such as wheat, rye, barley, etc. It is those who habitually live on *denatured* (that is, cooked and refined) foods who are liable to thyroid-gland trouble of some kind or other, other factors being present ; not those who eat much of their food in the raw or uncooked state.

Treatment.—As regards the treatment for goitre, this is essentially the same as that for *exophthalmic goitre*, for, as already explained, their underlying causes are identical in many ways, although they may differ from person to person in one way or another. In fairly simple cases of goitre, though, the *short fast* and period on the *restricted diet*, which begin the treatment for exophthalmic goitre, can be substituted by a week on *all-fruit* instead. This, of course, should be followed by the *full weekly diet* given in the Appendix, with further short periods on all-fruit at monthly intervals as required (say two or three days). Otherwise the treatment should be just the same as for exophthalmic goitre (except that there is not quite so much need for prolonged rest as in some cases of the former disease) ; and all that has been said regarding operations, injections, treatment by X-ray, gland extract, or iodine, etc., should be taken seriously to heart. No cure lies that way, only further trouble.

Hodgkin's Disease.—This is an affection of the lymphatic glands, causing swelling of these glands all over the body, as well as possible enlargement of the liver, kidneys, and spleen. The disease is entirely the outcome of malnutrition and wrong living generally, the whole system being in a highly toxic state ; and suppressive medical treatment of former childhood ailments plays a large part in its development, for the disease is most common amongst young adults.

Treatment.—Treatment for this disease should always be in the hands of a Naturopath where at all possible, as fasting and dietetic treatment are its only cure, together with other ameliorative natural methods, such as manipulation, eliminative baths, sun-ray treatment, etc.

Myxœdema.—This is a disease due to the withering or atrophy of the thyroid gland. The trouble may be influenced to a certain extent by heredity, especially where there is a family history of cancer, tuberculosis, asthma, or other serious disease, nervous or physical ; but its real underlying causes are to be found in a lifetime of wrong feeding and general wrong living, coupled with previous suppressive medical treatment of many years' standing by drug or knife, or both. The disease usually appears in middle life, and its symptoms include such undesirable features as enlargement of the body, dryness and yellowing of the skin, thickening of the hands and feet, together with broadening of the head and face, flattening of the nose, enlargement of the mouth, etc.

Treatment.—This complaint can now be kept in check by the use of *thyroxin* (thyroid extract) given under medical supervision. If, however, any real progress is desired in the eradication of the basic causes of the disease, it is essential for general Nature-Cure treatment to be instituted at the same time, *as well*. The treatment outlined for *exophthalmic goitre* earlier in the present section may be adopted with benefit in this respect.

Diseases of the Prostate Gland.—This gland, which has much to do with the development of the male sex life, is often the cause of much trouble in middle and later life, as its *inflammation* and *enlargement* both interfere with the action of the bladder and urethra, and so cause imperfect and too-frequent urination. The most frequent symptom is the constant desire to pass water, especially at night. The amount of urine voided is usually scanty, and is passed with difficulty. There is also a feeling of great discomfort in the region of the rectum and between the legs, as when enlarged the prostate gland presses on the rectum and other parts adjoining.

The cause of prostate-gland trouble is usually too excessive use of the sex organs in earlier life, especially masturbation ; but a general toxic condition of the system plus local irritation due to excessive cycle riding, horseback riding, etc., can cause its appearance in certain cases, especially if constipation is habitual. Indeed, constipation is one of its most potent predisposing factors in a way. Worry, over-work, etc., all play a part in the development of prostate-gland trouble.

Treatment.—The medical treatment for prostate-gland disease is the removal of the gland. As this is a most dangerous operation, and on the face of it a most undesirable one, the sufferer from prostate-gland trouble should never consent to such an operation if it can possibly be avoided. In the first place, it does not get rid of the cause of the trouble—only the effects ; secondly, the removal of the gland is a serious handicap to future mental, emotional, and physical well-being. The only real cure for prostate trouble lies in natural methods of treatment. Even if the condition is past complete cure, then a great deal can often be done towards overcoming it by the adoption of sane natural methods of treatment, of which rational dietetics and hydro-therapy are the two chief combined with manipulative therapy.

If the sufferer from prostate-gland trouble cannot enter a Natural-Cure institution for treatment or place himself under the care of a competent Naturopath, he should carry on at home as follows :

The best way to begin the treatment is to go on to an *exclusive fresh fruit diet*, as outlined in the Appendix, for from four to seven or ten days. Then the *full weekly dietary* should be begun and adhered to strictly thereafter. Further short periods on the all-fruit diet should be undertaken at monthly intervals from then on, say two or three days monthly. This will help matters considerably. The warm water enema should be used nightly to cleanse the bowels for the first few days of the treatment, and later if necessary ; whilst if constipation is habitual (as it generally is in these cases), the rules for its eradication given in Section 9 (page 275) should be put into operation forthwith.

The daily dry friction and sitz-bath—as given in the Appendix —should be undertaken regularly, as also the breathing and other exercises given therein ; whilst the hot Epsom-salts bath will be found most beneficial if taken twice weekly. Fresh air and outdoor exercise should form an essential part of the treatment.

As regards local treatment, the hot and cold sitz-bath (detailed in the Appendix) is most helpful indeed in cases of prostate trouble, and should be taken nightly (except on those nights an Epsom-salts bath is being taken) ; whilst hot and cold fomentations should be applied several times daily to the parts between the legs. (A piece of linen material is wrung out in hot water, and after folding small applied to the affected part for, say, three minutes ; it is then removed and replaced by a second and later a third application for the same length of time. After this, a cold application is put on. The applications should always be in the same order, viz., three hot, then one cold.)

Spinal manipulation is helpful in all cases of prostate trouble and there is also a method of electrical and finger massage, applied through the rectum, which is of value. Regular habits of living, simple food, and the avoidance of alcoholic beverages are essential to success in the treatment. All highly flavoured dishes, condiments, pickles, sauces, etc., should be avoided, as also strong tea and coffee. *The patient should drink as little fluid as possible during the day, and nothing after 6 p.m.*

The Spleen and its Diseases.—The spleen, as the chief gland of the lymphatic system, is one of the most important organs in the whole body Its chief work lies in the removal of waste matter from the blood and tissues, aided by the other glands which go to make up the lymphatic system, the lymph vessels, etc. When the body is in a very run-down and toxic state, the lymphatic system becomes over-worked, and if, through persistent wrong treatment by means of drugs and operations, the toxæmia becomes very profound, then it is quite likely that the spleen will become affected. Splenic anæmia and other affections of the spleen all arise from this cause. Enlargement of the spleen follows inevitably from the orthodox medical treatment of fevers and other acute diseases, and there is hardly a worse-used organ in the whole body than this unfortunate gland, what with present-day methods of living and present-day orthodox methods of medication. That it carries on to the best of its ability for as long as it can before giving in is a credit not to the individual concerned, or to his medical advisers, but to the innate powers of the body itself.

Treatment.—As regards treatment for diseases of the spleen, this should always be in the hands of a competent Naturopath, or, better still, in a Nature-Cure home. By rigorous fasting, dieting, and other natural methods, health can often be restored to the sufferer from even serious splenic disorders, providing always that the condition has not been allowed to develop too far or been interfered with too much by previous medical treatment. Cases are on record where the spleen as been *completely removed* by surgical operation as a " curative " measure ! Imagine what the effects will be upon the after-life of the luckless sufferer who has had such an operation performed upon him under the guise of "improving his health " ! Such are the methods, and such the colossal ignorance, of the men into whose hands the health of the nation is so trustingly and unhesitatingly placed !

DISEASES OF THE EYES

Blepharitis — Cataract — Choroiditis — Conjunctivitis — Glaucoma — Iritis — Keratitis—Retinitis—Styes—Trachoma—Ulcers of the Cornea.

PERHAPS the most important attribute of the whole human organism is that of vision. Without the ability to see, man would indeed be lost. We all know that the eyes are the special organs concerned in seeing and making the external world cognisable to us, yet it would tax the mental powers of the greatest scientist to tell us exactly *how* this phenomenon which we call " seeing " is actually brought about.

We know that the lens at the front of the eye throws the impressions of the external world on to the retina at the back of the eye, and that these impressions are in turn carried by the optic nerve to the brain. But just in what way these sense-impressions are transformed into sight itself is a complete mystery which no one has yet succeeded in unravelling.

However, this is neither the time nor the place for reflections upon the mysteries of sight ; what we are here concerned with is a description of the diseases which affect the eyes, and how they may be cured. Many people do not realise that diseases of the eyes and defective vision are not one and the same thing, but two entirely different categories of diseases, yet such is indeed the case. Diseases of the eyes occur as the outcome of pathological changes in the various eye-structures, resulting from disturbances of function both in the eye itself as well as in other parts of the body ; defective vision is the result not of such pathological changes, but of a disability of the eye *as a whole* to accommodate itself to the instinctive physiological act of seeing. Short-sight, long-sight, etc., are defects of vision ; cataract, glaucoma, iritis, etc., are diseases of the eye.

Obviously many diseases of the eye interfere with the processes of vision, and indeed sometimes succeed in preventing sight altogether. But that is only by the way, as it were. Primarily they are not to be classed with those conditions through which the eye is prevented from focusing for near and distant objects, and which give rise to what we call true defective vision.

In my book *Better Sight without Glasses* I have gone into the whole subject of defective vision, and shown how it is really caused, and how it may be overcome by simple natural methods of treatment. Defects there dealt with are : short sight (myopia); long-sight (hypermetropia); old-sight (presbyopia); astigmatism; squint (strabismus); and *cataract*. Cataract, being really a disease of the eyes and not a defect of vision, will be dealt with again in the present section; but those who wish for advice for the correction of the visual defects just mentioned are referred to the book in question for treatment. In any case, all those wearing glasses are advised to read what the book has to say with regard to the harmfulness of the present-day craze for spectacle-wearing, and of how impossible it is for people wearing glasses to regain normal sight whilst still wearing them.

A person with ordinary normal health may develop defective vision, because the root cause of this defect is *mental strain* ; but for diseases of the eyes to develop there must be something definitely wrong with the physical organism. We must never forget that the eye is part of the body, and as such must share in any deficiency or disturbance of function affecting the whole organism ; and, indeed, if we are going to put our finger on the causes of eye diseases, this is the most important fact of all. *We do not have to look to the eye itself for the causes of eye diseases, but to the body as a whole, of which it forms part !*

Medical scientists, in their usual short-sighted way, generally seem to think that because a disease affects the eye, therefore its cause can be found in something which has only to do with the eye itself, such as local irritation, prolonged eye-strain, etc. Such factors certainly play their part in producing diseases of the eyes, but they are only of secondary importance. Of infinitely more importance to the origin of eye diseases is the general bodily condition of the individual sufferer from these diseases and his past medical history.

It can be taken as axiomatic that no person who is in really good health can develop diseases of the eyes such as conjunctivitis, cataract, etc. A lowered vitality and a poisoned blood-stream due to wrong feeding and wrong living generally are always at the root of the trouble. Medical Science ignores these underlying factors ; that is why its treatment for eye diseases is so unsatisfactory. Constitutional treatment, and constitutional treatment only, can get rid of these diseases in a sane and satisfactory manner, leaving the sufferer in far better health than before, because of the thorough cleansing his system will have received as a result of the treatment.

Once the sufferer from eye disease can be made to realise that he must look to the state of *his whole body* for the cause of his eye trouble, then he is already half-way towards a successful cure. It is only ignorance of this vital truth which prevents him understanding his trouble and being able to grapple with it successfully. The attitude of orthodox Medical Science towards all eye diseases is such as to mask the origin of such diseases more or less completely from the view of the unfortunate sufferer, who, thus deluded and misled, allows himself to have all sorts of treatments performed upon him, which, if he knew the true facts of the matter, he would never dream of allowing at all. In common with its attitude to other diseases, the medical treatment for eye diseases is entirely suppressive and unnatural, and arises out of a complete inability to understand the primary causes concerned in the development of the conditions under treatment.

The most prominent of all eye diseases is cataract, and the medical treatment for this by operation is just as suppressive in character as any operation performed on any other part of the body. It is merely the *effects* of the trouble which are dealt with, not the causes at all. The constitutional condition of the sufferer, which is the key to the disease in the first place, is ignored entirely by such treatment, and indeed aggravated.

Nothing could show more clearly the truth of the Nature-Cure contention that the body is a unity and in disease must be treated as such than the gratifying successes achieved in the natural treatment for eye diseases, such treatment being directed almost exclusively towards the cleansing of the body as a whole, although, naturally, a certain amount of local treatment to the eye itself is required too.

Blepharitis.—This is a condition in which there is inflammation of the glands at the border of the eyelids, this latter trouble being also present in *styes*. The appearance of eyelids which are the seat of blepharitis are characteristic. They are red and swollen at the border, and yellowish crusts are constantly forming upon them, which rasp against the eyes and cause discomfort. In bad cases the hair-follicles are destroyed and the eyelashes fall out.

Treatment.—The cause of blepharitis is *constitutional*, it being the outcome of a lowered vitality and a poisoned blood-stream due to wrong feeding, general wrong living, etc., although local irritation to the eye and prolonged eye-strain are generally supplementary causative factors. Treatment for blepharitis must therefore be *constitutional* in character, rather than merely local, if the condition is to be definitely overcome. The application of ointments, salves, lotions, etc., is just useless where *a real cure* is concerned. The sufferer from blepharitis should turn to the treatment for *Conjunctivitis* given in the following pages and apply it to his own case. He will be more than gratified with the results obtained, both as regards the condition of his eyes and his health generally.

Cataract.—Just behind the iris, or coloured portion of the eye, is situated the lens, through which light travels into the interior of the eye. In cataract this lens becomes opaque, and so the entrance of light into the eye is more and more seriously interfered with as the condition develops. When no light-rays at all are allowed to enter the eye, through the opacity of the lens having developed accordingly, then blindness ensues. The medical removal of the lens (or the major portion of it) by means of surgical operation is taken to be the only way of getting over the trouble, as, when suitable glasses are provided after the operation, the sufferer from cataract can see fairly well to get about and carry on his ordinary avocation, whatever it may be.

Once we assume that if a cataract is forming in the eye of an individual then nothing can be done to prevent its future development, perhaps the medical attitude to the condition is justified. They wait until the cataract is "ripe" (this may take a few years to bring about), and then the cataract is removed, and that is the end of the matter. The fact that the unfortunate sufferer has had to go about for the intervening years with his sight growing dimmer and dimmer, and with the prospects of a fairly serious operation always before him as something inevitable, is considered a matter which cannot be helped in any way, things being as they are.

But things need not be as they are, if our medical scientists would concern themselves with the *causes* of disease, rather than just its effects. For one thing, we know that people suffering from diabetes or Bright's disease sometimes develop cataract; surely that fact itself should throw some light on to the genesis of the condition as a whole ? Cannot it be seen merely from this that constitutional factors are *always* concerned in the formation and development of cataract, whether diabetes or Bright's disease are present or not ? It only shows how blind our medical scientists are, and how incapable of adding two and two together to make four !

The root cause of cataract is a toxic condition of the system due to many years of wrong feeding and wrong living generally ; and constipation of many years' standing is almost always a predisposing factor in the case, just as it is with other highly toxic conditions, such as rheumatism, arthritis, etc. The blood-stream becomes full of toxic matter, and this is carried to all parts of the body to find lodgment in any spot available to it. If, through strain, too prolonged use of the eyes, local irritation, etc., the lens happens to become defective in tone with some people, the toxins will begin to exert their fateful influence there. As time goes on the condition becomes more serious, and then cataract commences to develop. This, in brief, is the real genesis of cataract. It is a silting up of the lens of the eye over a period of years, as the outcome of a general highly toxic condition of the system. The fact that practically all cataract sufferers are getting on in years, and have usually to their credit a past history of chronic disease plus many years of suppressive medical treatment by knife or drug or both, are facts that only show how true is the contention here made regarding the cause of cataract. (Cataract in children is the result of a diabetic condition of the mother during the pre-natal period.)

Treatment.—I do not want every sufferer from cataract to imagine from what has just been said that his trouble can be readily cured by natural treatment. If the cataract has been allowed to develop for many years and has become really deep-seated, then I am afraid nothing short of an operation will help matters. I am being quite candid here, as I do not wish my readers to have any false impressions as to what can or cannot be done in certain cases, even if natural treatment is employed.

But if cataract is in the early stages, then there is every possibility that the trouble can be got rid of by natural means ; and even in fairly advanced cases it can often be prevented from getting worse. (Surely this latter fact alone is worth something to the sufferer from cataract, haunted as he always is by the future prospect of a serious operation ?) By a thorough course of natural treatment the blood and tissues can be so cleansed that the trouble will disappear entirely in many early cases of cataract, whilst in many others it will be prevented from getting worse. Really long-standing and serious cases may have to face the possibility of an operation even if natural treatment *is* adopted ; but even so it is well worth a trial, for even if the cataract cannot be prevented from developing further in these cases, at least the general health of the sufferer will have been greatly improved by the treatment. This, no mere waiting for an operation can do for them.

Treatment by fasting, strict dieting, manipulation, eliminative baths, etc., will all be required by the sufferer from cataract who wishes to give himself every possible chance of cure ; and treatment in a Natural-Cure home or under the supervision of a competent practitioner would be by far the best, if carried out in conjunction with the general exercises and advice for strengthening the eyes and improving their visual power given in *Better Sight without Glasses*. But if this is not possible, then the patient can carry on at home for himself as follows :

Begin with a fast for from three to five days, as directed in the Appendix. Follow this with from seven to fourteen days on the *restricted diet* also given therein. The fast and period of restricted dieting over, the *full weekly dietary*—also given in the Appendix— can then be adopted, and it should be adhered to as strictly as possible from then on. Further short fasts and periods on the restricted diet should be undertaken at two or three-monthly intervals during the succeeding months, as required by the needs of the case.

The warm-water enema should be used nightly during the first week of the treatment, and afterwards as necessary ; whilst if constipation is habitual (as it generally is in these cases), the rules for its eradication given in Section 9 (page 275) should be put into operation forthwith. The daily dry friction and sitz-bath or sponge (outlined in the Appendix) should be carried out regularly, as also the breathing and other exercises given therein, so far as the patient is able to. The hot Epsom-salts bath is most valuable in cases of cataract, and two or three should be taken weekly if at all possible. The *closed* eyes should also be bathed night and morning with hot water containing Epsom salts (a dessert-spoonful of salts to a pint of hot water). Give the eyes a good bathing each time, and be sure the eyes are CLOSED all the time, not open. Always finish by rinsing with cold water.

Fresh air and gentle outdoor exercise are two essential factors in the treatment which must not be neglected ; walking is by far the best form of exercise to take. The exercises for relaxing and strengthening the eyes, as given in *Better Sight without Glasses*, should be put into operation in conjunction with the general treatment here given. PALMING and SWINGING are the most important of these where cataract is concerned, as also the *eye-muscle exercises* and *neck exercises*.

The diet factor is extremely important, and fruits and salads should form the major portion of the future dietary, these being Nature's cleansing foods. No white bread, sugar, refined cereals (such as rice, porridge, etc.), boiled potatoes, puddings, pies, heavy and stodgy and greasy foods, are to be taken. No tea, coffee, or alcoholic beverages ; no condiments, pickles, sauces, etc. Meat can be left out of the dietary entirely with every benefit, but at most should be eaten only *very* occasionally, and then in small quantities only. Eggs, cheese, or nuts can take the place of meat where mentioned on the diet sheet.

Choroiditis.—This is a condition in which the *choriod coat*, or middle layer of the three layers composing the wall of the eye-ball, becomes inflamed. Choroiditis may be one of two kinds—*suppurative choroiditis* or *exudative choroiditis*. The former condition is most serious indeed and follows sometimes in the wake of orthodox medical treatment for syphilis and other sexual diseases. The latter condition—*exudative choroiditis*—is the outcome of *constitutional* causes, similar to those responsible for *iritis*, and the sufferer is referred to the treatment for *Iritis* given farther on in the present section for treatment for his case.

Conjunctivitis.—This is a very common trouble indeed, and is caused by inflammation of the inner lining of the eyelids Its main feature is redness and swelling of the lids, accompanied sometimes by a feeling as though there were something in the eye. There is often a copious discharge of tears (or " watering "), and sometimes, in more serious cases, there is also pus formation. The medical belief is that conjunctivitis is due to " germ " infection or eye-strain. Certainly the evidence is clear that prolonged work under artificial light or excessive use of the eyes in one way or another predisposes towards the appearance of the trouble, but its root cause is systemic in origin, and is to be found in a general catarrhal condition of the system.

No one can develop conjunctivitis who is not in a condition of general toxæmia due to wrong feeding and wrong living generally. All talk of " germs " is just nonsense—a mere cloak to hide medical ignorance of the real cause of the trouble. The sufferer from conjunctivitis is one who is always having colds and other ailments indicative of a general catarrhal condition ; and as catarrh is a pathological condition essentially connected with the mucous membrane, or inner lining, of the nose, throat, etc., it simply means that this general catarrhal condition of the mucous membrane of the structures in question has spread to the mucous lining of the eyelids too, and affected them also. That is the whole secret of conjunctivitis—that, and nothing more, although one has always to keep in mind the possible accessory part played by eye-strain in bringing on the condition.

Treatment.—Once we realise the true cause of conjunctivitis, the uselessness of so-called " remedies " such as salves, ointments, etc., will be at once apparent to the intelligent reader. Treatment *must be* constitutional if it is to be effective at all. The sufferer from conjunctivitis usually eats far too much starchy and sugary food in the shape of white bread, refined cereals, boiled potatoes, puddings, pies, pastry, sugar, jams, confectionery, etc., etc. *These* are the root cause of his general catarrhal condition (and conjunctivitis also), especially when coupled, as they generally are, with the eating of excessive quantities of meat and other protein and fatty foods, the drinking of much strong tea and coffee, and the too free use of salt, condiments, sauces and other seasonings, etc. We can also add to the above citation a run-down condition of the system due to enervating habits and wrong living, and a tendency to excessive use of the eyes or undue eye-strain to complete the picture.

It will be obvious from the above that only a thorough *internal* cleansing of the system, with the adoption of a future rational scheme of diet, can help to get rid of conjunctivitis, once it has made its appearance. And the sufferer from the complaint who wishes to build up his whole system, as well as cure his conjunctivitis, should therefore carry on as follows.

Begin with from seven to ten days on the *exclusive fresh fruit diet* outlined in the Appendix. Those who have the trouble in a rather advanced form should have up to fourteen days on the all-fruit diet to begin with, or, better still, have a short fast for from three to five days, followed by seven to fourteen days on the *restricted diet* as given for the treatment for *Cataract*. The all-fruit diet or fast and restricted diet, as the case may be, should then be followed by the adoption of the *general weekly dietary* given in the Appendix.

Further short periods on all-fruit should be taken at monthly intervals during the next few months—say two or three consecutive days ; and in the more serious cases more short fasts and periods on the restricted diet should be taken at two- or three-monthly intervals as required. The warm-water enema should be used nightly during the first week of the treatment, and after as necessary ; whilst those with chronic constipation should put into effect the rules for its eradication given in Section 9, page 275.

The morning dry friction and sitz-bath or sponge, as given in the Appendix, are most essential, as are also the breathing and other exercises to be found therein. All these will help to build up the general health-level of the sufferer, and so help on the cure. The hot Epsom-salts bath is most valuable too in conjunctivitis, and one, two, or three should be taken weekly, according to the severity (or otherwise) of the condition. In addition, the *closed* eyes should be bathed night and morning with hot water containing Epsom salts (a dessertspoonful of salts to a pint of hot water). Be sure to keep the eyes CLOSED whilst so doing, and give them a good bathing each time. Always finish off by rinsing with cold water. Salves, ointments, etc., *must not be used* on any account whatsoever. Exposure of the *closed* eyes to the rays of the sun is very good indeed.

Fresh air and outdoor exercise are two essentials to the treatment which must never be overlooked, and the sufferer from conjunctivitis should be out in the open air as much as possible.

The eyes must be looked after carefully, and too much reading or close work under artificial light or bad lighting conditions should be discouraged. The exercises given in *Better Sight without Glasses* for relaxing and strengthening the eyes should be put into operation in conjunction with the general treatment here outlined. PALMING in particular is most helpful. The sufferer from conjunctivitis should do as much of this as possible during the day (three or four fifteen-minute periods at least, if not more). Also the cold-water splashing is very good too, as mentioned therein.

As already indicated, the diet factor is of extreme importance, and the more rigidly the diet-sheet given in the Appendix is adhered to, the better will it be in every way as regards quickness of cure, future general health, etc. The items of diet mentioned in the foregoing pages as being the direct causes of a catarrhal condition of the system such as white bread, sugar, much meat, strong tea, and coffee, etc., should be carefully excluded from the future dietary, and fresh fruits and salads MUST form the bulk of the foods eaten.

Glaucoma.—This is a condition in which there is tension in the, eye-ball as a result of the presence of excess fluid. The eye becomes hard as a consequence of this excess fluid within it, and feels hard to the touch, instead of soft and resilient, as in the normal state. One of the first symptoms of the onset of the condition is the appearance of haloes or coloured rings round distant objects when seen at night. The iris is usually pushed forward, and there is constant pain in the brow, the temple, the cheek, or other part near the eye. There is also gradual impairment of vision as the condition develops, and ultimate blindness may ensue if proper steps to deal with the disease are not inaugurated in the early stages.

Medical Science offers severe eye-strain or prolonged work under bad lighting conditions as the main cause of glaucoma, although it is sometimes admitted that a run-down condition of the patient has something to do with the onset of the trouble. But in reality the origin lies much deeper than that. The basic cause of glaucoma is exactly the same as that of cataract, i.e. a highly toxic general condition of the system due to many years of wrong feeding and wrong living, plus (usually) suppressive medical treatment of previous disease, by knife or drug, over a considerable period of time. Eye-strain is a supplementary factor only.

Treatment.—The medical treatment for glaucoma is operation, to relieve the internal pressure set up in the eye as a result of the presence of the excess fluid. This, however, does nothing to get rid of the *cause* of the excess fluid, merely of its effects. Consequently, even where an operation *has* been performed in glaucoma, it is no guarantee at all that the trouble will not return or affect the other eye. Until the cause of the excess fluidity is understood and dealt with, a real cure is not at all possible, and operations must be regarded as merely palliative at best.

The real treatment for glaucoma is *constitutional* in character, not merely local or palliative. When excess fluid appears in various parts of the body other than the eye, it is taken as being due to faulty functioning of the kidneys or other organs of elimination. Excess fluid in the eye is no exception to this rule in the eyes of the Naturopath, in the sense that it is taken to be a sign of derangement of bodily function due to a highly toxic general condition, plus imperfect local drainage of the eye. Of course, eye-strain and excessive use of the eyes in bad light, etc., are accepted as subsidiary causes. A general run-down condition of the system due to overwork, excesses of all kinds, etc., all contribute to the onset of the condition, which usually does not appear until the patient is well on in years.

The treatment for glaucoma, so far as Natural Cure is concerned, is no different from that for any other condition connotative of high toxicity; and the sufferer from the complaint is referred to the treatment for *Cataract* given in the preceding pages (page 217) for details as to how to carry on in his own case. Cases in the early stages should respond very well to the treatment, but more advanced cases may be beyond cure. Even so, in these latter, much can be done to build up the general health-level of the patient by the treatment, and for that reason alone it is well worth carrying out, even if a complete cure is not possible. In many such cases the trouble can at least be prevented from developing further. If the patient is in a run-down and generally " nervy " condition, then a period of complete rest in bed to begin the treatment is essential.

Iritis.—The iris, or coloured portion of the eye, is sometimes the seat of inflammation, and this condition is known as *iritis*. Iritis is a most painful malady, and left in medical hands may keep on for many months, leaving the sight of the sufferer much worse than it was before the trouble set in. This is merely because the real underlying causes of the inflammation have not been understood, and suppressive measures instead of eliminative measures have been used as a basis of treatment.

Iritis is primarily due to a highly toxic condition of the system *as a whole*, and unless the *whole system* is treated there is little hope of a successful termination to the complaint, so far as complete restoration of vision and general health of the eye are concerned. A person suffering from iritis is one who has a past medical history of disease of one kind or other extending over many years, and more often than not long-standing constipation is one of the prime factors involved. To treat the eyes only and leave this general toxic condition untouched is indicative of the short-sightedness of our medical practitioners when it comes to the practical cure of disease.

Treatment.—For the effective treatment of iritis the sufferer is referred to that for *Conjunctivitis* given in the preceding pages of the present section (page 219), beginning with the fast and *restricted diet*, instead of the *all-fruit diet*. Fasting and strict dieting are the main curative measures needed in these cases. (In acute cases a fairly lengthy fast may be necessary.) The use of the enema during the fasting period is most essential, as bowel trouble is one of the main predisposing causes of the condition. The full Epsom-salts bath and the bathing of the closed eyes with hot water containing Epsom salts, as described in the treatment for *Conjunctivitis*, are two most useful measures too. The eyes may be bathed three, four, or more times daily to begin with if desired, and less often as the inflammation decreases under the treatment. Hot fomentations applied *behind the ears* are also useful, and a cold pack can also be applied to the eyes at night. (See Appendix for details as to how packs are made.) *Palming*, as detailed in *Better Sight without Glasses*, is a most helpful procedure in iritis, and should be done several times a day for fifteen or twenty-minute periods.

Future strict attention to the diet, along the lines laid down in this book, is essential ; and care in the use of the eyes for close work, work under artificial light, etc., should be exercised for some considerable time to come. (Dark protector glasses may have to be worn during the attack.)

Keratitis.—The causes which will lead to the development of *keratitis*, or inflammation of the cornea of the eye, are very much the same as those for *iritis* just referred to. Keratitis is also indicative of a highly toxic condition of the system generally, although eye-strain, injury to the eye, etc., are of course superficial predisposing factors to its occurrence.

Treatment.—As regards treatment, the sufferer from keratitis is referred to that for *Iritis* just given above. Such treatment will not only cure his eye trouble, but build up his whole general health too.

Retinitis.—The retina is that portion of the internal eye-structure, situated at the back of the eye-ball, upon which the light-rays are reflected after passing through the lens into the eye. It is the most sensitive portion of the internal eye-structure, and is indeed only a continuation and development, in a way, of the optic nerve itself, which carries sight impressions to the brain. The retina is sometimes the seat of inflammation, and this condition is known as *retinitis*.

Retinitis is a sure sign of a highly toxic condition of the system generally, and the sufferer usually has some definite disease of one kind or other present in his system at the time of the development of the retinal trouble, such as diabetes, kidney disease, etc.

Treatment.—Obviously it is only by dealing with the disease at the *back of the retinitis*—Bright's disease, or whatever it is—that the unduly high toxic condition responsible for the development of the eye trouble in question can be got rid of ; and the sufferer from retinitis is therefore referred to the treatment given in this book for any particular disease which may have brought on the trouble in his case. In addition, he is referred to the treatment for *Iritis*, just previously given, for guidance in the carrying out of *local* treatment for his case. As much *palming* as possible (as outlined in *Better Sight without Glasses*) should be done daily in twenty-minute periods, or more, and the eyes should be rested completely for the period the inflammation is in evidence. (Dark glasses should be worn.) Only when the condition has fully cleared up should reading again be undertaken, and even then with care to begin with.

Styes.—Styes are due to inflammation of the sebaceous glands at the border of the eyelids. They are a sign of a toxic condition of the system, and usually make their appearance when the sufferer is rather " run-down " or below par generally. Eyestrain has also to be reckoned with as a subsidiary factor in bringing on the condition.

Treatment.—As regards treatment for styes, this should be along the lines of that for *Conjunctivitis* given earlier in the present section (page 220), both as regards general and local treatment. Only in this case hot fomentations can also be applied to the affected eye (or eyes) several times daily, as well as bathing with hot Epsom-salts water, etc.

The treatment here outlined will not only get rid of the present trouble, but, by building up the whole general health-level will effectually prevent future styes from forming. For once there is a tendency for styes to form, they will always tend to do so whenever the general condition of the sufferer is at a lower level than usual.

Trachoma.—This is a condition very common among the poor in many parts of the world. It is a very extreme form of *conjunctivitis*, and its root causes are defective nutrition and unwholesome living. Any attempt to treat trachoma other than by constitutional methods is doomed to failure by the nature of the case, yet treatments by salves, ointments, etc., seem to be the only methods Medical Science can devise for its removal, other than the attempt to "clean up" the general outward condition of the sufferer by the free use of soap, water, etc. Cleanliness of the external person is no doubt a very good thing, but it is cleanliness of the *internal* person which is most needed if trachoma is to be overcome effectively. It is the blood and tissues which must be scoured, not only the face and body.

Treatment.—The treatment for trachoma is exactly the same as that for *Conjunctivitis* (page 220), only in this case a fairly protracted fast will be required to start it. Further shorter fasts will no doubt be required at intervals, until the condition is quite cleared up. The use of the enema, the Epsom-salts bath, bathing the closed eyes with hot water and Epsom salts, etc., are all essential factors in the treatment. Exposure of the *closed* eyes to the rays of the sun is a most helpful measure too.

Cleanliness of bodily habits, cleanliness of living, and a rational scheme of diet in which fruits and salads play the most important part are the only sure ways in which to overcome trachoma—if it has not been allowed to develop too far, that is, in any given case.

Ulcers of the Cornea.—The cornea is the sort of window at the front of the eye which protects the pupil and iris. Not infrequently small ulcers appear upon the cornea, and give a great deal of trouble to the unfortunate sufferer. As with all other eye diseases, the cause of corneal ulcers is *systemic* in origin, and can be traced to wrong feeding in particular and wrong living in general.

Treatment.—For an understanding of how a toxic condition of the system can affect the eyes, the sufferer from corneal ulcers is referred to the sections on *Cataract* and *Glaucoma* in the preceding pages. And as regards treatment he should put into operation the advice given for the cure of *Iritis* (page 224) and *Keratitis* (page 224), adapting it according to the severity or otherwise of his own particular case.

Strict attention to the future dietary is essential if future recurrences of the trouble are to be prevented, and the whole general health-level should be built up by systematic exercise, hygienic living, etc. No drugs, lotions, etc., should be used as aids to treatment, the only local help to be employed being the frequent bathing of the *closed* eyes with hot water and Epsom salts, as advised in all other eye diseases, and the exposure of the *closed* eyes to the rays of the sun. *Palming,* as described in *Better Sight without Glasses,* is most helpful, and should be carried out several times daily, in fifteen- or twenty-minute periods

SECTION 8

DISEASES OF THE
EARS, NOSE, MOUTH, AND THROAT

Adenoids — Catarrh — Catarrhal deafness — Colds—Deafness—Defective teeth (dental decay) — Diphtheria — Enlarged tonsils — Gum-boils — Hay fever—Head noises — Leucoplacia — Mastoiditis — Menière's disease—Middle-ear disease—Pharyngitis—Polypi in nose— Pyorrhœa — Quinsy — Rhinitis — Sinusitis —Sore or inflamed tongue—Sore throat—Tonsillitis—Vincent's angina.

DISEASES of the ears, nose, mouth, and throat are amongst the most common of the diseases prevalent to-day. To understand the peculiar intimacy existing between the four structures named, and between them and other and more distant organs, such as the stomach and intestines, for instance, we must realise that they are all connected by one common factor—namely, *mucous membrane*. (Mucous membrane is the inner lining with which Nature protects all internal structures having orifices or openings on to the external surface of the body, and has protected the alimentary canal, or food-tract, all along its length in this way, the mouth and throat being the beginnings of this structure, which includes in turn the gullet, the stomach, the intestines, and the rectum.)

This mucous membrane or protective lining of the alimentary canal spreads out from the mouth and throat to include the nose and eyelids also, and by means of the Eustachian tubes, which connect the throat with the ears, it reaches as far as these latter organs too. (The Eustachian tubes are covered with mucous membrane for their whole length.) Thus all are intimately bound together.

It is of fundamental importance in the study of diseases of the ears, nose, mouth, and throat to understand the full significance of this close relationship existing between the structures named, and between them and the stomach and intestines, for it is from the habitual eating of food in excess of the body's needs (especially demineralised and refined food), as well as from the fermentation and decomposition of such food in the alimentary canal, that toxins are generated which Nature strives to throw off as *catarrh*, mainly through the medium of the mucous membrane lining the structures at the upper end of the canal, which, as already stated, are the mouth and throat, with their direct connection, the nose. Once a catarrhal condition has arisen, it does not take long before the ears too are affected—for reasons already stated—and the eyes may even become involved, as in conjunctivitis, as pointed out in the section on *Eye Diseases* (page 213).

228

We can see, therefore, that *wrong feeding* is a prime factor in the causation of diseases of the ears, nose, mouth, and throat. But a second and almost equally potent factor is the suppressive medical treatment of previous disease, especially *acute diseases* such as fevers. By means of fevers Nature attempts to throw off accumulations of toxic matter generated in the system (over a period of time) through general wrong living (dietetic and otherwise) ; and the orthodox medical treatment of these diseases simply disperses these same toxins into the various organs and structures of the body, to cause serious trouble later on, instead of allowing them to be eliminated as Nature intended.

To the seemingly " successful " orthodox medical treatment of childhood fevers, such as scarlet fever, diphtheria, measles, etc., can be traced to a most marked degree affections of the nose, ears, and throat which for no *apparent* reason (according to our medical scientists) spring up in after-life in the bodies of children thus treated. (Chronically enlarged tonsils and other lymphatic glands, other chronic throat affections, nasal troubles, and diseases of the ear, such as middle-ear disease, etc., can be traced in origin, *in very many cases*, to treatment by orthodox medical methods of childhood complaints, especially fevers.)

To the main causes of diseases of the ears, nose, mouth, and throat already cited, we can now add a third in the shape of medical ignorance of the function and value of the lymphatic glands and lymphoid structures which guard the entrance to the throat and surrounding parts, the best known of which lymphoid structures are *the tonsils*.

These organs, whose duty it is to remove waste matter and impurities from the upper part of the body, often become enlarged and inflamed as a result of the enormous amount of work they are called upon to perform in the bodies of the habitually overfed and unhygienically developed children and adults of our present era. But instead of this being regarded as a sign of a general toxic condition of the system, as it really is, it is declared by our medical scientists that these lymphatic structures have become diseased as a result of " external germ infection " (whatever that may mean), and are regarded as a potential menace to the health of the rest of the system so long as they are allowed to remain in the body. Thus has arisen the modern mania in medical circles for the removal of tonsils and other lymphatic glands on the slightest provocation (or without such provocation sometimes !), on the pretext that by so doing the health of the individual is being improved and future disease prevented.

Further to bolster up this indiscriminate tonsil-removing from both young and old (especially young), our medical leaders assure us that these guardians of the health of the upper body (as the lymphatic structures really are) are " useless organs " ! Our medical scientists always work upon the principle that if *they* do not understand the use of an organ or structure in the body, therefore it *has* no use, and Nature has simply put it there for no other purpose than to be a perennial source of menace to the future health of its " unfortunate " possessor. The same attitude is held with regard to the appendix on equally specious and unfounded grounds.

By removing tonsils, adenoids, and other lymphatic glands in the wholesale manner prevalent to-day, the medical profession is doing far more to undermine the future health of the individual concerned, on the pretext of safeguarding it, than one might at first be led to imagine. For, by such removal, the defences and detoxifying mechanism of the upper body are definitely impaired, and the work of keeping the upper body clear of toxins is thrown upon other and less capable structures. Thus the way is paved for the development of disease in all adjacent parts of the body, such as the nose, the ears, the chest, and sometimes even the brain. (Many cases of bronchitis, asthma, tuberculosis, mastoiditis, sinusitis, deafness, etc., etc., can be definitely traced in origin to the haphazard removal of enlarged tonsils and other lymphatic glands in early life.)

The fact that there is an *apparent* increase in health sometimes after the surgical removal of these glands, and that these other and more serious diseases develop at a later date, masks the direct connection between the two which in reality exists, thus lulling our short-sighted medical practitioners (and their trusting patrons likewise) into a falsely optimistic attitude with regard to the ultimate efficacy of the operation in question, which a real understanding of the facts does not in the least justify.

The part played by unhygienic habits, such as living and working and seeking amusement in habitually stuffy atmospheres, the wearing of excessive quantities of underclothing, drinking, smoking, and other excesses, lack of proper exercise, and such-like factors, must also not be lost sight of when considering the causes of diseases of the organs under discussion ; but these are merely subsidiary to the three main causative factors already discussed, which are : (1) wrong feeding habits ; (2) previous suppressive medical treatment of disease, especially infantile disease ; and (3) the modern medical craze for the removal of tonsils and other lymphatic glands.

We can now turn to the discussion of the various diseases themselves, and the natural methods necessary for their cure. Suffice it to say that all these measures are *eliminative* in their action, and *not* suppressive, as all orthodox medical methods of so-called " cure " are.

This point about *eliminative* as opposed to *suppressive* treatment is most needful of being understood clearly by all those who would follow out intelligently the treatments outlined in the following pages. For *suppressive* treatment simply means the forcing of the outward and visible manifestations and symptoms of disease back into the system, by means of the methods employed, with the *apparent* appearance of cure, but with the inevitable result of causing more deep-seated and lasting trouble later on. *Eliminative* treatment, however, means the actual removal of toxic matter from the system as Nature intends, and the direct helping of the system towards a condition of ultimate and lasting health.

It is worthy of note that in no class of disease is medical treatment so suppressive as in that for diseases of the kind we are about to deal with in the present section. The surgical removal of tonsils, the giving of drugs for the " curing " of colds, the administration of injections for the equally supposed " curing " of catarrh and hay-fever, nasal spraying, the painting of sore throats, etc., are all most significant examples of what is here meant by suppressive treatment. In none of these cases are causes dealt with and removed, but, instead, the superficial symptoms and effects of the trouble are got rid of merely. The patient is left definitely worse off by such treatment *in every way*, even though he may *seem* better for the time being. For this temporary improvement—for temporary it undoubtedly is—is purchased inevitably at the expense of the future health of the body. Health, real health, *cannot* be gained in these ways. The body refuses to be cajoled or tricked into health by the administrations of drugs or injections or such-like. Natural methods and natural methods alone, are the only sure way to health.

Adenoids.—The mucous membrane which lines the nose and throat contains what is called lymphoid tissue. In the introduction to the present section the reader has already been told what work such tissue is called upon to perform in helping to detoxify the blood and tissues generally. When the lymphoid tissue becomes overworked, as it habitually is in the system of the over-fed individual of to-day, this tissue tends to develop itself excessively, and often forms small masses and lumps at the back of the nose and throat. Such masses and lumps of lymphoid tissue are called *adenoids*.

Adenoids are therefore merely part of the lymphatic tissue of the nose and throat which has become more or less over-developed as a result of excessive work, and may be present in both young and old alike, but especially the young, because of the great amount of work lymphatic tissue is called upon to perform during the early years of life in safeguarding health. The presence of adenoids is therefore a sure sign of a general toxic condition of the system ; but, ignoring this underlying toxicity which is the real cause of the development of adenoid tissue, our medical scientists shout loudly for the immediate removal of adenoids (especially in the young), on the grounds that their presence is a direct menace to the future health of the individual by retarding development both physical and mental.

Now, it is quite true that the presence of adenoid tissues prevents proper breathing, because of the obstruction to the air-passages which follows ; but to ascribe to this one cause any retardation of development or any physical disability which may be present in the system at the time is just foolishness. Our medical scientists are ever on the look-out for some " scapegoat " upon which to pin the cause of disease, and tonsils and adenoids are the principal scapegoats in medical practice to-day, with the possible exception perhaps of the ever-elusive " germ."

The surgical removal of adenoids will lead to freer breathing—for a time ; but it can in no sense be looked upon as a curative measure —as a measure, that is, likely to lead to the future health of the individual concerned. The operation removes the adenoids, but what about the unwise feeding habits and general wrong habits of living which are the real root of the trouble ? These, the treatment ignores entirely ! The consequence is that disease in other tissues or structures in surrounding areas *inevitably* follows, leading to all sorts of troubles in later life (perhaps the nose is affected, perhaps the ears or chest, and so on).

Treatment.—It must be obvious to the intelligent reader by now that the only *rational* treatment for adenoids must be *constitutional*. It is only by a thorough cleansing of the system and the adoption of a sensible scheme of living—dietetic and otherwise—that a real cure can be effected. For such treatment will not only lead to the *natural* reduction of the adenoid tissue in time, but it will build up the whole system too—something which *no* operation could ever do.

For the effective treatment for adenoids the reader is referred to the treatment in the present section for *Enlarged Tonsils* (page 242). The causes of both are identical ; their treatment must of necessity be identical also.

Catarrh.—There is no disease condition more widespread among civilised races to-day than catarrh. Its cause, according to medical text-books, is wrapped in mystery. The weather, dusty or dirty atmospheres, " germ " infection, are all cited as possible causes of the trouble ; and as regards cure, there our medical scientists admit they can do nothing. According to them, catarrh is an *incurable* condition. Of course they proceed to dose their catarrh patients with medicines, and advise inhalants, spraying, and the like, or the cauterising of the membrane of the nose, or the surgical removal of pieces of the nasal bone in advanced cases, and now they are even trying germ inoculation ; but in their heart of hearts they admit to themselves that there *is* no cure for catarrh.

Why ? Simply because of all diseases catarrh is the one which will not submit to being pushed out of the way by the drugs and paraphernalia of modern medicine. It is a condition which persists in carrying on, in spite of all the wonderful " battle-array " that present-day Medical Science musters to its aid in its " fight " against disease.

Nothing could show more clearly the uselessness of modern medical methods of treating disease on the one hand, and medical ignorance of the real causes at work in the production of disease-conditions on the other, than the failure to cope with catarrh. For catarrh, of all diseases, is due to *wrong feeding* essentially ; and as wrong feeding is completely overlooked as a causative factor in the production of disease in medical circles the world over, hence the inability of Medical Science to devise a suitable treatment for the cure of catarrh, and its conclusion, as a consequence, that the disease is incurable. For it is by dietetic treatment, and dietetic treatment *only*, that catarrh can be overcome.

233

The sufferer from catarrh may submit to nasal operations, he may take all sorts of inhalants or use all kinds of sprays, but unless he radically alters his diet, no good whatsoever will come from his efforts. For the cause of his trouble lies precisely in the " unwholesome " food he eats, and in such over-abundant quantity. " Unwholesome " may sound strange to the catarrh sufferer who is accustomed to living on what he imagines to be the " fat of the land " ; but the word is here used in a sense not often ascribed to it. By " unwholesome food " is here meant food which has been refined or treated in such a way as to deprive it of all, or nearly all, of its essential vital elements.

The modern craze for refining foods, which has led to the universal use of white bread, white sugar, refined cereals, and white-flour products of all kinds, the modern habit of tinning and preserving food, the equally modern habit of having as much cooked food as possible, as opposed to uncooked—all these are leading people farther and farther away from a " wholesome " scheme of dietary (a *naturally* wholesome scheme of dietary, that is) towards an unnatural scheme of dietary which is the main causative basis of disease in the human body to-day, as pointed out consistently throughout the pages of the present book. When such demineralised and denatured foods are habitually consumed in quantities out of all proportion to the direct needs and requirements of the body, as they regularly are nowadays by those accustomed to their four or even five " good square meals " daily, the tissues of the body become engorged with excess food materials broken down into the form of acid waste products, and it is out of this condition that catarrh arises.

Although meat and other flesh foods are consumed in such great quantities in England and America to-day, it is the starchy and sugary foods which are eaten most, and these *always*, or nearly always, in their refined and demineralised state. Just think of the amount of white bread, boiled potatoes, refined cereals (such as porridge, rice, tapioca, etc.), biscuits, cakes, pastry, puddings, pies, etc., etc., that are eaten in the world to-day ! And of the white sugar, jams, marmalade, sweets, and chocolates likewise consumed ! It is the daily piling up of these excessive and unwanted starch and sugar food-products in the system (further enhanced by the presence of such inordinate quantities of meat and other protein foods, to say nothing of fats) which sets up the toxins which Nature attempts to expel mainly through the medium of the mucous membrane of the aliment-ary canal in the form of what we call *catarrh*.

Chronic catarrh does not usually develop in very early life, because the body is able, by means of periodic *colds* (which are really nothing but a form of *acute* catarrh), to cope with the toxins generated in the system as the result of excessive and unwise feeding habits ; but as wrong feeding habits continue, and cold after cold is suppressively treated, the body's powers of dealing with the condition get gradually undermined as the years advance, and it is at about the teens that the first signs of *chronic* catarrh generally appear. (It will thus be seen that catarrh is really nothing more than a drastic and protracted form of *body cleansing*, of which the " common cold " is merely an example in an *acute* form.)

Living and working in habitually stuffy atmospheres, smoking and drinking, the wearing of thick or excessive underclothing, improper care of the skin, lack of exercise, and many other factors besides, all help to lower the condition of the system and aggravate and intensify the catarrhal state. But *persistent wrong feeding*, as already described, is the main factor concerned all the time.

Treatment.—As regards treatment, it will of course depend upon how long the trouble has been in existence, and how old the sufferer is, as to the time it will take for results to be secured by natural treatment. But with patience and perseverance even the worst case of catarrh can be cured in time. The best way to proceed is as follows :

According to the severity and duration of the condition, from five to seven, ten, or fourteen days should be spent on the *all-fruit diet* outlined in the Appendix, as the first step in the treatment. Then the *full weekly dietary*, also given in the Appendix, should be adopted, and adhered to as strictly as possible thereafter. Further periods on all-fruit—ranging from two to four or five successive days —should be undertaken at monthly or two-monthly intervals during the succeeding few months, according to the needs of the case.

During the first few days of the treatment, and after if necessary the bowels should be cleansed nightly with warm-water enema or gravity douche ; and if constipation is habitual, the rules for its eradication given in Section 9 (page 275) should be put into operation forthwith. The daily dry friction and sponge or sitz-bath, as detailed in the Appendix, are necessary features in the treatment ; as are also the breathing and other exercises given therein. The hot Epsom-salts bath, once or twice weekly, is also a most useful measure, and should be regularly taken where at all possible.

The catarrh sufferer should be out in the open air as much as he can, and should always sleep with his bedroom well ventilated. He must take as much exercise as he can. No thick or heavy under-clothing should be worn in future ; the best kind is " Aertex " or " Lahmann " underwear, which allows the air to get to the skin. (Improved skin action is an important feature in the successful treat-ment of catarrh.)

As regards local treatment, cold water can be sniffed up the nose night and morning, a few drops of lemon juice being introduced into half a glass of water to act as an astringent. If the throat is affected, a cold pack (as described in the Appendix) can be applied nightly, and the throat gargled night and morning with warm water containing a little lemon juice. Drinking and smoking, if habitual, should be discontinued, of course. Regular habits of living are essential to the success of the treatment.

It would be well worth the while of every catarrh sufferer to read a good book on the diet question, for, as he or she will now realise, this is the real crux of the matter. The difference between *demineralised* and *denatured* food on the one hand, and natural wholesome food on the other, must be clearly understood. Fresh fruits and green salads should form the staple portion of the future dietary of the catarrh sufferer, and white bread, white-flour products, refined cereals (such as porridge, rice, etc.), boiled potatoes, cakes, puddings, pastry, white sugar, jams, and all forms of confectionery must be rigorously excluded from the dietary if a real cure is desired. *In very severe cases of catarrh* it is sometimes necessary to exclude *all* starchy and sugary food from the dietary for from three to four months (that is to say, even wholemeal bread, bananas, dried fruits, and honey—which are all natural wholesome foods—must be left out of the dietary for the time being : and, of course, potatoes too.) NO DRUGS, SPRAYS, OR GARGLES SHOULD BE USED AT ALL.

Catarrhal Deafness.—As already explained in the introductory remarks to the present section, catarrh often spreads to the ears, via the Eustachian tubes, and, once settled there, prevents hearing more and more as time goes on. The condition may become so severe eventually as to cause complete deafness, but in any case it is a most distressing complaint, because, in addition to great impairment of hearing there are often continual noises and crackings going on in the ears (as a result of the catarrh), which sometimes are of the most distracting and disturbing nature. There is often nothing to see in the external ear in theses cases, although sometimes there are deposits of wax being constantly formed. The trouble is all *internal* (that is, *within the ear*).

As regards causes, the sufferer from catarrhal deafness is referred to what has just been said with regard to the origin and development of *catarrh*. There is always a previous history of general catarrh, out of which the catarrhal deafness grows. Previous drug and operative treatment also often plays its part, and drugs such as quinine affect the condition of the ears very adversely. The use of quinine over any considerable period of time will definitely aggravate any catarrhal trouble present.

The medical treatment for catarrhal deafness is just as inadequate as that for ordinary catarrh, and it is to natural methods only that the sufferer from catarrhal deafness can look for alleviation of his condition. (I say advisedly *alleviation*, and *not* cure, for many cases of catarrhal deafness have progressed so far that a permanent cure is impossible. It is only in those cases which are in the comparatively early stages that a real cure is possible. But every case of catarrhal deafness can be benefitted *to a greater or less extent* by the adoption of natural methods of treatment.)

Treatment.—As regards general treatment, that for *catarrhal deafness* is exactly the same as for *catarrh* ; only in this case it would be advisable to begin the treatment with a fast for from three to five days, followed by a further ten to fourteen days on the *restricted diet* given in the Appendix, instead of the all-fruit diet. Further short fasts followed by periods on the restricted diet should be undertaken at, say, two- or three-monthly intervals, as the needs of the case demand. (Otherwise treatment should be just as for catarrh.)

As regards local treatment, a great deal can be done by *manipulative treatment* at the hands of a good Osteopath, especially if he employs *finger surgery* in his work. (Finger surgery is a method whereby the fingers are inserted into the mouth and the Eustachian tubes opened up. This is an excellent way of clearing these tubes of catarrhal matter which is blocking normal ear functioning. The method is not very common in England yet, unfortunately.)

Another useful form of local treatment is to wrap a hot-water bottle in a towel, place on the pillow when retiring, and then lie with each ear on it for, say, fifteen or twenty minutes each. Also, the more the tissues in and around the ears can be eased up and moved, the better. One way of doing this is by gentle massage around and behind the ears, and another is by the frequent opening and shutting of the mouth, as this stretches the internal ear structures and so relieves congestion. Opening the mouth as wide as possible several times, at intervals during the day, is a most useful procedure therefore, and should be practised consistently (although not to excess, of course !) by all sufferers from catarrhal deafness. Neck exercises (after the style of those given in *Better Sight without Glasses*) will also be very helpful. Electrical treatment is sometimes of good use in catarrhal deafness.

Perseverance with the foregoing will bring definite results in its train ; but, of course, advanced cases will take longer to show results than the less serious ones.

Colds.—The " common " cold is always with us—and no wonder, in this constantly overfed world of ours ! For the cold is Nature's simplest and oftenest-used cleansing agency. It is a natural *eliminative* measure pure and simple. It is Nature's way of removing surplus rubbish (toxic waste) from the system. All the world believes that we " catch " colds from each other, or from germs ; but although there is no doubt that a cold can be transmitted easily from one person to another, it is only because *both* individuals are in a food-clogged state and in need of a systemic cleansing.

No one who is perfectly clean and healthy *inside* can catch or develop a cold ; and the sooner people realise this, the better. Colds are pre-eminently the outcome of wrong feeding habits which have led to the clogging of the tissues with toxic waste, and any sudden lowering of the vitality serves as a means of bringing them into operation (getting wet through, getting run down, etc., etc.). The more one is addicted to colds, the more certain is it that that particular person is in a state of general toxicity due to wrong feeding and general wrong living.

To treat a cold in the usual way, by means of drugs, is just folly, from the Natural-Cure point of view. For all that such treatment does is to put a sudden stop to the eliminative process then taking place, and to force the toxic matter, which would thus have been eliminated, back into the tissues again. The cold is " cured " at the cost of the future health of the individual! (Only when *the cold* is understood in its true nature is this apparent, of course.)

Treatment.—The use of drugs in the treatment of colds is here exposed in its real light as a measure which makes for the future ill-health of the sufferer, even though they may appear to " cure " him at the time. The only real treatment for colds is *fasting*. For when we fast we aid Nature in her self-initiated task of body-cleansing —not hinder and thwart her as we do when we resort to drugs. A fast for from one or two to four or five days on orange juice (according to the severity or otherwise of the condition) is the finest way of dealing with a cold, with from two to three days on the *exclusive fresh fruit diet*—as outlined in the Appendix—to follow. The warm-water enema should be used daily to cleanse the bowels during the fasting period, and a hot Epsom-salts bath should be taken nightly, or every other night. If this is done, the cold will soon disappear, leaving the sufferer in *far better health than before,* because his system will have been *really* cleansed of toxic matter by the treatment.

If future colds are to be prevented, care of the body along sound health-building lines is essential, and in this respect nothing is more necessary than a sensible form of dietary. (The *weekly menus* given in the Appendix can be followed by all with every success in this connection.) If there is a condition of general catarrh associated with the constant catching of colds, then the treatment given for *catarrh* in the preceding pages should be put into full operation.

Deafness.—Deafness is a very common condition these days. Where its origin is not due to catarrh or actual disease of the ear, there may be a history of injury, shock, or previous disease in some other part of the body to account for it. (The taking of medicinal drugs such as quinine over a number of years helps materially in the development of ear troubles of all kinds.) Deafness can also appear from the psychological side (as a functional disability, that is, brought on by mental factors), and in these cases psychological treatment, at the hands of a competent psycho-therapist, can do a very great deal to rectify matters. Many cases of complete deafness have been cured in this way.

Where deafness is of catarrhal origin, the sufferer is referred to the treatment for *Catarrhal Deafness* just previously given. Where the deafness is due to loss of the ear-drum, through long-standing disease of the ears themselves, such as middle-ear disease, then I am afraid very little can be done to effect a cure. But a Natural-Cure regimen, along the same lines as that given for *Catarrhal Deafness*, will prove most helpful to the general condition of the sufferer, even if hearing cannot be restored by such treatment. (It is worthy of note that many cases of complete deafness have been cured by *spinal manipulation*, but in these cases the trouble has usually been due more to mechanical interference with hearing than to anything else.)

Defective Teeth (Dental Decay.—Defective teeth is one of the most common features of modern existence. Very few indeed would realise that it is the present-day dietary which is to blame for this, however, but such is indeed the case. A dietary of white bread, white sugar, refined cereals, cooked meat and cooked vegetables is sadly deficient in organic mineral matter, and if persisted in over a long period mineral starvation of the body occurs. To rectify this as far as possible within her means, Nature extracts some of the mineral matter from our teeth—the richest storehouse of organic mineral matter within the body—and uses it for the systemic purposes required. *It is thus that ental decay arises !*

The more impoverished and devitalised the dietary, the sooner will the teeth decay, therefore ; especially if cakes, pastry, puddings and pies, sweets and chocolates play a prominent part in the culinary habits of the person in question. To ascribe the decay to the eating of " mushy " food or to the eating of sweet foods, etc., as the doctor and dentist do, is only approaching the matter from the *outside* as it were ; such factors are merely superficial. The real *fundamental* cause, as here stated, is *ha itual wrong feeding*—that is, the habitual eating of demineralised and refined foodstuffs, with the almost total exclusion of natural unspoilt foods from the dietary.

Where children develop defective teeth early in life, it is not due primarily to the sweets, etc., they have been eating ; it is due to the fact that in pre-natal life—that is, when in their mother's womb—they were not given sufficient organic mineral matter to supply their developing bodies with the right kind of material for proper bone and teeth building. Hence decay at an early age. Thus it is an inadequate dietary (not in bulk but in organic mineral and vital content) on the part of the mother, during the pre-natal period, which is the real cause of defective teeth in children. (The fact that the mother's teeth often decay rapidly after childbirth is only another indication that the facts here being put forward are correct. For living on a demineralised dietary as she is, the mother is unable to supply the foetus with an adequate amount of organic mineral matter for proper bone and teeth building, and Nature makes up the deficiency as best it can, by extracting mineral matter from the mother's teeth.)

The first thing that strikes us about primitive races is their remarkably good teeth. This is solely because they *eat natural food*—food rich in organic mineral matter—and not the devitalised foodstuffs of more " civilised " and " enlightened " races !

Proposals to add sodium fluoride to public drinking water in an attempt to reduce the incidence of dental decay are misguided and fallacious. At best, the onset of dental decay may be deferred for a relatively short time, and at the worst there may well be a serious long-term health risk in the life-long consumption of a highly toxic chemical.

Treatment.—As regards treatment for defective teeth, there is not much that can be done really, once teeth have decayed, beyond having them attended to by a good dentist at regular intervals. But if further decay of the teeth is to be prevented, the only way to do this *effectually* is to adopt a scheme of dietary in which the organic food minerals are present in full abundance. For this purpose the *full weekly dietary* given in the Appendix is ideal.

Parents who would wish to preserve the teeth of their children as much as possible can only do so by looking after their dietary along the lines laid down in the present book, AND IN NO OTHER WAY.

Proper care of the teeth is essential, of course, and they should be brushed night and morning regularly. The use of abrasive toothpastes is not recommended. One of the best things to use for cleaning the teeth is *lemon juice*. (The brush is dipped in warm water first and then a little lemon juice is squeezed on to it.)

Diphtheria.—See section on *Fevers*.

Enlarged Tonsils.—In the opening remarks to the present section, and in dealing with tonsil troubles in the section on *Children's Ailments* (page 103), enough has been said already in the present book concerning the folly of removing enlarged or inflamed tonsils as a " curative " measure. The *cause* of the condition—which is *always* a toxic condition of the system, due to wrong feeding habits and general wrong living

—is completely ignored in these cases ; and the removal of the tonsils does nothing but weaken the defence mechanism of the organism, of which these lymphatic glands form an important part.

Without meaning in the least to be uncharitable, it must be obvious to all that so far as the general run of medical practitioners go, they are only too ready to seize upon any plausible-sounding excuse as the cause of disease within a given individual's system. If it isn't the " weather " it is " germs," or if not " germs " it is something equally external and superficial. So that it will be readily recognised that when a patient comes to the doctor with enlarged or inflamed tonsils, the doctor has here a ready " cause " for any more serious ills the patient may be suffering from. Everything is blamed on to the tonsils, and nothing on to the condition of the patient's system as a whole ! And so, what is merely one of the *effects* of ill-health is at once regarded as its *cause*. " Have your tonsils out," the doctor says, " and you will soon be quite all right " ; and the trusting patient does so, not realising in the least that his poisoned blood-stream—the real cause of all the trouble—will still go on infecting his tissues after the operation, as before.

The fact that so many people have had their tonsils out, only to find themselves in far worse health after the operation than before, is at last forcing itself upon the minds of the more enlightened members of the medical profession, and at the present moment there is quite a considerable body of prominent medical opinion strongly against the practice.* Curiously enough, some of those who now so vehemently oppose the practice of removing tonsils were the very ones who advocated it most strongly to begin with. This is also the case with appendix troubles. It seems that after a time a man does get to realise that the wholesale removal of seemingly " useless " organs or structures from the body is fraught with more danger to after-health than might at first sight be imagined ; especially so if he has himself been instrumental in removing several thousands of such organs or structures from the bodies of his patients ! Time brings wisdom even here !

But if there is a growing body of medical opinion against the surgical

* Mr. T. B. Layton, F.R.C.S., surgeon to the Throat and Ear Department of Guy's Hospital, in the *Lancet* for January 1934, says : " The operation for the removal of tonsils has a greater number of complications to life, to immediate illnesses, and to post-operative impairment of function, than any other operation of the same magnitude."

removal of tonsils, the vast mass of medical men are still wholly in favour of it ; and if the more sensible few are against it, they know of no really effective treatment to put in its place.

Treatment.—The only sound and logical treatment for enlarged, inflamed, or septic tonsils is *constitutional* treatment—that is, a regimen directed towards cleansing the system *as a whole*; for it is the whole system which is concerned in the production of the trouble in the first place. In the section on *Children's Ailments*, earlier in the book (page 103), will be found the home treatment for enlarged tonsils, where children are concerned ; here we will deal with adults suffering from the trouble. The best way to carry on is as follows :

From five to seven or ten days on the *all-fruit diet* outlined in the Appendix is the best way to start the treatment in not too serious or long-standing cases. Serious or long-standing cases should begin with a *short fast* for four or five days, followed by ten to fourteen days on the *restricted diet*, as given in the Appendix. In either case the *full weekly diet* outlined in the Appendix should then be begun, and adhered to as strictly as possible from then on. Further short periods on all-fruit—say two or three consecutive days—may be required in the less serious cases, at monthly intervals ; and in the more serious cases further short fasts followed by periods on the restricted diet may be necessary at, say, two- or three-monthly intervals, until the condition is quite cleared up. (With some people the tonsils may take much longer in clearing up than with others.)

The warm-water enema should be used nightly to cleanse the bowels during the first few days of the treatment, and afterwards as necessary ; and where constipation is habitual, the rules for its eradication given in Section 9 (page 275) should be put into operation forthwith. The daily dry friction and sponge or sitz-bath, and the breathing and other exercises given in the Appendix, form an essential part of the treatment, and should be carried out daily. Hot Epsom-salts baths, twice or three times weekly, will be found most beneficial.

A cold pack applied to the throat at night, and removed in the morning, will be most effective ; and the throat should be gargled night and morning with warm water containing a little lemon juice. (Cold packs are described in detail in the Appendix.) If the tonsils are very much inflamed, a good thing is to gargle several times a day with first hot water, and then cold. Any matter visible in the tonsils should be squeezed out and removed daily, by the aid of a suitable instrument—the end of a tooth-brush, etc. (See that this is quite clean before using.) On no account should medicinal gargles be used, and, most important of all, on no account should the throat be *painted* (this is a most harmful and suppressive measure).

Fresh air and outdoor exercise are two essentials to the treatment which must not be overlooked ; and regular and simple habits of living are equally essential to cure. Drinking and smoking, if habitual, must be rigorously excluded in future. As regards diet, all that has just previously been said to the sufferer from *catarrh* on this point should be borne in mind and acted upon by the sufferer from tonsil trouble also, as implicit adherence to a strict dietetic régime is necessary in all cases which look for a speedy cure.

In conclusion, when tonsil trouble has been overcome by natural methods, such as those outlined above, the gain in all-round general health is remarkable, as the whole system is dealt with by the treatment, and the *whole system* gains. Contrast this result with the surgical removal of tonsils ! There, the individual is left definitely far worse off as a result of the treatment than before, from the health point of view, even though, as in some cases, an *apparent* improvement is discerned for a short time afterwards ; for such apparent improvement is only temporary, and the system soon shows in unmistakable manner that its vitality and soundness have been materially affected by the treatment. Further disease, in other and perhaps more distant parts of the body, soon appears. But as this is connected in no way with what went before, either by doctor or patient, no one realises what real harm the operation has done. (To the surgical removal of tonsils can be traced the origin of many a case of deafness, middle-ear disease, or mastoiditis, many a case of chronic bronchitis or asthma, or other trouble, which seems to have sprung up for no possible reason at all !)

In all cases of tonsil trouble *spinal manipulation* can be fully recommended as a most useful adjunct to natural treatment.

Gum-boils.—See treatment for *Boils* (Section 2, page 130).

Hay-fever.—This disease is a catarrhal inflammation of the mucous membrane of the nose, eyes, and mouth. It is a most distressing complaint, causing the sufferer to have paroxysm after paroxysm of violent sneezing bouts (with copious watering of the eyes and other complications), which tend to leave him more and more exhausted as the trouble progresses. It usually puts in its appearance about June, at the time that the haying season commences, and is supposed by our medical scientists to be due to the irritating effects of hay particles and the pollen of flowers upon people having an especially sensitive mucous membrane of the nose, eyes, and mouth.

This, however, as is usual in all orthodox medical reasoning into the cause of disease, is a very short-sighted attitude indeed to adopt with regard to the origins of hay-fever. For no one seems to wonder why the person in question should have a super-sensitive mucous membrance or how it should have come about. It is simply taken for granted that some unfortunate people are just born that way, and so find themselves in after-life the victims of hay-fever, and that is all. Nothing could be more superficial and vague than that, surely, yet it seems to satisfy the hay-fever patients of the medical profession quite well, and they accordingly allow themselves to be persuaded not to stay in the country during the summer-time ; always to travel through the country—if such is necessary—with all windows of their car or railway-carriage closed ; and to be always inhaling or gargling or swallowing medicinal drugs or preparations of all kinds and descriptions, such being the only methods known to Medical Science of palliating the trouble. For cure there is none, from the medical point of view !

To anyone with any powers of constructive thinking it must be obvious that there *is* a reason, and a most definite reason, for this tendency on the part of some people to develop hay-fever—a reason our medical scientists know nothing of. For one thing, the hay-fever sufferer is always a catarrhal subject, which means that his system is in a food-clogged condition, and this in itself is sufficient to throw quite a deal of light upon the origin of the trouble.

The truth of the matter is this : Some people who are catarrhal subjects (people whose blood and tissues are surfeited with the toxins generated through years of unwise feeding habits) develop a super-sensitivity of the mucous membrane of the nose, eyes, and mouth, as a result of the chronic inflammation set up in those tissues over a period of time through the action of catarrhal toxins. This means that the mucous membrane is always in a state of incipient irritability, so that any continuous bombardment of small particles of dust, dirt, or such-like matter can set up a state of immediate and acute inflammation, which gives rise to the sneezing, watering, etc., which is characteristic of hay-fever. The fact that in the country in the summer-time there is always the pollen of flowers and hay particles floating about has given rise to the belief that it is these latter which are in some mysterious way definitely connected with the setting up of the condition ; but in reality any prolonged subjection of the individual concerned to an atmosphere where dirt and dust particles are prevalent will set up the trouble just as well.

The reason why what we call hay-fever usually arises only in the summer and autumn can be attributed to the fact that the warmer weather experienced then has the effect of inducing a more heated—and therefore more inflamed—condition of the membranes concerned than is the case in the colder months of the year.

Treatment.—Treatment for hay-fever by means of sprays, gargles, drugs, and the like is just a waste of both money and time. These merely attempt to get rid of the immediate effects of the trouble without in the least removing the causes. The only real cure for hay-fever lies in remedying the *underlying* catarrhal condition of the sufferer, which has led, as already pointed out, to the inflamed state of the membranes concerned and to their present excessive sensitivity.

The sufferer from hay-fever who wishes *really* to get rid of his trouble once and for all is advised to follow out the treatment given in the preceding pages for the overcoming of *catarrh*. He can be assured that by the assiduous carrying out of the treatment in question his trouble will definitely disappear in time, never to return—that is, if he strictly adheres to the general dietetic principles laid down in the treatment *when once cured*, and does not revert to his old ways of living.

Serious and long-standing cases of hay-fever are advised to begin with a fast for from three to five days, followed by ten to fourteen days on the *restricted diet* given in the Appendix rather than with the period on all-fruit. This latter is quite all right for the less severe cases. Further short fasts followed by periods on the *restricted diet* should be undertaken at two- or three-monthly intervals during the next year in these more serious cases. Whenever a hay-fever attack is on, the sufferer is advised to fast immediately, and to take a hot Epsom-salts bath every night for the time being. The enema should be used nightly too. If this is done, the attack will lose a great deal of its severity.

In the case of all hay-fever subjects it is always advisable to reduce the starchy and sugary foods to a minimum (in serious cases to cut them out entirely) during the months when they are most prone to an attack. Starches and sugars can be reintroduced in their normal amounts when the danger period is over. (Of course when the trouble is quite cured, there is no need to observe this rule strictly ; but even so, it is always best to be prepared and to take due precautions.) Starchy foods are bread, potatoes, cereals, bananas, and all flour products ; sugary foods are sugar, honey, preserves, and dried fruit.

A good thing for all hay-fever sufferers is to sniff cold water up the nose night and morning. A few drops of lemon juice may be introduced into the water. This is the best way to improve the tone of the membranes affected.

Head Noises.—Head noises are usually associated with *catarrh of the ear*, but may be due to *high blood-pressure* or other causes. The taking of medicinal drugs, especially quinine, over a period of years often induces noises in the head, such drugs having a very harmful effect indeed upon the internal ear structure.

Treatment.—Where head noises are associated with catarrh of the ear (or with previous drug treatment), the treatment for *Catarrhal Deafness* given in this section (page 237) should be carried out. Where the underlying cause is *high blood-pressure*, the sufferer is directed to the treatment for that complaint in the section on *Diseases of the Blood and Blood-vessels* (page 169). Where the cause is unknown, a Naturopath should be consulted with a view to discovering the cause and prescribing suitable treatment.

Leucoplacia.—These are white patches or sores upon the tongue and although from the medical point of view they are directly caused by irritation to the tongue through pipe-smoking, ill-fitting artificial teeth, etc., from the Nature-Cure point of view there is always an underlying toxic condition of the system to be counted upon where leucoplacia is present.

Treatment.—Treatment for leucoplacia should be *constitutional* rather than local, although of course a certain amount of local treatment is required too. But the emphasis is on the constitutional aspect of the treatment rather than upon the local. Medical treatment for this condition is purely local, and suppressive, and is both harmful as well as unsound, the strong drugs always used for the purpose of

247

removing the sores doing much damage to the system. The sufferer from leucoplacia is advised to consult a Naturopath with a view to treatment for his condition. If this is impossible, the treatment for *pyorrhœa*, given in the succeeding pages, will be found most helpful in his case. (Of course, anything tending to set up constant irritation in the mouth should be got rid of or stopped, as the case may be.)

Mastoiditis.—The mastoid bone is situated behind the ear, and is directly connected with the middle or internal ear. Thus it is linked up with the nose, mouth, and throat too ; for, as we have already seen, these structures are all intimately connected with the ears. Disease of the mastoid bone often occurs, and is sometimes a very serious condition indeed by virtue of the nearness of the structure named to the brain.

The cause of mastoid trouble is *in every case* a highly toxic general condition of the system, plus previous suppressive medical treatment of one kind or another (either for ear trouble, for tonsils and adenoid trouble, for childhood fevers, etc.). In fact, *mastoiditis*, as inflammation of the mastoid bone is called, is a shining example of what happens when the defence and eliminative mechanisms of the system are persistently interfered with over a period of years, under guise of improving the patient's health, by means of operations and drug treatment. The toxins which the system has been trying vainly to throw off during all this time are thrust farther and farther back into the tissues, and it is structures like the mastoid bone which are finally called upon to lodge the toxins Nature has been endeavouring to get rid of, but which Medical Science always persists in forcing back into the system again.

The sufferer from mastoid trouble can take it for granted, therefore, that his trouble is not " spontaneous " in any way ; it has not suddenly emerged out of thin air. It is the direct and logical outcome of a highly toxic condition of the system, plus suppressive medical treatment of former disease. That and nothing more.

Treatment.—The medical treatment for mastoiditis is operation. This calls for skilled handling, and sometimes has fatal results. But be it noted that the fatal termination to the operation is not due to the disease as such, but to the way in which the operation has been performed. For the structures which divide the mastoid from the brain are cut into on these occasions during the performance of the operation, and pus allowed to enter the brain area, with the aforesaid fatal results.

In any case, if the operation for mastoid trouble *is* successful, the patient is left with the underlying toxicity of his system still undealt with by the treatment. It is merely *the effects* of the trouble which are removed, not *the causes*. The only sane and logical treatment for mastoiditis is *constitutional* treatment—treatment, that is, which cleanses the system *as a whole,* and so gets rid of the real fundamental causes of the trouble.

The sufferer from mastoiditis is referred to a competent Naturopath for treatment for his case, where such personal treatment is at all possible. If not procurable, then the treatment for *middle-ear disease,* given in the following pages, can be adopted with very good results, the part behind the ear having hot fomentations applied to it several times daily whilst the swelling lasts. But again it must be stressed, personal treatment is by far the best, as in serious cases a fast of a week or longer may be necessary to begin with.

Spinal manipulation and sun-ray treatment are two very useful adjuncts to natural treatment in these cases. It is worth noting that during the natural treatment for mastoiditis the matter usually discharges itself through the ear.

Menière's Disease.—This is a condition in which the semi-circular canals of the internal ear are affected, and dizziness or vertigo is its outstanding symptom. The sufferer finds it difficult to balance himself when walking, and partial deafness and ringing in the ears are present in varying degrees. The disease is a difficult one to deal with, and is most often the outcome of previous suppressive medical treatment of disease, especially influenza or other acute toxic condition. Natural treatment, by fasting, strict dieting, manipulation, eliminative baths, etc., is the only possible hope of cure.

Treatment.—Where the sufferer from *Menière's disease* cannot undertake treatment in a Natural-Cure institution or under the personal care of a competent Naturopath, he will find the treatment for *middle-ear disease,* in the following pages, of real help to him. But, as already stated, personal treatment is by far the best in these cases, especially institutional treatment.

Middle-ear Disease.—In this disease there is inflammation of that portion of the ear directly behind the ear-drum, with discharge of matter into the outer ear. As the trouble progresses, the inner ear becomes more and more seriously affected, and hearing more and more impaired. The drum-membrane is always perforated in middle-ear disease.

To understand the cause of middle-ear disease the reader must turn to the introductory remarks made at the beginning of the present section. For middle-ear disease is the direct outcome of previous suppressive medical treatment of one form or another. Either it is due to suppressive treatment of childhood fevers or to operations for the removal of tonsils or adenoids or similar cause. When middle-ear disease occurs, it simply means that toxins which Nature has been trying to throw off through the medium of the usual channels of elimination (or through special channels) have been diverted back into the system again through wrong medical treatment, and have taken up permanent lodgment in the inner-ear structure to cause the continual suppuration and discharge associated with the disease thereafter. The way for this to take place is made easy because of the Eustachian tubes, which connect the ears with the throat and nose, toxic matter from these structures thus being enabled to pass quite easily into the middle-ear and to collect and suppurate there.

Treatment.—Orthodox medical treatment for middle-ear disease is just useless where a real cure is concerned. It is only a thorough course of *internal cleansing treatment* which can get rid of the toxins at the root of the trouble and clear up the discharge for good and all. Where the sufferer from the condition cannot undertake treatment under a Naturopath, he should carry on as follows :

The first thing to realise is that no drugs or medicinal agents of any sort are to be used in future for cleansing the ears. The treatment is to be purely natural. The patient should begin with a *short fast* for four or five days, as directed in the Appendix, and follow this with fourteen days on the *restricted diet*, also given therein. Then the *full weekly dietary* given can be adopted, and adhered to regularly thereafter. Further short fasts followed by periods on the restricted diet should be undertaken at two- or three-monthly intervals, until the discharge has quite cleared up. (Children and comparatively early or slight cases can begin with from five to ten days on the *all-fruit diet* given in the Appendix, instead of the fast and restricted diet, with two or three consecutive days on all-fruit at monthly intervals thereafter, until the condition rights itself.)

The warm-water enema or gravity douche should be used nightly to cleanse the bowels during the first few days of the treatment, and after if necessary ; whilst if constipation is habitual, the rules for its eradication given in Section 9 should be put into operation forthwith. The daily dry friction and sitz-bath or sponge (given in the Appendix) are essentials to the treatment, as is also the hot Epsom-salts bath twice weekly. Fresh air and outdoor exercise are necessaries too. (The breathing and other exercises given in the Appendix should also be gone through daily.)

As regards local treatment, the ear should be wiped out daily with a little cotton-wool steeped in warm water, and kept scrupulously clean. Every night on retiring a hot-water bottle should be wrapped in a towel and applied to the affected ear for, say, twenty minutes— both ears if necessary for an equal length of time. (It is best to place the wrapped bottle on the pillow and lie on it with the ear pressed to the bottle.) Also a very good thing to do is to apply hot and cold fomentations several times daily to *the back of the ear* (not the actual ear itself, but the part *where the ear joins the head*). A piece of material is wrung out in hot water and applied to the part mentioned for two or three minutes ; it is then removed and a second application applied for the same length of time. After this a third is applied and then removed, and a cold application put on. Always work in this order : three hot applications, one cold.

Gentle massage and stroking of the part behind the ear is very useful ; and the opening of the mouth as wide as possible, several times a day, is a good thing too, as this tends to loosen up and stretch the internal ear tissues, and so to ease congestion. Spinal manipulation is a very useful adjunct to natural treatment in all cases of ear trouble, and the regular daily performance of neck exercises, similar to those given in *Better Sight without Glasses*, will also prove beneficial.

The diet factor is one that needs the most careful consideration if the discharge is to be cleared up finally, and all that has been said in the present book as regards sensible dietetics should be paid careful attention to. White bread, refined cereals such as porridge, polished rice, etc., boiled, mashed, or fried potatoes, sugar, jams, confectionery, tinned foods, rich cakes, pastry, puddings and pies, and all heavy, greasy, or stodgy dishes should be strictly avoided in future. The diet should be as clean and wholesome as possible, with fruits and salads as the main ingredients. Meat and other flesh foods can be left out of the dietary with benefit ; they can be substituted on the diet-sheet by eggs, cheese, or nuts. Condiments, sauces, pickles, etc., should never be taken in future ; neither should coffee nor alcoholic liquors. Tea should be *very* weak, and very little taken, if at all. Strong tea is most detrimental.

If the trouble has not been allowed to develop too far in the first place, then the sufferer from middle-ear disease who carries on as directed above can rest assured his trouble will gradually disappear in time ; but of course patience and perseverance with the treatment are two essentials to ultimate success. The regimen will make a vast improvement in all-round general health too.

Pharyngitis.—This is an inflammation of the mucous membrane of the throat, affecting the voice and causing huskiness of speech, etc. Pharyngitis is often directly allied to chronic bowel trouble, but in any case is the outcome of a general toxic condition of the system as a whole. Previous suppressive medical treatment of disease (especially fevers) is a big factor in its appearance in certain cases, and the usual medical treatment for the condition, by means of gargles, sprays, etc., only tends to make the trouble chronic.

Treatment.—Treatment for pharyngitis which would be *really effective* must be constitutional rather than local. For an acute attack nothing is so efficacious as a *fast*. A fast for three or four days on water is the finest thing (a glass of warm or fairly hot water every two hours throughout the day). The warm-water enema should be used nightly to cleanse the bowels during that time. A cold pack should also be applied to the throat at night, and at three-hourly intervals during the day, too, if required. (See the Appendix for details as to how the pack is made and applied.) A hot Epsom-salts bath can be taken every other day whilst the attack lasts.

When the acute symptoms have subsided, a day or two on the *exclusive fresh fruit diet*, given in the Appendix, can be undertaken to follow the fast, and after that the *full weekly diet*, also given in the Appendix, can be gradually adopted and adhered to strictly there-after. The breathing exercises outlined in the Appendix should be performed regularly daily, in conjunction with the dry friction and sponge, and a definite attempt must be made to prevent further attacks by building up the tone of the whole system by adopting a plan of general health-building along the lines laid down in the treatment for *catarrh*.

Smoking and drinking, if habitual, should be definitely discontinued, as also all other habits tending to enervate the system. No medicinal preparations *of any kind* should be used ; but the throat can be gargled several times daily with warm water containing a little orange or lemon juice, during the treatment, if desired.

For *chronic pharyngitis* a course of general treatment, such as that given for *catarrh* in the preceding pages, will be found to provide the most beneficial results.

Polypi in Nose.--Polypi in the nose are merely outgrowths of the nasal mucous membrane. They arise only in those who are catarrhal subjects, and their formation is a sure sign of the general catarrhal state within. Their removal by surgical means is no doubt the simplest method of dealing with these growths, but such treatment does nothing to get rid of the underlying catarrhal condition which is the real cause of the trouble, and so does not prevent in the slightest the appearance of further polypi at some future date—something which very often occurs.

Treatment.—The natural treatment for *catarrh* given in the preceding pages of the present section will get rid of the underlying catarrhal state which is the real cause of the appearance of polypi in the nose, and will lead to the gradual disappearance of the polypus too, if that has not been allowed to develop too far before treatment is begun. If the polypus is one of long standing, however, then there *might* be need for an operation ; but even so, the treatment for catarrh already referred to should be put into operation forthwith. For only in this way can the sufferer build up his health and prevent further polypi forming.

For strengthening and toning up the mucous membrane the sniffing of cold water up the nose, several times daily, is a very useful thing (squeeze a few drops of lemon juice into the water) ; whilst the application of hot and cold fomentations over the area where the polypus is, is a most helpful procedure too, and should be done several times daily if at all possible. (The method by which these applications are applied is outlined in the treatment for *middle-ear disease* in the preceding pages.) Spinal manipulation and sun-ray treatment are both most valuable in cases of polypi, in conjunction with natural treatment.

Pyorrhœa.—This is a disease of the teeth-sockets, and is very prevalent indeed these days. It is the membrane surrounding the teeth-roots which is affected, with loosening of the teeth, pus formation, and shrinkage of the gums. According to the dentist and the doctor, it is " germs " which are the cause of pyorrhœa, and all that can be done from their point of view is to extract the affected teeth, and, by means of germicides, prevent the trouble from spreading further.

This attitude to pyorrhœa is completely wrong, however. Pyorrhœa is *not* due to germ infection ; it is merely one of the many forms of *acidosis* with which our present-day humanity is afflicted, as a result of the wrong feeding habits of to-day. As has been pointed out again and again in the present book, a dietary of white bread, refined cereals, much meat, white sugar, cooked vegetables, etc., etc., *always* leads to the swamping of the blood and tissues with acid waste matter, and to the development of disease in one form or another. Pyorrhœa is merely one of the many forms this swamping of the system with acid impurities (acidosis) takes. The sufferer from pyorrhœa can take it that his blood and tissues are in an excessively acid condition, and that his trouble is due solely to errors in diet, and *not* to " germs " or other hypothetical factors.

Treatment.—It must be obvious from the foregoing that no treatment for pyorrhœa can be effective which does not seek to cleanse the blood and tissues of the acid impurities which are at the root of the trouble. The extraction of teeth affected with the disease does nothing to clear up the systemic toxæmia which is the underlying factor concerned, and the pyorrhœa sufferer who has had his teeth removed and is now wearing false dentures can rest assured that disease in some form or other—other than pyorrhœa—will soon be knocking insistently at his door. It must be so, simply because the toxic matter which caused the pyorrhœa, and which his present feeding habits only intensify in quantity, is still present in his system all the time.

The only effective treatment for pyorrhœa is therefore *constitutional* treatment ; and the sufferer is advised to proceed as follows : Begin with a *short fast* for from three to five days, and follow this with ten to fourteen days on the *restricted diet* given in the Appendix. After this the *full weekly dietary*, also given in the Appendix, should be adopted, and adhered to strictly thereafter. Further short fasts followed by periods on the restricted diet may be required at, say, two- or three-monthly intervals in certain cases, depending upon the initial severity of the condition. (Some really serious cases may need a protracted fast to begin with.)

The bowels should be cleansed nightly during the first few days of the treatment with the warm-water enema or douche, and afterwards if necessary ; and where constipation is habitual, the rules for its eradication given in Section 9 (page 275) should be put into operation forthwith. The daily dry friction and sitz-bath or sponge, and the breathing and other exercises given in the Appendix, should be made a definite part of the morning routine ; and a hot Epsom-salts bath should be taken twice weekly from now on.

As regards local treatment, the teeth should be cleansed night and morning with a little lemon juice squeezed on the tooth-brush (after the latter has been dipped into warm water), and the mouth should be well rinsed afterwards with warm water containing lemon juice also. The forefinger of the right hand should be rubbed gently over the gums for a minute or two after each brushing. NO MEDICINAL OR PATENT PREPARATIONS OF ANY KIND ARE TO BE USED. NO TOOTH-PASTES.

As already indicated, the diet factor is essentially the whole crux of the matter where real cure is concerned, and all that has been said on this subject in the present book—and in the author's book *Your Diet in Health and Disease*—should be read through carefully and taken to heart by the sufferer from pyorrhœa. Fresh fruits, green salads, wholemeal bread, *properly cooked* vegetables, eggs, cheese, nuts, and milk should form the basis of the future dietary. White bread, white sugar, and all refined and tinned foods must be completely given up. Meat and other flesh foods can with great benefit be left out of the future dietary, and those who are able and willing to do without such foods altogether, to help on their cure, can substitute egg or cheese or nuts for flesh foods where mentioned on the weekly diet-sheet given in the Appendix. Condiments, sauces, etc., are *taboo* ; as also are coffee, alcohol, and strong tea.

Quinsy.—This is a condition in which an abscess forms upon a tonsil. It is a very painful condition indeed, and is entirely the outcome of a highly toxic condition of the system generally, with habitual constipation as its most potent predisposing cause. In really severe cases the abscess may have to be lanced by a medical practitioner, but as regards general treatment, that given for *Tonsillitis* in the succeeding pages should be put into operation in its entirety. This is the quickest and surest way back to health for the quinsy sufferer. No other medical treatment *of any kind*, other than lancing in the more serious cases, should be tolerated at all (no spraying, etc.).

Rhinitis.—This is a very extreme form of catarrh of the nose, and is a very difficult condition to deal with because of the serious degenerative changes which have taken place within the nasal structure. All that has been said about *catarrh* and its treatment (in the preceding pages of the present section) should be studied carefully by the sufferer from rhinitis, but in his case it would be far more satisfactory if personal naturopathic treatment were sought. Such treatment is always best, because of the additional curative measures which can be employed—curative measures which one carrying on at home must of necessity do without. (A fairly long fast, to start the treatment, would be far the best in these cases, with further shorter fasts at intervals, as required.)

Sinusitis.—The nasal sinuses, being connected with the nasal passages, are liable to disease emanating from the nose or throat. Operations for the removal of tonsils and adenoids have a great deal to do with the development of diseases in the nasal sinuses, as has also previous suppressive medical treatment for fevers, persistent colds, catarrh, etc. When the nasal sinuses become chronically inflamed, they are the cause of much pain and suffering to the unfortunate individual concerned, and treatment along orthodox medical lines for the cure of the trouble is far from satisfactory, to say the least !

For the effective treatment of *sinusitis* or other affection of the nasal sinuses the sufferer is referred to the treatment for *Catarrh* given in the preceding pages of the present section. Along its lines, and its lines *only*, does his real cure lie.

As regards local treatment for the alleviation of pain, hot and cold compresses to the affected areas will be most beneficial. A piece of linen material or a towel is wrung out in hot water, applied over the painful area or areas for, say, two or three minutes, and removed. A second and then a third hot compress are then applied for the same length of time, and then a cold application is put on. This can be done several times daily if desired. Always work in the same order : three hot applications, one cold. *Manipulative treatment* and *artificial sunlight treatment* can be recommended in all cases of sinusitis.

Sore or Inflamed Tongue.—Sore or inflamed tongue is usually a sign of excess acidity of the stomach due to wrong feeding habits, especially the over-consumption of starchy and sugary foods.

As regards treatment, the sufferer is referred to *Hyperacidity* and its treatment in Section 9 (page 293). In cases where it is found that fruit or fruit juices tend to accentuate the trouble, the best procedure regarding treatment is to have a fast for from two to four days, having a glass of warm water every two hours during the day and to follow this with a period on the *milk diet,* as outlined in the Appendix. When on the milk diet not more than four pints of milk should be taken in all, beginning with about two pints the first day, and gradually increasing up to four pints daily. The warm-water enema should be used daily during the first few days of the fast and milk diet, and every other day thereafter as required. The period to be spent on the milk diet will, of course, depend upon the condition of the tongue. As soon as the tongue has improved sufficiently, the *full weekly dietary* given in the Appendix should be begun. Treatment should otherwise be exactly as for *Hyperacidity* as outlined in Section 9 (page 293)

Further short fasts with periods on the milk diet may be required in certain cases, at intervals of, say, a month to six weeks.

Sore Throat.—See *Tonsillitis* below.

Tonsillitis.—Tonsillitis or acute sore throat, is really acute inflammation of the tonsils, the almond-shaped bodies situated on either side of the throat, or pharynx. If the reader has read with care what has been said at the beginning of the present section regarding the work of the tonsils and how they become diseased, he will realise that tonsillitis is nothing more than the direct outcome of a toxic condition of the system generally, brought to a head by a sudden lowering of vitality resulting from exposure, sudden chill, etc. In this connection nothing predisposes more towards throat affections of this kind than *chronic constipation.* A tendency towards recurrent attacks of quinsy and tonsillitis is almost always associated with this condition, as toxins which should have been ejected from the system in the ordinary way are reabsorbed into the blood-stream because of the constipated condition of the individual concerned, thus throwing more and more work upon the detoxifying mechanisms of the system, of which the tonsils are one of the foremost.

Treatment.—Treatment for sore throat or tonsillitis along orthodox lines, by means of painting, gargling, spraying, etc., is both harmful and suppressive. It does nothing to rid the system of the toxins at the root of the trouble ; it merely forces these toxins back into the system to cause more serious trouble later on. The only sane and logical treatment for tonsillitis is a *cleansing* one—treatment which will rid the system once and for all of the underlying toxic matter which is at the root of the trouble. The condition will then be overcome in the shortest possible time, whilst the general health of the individual concerned will be very much enhanced by the treatment and *not further impaired*, as it would be under orthodox medical treatment.

The sufferer from acute sore throat, or tonsillitis, is advised to carry on as follows : *Fast* for as long as the more serious symptoms continue. This may be from two to four or even five or six days, according to the severity of the condition. NOTHING BUT WATER AND ORANGE JUICE SHOULD BE TAKEN DURING THAT TIME. NO MILK ; NOTHING ELSE AT ALL. The bowels should be cleansed daily with the warm-water enema or douche during that time—twice daily in the more serious cases. A cold pack—as described in detail in the Appendix—should be applied to the throat at two-hourly intervals during the day, and one at night too (this latter should be removed in the morning). The throat may be gargled several times daily with warm water ; but nothing else should be used. A hot Epsom-salts bath may be taken every day, or every other day, with good effect.

If the patient is kept quiet, and the foregoing treatment carried out, the most serious attack of tonsillitis or sore throat can be weathered quite easily. As the symptoms subside, then the *all-fruit diet* given in the Appendix can be adopted for a few days, and after that the *full weekly dietary* given therein. This full weekly dietary should be adhered to strictly thereafter, if further trouble of the same kind is to be prevented. The daily dry friction and sitz-bath or sponge and the breathing and other exercises given in the Appendix should all form part of the daily health regimen, once the patient is convalescent. A hot Epsom-salts bath once or twice a week can be taken regularly from then on with every benefit too.

Remember : *No medicinal preparations or drugs of any kind are to be taken or employed in any way.*

Pineapple juice—the juice of *fresh* (not tinned) pineapple, that is— is most valuable in all throat affections of the kind we are discussing. Spinal manipulation is extremely beneficial in all cases of tonsillitis and allied ailments. For chronic sore throat see treatment for enlarged *Tonsils* (page 242).

Vincent's Angina.—This is a rather serious inflammatory condition affecting the mucous membrane of the tonsils and throat, and is due to a highly toxic general condition of the system. Treatment should be as for *Tonsillitis*, although the initial fasting period will no doubt have to be considerably longer to enable the infection really to clear up.

Where possible, personal naturopathic advice should be sought.

DISEASES OF THE STOMACH AND INTESTINES

Acid stomach—Appendicitis — Cancer—Cholera— Colic— Colitis — Constipa-
tion—Diarrhœa—Dilatation of the stomach — Dropped stomach — Duodenal
ulcer — Dysentery — Dyspepsia — Enteric fever—Fissure of anus—Fistula—
Flatulence — Gastric catarrh — Gastric ulcer— Gastritis (Acute) — Gastritis
(Chronic) — Hæmorrhoids (Piles)— Heartburn — Hyperacidity — Indigestion
(Acute) — Indigestion (Chronic) — Intestinal catarrh — Loss of appetite —
Ptomaine poisoning—Typhoid.

WHEN we consider that all the food we eat has to be dealt
with in that part of the human organism known as the *alimentary canal*, then the reason for the great prevalence of diseases of the
stomach and intestines will be at once apparent, for the alimentary
canal is made up principally of the stomach, or food-bag, and the
intestines.

We eat primarily in order that we may live, but the modern world
has almost lost sight of this most elementary fact. With a great
number of people nowadays it is a question of living in order that
they may eat ; and even if this is not actually the case with others,
the eating of food has become an habitual matter, a matter dictated
solely by routine, and bearing no relationship whatsoever to the
direct needs of the body, which it is the true and primary function
of food to subserve.

It can be accepted as a fact that the average person to-day eats
two or three times as much food as his body really requires, especially
sedentary workers. (All this without any reference as to whether the
food is really *good food*, as measured by Natural-Cure standards.)
The inevitable result is that the organs most affected by this persistent
influx of food—the stomach and intestines—are perpetually at a
disadvantage where normalcy of condition and tone are concerned.
They are ever on the brink of breaking down under the continuous
strain imposed upon them by their blissfully ignorant owners, who
go on eating their four or five meals a day, year in and year out, in
the fond belief—fostered by those in medical and social authority—
that the more food they eat the better is it for their future health and
strength !

This is hardly the place to enter into a full discussion of present-day
food fallacies, it has all been gone into thoroughly in the author's
book *Your Diet in Health and Disease* ; but the upshot of modern

food habits and theories is to land the peoples of present-day civilisation with a variety and accumulation of diseases of the organs of digestion and elimination such as no previous period in history can equal (The advertisements for " cures " for indigestion and constipation that appear in never-ending succession in every newspaper and periodical one picks hold of more than bear out this statement, if the reader's own experience with family and friends does not already bear it out to the full.)

Now, what steps does the medical profession take to deal with this inordinate amount of disease of the stomach and intestinal tract ? We find that its treatment resolves itself down to one of *palliation* pure and simple. No attempt is made to get down to the *real cause* of the trouble—the extravagant amounts of food habitually eaten, and in all kinds of unwise combinations—but the patient is merely given medicine to help overcome the *immediate symptoms* of his complaint, and that is all. Has any sufferer from indigestion or constipation ever been cured—*really* cured—by medical treatment ? These diseases, simple as they are, are quite incurable by orthodox medical methods of treatment, simply because the real underlying cause of the condition, *wrong feeding*, is not affected in the slightest by it. (Dietetic treatment, of a kind, is attempted in certain cases of stomach and bowel trouble, but this is always secondary to the drug treatment employed, and is of no real curative value, as it is entirely unrelated to any of the principles of rational dietetics.)

In no section of disease is the medical record so poor and ineffectual as is its record for the treatment of diseases of the kind we are discussing in the present section ; and conversely, in no section of disease is the Natural-Cure record so bright and shining as is its record for the treatment of these same diseases. Why ? Simply because in the natural treatment the real cause of the trouble is recognised and removed ; whilst in the medical treatment the real cause is ignored or neglected, and the regimen is turned merely towards the end of getting rid of superficial symptoms.

The patient suffering from stomach or bowel trouble, who has been taking medicines for years, often finds himself on the operating-table eventually as a result thereof. And does this last desperate attempt to get rid of his ailment *cure* him ? It patches him up perhaps for a time, only to leave him all the more a chronic invalid thereafter in ninety-nine cases out of a hundred And this because the only factor which can *really* turn the scale—the food factor—is persistently neglected all the time.

Look at it in whichever way you will, there is no possible hope for the sufferer from stomach or intestinal trouble who leaves himself in medical hands. His symptoms may be masked and palliated for a time ; drug treatment and operations may lead him to think that he is getting over his trouble ; but in the end he will have to face the blunt fact that he is definitely worse off in health (both as regards the actual trouble he is being treated for and general health too) than when he first came under treatment. His only pathway to cure —to real and *permanent* cure—lies along natural lines. These, and these only—as results more than prove.

Having given the sufferer from stomach or bowel trouble this assurance that under natural treatment his health can—in whole or in great part—be restored in the majority of cases, even if he has spent years vainly seeking for cure at the hands of orthodox medicine, we can now proceed to outline the actual treatments themselves. The results obtained will be more than gratifying.

Acid Stomach.—See *Hyperacidity* (page 293).

Appendicitis.—We are all accustomed to hearing of people " suddenly " developing appendicitis, and being rushed off to the hospital for an immediate operation, and their lives thus saved. But if one knows something about the inside workings of these matters, the facts are not quite as they appear to be.

The modern medical craze for removing appendices almost rivals that for the removal of enlarged tonsils ; and many people accept an appendicitis operation as something more or less inevitable, and feel quite in the fashion thereby. But if the medical profession would delve a little more deeply into the causes of appendicitis than it now does, and realise how inevitably appendix trouble is linked up with bowel sluggishness and constipation, it might hesitate a little before condemning its appendicitis patients out of hand to the knife, and imagining that it is bringing them back to sound health thereby. It *might* ; but I very much doubt it even then. For the medical outlook is so befogged by the germ theory of disease that when it comes to a question of following out the various disease-processes through all their various stages of cause and effect, the medical mind seems quite incapable of the task.

Appendicitis is *not* something which attacks you suddenly out of thin air, as it were, as a result of germ infection. That is merely a cock-and-bull story invented by the medical profession to hide its own colossal and complete ignorance as to the real causes of the trouble. No sufferer from appendicitis caught his disease " out of the blue." It was the direct outcome of a toxic bowel condition which has its origins far back in the patient's medical history, and the habitual taking of aperient medicines has more to do with its development than most people would care to realise.

The appendix is a small organ or structure placed at the very beginning of the large intestine (or colon), and any extensive accumulation of waste matter in the colon over a period of time can lead to the development of appendicitis, which disease is nothing more than an attempt on the part of Nature to localise and " burn up " the toxins in question. (Inflammation of the bowel lining, due to the habitual taking of aperient drugs, is a most potent predisposing factor in the setting up of appendicitis.) It is quite true that when the appendix is affected there is germ activity present, but this is the *result* of the condition, *not* the cause ! (Just the same as when there is an accumulation of filth in a dustbin, all sorts of parasites seem to appear automatically. They are not the *cause* of the filth surely ? They are merely developed there *as the outcome* of the presence of the filth.)

When the appendicitis sufferer realises that his trouble is due to past wrong living—for constipation and bowel sluggishness are the direct outcome of wrong feeding habits, plus enervation of the system —he will have made a definite step towards a correct understanding of the cause of his condition. But he will say here, " How is this knowledge going to help me ? Surely now that I *have* appendicitis the only way to cure it is by operation ? " The removal of the diseased appendix by means of surgical operation is not a *cure* for the trouble by any means. For the original condition which was the cause of the appendix trouble in the first place—the chronic constipation and toxic bowel condition—has not been improved in any way by the operation. Indeed, it has been made worse, as the appendicitis victim finds out to his cost after the operation.

The surgical removal of appendices does nothing to cure the underlying bowel trouble ; it does nothing to improve—in the real sense— the patient's health. But it certainly puts fees—and often fat fees— into the pockets of operating surgeons. Hence the popularity of such operations among those self-same surgeons, whose advice in these matters the public accepts with such touching and childlike trust and confidence. Then again, if a person is in acute pain he will consent to anything if he is promised relief from his sufferings thereby.

This is not to say that all surgeons are actuated by purely pecuniary motives, but even in medical circles it is admitted that there is far too great a tendency for operations in general to be advised, and most especially where appendices and tonsils are concerned. Some medical authorities go so far as to say that at least fifty per cent. of all operations performed nowadays are unnecessary ; and this from men who believe in the efficacy of operations as a means to restored health !

The only real cure for appendicitis is *fasting*. The fast—Nature's safest and most simple curative measure—is the one sure road to cure in all appendix troubles. Why, then, does not the medical profession make use of it ? Merely another example of its steadfast and purblind refusal to accept any curative measure—*however provedly successful*—that does not emanate from within its own closed circle of ideas.

Treatment.—Many hundreds of cases of appendicitis have been cured by Naturopaths simply through the agency of the fast. It is very difficult for many, however, to secure the services of a qualified Naturopath at these times, so that the following outline of home treatment will be of the utmost service to them. Appendicitis brings with it a state of great nervousness and fear both in the minds of the sufferer and friends ; but if the natural treatment to be outlined herewith is carried into operation without delay, then no fear as to the ultimate consequences need be maintained.

To begin with, the patient should be kept as quiet as possible, and nothing but sips of water given to drink. Hot compresses can be placed over the painful area several times daily. An enema, containing about a *pint of warm water*, can be given each day for the first two or three days, to cleanse the lower bowel; but only if it can be taken with comfort by the patient, not otherwise.

About the third day the condition should have eased sufficiently for a full enema to be given, containing about three pints of warm water; and this should be repeated daily thereafter until all pain and inflammation have subsided. From the third day onwards fruit juices, as well as water, can be given the patient.

Nothing more than the above simple treatment, sensibly applied is needed to overcome an appendicitis attack, and as soon as convalescence develops the *all-fruit diet* given in the Appendix can be adopted. (Do not be in too great a hurry to give food. It is better to fast the patient for a day or two longer than less !) After a few days of this diet the *full weekly dietary*, also outlined in the Appendix, can be then gradually begun, and it should be adhered to faithfully thereafter. If there is still a tendency towards constipation, the rules for its eradication given in the following pages of the present section should be put into operation, and the enema used on occasion as necessary. The breathing and other exercises given in the Appendix, together with the morning dry friction and sitz-bath or sponge, should be incorporated into the daily régime as soon as the patient feels sufficiently recovered.

A scheme of clean and sensible living—early hours, no excesses, etc.—and the adoption of the advice given in the foregoing paragraphs, and in a few weeks the erstwhile sufferer from appendicitis will be a far healthier person than for many years before ; and in addition, his appendix—a *most useful* little organ employed by Nature in the work of detoxifying the colon and lubricating the faeces—will be retained in his system in as healthy a condition as possible, instead of reposing—as in all probability it would have been—in the specimen bottle of some operating surgeon !*

SPECIAL NOTE RE PERITONITIS.—Where peritonitis sets in after appendicitis, it is the operation which is to blame, never the disease itself. Appendicitis treated along natural lines can never develop into peritonitis.

Cancer.—Cancer is the dread disease of to-day, the disease spoken of with bated breath by all. It is the veritable " white scourge " of our times, and, as statistics plainly indicate, is steadily on the increase in all civilised countries, in spite of all the efforts made by the medical profession to keep it in check.

Despite the expenditure of millions of pounds in research work, modern Medical Science has not yet discovered the cause of cancer. And it never will, even though many millions more are expended, if it continues its researches along the same lines as now.

No amount of work in laboratories, among test-tubes or upon dumb animals, will reveal the cause of cancer. That cause is only

* For treatment of *Chronic Appendicitis*, see treatment for *Colitis*, page 270.

to be found in an examination of the previous life-history of *the sufferer from the disease himself* ; in an examination of his past medical history and general habits of living. Cancer is not the result of infection by a germ; it is not caused by accident or chance; it is the direct outcome of a lifetime of wrong living—dietetic and otherwise—plus prolonged suppressive medical treatment, by drug and knife, for one disease after another.

If a person is suffering from cancer, then that person can rest assured that the disease has only developed in his system as a result of the breaking down of the body's powers of resistance as a culmination to a prolonged and insidious attack upon the health of the organism by a combination of all (or some) of the following health-destroying factors :

(*a*) A lifetime of wrong feeding (a more than usual subsistence upon the demineralised and devitalised white bread, sugar, and cooked and refined food dietary of to-day).

(*b*) Chronic constipation—leading to the taking of excessive quantities of purgative drugs.

(*c*) The using up of the body's powers and forces through overwork, excessive worry, fear, morbid and destructive thinking, indulgence in excesses of all kinds, etc.

(*d*) Previous suppressive medical treatment by knife and drug for one disease after another.

(*e*) Improper care of the body, bodily organs, and functions generally, especially the generative organs in the case of women.

From the above combination of causes are the seeds for the development of cancer sown within the system, and the organ finally selected for the appearance of the disease is usually one which has been subjected to prolonged and persistent irritation of one kind or another. (It must be stressed again that cancer is not something which appears quite suddenly within the organism ; it is the outcome of a series of factors making for the gradual deterioration of the body's powers of resistance, and is a process of gradual development, although the actual appearance of the cancer itself at the end of the process may seem to be quite a sudden affair.)

Treatment.—Whether it be cancer of the stomach or rectum, or cancer of the liver, etc., the genesis of the complaint is all the same ;

and medical treatment by means of operation or X-ray or radium is just futile. Such methods do nothing to get rid of the real causes at work in the development of the disease, and are really destructive in their ultimate effect, however much they may appear to palliate matters for the time being.

A most insidious feature of present-day medical methods of dealing with cancer by operation is the removing of all lymphatic glands in the vicinity of the area affected. This is carried out on the assumption that these glands serve as a medium for the spread of the disease to other organs ; but the whole thing is monstrously nonsensical—yet another sign of medical inability to understand the immensely valuable part played by the lymphatic glands in guarding the body from auto-intoxication. All that such treatment does is to weaken yet further a defence mechanism already far too weak to carry out its allotted task satisfactorily.

Cancer of the breast is the only form of cancer that seems to respond at all to operation, the patient being comparatively well thereafter. But if the principles underlying the development of the disease are understood, it will be realised that such treatment has done nothing to build up the health of the individual concerned ; nor has it done anything to prevent cancer developing in any other organ at a later date.

If the cancer patient is to be cured at all—*really* cured—it is only by natural methods of treatment that this can be effected. *By the removal of causes*—if such be at all possible in any given case. It does not do to raise the hopes of the cancer sufferer too high, for if the condition has developed at all far, a cure is well-nigh impossible ; but in the comparatively early stages a great deal can be done to effect a cure by thoroughly applied natural treatment. Fasting, strict dieting, manipulation, eliminative baths, sunray treatment, etc., will all be required, and obviously the best place for the carrying out of this is a Nature-Cure home. Failing this, the cancer sufferer should place himself at once under the care of a competent Naturopath for treatment. Self-treatment, at home, is not desirable for a number of reasons, where cancer is concerned.

There are several authentic instances on record where cancer has been cured by natural methods, but no doubt the disease was not very far advanced in all these cases, as the writer doubts very much whether a complete cure would have been possible otherwise.

Cholera.—See section on *Fevers* (Section 13, page 404).

Colic.—This is the name given to sharp, shooting pains in the intestines. Its cause, most often, is the eating of incompatible or wrongly combined foods, and the following simple treatment will be quite sufficient to set things right in all ordinary cases.

Treatment.—The patient should drink nothing but warm water for twenty-four hours—longer if necessary—and the bowel should be cleansed once or twice during that time with a warm-water enema. A hot-water bottle or hot flannels can be placed over the painful area, and the patient rested in bed. If this is done, any ordinary attack of colic will soon pass off, and strict attention to diet thereafter, along the lines consistently laid down in the present volume, will prevent the occurrence of future attacks.

Where the pain persists in spite of the above treatment, a Naturopath should be consulted, as there will most likely be some other factor concerned in the causation of the trouble, which only personal examination will reveal. In any case, the safest procedure is to carry on with the water fast, using the enema daily or twice daily meanwhile.

Colitis.—Colitis means inflammation of the colon or large intestine, and is of two kinds : *ulcerative colitis* and *mucous colitis*. To understand the cause of colitis it is necessary to realise that the lining of the colon is of sensitive mucous membrane, and only prolonged irritation of this delicate mucous lining of the colon can develop into colitis. The two great factors concerned in the setting up of this continuous irritation of the lining of the colon which ultimately leads to colitis are *chronic constipation* and the *purgative habit*.

When, through habitual wrong feeding habits, the colon can no longer perform its function properly, and becomes sluggish, constipation arises, and faecal deposits accumulate around the walls of the colon and set up irritation there ; and the purgative drugs taken to combat this condition only succeed in making this irritation of the lining of the colon worse, in proportion to their strength, as explained in the treatment for *Constipation* farther on in the present section.

The more that meat and other flesh foods form a part of the dietary of such a person, the more will putrefactive matter form in the colon, and the worse therefore will be the effects on the general condition of the colon itself. It is because of the combination of all these factors that colitis ultimately appears, generally.

It is often assumed that the eating of foods containing "roughage" is a prominent cause of colitis, but this is owing to the lining of the colon being in such a devitalised state to begin with, because of the factors previously mentioned. Foods containing a large percentage of natural roughage, such as fruits, vegetables, wholemeal bread, etc., can never be the *cause* of colitis, although if colitis is once present they may serve to aggravate matters. As a matter of fact, an abundance of natural foods such as fruits, vegetables, wholemeal bread, etc., in the dietary *to begin with* would have effectually prevented the appearance of colitis in after-life, because these foods are the foods given us by Nature for the very purpose of keeping the intestines and colon clean and healthy by virtue of the scouring that they give to the structures named in their passage through them. The more roughage food contains, the more will it aid in the work of the colon and promote healthy functioning—not interfere with it, as so many believe. Given a colon that is *already* in a devitalised condition, however, then foods containing much roughage may tend to aggravate the poor condition of the colon and increase the tendency to colitis, *but only because the colon, in its present unhealthy condition, is not in a fit position to deal with them adequately.*

Previous suppressive treatment of disease by means of drugs and operations may tend to bring on colitis in certain cases, in conjunction with other systemic factors already dealt with ; whilst a general catarrhal condition of the whole system is usually an underlying factor in all cases of colitis. (For an understanding of how a catarrhal condition arises, the reader is referred to the treatment of *Catarrh* in Section 8, page 233.)

Once the cause and nature of colitis are understood and recognised in their true light, then the means to be employed for the eradication of the trouble are relatively simple. The first thing needed is to institute treatment which will cleanse the colon and the whole intestinal tract, and allow the inflamed mucous membrane to heal. Then a strict diet of natural foods must be followed, and before long the erstwhile sufferer from colitis will begin to believe that he was never afflicted with such a painful and debilitating malady. Unfortunately for most people, it is orthodox medical treatment which they have to adopt in their case if they develop colitis, and the medical attitude towards the disease is such that the trouble is more often than not aggravated rather than lessened by the treatment.

To Medical Science colitis is a disease due to " germ infection," and by means of bowel wash-outs with highly suppressive drugs the medical profession seeks to cure the condition. These methods often succeed in making the disease *chronic* ; but even if they appear to be successful in suppressing or checking the trouble for the time being, they are never in the least degree curative in the real sense. The toxic matter Nature was trying to eliminate through the medium of the bowel lining (mucous membrane) is forced back into the system again by such treatment, and this being so, the colitis is always likely to break out again at some future time.

Another feature about the orthodox medical treatment for colitis which adversely affects the patient's future health is the ruling out of all foods containing roughage from the diet. As such foods as wholemeal bread, fruits, and green vegetables are included under this heading, the unfortunate colitis sufferer soon finds himself in a very mineral-starved condition as a result of such feeding, with the possibility of *acidosis* in one or other of its more serious forms as a very likely complication to his present bowel trouble !

Treatment.—As already pointed out, when once colitis is recognised in its true light, then the treatment required for its cure is relatively simple, fasting and strict dieting being the two great essentials required. Really serious cases may need a fairly lengthy fast to begin with, to enable the inflamed colon to regain normal tone, but ordinary cases should proceed as follows :

Begin with a *short fast* for from three to five days, as directed in the Appendix, and then continue with the *full milk diet* as outlined therein, remaining on this for two to four weeks as deemed necessary. Rest as much as possible the while. Then begin on the *full weekly dietary* as given in the Appendix, but substituting stewed fruit for fresh fruit, at first, and steamed vegetables or vegetable broth for salads, until able to deal with these raw foods satisfactorily. These may be included gradually in the diet later, as the condition of the bowel improves. Further fasts and periods on the milk diet may be necessary, at intervals of two to three months, according to the way the case is progressing. Sufferers must use their discretion here of course.

During the fast, and after if necessary, the bowels should be cleansed nightly with the warm-water enema or gravity douche; this can be discontinued as soon as the bowels begin to function naturally as a result of the treatment. If it be necessary to use the enema after the first week, it can be used every *other* night from then on. The dry friction and sitz-bath detailed in the Appendix should be taken every morning in conjunction with the scheme of general exercises also outlined therein; and a hot Epsom-salts bath should be taken twice weekly. A hot and cold sitz-bath should be taken *every night*—except on those nights when an Epsom-salts bath is being taken—until the trouble has quite cleared up. (See the Appendix for details of the hot and cold sitz-bath and Epsom-salts bath.)

By carrying on in the manner outlined above, the sufferer from colitis will soon be on the path to health again, but the strictest attention to the future dietary is essential if trouble of the same nature is to be prevented. No condiments, seasonings, or sauces of any kind are to be taken, and the foods to be most careful of are flesh foods-meat, fish, etc.—as these are the most putrefactive of all, and so most prone to affect the colon and set up irritation and rekindle inflammation there. Foods which have a *detoxifying* and *cleansing* effect upon the intestines on their passage through—such as fruits and vegetables— *are most essential of all to the future dietary*, despite the horror with which such foods are viewed by the medical profession where colitis is concerned. (Flesh foods can with benefit be left out of the dietary altogether, and their place taken by eggs, nuts, or cheese.) Sugar and all white-flour products are also extremely harmful in all cases of colitis.

NOTE.—It is quite possible that many sufferers from colitis will not be able to eat fruits and salads with comfort *right away*, but after the initial fast and period on the milk diet they should find such foods much easier to get on with, if eaten as directed in the diet-sheet; but remember what has already been said on this point in the preceding remarks. The colon should have lost most of its inflamed condition by then, and fruits and salads will be much more easily tolerated— and even welcomed. For cleansing the bowel, nothing but warm water should ever be employed. *No medicinal agents or drugs of any kind should be used.*

271

Constipation.—Constipation is not a disease, it is a condition of malfunctioning. But although not a disease in itself, constipation is the fruitful source of many of the most dreadful diseases of to-day, as well as many of less serious import. Appendicitis, rheumatism, arthritis, high blood-pressure, cancer, cataract, are only a few of the diseases in which constipation is an important predisposing factor ; but it is latent in almost every type of disease-condition which one cares to examine. Then there are the lesser and more immediate effects of constipation, such as listlessness, lack of concentration, persistent headaches, etc., etc.

All the evils connected with constipation arise out of what we call *auto-intoxication*. The sufferer from constipation always retains in his bowel an unusually large accumulation of faecal matter, and it is the reabsorption of the toxins generated in the bowel by the continued presence and putrefaction of this same faecal matter—which in the ordinary course of events Nature would never have allowed to remain there—which sets up the auto-intoxication referred to.

What causes constipation in the first place ? The answer to this is twofold : (1) a dietary consisting of denatured and refined foods ; (2) nerve enervation resulting from nerve strain, overwork, excesses of all kinds, lack of proper physical exercise, and all other habits and practices which lower the tone of the system. In other words, the cause of constipation is *wrong feeding* aided by *general wrong living !*

In their natural state all foods contain a fairly large percentage of " roughage," or so-called waste matter—waste matter in the sense that the body makes no use of it in the passage of the food through the digestive tract, and eliminates it through the bowel after the nutrient elements of the food have been absorbed. Now, this roughage is most essential in preserving the natural balance of foods, and also in helping on *peristalsis* (the natural rhythmic action by means of which food is passed down the alimentary canal). It will thus be seen that this roughage—this *indigestible* portion of all food—indigestible in the sense that it is not absorbed—is essential to the proper functioning of the system, and especially to the business of the intestines in their work of digestion and elimination.

It is because so very much of the food we eat to-day is deprived of its roughage before eating that constipation is the curse we know it to be amongst civilised races the world over ! Not among primitive

or savage races, mark you ! Savage man does not suffer from constipation. His food is not deprived of its natural roughage before eating !
Constipation is one of the many " blessings " conferred upon man
by the ever-onward march of " Civilisation " and " Progress."

The usual white-bread, cooked-meat, and boiled-vegetable dietary
of to-day is very deficient in natural bulk (roughage). The bran and
rougher portions of the wheat berry are all removed in the milling of
white flour ; the skins of vegetables and fruits are invariably removed
before cooking, and the said foods yet further devitalised by the cooking
process ; meat or other flesh foods that have been boned and bled
and then prepared for the table are likewise in a very " unbalanced "
and therefore unnatural state ; and so we can go on right through the
whole list of foods used in the dietary of the average individual of
to-day. They are all unbalanced ; they are all unnaturally *concentrated*
because of the absence of the natural elements which modern food-
refining and obsolete cooking methods have destroyed or removed from
them. Where natural balanced foods such as raw fruit and raw vegetables *are* eaten, the quantity is so small in comparison to the rest
as to be quite negligible.

Not only is a diet of the usual kind unbalanced and concentrated,
and thus heading straight for constipation because of the absence of
natural roughage and bulk ; it is a diet which makes for *overeating*
too. Because when foods are consumed in their natural state, and
the roughage included in them, we cannot eat so much of these foods
as we can when they have been subjected to the refining and cooking
process and the roughage and other elements removed. The consequence is we eat far too much of these foods, and overload our systems
with a mass of highly concentrated starchy, sugary, protein, and fatty
food-elements which are not in the least what the system really needs
for its sustenance and repair. When we consider further that these
same refined and cooked foods are also sadly deficient in organic
mineral and vital elements (mineral salts and vitamins), when compared with natural uncooked foods, we can see that the almost certain
possibility of constipation which confronts the individual eating in the
conventional way is far from being the sum-total of the evils likely
to befall him if he persists, year in and year out, with his unnatural
and debased dietary, for such indeed it is.

I have pointed out that the usual refined and cooked food dietary
of to-day makes for overeating, and thus enhances yet further the

inherent constipating quality of the dietary, because of the clogging of the system which goes on. If the individual in question is an outdoor worker or takes plenty of exercise, the evil is not so great ; but where sedentary workers are concerned, the troubles consequent upon living in such a way are surely apparent ? And when overwork, worry, indulgences of all kinds, late hours, etc., etc., come along to complicate matters, is it any wonder that the person so situated should become a victim to chronic disease, of which constipation is the starting-ground and basis ? Living on the wrong food and using up one's nerve force unduly are tantamount to burning the physical candle at both ends, and surely it is small wonder that disease is the reward of such living ? Thus Nature takes her toll for the transgression of her laws governing life and well-being.

Not by the longest stretching of the imagination can the taking of laxatives for constipation be called curative. The bowels are *forced* into action by the methods employed, but the possibility of a return to normal bowel action is rendered more and more remote the longer the purgative habit is persevered with. People so treated go on from bad to worse, and usually end up by becoming so constipated that they often cannot obtain a bowel movement for days on end, even with the daily use of the strongest purgative drugs available. Thus in the long run the remedy proves worse than the disease.

Over the years it has come to be considered quite " natural " for people to take laxatives and purgatives. The habit of " taking something to keep the bowels open " has become almost universal, and is considered in the light of something *healthful,* something making for the future health of the individual. And so, backed by a gigantic Press campaign, and with slogans such as "*Take So-and-so and be* HEALTHY!" proprietary medicine vendors have been enabled to become millionaires by the instillation into the public of a habit, medical in origin and fundamentally pernicious, which assures them that by so doing they are freeing themselves from the evils of constipation and building up " health," whereas, in reality, they are making themselves more and more its slave by such practices !

It is desirable for the reader to understand what the real action of purgative drugs is, and how a bowel action so obtained is in no way comparable with a natural action. When a purgative such as Epsom salts, for instance, is introduced into the intestines, its presence is a constant irritation to the delicate mucous lining of the bowel. The intestines *react against* the salts, and in forcing the salts out of the system a bowel action necessarily takes place. The action is brought about by the expulsion of the salts, which the body regards as foreign matter unsuitable to it. It can thus be seen that the more the purgative habit is presevered with the weaker will the intestines become, by having continually to *flog themselves into action* to throw off the drugs daily thrust upon them by an unsuspecting owner, who has been led to imagine that by so doing he is bringing " health " to his system.

The more purgative drugs are used, the weaker do the intestines become, and the more sluggish is their action in consequence. This means that stronger and stronger drugs have to be resorted to, to obtain a movement. Thus does the initial constipation become more and more serious by the habitual use of such " aids " to bowel action. Whether the purgatives used are mineral or vegetable in origin does not matter in the least. The bowel action they produce is merely one of *reaction against them* all the time, with further weakening of bowel action as a direct consequence. Salts or senna, cascara or calomel, liquorice or jalap, they are all in the same class as purgative drugs, albeit some are less forceful—and therefore less harmful—than others. It is merely a question of degree.

Treatment.—Having shown that the drug treatment for constipation is likely to produce the most harmful results in the long run, by virtue of the deleterious effect upon the bowel produced by the incessant necessity of having to expel the bowel-content in an effort to get rid of the drug employed, let us now turn to the natural treatment for the condition. The natural treatment for constipation *really* cures the condition, for it sets out to remove the causes responsible for the trouble in the first place, and not just to flog an unwilling bowel into action. To see people who have been constipated for years getting two and even three quite natural movements daily is no new thing to the practitioner of natural methods of treatment. Such results are not extiaordinary or miraculous ; they are merely the logical outcome of a scheme of treatment designed to overcome (or get rid of) the root causes of the trouble, and so set the bowels working naturally once more of their own accord—something which they have been wanting to do all the time, but which they have been prevented from doing by the unwise feeding habits and general wrong habits of living of their owner.

To begin the treatment, the whole digestive tract must be given a complete rest for a few days, and the intestines thoroughly cleansed ; and for this purpose the *all-fruit diet* outlined in the Appendix is most useful, as it gives the stomach a rest from hard digestive work and at the same time gives the whole intestinal tract that thorough scouring which it so very much needs. In all ordinary cases of constipation, say seven to ten days on the *all-fruit diet* would be the best way to begin the treatment. (In long-standing and stubborn cases it would be best to have a *short fast* for, say, four or five days, and to follow this with ten to fourteen days on the *restricted diet* outlined in the Appendix, instead of going on to all-fruit.) Then, in either case, the *full weekly diet*, also outlined in detail in the Appendix, can be begun, and should be adhered to as strictly as possible thereafter.

In some cases further short periods on fruit, or further short fasts followed by a period on the restricted diet, may be required at intervals of a month or two. This must be left to the patient to decide for himself, according to the progress being made in the meantime. Obviously, those who have been taking strong purgative drugs for many years will take longer to put right than others.

A most essential feature of the treatment is the use of the warm-water enema or gravity douche. The enema or douche is *not* a cure for constipation. It is used merely for the time being to cleanse the bowels of faecal matter. It is the simplest and safest means known to the Natural-Cure practitioner of securing this desired result. That is why it is employed. Some people imagine from the great use made of the enema in natural treatment that it is regarded, if not as a " cure " for constipation, at least as a method of cleansing the bowels which can be continued without harm almost indefinitely. This conclusion is erroneous. Besides not being able to *cure* constipation, the *protracted* use of the enema produces enervation of the bowel, and is therefore definitely harmful. In short, used *judiciously*, the enema is a most useful appliance ; used *injudiciously*, it is not !

With these few preliminary remarks concerning the use and misuse of the enema, we can now go on to the part it should play in the natural treatment for constipation. From the time the treatment is begun, the enema should be used *nightly* for the first week to cleanse the bowels, and then *every other night* thereafter until at least one natural movement is being obtained daily. It should then be at once discontinued, and never used again unless, for some reason or other, constipation should return at any future time. It should always be resorted to on those occasions. IN NO CIRCUMSTANCES SHOULD PURGATIVES OR LAXATIVES OF ANY KIND BE TAKEN IN FUTURE.

In persons with long-standing constipation the muscles which control bowel action have become so atrophied through long neglect and misuse that they will require some little additional treatment to make them work. That is why all those undertaking the treatment for constipation should carry out the following little " rite," or custom, and continue with it for several months to come—until, in fact, they are assured of two really good bowel movements daily, which is the goal aimed at.

The custom, or " rite," is as follows : Every day at 9 a.m. and, say, 7 p.m. the patient should attend stool, and an attempt should be made to evacuate the bowels. The patient should not force too hard, but a certain amount of gentle pressure should be exerted so as to " coax " the muscles controlling bowel action into operation. Of course a movement of the bowels will not take place every time (or any time perhaps for the first two weeks or so), but that does not matter. The twice-daily attendance at stool will bring about the desired results in time, providing always, of course, that the full scheme of treatment here outlined is being carried out faithfully at the same time.

In addition to correct diet, there is also need of other measures to tone up the system and build up its muscular power. For this purpose the daily dry friction and sitz-bath or sponge, and the scheme of physical and other exercises outlined in the Appendix, should be gone through religiously every morning. A good walk, of several miles daily, is also a most necessary adjunct to the treatment, where it can possibly be managed. A hot Epsom-salts bath, as detailed in the Appendix, should be taken once or twice weekly for the next few months. This will prove most beneficial. Regular habits of living, early hours, etc., are essential factors to the success of the treatment. *Future strict attention to diet is absolutely indispensable,* and all that has been said to the sufferer from *catarrh* on this point, in the preceding section, should be carefully noted and taken to heart.

SPECIAL NOTE.—Those who do not know how to use the enema will find full details in the Appendix at the end of this book.

Diarrhœa.—Diarrhœa is one of Nature's eliminative actions. It is a simple case of the throwing off of unwanted material by the intestines in the quickest possible manner. Whatever the cause of diarrhœa—usually dietetic errors—it is the worst thing possible to " take something " to stop it. What we have to do is to *aid* Nature in her eliminative attempt, not thwart her by stopping the action of the bowels.

Treatment.—When diarrhœa is present, the patient should be kept in bed and the warm-water enema used to cleanse the bowels. No food or drink (except water) should be given until the diarrhœa has quite ceased, and then only fresh fruit should be given for the following day. The enema should be used as needed for the day or two following the attack. Rest in bed, abstention from food, and the use of the enema are the three essential requisites for the curing of diarrhœa. It will pass off in the quickest possible time if such treatment is employed. (Where diarrhœa is part of the development of a fever or other complaint, the disease in question should be dealt with along the lines laid down in the present book.)

Dilatation of the Stomach.—Dilatation of the stomach is caused through the continual overloading of the stomach with food and drink. The stomach begins to swell in size and lose its power of digesting food, and constant fermentation and eructation of gas are the consequences, aided by chronic constipation. To attempt to treat the condition by means of medicines designed to " aid " digestion is just useless. Such treatment does nothing to get rid of the wrong feeding habits responsible for the cause of the condition in the first place, and it yet further weakens a stomach already hardly able to carry on its work, because of the ultimately irritating and lowering effect upon the delicate stomach lining of the drugs employed. (See treatment for *Chronic Indigestion*, page 294, for the effects of drugs in the treatment of stomach ailments.)

Treatment.—The only effective treatment for dilatation of the stomach is twofold : (1) that which aims at cleansing the stomach and intestines, and introducing more sensible feeding habits ; (2) that which helps to tone up the internal musculature of the body, and so helps the stomach to return to its normal powers and functional ability. For the correct treatment for dilatation of the stomach the reader is referred to that for *Dropped Stomach* to follow, which is on exactly the same lines.

Dropped Stomach.—When dilatation has progressed far enough, the stomach is forced out of its natural position and drops lower and lower down into the abdominal cavity, causing more and more disturbance to the organs and structures around it, the first structures to suffer being the intestines. Thus, in addition to pain and discomfort, chronic constipation is one of the foremost features connected with dropped stomach, and there is also persistent fermentation and gas eructation to affect the sufferer because of the inability of the stomach to carry on its work of digestion properly.

To advise the taking of medicines to " tone up " the stomach and increase its digestive powers is just a waste of time. Nothing definite is gained in this way. Indeed, the stomach lining is permanently weakened by the irritating effect of the drugs used. (See treatment for *Chronic Indigestion*, page 294, for notes on the effect of drugs in stomach ailments.) Neither is the advice usually given by the medical profession to eat small but frequent meals any good either. This only serves to make the chronic indigestion more pronounced, for before one meal is fairly digested, the stomach is called upon to deal with another, and so on. The wearing of surgical belts is sometimes a help in extreme cases, but there is nothing to be gained from their wear from a curative point of view. Most people find them most uncomfortable, and would rather not wear them than have to put up with them continually.

Treatment.—As indicated in the treatment for *Dilatation of the Stomach*, the cure for dropped stomach and dilatation is twofold. The whole digestive and intestinal tract must be cleansed, and proper feeding habits introduced, and the stomach must be brought back to proper shape, position, and power by the introduction of a system of exercises which will build up the internal musculature of the body. Many seemingly hopeless cases of dropped stomach and dilatation have been cured in this way.

To begin the treatment, the sufferer should go on to an *exclusive fresh-fruit diet* for from five to seven or ten days, as detailed in the

Appendix. (If the sufferer is very much affected by constant eructation of gas, it would be wise to *precede* the all-fruit period with a day or two on water only—a glass of hot water every two hours throughout the day.) Really serious and long-standing cases should begin with a fast for four or five days, and follow it with ten to fourteen days on the *restricted diet* outlined in the Appendix.

After the period on all-fruit (or the fast and restricted diet as the case may be), the *full weekly dietary* given in the Appendix should be begun and adhered to as strictly as possible thereafter. Further short periods on all-fruit, at monthly intervals (say two or three days each time), or further fasts and periods on the restricted diet at two- or three-monthly intervals, may be required in certain cases. This the patient must decide for himself, according to the progress being made.

From the time the treatment is begun, the bowels should be cleansed nightly with a warm-water enema or gravity douche, and the rules for the eradication of *constipation* given in the preceding pages of the present section should be put into operation forthwith. The dry friction and sponge or sitz-bath and the breathing and other exercises given in the Appendix should be gone through daily, and a hot Epsom-salts bath taken every week. Rupture is primarily due to a weakening of the internal musculature of the abdomen—that internal musculature which keeps the abdominal organs and structures in position—and so the natural treatment for this, by means of properly graded exercises, is the ideal thing for the sufferer from dropped stomach too.

The patient should take things very easily and quietly for the time being, and no medicines of any kind should be taken in future. A most useful thing is to rest for, say, half an hour, two or three times during the day, with the legs raised higher than the rest of the body. For this purpose the patient lies on a couch with the legs raised about eighteen inches by placing cushions under them. Or else he can sit on one chair with the legs placed on a chair facing, if the former is impracticable. An occasional day or half-day's rest in bed, in the foregoing position, is most helpful in all cases of dropped or dilated stomach.

The diet factor is most important, and the dietetic rules consistently emphasised in the present book should be carefully followed. Eating and drinking together at meals should never be permitted. Drinks should be taken from an hour to half an hour before a meal is due.

Duodenal Ulcer.—When food is taken into the stomach, it is acted upon by the gastric juices and is then passed into the small intestine for further digestion. By the time the bile, from the liver, and the pancreatic and intestinal juices have been added, the gastric juices are no longer of the same strongly acid character as before, and so their corrosive action is checked. It is because only the stomach and the first portion of the small intestine, or duodenum, are subject to the direct action of the gastric juices, and not the rest of the alimentary canal, that these parts are peculiarly subject to the formation of ulcers, known as *gastric ulcers* and *duodenal ulcers* respectively.

It is not the strongly acid or corrosive quality of the gastric juices as such which is responsible for the formation of the ulcers in question, otherwise everyone would have ulcers of this nature constantly forming. It is only those who have persistently misused their stomachs over a period of years, and so lowered the tone of the protective stomach and duodenal lining, who find themselves the victims to such ulcers. As gastric ulcers and duodenal ulcers are exactly the same as regards genesis, development, and treatment, the whole question will be found discussed in full under the heading of *Gastric Ulcer* farther on in the present section (page 287). The sufferer from duodenal ulcer is therefore referred to *Gastric Ulcer* for an understanding of its causation and the effective natural treatment for his case.

Dysentery.—Dysentery is a rather serious condition affecting the large intestine, and is to be met with in hot seasons or tropical climates. Fever, accompanied by ulceration and inflammation of the bowel, is the chief characteristic of the complaint, together with the passing of blood, mucus, etc., from the bowel. The condition is a most distressing one, and if left in medical hands is always likely to recur, or lead to complications connected with the bowel and digestive tract generally.

The cause of dysentery according to orthodox medical views is *germ infection*, but this is only another instance of the cart being put before the horse in medical reasoning. The germs which are *supposed* to be the cause of dysentery only develop in the colon as a result of the putrefaction there of excessive quantities of animal protein food, and it is to the eating of excessive amounts of flesh food in hot weather or tropical climates unsuited for the digestion of such food that we must look for the cause of dysentery, *not to germs* ! The Englishman who goes out to India, say, and eats meat three times a day in a sweltering climate, is asking for trouble, especially if he suffers from habitual constipation. The food is not evacuated from the intestines as quickly as it should be ; it putrefies there ; and bowel trouble of some kind is the result. If the condition is really serious, then dysentery may set in.

Treatment.—To treat dysentery by means of drugs or injections is not in the least going to get rid of the trouble in the way Nature desires. Such treatment only renders chronic bowel trouble almost inevitable. The only sane regimen for dysentery is *fasting*. The sufferer should fast as long as the acute symptoms are present, having the bowels cleansed twice daily with the warm-water enema. (During the fasting period fruit juices and water are the only things to be taken.) The fast should be continued for a day or two longer than absolutely needed—it is always best to carry on longer rather than less than is necessary—and then the *all-fruit diet* mentioned in the Appendix can be adopted for a few days, after which the *full weekly dietary* mentioned therein can be gradually embarked upon.

When the sufferer has reached the convalescent stage, he can then carry on, as regards general treatment, as indicated in the treatment for *Colitis*, earlier in the present section (page 270).

Flesh foods of all kinds should be avoided as far as possible in the future, the dairy products, such as eggs, cheese, and milk, being far safer to eat in every way. The best protein food for hot climates is nuts. Alcohol in all its forms should be strictly avoided, and especially should no quinine be taken in future. Correct feeding, and not dosing with quinine, is the sure preventive of tropical diseases. Quinine upsets the action of the whole system, and is a most pernicious drug, affecting as it does the working of the heart, liver, and the aural apparatus. (For further remarks *re* quinine see section on *Fevers*, with special reference to *Malaria*, page 417.)

SPECIAL NOTE.—If salads are difficult to obtain in certain countries, then *fresh ripe fruit* should form the major proportion of the daily dietary.

Dyspepsia.—This is a form of nervous indigestion very much to be met with in all civilised countries these days. Wrong feeding and unwise habits of living are its two main causes. For the stomach to digest food properly, it must be supplied with sufficient nerve force to carry out its task. People who are of the worrying type, or who are " always in a hurry," or are run-down or nervy, or overworked, etc. (those, too, who indulge in excesses of all kinds) are either always depleting their system unduly of nerve force or else are not able to generate sufficient of such force for the body's necessary tasks. The result is that the efficiency of the whole system suffers, and especially the efficiency of the stomach. If the food habitually eaten is badly combined and deficient in proper natural balance, is it any wonder that such people develop dyspepsia sooner or later in life ?

To try to rectify such a condition by the administration of various kinds of drugs is sheer futility ; the only therapeutic measures which will set the trouble right are : correct diet and a rectification of the wrong habits of living involved. The nervous system must be given a chance to recuperate and build up its powers afresh, and a régime of feeding must be instituted which will effectually prevent the stomach being overtaxed by the introduction of badly combined foods and incompatible food mixtures. Once the dyspeptic can see this point clearly (and surely it is clear enough !), then the rest is more or less easy. I say advisedly *more or less* easy, for although in the present book a proper system of diet, exercise, etc., has been outlined for the dyspeptic which will build up his system afresh and tone up and recondition his digestive organs, the rest remains with himself *all the time.* It is *he* who must set about rectifying his wrong habits of living—his late hours, his inordinate tea or coffee drinking or smoking, his habit of worrying over every little thing, etc., etc. ; *no one else can do it for him !* But he can rest assured that if he will only take himself in hand in this way, and organise his life upon the lines of more rational living, the results in terms of better health will repay him over and over again for the effort required.

Treatment.—With the above remarks in mind, the dyspeptic can turn to the treatment for *Chronic Indigestion* given in the following pages of the present section (page 297), and follow out the treatment outlined therein, with every confidence as to its ultimate success, not only as regards the overcoming of his stomach trouble, but also the healthy reorganisation of his whole system generally. The treatment for *Neurasthenia* in the section on *Diseases of the Nervous System* (Section 5, page 192) should also be studied carefully by the sufferer from dyspepsia. He will find a great deal of help there.

Enteric Fever.—See section on *Fevers* (Section 13, page 404).

Fissure of Anus.—This is a fissure or crack in the mucous lining covering the muscle situated at the end of the bowel, which is concerned in the work of emptying the bowel content. It is a most painful affliction, and is the outcome of persistent straining at stool, as a result of chronic constipation and the purgative habit. Often hæmorrhoids (or piles) are present at the same time, as a result of the same causes, and this makes the condition relatively worse so far as pain and discomfort are concerned.

Treatment.—Obviously the only sure way to cure the fissure, and prevent the occurrence of further trouble of the same kind, is to get rid of the chronic constipation which is at the root of the whole matter. No amount of palliative treatment by means of drugs can achieve this end ; nor can surgical operation succeed in so doing, however much it may relieve matters at the time. The sufferer from fissure is referred to the treatment for *Fistula*, given in the following pages, for the only sane and natural method of curing his condition. Not only will the fissure be cured in time by such treatment, but the underlying chronic constipation too ; without the overcoming of which, a return of trouble of a similar kind would be almost inevitable. (Read also the remarks on the purgative habit in the treatment for *Constipation*, page 275.)

Fistula.—Fistula is an abscess upon the rectum, and, like a fissure, is a most painful affliction. Its cause is chronic constipation in every case, the poisons from putrefactive bowel material being retained over-long in the bowel, and forming into the abscess in question. Treatment for the condition by means of operation—which is the usual one favoured in medical circles—does nothing to get rid of the underlying constipation which was the cause of the fistula in the first place, and so does nothing to prevent the occurrence of further bowel trouble later on—something which is more or less certain to occur.

Treatment.—The only sane and logical treatment for fistula is by natural methods, which will get rid of the underlying constipation and remove the excess toxic matter thus constantly being formed. Such natural treatment may take longer to achieve results than spectacular medical methods, but once achieved, these results are far more certain and lasting in every way. The way to begin the treatment is as follows :

Commence with a fast for from four to seven days, according to the severity of the case. The fast should then be followed by seven to fourteen days on the *restricted diet* outlined in the Appendix. After the fast and restricted diet, the *full weekly dietary* given in the Appendix can be begun. A further fast and period on the restricted diet may be necessary in some cases, a month or so after the first period of fasting and restricted dieting has been completed, and perhaps yet a third period still later. (This can be left to the patient to decide, according to the progress being made.)

From the time the treatment is begun, the warm-water enema should be used nightly to cleanse the bowels, and the rules for the eradication of *Constipation* given under that heading in the present section (page 275) should be put into operation forthwith. The daily dry friction and sitz-bath should also form a regular feature of the treatment (see Appendix), as also the scheme of physical and other exercises outlined therein.

A hot Epsom-salts bath should be taken three times weekly for the first month, and twice weekly thereafter ; and a hot and cold sitz-bath should be taken every night (for the time being), except on those nights on which an Epsom-salts bath is being taken. (Details of the Epsom-salts bath and hot and cold sitz-bath will be found in the Appendix.)

The affected part should also be bathed several times daily with hot and cold fomentations. A piece of linen material is wrung out in hot water and applied for two or three minutes, then a second and later a third for the same length of time ; after which a cold application is applied. Always work in this order, viz. three hot, one cold application.

Spinal manipulation—if at all procurable—is of assistance in these cases ; but such auxiliary treatment, although most helpful, is by no means essential. The main scheme of treatment advised above will achieve all the results required in time, with perseverance.

Future attention to diet is most essential. Tea, coffee, alcohol, and all condiments, etc., must be avoided. Meat and other flesh foods should be left out of the future dietary *as far as possible*, and their place taken by the dairy products, eggs, cheese, and milk. Fruits and salads *must* form the bulk of the future dietary.

Flatulence.—Although a certain amount of flatulence is possible to everyone, serious or persistent flatulence is a sign of disturbed digestion, and is due to the habitual eating of unwise food mixtures and combinations. By means of the gases thus thrown off, Nature strives to rid the system of the fermenting elements which are interfering with proper digestion. The taking of bicarbonate of soda or other medicinal preparations, for purposes of securing relief, is not the way to cure the trouble, but to make it chronic. Such methods only relieve effects at best ; they never get rid of *causes*.

For the natural treatment of flatulence, which is a usual accompaniment to *chronic indigestion*, the reader is referred to the treatment for that condition in the following pages of the present section.

Gastric Catarrh.—Gastric catarrh is essentially a form of disease due to wrong feeding. Through habitual eating of excessive amounts of food materials, aided by the consumption of equally excessive quantities of liquids, the mucous lining of the stomach becomes affected in tone and its normal action is interfered with. When strong tea, coffee, alcohol, strong condiments, sauces, pickles, etc., etc., form a regular feature of the dietary, the mucous lining begins to become seriously irritated, and to protect itself it throws off excessive quantities of mucous, which interfere yet further with normal digestion, and in this way catarrh of the stomach arises.

Although catarrh of the stomach may be allied in the same individual with catarrh of the nose and throat, it is not the outcome of the dropping of mucus from the nose and throat into the stomach as many believe. The point is that wrong feeding habits which will set up nasal catarrh can also set up gastric catarrh in the same person.

Treatment.—The taking of medicinal drugs for the relief of the condition, whilst at the same time carrying on with the same unwise feeding habits which have set up the trouble in the first place, is obviously not the way to secure a permanent cure. The only real remedy for gastric catarrh lies in a thorough cleansing of the whole digestive tract and the adoption of a scheme of diet which will allow the stomach lining to normalise itself, instead of becoming more and more irritated. For such a scheme of treatment the reader is referred to that for *Chronic Indigestion*, to be found in the following pages of the present section (page 297). If such treatment is followed consistently, not only will the stomach trouble be cured, but the whole general health will be greatly enhanced.

Gastric Ulcer.—The only foods which are really digested in the stomach are protein foods, i.e. meat, fish, cheese, eggs, nuts, milk, etc. Starches and fats are not affected by the gastric juices, and have to pass through into the intestines for final digestion. (The digestion of starchy foods is really begun in the mouth, through impregnation with the saliva, but their final digestion is completed in the intestines.) When the stomach is continually overloaded with a mass of demineralised starchy foods in the shape of white bread, boiled, mashed, or fried potatoes, refined cereals of all kinds, puddings, pies, etc., etc., this starchy mass has to wait behind until the protein portions of the meal—the meat, fish, eggs, etc.—have been digested, to be itself enabled to pass into the intestines for final digestion. The result is that where there is constant bodily stagnation through sedentary work, lack of exercise, etc., fermentation and souring readily occur in the stomach, because of the presence of all this stagnant mass of undigested starchy food lying by whilst the proteins are being acted upon by the gastric juices, and acids of fermentation of various kinds are constantly formed. (The more hastily these same starchy foods are eaten, the more readily does fermentation occur, because they will have had little or no time to be acted upon by the saliva when in the mouth—a process most necessary to thorough starch digestion.)

When we realise that sugary foods (especially the demineralised kind, such as white sugar, jams, etc.), although more or less directly absorbed into the blood-stream when taken into the stomach, yet further intensify the fermenting and souring propensities of starches when present in conjunction with proteins (as also do condiments, sauces, pickles, etc.), we can begin to see something of the reason why stomach troubles in general, and ulcers of the stomach in particular, occur so frequently in these days of indiscriminate feeding.

The acids which form during the fermentation and souring of starchy and sugary foods in the stomach have a most detrimental effect upon the delicate stomach lining (as also do condiments, sauces, strong seasonings, etc.), especially in the case of those whose general health-level is very much below par, as a result of general wrong living and other factors. And these acids of fermentation, together with the gastric juices—which are intensely acid in reaction—sometimes succeed in eating right through the surface layer of this protective stomach lining, and thus begin the formation of a stomach ulcer. Once the ulcer is started in this way, all food of starchy and sugary origin—to say nothing of highly spiced foods, seasonings, etc.—only serve to aggravate the trouble, and, if not checked in time, the ulcer succeeds sometimes in boring right through the stomach walls into the peritoneum, in which case serious complications occur.

The chief symptoms of ulcers of the stomach are intense pain, vomiting, and occasional hæmorrhage. The pain is the most consistent symptom, and may come on from half an hour to two hours after eating. Those with duodenal ulcers experience exactly the same symptoms, only in their case the pain is felt a little to the right of, and above, the navel, instead of in the stomach itself.

Treatment.—If gastric and duodenal ulcers are treated surgically, the fundamental cause of the trouble—the wrong feeding habits of the individual—are left entirely unaffected, whilst the already defective stomach tone is rendered yet more defective by the operation. And so the appearance of further ulcers, or even more serious stomach trouble of other kinds, is definitely encouraged rather than checked by such treatment. Merely to cut out the ulcer and " leave it at that " can hardly be called *curative* treatment.

In many cases, nowadays, treatment by means of special diet is being tried in medical circles for the overcoming of gastric and duodenal ulcers ; but as the treatment also includes the regular taking of alkaline powders to neutralise the excessive acidity present, such treatment is hardly likely to lead to good results in the long run, however efficacious it may appear to be temporarily. What we have to do is to *get rid of* the underlying acidity altogether, not neutralise its effects by introducing alkaline chemicals into the stomach. Then again, these alkaline powders prevent the digestion of protein foods from taking place in the normal manner, because all protein food, such as eggs, meat, fish, etc., needs an *acid* medium for its digestion, and the alkaline powders make the stomach content predominantly alkaline ; and further, the continual taking of alkaline powders or alkaline medicines leaves a growing residue of chemical salts in the system, which has a most deleterious effect upon the kidneys after a time.

Again, the diet prescribed by medical advisers for patients with gastric or duodenal ulcer is the reverse of that which would be prescribed under natural treatment. This usually consists of eggs, milk, white bread, fish, milk puddings, etc., and leaves out entirely fruits, green vegetables, etc. The result of living on such " invalid's " fare—plus thrice-daily doses of alkaline powders—is that even if the ulcer *is* cured by such treatment (an extremely doubtful premise), the unfortunate patient invariably begins to find himself suffering from constipation and allied ailments because of the clogging nature of the dietary advised.

If the sufferer from gastric or duodenal ulcer cannot enter a Nature Cure establishment for treatment or obtain the personal services of a Naturopath, he should carry on at home as follows :

Begin with *a fast* for from three to five days, as outlined in the Appendix, and then go on to the *full milk diet* outlined therein for a further two to four weeks, as found to be necessary. Rest as much as possible the while. Thereafter adopt the *full weekly dietary* as indicated, but substituting stewed fruit for fresh fruit, at first, and steamed vegetables or vegetable broth for salads, until able to deal all right with these raw foods. These can then be gradually introduced into the dietary as digestive powers improve. Further fasts and periods on the milk diet may be necessary, at intervals of two to three months, according to the severity of the case. Patients must use their discretion here, of course.

During the first week of the treatment the bowels should be cleansed nightly with a warm-water enema or gravity douche, and every other night thereafter as necessary ; and where constipation is habitual, the rules for its eradication given earlier in this section should be put into operation forthwith. The daily dry friction and sitz-bath or sponge and the breathing and other exercises given in the Appendix should form a regular feature of the morning routine, and a hot Epsom-salts bath should be taken twice weekly for, say, two months or so, and once weekly thereafter.

Fresh air and outdoor exercise are two essentials to the treatment which must not be overlooked, but exercise should be graduated according to how the patient is feeling under the treatment. (As he feels himself getting better, so he can do more and more, etc.) *No medicines or powders of any kind are to be taken.* Correct diet is a most essential factor *after*, as well as *during*, treatment, and no white bread, sugar, white-flour products, refined cereals, boiled or mashed or fried potatoes, puddings or pies, or such-like food should be eaten in future ; no condiments, pickles, sauces, vinegar, etc. ; no strong tea or coffee ; no alcoholic beverages. (No tinned or preserved foods either.) Meat and other flesh foods must be eaten very sparingly indeed, in accordance with the weekly diet-sheet. Sweets or confectionery of any kind are strictly taboo.

Spinal manipulation, where procurable, is highly recommended in all cases of gastric and duodenal ulcer.

Gastritis (Acute).—Acute gastritis—or acute inflammation of the stomach—may arise from a number of causes, but indiscretions with regard to diet are always the main predisposing factors in its appearance. The habitual eating of too much food or of badly combined or badly prepared food, the drinking of excessive quantities of strong tea and coffee or alcoholic liquors, the habitual use of large quantities of condiments, sauces, etc., etc., are all to be counted as decisive factors making for the appearance of an attack of gastritis. The onset of the condition simply means that the stomach has had far more to put up with than it can bear, for some considerable time past, and has at last " thrown up the sponge " temporarily and " gone on strike " in protest against the foolish and indiscriminate manner in which it has been fed and treated.

Treatment.—When an attack of acute gastritis develops, there is pain and fullness in the stomach, with vomiting of partly digested food, mucus, etc. ; also headache, fever, and diarrhœa, followed by constipation. All this denotes a complete upheaval of the digestive system, and what is needed is obviously a *fast*. To attempt to treat the condition by means of medicines is just a waste of time where a real cure is concerned, for such treatment, even if it succeeds in putting the patient right for the time being, can never get rid of the underlying stomach weakness which was responsible for the setting up of the condition in the first place. And if the patient persists in his usual wanton food habits, then further attacks of gastritis are bound to occur from time to time, with every possibility of the condition becoming chronic.

The sufferer from acute gastritis should fast for as long as the acute symptoms of his trouble last, having just warm water to drink. The fast may have to proceed for from one to four days or more, according to the severity or otherwise of the condition. When things have begun to normalise themselves again, and the patient feels like eating, the *all-fruit diet* given in the Appendix can be adopted for a further two or three days, after which time the *full weekly dietary* also given therein can be gradually embarked upon.

From the time the treatment is begun, the bowels should be cleansed nightly for at least a week ; and where constipation is habitual, the rules for its eradication given in the present section should be put into operation as soon as practicable. The daily dry friction and sitz-bath or sponge and the breathing and other exercises given in the Appendix should form a regular feature of the morning routine, once convalescence has been reached ; and a hot Epsom-salts bath should be taken once or twice a week regularly from then on.

If further attacks of gastritis are to be prevented, the general dietetic advice given in the present book should be taken seriously to heart. No condiments, pickles, sauces, vinegar, strong tea or coffee, or alcoholic liquors should be taken in future ; also no sweets or confectionery of any kind should be eaten, and no pastries, rich cakes, etc. *Lastly, and most particularly of all* : No MEDICINES OF ANY KIND, OR PILLS, POWDERS, ETC., SHOULD EVER BE TAKEN ON ANY ACCOUNT. (See treatment for *Chronic Indigestion*, page 297, for notes on the effects of drugs upon the stomach and system generally.)

Gastritis (Chronic).—If repeated attacks of acute gastritis or indigestion are treated by medicines in the usual way, and the unwise feeding habits which are responsible for the setting up of the trouble are allowed to go unchecked (see remarks on this point in treatment for *Acute Gastritis* just previous), then chronic gastritis will appear in time. This is a condition in which the stomach lining is in a constant state of irritation and inflammation, and no amount of drug treatment is going to put it right, for two reasons : firstly, because the food and feeding habits of the sufferer are such as further to irritate and inflame the delicate stomach lining all the time ; and secondly, because the drugs used to " cure " the condition only succeed at best in masking and palliating symptoms, at the cost of further injuring and debilitating the stomach lining itself, because of the deleterious chemical substances contained in the medicines, powders, etc., used to " regulate " or " soothe " stomach activity.

Treatment.—It must be obvious to the sufferer from chronic gastritis who looks at the matter from an intelligent angle, that his trouble can only be overcome by first giving his digestive system a thorough cleansing, and then adopting a scheme of feeding which will adequately nourish his system, whilst at the same time allowing the stomach to recondition itself. Such a scheme of treatment will be found under the heading of *Chronic Indigestion*, farther on in the present section, and to that the sufferer from chronic gastritis is advised to turn for effective treatment for his case.

Hæmorrhoids (Piles).—This is a condition in which the veins of the rectum become dilated (or varicose) as a result of constant straining at stool, following on constipation and the purgative habit. In some cases the veins burst and what is known as " bleeding piles " results. Treatment for hæmorrhoids along orthodox medical lines consists in operation or injection treatment. In either case the underlying cause of the condition is not in the least affected by such treatment, so that further trouble of the same kind may be expected to occur again at any time, whilst habitual constipation becomes more stubborn.

Treatment.—For the effective treatment for hæmorrhoids, or piles the sufferer is referred to the treatment for *Constipation* earlier in the present section (page 275). As constipation and consequent straining at stool are the cause of the trouble, it must surely be obvious that only by rectifying this condition can piles be effectively overcome.

As regards local measures, the best thing is to inject the juice of a lemon in a pint of cold water into the rectum every day (and leave in for ten minutes) whilst the piles are irritating (not afterwards), and to have a cold sitz-bath every morning with the daily dry friction bath. In severer cases the hot and cold sitz-bath, outlined in the Appendix, can be taken nightly for the time being. No ointments or salves of any kind should be used, but if the piles need soothing at any time, *cold-water compresses* are the best thing for this.

Heartburn.—This is a condition associated with indigestion, and is due to excessive acidity of the stomach. (See *Hyperacidity*, below). For the effective treatment for heartburn see treatment for *Chronic Indigestion* farther on in the present section.

Hyperacidity.—This is a condition which arises in the stomach purely as a result of the habitual eating of excessive quantities of refined starchy and sugary foods, and has nothing whatever to do with the excessive secretion of hydrochloric acid by the glands of the stomach, as the medical profession believes. When such excessive quantities of starchy and sugary foods are eaten—as they always are —in conjunction with protein foods (meat, fish, eggs, cheese, etc.), the proteins are digested first, whilst the starchy food (the bread, porridge, pastry, puddings, etc., etc.) is left to ferment and acidify in the stomach before passing on into the intestines for digestion. It is out of this condition that hyperacidity arises, and it is made much worse by the presence in the stomach at the same time of sugar and sugary foods. (See remarks at the beginning of the treatment for *Gastric Ulcer*, page 288, for a full explanation of this.)

From the above it must be obvious that to try to cure hyperacidity by taking alkaline medicines or powders is a completely fallacious procedure. Such treatment can only palliate matters at best, because so long as the wrong feeding habits responsible for the setting up of the trouble go on, so will the excessive acidity continue to make itself felt. Besides, the habitual taking of such " remedies " as above mentioned seriously interferes with proper digestion (as will be explained in the treatment for *Chronic Indigestion*) ; and further, the chemical residue they leave behind in the system has a most deleterious effect upon the kidneys in time, to which organs such residue is carried eventually for final elimination.

Treatment.—For the effective treatment for hyperacidity (or acid stomach), which is a condition bound up intimately with indigestion, the sufferer is referred to the treatment for *Chronic Indigestion* to follow.

There is a popular belief that the eating of fruit *increases* acidity of the stomach. This is quite wrong, as a few days on the exclusive fruit diet will soon show. However, the eating of *unripe fruits* or acid fruits *with starches* tends to increase acidity, if there is already a tendency in that direction.

Indigestion (Acute).—Acute indigestion arises from dietetic indiscretions pure and simple, although a run-down condition of the system, nerve strain, worry, etc., can all play their part in precipitating an attack. The eating of too much food, the hasty eating of food, the eating of badly prepared or ill-assorted combinations of food, can all bring on an attack of acute indigestion, especially if the stomach is below par. To attempt to deal with such a condition by taking medicines, etc., is not the way to clear up the trouble satisfactorily, but to render future attacks of indigestion more and more likely to occur. For such treatment pays no attention to the wrong feeding habits which have set up the trouble in the first place, neither does it give the stomach that thorough cleansing which alone can bring it back to normalcy of function and tone.

Treatment.—The only sane and effective treatment for acute indigestion is *fasting*. The sufferer should fast as long as the acute symptoms last—perhaps a day (or even two), perhaps less—and have nothing but *hot water* to drink during the time. When the acute symptoms have subsided, the *all-fruit diet* given in the Appendix can be adopted for a further day, after which the *full weekly diet* outlined therein can be embarked upon. The more closely the said diet is adhered to thereafter, the more certain is it that future attacks of indigestion will be prevented.

The warm-water enema should be used nightly during the fast, and for a day or two afterwards if necessary ; and once the patient has fully recovered, the advice *re* future living and general welfare of the body given· below in the treatment· for *Chronic Indigestion* should be carefully followed. Where the attack is very mild, the missing of a meal or two and the sipping of hot water is all that is required.

Indigestion (Chronic).—Chronic indigestion is the commonest of all the " family ailments " of to-day (constipation perhaps excepted), as the patent-medicine advertisements one sees on every side more than testify. The cause of the trouble is *habitual wrong feeding,* and is aggravated, rather than helped, by the taking of medicinal drugs for the purpose—so-called—of " curing " the condition. When we think of the way people persistently overload their stomachs, day after day, year in and year out, with the most ill-assorted variety of foods, drinks, condiments, etc., it is surely not very surprising that the stomach becomes defective in function in time, as a result of such treatment. The stomach is a wonderful piece of natural mechanism, but it *is* only a piece of mechanism after all, so who can wonder that it should break down more and more completely, as the years advance, under the colossal strain imposed upon it as a result of modern feeding habits ?

Overfeeding and persistent wrong feeding apart, the most potent cause of indigestion is the habitual eating of starchy and protein foods together. If one is in really good health and leading an active outdoor life, the eating of protein and starchy foods together habitually may not cause any inconvenience to the digestive organs; but most people are *not* in really good health, and do *not* lead active outdoor lives, and so the more they get on in years the more are they likely to incur digestive troubles as a direct result of such promiscuous mixing of foods. (Protein foods are meat, fish, eggs, cheese, etc.; starchy foods are bread, potatoes, porridge, pastry, puddings, etc.)

As explained in the treatment for *Gastric Ulcer*, starchy foods are not digested in the stomach at all; their digestion is begun in the mouth and finished in the intestines. Proteins are the only foods digested in the stomach. Thus when starchy and protein foods are habitually eaten together, the starches have to wait in the stomach whilst the protein portion of the meal is dealt with, before being allowed to pass through into the intestines for final digestion. It is from this cause that fermentation and souring of food (with indigestion, eructation of gas, etc.) occurs in the stomach, a condition made worse by the presence of sugar and sugary foods. The eating of acid fruits and starchy foods together also predisposes towards fermentation and indigestion.

The habit of eating and drinking together is another of the causes of indigestion, as when liquids are drunk at the same time as food is eaten it means that the digestive juices will be diluted in strength and their potency diminished accordingly. Then another big factor in the setting up of indigestion is the eating of condiments, pickles, sauces, etc., with meals. Such articles of diet have a most deleterious effect upon the delicate stomach lining, especially pepper, vinegar, and highly spiced and "piquant" flavourings. The free use of table-salt also predisposes towards stomach trouble in after-life, because mineral salt is not a commodity the body can deal with properly (it is vegetable salts from proper natural food that is required), and mineral salt taken to excess becomes a hindrance to stomach functioning in time.

Another factor responsible for much digestive trouble is *eating between meals*, as also is the eating of meals at too frequent intervals. Food requires at least five hours to be completely emptied from the stomach, so that the eating of too frequent meals, or "snacks" between meals, means that the stomach will be called upon to start the digestion process all over again whilst there is still undigested or partly digested food present in it.

We can see therefore that, quite apart from the eating of the wrong kind of food as measured by Natural-Cure standards, it is essentially *the general feeding habits* of the people of modern civilisation which bring in their train the almost certain liability to indigestion which appears as the individual grows up. (Children seem able to deal with all sorts of things in the food line which grown-ups cannot ; but they pay the penalty for such food follies sure enough in later life.) Now, with all this in mind, when we turn to the medical treatment for indigestion and digestive disturbances generally, what do we find ? We find that, with perhaps one rare exception here and there, the vast majority of medical men confine themselves solely to trying to get rid of the superficial symptoms and effects of the trouble by means of medicines, powders, etc., without in the least attempting to rectify the crass feeding habits which are in every case the real cause of the trouble.

How can such treatment be called *curative,* on the face of it ? *It never is !* That is why the medical profession is unable to rid the world of digestive troubles, which troubles are the easiest to rectify, if only the right methods of procedure are adopted for their cure.

Not only does drug treatment fail to cure indigestion and allied ailments, *it succeeds in making these troubles worse in time !* Medical men think that by giving medicines or powders to their patients they can neutralise the excessive acidity set up in the stomach through wrong feeding, or get rid of pain or " wind " or stimulate a sluggish stomach into activity, etc. But such measures are never curative in the real sense, because they never remove causes ; and they only succeed in temporarily removing the effects of the trouble, *if at all,* at the cost of definitely impairing the health of the stomach, and so making permanent the very condition they were employed to " cure," as we shall now see.

For instance, when bicarbonate of soda is habitually taken to relieve the effects of gas in the stomach or to reduce excessive acidity, there is a continual residue of chemical matter left behind in the stomach which definitely impairs stomach action and affects the stomach lining ; further, this chemical residue is carried eventually to the kidneys by the blood-stream, to be finally eliminated from the system. But its presence in the kidneys is a source of constant irritation to these delicate organs, and many cases of kidney disease can be definitely traced, in great part, to the excessive use of bicarbonate of soda or other alkaline powders or drugs for the so-called " curing " of digestive troubles. The same remarks apply to the bismuth medicines and other medicines—patent or otherwise—taken for indigestion.

Another most important fact about the action of drugs in the treatment of indigestion is this : By correcting the excessive acidity which is the main feature of indigestion and allied troubles, the medicines used turn the stomach-content preponderantly alkaline. Now, for protein foods to be digested the stomach must be acid in reaction (as already pointed out) ; thus when alkaline medicines are taken after meals it means that the protein portion of the meal—the meat, fish, eggs, cheese, etc.—will not be properly digested, but will pass through into the intestines either undigested or partly digested, and so will not be adequately utilised by the system. Not only does this mean that such food will be incapable of proper assimilation, but it means that the function of the intestines will be definitely disturbed, and so constipation will become a more and more noticeable factor in the case.

Such, then, is the " value " of drugs in the treatment of indigestion and other stomach ailments ! No wonder indigestion is incurable by orthodox medical methods of treatment ! And no wonder patent-medicine vendors continue to thrive and wax fat on the victims of such medical treatment, who turn to them in despair for that cure of their ills which Medical Science, with all its boasted attributes, cannot give them !

Treatment.—As already pointed out, the only effective treatment for chronic indigestion, gastritis, flatulence, hyperacidity, etc., is, *firstly*, a thorough cleansing of the digestive tract ; and *secondly*, the adoption of a sensible dietary and common-sense scheme of future feeding and living. *In no other way can these troubles be permanently cured.* The sufferer from stomach troubles of the kind here mentioned should take his case in hand along the following lines (he will be more than satisfied with the results obtained if he does so).

From four to seven or ten days on the *all-fruit diet*, outlined in the Appendix, is the best way to begin the treatment, the period on all-fruit being graduated to suit the needs of the case. (Really serious and long-standing cases should begin with a *short fast* for from three to five days, followed by ten to fourteen days on the *restricted diet* given in the Appendix.) Then the *full weekly dietary*—also given in the Appendix—can be begun, in either case, and adhered to *strictly* thereafter. Further short periods on all-fruit at monthly intervals— say of two or three days—or a further short fast and period or two on the restricted diet at two- or three-monthly intervals, may be required in certain cases, according to the progress being made.

Where flatulence is habitual and severe, it would be wise to precede the all-fruit diet, where adopted, by a day, or even two, on water only, having a glass of hot water every two hours during the day.

For the first few days of the treatment the bowels should be cleansed nightly with the warm-water enema or gravity douche, and every other night thereafter as necessary ; and where constipation is habitual, the rules for its eradication given earlier in the present section should be put into operation forthwith. The daily dry friction and sponge or sitz-bath and the breathing and other exercises given in the Appendix should form a regular feature of the treatment ; and a hot Epsom-salts bath should be taken every week. Fresh air and outdoor exercise are essential, and efforts should be made to indulge in a fairly long and brisk walk every day.

Not only is future careful attention to diet necessary, along the lines consistently laid down in the present book but the sufferer from indigestion must bear in mind the following rules *re* eating consistently :

(1) Never eat and drink together. Drinking should be done half an hour before or three hours after a meal.

(2) Never hurry through a meal, and masticate your food as thoroughly as possible. Never eat " mushy " foods, such as porridge, milk puddings, etc., which cannot be so masticated ; eat your food as crisp and dry as possible.

(3) Never eat to repletion. Always leave the table feeling that you could eat more.

(4) Never eat between meals, and allow five hours to elapse between one meal and the next. (Meals at, say, 8 a.m., 1 p.m., and 6 p.m. would be best.)

(5) Never sit down to a meal feeling worried, over-excited, over-tired, in a temper, etc.

(6) Never use condiments, sauces, seasonings, etc., with your food. Never drink strong tea or coffee or alcoholic beverages.

(7) Always come to a meal really ready for it. If appetite is lacking, do not try to " coax " it by means of dainty tit-bits, relishes, etc. Miss a meal, or two even, or fast a day if necessary, until real appetite returns.

(8) Eat only *genuine natural foods*. Never eat tinned, preserved, potted, or refined foods. (This latter item includes such articles of diet as white bread, white-flour products, white sugar, jams, confectionery, etc.) Never boil vegetables, always steam them. Never peel and boil vegetables such as potatoes, carrots, etc., keep the peel on and either bake or steam them. (In this way you preserve the invaluable mineral salts these vegetables contain, and which ordinary cooking methods lose.)

(9) Never eat fried or greasy foods. Never eat bread or other cereals with acid fruits ; never eat fruit tarts, fruit pies, etc. Never eat *unripe* fruit.

(10) Keep protein and starchy food apart as far as possible. Such foods can be eaten together *occasionally*—as detailed in the diet-sheet given in the Appendix—but not as a general rule.

(11) Take no medicines, powders, or drugs of any kind from now on.

(12) If affected by flatulence at all seriously, sip some hot water slowly, and, if necessary, miss a meal or even two.

If the sufferer from chronic indigestion and allied ailments will carry on as herein directed, his trouble will soon be on the way to complete disappearance ; not only so, his whole general health will be greatly enhanced by the treatment, and many useful years added to his life. Such are the benefits of Natural Healing !

Intestinal Catarrh.—See *Colitis* (page 268).

Loss of Appetite.—Loss of appetite is a symptom of deranged digestion, and instead of trying to cajole back his appetite by means of tasty dishes, appetising tit-bits, etc., or by taking doses of stomach tonics, " pick-me-ups," etc., the sufferer from the condition should go without food altogether until normal appetite returns. It may mean missing a meal, or two meals, or even three, or fasting for a day or so ; but that is the only way to ensure a *real* appetite for food in future. In this overfed world of ours most people could do with going without a meal several days a week at least—if not every day ; and some could do well with a fast-day every week !

The only sound dictum in the matter is : *Never eat unless hungry If not hungry for a meal, then go without it.*

Ptomaine Poisoning.—This is a condition due to the eating of putrefactive food, or food which has putrefied upon entering the stomach. Treatment should be the same as for *Acute Gastritis* (page 290), only in this case the initial fasting period will have to be longer. See also Appendix B *for First Aid Treatment.*

Typhoid.—See section on *Fevers* (Section 13, page 404).

DISEASES OF THE HEART, LUNGS, BRONCHIAL TUBES AND LARYNX

Angina pectoris—Asthma—Bronchial catarrh—Bronchitis (acute)—Bronchitis (chronic)—Coronary thrombosis—Cough—Dilatation of the heart—Endocarditis—Enlargement of the heart—Emphysema—Empyema—False angina pectoris—Fatty heart—Heart disease—Hypertrophy of the heart—Laryngitis — Myocarditis — Pericarditis — Pleurisy—Pneumonia — Pulmonary tuberculosis (consumption)—Tachycardia—Valvular disease of the heart.

DISEASES OF THE HEART

DISEASES of the heart—the most important and hardest-working organ in the body—are exceedingly common these days, and instead of showing signs of decreasing under medical methods of treatment, as one might expect or hope, these conditions show a steady tendency to become more and more prevalent as the years advance. There is, however, not such a great deal of cause for wonder in all this, when once the true facts of the matter are understood ; for it is to medical treatment *itself* that by far the largest percentage of cases of heart trouble of all kinds is due.

Let me make this point quite clear. As has already been pointed out in various places in the present book, when acute diseases such as fevers are treated along orthodox medical lines, the disease is not cured by such treatment, but is suppressed. This means that the toxins Nature is endeavouring to throw off through the medium of the disease are forced back again into the tissues to form the basis for future disorders of the *chronic* type. Now, in all such treatment of acute disease the heart is likely to be affected by the suppressive measures employed, not only through the actual forcing back of toxic matter into the system, but through the medium of the drugs employed to " cure " the fever.

For the drugs used by the medical profession for reducing fevers (called *antipyretics*) reduce temperature *at a cost*—the cost of affecting heart action and often permanently damaging the heart structures. Especially is this fact noticeable in the treatment of scarlet and rheumatic fever ; but the damage caused to the heart is never ascribed to the drugs used, always to the fever. In the case of rheumatic fever the trouble is still more complicated by virtue of the drugs used for neutralising the acid effusions into the joints which are a characteristic feature of this disease. Such drugs (called *salicylates*)

301

seriously affect the heart lining and pave the way for the permanent and often serious heart trouble which usually follows in the wake of the orthodox medical treatment of rheumatic fever. The heart affection is *not* due to the action of the fever as such, *but to the drugs employed in the treatment of the fever.* (Rheumatic fever treated along natural lines leaves no harmful after-affects whatsoever.)

The taking of aspirin and other drugs for deadening nerve pain, the taking of drugs of many other kinds for the medical treatment of diseases of one kind or another, all have a definitely harmful effect upon the heart; so, all in all, who can wonder that heart troubles are such a common feature of present-day life, in this drug-soaked world of ours, and that the medical profession seems powerless to do anything really effective in the matter?

The habitual taking of drugs of all kinds, and *especially* the drug treatment of acute diseases such as fevers, are here cited as the main causative factors in the setting up of diseases of the heart as met with in the civilised world to-day; but there are other factors which can and do play their part in originating heart troubles. Among these other factors none is so important as *wrong feeding*

When we realise that the blood is always passing to and from the heart (ceaselessly, night and day), we can see at once that if the blood-stream is continually being clogged with waste matter in its passage round the body, then a certain amount of this same waste matter will tend to accumulate in and around the heart structures; that is why the excessive and high-protein and starch diet of to-day predisposes inevitably towards defective condition and action of the heart. The more meat, white bread, white sugar, etc., that is eaten habitually, the more will the blood-stream be clogged with waste matter, and the more will heart action suffer, especially as middle-life approaches.

The habitual drinking of strong tea, coffee, and alcoholic liquors also affects heart action adversely, because of the alkaloids and other harmful elements contained in these beverages and which get into the blood; and excessive smoking also affects heart action for the same reason. Then there is severe strain, overwork, nerve exhaustion, excesses of all kinds, etc., etc., to be considered too in the setting up of heart troubles, such factors inevitably tending to accentuate the deleterious effects of the other factors already referred to in the foregoing paragraphs.

Having considered the main factors concerned in the inception of heart diseases, as enumerated above, let us now turn to the medical treatment for such diseases. We have already mentioned the part played by drug treatment in the commencement of heart troubles, yet it is by the use of still more drugs that the medical profession tries to treat these diseases. Is it any wonder, then, that such treatment is ineffectual in curing heart troubles, and that cases of chronic heart disease are becoming more and more numerous in our midst every year ?

There are certain drugs known to Medical Science which have a definite effect upon heart action : for instance, *digitalis* retards heart action, *strychnine* increases heart action ; and it is by means of drugs of this nature (all of them highly dangerous !) that the medical profession tries to effect the " cure " of heart diseases. On the face of it such treatment is not curative ; at best it can only temporarily reduce or remove symptoms ; it cannot affect causes at all. Indeed, the taking of drugs of this nature over a period of time inevitably tends to make any heart condition *worse*. No wonder, then, that heart troubles are regarded in medical circles as the most incurable of all disease conditions ! Anyone whose heart *does* get better under drug treatment does so *in spite of*, not because of, the treatment !

So much, then, for the medical treatment of heart troubles ! What is needed is a regimen which will tend *to remove causes*, so far as this is possible in any given case—not to tamper with symptoms. *And that is just what natural healing sets out to do.* Some cases of heart disease will have had the heart structure so damaged that a cure will be impossible in any circumstances ; others, again, will have sustained only slight damage to the heart structures, or the trouble will be functional rather than organic (cases will necessarily differ from person to person in severity, effect, etc.) ; but no matter what the cause of the trouble or the extent of the damage done to the heart, every sufferer from heart disease can be helped on the road to recovery, in greater or lesser degree, by *natural treatment*.

It is not our wish to hold out too high a hope for the sufferer from serious heart trouble, for we have already said that where the heart structures are seriously damaged, a cure is impossible in any circumstances ; but where the damage to the heart structures is comparatively slight, or where the trouble is functional or due to constitutional factors, a complete cure by means of natural methods of treatment

303

is quite within the bounds of possibility, as records of cases treated along Natural-Cure lines amply testify. But even where the valves are seriously damaged, and a real cure is impossible, quite a lot can be done to alleviate the condition of the sufferer by natural methods of treatment.

It has already been pointed out that every particle of blood circulating through the body has to pass through the heart countless times during the day and night, so it must be obvious that a scheme of treatment which aims at purifying and cleansing the blood and tissues of toxic matter MUST definitely affect heart action and the health of the heart in no uncertain way. That is why natural treatment with its *eliminative dieting* can do so much for the sufferer from heart troubles. By regulating the amount and kind of food eaten, more can be done to relieve and improve the condition of a badly working or defective heart *than by any other method*.

Putting a stop to the drug habit, and the avoidance of all habits and practices tending adversely to affect heart action, such as drinking, smoking, the too free use of strong tea, coffee, etc., will all help on the cleansing work being performed by the dietetic part of the treatment ; and carefully graduated exercise, sun and air baths, and other natural curative measures can all play their part in the building up of the heart and system generally in those affected by heart troubles. *Manipulative treatment* is especially beneficial in all forms of heart disease, when performed in conjunction with a full scheme of natural treatment, by a skilled Osteopath or Naturopath.

Owing to the fact that fasting and strict dieting may tend to have a temporarily adverse effect upon the heart in certain cases, the treatment for heart troubles should always be in the hands of a skilled Naturopath or should be undertaken in a Natural-Cure home where at all possible. But if such personal treatment is not procurable, then the sufferer can take his case into his own hands with the most beneficial results by following the advice for the treatment of his own particular complaint to be found in the present section. (Of course, one cannot expect too much in the way of progress to begin with in long-standing cases, but patience and perseverance with the treatment will bring their due reward.)

DISEASES OF THE LUNGS AND BRONCHIAL TUBES

To understand something of the origin of diseases of the lungs and bronchial tubes we must always bear in mind the following phsiological facts: the oxygen needed by the body for the work of metabolism is drawn into the system through the bronchial tubes and lungs; it is carried by the blood-stream to every part of the body; and the carbon dioxide formed in the tissues as a result of the oxidising process is then brought back to the lungs by the blood-stream and ejected from the system.

Now, it is because the blood-stream is continually bringing *other* impurities (as well as carbon dioxide) with it from the tissues to the lungs that we find the lungs and bronchial tubes so often the seat of disease. For if the tissues of the body are continually being clogged with an excess of waste material due to habitual wrong feeding habits, then more and more of this waste matter will tend to find its way to, and collect in, the lungs and bronchial tubes as the years advance; and this is the main reason for the prevalence of diseases of the chest amongst the persistently wrongly-fed and overfed populations of the present-day world.

It would seem that the waste residues from starchy and sugary foods *in particular* are attracted to the lungs and bronchial tubes; so that the more these foods are indulged in, the more likely is the individual concerned to be afflicted with chest complaints. Then, again, the large bronchi and smaller bronchial tubes are lined with mucous membrane, so that these structures often become the seat of catarrh, either directly or else through contiguity with the mucous membrane of the mouth, nose and throat. (See Section 8, page 228, for an understanding of what catarrh rally is and how it arises in the system.)

Thus *habitual wrong feeding* is the main causative factor responsible for the setting up of diseases of the lungs and bronchial tubes, and this even holds good where *tuberculosis* is concerned, as we shall see when turning to the treatment for that condition farther on in the present section. The medical profession attributes diseases of the chest to "the weather," to "germs," or other extraneous factors. and leaves it at that; although it speaks of lack of fresh air, improper breathing, and other environmental factors as playing a part in the setting up of these diseases in certain cases. There is no doubt that living and working in an habitually stuffy atmosphere predisposes to the commencement of chest complaints; but without the presence of toxic matter accumulated in the lungs and bronchial tubes through wrong feeding habits, such diseases *could never develop*. Lack of exercise, the wearing of too much clothing, especially underclothing (leading to the impeding of skin action), and the inability to use the lungs to their full capacity in breathing, are all cogent factors to be considered when dealing with diseases of the lungs or bronchial tubes ; but all in all, the main emphasis MUST be laid on the food factor all the time. The part played by the suppressive medical treatment of former disease—especially colds, fever, and childhood complaints such as whooping-cough, etc.—must also not be lost sight of in seeking for the cause of chronic chest diseases.

Medical treatment for diseases of the sort we are here discussing is lamentably ineffectual. Asthma and chronic bronchitis, for instance, are two chest complaints which defy medical methods altogether where a permanent cure is concerned. Even with regard to tuberculosis, it is only the fresh air and outdoor living which have helped to keep down that dread disease to a certain extent under medical treatment, *not* drug treatment. But under natural methods of treatment the cure of the first two disease-conditions here referred to is by no means an uncommon thing. No case of asthma or chronic bronchitis (no matter of how long standing) need be considered entirely hopeless where there is a possibility of securing adequately prescribed natural treatment.

Of course, with regard to tuberculosis the chance of permanent cure will differ from case to case (according to age, duration of the disease, extent of the damage done to the lung tissue, etc.) ; but all in all, the sufferer from this dread disease can look to Natural Cure with greater hope of final recovery from his affliction than to any other system of treatment. Many cases have been completely cured by Natural-Cure methods.

To begin, then, with the treatment for diseases of the heart, lungs, etc.

Angina Pectoris.—Angina pectoris really means sharp pain in the chest ; " breast-pang," it is sometimes called. The term is applied to a group of symptoms rather than to a well-marked disorder, though the condition is usually associated with disease of the heart, especially of certain of the arteries by which the heart itself is nourished, or with disease of the aorta, the great blood-vessel which leads directly out of the heart.

When an attack comes on, the symptoms are most alarming. There is agonising pain in the region of the breast-bone, with a sense of constriction in the chest, as if one were being screwed in a vice. The pain radiates into the back, shoulders, and arms, particularly the left arm. The attacks are brought on by various causes, such as the hasty eating of a meal, the eating of too much food at a meal, sudden over-exertion, intense excitement or emotion of any kind, etc.

After an attack there is usually the belching of gas from the stomach, or vomiting, or the bowels move, and then the patient gets relief. Constriction of the arteries around the heart is the physiological cause of the attack.

Treatment.—True angina pectoris can only arise in those who are definitely suffering from heart disease. There is a *false* angina, in which the symptoms are very similar to the true, but the cause in this case is *nervous*, and people whose hearts are in quite good condition can be affected by it. (See *False Angina* farther on in the present section, page 318.)

In cases of true angina pectoris, the taking of drugs only causes the condition to become more and more chronic. What is needed is *constitutional treatment*—treatment, that is, which will serve to build up the general health-level of the patient, and at the same time cleanse the heart and its surrounding tissues of toxic matter, and so pave the way for more healthy heart action. By following out the treatment for *Valvular Disease of the Heart*, given farther on in the present section (page 331), the sufferer from angina pectoris can do more for himself in every way as regards lessening the number and severity of future attacks, building up of general health and heart action, etc., than by any other means.

On no account should drugs be taken in future, and great care should be used to see that there is no overeating or hasty eating at meals, as digestive disturbances are a most potent factor in the setting up of attacks. It is best to eat very lightly and sparingly in all cases of true angina. Then again, all habits and practices tending to over-excite or over-stimulate the system should be carefully avoided, and the patient should live as quiet and simple a life as possible. Smoking and drinking are two habits which should be absolutely taboo in all cases of angina pectoris.

When an attack is on, the only thing that can be done to give relief is to apply hot towels over the heart region. This will tend to relieve

307

the constriction of the arteries around the heart, which is the real cause of the setting up of an attack.

Asthma.—An attack of asthma is an agonising experience, and none there are who would willingly go through a further attack if they knew of any means whereby such attacks could be averted. Unfortunately for the asthma sufferer, Medical Science offers no means of treatment whereby the condition can be *really cleared up* and the possibility of future dread attacks banished once and for all. Medical methods of dealing with the disease centre solely around the employment of certain drugs to bring relief to the sufferer *during an attack*, and no more. But such drugs are highly dangerous in the extreme, and the relief they bring is purchased at the cost of the further deterioration of the health of the sufferer. So that asthma treated along orthodox medical lines invariably tends to become worse and worse under treatment.

Happy, however, is the asthma sufferer who comes into touch with natural methods of treatment, for by such treatment his condition unless very severe and of long standing—can be very much improved, if not definitely cured, in a large number of cases. Natural treatment does not aim at just trying to palliate the effects of an asthmatical attack ; it aims at purifying the system of the toxic matter which is at the root of the trouble, and so effectually preventing the occurrence of further attacks. At the same time the whole general health-level of the sufferer is built up by the treatment, and many an erstwhile sufferer from asthma has been heard to declare that Natural Cure has made a completely new man of him, as well as ridding him of the nightmare of ever-recurring asthma attacks.

Asthma may be connected with other respiratory diseases in the same person, such as bronchitis, tuberculosis, etc., but many people suffer from asthma who have no other sign of serious chest complaint of any kind. Thus it can be seen that it is not chest trouble *as such* which is needed to set up an asthmatic condition in any given individual.

The whole point about asthma is that it is a nervous condition affecting the breathing of the sufferer, and can be brought on from a variety of constitutional causes, the chief of which is *disturbance of function of the digestive organs*. The stomach and bronchi and bronchial tubes are connected by the *vagus nerve*, and by reflex action digestive disturbance can so affect the bronchi and bronchial tubes that the passage of air through them is restricted, and an asthmatical attack precipitated. Obviously, a catarrhal condition of the bronchial tubes will tend to make the appearance of asthma more likely than otherwise, and a highly nervous and run-down condition of the system will also conduce to its development.

Still, no matter what combination of causes there may be acting together to set up asthma in any given individual, the method by which the trouble should be tackled is quite simple and obvious really. What is needed is a thorough internal cleansing of the system (especially of the digestive organs and air apparatus), and the building up of the tone of the whole organism. In this way the asthma bogy can be laid completely in many cases, providing other serious complications do not happen to be present.

Treatment.—As has just been pointed out, treatment for asthma *must be constitutional* to be effective at all. And if the asthma sufferer cannot undertake treatment at the hands of a duly qualified Naturopath, he should carry on at home for himself along the following lines. Good results are assured if he continues with patience and perseverance.

To begin with, a short fast for from three to five days should be undertaken as directed in the Appendix at the end of the book. This should be followed by from ten to fourteen days on the *restricted diet* also outlined therein. Then the *full weekly diet* given in the Appendix can be adopted, and should be adhered to as strictly as possible thereafter. Further short fasts and periods on the restricted diet may be required in certain cases at intervals of, say, two or three months or so. This will, of course, depend upon the progress being made.

From the time the treatment is begun the bowels should be cleansed nightly with a warm-water enema or gravity douche ; and where constipation is habitual, the rules for its eradication given in Section 9 (page 275) should be put into operation forthwith. A daily dry friction and sponge should form a regular feature of the treatment, together with the consistent daily performance of the breathing and other exercises given in the Appendix. A hot Epsom-salts bath should also be taken twice weekly, where at all possible.

Fresh air and gentle outdoor exercise are essentials to the success of the treatment, and the sufferer should spend as much of his time as possible out of doors. The diet factor is extremely important, and great care should be taken to see that there is no danger of digestive disturbance occurring through overeating, the eating of badly combined foods, etc. White bread, sugar, jams, confectionery, rich cakes, pastry, puddings and pies, boiled or mashed potatoes, refined cereals, and milk puddings should all be strictly avoided in future, and very little meat or other flesh food should be eaten. The diet should consist mainly of the natural cleansing foods, i.e. fruits and vegetables. No strong tea or coffee should be taken, also no alcoholic beverages ; and all condiments, pickles, sauces, etc., should be strictly avoided. Smoking is taboo.

As regards local measures, when an attack is coming on the sufferer should sip some hot water slowly, sitting at the same time, if possible, with his feet in a bowl of hot water. Hot cloths, wrung out and applied to the chest, are also beneficial ; or alternate hot and cold cloths. *No drugs of any kind should be taken*, unless absolutely essential for the relief of an attack. *Spinal manipulation*, at the hands of a competent Osteopath or Naturopath, will be immensely valuable in all cases of asthma, if carried out in conjunction with the scheme of home treatment outlined above.

Bronchial Catarrh.—The bronchi and bronchial tubes are lined with mucous membrane and so are liable to the setting up of catarrh, as catarrh only shows itself where there is mucous membrane. For an understanding of what catarrh is and how it may develop in the system, the sufferer from bronchial catarrh is referred to Section 8 (page 233) of the present book ; and as regards treatment for his case, he should follow out that given in the section in question for *Catarrh* (page 235).

Bronchial catarrh may arise either directly or through the spread of catarrh from the mouth and throat ; but in either case the root causes of its development are the same, and the treatment identical. (For the loosening up of catarrh in the bronchi and bronchial tubes, the *cold pack* is very beneficial. It should be applied nightly to the chest. See Appendix for details.)

Bronchitis (Acute).—Bronchitis means inflammation of the mucous membrane lining the bronchi and bronchial tubes. It is the outcome of a catarrhal condition of the bronchial tubes and system generally, and is nothing more than a " chest cold."

If the sufferer from acute bronchitis will turn to Section 8 (page 233) and see what has been said in that section *re Catarrh* and *Colds*, he will soon realise what the underlying cause of his trouble is. His bronchitis is directly the result of *wrong feeding habits*, which have loaded the system with toxic matter and led to the collection of such waste toxic matter in the bronchial tubes, the trouble being brought to a sudden head by a lowering of the vitality through a chill, exposure, overwork, a run-down condition of the system, etc., etc.

When we realise what bronchitis is due to, the treatment is obvious. We have to allow the toxic matter responsible for the setting up of the trouble an opportunity to *eliminate itself* from the system, and so help Nature in the body-cleansing work she has in hand. For, strange as it may seem to many people, all acute diseases are attempts on the part of Nature to rid an over-clogged system of toxic matter. And acute bronchitis is no exception to the rule.

Treatment.—To treat an attack of acute bronchitis by means of drugs will only mean that the cleansing scheme Nature had in hand will be thwarted and the toxic matter in question thrust back into the tissues again, to sow the seed for the development of chronic bronchitis or even more serious chest disease later on, especially if former attacks have been treated in the same way. The only sane and logical treatment for acute bronchitis is as follows :

The sufferer should *fast* on orange juice and water for as many days as the acute symptoms last, using the warm-water enema nightly to cleanse the bowels. When the fever and other acute symptoms have subsided, the *all-fruit diet* given in the Appendix can be adopted for a further two or three days, and then, if convalescence is definitely established, the *full weekly dietary* also given in the Appendix can be gradually embarked upon.

A hot Epsom-salts bath every night or every other night will be most beneficial during the acute stages of the attack, and a cold pack can be applied to the upper chest several times daily, and one at night too. (See the Appendix for details as to how the packs are applied.) Hot towels, wrung out and applied over the upper chest, are also most helpful. After applying, say, three hot towels in turn for two or three minutes each, one should always finish off with a cold towel. These applications can be made several times daily in preference to the packs if desired. Both are efficacious in giving relief.

When the erstwhile sufferer from acute bronchitis is fully recovered, he should then take up a regular system of health-building, such as that given in the treatment for *Chronic Bronchitis* to follow. In this way not only will he effectually prevent further attacks of the same kind, but he will give his whole system a much-needed toning-up and rejuvenation. ON NO ACCOUNT SHOULD DRUGS OF ANY KIND BE TAKEN OR USED.

As wrong feeding is directly responsible for the setting up of the trouble in the first place, the more the dietetic advice given in the treatment for *Chronic Bronchitis* is carried out, the better will the results in future general health be in every way.

Bronchitis (Chronic).—As has already been pointed out in the introductory remarks to *Diseases of the Lungs and Bronchial Tubes* given at the beginning of the present section, it will be seen that wrong feeding habits are the main predisposing cause in the setting up of chest complaints of all kinds. Of none is this more so than of bronchitis, and if repeated attacks of *acute bronchitis* are treated along orthodox lines, and the same old wrong habits of feeding persisted in, then chronic bronchitis will not take long to develop.

It has already been said that the lungs and bronchial tubes seem to have a special affinity for the waste matter left in the system after the habitual eating of excessive quantities of starchy and sugary foods ; and most especially is this so if the starchy and sugary food eaten is of the *demineralised* or *refined* kind, as it is in almost every case to-day. When white bread, cakes, porridge and other refined cereals, boiled potatoes, pastry, puddings, pies, etc., etc., are habitually consumed, in conjunction with equally excessive quantities of sugar, jams, and other sugary foods, then nothing is so likely as that catarrh or bronchitis will arise in time. Especially will this be so where equally excessive quantities of meat and other flesh food and fatty foods are eaten daily—as they generally are—in conjunction with the articles of diet enumerated above.

It does not follow that *everyone* who eats and lives in the above manner will develop bronchitis or catarrh ; some persons' constitutions may be such that they will develop a *rheumatic tendency* or a tendency to *neuritis* or other form of *severe acidosis*. But the whole point is that the individual living in this way *must* develop disease of *some* sort in time ; and if his chest is weak through wrong breathing habits, excessive smoking, living or working in habitually stuffy atmospheres, suppressive treatment of former diseases, etc., then it is most likely of all that bronchitis will be the form disease will take in his system. *Overclothing of the body* (especially the wearing of too thick underwear) is also a predisposing factor to be considered in the setting up of bronchitis.

Treatment.—The sufferer from chronic bronchitis will have learnt ere reading this book that Medical Science can offer him nothing in the way of cure for his condition. That is simply because the real underlying cause of his trouble—*his wrong feeding habits*—are entirely ignored by medical treatment. Drugging for chronic bronchitis is just a waste of time and money ; more, it is likely to make the condition worse in time, because of the suppressive character of the drugs employed. The only logical and sane treatment for chronic bronchitis is that which aims at setting right the dietetic and other mistakes which have caused the condition to develop. In no other way can a cure be effected. And by means of *constitutional treatment* based on these lines many cases of chronic bronchitis which have been given up as " incurable " by the medical profession have been restored to health and fitness once more by Natural-Cure methods.

If the sufferer from chronic bronchitis will now leave off taking medicines—patent or otherwise—and will carry on in his own case in the manner here to be described, he will soon be able to convince himself, in the only real way possible, of the curative powers inherent in natural methods of treatment.

Comparatively mild cases can begin with from five to seven or ten days on the *all-fruit diet* outlined in the Appendix ; more serious and long-standing cases should begin with a short fast for four or five days, followed by ten to fourteen days on the *restricted diet* given in the Appendix. In either case the *full weekly diet*, also given in the Appendix, should then be adopted, and should be adhered to as strictly as possible thereafter.

Further short periods on the all-fruit diet—say two or three consecutive days at monthly intervals—or further short fasts and periods on the restricted diet at two- or three-monthly intervals, may be needed in certain cases, according to the progress being made. The patient must decide this for himself, using his own discretion in the matter.

The daily dry friction and sponge, together with the breathing and other exercises outlined in the Appendix, should form a regular daily feature of the treatment ; and a hot Epsom-salts bath should be taken twice weekly from now on. For the first few days of the treatment, and after if necessary, the bowels should be cleansed nightly with a warm-water enema or gravity douche ; and where constipation is habitual, the rules for its eradication given in Section 9 (page 275) should be put into operation forthwith.

Fresh air and outdoor exercise are two essentials to the treatment which must not be neglected, and a good walk should be taken every day where possible. The diet factor is of the utmost importance, and the demineralised and refined foods already mentioned as being instrumental in the setting up of catarrh and bronchitis should be left severely alone. The bulk of the future dietary MUST be made up of fresh fruits and vegetables. Bread—even if wholemeal—should not be eaten more than once a day (with the salad meal). Strong tea, coffee, and all condiments, pickles, sauces, etc., should be strictly avoided. No alcohol should be taken, and smoking, where habitual, should be cut out entirely if the best results from the treatment are to be achieved. No extraneous factor affects the bronchial tubes so adversely as habitual smoking.

For easing up phlegm or mucus in the chest, nothing is so valuable as the cold pack (for details of which see the Appendix). A pack should be applied to the chest every night on retiring, and removed in the morning. Where at all procurable, *spinal manipulation* is most beneficial indeed as an adjunct to the natural treatment for chronic bronchitis. ON NO ACCOUNT SHOULD DRUGS OR MEDICINES OF ANY KIND BE TAKEN.

Coronary Thrombosis.—This is a very prevalent type of heart disorder nowadays, and it is the cause of many deaths of even middle-aged people. The cause is thickening of the coronary arteries which supply the heart with blood, due to a toxic condition of the system generally. A blood-clot forms in one of these arteries, and a blockage occurs, which is the cause of the attack. Treatment by orthodox medical methods may give relief, and such alleviation may sometimes give the impression that a complete cure has been effected; but the patient is seldom really well thereafter. Under Nature Cure methods, however, much better results are usually achieved in the treatment of this type of condition, which should follow the lines of that given for *Angina Pectoris,* to which the disease is very closely allied.

Cough.—Coughs are very common these days, and it is surprising how ignorant as to their real origin are both medical men and laymen alike. Of course, a cough may be set up through irritation of the throat from habitual smoking, etc., or there may be what is known as a "stomach cough" due to digestive disturbance, but the cough referred to here is the *common chest cough.*

If one listens to a doctor speaking, one would imagine that a cough can develop in the chest merely as the result of "the weather" or such-like seasonal cause ; but this is ascribing a cause to the condition which is no cause at all, but merely an excuse or invention to hide ignorance of the real truth of the matter. Where there is a cough there is phlegm ; and where there is phlegm there is catarrh ; and where there is catarrh it means that the bronchial tubes are clogged up with waste matter brought into the system through the medium of wrong feeding habits. Thus the sufferer from a cough has only *himself* to blame for the setting up of his trouble ; it is no good putting the blame on to outside factors—which cannot defend themselves !— such as "the weather."

Why do coughs generally arise in winter and not at other seasons ? Because the average individual usually eats more heavily than ever of the catarrh-forming foods (white bread, meat, sugar, porridge, potatoes, puddings, pies, etc.) in the colder months of the year ; because he tends to overclothe himself with heavy under-garments and other garments at that time, and so prevents proper aeration of the skin ; because there is a lack of sunshine and other life-quickening factors during the winter months ; and finally, because this same average individual spends nearly all his time indoors or in stuffy atmospheres and so does not get enough pure air to breathe or sufficient exercise.

There may be one or two other factors concerned in the setting up of a cough in winter, but we need not concern ourselves with them here. We have given enough reasons already, surely, to satisfy the intelligent reader that coughs do not appear "out of the blue" as it were, but are the direct outcome of certain definite physical and physiological factors.

Treatment.—Having realised that a cough is merely a symptom of a catarrhal condition of the bronchial tubes, in which the mucus, or "phlegm," is being audibly stirred up and expectorated from the system, the reader can surely now see that in the circumstances *a cough* is really a good thing. It is a move towards health—an attempt to force toxic matter out of an overloaded system. What we have to do, therefore, is to *help on* the cleansing work, not to hinder it by means of suppressive drugs in the form of medicines—patent or otherwise—designed to *stop the cough*.

People think that if they can take something to "stop" a cough, then it is quite all right. But in stopping the cough they have left the toxic matter responsible for its setting up *still in the system*, to cause further coughs and perhaps more serious chest trouble later on. Especially will this be so if the same old wrong feeding habits as of yore are continued with—as they inevitably will be—in complete ignorance as to the vital part they play in the matter.

For the only really *effective* treatment for a cough the sufferer is referred to that for *Bronchitis* just previously given. If the cough is a severe one the treatment for *acute* bronchitis should be followed out ; but if the cough is of a less serious nature or of the chronic kind, the treatment for *chronic* bronchitis should be adopted.

Dilatation of the Heart.—Dilatation of the heart is closely related to enlargement or *hypertrophy* of the heart, and is an almost inevitable development from the latter condition. In hypertrophy the heart is increased in size by the enlargement of one or both of its lower chambers, or ventricles ; and it compensates for its defective condition by an increase in muscular volume or strength. Dilatation occurs when this process of compensation has deteriorated and is no longer sufficient to enable the heart to carry on adequately.

As compared with hypertrophy or enlargement of the heart, it will thus be seen that dilatation is a condition of decided weakness and danger ; and shortness of breath after the slightest exertion, disturbed sleep, more or less continual discomfort in the region of the heart, palpitation, etc., etc., are its accompanying symptoms.

Treatment.—The sufferer from dilatation of the heart can look to no help in any real sense from orthodox drug treatment ; such treatment but serves to make his condition more and more chronic as time goes on. The only sane and logical treatment for dilatation of the heart is along the lines of that given for *Valvular Heart Disease*, to be found farther on in the present section (page 331). By carefully following out the advice there given, the sufferer from dilatation can look for quite a decided improvement in his condition, although a complete cure can hardly be hoped for from the very nature of the case.

Endocarditis.—This is a condition in which there is inflammation of the membrane which lines the cavities of the heart, and particularly of that portion which covers the valves. The disease may be acute

316

or chronic, and is positively associated with a highly toxic condition of the system, particularly with fevers. Endocarditis usually leads to definite disease of the heart, generally to disease of the mitra valve.

As has already been said, endocarditis is associated with a highly toxic condition of the system, and is often a complication in fevers, especially rheumatic and scarlet fever ; but in these latter cases it is not the toxicity of the system as such, so much as the drug treatment employed to " cure " the fever, which leads to the development of the endocarditis and subsequent heart disease, as we have already pointed out on more than one occasion in the present book. Still, toxin poisoning of the heart structures—due to a condition of high systemic toxicity—can, and often does, play a part in the development of endocarditis (apart from drug treatment), the heart being affected by the toxins carried to and from it by a heavily toxin-laden bloodstream. As usual in all these cases, *wrong feeding habits* are the main predisposing factor at work all the time behind the setting up of the toxic condition in question.

Treatment.—Treatment for endocarditis should be in the hands of a competent Naturopath *where at all possible* ; for although fasting and strict dietetic treatment are indicated, the heart, in certain cases, owing to its weakened condition, may not be able to stand the strain imposed upon it by rigorous eliminative treatment. But if personal naturopathic attention is not available in any given case, treatment should be along the lines of that for *Valvular Disease of the Heart,* to be found farther on in the present section (page 331).

Enlargement of the Heart.—See *Hypertrophy of the Heart* (page 319).

Emphysema.—Emphysema is a condition which arises in the lungs of those who have put great strain upon these organs in the violent efforts of asthma, the hard coughing of bronchitis or tuberculosis, etc. It is brought about by the bursting of some of the air-vesicles in the more minute bronchial tubes, and leads to great softening of the lung-tissue with retention of excess air. Treatment for the condition should be as for the disease with which it is associated.

When doing breathing exercises, the emphysematous patient should stress the *expiratory* movements more than the *inspiratory*—that is to say, he should stress the *expelling* of the air from the lungs, and not so much the inhaling of air.

Empyema.—When pleurisy lasts a long time and suppuration sets in in the pleural membrane, the condition is known as *empyema.*

The condition could never arise if the pleurisy had been properly treated in the first place, and is merely a further indication—if such were needed !—of the inability of orthodox medical scientists to understand and deal effectively with the phenomena of disease in the human system.

Medical treatment for empyema is surgical, and in the circumstances such treatment is very useful ; but such surgical measures *cannot* cure the underlying toxic condition of which the empyema is only a feature. For the effective treatment for empyema the reader is referred to that for *pleurisy* farther on in the present section. If such a régime had been adopted in the first place—or better still, if the pneumonia from which the pleurisy usually arises had been treated along natural lines in the first place—*empyema could never have arisen.*

False Angina Pectoris.—Symptoms very similar to those experienced in *angina pectoris* are sometimes felt by people who have no definite disease of the heart structures, and who therefore cannot be suffering from *true* angina pectoris. This condition is known as *pseudo-angina* or *false angina*, and is nervous in origin. It is the outcome of nerve strain or tension in a toxic system, and wrong feeding, overwork, excessive strain, worry, etc., etc., can be cited as predisposing factors in its occurrence.

Treatment.—Where the sufferer can be sure that his symptoms are due to *false angina* and not *true angina*, a scheme of systemic cleansing treatment is all that is required to put him right. He should begin with from four to seven days on the *all-fruit diet* outlined in the Appendix, and follow this with the *full weekly dietary* also outlined therein. This full weekly dietary should be adhered to as strictly as possible from then on. Further short periods on all-fruit —say, two or three days at a time at monthly intervals—may be required, for the next few months or so, in certain cases.

The bowels should be cleansed nightly with a warm-water enema or gravity douche during the first few days of the treatment, and after if necessary ; and if constipation is habitual, the rules for its eradication given in Section 9 (page 275) should be put into operation forthwith. A daily dry friction and sitz-bath or sponge, together with the regular performance of the breathing and other exercises given in the Appendix, should form a regular feature of the treatment. A hot Epsom-salts bath should be taken once or twice weekly where possible.

If hot baths affect the heart at all, the baths should not be taken too hot, but just comfortably so.

The patient should see that he leads a quiet, normal existence, and all excitement and nerve strain should be avoided as far as possible. Fresh air and outdoor exercise should form a definite feature of the treatment, but moderation in exercise is needed in the early part of the regimen at least. *No drugs of any kind should be taken*, and strong tea or coffee or alcoholic beverages should be strictly avoided. Smoking, where habitual, should be discontinued Great care with the future dietary is essential, and white bread, sugar, pastry, puddings, pies, boiled potatoes, refined cereals, all greasy and heavy dishes, much meat, and all condiments should be avoided. Fruits and salad should form the bulk of the daily dietary.

The hasty eating of meals, hurrying away to work or to do violent exercise directly after a meal, and the eating of meals late at night should be carefully guarded against.

Fatty Heart.—This is a condition in which there is a deposit of fat between the sac which contains the heart and the heart muscle. The trouble is directly associated with obesity, and is dietetic in origin, being attributable to over-indulgence in food and drink. Shortness of breath on exertion and a feeling of distress or oppression in the region of the heart are its most marked symptoms.

Treatment.—Obviously the only treatment for fatty heart that will cure the condition is *constitutional treatment* ; and if the sufferer will carry out that for *Obesity* given in Section 14 (page 428) of this book, not only will his heart trouble be removed in time, but his whole general health will be greatly enhanced—surely a prize well worthy of the efforts entailed in its getting !

Heart Disease.—See *Valvular Disease of the Heart* (page 330).

Hypertrophy of the Heart.—Through excessive strain, such as in athletics, the heart often becomes enlarged or hypertrophied ; but this is not the only factor concerned in the case. A toxic condition of the system due to wrong feeding habits is always back of the condition, no matter what the actual superficial factors active in the setting up of the enlargement may be. Arteriosclerosis, Bright's disease, affections of the lungs, etc., etc., can all lead to a condition of hypertrophy of the heart.

Where there is hypertrophy, it means that in attempting to carry on its full activities under a condition of strain or effort, one or both of the lower ventricles of the heart have become enlarged to enable it to carry out its added work. Such action is known as " compensation," and some cases of heart enlargement or hypertrophy are so well compensated that there is little or no sign of any visible heart trouble. Others, on the other hand, have symptoms of throbbing or heaviness around the heart, and there may be dizziness, headache, noises in the head, etc. The more pronounced these symptoms become, the more certain is it that compensation is failing, and that the condition is progressing towards *dilatation*.

Treatment.—Sufferers from enlarged or hypertrophied heart can achieve excellent results under natural treatment, especially if the case is taken in the early stages. If treatment cannot be carried out under the personal direction of a Naturopath, the patient should proceed for himself along the lines indicated for *Valvular Heart Disease* farther on in the present section (page 331). Such treatment, graduated to suit his own case, will give the most beneficial results.

Laryngitis.—The larynx, or " voice-box," is situated in the throat, at the head of the windpipe, and is yet one more example of the marvellous ingenuities of mechanism embodied by Nature in the human organism. Like the windpipe, bronchi, and bronchial tubes, from which it is a continuation, the larynx is lined with mucous membrane, and *laryngitis* is the term applied to an inflammatory condition of this mucous membrane or lining of the larynx.

In common with all other inflammatory conditions, a toxic condition of the system (due to wrong feeding habits mainly) is at the root of laryngitis, and long-standing constipation is often a very potent factor in the frequent recurrence of the trouble. People who have to do a great deal of talking or singing, or who smoke or drink a great deal, are more likely to be subject to laryngitis than others. (The suppressive medical treatment of childhood ailments, especially fevers, often predisposes towards a susceptibility to laryngitis.)

Treatment.—As regards general treatment for laryngitis, the sufferer is referred to that for *Acute Bronchitis* given earlier in the present section (page 311). Such a scheme will put him right in the quickest possible time. As regards local treatment, the throat should be gargled several times a day with warm water and a little orange juice, and cold packs should be applied frequently daily and one at night (as directed in the Appendix at the end of the book). ON NO ACCOUNT SHOULD DRUGS OF ANY KIND BE TAKEN

Myocarditis.—This is the term used to denote inflammation of the muscle of the heart. The condition may be acute or chronic and leads to progressive degeneration of the heart muscle with greater or lesser impairment of heart action. A highly toxic condition of the system, due to wrong feeding habits and general wrong living, is the main predisposing cause in the setting up of myocarditis, the suppressive medical treatment of previous disease of one form or another being also a factor not to be lost sight of.

Treatment.—Myocarditis is a condition which needs careful watching, and very good results can be obtained in many cases by natural treatment. *Drug therapy for the disease is just useless.* The sufferer from myocarditis is advised to secure the services of a competent Naturopath for his case where at all possible ; but if this is not practicable, he should carry on as advised in the treatment for *Valvular Disease of the Heart*, farther on in the present section (page 331).

Pericarditis.—Pericarditis is the name applied to inflammation of the pericardium, or membranous sac in which the heart is enclosed. Pericarditis is very often a complication to the medical treatment of fevers, due to the suppressive nature and deleterious action of the drugs employed. Pericarditis may also appear in connection with the medical treatment for other diseases which have been treated suppressively.

Treatment.—If disease was rightly understood and always treated sanely, conditions such as pericarditis would never develop. The condition can only arise during an acute disease or other serious toxic condition, where the heart is affected by the toxins forced back into the blood-stream as an outcome of treatment by suppressive drugs or other medicinal agents.

Where present, pericarditis needs nothing more than the Natural-Cure treatment for the disease with which it is associated. Pain may be relieved by the application of hot compresses over the heart area or by the alternative application of hot and cold compresses.

Pleurisy.—Pleurisy means inflammation of the pleura, or the membrane covering the walls of the chest cavity (in which the lungs are contained). The disease may appear on its own, but is usually a complication to the medical treatment for pneumonia. If pneumonia or other serious chest diseases were treated *in a proper manner* to begin with, pleurisy could never develop. For it is only when toxic matter is prevented from being eliminated from the lungs during a period of high toxicity, by suppressive medical treatment, that the condition of the lungs becomes such that the pleura is involved and pleurisy sets in.

Treatment.—Where present, the only sensible treatment for pleurisy is *fasting*, to enable the toxic matter present in the pleura to be absorbed and eliminated by the system. And the sufferer is referred to the treatment for *Pneumonia*—to follow—for an understanding of how to carry on in his particular case. If such natural treatment is adopted, there will be no fear of further complications of any kind occurring, and in addition the whole system will be built up by the treatment.

Pneumonia.—Pneumonia is a serious acute disease or fever affecting the lungs, and although Medical Science ascribes its presence to germ infection, its true cause is to be found in a highly toxic condition of the system, especially of the lungs and air passages. As in all toxic conditions affecting the health of the system, wrong feeding habits and general wrong living are the main factors concerned in the development of pneumonia in any given case, but suppressive medical treatment of previous disease *plays a very big part in the matter too* (especially the medical treatment of influenza !) It is safe to say that no person could develop pneumonia whose tissues were really clean and wholesome and whose lungs were not silted up with waste matter.

The actual starting cause of an attack may be a chill, exposure, etc., etc., but without this underlying toxicity of the lungs and system generally the disease could never develop. Germs are merely superficial agents in the matter, and only arise as a *result* of the toxic condition in question, not as its cause. The driving back of toxic matter into the system, and its collection in the lung tissue as a result of the suppressive treatment of acute toxic conditions such as influenza, etc., often leads directly to the setting up of pneumonia.

Treatment.—Treatment for pneumonia along Nature Cure lines is no different from that for any other acute disease or fever, and the reader is therefore referred to the section on *Fevers* (Section 13, page 404) for full details as to how the disease should be treated.*

* The treatment of pneumonia by the use of antibiotic drugs only serves to get rid of the superficial germ effect, leaving the underlying causes completely untouched. Thus, although the patient may appear to be cured quite rapidly, a recurrence of the trouble may be expected in the near or distant future, and of a more severe nature. Also, the respiratory tissues are affected adversely by antibiotic treatment, and the lungs tend to lose their elasticity, thus paving the way for *emphysema* to develop in many cases. In the author's view, the antibiotic treatment of chest diseases has a great deal to do with the subsequent development of lung cancer. Smoking is only a secondary factor.

Pulmonary Tuberculosis (Consumption).—Pulmonary tuberculosis or *consumption of the lungs*, is one of the most dreaded of diseases, and is known universally as the " white plague," because of the colossal amount of mortality it has brought in its train. Yet, in spite of the seriousness and often malignancy of the disease, it is a curious and most significant fact that tuberculosis is the *only one* of the serious chronic diseases which beset civilised man to-day of which Medical Science has in some measure been able to check the advance, merely because it has abandoned drug treatment as the chief agent employed in dealing with the condition, and relies more on the healing value to be found in those purely natural agents, *fresh air* and *sunshine*— a fact surely worth pondering upon !

Tuberculosis is supposed to be due to infection by the *tubercle bacillus*, and although many parts of the body may be affected, it is the lungs which are the usual seat of the disease. Bad housing and wretched conditions of work, lack of sunshine and fresh air, the devitalising of the system through excess and abuse, overwork, defective nutrition, etc., etc., are all given as predisposing factors in the development of tuberculosis by our medical scientists, it being realised that a devitalised and impoverished state of the system is necessary before the germ can become active.

The germs of tuberculosis may be either inhaled or introduced into the system through food, we are told, and one of the most potent sources for the spread of the disease, according to orthodox medical views, is *cow's milk*, especially with regard to tuberculosis in children ; for the domestic cow is very prone to become the victim to tuberculosis under modern dairy-farming conditions. Now, this fact that cows can, and do, develop tuberculosis when taken away from a natural state of living and feeding and subjected to an artificial and unnatural existence, points the way more clearly than any other single factor to the *real causes* underlying the development of tuberculosis, not only in animals, but in man as well, as we shall soon see.

We are told by our medical authorities that tuberculosis is a disease due to germ infection, yet even these self-same authorities admit that the disease will not take root in any and every person's organism indiscriminately, but depends upon a considerable devitalisation of the system beforehand for its development. *The fact is that it is this devitalisation of the system which is the chief factor concerned all the time, and not the germs !* Not only are we all exposed to infection by the tubercle bacillus at every turn, we actually have these germs within our system *all the time*, without the slightest apparent harm in the great majority of cases. It is only where the vitality of the organism has been brought to a low ebb, through various causes, that the germs begin to assert their sway and tuberculosis is said to be beginning. It is the devitalisation which comes first always, and the germ activity afterwards as a direct consequence.

No, the fact is that all of us have seeds for the development of tuberculosis within us in greater or less degree. The germs do not attack us; they are already housed within us, and will do us not the slightest harm, providing we have not depleted our vital forces in such a way as to make their propagation possible. If we *have*, then the development of tuberculosis within us will begin, whether we have been exposed to germ infection or not.

As to what the real fundamental cause is which will so deplete the system as to allow the tubercle bacillus an opportunity to develop and set up tuberculosis, let us return to our point *re* the domestic cow, which we said would show where the trouble lies. In his work as a food investigator, Alfred McCann, the great American food scientist and author of *The Science of Eating*, proved over and over again that tuberculosis in domestic animals is the direct outcome of the artificial manner in which these animals are fed. If cows are fed on grass, hay, etc.—their *natural* foods—they *cannot* develop tuberculosis; it is only when they are kept in dairies and fed on all kinds of "manipulated" and "concocted" feeds that tuberculosis arises after a time.

The whole thing is quite simple, and starts in this way. Instead of being allowed to eat natural foods containing all the minerals and other vital elements necessary for the healthy upkeep of the body, the cow in many dairies—especially in winter-time, and more so in the United States than in England—is given artificially prepared foods which are very deficient in mineral and vital properties. The result is that the cow's tissues tend to become more and more starved of these essential elements to health the longer it is fed in this way, and as it is under a constant strain all the time by virtue of the fact that it is forced to provide milk far out of all proportion to what it naturally should do, the animal's system becomes so devitalised in time that the tubercle bacillus has an easy ground for growth, and the seeds for the development of tuberculosis are readily sown. The trouble is made all the more acute because in its milk the cow has to furnish a large amount of mineral and other vital matter which it is itself being denied from the food supplied to it, so that the deterioration of its tissues goes on at a far greater rate than would otherwise be the case, and tuberculosis develops the more readily.

A bullock fed in the same way as a dairy cow would stand far less chance of developing tuberculosis than the cow because of the fact that there would not be this continual drain on its vital powers for the production of milk containing essential elements which its food has not supplied to it, and which its own tissues have had to give up as a consequence. Herein lies the tragedy of the domestic cow ! *In exactly the same way many a nursing mother living on the devitalised foodstuffs of the present era develops tuberculosis.* Not having received an adequate supply of natural mineral matter and other vital elements from her food during pregnancy, her steadily depleting store of these same elements has been drained from her own tissues for the needs of the growing child within her ; and after the birth of the child and the strain of nursing and giving an adequate supply of milk to the infant, tuberculosis comes along to claim yet another victim. Especially is this so after the second or third child in those living habitually on a vitally impoverished dietary.

The main cause of tuberculosis is therefore *mineral starvation of the tissues of the body, due to an impoverished dietary* ; and the chief mineral concerned is *calcium.* Indeed, tuberculosis is in many ways a *calcium-deficiency disease,* for there can be no breakdown of tissue and no tubercular growth where there is an adequate supply of organic calcium in the said tissues. In many post-mortem examinations, those making the autopsy have been surprised to find unsuspected tubercular lesions which have been healed automatically, as it were, by the natural defence mechanism of the body, the healing having been brought about by what is known as the " calcification " of the lesion. That is to say, the body has " walled up " the lung area infected by the tubercular bacilli and prevented its spread by means of the use of the organic calcium at its disposal. Thus, not only is an adequate supply of organic calcium in the system—together with other organic mineral matter—a sure preventive of the development of tuberculosis, but organic calcium is the chief therapeutic agent needed for the overcoming of tuberculosis when once the disease has taken hold upon the system.

There is no doubt that living and working in habitually stuffy or badly ventilated atmospheres is conducive to the development of tuberculosis, as is also abuse or misuse of the system generally ; *but the main predisposing cause* all the time is mineral starvation of the tissues of the body through an inadequate dietary, as already pointed out. This does not mean to say that the dietary has been inadequate when measured by mere bulk standards, but when measured according to the amount of organic mineral and other vital matter it contains. Thus many people eating four or five meals a day may be having an inadequate dietary when judged from this standard, whereas from the ordinary conventional point of view their dietary is full and abundant in every way. And the sort of dietary we are here referring to is precisely that same white bread, refined-cereal, white-sugar, cooked-meat and cooked-vegetable dietary so prevalent throughout civilisation to-day.

But over and above mineral starvation of the tissues of the body as a result of living upon a dietary in which the food minerals and other vital elements are almost altogether lacking, there is yet another factor to be considered in every case where tuberculosis sets in, and that is something entirely to do with the *psychical* (and *not physical*) " make-up " of the individual concerned. It would seem with tuberculosis (in human beings at least), as with cancer, that there is needed a *negative attitude* —a sort of *non-vital* attitude—*towards life* on the part of the individual concerned, before malnutrition and the other physical factors already referred to can pave the way for the development of the disease in the said individual's system. And, of course, with regard to tuberculosis of the lungs, the part played by habitual colds and catarrh treated suppressively, and by bronchitis, pneumonia, and other chest and throat affections treated by drug and knife, has always to be considered, such treatment inevitably tending to lower the tone and lead to the high toxicity of the lung tissue, a condition very favourable to the later development of tuberculosis.

Treatment.—The cause of tuberculosis has here been made clear as being fundamentally due to the impoverishment of the tissues of the body of essential organic mineral elements—particularly calcium —as a result of living upon an habitually demineralised and devitalised dietary. But the part played by bad environmental conditions, misuse and abuse of bodily powers, and the suppressive medical treatment of former disease (especially chest disease such as bronchitis, pneumonia, etc.), has also not been lost sight of. Further, a *negative attitude to life,* on the part of the individual affected by the disease, has also been cited as a most important predisposing factor on the psychical side. One must also remember that certain individuals inherit a *tendency* towards the development of the disease. The tubercular bacillus itself is therefore only a very late-comer on the scene, as it were ; it puts in its appearance when all the spade-work has been performed by the other factors above named. But once the disease begins to take hold (with its accompanying symptoms of hacking cough, emaciation, night sweats, heightened temperature, etc., etc.), then of course the germ takes more and more of the lime-light upon itself, until it appropriates the whole centre of the stage eventually, and all other factors fade inconspicuously into the background.

With regard to the medical treatment for tuberculosis, we have already said a certain amount of good work has been done by means of open-air treatment, in which fresh air and sunlight play the most important parts. But such treatment is very rarely sufficient to cure the disease on its own ; what is needed is proper dietetic and other health-building help along natural lines *as well*. The medical view with regard to the dietetic treatment for tuberculosis appears to be that the patient should be made to eat as much " nourishing " food as possible, in order to " build up his strength " and so " fight the germ." But such a dietetic règime is the reverse of that really needed, as the foods given are *themselves* of the same devitalised and demineralised kind as those here cited as the real underlying cause for the setting up of the condition.

White bread, white-flour products, refined cereals such as porridge rice, barley, etc., milk puddings, boiled and mashed potatoes, boiled vegetables, cooked meat, white sugar, etc., etc., are all foods which are deficient indeed in organic mineral and vital matter, yet these are the very foods upon which the consumptive is told to " feed up " in order to build up his strength " to fight the germ of tuberculosis." No wonder the fight is a losing one in great numbers of cases ! There is no doubt that sanatorium treatment for tuberculosis owes ninety-nine per cent. of its failures to crass ideas about feeding— ideas which only perpetuate the old fallacies regarding food, and which lead many a consumptive to an early grave who would be otherwise saved.

There is much talk these days of new treatments for tuberculosis— drug and otherwise—from orthodox (or unorthodox) sources, many of them of the most weird nature ; but no system of medication will prevail in which the dietetic factor is either overlooked or misunderstood. *An all-round scheme of dietetic and vitality-building treatment along natural lines is the only sure road to success in tuberculosis,* as the many cures achieved by Natural-Cure practitioners the world over in this dread disease testify. But the case must be in the comparatively early stages for the best results to be secured ; long-standing cases may be past cure because of the great deterioration of lung tissue that will have taken place here. Even so, in these latter cases, quite a great deal can be done by natural treatment properly applied.

Treatment in a Natural-Cure institution is of course by far the best in all cases of tuberculosis ; but failing this, the sufferer should try his utmost to carry on under the personal supervision of a competent Naturopath. *Personal treatment is far and away the best.* However, if the sufferer is unable to secure such individual treatment he can carry on as follows with every hope of achieving satisfactory results with patience and perseverance, providing, of course, his trouble has not been allowed to develop too far or there are not too many subsidiary complications.

To begin the treatment the best thing is to have three or four days on the exclusive *fresh fruit diet* outlined in the Appendix. This should then be followed by a period on the *fruit and milk diet* also outlined therein. This fruit and milk diet should be carried on with for from three to six or eight weeks, according to the progress being made, the quantity of milk taken daily being gradually increased up to, say, six to eight pints daily relatively to the capacity of the patient. Then the *full weekly dietary* outlined in the Appendix can be begun, and should be adhered to strictly thereafter. Up to two pints of milk can be added to this full dietary daily. Further periods on the all-fruit diet followed by fruit and milk should be taken at intervals of, say, two months or so, according to the needs of the case.

It has been pointed out that tuberculosis is a disease due primarily to mineral starvation of the tissues of the body, and that the chief mineral concerned is *calcium.* Milk is the finest food medium for the supply of organic calcium to the body, and that is why it is so much used in the natural treatment for tuberculosis. But the milk should always be *fresh* and *unboiled*—NOT BOILED. Never mind about the "germs" in unboiled milk ; build up the tone of the system along approved natural lines and the erstwhile sufferer from tuberculosis can snap his fingers at germs. Besides, unboiled milk contains many vital properties necessary to the building up of the system which boiled milk has lost. *That is why unboiled milk is the milk required.* And the fresher and more direct the supply, the better.

Instead of the fruit and milk diet outlined above, the *full milk diet* can be tried by some with equally good or even better results. Cases vary, and what suits one best may not quite suit another. In this connection there is a short fast for from three to five days to begin with, on orange juice and water, and then the *full milk diet* given in the Appendix is begun and adhered to for from four to six weeks. The *full weekly dietary* with two pints of milk added daily is then begun, as advised above, with further short fasts and periods on the milk diet at two-monthly intervals thereafter as the case requires.

During the first few days of the treatment the bowels should be cleansed nightly with the warm-water enema or gravity douche, and afterwards if necessary ; and where constipation is habitual, the rules for its eradication given in Section 9 (page 275) should be put into operation forthwith. The morning dry friction and sponge outlined in the Appendix should form a regular feature of the treatment, and the breathing and other exercises also outlined therein should be gone through in conjunction with them. As regards breathing exercises, these should be done very gently and carefully at first, so as not to put too much strain upon the lungs. A hot Epsom-salts bath, taken once or twice a week, will be a very useful adjunct to the treatment.

The tuberculosis sufferer should see that he has as much fresh air and gentle outdoor exercise as possible, but he should not overtax his strength in any way. He should sleep with a good current of fresh air in the bedroom, and outdoors in summer where at all possible. All devitalising habits and practices should be discontinued, and early hours and simple living instituted as the main routine of living. Smoking and drinking, where habitual, must be rigorously excluded.

The dietary must consist of fruits, vegetables (raw and conservatively cooked), milk, wholemeal bread, butter, eggs, nuts, and cheese mainly, as these are the foods richest in organic calcium and other organic minerals. Meat should be eaten very sparingly indeed, and all devitalised foods such as white bread, white sugar, refined cereals, milk puddings, puddings and pies, tinned and preserved foods, etc., rigorously avoided. No strong tea or coffee, and no condiments, pickles, sauces, etc., should be taken. On no account should drugs of any kind or so-called " nourishing foods "—patent or otherwise—be taken.

The mental factor is of very great importance in all cases of tuberculosis, and that is why personal treatment is always best. The patient receives support and encouragement from the practitioner all the time. But even with those carrying on on their own, the right mental attitude should soon be attained once the true facts concerning the cause and cure of the disease (as outlined herein) are understood. It is the fear and uncertainty connected with tuberculosis which have such a depressing effect upon the patient, quite apart from his own negative attitude psychologically (which we have already alluded to as being a predisposing factor in the setting up of the trouble in the first place). Once let the patient realise that he is on the right road towards cure—*as he will if he adopts natural treatment*—then the right mental attitude will come of its own accord.

SPECIAL NOTE.—Under medical treatment, *hæmoptysis* (the spitting of blood) is regarded as a very bad sign indeed. When natural treatment has been undertaken, the spitting of blood is often a sign of progress, and should not be regarded with alarm by the sufferer, other things being favourable.

Tachycardia.—Tachycardia means rapid action of the heart. This may arise from a variety of causes, all of them systemic in origin. If the patient cannot connect the rapid heart action with any disease-condition he is suffering from, or has been suffering from, a course of general treatment along the lines of that for *false angina*, given in the preceding pages, should be carried out. Smoking is often a most potent cause of tachycardia.

Valvular Disease of the Heart.—Valvular disease of the heart may be of various kinds, ranging in degree from very serious to comparatively slight. In valvular heart disease the valves which shut off the heart chambers one from another, or which shut off the great arteries leading from the heart itself, have become either too large or too small, thus interfering with the proper passage of the blood to and from the heart, with greater or lesser disturbance of bodily function.

The greatest predisposing factor towards the setting up of valvular heart disease is inflammation of the heart lining (endocarditis) ; and this, as has been pointed out in discussing endocarditis earlier in the present section, is most often the outcome of the suppressive drug treatment of former disease, especially acute disease (or fevers), such as rheumatic fever, scarlet fever, etc. The part played by *toxin poisoning* in the development of endocarditis has also been mentioned, such toxin poisoning being the direct outcome of a highly toxic condition of the blood and system, as a result of wrong feeding habits and unhygienic habits of living.

However, the chief underlying *causes of all heart troubles in general* have been made perfectly clear and fully discussed in the introductory pages to the present section, and these same introductory pages should be read *carefully* by every sufferer, not only from actual heart disease itself, but from all other heart affections, such as hypertrophy, dilatation, myocarditis, etc., as the general remarks there made apply to all cases of heart trouble, no matter of what kind or origin. The only thing is that in certain instances one of the points raised may need stressing more than another, according to the particular and peculiar circumstances of the case.

In the pages above referred to, not only was the origin and development of heart troubles clearly explained, but the value of drug treatment was exposed in its true light, and the sufferer from heart affections was assured that only under natural methods of treatment could he hope for any lasting improvement in his condition. He was further advised to seek personal naturopathic treatment where at all possible, because of certain facts which were made clear.

It is fully realised, however, that there will be many who will find it impossible to secure personal treatment for their case, and these can carry on along the lines here to be laid down, with every hope of securing beneficial results, no matter what their heart trouble may be, providing, of course, that the condition has not been allowed to develop too far before natural treatment is begun.

Treatment.—In outlining a scheme of home treatment for heart troubles one has always to bear in mind that some sufferers from heart affections can undertake a far more rigorous scheme of treatment than others. For instance, those with only slight hypertrophy or slight V.D.H. might be able to undertake quite a strict scheme of fasting and other eliminative treatment without undue strain upon the heart itself; but others, on the other hand, with myocarditis or dilatation or pronounced V.D.H., will find it impossible to do much in the way of very strict treatment, because the strain would be more than their weakened heart structures could be safely called upon to withstand successfully. That, indeed, is the real reason why personal treatment is so much to be desired in heart troubles ; each patient can have the treatment definitely arranged to suit the needs of his own special case. But we shall get over the difficulty here, to a very great extent, in the following manner.

The great thing in all cases of heart trouble is a *cleansing diet*, for as already explained, the cleaner and purer the blood is as it passes to and from the heart, the less will be the toxicity set up in the heart structures, and the easier will it be for the heart to carry out its function. So that the first essential for all those undertaking treatment is to place themselves *at once* upon a *natural cleansing dietary*, and to cut down very much (or exclude altogether as the case may be) the consumption of meat, bread, sugar, puddings, pies, rich cakes, all heavy and stodgy dishes, fried foods, and other highly toxin-forming food materials which throw a great burden upon the system in general and the heart in particular. For this purpose the *full weekly dietary* given in the Appendix can be followed with the most beneficial results by each and every sufferer from heart affections, no matter of what nature or how long duration his trouble might be.

The next step is to cut out the drinking of tea, coffee, alcohol, or other highly stimulating beverages, and to stop altogether the use of condiments, pickles, sauces, etc. Articles of diet such as these either directly affect the working of the heart or tend to make the toxicity of the blood worse than it otherwise would be, and so indirectly affect the heart's activity. Of course, where smoking is indulged in, that must be stopped altogether, or very much reduced, according to the severity or otherwise of the case. It is, however, by far the best thing to cut out smoking *entirely* in all cases where the heart is affected.

Having brought the dietary on to a new and cleaner basis, and removed the harmful effects upon the heart of stimulating drinks, etc., the sufferer from heart trouble will soon begin to find a definite improvement in his condition, commensurate, of course, with the severity and duration of the complaint. He can then begin to introduce a fast-day or a day on the *all-fruit diet* outlined in the Appendix, at intervals of, say, a fortnight. (For the fast, hot water and orange juice may be taken.) It will be quite easy for those with even serious heart trouble to stand a fast for a day, or a day on the all-fruit diet, every fortnight ; and those with less serious heart conditions can have both a fast-day *and* a day on fruit to follow, at these times, or a fast-day one week and a day on fruit the next. All this will assist very greatly indeed in clearing up toxic matter in the system, and so helping on heart action, whilst at the same time it will prevent the heart from becoming affected by the treatment.

The foregoing is the manner in which all sufferers from more or less *serious* heart trouble should carry on, then : go on to the weekly dietary outlined in the Appendix and then have a day's fast or a day on fruit—or both—at regular fortnightly intervals thereafter, as described above. If desired, a day's fast or a day on fruit can be taken as a preliminary to beginning on the weekly dietary ; and many will be able to undertake both a fast-day *and* day on fruit before beginning the new diet. It all rests with the individual to decide for himself according to the special circumstances of his case. The great thing is not to do too much in the way of fasting or strict eliminative dieting *at a time*, but to spread it out at intervals, over a period, as directed.

Of course, there will be those with comparatively slight heart disease or other heart trouble who could quite easily undertake a short fast of three or four days, or a similar period on the *all-fruit diet*, to begin the treatment, and who could have further short fasts or periods on all-fruit at monthly intervals thereafter as needed. But the great thing is never to overtax the system at these times. but just to carry on as long as the patient feels he comfortably can. There are some sufferers from heart trouble who could undertake a fast for a week with ease, and with the greatest benefit to themselves. It is all a question of what each separate individual is capable.

The great point for the sufferer from heart disease or other heart trouble to realise, then, is that (commensurate with his powers and graduated thereto) the more fasting and strict eliminative dieting he can carry out (apart from the regular following of the weekly dietary), the more quickly will curative results be secured in his particular case ; for *nothing* helps so much in the cure of heart disorders as treatment of the nature here referred to. That is why the medical regimen for heart troubles—apart from the definitely harmful after-effects of drugs—is so ineffectual. The diet factor is ignored all the time, and the patient is allowed to eat all sorts of foods which are the very worst possible for him where the health of the heart is concerned. The more the dietary approximates towards a fruit and salad basis, the cleaner will it be, and the better will the heart be able to function.

It is of great importance in all heart affections to avoid indigestion and allied ailments, for such troubles tend to affect the heart very much (through pressure of wind, etc.). It is therefore always best to eat very sparingly, and to leave the table after a meal feeling that you could easily eat more. Never eat to repletion. For the same reason, it is never wise to eat a meal late at night; let the last meal be at least three hours before retiring. Avoid all white-flour products, refined cereals, milk puddings, and other mushy foods; avoid sugar in all forms. Another dietetic point worth bearing well in mind is that it will always pay the heart sufferer to replace meat or other flesh foods, where mentioned in the menus, by either egg or cheese or nuts, where at all possible. ON NO ACCOUNT SHOULD DRUGS OF ANY KIND BE TAKEN.

It is always best to use the warm-water enema or gravity douche to cleanse the bowels nightly during the first few days of the treatment, and afterwards as necessary; whilst if constipation is habitual, the rules for its eradication given in Section 9 (page 275) should be put into operation forthwith. The morning dry friction and sponge outlined in the Appendix should be taken daily by all those capable of it, whilst the breathing and other exercises (also outlined in the Appendix should be gone through in conjunction with them, so far as is possible without straining or overtaxing the heart. These exercises should be done very gently at first and more vigorously as the patient improves. (Some will have to leave the exercises out altogether; each person must use his own discretion here.) It is a mistake to think that sufferers from heart troubles should not take much exercise, though it should never be really strenuous, but of a gentle kind. Walking is the best exercise of all.

Those who can stand a hot bath fairly well should have a hot Epsom-salts bath every week, as part of the treatment, but the bath should not be taken too hot in any case.

If the sufferer from valvular heart disease (or other heart trouble) carries on as here directed, progress is bound to follow, even in really long-standing cases; but of course the rate of progress will depend in every case upon the nature of the heart lesion, its duration, etc. The longer the treatment is persevered with, the better will the results be in every case.

As a general rule, the patient under treatment should take things fairly quietly and easily, and have plenty of rest daily. Early hours and no excesses must be the order of the day, and excitement and prolonged nervous or physical strain must be carefully avoided.

Spinal manipulation, where at all procurable, is very much to be recommended in all cases of heart trouble.

SPECIAL NOTE.—Where drugs for the heart have been taken over a long period, they may be left off *gradually*, and not all at once.

DISEASES OF THE LIVER, GALL-BLADDER, KIDNEYS, BLADDER AND PANCREAS

Abscess on the liver—Biliousness (" Bilious attack ")—Bright's disease—Cancer of the liver—Cirrhosis of the liver—Congestion of the kidneys—Cystitis—Diabetes (Insipidus)—Diabetes (Mellitus) — Dropsy — Gall-stones — Hæmaturia — Inflammation of the bladder — Inflammation of the gall-bladder — Jaundice — Movable or displaced kidney — Nephritis (Acute) — Nephritis (Chronic)—Pyelitis—Sluggish, enlarged, and torpid liver—Stone in the kidney or bladder—Tubercular kidney.

THE LIVER

THE liver is one of the most important and vital organs of the body. Indeed, in many ways, it is *the* most important of all. Its functions are of supreme importance to the life of the organism both in health and disease, and indeed, if the medical profession but knew it, it is the liver which is called upon more often than not to deal with the drugs forced upon a somewhat defenceless organism under the guise of restoring the said organism to health through the medium of medical treatment. For the liver is the great barrier within the system to the inroads of foreign and deleterious substances which would seriously affect the working of the system as a whole if allowed undisputed entry ; and—all unknown to either the drug victim or his medical advisers—many a battle is fought out within the confines of the liver between the drugs of orthodox medication and this great defence mechanism of the body. But more of this anon ; let us proceed first with our general remarks concerning the liver.

Briefly stated, the general functions of the liver are : (1) to produce bile ; (2) to store glycogen, or animal starch ; (3) to excrete waste products. Although of its three main duties each is of vital consequence to the organism as a whole, the secretion of bile is perhaps the most important of all the liver functions. Bile is both a secretion and an excretion ; it is a secretion concerned in the emulsification and assimilation of fats in digestion, and it aids, in some degree, the peristalsis of the bowels. Bile is also an excretion, inasmuch as it breaks down and disposes of blood pigments, together with a certain quantity of the waste of protein metabolism.

With regard to its second function, the storage of glycogen, or animal starch, the liver is constantly involved in the assimilation of starches. After starches and sugars have been rendered fit for absorption by the digestive processes, they are taken via the blood-stream to the liver, and there a certain amount is converted into glycogen, to be stored up for the future needs of the body, only a very limited amount of sugar being allowed in the blood at any one time. When the body is in need of a new supply of sugar for its work, a certain quantity of the glycogen in the liver—which has been stored up—is reconverted into dextrose (sugar) and allowed to enter into the circulation, thence to be utilised by the tissues.

The liver has also a great deal to do with protein metabolism. When protein foods are broken down in the system (digested), they are converted into what are known as amino-acids, and when too much protein food has been eaten, a large proportion of these amino-acids of protein digestion are carried to the liver, there to be broken down into urea—together with other nitrogenous wastes of the system—and finally eliminated through the kidneys in the urine. This point is of vital importance to the understanding of the cause of a large percentage of liver disorders, and of kidney disorders too ; for the more meat, fish, eggs, cheese, and other protein foods are included in the daily dietary, the more excess protein will there be for the liver to break down into urea and get rid of via the kidneys, and the more will these two organs be adversely affected both in health and functional ability in consequence.

It will thus be seen that the liver is the chief organ concerned in preserving the balance of nutrition of the body, and it also acts as an important defence against poisons generated in the system either in the normal course of bodily functioning or in abnormal conditions of such functioning. Further, and as already mentioned, it is the great defender of the body against the inroads of medicinal drugs. It will thus be seen that if, for any reason, the liver fails to carry out its allotted tasks, the system as a whole will immediately suffer as a direct consequence in many and varied ways.

It will be obvious from the foregoing that the liver is an organ which is subjected to a continual strain all the time because of the variety and importance of the functions it is called upon to perform in the vital economy of the system ; and it will be equally obvious, surely, that where there is constant overfeeding and other dietetic indiscretions, the liver will be made to bear the immediate brunt of such living, with consequent malfunctioning and subsequent disease.

But the relationship between diseases and disorders of the liver and wrong feeding are yet further intensified by the chronic constipation which usually accompanies such wrong feeding habits ; for where there is chronic constipation there are always large quantities of toxic material forming in the bowel, and as a means of safeguarding the health of the system these toxic materials are carried by the *portal vein* to the liver, to be dealt with as best that organ can, in its rôle of defender of the health of the organism. Thus where there is chronic constipation, the liver will be constantly swarming with bacteria and toxins which it will have to destroy or neutralise, in addition to its other functions.

Then again (and as already pointed out), in addition to its liability to disease from the sources just referred to, the liver is the great barrier to the entry of drugs into the system proper, and so drugs taken for the supposed " curing " of stomach or bowel or other disorders have more often than not to be dealt with by the liver and ultimately taken care of there, to the yet further detriment of the said organ. (In the drug treatment of fevers the liver is practically always affected and often permanently enlarged as a direct result of such treatment.) And finally, when the liver *itself* succumbs to all these factors acting against it, it is subjected to yet further drug treatment *on its own behalf*, in the belief that by so doing it can be brought back to normal functioning again ! No wonder liver disorders continue to grow in our overfed and drug-drenched world !

The drugs most frequently employed in the orthodox treatment of liver disorders are those which contain mercury—such as calomel —it having been observed by the medical profession that such drugs have a very strong effect indeed upon the liver, and it being assumed accordingly that such effect must of necessity be beneficial. But in reality this result upon the liver of calomel and other mercurial drugs is due to the fact that such drugs are instinctively recognised as being in the highest degree harmful to the health of the organism, and so the liver makes desperate efforts to deal with them and counteract their effect. The doctor believes that his mercurial drugs are forcing the liver to act naturally again, where it has been torpid or sluggish before ; but in truth the liver has simply been goaded into unnatural and forced activity in its efforts to deal with the drug. This explains the use of mercurial compounds in the medical treatment of liver disorders. The whole thing is based upon a complete misunderstanding as to what effect drugs have upon the system in general and upon the liver in particular. Instead of the liver being improved in function by such treatment, it is simply left all the more exhausted after its enforced activity in dealing with the drug.

The habitual drinking of alcoholic liquor also very adversely affects the working of the liver, because in its rôle as defender of the system the liver is called upon to deal as best it can with alcoholic poisons too ; and much liver trouble in later life can be directly traced to that one cause alone. Again, the constant use of condiments, sauces, seasonings, and spicings of all kinds tends to upset liver functioning too, quite apart from any of the other factors already mentioned, because the liver is ultimately called upon to deal with the end-products of such embellishments of the daily dietary, to its own cost,

So much, then, for our general survey of the liver, its functions. and the potential sources (and causes) of the diseases it suffers from. As the intelligent reader will have fully grasped by now, apart from general factors affecting the health of the organism as a whole, such as lack of exercise, nerve enervation due to excesses of all kinds, overwork, etc., liver disorders and diseases owe their origin to two main causative factors : (1) to wrong feeding habits on the part of the individual concerned, especially over-feeding and over-indulgence in drink ; (2) to the suppressive drug treatment of former disease of one kind or another As to the method or methods by which such disorders and diseases of the liver can be overcome, the reader has only to turn to the treatments given in the present section, and to follow such treatments out carefully, for the path to health to be opened up to him, even though under orthodox medication his condition has been getting gradually worse for years. Drug usage for liver troubles never removes causes and inevitably tends to make the condition of the sufferer worse in time, by virtue of the drugs employed ; natural treatment for liver troubles *actually removes causes*, and so paves the way for that return to real health which can only follow in its wake.

THE KIDNEYS

If not quite as important as the liver, the kidneys are of the greatest significance in the maintenance of bodily health and well-being. They are the organs through which a great part of the refuse and waste matter piled up in the body during the course of bodily activity and functioning are removed, or *eliminated* ; and any breakdown in their activity will have the direst consequences where the health and efficacy of the organism are concerned, as the sufferer from kidney trouble soon finds to his cost.

The kidneys are two bean-shaped organs situated in the back part of the abdominal cavity on either side of the spine. They lie partly above, and partly below, the waist-line. From the centre, or concave side, of each kidney a tube originates, which terminates in the bladder. The two tubes are termed ureters, and they serve to convey the urine from the kidneys to the bladder.

The interior of the kidneys consists of a complicated system of tiny tubules and other structures, which form a filter for the purification of the blood. Waste material of the system, such as urea, acids, salts, ptomaines, and so on, are removed from the blood by the kidneys and, in solution in water, are discharged as urine through the ureters, bladder, and urethra. When in a healthy state the kidneys purify the blood, excreting the urea, salts, and toxins only. The presence in the urine of such nutritive substances as sugar, albumen, and mineral elements shows an abnormal condition of the organs, and usually is a prelude to destructive changes within the kidneys themselves.

It has already been pointed out in dealing with the liver that excess protein is broken down by that organ into urea, and is thence passed on to the kidneys to be excreted in the urine. Thus the most potent cause for the setting up of kidney trouble is at once made manifest. A dietary in which meat, fish, eggs, cheese, and other high protein foods are very prominent, and in which there is also excessive consumption of demineralised starchy foods, sugars, and fats, is one which will tend markedly towards the development of kidney disease in later life, because of the great strain that will be imposed upon the kidneys in dealing with the waste products arising in the system from such continual unwise feeding habits. And in this respect the usual white-bread, white-sugar, boiled-potato, porridge, pudding-and-pie dietary, of to-day, with its bacon and eggs for breakfast and meat and fish once or twice a day as well, is the dietary most likely of all to set up kidney trouble, which said kidney trouble usually shows itself when the victim of such an injudicious régime is just beginning to get on in years.

It usually takes time for the kidney structures to break down and for kidney disease to appear, but previous drug treatment for disease of one kind or another—especially fevers, influenza, and other acute diseases—through the serious damage to the kidney structures which often ensues as a direct result of such suppressive treatment, is a most potent factor in the setting up of that permanent kidney weakness which tends ultimately towards the development of chronic kidney trouble. Kidney disease *in the acute form* often arises, indeed, as a *direct* complication of the medical treatment of acute conditions of the kind just referred to, the kidneys being seriously affected by the forcing back of toxic matter into the system through the agency of the drugs employed, as well as being affected directly by the drugs themselves.

The habitual taking of medicines (and chemical agents of one kind or another) over a period of years, for the alleviation of indigestion and stomach troubles in general, also tends to affect the kidneys adversely ; for it must always be borne in mind that it is the kidneys which are ultimately called upon to deal with (and eliminate if possible) the waste residues and end-products of the interaction of all drugs and chemical substances taken into the system for the purpose (so called) of " curing " or " getting rid of " the systemic manifestations of disease. Many of these chemical substances the kidneys find it extremely hard—sometimes impossible—to deal with satisfactorily ; their continued presence is a source of constant irritation to the delicate kidney structures ; and so future kidney disease is readily precipitated. For instance, when chemical agents such as bicarbonate of soda are taken for the relief of indigestion, heartburn, etc., a residue of chemical matter is left behind in the stomach which is ultimately carried to the kidneys by the blood-stream for excretion. When such chemical agents are taken habitually, over a period of years the kidneys find it harder and harder to withstand the irritating effects upon them of the chemical end-products thus generated in the system, and so one more potent factor in the development of future kidney disease is thus made clear. The same remarks apply with equal force to the habitual taking of aspirin and other " headache removers," pain-killers, etc.

We have stated that wrong feeding, previous suppressive drug treatment of disease (especially acute disease), and the habitual use of indigestion mixtures, " pain-killers," etc., are all directly concerned in that undermining of kidney efficiency which ultimately leads to definite disease of the kidney structures (which disease usually appears in middle or later life) ; but there are other factors which must be mentioned too. Among these, the habitual drinking of strong tea and coffee and alcoholic liquors, and the too-free use of condiments, sauces, seasonings, etc., are the most important. Tea and coffee are known as *diuretics* (a medical term applied to certain drugs which excite or increase kidney functioning) ; this simply means to say that tea and coffee have the power to increase the activity of the kidneys, because when tea and coffee are taken, the kidneys have to work harder than they should do in order to get rid of the irritating effects of the purins and toxins contained in these beverages. Thus when tea and coffee drinking is indulged in to excess (especially strong tea and strong coffee), the kidneys are bound to suffer in general health and functional ability. The same with alcoholic liquors too. The kidneys and liver are both very adversely affected by the habitual consumption of such beverages. As for condiments, seasonings, etc., here again both kidneys and liver share alike in loss of functional ability in having to deal with and get rid of the deleterious end-products of such " embellishments " of the daily dietary.

In addition to the factors enumerated above, as being potent causative factors in the setting up of kidney disease, it is well to bear in mind that the kidneys are organs of elimination, so that any falling off in the efficacy of any of the other eliminative organs—the skin, the bowels, and the lungs—will tend automatically to throw extra work upon the kidneys. Lack of exercise and fresh air and habitual constipation will all play their part in helping on the appearance of kidney trouble in the individual concerned.

As regards the medical treatment for diseases of the kidneys, we have already said that previous suppressive drug medication of disease plays a big part in the setting up of future kidney trouble, so how shall further drugs cure such conditions when present ? As one might expect, medical therapy for kidney diseases has proved itself so ineffectual that any serious kidney trouble is generally regarded in medical circles as *quite incurable*. No attempt being made to get rid of causes, obviously the condition remains " incurable " under orthodox treatment, especially as the drugs employed only tend to increase the kidney weakness !

As for treatment for kidney disease by operation, that is a most dangerous procedure, and at best is only palliative. *Causes are not removed in the slightest by such treatment*, and as the patient is allowed to go on after the operation living in the same old wrong way as before (and, if a kidney has been completely removed, with only one kidney to keep his system clear of toxic matter), what possible hope of future restoration to health can there be in such cases ? Stones in the kidney removed by operation always tend to return, simply because the cause of the trouble—*which is systemic*—is there just as much *after* the operation as before!

Now, although kidney disease is regarded so gloomily in orthodox medical circles—and quite rightly so, judging by the results obtained in treatment !—natural treatment for kidney trouble gives the most marked and astonishing results. For the kidneys respond very quickly indeed to any treatment which *aids* them to achieve normal functioning, instead of *hindering* and *suppressing* it. Fasting and strict dieting are the two chief agents employed in the natural treatment for kidney disease, and by their aid many hundreds of people, condemned to a life of chronic invalidism under medical hands, have been restored to health and fitness once more. Except with regard to advanced or extreme cases, the treatment for kidney disease given in the present section should bring renewed life and health again to many a sufferer who has despaired of ever recovering from his complaint.

Abscess on the Liver.—In discussing the liver and its functions in the opening pages of the present section it has been pointed out that if constipation is habitual, the liver is called upon to get rid of (or take care of) as best it can the toxins and bacteria brought to it from the bowel by the *portal vein*. When the liver is already very much overworked and below par, the net result of this often is that an abscess forms in the liver tissue, which is the only way Nature can devise of disposing, temporarily, of these toxic bowel substances.

Treatment.—If people are going to let their system get into such a state that an abscess on the liver forms, then operative treatment *may* be the only thing left to do in the circumstances ; for by that time the condition of the whole system would have been allowed to deteriorate so far that natural curative agencies might well be powerless in the matter. But it must be understood that such surgical treatment *has done nothing at all to remove the causes of the abscess*, and unless the patient is prepared to take himself in hand along natural lines thereafter, further serious trouble of one kind or another is bound to be his lot sooner or later.

The only sound advice to give, therefore, is not to let the system get into such a state that an abscess on the liver can form ; but if one *has* formed, then naturopathic advice should be sought *at once.* Even if an operation cannot be prevented, at least the patient can be placed upon a proper scheme of living afterwards and much future serious trouble obviated.

Biliousness ("Bilious Attack").—Although the public are as a general rule so grossly ignorant as to the effects of wrong feeding upon the health of the system, they have yet learned to regard a "bilious attack" as the penalty to be paid by erring man for the grosser kind of dietetic indiscretions. The eating of too rich food, of too much food at a meal, of badly assorted foods, etc., etc., may all lead to the development of a "bilious attack" in those whose systems are in an habitually food-clogged condition, and chronic constipation is one of the most potent predisposing factors in the case. An overworked and congested condition of the stomach and liver, with interference with the bile secretion of the liver, lead directly to an attack.

Treatment.—The only obvious treatment for a condition such as biliousness is total abstention from food for the time the unpleasant symptoms connected with an attack last. The patient should take nothing but warm water, or orange juice and water, for a day or two, and follow this with a further one or two days on the *exclusive fresh fruit diet* given in the Appendix. During this time the bowels should be cleansed nightly with the warm-water enema or gravity douche. After the all-fruit period, the *full weekly dietary* given in the Appendix should be adopted, and if this is adhered to rigidly thereafter, further bilious attacks will be a most rare occurrence indeed.

Those who have been prone to biliousness over a long period should put into operation a full scheme of general treatment along the lines of that given for *Sluggish or Torpid Liver* (page 366) farther on in the present section. ON NO ACCOUNT SHOULD DRUGS OF ANY KIND BE TAKEN.

Bright's Disease.—See *Nephritis (Acute and Chronic)*, farther on in the present section (page 360).

Cancer of the Liver.—See *Cancer* (Section 9, page 265).

Cirrhosis of the Liver.—This is a condition in which there is progressive breaking down of the liver cells, the liver gradually contracting in size and becoming hard and leathery. Cirrhosis is a most serious state, and if allowed to progress leads ultimately to the death of the sufferer. The excessive use of alcohol over a period of many years, is the most potent causative factor in the development of cirrhosis but food excesses in general and the habitual taking of quinine over a length of time in tropical climates can also be cited as important factors in some cases. Drug treatment for syphilis, fevers, etc., can also play its part in leading to the future development of cirrhosis of the liver.

Treatment.—Cirrhosis of the liver is a condition generally looked upon in orthodox medical circles as being incurable, and not much can be expected even from natural methods unless the case is taken in hand in the fairly early stages. Institutional treatment is always best; but if this is impossible, the patient should endeavour to carry on under the personal supervision of a competent Naturopath.

Where neither institutional nor personal naturopathic guidance is possible in any given case, treatment should be along the following lines: Begin with a fast for from three to five or seven days (according to the ability of the patient), and follow this with the *fruit and milk* diet given in the Appendix for a further two weeks to a month. Then a *full weekly dietary,* as given in the Appendix, should be adopted. Further short fasts and periods on fruit and milk should be undertaken at intervals of, say, a month thereafter, as required.

The warm-water enema should be used during the treatment as needed, and the scheme of baths, exercises, etc., given in the treatment for *Sluggish Liver* farther on in the present section (page 366) should be undertaken as far as possible in conjunction with the dietetic treatment here advised. All habits of eating, drinking, etc., which have led to the development of the trouble in the first place must be rigorously tabooed in future. Rest, quiet, simple food, early hours, and no excesses are essential to the success of the treatment. *On no account must any drugs be taken.*

Congestion of the Kidneys.—Congestion of the kidneys is generally the first stage in the development of kidney disease. Owing to some (or all) of the factors referred to in the introductory remarks on the kidneys in the opening pages of the present section (such as wrong feeding, excessive drinking, the habitual taking of medicinal drugs, etc., etc.), there is a gradual accumulation of systemic poisons, disease products, and drug poisons in the kidneys over a period of years, and congestion arises from these morbid deposits obstructing the flow of the blood through the tiny capillaries of the kidneys.

The symptoms of congestion of the kidneys (which is a simple acute inflammatory condition) are : pain over the region of the kidneys, constant desire to pass water, and high specific gravity and high colour of the urine.

Treatment.—If this simple *renal hyperœmia* (congestion of blood in the kidneys) were treated by natural methods right away, the successive stages of acute and chronic kidney disease which usually follow the orthodox treatment of the condition would be entirely avoided. But this first simple inflammatory crisis denoted by congestion of the kidneys is treated at once by suppressive drugs, and so chronic kidney disease is more often than not the final result. (There are cases, of course, where patients have completely recovered after being treated along medical lines for congestion of the kidneys, but this has been *in spite of,* and not because of, the drug treatment employed ; the inherent high vitality of the patient has helped to defeat the suppressive action of the drugs employed, and brought about a natural cessation of the trouble.)

The proper treatment for congestion of the kidneys is *fasting.* The patient should be fasted on water and orange juice for as long as the acute symptoms last, and the warm-water enema should be used nightly during that time. Then the *all-fruit diet* given in the Appendix can be adopted for a further few days, and finally the *full weekly dietary,* also outlined in the Appendix, can be begun when convalescence is well advanced. This full weekly dietary should be adhered to rigorously thereafter if future kidney trouble is to be effectively prevented and sound health achieved.

During the fasting period hot Epsom-salts baths will be most effective if given every day or every other day, and wet packs should be applied over the kidney area several times daily and one at night. (See Appendix for details as to how the packs should be applied.) After the Epsom-salts bath the patient should be sponged down with cold or tepid water before being put back to bed. Complete rest is essential until convalescence has been reached. *No drugs whatsoever are to be taken.*

If the foregoing simple treatment is carried out, not only will the kidney congestion be overcome, but the patient will be in far better health after it than for many years before, because of the thorough

346

cleansing his system will have received. Contrast this with the effect of drug treatment in a similar case !

Cystitis.—Cystitis means inflammation of the bladder. It is usually the mucous membrane of the bladder which is affected, but sometimes the deeper structures are involved too. Cystitis may be acute or chronic, and if treated along orthodox medical lines may never clear up finally, but hang on and on to make the future life of the patient a sheer misery in many cases. Germ infection is usually cited as the predisposing cause of cystitis by the medical profession, but this means nothing really. Germs can only flourish in a suitable soil, and unless the patient has a system full of toxic matter (and more especially a bladder which is in a highly toxic condition), an inflammatory condition such as cystitis could never arise, no matter how many millions of germs there might be present.

Although there may be various minor extraneous predisposing causes, such as a chill, etc., which may precipitate an attack in any given case, a highly toxic condition of the system due to wrong feeding and general wrong living is at the real root of cystitis in all cases ; and previous suppressive medical treatment for acute diseases such as fevers, influenza, etc., often plays a big part in the setting up of the trouble (as does also chronic constipation).

Treatment.—As already observed, treatment for cystitis along orthodox medical lines, by means of bladder wash-outs, drugs, etc., is never really successful. Of course many cases *seemingly* recover under such treatment, but the patient is always liable to the future recurrence of attacks ; others never recover to any extent at all, and are doomed to much misery and pain thereafter as a result of the treatment employed.

The only correct treatment for cystitis is *fasting* for as long as the acute symptoms last. The patient should be kept in bed and given only orange juice and water during that time, and the warm-water enema or gravity douche used nightly to cleanse the bowels. When the acute symptoms have disappeared, then the *all-fruit diet* given in the Appendix can be adopted for a day or two, to be followed by the *fruit and milk* diet also detailed therein. When on the fruit and milk diet not more than two pints of the latter should be taken daily for the first few days, and up to three pints can be taken later on. The patient should have just enough milk to satisfy his need for sustenance.

If the foregoing treatment is persevered with, the cystitis will clear up completely, and then the *full weekly dietary* outlined in the Appendix can be gradually embarked upon, and should be rigorously adhered to thereafter if future bladder trouble of any kind is to be prevented.

If constipation is habitual—as it often is in these cases—the rules for its eradication given in Section 9 (page 275) should be put into operation, and the daily dry friction and sitz-bath and physical and other exercises given in the Appendix should be performed regularly as soon as convalescence has been reached. A hot Epsom-salts bath should be taken twice weekly.

During the acute symptoms a hot and cold sitz-bath should be had two or three times daily (the chill being taken off the cold sitz-bath in certain cases if necessary), and hot applications can be applied over the bladder area several times daily too. A towel is wrung out in hot water, applied for two minutes, then removed and a second towel applied, and later a third. A cold towel is applied to finish off. Always work in this order : three hot, one cold application. (For details of the hot and cold sitz-bath, see the Appendix.)

ON NO ACCOUNT SHOULD ANY DRUGS OF ANY SORT BE USED, OR BLADDER WASH-OUTS OF ANY KIND.

Future care with regard to the dietary is most essential, and white bread, white-flour products, sugar, boiled potatoes, refined cereals, milk puddings, pastry, puddings and pies, and all heavy, stodgy, and greasy foods must be rigorously excluded from the future dietary. Meat can with benefit be left out altogether, too, as also other flesh foods, and their place taken by eggs, cheese, or nuts, where flesh foods are mentioned on the diet-sheet. Tea, coffee, and alcohol should also be strictly avoided in future, and all condiments, pickles, sauces, etc.*

Diabetes (Insipidus).—Diabetes may be of two kinds, *diabetes insipidus* and *diabetes mellitus*. The latter kind is the more serious of the two, and is the one commonly known as *diabetes*. *Diabetes insipidus*, the form of diabetes that we are here considering, is characterised by the passing of great quantities of urine—urine that is almost colourless. Although great physical exertion may be the cause of the trouble in certain cases, the disease is most often nervous in origin ; and injury to the nerve centres in the brain and spinal cord, excessive emotionalism, overwork, brain-fag, etc., etc., may all bring on the complaint.

* For *Chronic Cystitis*, treatment should be as for *Nephritis (Chronic)*, p. 363.

Treatment.—As regards treatment for diabetes insipidus, the patient should be kept very quiet, rested in bed, and a *short fast* for three or four days undertaken as directed in the Appendix at the end of the book. The fast should then be broken as directed, and a period of from seven to fourteen days spent on the *restricted diet*, also outlined in the Appendix, according to the severity or otherwise of the case. Then the *full weekly dietary* given in the Appendix can be begun. Further fasts and periods on the restricted diet may be required at intervals, in some cases, before the trouble finally clears up.

During the fast, and after if necessary, the bowels should be cleansed nightly with the warm-water enema or douche, and where constipation is habitual, the rules for its eradication given in Section 9 (page 275) should be put into operation forthwith. The morning dry friction and sponge or sitz-bath and the breathing and other exercises given in the Appendix, should be performed regularly daily by the patient as soon as well enough. Hot Epsom-salts baths three times weekly will be most beneficial, as will also ordinary hot baths. Sun and air bathing will also be highly valuable.

Complete rest and careful treatment along the lines laid down should lead to the best results in most cases, but, if procurable, *manipulative treatment* would form a most useful adjunct to the régime. Strain, excitement, and arduous mental or physical work should be carefully guarded against when once the patient has recovered. *No drugs of any kind should be taken during treatment.* Tea, coffee, alcohol, and all condiments, sauces, etc., must be rigorously excluded from the future dietary, also sugar.

Diabetes (Mellitus).—This is the common form of diabetes, where there is sugar present in the urine. In the ordinary course of events, when starches are digested in the small intestine, the resultant glucose (sugar) is carried by the blood to the liver, and only a certain small amount is allowed to remain in the blood at any one time. (See description of the work and function of the liver in the opening pages of the present section.) In diabetes mellitus, however, more than this minimum amount of sugar remains in the blood, and the kidneys get rid of as much of the excess as they can by excreting it in the urine.

It is generally supposed that in diabetes the pancreas is at fault, because the pancreas secretes a fluid which plays an important part in the digestion of starches and sugars ; but the disease is really one of faulty nutritional balance, following on a breakdown of the whole nutritional system of the body, in which the liver and other vital organs are involved just as much as the pancreas. The trouble is far more *systemic* in origin than the failure of any particular organ, and takes many years to develop. Long-continued unwise feeding habits, enervation of the system through excesses and indulgences of all kinds, protracted worry, overwork, etc., and suppressive medical treatment of former disease are the chief predisposing factors concerned in the setting up of this systemic disturbance of nutritional activity which we call *diabetes*.

It is often assumed that it is just overeating of starchy and sugary foods which is basically responsible for the breakdown in nutritional balance leading to diabetes, but as a matter of fact it is through subsistence on a dietary in which both proteins and fats, *as well as* starches and sugars, are present in great over-excess, that the trouble ultimately arises (in conjunction with the other factors just previously named).

We have stated again and again in the present book that at the bottom of practically every form of disease lies the white-bread, white-sugar, meat, boiled-potatoes, cooked-vegetable, pastry, pudding-and-pie dietary of to-day ; but why such a form of diet, aided by general wrong living (and often environmental factors) should lead to high blood-pressure and kidney trouble in one person, asthma and bronchitis in another, and diabetes in a third, it is impossible to say. All we know is *that this is actually the case,* and it can only be supposed that the constitutional make-up of the individual (and possibly hereditary tendencies) play the final part in determining just what form disease will take in any particular case. Still, the great point is that if people *do* eat and live in the way mentioned above, disease in one form or another is *bound* to be their lot ; and the more such disease is suppressively treated by drugs, operations, etc., the more will chronic conditions of the type of diabetes, kidney disease, asthma, bronchitis, etc., be their ultimate lot. It is a most significant fact, but the more readily Medical Science devises means of suppressing colds, chills, fevers, influenza, etc., the more do chronic diseases of the kind here referred to grow, as witnessed by present-day disease statistics !

Treatment.—Since the discovery of the insulin treatment for diabetes the public have been led to believe that here at least the medical profession have vindicated their right to be considered as the " Nation's saviours from disease ! " ; but, as a matter of fact, nothing proves more conclusively than the insulin treatment for diabetes the contention made again and again in the present book that medical usage does nothing to remove causes and really cure disease, but merely tampers with and removes or suppresses symptoms.

The insulin treatment for diabetes takes no notice of causes, but merely tries to get rid of *the effects of diabetes*. It can never be claimed to be curative by the widest stretch of the imagination, for in the great majority of cases it has to be taken regularly *for ever after*, once it has been begun. When the insulin craze first started, the public were led to believe that insulin was a *positive cure* for diabetes, and the Press went wild with excitement over this " wonderful discovery of modern Medical Science." But sad disillusionment was in store for those diabetics who believed what they were told. Many a poor wretch has been turned into a human pin-cushion as a result of having daily insulin injections for the rest of his life, as a " cure " for his diabetes ! (Of such are the cures of Medical Science made !)

Not only is insulin not a cure for diabetes, but the dietetic treatment carried out at the same time is so ill-arranged and unbalanced that many a sufferer from diabetes finds himself the victim of all sorts of other ailments—as well as his diabetes—as a result of such a régime. Constipation and indigestion are the least of the evils attendant upon the orthodox dietetic treatment for diabetes, carried out in conjunction with insulin injections.

As we have said, the Press went hysterical over the wonders of insulin, but now that it has been proved definitely to be no cure for diabetes, nothing is said on that point. The poor diabetic is still made to believe that in insulin lies his only saviour from his disease— until he tries it and finds out what insulin treatment really means ! Besides, Medical Science knows of nothing else to put in its place, so insulin treatment it must be, even though it has so sadly failed to come up to the high expectations held out for it in the first place.

The sufferer from diabetes who places himself under Natural-Cure treatment is in an entirely different position from the insulin-riddled patient of orthodox medicine. When treated by fasting and strict dieting, diabetes (if not too chronic) can eventually be got rid of; it is *really cured* that way, not just temporarily alleviated, as when insulin is used. That is because under natural treatment the *actual causes* of the disease are removed and the whole health-level of the patient built up. But no word appears in the Press about the wonders of the fasting treatment for diabetes—or the fasting treatment for any disease, for that matter ! Natural Cure has to fight its way unaided by any gratuitous publicity of the sort that is so lavishly bestowed upon the medical profession. But still, publicity or no publicity, it is results that count, and that is where Natural Cure scores all the time, not only with regard to diabetes, but with all diseases in general.

Treatment in a Natural-Cure home, or under the personal super-vision of a competent Naturopath, is always best in diabetes, especially if insulin treatment has already been or is being taken ; for insulin renders the curative work of the Natural-Cure régime far harder to carry out than if it had never been used. (Indeed, in some cases it makes a cure impossible.) But in all ordinary cases the sufferer can carry on quite well at home, along the following lines, if personal treatment is not possible in his particular case. Those who are taking insulin, and who wish to carry out the treatment, may do so, of course, but must take special note of the remarks made on page 354.

The diabetic sufferer should begin with a short fast for three or four days, having nothing but orange juice and warm water during that time. Then a further two to four days should be spent on the *all-fruit diet* given in the Appendix. (Rather serious cases will need a longer fast, say up to seven days, before beginning on the fruit diet.) After the fast and period on all-fruit, the *fruit and milk diet* given in the Appendix should then be adopted, and should be adhered to until all traces of sugar have disappeared from the urine. In cases where the latter has cleared during the fast or all-fruit period—which it very often will do—the fruit and milk diet can be omitted.

The fruit and milk diet can be carried on from a few days up to three or four weeks in some cases, as needed, the amount of milk taken daily not exceeding four pints, however. If the urine has not cleared by that time in any given case, then a further short fast and period on all-fruit will be needed, with an added period on fruit and milk to follow. But these will be exceptional cases, however ; most cases will have quite cleared up by that time.

When the urine is free of sugar, then the diabetic can begin on the *full weekly dietary* given in the Appendix, but *all bread, potatoes, and dried fruit* should be omitted from the dietary for at least a fortnight to a month. If the patient's condition continues to improve, and no further sugar appears, then these articles of diet can be gradually reincluded in the dietary at the end of that time, as outlined in the menus in question. In any case, no sugar at all should be taken in future ; if any sweetening substance is needed for any purpose at all, such as stewing fruits, etc., a little honey should be used—nothing else.

If for any reason sugar should reappear in the urine at any time, a further short fast followed by fruit and milk should be undertaken at once, until the urine is quite clear again.

During the fast, and after if necessary, the bowels should be cleansed nightly with a warm-water enema or gravity douche ; and where constipation is habitual, the rules for its eradication given in Section 9 (page 275) should be put into operation forthwith. A daily dry friction and sitz-bath or sponge, as directed in the Appendix, should be taken regularly ; and the physical and other exercises also given in the Appendix should be gone through daily in conjunction with them. A hot Epsom-salts bath should be indulged in two or three times weekly to begin with, and less frequently later. Whilst the diabetic condition lasts, frequent warm baths are very good, say every other day. Sun and air bathing is also most beneficial, if procurable in any given case.

All habits and practices which have led to the enervation of the system must be discontinued, and the " worry habit " in particular must be guarded against. (For helpful suggestions on this point, see the treatment for *Neurasthenia* in Section 5, page 192.) A simple scheme of living, with early hours and no excesses, must be instituted. The diet factor is of the utmost importance, and no white bread, white-flour products, sugar, boiled potatoes, pastry, puddings or pies, milk puddings, refined cereals (such as rice, tapioca, porridge, etc.), are to be taken in future ; no strong tea, or coffee or alcohol ; no condiments, pickles, sauces, etc. Meat and other flesh foods must be eaten very sparingly indeed, as also butter and other fats or oils. No cream should be taken at all, and no animal fats such as lard. Fresh fruits and salads MUST form the main bulk of the future dietary.*

* A watchful eye must always be kept on bread (even if wholemeal) and dried fruits, as these are danger foods for the diabetic and must always be eaten sparingly.

Fresh air and gentle outdoor exercise such as walking should form an essential part of the treatment, and a walk of three or four miles every day can be recommended to all patients capable of it as a very good thing indeed.

SPECIAL NOTE RE INSULIN.—As already remarked, where insulin has been used it makes natural treatment far more difficult to achieve a cure than if none had been taken. Those who have taken insulin over a period of time but have since stopped its use may, however, still carry on as directed. It is those who are *still taking insulin* who need the most care in treatment. These are, therefore, again strongly advised to carry out the regimen under the expert guidance of a Naturopath *where at all possible*. If this cannot be done in any given case, then the following is the best way to proceed as regards an average case:

Instead of starting on the fast as instructed for the ordinary diabetic sufferer, those who are using insulin *should begin on the full weekly dietary given in the Appendix, but reducing to a minimum bread, potatoes, and dried fruit*. The quantity of insulin being taken should then be steadily *decreased* over a period of from one to two months, until none is being taken at the end of that time. Thereafter, if conditions are favourable, the full scheme of treatment as outlined can be embarked upon.

Dropsy.—By the term "dropsy" is meant the effusion of fluid into the tissues or cavities of the body. Dropsy is a feature of many diseases, and is due to obstruction to the free circulation of the blood and lymph and consequent impaired elimination. Dropsy is often connected with kidney disease, and where present usually indicates that the condition is rather serious. As regards treatment for dropsy, this should be as for the trouble with which it is connected, as detailed in the present book. As the diseased organic condition is cleared up through natural treatment, so the dropsical affection connected with it will clear up too. In general, fasting, hot baths, and all methods for *increasing elimination* are indicated where dropsy is present.

Gall-stones.—Attached to the lower surface of the liver is a small sac known as the gall-bladder, which serves as a reservoir for bile not required for use by the liver. When there is a general catarrhal condition of the system, with overwork and sluggishness of the liver, the bile often becomes thickened, and given a nucleus of cell débris to form around, gall-stones may begin to appear in the gall-bladder.

Gall-stones cannot appear out of " thin air," as it were; neither are they the result of bacterial infection. They are simply and solely the results of many years of wrong feeding habits and general wrong living (plus previous suppressive treatment of disease) which have led to a toxic condition of the system in general, and of the liver and gall-bladder in particular. Chronic constipation is a most important predisposing factor. Gall-stones often take many years to collect, and they may be very small or they may be quite large in size. A large stone may block the bile-duct and lead to an attack of jaundice, or it may actually succeed in passing through the duct into the intestines, causing excruciating agony to the unfortunate sufferer in its passage the while. Smaller stones are often passed without difficulty into the intestines and out of the system in this way, their appearance in the faeces being that of sand in larger or smaller particles. The general symptoms connected with gall-stones are: sharp pain in the region of the lower right ribs (especially on pressure), flatulence, constipation, vomiting, loss of appetite, general sluggishness, etc.

Treatment.—Where a case has been allowed to run on for a long time, and the gall-stones have grown to a large size, it is quite possible that nothing short of an operation will be required to get rid of them. But please note that such surgical treatment is only recommended *in extreme cases,* and at best is only palliative. For nothing is done by such treatment to get rid of the underlying toxicity of the system and liver sluggishness which are responsible for the setting up of the trouble in the first place, and so further stones can form just as easily *after* the operation as before—unless the gall-bladder is taken away, in which case the patient's system will suffer as a result of such treatment, especially the functioning of the liver, which depends upon the gall-bladder for the storage of excess bile, and so will be working at a distinct loss thereafter.

Having said that surgical treatment may be necessary in advanced and serious cases of gall-stones, and having pointed out that such treatment does nothing to remove *the causes of the trouble* or to improve the general health of the patient in a permanent way, we can definitely say that the only way in which gall-stones can be *really cured* is through the agency of natural treatment. By this we mean that under natural treatment *the stones can be dissolved and passed out of the system, and the underlying causes responsible for their occurrence finally removed, thus making it impossible for further stones to appear.* (Something quite different from surgical treatment !)

Where at all possible, treatment for gall-stones should be in a Natural-Cure home, as a fairly long fast may be required in certain cases. Failing this, the services of a competent Naturopath should be secured to supervise the treatment. If either institutional or personal naturopathic treatment is not possible in any given case, it should be along the following lines :

To begin with, a fast for from four to seven days should be undertaken, as described in the Appendix, the duration of the fast depending upon the severity (or otherwise) of the case. After the fast the *restricted diet*, also given in the Appendix, should be begun and adhered to for a further ten to fourteen days. Then the *full weekly dietary* also outlined therein can be adopted.

It may be necessary in certain cases to repeat the process of fast and restricted diet at intervals of, say, six to eight weeks ; this must be left to the patient to decide for himself, at his own discretion, according to the progress being made.

During the fast, and after if necessary, the bowels should be cleansed nightly with a warm-water enema or gravity douche, and the rules for the eradication of constipation given in Section 9 (page 275) should be put into operation. The daily dry friction and sitz-bath or sponge, and the breathing and other exercises given in the Appendix, should be gone through regularly daily, as far as possible, in conjunction with the dietetic treatment. A hot Epsom-salts bath, as detailed in the Appendix, should be taken twice weekly, where at all possible. If there is any pain over the gall-bladder area, hot compresses may be applied several times daily, or a hot-water bottle, whilst a cold pack may be applied at night. (See Appendix for details of these packs.)

The patient should take things very quietly and easily during the first few weeks of the treatment, and plenty of rest is essential. On no account should any drugs or medicines OF ANY KIND be taken. Olive oil is considered to be of great therapeutic value in the treatment of gall-stones, but we do not think its use especially advantageous. Cases that have supposedly been cured by the administration of olive oil have generally not been cases of gall-stones at all, but of inflammation of the gall-bladder, with which gall-stones is often confused in diagnosis. The deposits in the faeces supposed to be broken-down fragments of gall-stones are really particles of olive oil more often than not !

Manipulative treatment, at the hands of a good Osteopath or Naturopath, would be most valuable in conjunction with the treatment here outlined, as would also artificial sunlight and sun and air bathing.

The diet factor is of extreme importance, and fruits and salads *must* form the major portion of the future dietary when cured, as it is only by their aid that the fluids and secretions of the body can be kept clean and wholesome, and the possibility of further gall-stones thus effectually prevented. Tea, coffee, and alcohol must not be taken in future ; neither should any condiments, etc. All demineralised and " foodless " foods, such as white-flour products, white sugar, refined cereals, etc., must be strictly avoided, as must also all heavy and greasy dishes, all fried foods, stews, puddings, pies, etc. Very little in the way of butter or fats of any kind should be taken, too, and cream should be left out entirely from the future dietary, as also all animal fats, such as lard, suet, etc. Meat and other flesh foods must be eaten very sparingly indeed.

Hæmaturia.—Hæmaturia means blood in the urine. Blood may be present there from various causes, most generally from disease or injury to either the kidneys, ureters, bladder, or urethra. The passage of a stone from the kidney towards the bladder may produce hæmaturia sometimes, and prostate-gland disease may also bring on the condition. Certain poisonous drugs may produce hæmaturia, and the complaint is very common in acute eliminative crises such as fevers.

Treatment.—The presence of blood in the urine may or may not be serious. It all depends upon the condition with which it is associated. As regards treatment, it is obvious that it is only by finding out the cause, and treating this, that the hæmaturia can be cured If no cause can be ascertained at all, and there is no pain or other untoward symptom, a few days' fast followed by a further few days on the *all-fruit diet* outlined in the Appendix should soon clear up the trouble. A morning cold sitz-bath, and a hot and cold sitz-bath every night, whilst the bleeding lasts, will also help materially in clearing the urine. The warm-water enema should be used nightly during the first few days of the treatment, and after if necessary. (Sitz-baths are described in detail in the Appendix at the end of the book.)

Inflammation of the Bladder. See *Cystitis* (page 347).

Inflammation of the Gall-bladder.—Like gall-stones, inflammation of the gall-bladder is the outcome of a toxic condition of the system leading to faulty and sluggish liver functioning, as a result of wrong feeding habits, general wrong living, the suppressive medical treatment of former disease, habitual constipation and the purgative habit, etc. It is often associated with gall-stones and with other disorders connected with the liver and its adjacent organs. Treatment for inflammation of the gall-bladder should be along the lines of that for *Gall-stones* given earlier in the present section (page 355), for only by a thorough cleansing of the system and the reorganisation of liver functioning along the lines of treatment there indicated can the trouble be removed and health restored to the sufferer. (Many cases diagnosed as gall-stones are really only cases of inflammation of the gall-bladder.)

Jaundice.—Jaundice is really a group of symptoms rather than a disease. It is produced through obstruction to the passage of bile from the liver, the bile being retained and passed into the general circulation, instead of into the small intestines to complete the work of digestion, as it would do in the ordinary way. The cause of the obstruction may be a simple catarrhal or inflammatory condition occluding the bile duct, or a gall-stone, or a tumour or other toxic factor.

The characteristic feature connected with jaundice is the yellowing of the skin, and particularly of the whites of the eyes, this being due to the presence of the bile in the blood, as a result of the obstruction in question stopping its passage into the intestines. A further result of the bile being prevented from entering the small intestines is that in jaundice digestion (especially that of fats) is very much interfered with, and so there is alternating constipation and diarrhœa, with clay-coloured stools.

Treatment.—Treatment for jaundice must obviously be *fasting*. The patient should be fasted on orange juice and water for as long as the acute symptoms last. This may be from three to seven days or longer, according to the severity (or otherwise) of the case. When the acute symptoms have fully subsided, the *all-fruit diet* outlined in the Appendix can be adopted for a further three to five days, and then the *full weekly dietary* also outlined therein can be gradually embarked upon. The bowels should be cleansed nightly with the warm-water enema or gravity douche during the fast, and after if necessary, and a hot Epsom-salts bath or ordinary hot bath can be taken every day with great benefit.

If the foregoing treatment is faithfully carried out, and the patient rested in bed the while, the attack will clear up in the quickest possible time, leaving the sufferer in far better health than before, owing to the thorough cleansing his system will have received as a result of the treatment.

When a full diet is begun, all fats and oils should be avoided for the first fortnight or so, but butter and olive oil can be included thereafter, as directed on the diet-sheet; these should always be in fairly small quantities, however.

The general remarks regarding diet made to the sufferer from *gall-stones*, in the treatment for this condition earlier in the present section, should be carefully studied after recovery from jaundice. The strict observance of these general dietetic rules is most important if future attacks of jaundice are to be effectually prevented.

SPECIAL NOTE.—Where jaundice is caused through gall-stones, tumour, etc., treatment should be in the hands of a competent Naturopath if at all possible.

Movable or Displaced Kidney.—When the tissues surrounding the kidney, and which keep it in place, become thin and weak, as a result of a devitalised condition of the system in general, it is quite possible that the kidney may be forced out of place if subjected to much strain. The condition is known as *movable kidney*, and is a fairly common occurrence these days, especially among women.

The means usually employed to deal with movable kidney are stitching it back in its rightful place or else the prescription of a surgical belt. In neither of these cases is the real underlying cause of the trouble dealt with, i.e. the weakened condition of the abdominal muscles and of the abdominal structures in general, and so results are far from satisfactory. The only sensible procedure to adopt where movable kidney is concerned is a scheme of general health-building treatment, in which *exercise*, especially of the abdominal muscles, occupies a prominent place. In this way the weakened bodily condition can be gradually overcome and the kidney induced back towards its normal position. In addition, the whole general health of the sufferer will be greatly enhanced by such an all-round régime. Manipulative treatment (at the hands of a good Osteopath) would be most helpful as an adjunct.

All exercise which tends to strengthen the abdominal muscles will be very useful in these cases, and in this connection the reader is referred to the remarks *re* special curative exercises at the end of the treatment for *Dropped Stomach*, in Section 9 (page 279). The scheme of physical exercises given in the Appendix at the end of this book (as well as the friction bath, sitz-bath, etc.) will also be most helpful.

Nephritis (Acute).—Nephritis, or inflammation of the kidneys, is a serious disease-condition, and may be either acute or chronic. The common term applied to the complaint is " Bright's disease," but really Bright's disease refers to the chronic forms of nephritis, and not to the acute form.

The causes underlying diseases of the kidneys in general have already been discussed at length in the introductory pages at the beginning of the present section ; there the reader has been shown the various factors leading up to kidney disease : wrong feeding, excessive drinking, the suppressive medical treatment of former disease, the habitual use of chemical agents of all kinds for the alleviation of indigestion and stomach ailments in general, the too free use of aspirin and other drugs as " pain-killers," etc. A combination of some or all of these factors is at the root of nephritis, either in the acute or chronic forms.

To show how close the relationship between the suppressive drug treatment of disease and nephritis may be, one has only to observe how common it is to find nephritis setting in as a direct complication to the medical treatment of fevers such as scarlet fever, rheumatic fever, etc. The toxic matter forced back into the system as a result of such treatment, combined with the drugs employed, cause an intolerable strain to be placed upon the kidneys in their work as the chief eliminative organs of the system, and so nephritis occurs as a direct result in many cases. (It is worth while repeating again at this point, at the risk of somewhat boring the reader perhaps, that if a fever or other acute disease is treated along Natural-Cure lines, by fasting, etc., complications of the kind such as nephritis can never occur.)

Again, with regard to nephritis, it was pointed out in the treatment for *Congestion of the Kidneys*, earlier in the present section (page 346), that if this condition is treated by means of suppressive drugs, nephritis is very often the result, for exactly the same reasons as those given above.

Acute nephritis is usually characterised by pain in the kidneys extending down the ureters, and by fever, with dull pain in the back. The urine is scanty and highly coloured. Dropsical swellings appear as the inflammatory process continues, and destruction in the capillary blood-vessels and tubular structures cause albumen and blood to leak into the urine.

Treatment.—Treatment for acute kidney disease is essentially *fasting.* By means of the fast the toxins and systemic impurities responsible for the setting up of the inflammatory kidney condition are removed in the quickest and safest possible manner, and the way to future health thus paved. If drug treatment is resorted to, and the acute inflammatory condition suppressed, all sorts of untoward complications may arise, and, more often than not, chronic Bright's disease is the final result.

The sufferer from acute nephritis should be fasted on orange juice and water for as long as the acute symptoms of his condition last. (See the Appendix for details of how to carry out the fast.) The fasting period may have to extend for a week or ten days, or even longer in some cases. Then the *all-fruit diet* outlined in the Appendix should be adopted for a few days, after which—if convalescence is assured—a further time can be spent on fruit and milk, and then the full *weekly dietary,* also outlined in the Appendix, can be gradually embarked upon.

The warm-water enema or gravity douche should be used nightly during the fast, and after as necessary; whilst if constipation is habitual, the rules for its eradication given in Section 9 (page 275) should be put into operation as soon as practicable. All measures which will relieve the kidneys of work by increasing elimination through other channels will be of value in the treatment of acute nephritis, and so hot Epsom-salts baths should be taken every day, or every other day, whilst the acute symptoms last, where possible (or else ordinary hot baths can be taken), to induce elimination through the skin as much as possible. (After any hot bathing the patient should be sponged down with cold or tepid water before being put back to bed.)

Body packs will also be most beneficial in the treatment of acute nephritis, for the purpose of inducing increased skin elimination, and these should be applied two or three times daily, in accordance with the instructions *re Cold Packs* to be found in the Appendix at the end of the book. (A fairly large sheet should be used, so that it can be wound right round the whole trunk.)

If the foregoing treatment is faithfully carried out, and no drugs taken, then the patient should soon be on the way to health again, with his whole body in a far cleaner and healthier state than before, as a result.

As regards general rules *re* living, exercise, and diet thereafter, the patient should turn to the remarks made on these points in the treatment for *Chronic Nephritis*, to follow.

Nephritis (Chronic).—Chronic disease of the kidneys, or *Bright's disease*, may be divided into two classes—*parenchymatous* and *interstitial nephritis*. The former affects more particularly the tubules of the kidneys, and is characterised by dropsy and by large quantities of albumen and casts in the urine. The latter form of chronic nephritis is characterised by atrophy and thickening of the connective tissues of the kidneys, with high blood-pressure, hypertrophy of the heart, changes in the blood-vessel walls, etc.

In the *parenchymatous* type the kidney becomes greatly swollen and assumes a pure white colour. It is known as the *large white kidney*. The walls of the tubules are dilated and thickened with cells and casts. This stage is followed by atrophy and contraction of the whole organ. The kidney becomes smaller, and is known as the *small white kidney*. The patient has persistent dropsy, which first appears under the eyes, but it is soon general over the body. The condition is also attended by intestinal disorders, continual and progressive anæmia, and loss of weight and strength. The disease is of a very stubborn nature, and if left in medical hands grows steadily worse and worse; it is only by properly applied natural treatment and natural living that its course can be checked, and, if degenerative changes have not developed too far, ultimately cured.

The predisposing factors contributing towards the setting up of *parenchymatous* nephritis are those for kidney disease in general, as given in the introductory talk on the kidneys in the opening pages to the present section. The most important are: wrong feeding (i.e. the habitual overeating of protein, starchy, sugary, and fatty foods), alcoholism, sexual diseases, indulgences and excesses of all kinds, worry, overwork, etc., and many forms of drug poisoning. As a matter of fact, any habit or way of living which reduces the vital powers of the body contributes towards the accumulation of toxins in the system, and so helps on chronic kidney trouble. Medical Science admits that the excessive consumption of meat and other protein foods has much to do with the creation of kidney diseases, but it seems quite unable to recognise other equally important causative and contributive factors.

In *interstitial nephritis* the patient complains of loss of strength, anæmia, and intestinal disorders. The pulse exhibits very high tension. The blood-pressure is usually increased, the heart enlarged, and there is frequently palpitation and dizziness. The sight may become affected, and partial or total blindness develop. The urine is pale in colour, increased in quantity, and of low specific gravity. The quantity of urine varies and may disappear altogether at times.

Treatment.—If treatment is left in medical hands, then the sufferer from either form of Bright's disease stands very little hope of recovery. Indeed, his condition is regarded as hopeless from the start. Under natural treatment, however, many are the sufferers from chronic nephritis who have been restored to health after having been given up as quite incurable by the medical profession. Of course, curability depends in every case upon how far the disease has been allowed to progress before natural treatment is begun. Where chronic destruction and atrophy of the organs has been allowed to go on for a long time, then it may not be possible to effect a complete cure. But even so, in these advanced and long-standing cases, if a complete cure is not attainable, a great deal can be done to improve the condition of the sufferer by means of properly applied natural treatment.

As regards treatment for Bright's disease, this should be in a Natural-Cure home or under the personal supervision of a competent Naturopath, *where at all possible*; for to achieve the best results treatment will have to be regulated strictly in accordance with the patient's capacity to carry out a scheme of strict elimination. For it must be realised that in all eliminative activity the kidneys are called upon to carry out a large part of the work, and if they are much diseased, this will mean that they must be carefully nursed during treatment and not exposed to too much eliminative work at a time.

However, if personal treatment is not possible in any given case, the sufferer from Bright's disease can carry on along the following lines on his own behalf, with every hope of achieving the most beneficial results from the treatment.

To begin with, a short fast for three or four days should be undertaken, as directed in the Appendix. This should then be broken as directed, and a further seven to fourteen days should be spent on the *restricted diet* outlined in the Appendix. (This restricted diet should be proceeded with for as many days as possible, as the longer it can be continued, the better it will be.) Then the *full weekly dietary*, also outlined in the Appendix, can be begun and adhered to as strictly as possible thereafter.

Further short fasts followed by periods on the restricted diet should be undertaken at intervals of two or three months, until such time as the kidney condition will have begun to normalise itself.

During the fast, and after if necessary, the bowels should be cleansed nightly with a warm-water enema or gravity douche ; and where constipation is habitual, the rules for its eradication given in Section 9 (page 275) should be put into operation forthwith. The daily dry friction and sitz-bath or sponge detailed in the Appendix should be undertaken every morning from the time treatment is begun, and the breathing and other exercises also outlined therein should be gone through daily in conjunction with them. A hot Epsom-salts bath should be taken twice weekly, where at all possible, and a hot and cold sitz-bath, say three nights weekly (see Appendix for details). Cold packs to the kidneys will be beneficial in some cases.

Fresh air and outdoor exercise will be of great benefit in all cases under treatment, and where possible the patient should have a walk for at least two miles once or twice a day. There is no need to exert oneself when taking exercise; the walking may be fairly leisurely; but it is good to get the whole system into full movement. The sufferer from Bright's disease should never try to exert himself when doing anything; he should take his time and avoid all hurry and excitement. He should make it a practice to do everything quietly and without effort. " No hurry and no worry " should be his watchword.

Smoking and drinking, where habitual, must be completely given up, and early hours and no excesses must be the rule. No drugs of

ANY KIND should be taken at all. The diet factor *is of the utmost importance*, and the following facts must be persistently borne in mind.

No white bread, sugar, cakes, pastry, puddings, or pies are to be eaten ; no refined cereals, such as porridge, etc. ; no boiled or mashed or fried potatoes ; no greasy, heavy, or fried foods ; no stews, " hot-pots," etc. ; no cream ; very little butter or fats of any kind. Tea and coffee must not be taken at all in future ; neither should condiments, pickles, sauces, etc. Meat should be kept out of the dietary as much as possible, as also other flesh foods too, and egg or cheese or nuts can be substituted with advantage for meat or fish where mentioned in the weekly dietary outlined in the Appendix. Meals should be as small as compatible with hunger, and eating and drinking should be done apart, except in the case of fruit and milk.

If the sufferer from Bright's disease carries on in the manner indicated above, the path to returning health will be opened up to him, despite the medical belief in the incurability of his complaint. Of course, it is only those in whom the disease of kidney tissue has not been allowed to progress too far who can hope for complete ultimate cure ; but, as already pointed out, even in advanced cases a great deal can be done to improve the sufferer's condition by perseverance with a scheme of treatment such as the foregoing.

In all cases of Bright's disease a course of *manipulative treatment* at the hands of a competent Osteopath or Naturopath is strongly recommended.

Pyelitis.—Pyelitis may be of two kinds : a simple catarrhal inflammatory condition affecting the kidneys, in which there is a certain amount of mucus passed in the urine ; and a serious suppurative inflammatory condition, in which case there is pus present in the urine. The disease is a highly toxic one, due to a poisonous state of the system in general, and treatment should be in the hands of a Naturopath where at all possible. Failing this, the scheme of home treatment for *Nephritis* (acute and chronic), given in the present section (page 361), can be put into operation with good effect. (Stone in the kidney may be the cause of pyelitis in certain cases.)

Sluggish, Enlarged, and Torpid Liver.—From what has been said regarding the functions of the liver in the opening pages of the present section, it will be seen that the liver is the hardest-worked organ in the body. Is it any wonder, then, that the liver should become overworked and out of condition in those who persistently misuse their body and bodily functions? Overeating is the greatest factor concerned in the development of liver troubles of all kinds, especially where combined with sedentary occupation and consequent lack of exercise; and habitual constipation and "liverishness" may be said to go hand in hand.

The reason why constipation should play such a large part in the development of liver disorders has been made clear in the opening remarks on the liver and its functions already referred to, and it must be stressed again that drug treatment for previous disease—especially drug treatment for fevers—has much to do with the setting up of liver trouble in later life. Excessive drinking and excesses of all kinds play their part in breaking down liver efficiency.

Liver sluggishness and liver troubles are very common in. tropical climates amongst white people. This is the outcome of the unwise feeding habits indulged in by such persons in such climates (especially the eating of two or three meat meals a day !), as well as the habitual taking of quinine as a preventive of malaria and the excessive spirit drinking which usually goes on. It is the climate which is blamed, but it is the people themselves and their unwise habits and practices which are at fault all the time.

Treatment.—From the very nature of the case it must be obvious that only constitutional measures applied to the *whole system* can hope to restore liver functioning in those whose liver is working below par. Drugs to stimulate liver action only succeed in making matters worse in the long run, instead of better (for reasons already given in the introductory remarks on the liver previously referred to). It is only by giving the *whole system* a thorough cleansing and adopting a rational scheme of feeding and living thereafter, that normalcy of liver function can be secured. All those who wish to put their liver in proper working order, therefore, and to build up their whole general health-level at the same time, should carry out the following scheme of home treatment. Results will more than repay them for the effort entailed.

Begin with from five to seven or ten days on the *exclusive fresh fruit diet* outlined in the Appendix. (Obviously the time to be spent on the fruit diet must depend upon the condition of the case; but in general it can be said that the longer the fruit diet can be persisted with by any given patient, the better it will be.) Then the *full weekly dietary*, also outlined in the Appendix, should be begun, and adhered to as strictly as possible thereafter. Further short periods on the fruit diet—say two or three consecutive days at a time—should be undertaken at monthly or two-monthly intervals, according to the needs of the case.

During the all-fruit period the bowels should be cleansed nightly with a warm-water enema or gravity douche ; and where constipation is habitual, the rules for its eradication given in Section 9 (page 275) should be put into operation forthwith. The morning dry friction and sitz-bath or sponge, and the breathing and other exercises outlined in the Appendix, should form a regular daily feature of the treatment. Where possible, a hot Epsom-salts bath should be taken once or twice weekly.

Fresh air and outdoor exercise are two most important essentials to the treatment, and the sufferer from liver troubles should try to have a four or five-mile walk every day at a good pace. The more exercise he can take—within reason, of course—the better for him. Smoking and drinking, where habitual, should be taboo from now on, and no drugs OF ANY KIND should be taken. Early hours and no excesses should form the order of the day.

The future diet is of the utmost importance, and fresh fruits and salads *must* form the bulk of the dietary, as advised in the weekly diet-sheet. These are Nature's cleansing foods, and the " livery subject " needs them more than most people. Strong tea and coffee must not be taken in future ; neither should condiments, pickles, sauces, etc. The diet should be as plain and simple as possible, and there should be no eating and drinking together (except in the case of fruit and milk). All white-flour products must be deleted from the dietary, all refined cereals, white sugar, tinned and potted foods, all heavy, greasy, and stodgy dishes, all fried things. Fatty foods must be eaten very sparingly indeed ; no cream and no animal fats (except a little butter) should be taken. Meat and other flesh foods should be cut out as much as possible.

Spinal manipulation, at the hands of a competent Naturopath, will be most beneficial in conjunction with the scheme of treatment here outlined. Sun and air bathing can be recommended to all who can avail themselves of their curative value.

Stone in the Kidney or Bladder.—Stone in the kidney is a very painful affliction, and pain is most intense when a stone is on its way from the kidney to the bladder in its passage down the ureter. Stones may form in the bladder quite independently, as well as being brought there from the kidneys.

The cause of stone in the kidney or bladder is purely dietetic in origin. The stones are only the collection of systemic refuse and toxic matter around a nucleus, and so long as the blood brings systemic impurities to the kidneys for expulsion in the urine, so long can stones continue to form. The uselessness of attempting to deal with the condition by means of operations must be apparent therefore. The operation removes the stone (or stones) that may be present at any given time, but their further accumulation is not in the least prevented by such treatment, because the underlying factors involved have not been affected in the slightest by the operation. That is why so many people who have been operated on for stone in the kidney or bladder have the shadow of further operations always hanging over them.

Stones are composed of crystals of phosphate or oxalate of lime mainly, which are precipitated out of the urine whilst in the kidney or bladder, and the presence of these toxic products shows quite clearly how much the blood is clogged with toxins and impurities accumulated in the system through unwise feeding habits. Not all people are liable to the formation of stones—it seems that there is a certain tendency in some towards their formation, owing to inherent constitutional peculiarities ; but the cause of their origin is no mystery once the true relationship between wrong feeding and disease is understood.

Treatment.—As already stated, operation for the removal of stone in the kidney or bladder is never curative in the real sense, because the possibility of the future recurrence of stones is in no way prevented by the treatment. The only way in which *really to cure* the condition is by a thorough course of systemic cleansing treatment, in which fasting and strict dieting play the most important part. Many cases of stones (*renal calculi* is their medical name) have been cured by natural treatment, and the sufferer is advised to secure help at a Natural-Cure home where at all possible. Fairly prolonged fasting may be required in certain cases, and that is why institutional treatment is always best. As opposed to an operation, not only is the cause of further stones effectually removed by natural treatment, but the whole general health-level of the patient is greatly enhanced.

Of course it cannot be denied that in advanced cases, where stones are very large, operation may be necessary because of the difficulty of breaking down the stones and removing them from the system under natural treatment, but the latter should always be tried first. In any case, future strict diet along natural lines, after the operation, will be most essential to prevent further stones forming.

Those who cannot carry out treatment in a Natural-Cure home (or under personal naturopathic advice and attention) should carry out a scheme of home treatment along the lines of that for *gall-stones* given earlier in the present section. Such a scheme will prove most beneficial in all cases. *Manipulative treatment* would be most effective if carried out in conjunction with that here advised.

SPECIAL NOTE RE DIET.—There is a common belief that because stones in the kidney and bladder contain oxalates, therefore any food which contains oxalic acid is no good for the sufferer from this afflic-tion. This is an erroneous idea, and the fact that most medical men believe in it is quite as it should be, given the average medical ignorance concerning dietetics. The point is that the oxalates which go to make up stones in the kidney or bladder are the *end-products of systemic activities*. They are the waste refuse of the using up of food in the system, and are due to a preponderance of such foods as meat, fish, eggs, bread, sugar, etc., in the dietary; whereas the oxalic acid in tomatoes or spinach, for instance, is a natural organic product which cannot possibly do harm to the system. It is broken down as soon as digested and does not reach the kidneys in the form of oxalic acid.

Tubercular Kidney.—When the system is in a very low state vitally, the kidneys may be so undermined that tuberculosis can affect them. To remove a tubercular kidney—as is the practice of the medical profession—does nothing to get rid of this systemic ill-health ; indeed, it tends to make the general health of the sufferer worse, because only one kidney is left to carry on the work of the body. The one sane and logical regimen for tubercular kidney is natural treatment, and institutional treatment should be undertaken by the sufferer where at all possible. Fasting, strict dieting, eliminative baths, sunray treatment, manipulation, etc., will all be required in the case. Where such supervision is not possible, much can be done for the patient by the carrying out of the scheme of treatment for *Nephritis* (*Chronic*) given in the present section (page 363).

The general remarks on tuberculosis, made in Section 10 (page 326) in the treatment for *Consumption,* should be studied carefully by the sufferer from tubercular kidney; they apply with equal force to his case too.

DISEASES OF THE MALE AND FEMALE
SEX ORGANS

Amenorrhœa—Concerning childbirth—Displaced (or dropped) womb—Dysmenorrhœa — Excessive menstruation — Gonorrhœa — Growths in the womb (and breast)—Hydrocele—Impotence—Leucorrhœa—Loss of sexual power—Menorrhagia—Milk leg—Nocturnal emissions (involuntary night losses)—Painful menstruation—Prostate-gland disease—Puerperal fever—Scanty menstruation—Self-abuse—Stoppage of menstrual flow—Syphilis—Varicocele—Venereal disease—Woman's change of life.

DISEASES of the male and female sex organs can roughly be divided into two groups : those of venereal origin (to which group the great majority of diseases of the male sex organs belong) ; and those peculiar to women, and known generally as "women's ailments." We shall therefore deal with venereal disease first, and then with the diseases peculiar to women.

VENEREAL DISEASE

Venereal disease is not a subject which is generally discussed in the open, as it were, because of the horror and loathing with which such disease is looked upon by the world in general. It is not the purpose of the writer of the present book to go into the ethics surrounding the question of venereal disease, but what he would like to point out is that quite apart from the manner in which the disease is contracted, a great deal of this horror and loathing with which venereal disease is surrounded is due to the fact that it is generally regarded as bringing with it all sorts of unnameable and terrible afflictions in after-life to the body and mind of the person affected—afflictions which the medical treatment for the disease does its best to get rid of or prevent, but which persist in appearing in a great number of cases nevertheless.

If the public once knew that a disease such as syphilis is *quite amenable to successful treatment and complete cure* (as it is if treated along Nature Cure lines), leaving no ill after-effects whatsoever to mar the future life and happiness of its victim, then the writer is quite sure that most of the before-mentioned horror and loathing surrounding the disease would tend to disappear. There is no denying the fact that if such a dread disease as syphilis lost its terror for mankind in general it might lead to an intensification of promiscuous sexuality ; but that is not a point for those engaged in the natural healing art to

371

discuss. Sufficient for them if they know quite definitely that syphilis *can be cured*, and *completely so*, by natural methods of treatment, and to make that fact known as far as they possibly can.

We have enough people doomed to a life of utter misery and hopelessness through having contracted venereal disease which medical methods have failed to cure—many quite innocent sufferers (especially wives !) ; and quite apart from all so-called moral and ethical factors these persons should know that their miseries are in reality quite unnecessary, and the result of mistaken methods of cure on the part of those who have been appointed by society to deal with their condition. If promiscuous sexuality should flourish amongst those who have no self-control or real feeling about sex if the terrors surrounding venereal disease are removed, that is their fault entirely and not the fault of those who would like to rid the world once and for all of a loathsome scourge which is always eating deeper and deeper into the vitals of society.

And then think of the innocent children whose bodies have been malformed and misshapen through being so unfortunate as to be born of parents one or both of whom has had venereal disease which orthodox methods of treatment have not cured. Surely for their sake alone the disease (or rather its mind- and body-destroying after-effects) should be erased once and for all from the book of life, if such can be done. And it CAN BE DONE if right methods of treatment are adopted in every case, and not ruinous and suppressive medical methods.

When the famous " 606 " treatment for syphilis was introduced, it was thought that here was a sure " cure " for syphilis. But the cure merely consisted in the injection into the body of the victim of doses of metallic drugs of very high potency, which, by suppressing the superficial effects of the disease, were deemed to have effected a " cure " thereby. But the medical profession to-day is not so sure even of this superficial efficacy of " 606," or the various preparations of arsenic and other metals founded on it. The dreaded after-effects still tend to appear.

All that the medical profession is intent on in its treatment of syphilis is that the various superficial manifestations connected with the disease should disappear, and that the blood should show a negative reaction when tested by the Wassermann test. But that does not mean that the sufferer has been *cured—really cured* ; it simply means that the active manifestation of the disease in the victim's system has been stopped for the time being, through the suppressive action of the drugs employed. *The disease-poisons plus the metallic drugs employed are still left in the patient's system to work stealthily upon his tissues and structures as the years go on, and that is why under such treatment the dreaded after-effects connected with syphilis appear.*

It can be said quite definitely that if syphilis is not treated by suppressive drugs in its initial stages, and suppressed, then there would be no fear at all of the often dreadful after-effects which arise in cases so treated—after-effects such as paralysis, insanity, etc. The drugs used in such medical treatment—mercury, arsenic, etc.—have a most destructive effect upon the tissues and structures of the body, especially upon the nervous tissues ; and to their presence in such large quantities in the system of the victim, through the agency of the treatment employed, is most of the serious (and often fatal) nervous and mental trouble due, of which the sufferer from venereal disease goes in such fear in after-life.

The foregoing is a very serious indictment indeed, and one which cannot be made without absolute assurance as to its truth. The fact is that, in common with its inability to understand how disease in general should be treated, the medical profession has carried its suppressive views into the treatment of venereal disease too, and, owing to the strength and quantity of the deleterious drugs employed, the after-effects are so very much more serious than with other diseases treated along similar suppressive lines. That the damage is laid at the door of the disease, and not at all upon the treatment, is due not to any desire to escape from the blame attaching to its own actions on the part of the medical profession, but to a quite genuine and sincere belief on its part that *it is so.* It is firmly convinced that its treatment is the best possible in the circumstances, and that it is doing all possible for the future health and welfare of the patient. It is just a matter of ignorance pure and simple—ignorance on the part of the doctor, and ignorance on the part of the patient. That such ignorance brings misery and suffering in its train is unfortunate, but it is all part of the price man has to pay for not understanding the laws of his own body and the manner in which ill-health should be overcome.

The faith that is put in the Wassermann test by the medical profession is in itself very childish indeed, for nothing is certain about the test, and people with diseases other than syphilis can show a positive Wassermann reaction when tested.

The only sure and safe way of treating venereal disease, and the way practised by the ancients, is FASTING. Perhaps it will sound incredible to some, but through the agency of the fast any case of syphilis or gonorrhœa can be *completely cured*, and not only will any possibility of dreaded after-effects be prevented by such treatment, but the whole general health-level of the patient will be greatly enhanced because of the thorough internal cleansing his system will have received as a result of the treatment. The truth of this has been proved over and over again in natural treatment, and surely the world should know of it. But, strange to say, no practitioner of Natural Cure in this country is allowed (by law) to treat diseases of venereal origin. Only authorised members of the medical profession can do so. Thus arises a situation by which those who *can* cure such diseases are prevented from doing so by the law of the land, whilst those who cannot really cure such diseases, and who often cause irreparable harm to the bodies of their patients through their treatment, are the only ones allowed by the State to do so ! Strange indeed are the anomalies of life !

In many States of the United States Naturopaths are quite free to treat venereal disease, and many books by leading American Naturopaths have been written on the subject ; but the fact remains that in England we are not allowed to do so. The subject will be dealt with only in the broadest and most general way, therefore, in the present section, as explicit instructions regarding treatment are not permissible under existing conditions. What *is* said, however, will, it is hoped, prove of the greatest possible value to many unfortunate sufferers from venereal disease who have never before heard of Nature-Cure treatment in relation to their affliction.

WOMEN'S AILMENTS

Having shed some much-needed light upon the subject of venereal disease, it is now time to say something about the second group of diseases connected with the sex organs—namely, those concerned exclusively with women and known as " women's ailments."

Diseases connected with the female sex organs are growing steadily year by year, despite all the efforts made by the medical profession to deal with them, and until something of their real origin is understood by women in general, there is no doubt that such diseases will continue to grow more and more rapidly as the years advance. The first thing to realise with regard to the origin of " women's ailments " is that the female sex organs are delicate structures, and so situated that they are easily interfered with by the structures above and around them ; and the second thing to realise is that through the menstrual flow Nature has found a means of getting rid of a great deal of toxic matter from the female system which is denied to the opposite sex. When women begin to relate womb and ovary troubles to the general health of the body, and to the way in which they carry themselves and live, then they will have taken the first step in an understanding of how womb troubles arise, and in what direction their intelligent treatment lies.

The medical profession, in its usual short-sighted way, sees no connection, as a general rule, between the feeding habits and ways of living of its women patients and the disorders of the sex organs they suffer from. Yet the connection is most patent, once a little thought is brought to bear upon the subject. For instance, the uterus (womb) is situated in such a position that if the intestines are continually distended with gas or an over-accumulation of food materials, there is constant downward pressure upon the womb and its surrounding tissues, and this is further accentuated if constipation is habitual, because of the pressure from behind exerted by an over-filled colon. Thus we can at once see that displacement of the womb and other womb troubles (through the resultant pressure, cramping, and congestion that take place) are clearly related to wrong feeding habits and their correlated physiological disturbances.

Then, again, all tight-fitting garments, especially corsets, tend to restrict the free play of the internal organs, and automatically throw extra downward pressure upon the womb and its surrounding structures, thus accentuating the pressure, cramping, and congestion referred to just previously ; whilst continual standing or sitting in a stooped position has an exactly similar effect. Slackness of the internal muscles of the abdomen, through lack of exercise, bodily weakness, etc., by not holding the womb and adjacent structures firmly in position, tends greatly to facilitate the harmful effects of the other facto.·s enumerated.

It will thus be seen that the way a woman carries herself, the condition of her body, the kind of garments she wears, and *especially* the condition of her abdominal organs in relationship to her feeding habits, are all factors of prime importance in studying the causes of womb troubles—factors which, with a little common sense and a knowledge of physiology, will be readily admitted by everyone who looks at disease as not so much a local affair as the logical result of various causes affecting the health and condition of the organism as a whole.

But beside these more or less obvious factors there are others more deep-seated concerned in the development of womb troubles which only an understanding of the way in which the body works during disease can make clear to one.   In the Natural-Cure philosophy it is realised that all disease is a move on the part of the body towards self-cleansing (as previously explained in the theoretical portion of the present book) ; and it is also realised that Nature tends to take advantage of any lowering in the vitality of the individual or any chance happening (such as accident or injury) to find an avenue for the removal of toxic matter from the system.   (The festering of a cut is a good example of this.)   Thus we can readily understand how the menstrual flow is utilised by Nature as a safety-valve in its efforts to preserve the health of the female organism.

When menstruation begins at puberty in connection with the female function of ovulation (or the passing of the female ovum from the ovary to the womb ready for impregnation), a free avenue for the removal of toxic waste material and systemic impurities is thus opened up in the female system ; and Nature tends to take more and more advantage of this extra eliminative outlet in the bodies of those women who are in a low state of health and whose blood and tissues are surcharged with toxic matter.   This fact, taken in relation with the other things previously named, is sufficient to explain the whole mystery of painful and excessive menstruation and, indeed, menstrual troubles in general.   When a woman is subject to these troubles, then it can be taken as certain that her general health-level is well below par, that her sex organism is in a toxic condition, and that, however painful the process may be, the menstrual flow is being utilised by Nature for the purpose of systemic purification, so far as lies within its power.

Of course, if the wrong habits of living—especially wrong feeding habits—which have set up the systemic toxicity in the first place are continued with, as they invariably are, then the menstrual outlet utilised by the natural forces of the body can never succeed in correcting matters ; and so the trouble goes on and on indefinitely, and is only made more deep-seated and chronic by medical efforts to deal with it through the suppressive agency of surgery, drugs, and the like. The trouble is *systemic* in origin, and can only be tackled at its source ; to deal with it as a purely local matter, as the medical profession does is just useless. (It may be mentioned here in passing that the habitual taking of so-called " remedies "—medical and otherwise—for the alleviation of menstrual ailments *always* tends to complicate matters, and often leads directly to the development of growths in the womb and other serious trouble.)

It is generally considered that scanty menstruation or premature cessation of the menstrual flow is a sign of general ill-health in women ; but this is not necessarily so. There is a view put forward by Dr. Shelton, the eminent American Naturopath, that the less a woman menstruates the better her health is, and that the cessation of the flow altogether in the fairly young is a very good thing indeed, rather than something to be deplored, as is generally the case. He bases this rather unorthodox view upon the conclusion, arrived at by himself, that all menstruation is a form of *vicarious elimination* (an attempt on the part of Nature to remove a tendency to chronic blood congestion in the female sex organs, owing to faulty carriage and faulty living on the part of civilised woman) ; and so he concludes that the less a woman menstruates the less her body is in need of this monthly cleansing process. The writer of the present book, although leaning somewhat towards this view, cannot think that the whole menstrual process is purely of the nature ascribed to it by Dr. Shelton (although there is much vicarious elimination connected with it, as he has himself already pointed out) ; but he certainly does think that scanty menstruation or the premature cessation of menstruation is nothing at all to worry about *in any woman who is otherwise healthy*. If her general health-level is poor, however, and she is subject to other disease-manifestations, then the scantiness of the flow or its premature complete cessation undoubtedly shows that the sexual organism is not functioning as it should.

We have stated that the various factors concerned in the development of the commoner forms of women's ailments are all systemic in character ; this applies equally to those of a more serious nature, such as growths, etc. A system full of toxic matter means a blood-stream always in a highly toxic condition, and when there is a state of chronic congestion and cramping of the womb and its surrounding structures—for the reasons already pointed out—there is every likelihood of growths forming in the womb, because of the difficulty of getting rid of congested blood and morbid deposits. Especially is this so where there has been much previous drug treatment, curetting, etc. There is no doubt also that the stoppage of the menstrual flow at the " change of life " tends towards the formation of growths in the womb, especially cancer, for the following reasons.

We have said that Nature makes use of menstruation for the purpose of getting rid of a great deal of waste matter and systemic refuse from the female organism ; when menstruation ceases, this process of extra elimination has perforce to cease too. That means that many women who can well do with it will now be debarred from this additional outlet for the toxic matter which their system is steadily piling up, and so more and more of this morbid material will collect in the womb, with the result that growths, both cancerous and non-cancerous, will tend increasingly to appear. (All this applies to the breast too, for the breast and womb are intimately connected in the female.)

Of course, in dealing with the causes of women's ailments, one must not overlook the part played by uncleanly habits, by unskilful handling of childbirth, and by excessive child-bearing in the setting up of these troubles ; and also one must not overlook the growing part played in the development of such ailments by wilful abortion, excessive sexuality, sex perversion, and modern methods of contraception. There can be no doubt that the introduction of " birth control " amongst civilised races is doing much to accentuate the liability of modern woman towards the development of ailments of the sex organs.

Having given this brief survey of the causes and factors relating to the setting up of women's complaints, it is worth while just briefly turning our attention to the methods employed by the medical profession to deal with them. We have already said that the medical mind always seems to regard each organ or part of the body as something more or less separate from each other part, and this same short-sighted view is held to a remarkable degree with regard to ailments of the nature we are here discussing. The practitioners of orthodox medicine *cannot* seem to relate these diseases with factors concerning

the health and condition of the female system *as a whole*, and so treatment for women's ailments is entirely local in character, and, as usual
with all medical usage, highly suppressive in action. It can safely
be said that *very few women indeed* have derived any real lasting
benefit for womb or ovary trouble at medical hands.

Apart from the free use of drugs for the alleviation and masking
of symptoms, surgery seems to be the most-used medium of procedure
in treating these cases; and many a woman has had cause to regret
having allowed herself to be operated on without having any idea as
to what was to be done to her and how it would affect her after-life.
Of course these women feel that the doctor knows all there is to know
about the matter, and that whatever he advises is bound to be for the
best; and so they give their consent to the removal of womb and
ovaries without realising in the slightest what the consequences may be.
Neither does the medical profession seek to enlighten them.

This is not to say that the doctor or surgeon wilfully attempts
through the medium of the treatment employed to pull down instead
of build up the future health of his patient ; he can see no other way
of dealing with these troubles than through the removal of the whole
or part of the female sex apparatus. He realises that such removal
may affect very severely the future nervous and mental life of the
patient, but he is doing the best he knows according to his lights to get
rid of the patient's *present* trouble. He sincerely hopes, of course, that
her future health will also be improved thereby, but if it is not, then he
cannot see that he is to blame in the matter. He has done his best,
and that is all.

It must be remembered that the sex organs are the most vital
part of the human being, both male and female ; and any tampering
with such organs, and especially their removal, is bound to have the
profoundest repercussion upon the nervous and mental health of the
individual. For once these life-centres are removed, then a great
part of the individual's life-flow departs too. (He or she is now no
longer a *complete* human being in *every* sense of the word.) Again,
the whole nervous apparatus in the neighbourhood of the sex organs,
which is very delicate and fine in structure, is very much cut about
at these operations, and so normal nervous functioning is further
interfered with from this source too. The woman who undergoes
an operation for womb removal is told that it is the only thing that

can be done in the circumstances, and that although she will no doubt be very depressed for a few months after the operation, she will feel ever so much better thereafter. But how the patient's health is going to be restored to her through having her whole sex-life shattered is hard to see, even from the most optimistic reasoning ; and results more than bear out the truth, here stated, that such operations do an infinite amount of harm to the future life and health of many women so treated.

There was a time when ovaries were completely removed, but that is no longer done to-day, because it was found that women so treated went insane eventually. Now a small part of the ovary is left in to prevent this terrible occurrence. Surely this shows how close is the relationship between these delicate sex organs and the life, both mental and physical, of the individual, and how dangerous it is to meddle with them through the medium of present-day surgery.

The only logical treatment for women's ailments, as the intelligent reader can now see, is treatment aimed at restoring the health and functional powers of the WHOLE ORGANISM. That is the ONLY way to get rid of these troubles in any real sense. Through the medium of natural treatment, scientifically applied, many thousands of women are possessors of sound health to-day who were told by their medical advisers that they could never possibly get well again unless they consented to operations for the removal of all or part of their sexual organism. These women have been completely cured by natural treatment, *and the whole sexual organism retained intact !*

In the present section the home treatment for women's ailments is given in full detail, and by their aid many a woman who has tried in vain to be cured of her complaint at the hands of orthodox medication can restore herself to eventual sound health and fitness (providing her condition has not been allowed to develop too far, or been interfered with to any serious extent by previous medical treatment). Really long-standing and serious cases would best be treated at a Nature Cure establishment, or under the personal care of a competent Naturopath, because of auxiliary treatment (in the form of manipulation, ray-therapy, etc.) which will be needed in such cases, not to speak of prolonged fasting and strict dietetic treatment.

Amenorrhœa.—Amenorrhœa means stoppage or interruption of the menstrual flow. As already pointed out in the introductory remarks on women's ailments made in the preceding pages, temporary cessation or even complete stoppage of menstruation in otherwise quite healthy and normal young women may be quite a good sign, and may even denote a high state of health, for reasons already given. But this obviously is not the case where the stoppage arises in connection with a debilitated and devitalised condition of the system. In these cases stoppage of the menstrual flow is indicative of debility of the whole sex organism.

Causes contributing towards this condition are : anæmia ; worry, grief, fright, or other serious emotional disturbance ; malformation of the womb ; tuberculosis ; womb displacement ; debility, especially after serious illness.

Treatment.—As regards treatment for amenorrhœa, this should obviously be directed towards the rectification of the disease-condition responsible for the setting up of the trouble in the first place ; and treatment should be as for this primary disease-condition as outlined in the various sections of the present book (where it is due to malformation of the womb, personal advice from a Naturopath is advisable). Where there is no definite disease or bodily condition which can be adduced as responsible for the stoppage, or where it is due merely to a general all-round debilitated condition of the system, or to emotional factors, then a course of general health-building treatment, as that for *Leucorrhœa*, given farther on in the present section (page 393), should be carried out.

If serious emotional disturbance, such as prolonged worry, grief etc., is concerned in the setting up of the trouble, then an initial period of quietness and rest will be essential to the carrying out of the treatment. A complete change of scene will also help greatly in securing the best results in these cases. All excitement, excessive mental strain, study, etc., should be avoided for some considerable period. (For the relief of pain in the pelvic region at the time when menstruation is normally due, see treatment for *Dysmenorrhœa*, page 387.)

Concerning Childbirth.—Although childbirth in a general way does not come under the heading of a disease-condition, so many women suffer unduly at these times nowadays that some consideration of the subject seems necessary in the present book. Childbirth should, in the ordinary way, be a purely natural function attended with very little pain or discomfort on the part of the woman concerned. It is so to-day still with primitive races, but the more civilised we become, the more women appear to find the bearing of children a task fraught with grave risk and suffering and attended by all sorts of minor or serious after-effects. *This is solely the result of modern ways of living and eating on the part of the civilised woman, especially her habits with regard to food.* The more the diet consists of denatured white-flour products, white sugar, refined cereals, much meat or other flesh foods, etc., during pregnancy, the larger does the fœtus become in the womb, and the harder therefore does the process of childbirth become. If one adds to this poor tone and development of the internal musculature of the modern woman, as a result of lack of exercise, unhygienic habits of living, and restrictive garments, then most, if not all, of the causes of the suffering experienced by the civilised woman of to-day in bringing children into the world will be readily understood.

It is generally assumed that the larger the baby is at birth, the " bonnier " and healthier it is; but this is quite wrong. Examination of the babies of primitive women or of the offspring of wild creatures shows us that at birth the natural tendency is for the young to be little more than skin and bone, and with the very minimum of flesh on them. This is as it should be, as in this way the progress of the unborn fœtus to the external world is made as easy as possible, with the minimum of difficulty to the mother. On the other hand, the more a child weighs at birth, above a certain minimum, the harder will it be for the mother to deliver it in comfort, because of the cramping and congestion that are bound to take place during the birth-process, through the undue size of the infant.

The weight of the baby should be about $6\frac{1}{2}$ to 7 lb. at birth; but we often hear of babies of 9 or even 10 lb. born, and we are informed of this fact with immense gusto by proud fathers and mothers. But imagine what that must mean to the mother, in agony and suffering, in striving to bring so large an infant into the light of day! Such a child is covered with unnecessary fat and watery tissue, which is nothing more than waste matter really, and an impediment to health; and it is not uncommon to find such infants shrinking in a few weeks to 2 or even 3 lb. less than the birth-weight, thus showing conclusively that it was not solid flesh they had on their little bodies (as their fond parents imagined), but just unhealthy tissue which had been built up as a result of the unwise feeding habits and general systemic toxicity of the mother during pregnancy.

Then again, to deliver a child properly, the muscles of the womb and pelvis generally must be in good condition, and they can only be so if plenty of walking and other exercise is taken daily, which most pregnant women do *not* do, in accordance with medical advice on the subject. They are told to eat what they fancy, and to do as little as possible during the period of pregnancy, and so it is surely little wonder that the woman of to-day dreads a confinement, because of the suffering she is likely to endure as a result of it, instead of welcoming it as an experience to be valued above all others in life by any true woman.

To make childbirth safe and easy, the great factor is *proper diet* The idea of " eating for two," which is so prevalent, is as absurd as it is dangerous, as it is this which so often leads to the overfeeding resulting in an unusually heavy baby, with consequences often disastrous to the mother. The diet during pregnancy should consist of *natural, vital foods*, and as little as possible of the denatured food-products of our present era. The unborn child will require a large amount of organic mineral matter from its mother, for the purposes of bone and tissue building, and this can only be supplied through the agency of natural foods such as fruits, raw vegetables, wholemeal bread, milk, etc. White bread, sugar, meat, puddings, pies, etc., are very deficient in organic mineral matter, and it is because of this that so many mothers suffer after childbirth from loss and decay of teeth, general debility and other ailments, and often consumption (as pointed out in Section 8 in dealing with *Dental Decay* (page 240), and in Section 10 in dealing with *Consumption* (page 322). When the mother's diet is deficient in organic mineral matter, the mineral stores in her OWN tissues are filched from her by Nature for the purpose of building up the unborn child within her, and thus her health is progressively undermined at each succeeding childbirth, because the health of the organism depends *to a very great extent indeed* upon the amount of organic mineral matter present within it, as repeatedly pointed out in the present book.

As regards a suitable diet for the expectant mother, the *full weekly dietary* given in the Appendix at the end of the present book can be followed with every confidence of securing a safe and easy childbirth and a healthy child. During the first five or six months of pregnancy the dry friction and cold sponge outlined in the Appendix should be taken daily, and the breathing exercises therein outlined also gone through. After that time the sponge may be taken tepid, and exercises gradually modified or suspended altogether. A good walk should be taken daily right up to, say, the end of the eighth month, and all ordinary household duties can be engaged in. It is a great mistake just to lie about and do nothing or next to nothing during the months preceding childbirth. As already pointed out, it makes the process of child-bearing far harder than it otherwise would be.

Of course, exercise should always be well within the capacity of the prospective mother, and all undue strain, worry, or excitement should be avoided.

As regards the feeding of children after birth, this is dealt with in the Appendix at some length. The diet of the mother for the first two days after confinement should be just fresh juicy fruits with perhaps a little cold or just warm milk ; a salad with thin wholemeal toast and butter, with a little stewed fruit to follow, may be added the next day ; and then the diet should be gradually extended day by day thereafter, until it approaches the pre-natal diet before mentioned. Milk puddings and "mushy" foods in general should be strictly avoided, and if constipation is present, the warm-water enema should be used. No aperients.

With regard to the pre-natal diet, it is essential that no white bread or white-flour products should be eaten ; no sugar, jams, confectionery, pastry, etc. ; no puddings or pies ; no heavy, greasy, or stodgy foods ; no fried foods ; and very little meat or other flesh foods. Strong tea, coffee, and alcohol should be strictly avoided ; also condiments, pickles, vinegar, etc.

If the foregoing advice is taken to heart and acted upon by the expectant mother, then she need have little fear as to the outcome of her efforts in bringing a further new life into the world to help share its joys and burdens.

Re CONSTIPATION.—Where constipation is habitual, pregnancy is always rendered more difficult as a direct result, because of the extra pressure and cramping in the pelvic region caused by an over-filled colon. For the treatment of constipation the sufferer is referred to that in Section 9 (page 275). Any prolonged fasting treatment during pregnancy is unwise, but two or three days on the *fruit* diet, at monthly intervals, during the first few months of pregnancy, is quite in order.

RE MORNING SICKNESS.—Morning sickness is a most common feature during the early months of pregnancy, but that is purely because of the unhealthy state of the modern woman's digestive system and system generally. If proper methods of feeding and living were instituted, then morning sickness would tend to become less and less common, until it would disappear altogether in due time. If morning sickness is very severe, a fast for a day, with the use of the enema, would be a good thing, or a day or two on fresh juicy fruit only. The sipping of hot water, or hot water and lemon juice, is helpful during attacks.

Displaced or Dropped Womb.—Displacement or dropping of the womb is a very common occurrence indeed these days, and the various factors contributing to its development have already been dealt with in the introductory pages to the present section. These are, briefly : continual distension of the intestines with gas or excess food materials, leading to constant downward pressure on the womb ; chronic constipation, leading to pressure from behind from an over-filled colon ; tight clothing, especially tight corsets ; constant stooping ; and a weakened condition of the internal muscles of the abdomen, through lack of exercise, bodily weakness, etc. Of course, the part played by unskilful handling of childbirth in the later development of displacement of the womb must not be overlooked—it is a most important factor sometimes ; and the part played in the setting up of the trouble by severe strain or heavy lifting is also of great importance too. Womb displacement is generally the outcome of a combination of some (or all) of the factors here named.

The condition is one which has a very lowering effect upon the health of the sufferer, through the constant pain and dragging which go on, and medical methods of treatment by means of the wearing of rings or operation for the stitching back of the womb into place are far from satisfactory. These measures are merely palliative. What is needed is to get rid of the *causes* of the trouble, so far as this is possible in any given case, and so to build up the tone of the internal muscles of the abdomen that the womb can be brought back naturally into place. This has been accomplished successfully many times in the course of natural treatment.

Treatment.—Treatment for displaced womb must consist mainly of correct diet and exercise—diet to remove any intestinal causes of the trouble, and exercise to build up the internal musculature of the body. Of course, any tendency towards tight lacing, constant stooping, heavy lifting, etc., must be carefully guarded against, once a natural régime is undertaken, as these will automatically tend to hold up the success of the treatment.

The sufferer should begin with from four to seven days on the *all-fruit diet* outlined in the Appendix. This should then be followed by the adoption of the *full weekly dietary*, also outlined therein. Further short periods on the all-fruit diet should be undertaken at monthly intervals as necessary (say two or three consecutive days each time).

During the first few days of the treatment the bowels should be cleansed nightly with a warm-water enema or gravity douche, and afterwards as necessary ; whilst, where constipation is habitual, the rules for its eradication given in Section 9 (page 275) should be put into operation forthwith. The daily dry friction and sitz-bath given in the Appendix should be gone through regularly every morning, in conjunction with the breathing and other exercises given therein. A hot Epsom-salts bath should be taken once or twice weekly where at all possible.

For toning up the structures surrounding the womb the hot and cold sitz-bath described in the Appendix is also of great value, and should be taken three or four nights weekly where possible.

Lying on a couch with the legs raised higher than the rest of the body is very helpful indeed in relieving pain and discomfort from a displaced womb, and this should be done for from half an hour to an hour two or three times daily. (The feet should be raised about eighteen inches by placing cushions under them.) When this is not possible, the patient can sit on a chair with the feet on another chair facing. The more this can be done *during the day*, the better will it be in every way.

It has been emphasised already that exercises for strengthening the abdominal muscles are most helpful in naturally correcting womb displacement, and a set of exercises which can be specially recommended for this purpose are to be found in a book by Harry Clements, N.D., called *Self-Treatment for Hernia*. These exercises are really most valuable for cases of womb displacement too, and every sufferer is advised to get the book therefore.

Great care with the future diet is most essential in all cases of womb displacement, because of the part so often played in the setting up of the trouble by distension of the intestines and an over-filled colon ; and it is always best to *undereat* rather than *overeat* in all these cases. Whenever there is any distension present during the treatment, a fast for a day or a day on the all-fruit diet should soon set the trouble right. No heavy or stodgy foods should be eaten, and especially no puddings or pies or milk puddings. Fruits and salads MUST form the bulk of the dietary.

Dysmenorrhœa.—Dysmenorrhœa, or painful menstruation, is a very common occurrence indeed these days, and, as already pointed out in the introductory remarks on the subject of women's ailments at the beginning of the present section, the condition is directly traceable to a toxic condition of the system in general, and of the sex organs in particular. The pain may be felt either before, during, or after the flow, and the causes mainly responsible for the setting up of the trouble are a debilitated and toxic condition of the system due to wrong feeding, general wrong living, nervous exhaustion, etc. ; inflammation and congestion of the vagina and/or uterus ; ovarian disease ; flexion of the womb or narrowing of the uterine passage ; catarrh of the womb. As a rule, when the pain is felt three or four days before the flow, it is considered that the ovaries are the seat of the trouble ; when it occurs just previously, it may be due to uterine contraction (which is the commonest form) ; when the pain continues for some time after the flow, there is usually some inflammation of the parts concerned.

Treatment.—Treatment for painful menstruation by means of drugs to deaden pain or by curetting, etc., is not of the slightest good. Such treatment never removes the *causes* of the trouble and only makes matters worse in the long run. The only sound cure for dysmenorrhœa is *treatment directed towards the removal of causes*—that is, one that will remove the systemic toxicity underlying the trouble and build up the health of the patient generally.

As regards a general scheme of treatment to follow, the sufferer from dysmenorrhœa can do no better than carry out the scheme given for *Leucorrhœa* farther on in the present section (page 393). Such a course of treatment will produce the most beneficial results in time, but of course it must be expected that long-standing cases will take longer to show results than cases in which the trouble is just beginning to manifest itself. In all cases of dysmenorrhœa *spinal manipulation*, at the hands of a good Osteopath or Naturopath, can be fully recommended as a most advantageous adjunct to the treatment.

Measures very useful for relieving pain during an attack are hot and cold compresses and the hot and cold sitz-bath. When applying the hot and cold compresses, a towel should be wrung out in hot water and applied as hot as can be borne, then, when the parts are thoroughly heated, it is removed, and a towel wrung out in cold water applied ; repeat if necessary. This can be done as many times during the day as required, and can be applied to either the painful area or the lower spine. The hot and cold sitz-bath is described in detail in the Appendix, and will prove most beneficial in many cases of dysmenorrhœa. If a hot and cold sitz-bath cannot conveniently be taken, the hot sitz-bath alone will be most helpful very often. The hot sitz-bath is made by placing about five inches of hot water in an ordinary bath or in a hip-bath. The patient just sits in it for from five to ten minutes. Always finish off by sponging with cold water.

Where the trouble is caused through flexion of the womb, the treatment here outlined will alleviate matters ; but obviously a complete cure can only be looked for when the flexion has been removed. Where the painful menstruation is due to a narrow or constricted uterine canal, marriage and motherhood often cure the condition ; but this *does not mean* that all cases of painful menstruation, *no matter what the cause*, can be cured in the same way, as is often hinted by medical advisers. Even with this latter affection the scheme of treatment here outlined should be followed out as directed ; it will prove greatly beneficial in every way. IN NO CIRCUMSTANCES MUST DRUGS OF ANY KIND BE TAKEN.

Excessive Menstruation.—See *Menorrhagia* (page 395).

Gonorrhœa.—This condition is an acute inflammatory disease connected with the sex organs, and under orthodox suppressive medical treatment often leads to serious disease in other parts of the organism. To say that the disease is cured through the institution of treatment which merely stops the discharge is very short-sighted reasoning indeed, and that is why so many people so treated have to face all sorts of complications in after-life (to say nothing of the risk of infecting others).

Treatment.—As already pointed out in the remarks on venereal disease at the beginning of the present section, this form of venereal disease is readily curable by means of *fasting treatment*, which leaves no harmful after-effects and no possibility of infection to others behind it. As also pointed out in those same introductory remarks, Natural-cure practitioners in this country are debarred by law from giving personal treatment in such cases, but treatment by Naturopaths is quite legal in the U.S.A., and excellent results are being obtained there along these lines.

As explicit instructions *re* treatment are not permissible, the sufferer from gonorrhœa is referred to the remarks on *Syphilis*, farther on in the present section (page 399). The treatment for both conditions is identical.

As regards a general health-building plan to follow after recovery, the scheme of treatment for *Hydrocele*, given farther on in the present section (page 391), will give the most beneficial results.

Growths in the Womb (and Breast).—The various factors contributing towards the appearance of growths in the womb (and breast) have already been discussed in the general survey of women's ailments made in the introductory pages of the present section. As there pointed out, a toxic condition of the system due to wrong feeding habits and general wrong living is always at the root of the trouble, but some (or all) of the other factors alluded to in the pages in question will play their part in the ultimate setting up of the condition. As already explained, the cessation of the menstrual flow in women and the appearance of growths—either benignant or malignant—in the womb have a very strong relationship to each other ; whilst the part played by tight clothing, uncleanly habits, excessive sexuality, wilful abortion, the taking of so-called " remedies " for menstrual disorders, previous surgical treatment, and *especially* the part played by modern contraceptual methods, must also be stressed.

Treatment.—Treatment for growths in the womb or breast should be in a Nature Cure home or in the hands of a competent Naturopath *where at all possible*. Fasting, strict dieting, manipulation, sunray treatment, and all measures for cleansing and improving the condition of the system will be required in these cases. For only in this way can the morbid matter constituting the growth be removed from the system—by absorption and elimination. To undergo an operation for the removal of a growth in the womb may get rid of the growth for the time being, but it does not remove causes, and so there is nothing to prevent further growths occurring later on. That is the whole fallacy behind medical methods of treatment. (Incidentally this explains why sometimes a growth appears in the womb after a growth has been surgically removed from the breast, and *vice versa*. The two structures are so intimately connected that suppressive treatment applied to one often directly affects the other.)

As regards cancer of the womb and breast, the reader is referred to the remarks on *Cancer* made in Section 9 (page 265). In these cases early treatment is always imperative if the trouble is to be really overcome, otherwise the condition may be beyond cure.

For those who cannot undertake personal treatment for growths in the womb or breast, the following scheme should be carried out at home. Even if it is not able completely to remove the trouble in certain cases, the treatment is bound to do a great deal of good.

Begin with a *short fast* for from three to five days (more if possible, and if the condition warrants it), as directed in the Appendix. Break the fast as also directed therein, and then the *restricted diet* given in the Appendix can be adopted for a further ten to fourteen days, after which the *full weekly dietary* also outlined therein can be begun. This full weekly dietary should be adhered to as strictly as possible from then on, with further short fasts and periods on the restricted diet, as necessary, at intervals thereafter, say every six weeks to two months or so, according to the severity (or otherwise) of the case.

During the fast, and after if necessary, the bowels should be cleansed nightly with a warm-water enema or gravity douche; whilst if constipation is habitual, the rules for its eradication given in Section 9 (page 275) should be put into operation forthwith. The morning dry friction and sitz-bath detailed in the Appendix should be undertaken daily, as also the breathing and other exercises. A hot Epsom-salts bath should be taken twice weekly where possible.

A hot and cold sitz-bath (details of which are given in the Appendix) should be taken every night, except on those nights on which an Epsom-salts bath is being taken, by those with growths in the womb; those with growths in the breast should apply hot fomentations several times daily as follows : Wring out a towel in hot water, and apply for, say, two or three minutes, then remove and apply a second towel, and later a third. Then put on a cold towel to finish off. Always work in this order : three hot, one cold. Gentle massage of the affected breast, after each series of bathing, will also be helpful. Sun and air bathing, where at all possible, will be most beneficial too.

The utmost cleanliness with regard to the sex organs must be maintained, and where the growth is in the womb, a vaginal douche may be used two or three nights weekly. Use only warm water for this : no medicinal preparations whatsoever. Gentle massage of the abdomen and pelvic region will be very useful.

ALL COLD BATHING SHOULD BE SUSPENDED DURING THE MENSTRUAL PERIOD.

Future strict attention to the dietary is most essential, and fruits and salads—Nature's cleansing foods—*must* form the bulk of the food eaten. No white bread or white-flour products, no sugar, no pastry, puddings, or pies, no refined cereals, no cream, or greasy or heavy fatty foods, and no boiled or mashed potatoes are to be taken in future. Meat and other flesh foods can with benefit be left out of the dietary entirely, and their place taken in the weekly menus by eggs or cheese or nuts. All tinned and potted foods must be avoided, as also strong tea or coffee or alcohol, and all condiments, pickles, sauces, etc.

The patient should have as much fresh air and gentle outdoor exercise, such as walking, as her condition will allow. *Osteopathic treatment* is strongly recommended.

Hydrocele.—This is a condition in which there is fluid and swelling in the testicles and scrotum. (One testicle is affected usually.) The superficial cause of the trouble may be a knock or a strain, but a toxic condition of the system is always at the root of the matter, this systemic toxicity being due to wrong feeding habits, general wrong living, suppressive medical treatment of former disease, etc. Sexual excess and abuse is also an important factor in some cases, through the degeneration of the sex organism which follows. The condition is one that often interferes greatly with walking, etc., and a suspensory bandage is generally advised by the medical adviser of the sufferer to overcome this.

Treatment.—Tapping is the method usually resorted to for getting rid of the fluid in hydrocele, but that does not get rid of the *cause* of the trouble, only its effects. The only way in which the condition can be *really* dealt with successfully is through constitutional treatment aiming at removing the underlying toxicity of the system, which is at the root of the trouble. The sufferer from hydrocele should therefore carry on as follows :

Begin with from four to seven or ten days on the *exclusive fresh fruit diet* outlined in the Appendix. (The longer the initial period spent on the all-fruit diet the better.) This all-fruit period should then be followed by the adoption of the *full weekly dietary* also outlined in the Appendix. Further short periods on the all-fruit diet should be undertaken at monthly intervals as required, say two or three consecutive days each time.

During the all-fruit period the bowels should be cleansed nightly with a warm-water enema or gravity douche, and if constipation is habitual, the rules for its eradication given in Section 9 (page 275) should be put into operation. The morning dry friction and cold sitz-bath detailed in the Appendix should be undertaken daily, in conjunction with the breathing and other exercises given therein. A hot Epsom-salts bath should be taken once or twice weekly where at all possible.

The hot and cold sitz-bath also detailed in the Appendix will be very helpful in this case, and should be taken every night, except on the nights an Epsom-salts bath is being taken. The affected part can also be bathed daily with alternate hot and cold compresses if there is any pain present. (A piece of material is wrung out in hot water and applied, then removed, and a piece of material wrung out in cold water applied, and so on.)

Every effort should be made to build up the general health-level to the highest degree, and fresh air and outdoor exercise are essentials to the success of the treatment. Sun and air bathing, where possible, are strongly recommended. The diet factor is of the utmost importance, and fruits and salads MUST form the main basis of the future dietary. No alcohol, strong tea, or coffee is to be taken in future ; no condiments, pickles, sauces, etc. Smoking, where habitual, should be cut out entirely, or else reduced to the very minimum. All habits and practices tending to lower the tone of the body should be studiously avoided in future, especially sexual abuse and excess.

Unless the condition is of long standing, the foregoing treatment should soon begin to show its beneficial effects, and the whole general health-level of the sufferer will be greatly enhanced at the same time.

HEAVY LIFTING AND STRAIN SHOULD BE AVOIDED AS FAR AS IS POSSIBLE. The wearing of a suspensory bandage is often useful.

Impotence.—See *Loss of Sexual Power* (page 395).

Leucorrhœa.—Leucorrhœa is the name given to the milky-white vaginal discharge experienced by many women, and known commonly as " whites." The trouble is a most annoying one, and is connected essentially with a devitalised and toxic condition of the system generally. That is why treatment by means of drugs or surgery cannot possibly be successful in these cases, the constitutional factors at the back of the trouble not being affected in the slightest by such treatment.

A general toxic condition of the system due to wrong feeding habits, and often accentuated by chronic constipation, is always at the root of the trouble ; but all factors (mental, emotional, and physical) which tend to lower the tone of the body and reduce its efficacy can help to set the condition in operation.

Treatment.—It must be obvious that treatment for leucorrhœa *must* be applied to the system as a whole, and not to any one part, if a cure is to be effected. It is only by the adoption of soundly devised constitutional treatment designed to build up the *whole general health-level of the sufferer* that the systemic toxicity responsible for the setting up of the discharge can be removed. Incidentally, such treatment will not only remove the leucorrhœa, but will place the feet of the sufferer firmly upon the road that leads to sound and lasting health.

To undertake such a scheme of all-round health-building treatment, the sufferer from leucorrhœa should carry on as follows : Begin with from four to seven or more days on the *all-fruit diet* outlined in the Appendix. Stay on this all-fruit diet for as many days as you can— the longer the better—and then the *full weekly dietary* also outlined in the Appendix can be begun. This weekly diet-sheet should be adhered to as strictly as possible from then on. Further short periods on all-fruit, say two or three consecutive days, can be undertaken at monthly intervals, according to the needs of the case.

In those cases where the sufferer is anæmic, very much under weight, or in a very debilitated condition, a period should be spent on the *fruit and milk diet* (given in the Appendix) after the all-fruit diet and before going on to the full weekly dietary.   If the fruit and milk diet is agreeing very well, it may be proceeded with for from a fortnight to a month with every benefit.   Further periods on all-fruit followed by fruit and milk may be required in these cases at intervals of, say, two months or so.

During the first few days of the treatment the bowels should be cleansed nightly with a warm-water enema or gravity douche, and after as necessary ; whilst if constipation is habitual, the rules for its eradication given in Section 9 (page 275) should be put into operation. The morning dry friction and sitz-bath outlined in the Appendix must form a regular feature of the treatment, and should be carried out daily in conjunction with the breathing and other exercises also given therein. A hot Epsom-salts bath should be taken once or twice weekly where at all possible.

The hot and cold sitz-bath detailed in the Appendix will be most beneficial in these cases, and should be taken four or five nights weekly where practicable.   A vaginal douche may be used occasionally* to cleanse the vagina whilst the discharge continues.   Use only warm water for this.

The utmost care of the body, combined with scrupulous cleanliness of habits, is essential to the success of the treatment, whilst as much fresh air and outdoor exercise as possible should be taken daily.   The open-air deep-breathing exercises given in the set of breathing exercises detailed in the Appendix are especially important and should be practised daily whilst walking in the open air.   As part of the general effort being made to bring the whole body to the highest pitch of health and efficiency, sun and air bathing, where at all possible, can be strongly recommended.

The diet factor is of the utmost importance, and the general views *re* diet expressed in the present book should be taken seriously to heart.   Fruits and salads—Nature's body-cleansing and health-restoring foods—*must* form the bulk of the future dietary.   No white bread or white-flour products, sugar, confectionery, rich cakes, pastry, puddings or pies, milk puddings, refined cereals (such as porridge,

* About once or twice weekly or so.

etc.), cream, rich, heavy, or greasy foods are to be taken in future. Very little meat or other flesh foods. No tinned or preserved food. No strong tea, coffee, or condiments, pickles, sauces, etc., are to be taken. Smoking, if indulged in, should be given up, and alcoholic beverages, if formerly taken, should be studiously avoided.

IN NO CIRCUMSTANCES SHOULD ANY DRUGS BE TAKEN. *During the menstrual period all cold bathing can be suspended.* Where procurable, *spinal manipulation* can be very strongly recommended as a most useful adjunct to the treatment.

Loss of Sexual Power.—Loss of sexual power, or impotence, in men, is quite a common occurrence, and its usual causes are abuse or misuse of the sexual organism over a long period, together with a devitalised condition of the system in general. Although most cases of impotence are of the above-mentioned nature, there are certain cases, however, in which the condition is due to previous drug treatment of disease, especially the taking of bromides, whilst in others the causative factor is psychological. The trouble in these latter cases develops out of a fear in the mind of the sufferer that he cannot perform the sexual act, although it is quite possible that he *can* do so if he can overcome this mental inhibition.

As regards treatment for impotence, a scheme of treatment along the lines of that for *Hydrocele* given earlier in the present section (page 391) will do much towards restoring sexual function, but of course the results achieved will all depend upon the age, condition, etc., of the sufferer. Long-standing cases will obviously not get such good results from the treatment as comparatively early cases ; and younger men will naturally tend to do better than older men. Where the trouble is of psychological origin, as above mentioned, treatment should be just the same, but in these cases advice from a qualified Psycho-therapist would be highly desirable. The taking of drugs or so-called " remedies " for these conditions is not only useless but dangerous. Osteopathic treatment is often helpful.

Menorrhagia.—Menorrhagia is the medical name given to excessive menstruation. Of course one must remember that what is excessive to one individual may not be so to another ; but in general we can say that if the loss occasions weakness and interferes with ordinary activities, then it may be considered abnormal.

There are a variety of causes which may be responsible for the setting up of the trouble ; but if the remarks made at the beginning of the present section have been thoroughly understood, the reader will readily perceive that a toxic condition of the system is at the root of the matter in every case, such systemic toxicity being due to wrong feeding habits, general wrong habits of living, previous suppressive drug treatment of disease, etc., etc.

Menorrhagia is the trouble that leads to a great deal of experimental treatment at the hands of the medical profession—experimental treatment which does more harm than the actual condition itself. Such treatment centres entirely upon symptoms—upon checking the excessive flow—and pays no attention to causes at all. When it is realised that the excessive menstruation is part of an attempt on the part of the body to rid itself of excess toxic materials, it must be obvious that such suppressive treatment must lead to a great deal of future harm to the system, and to serious disease of all kinds, even though it may be successful temporarily in checking the excessive flow.

Treatment.—Treatment for menorrhagia such as we have here been referring to is essentially short-sighted in every way. What is needed is a scheme that will thoroughly cleanse the system of toxic material and so get rid of the causes *behind* the excessive flow. Only in this way can the trouble be really overcome and sound health built in the individual concerned.

The sufferer from menorrhagia who would like really to get rid of her trouble and build up her general health at the same time should carry out the scheme of treatment for *Leucorrhœa* given just previously in the present section. Such a regimen MUST help her on the road to recovery, because it deals with essential causes and removes them, and does not merely tamper with symptoms. (For the relief of pain during menstruation, see treatment for *Dysmenorrhœa*, page 387.)

Milk-leg (White-leg).—This is a condition which sometimes arises in women after childbirth, and is caused by the formation of a blood-clot in one of the great veins of one or both legs. As regards treatment, if this cannot be under the personal care of a Naturopath, it should be as for *Phlebitis*, given in Section 4 of the present book (page 171).

Nocturnal Emissions (Involuntary Night Losses).—Nocturnal emissions, or *involuntary night losses*, are a common occurrence amongst young men, and need not cause the slightest alarm if they occur not more than, say, once every ten days to two weeks. They are quite a natural phenomenon in every way. If they occur excessively, however—say three or four times weekly—they are a sign of sexual weakness, and steps should be taken to deal with the matter by carrying out a scheme of health-building treatment along the lines for *Hydrocele* given in the present section (page 391). It will be generally found that the frequent occurrence of night losses goes with the practice of *self-abuse*, and what has been said in the present section (below) on that score should be taken seriously to heart by the sufferer.

Painful Menstruation.—See *Dysmenorrhœa* (page 387).

Prostate-gland Disease.—See Section 6 (page 210).

Puerperal Fever.—Puerperal fever, or childbed fever, is a condition which sometimes arises as a result of uncleanliness of conditions during and just after childbirth. But it must be realised that a toxic condition of the system of the patient herself is always at the back of the trouble. As regards treatment for puerperal fever, this should be exactly as for any other fever treated along natural lines (see Section 13, page 404). If treatment is carried out along these lines, there is no safer or surer way of securing recovery in these cases.

Scanty Menstruation.—See *Amenorrhœa* (page 380).

Self-abuse.—Self-abuse, or masturbation, is a practice common enough among young people to-day, but one which it is customary to avoid speaking about as far as possible. There seems to be a veritable conspiracy of silence on all sides about the matter, yet the practice is one which is pernicious in the highest degree where the future health and well-being of the individual are concerned.

Most young people secretly learn the habit when quite ignorant as to what its ultimate effects upon the system are, and there is no doubt at all that all the silence in which the subject is veiled on all sides adds much to the damage done by the habit—a silence due to the unwillingness of responsible people, such as parents, teachers, etc., to discuss the matter in any way.

It is not for the writer to moralise about the matter, and there can be no doubt that under present conditions of living a normal sex life is debarred from large numbers of young people, but to resort to the habit of self-abuse is no way out of the difficulty. That some responsible people (even doctors) sometimes regard the practice as a kind of safety-valve for suppressed sex, and look upon it as one way out of our present-day sex perplexities, only makes the trouble all the more serious. People who talk in this way cannot have the slightest idea of what the ultimate effects of the habit are. Only those who, like the writer, are brought into frequent contact with the victims of this pernicious habit, and are called upon to try to alleviate as far as they can its destructive effects upon the minds and bodies of the individuals concerned, can say how much misery, ill-health, and suffering the habit of self-abuse brings in its train. That the ill-effects sometimes take years to show themselves makes the practice all the more disastrous.

Treatment.—The individual who has brought himself upon the road to mental and physical bankruptcy through the practice of self-abuse can do much to recapture his lost health and vitality, however, if he will take himself in hand and follow out a scheme of well-planned natural health-building treatment. Such treatment as that for *Hydrocele*, given in the present section (page 391), can be followed by all victims of self-abuse with nothing but the most beneficial results, both mental and physical. But of course it stands to reason that the habit itself must be definitely broken, or else the treatment cannot possibly achieve the results desired.

As regards the breaking of the habit, if the sufferer will keep constantly in mind the price he is paying in terms of future health for its practice, and can bring himself to realise that he can be master of himself if he but tries, then the habit will not be long in being broken. It is just a question of determination and loyalty to one's better self; of saying to oneself, " I *can* overcome this habit which is sapping my life and vital powers, and I *will*."

It is the nervous system which is most affected by the practice, so that the more the sufferer can bring rest, quietness, fresh air, and sunshine to his aid in carrying out the scheme of treatment advised, the better will the results be in every way. Above all things, it does not do to be morbid or introspective about the matter, and to be always accusing and blaming oneself for what has happened. The habit is usually contracted in pure ignorance, and there is no moral blame attaching thereto. Let the sufferer realise that what is past is past, and that what we have to do is to look to the future and plan and build for that. If he will stop self-recrimination and do that, then he can regain for himself a very great deal of what he thought for ever lost.

SPECIAL NOTE.—All literature of an unhealthy and suggestive nature should be avoided, and an attempt made to keep the mind as clean as possible. One way of preventing oneself thinking too much about anything is to engage the body busily in hard manual work such as gardening, sawing, etc. This will serve a twofold purpose, because it will not only take the sufferer's mind away from morbid and unhealthy thoughts and imaginings, but will help still further to build up his health and vital powers through the physical exercise involved.

Stoppage of Menstrual Flow.—See *Amenorrhœa* (page 380).

Syphilis.—As already stated in the introductory pages to the present section, syphilis is *quite curable* by means of natural treatment, leaving none of the dreaded after-effects so common to orthodox methods of " cure." As also pointed out in the remarks in question, the Nature Cure practitioner in this country is not allowed by law to take on the treatment of syphilis, but it can be stated again, for the benefit of sufferers, that the cure lies in FASTING, pure and simple.

The following extract, with regard to the natural treatment of syphilis, is taken from the book *Direct Paths to Health*, by Major R. Austin, M.R.C.S., L.R.C.P. (published by the C. W. Daniel Co., Ltd., of Ashingdon, Rochford, Essex). Major Austin was a doctor in the Royal Army Medical Corps, but, realising the futility of orthodox medical methods of treatment, became a practitioner of Nature Cure instead. It was because of his holding an orthodox medical degree that he was able to treat cases of venereal disease, whilst other Nature Cure practitioners are not. On page 83 of his book he says:

" Sex diseases are not exactly pleasant topics to talk or write about but their importance is sufficient justification for plain speaking. I will therefore describe one bad case of syphilis as an example of what I have done by simple means to help Nature in bringing about a cure in other cases of the disease.

" Mr. A., aged twenty-seven, came to me suffering from tertiary syphilis. The classic drugs had been used, including mercury and ' 606 ' (known now under various names, such as salvarsan, neo-salvarsan, arsenobenzol, all being similar and based on arsenic), but it had not stopped the ravages of the disease. His face and body were covered with rupial eruptions—ulcers covered with a scab—and the odour from his body was most unpleasant.

" I prescribed a fourteen days' fast with a saline purge daily, plenty of water and as much strained orange juice diluted with water as he liked to drink during the day. At the end of the fourteen days he was allowed two meals a day, one of them consisting of nothing but properly cooked vegetables and some butter, and the other of milk and fresh fruit.

" In six weeks from the date of commencing the treatment all the eruptions had disappeared, as well as the foul odour of the body, and he was feeling remarkably well and has remained so ever since.

" After the first six weeks he was allowed a little animal food at one of his two daily meals. Needless to say, systematised exercises also formed part of his daily régime."

Major Austin further says : " The treatment of syphilis by fasting is by no means new ; indeed, I got the idea from Dr. Oswald's book, *Fasting, Hydropathy, and Exercise,* in which he says : ' A germ disease as virulent as syphilis and long considered too persistent for anything but palliative methods of treatment (by mercury, etc.) was radically cured by the fasting cure, prescribed in the Arabian hospitals of Egypt, at the time of the French occupation.'

" . . . Knowing what excellent results can be obtained without using drugs which impair the health and sometimes blind or even kill the patient, I never now advise their use."

For the guidance of readers it can be said that perhaps the best book on the natural treatment for venereal disease is that by Dr. Tilden, the eminent American Naturopath.

Varicocele.—This is a condition in which the veins around the testes become knotted and thickened. The trouble is brought on in every case through excessive abuse or misuse of the sex organs. As regards treatment, this should be exactly along the lines of that for *Hydrocele* as given in the present section (page 391). Such a scheme of treatment will not only help to diminish the varicocele and overcome its effects, but will also greatly enhance the general health of the sufferer. A suspensory bandage may be worn in cases where there is a dragging feeling in the groin, pain, etc.

Of course it goes without saying that the habits responsible for the setting up of the trouble in the first place must be discontinued before treatment is begun.

Venereal Disease.—See introductory remarks to the present section also *Gonorrhœa* (page 388) and *Syphilis* (page 399).

Woman's Change of Life (the Menopause).—When the menstrual flow in women ceases, it means that the child-bearing period is finally over, and the passage towards the third and last phase of life—that of old age—has begun. This change in the sex life of women is a perfectly natural phenomenon, and as such should not affect to any extent at all the general health and well-being of the individual concerned ; in the normal healthy woman the " change " should take place with little or no outward sign.

There are a great many women, however, who are *not* healthy whose health is always below par, and in these cases the " change " often leads to all kinds of physical and emotional disturbances of function, and sometimes even to definite disease of some kind or other. To understand *why* this should be, the reader should turn to the remarks on menstruation in the general discussion of women's ailments at the beginning of the present section. It was said there that the menstrual flow was utilised by Nature as a form of safety-valve, as an extra eliminative channel for the removal of toxic material from the bodies of women whose health was below the normal as a result of unwise feeding habits and general wrong habits of living ; and it was also pointed out that when the menstrual flow ceased, many women developed growths or other diseases of the sex organs as a direct result of the " drying up " of this additional eliminative outlet. It is for precisely this same reason that so many women begin to suffer from all kinds of distressing physical, nervous, and emotional symptoms and manifestations when the " change " arrives ; *but only because the bodily condition of the sufferer is already below par, and* NOT *because of anything inherent in the " change " itself.*

Now, with regard to the orthodox medical view about the matter, it has often been pointed out in the present book that the medical profession has a penchant for picking out " scapegoats " on which to hang the causes of diseases for which no definite physical cause can be discovered. The tonsils and the appendix are two examples known to all. But woman's " change of life " is another, and one that is being increasingly used every year. It is so convenient and handy to say to one's women patients who are around the forties and are suffering from this or that disease : " Oh, yes, it is the ' change ' that is responsible." It saves all further need for finding out *what*

EVERYBODY'S GUIDE TO NATURE CURE

really is the cause of the trouble, and gives that air of finality and definiteness to the decision which always impresses the patient.

That this use of the " change " as a convenient scapegoat for the cause of diseases in women in middle life should lead all women to regard it with dread and apprehension, and to invest this perfectly natural and innocent phenomenon with a sinisterness which it does not in the least possess, only adds to the potency of the medical claim. The vicious circle is thus completed !

The Naturopath has to deal continually with cases of disease unsuccessfully treated by the medical profession, and on asking what the patient has to say regarding medical opinion as to the cause of the trouble, *in nearly every case where the patient is a woman approaching or in middle life*, he is told that it is the " change " which has been named by her medical adviser as the cause of her condition of ill-health. (" Oh, yes, it is due to the change.")   The woman is thus led to believe that her disease is something which " happened " to her as a result of causes quite beyond her control, and which it is more or less impossible to rectify, and so she is led farther and farther away from an understanding of what the real causes of her trouble are and how the condition may be overcome.   It is only when she comes into contact with natural methods of treatment, and with Natural-Cure views about disease, that she realises that she has been led to ascribe to a perfectly natural phenomenon the cause of a condition entirely due to her own unwise habits of feeding and living, combined (most likely) with previous suppressive medical treatment in the form of drugs, operations, etc.

We have said that the medical profession is all too prone to use the " change " as a convenient cloak to its ignorance regarding the real causes of the diseases its women patients suffer from, and to give it a sinisterness which it does not naturally possess ; but that does not mean to say that the " change " is not to blame sometimes. We have said ourselves that it is, and have given definite reasons *why* it is.   It is this ascribing every and all disease to the " change " on the slightest provocation, where middle-aged women are concerned, that we are so much up against.   We must repeat, therefore, that the " change of life " is a purely natural phenomenon, and that in the normally healthy woman it should have no ill after-effects *whatsoever* ; but where a women is *not* in good health, then the "change" *may* bring all sorts of complications in its train.   In these cases *it is not the " change " as such which is to blame, therefore, but the bodily condition of the patient.*

Where a woman is affected by the " change of life " to any marked extent, it is a sure sign that her body is in a toxic condition and in need of a thorough cleansing. To restore her to a condition of health again, she will need to undergo a course of natural health-building treatment, and to that end nothing could be better than the scheme of treatment given for *Leucorrhœa* in the present section (page 393). Such a scheme of cleansing and health-rebuilding treatment will help her to overcome her difficulties in the shortest possible time, and add many useful years to her life.

FEVERS (ALSO INFLUENZA)

Chicken-pox— Diphtheria — Enteric fever — Influenza — Malaria — Measle (also German measles)—Meningitis—Pneumonia—Rheumatic fever—Scarle fever—Smallpox—Typhoid fever—Typhus fever (Yellow fever, Cholera, etc.)

TO the ordinary individual brought up on orthodox views about the matter, a fever is something which we " catch " from a germ, and has nothing whatever to do with what has gone before in the life-history of the individual concerned. Mr. A. is quite well and healthy to-day, and yet to-morrow he is down with typhoid, or pneumonia, or what not. " Purely the result of germ infection," the doctor says, and everyone believes it implicitly.

But the reader will not have gone far in the present book before he will have come to realise the superficiality and speciousness of such thinking about disease. No one can " catch " a fever who has not a ready soil for the propagation and development of the germ within his own body in the shape of accumulated systemic refuse and toxic material brought there through wrong feeding habits and general wrong living. As pointed out again and again in the present book, if a person is absolutely clean and wholesome INSIDE, then no germ disease of any kind can arise within the system. It is only in those whose systems are *unwholesome inside* that such diseases can develop. Whether the disease originates spontaneously or through contact with others does not matter in the least.

A fever, then, can only develop within the systems of those who are in a state of *internal uncleanliness*, and far from the fever being something inimical to health and likely to lead towards the death of the patient if not checked in time, as is generally believed, it is nothing but an attempt at self-cleansing on the part of the natural forces within the body of the individual concerned, and a direct move towards health and self-regeneration. This may sound very startling to the uninitiated, but once the theoretical portion of the present book has been read and understood, everything is quite plain and clear. *Fevers are acute diseases, and all acute diseases are direct manifestations of the self-cleansing and health-restoring activities of the body. Allow the fever to run its course in a natural manner, and the individual concerned will be in far better health in every way after the fever than before,*

*because his whole system will have undergone nothing short of a natural
" spring-cleaning."*

Contrast this attitude towards fevers with the orthodox view.
To the medical mind a fever is a most serious disease-condition
brought about through the agency of unseen but deadly germs—a
state which must be fought " tooth and nail " in order to save the
life of the individual concerned. A deadly war has to be waged *at
once* between the " life-saving " sera and drugs of orthodox medication and the potent death-dealing germs always prowling about the
universe, the battle-field being the body of the unfortunate sufferer.
If, " through the mercy of God," medical skill prevails, and the
death-dealing germs are destroyed, then the victim will have had his
life saved as a result of the blessings of orthodox medicine !

Unfortunately for those who like melodrama, even with regard
to disease (with the germ as the villain of the piece, and the doctor
as the hero, fighting with drug and serum to save the unfortunate
victim's life), this view of fevers and their treatment is not only
utterly wrong, but it is the bringer of untold harm to thousands upon
thousands of luckless sufferers dealt with in this way. For when
fevers are treated by drugs and sera, their natural self-cleansing
activity is *suppressed*, and the toxic matter which the natural forces
of the body were endeavouring to throw off through the medium of
the fever are forced back again into the tissues and internal structures,
where, plus the drugs and sera administered by the doctor, they sow
the seeds for the development of disease of a more lasting and insidious
kind—to wit, *chronic disease* (as pointed out clearly in the opening
chapters of the theoretical portion of the present book). What the
doctor calls a " cure " is nothing more than a checking of this natural
attempt at self-cleansing ; and even if no direct complications set in
(as often happens !), and the individual feels quite all right for the
time being, he often wonders why he suddenly finds himself the
victim of this or that disease thereafter for no apparent reason at all.
(And no doubt the doctor wonders too !)

The fact that so many complications arise out of the orthodox
medical treatment of fevers—complications sometimes of the most
serious nature—shows only too clearly what is going on within the
body as a result of the suppressive nature of the treatment employed.
Such complications simply mean that this or that vital organ or
structure is being swamped with toxic material and drug poisons

as a result of wrongly thought-out and wrongly applied measures of treatment, and has succumbed under the pressure. (That is why kidney and heart disease follow so often in the wake of fevers treated in the orthodox manner.) Indeed, on this question of complications alone, Medical Science stands convicted as totally misunderstanding the nature and treatment of fevers, because when a fever is dealt with along natural lines, COMPLICATIONS CANNOT OCCUR.

When fevers are understood in their true light as natural attempts at self-cleansing, their treatment is a simple matter. No doubt the symptoms and the general condition of the patient give cause for genuine alarm to relatives and friends ; but when we realise that all that is taking place is that waste matter and morbid deposits are being " burned up " in the tissues preparatory to a complete rejuvenation of the system, then one can take matters more philosophically, and carry out what has to be done with calmness and sureness, knowing with certainty that all will come right in the end.

One of the great besetting sins of all people is that they think that as soon as someone is ill something *must* be done for the patient. The doctor is hurriedly sent for, he comes into the sick-room, the anxious parents or relatives of the sick person are there waiting for him, and of course he is expected to do *something* right away to save the patient from further suffering. Even if he does not know what is wrong or what treatment to pursue, he still must do something to satisfy the touching faith in his prowess of those present. It is because of this that doctors often have to carry out all sorts of measures and give all sorts of things that even they do not consider needful to the case, simply because something spectacular is expected of them

This sort of attitude is not the one for those who would carry out a scheme of natural treatment in a case of a fever. For it is precisely in these cases that *nothing* must be done—or, if anything, very little. The fever is a natural crisis, and all that the work of healing consists in is helping it to run its course completely and so carry out its allotted task, to the ultimate and lasting benefit of the sufferer.

The great thing in the treatment of all fevers is FASTING. It is by withholding all food from the patient that the natural cleansing activity taking place can be hastened to its healthful conclusion in the shortest possible time and with the greatest lasting benefit to the patient. It is because the medical profession *will not learn this fundamental fact*, and in addition to drugging them, persists in feeding its fever patients " to keep up their strength " (as far as they can be fed !), that the medical treatment for fevers is so unsatisfactory. Indeed, it can be said that most of the complications that arise out of the orthodox treatment of fevers are due more to the crass feeding that takes place during the fever than to any other single factor. The patient's system does not want the food—the last thing in the world the patient wants is to eat !—and so, merely so much more waste matter is added to the pile of refuse already being burned up in his tissues. The consequence is that the patient's temperature continues to rise (or refuses to come down), and this or that trouble sets in.

We have said that the last thing the fever sufferer wants to do is to eat, and this antipathy for all food during the course of the fever supplies the natural clue to the method of treatment required. The patient's instincts tell him to avoid food, and the avoidance of food is the key to the whole matter so far as cure is concerned. Let him only keep away from food, as his instincts demand, and the fever will soon have carried out its allotted task and all will be well again. Surely the whole thing is simple when we see it in the right light ?

A most curious thing is that fasting treatment is often employed by the medical profession for the cure of typhoid fever, with excellent results ; yet they *cannot* bring themselves to see that the same procedure will achieve equally excellent results with regard to other fevers too—indeed with all fevers. (The reason why the patient is fasted in typhoid is because it is realised that any food taken will only aggravate the condition of the intestines, where ulcers have formed as a result of the fever.) But if a patient can be fasted for two or three weeks for typhoid with nothing but the best results, why hesitate to use this same mechanism of cure for other fevers ? No, the medical mind *cannot see that all fevers are due to the same cause, and that treatment must be identical to secure the best results.* They *must* have one treatment for one thing and another treatment for another. They could not possibly bring all medication down to the same thing. That surely would make the practice of medicine far too easy !

It is worthy of note that fevers are most common in the young ; this is because the vitality of the child is so much more in proportion to that of the adult. He has not yet frittered away his birthright of health on this form of wrong living or that. Every case of fever amongst children is due basically to the one thing: WRONG FEEDING (as pointed out in the section on *Children's Ailments*, page 93).

PLAN OF TREATMENT FOR ALL FEVERS

Having given this introductory talk on the origin and treatment of fevers, we can now proceed to give an outline of the general measures required for their effective treatment along natural lines. Although this or that organ or structure may be specially involved in any particular kind of fever—as, for instance, the small intestines in typhoid, the lungs in pneumonia, etc.—at bottom all fevers are due to the same cause, SYSTEMIC TOXÆMIA—and treatment is therefore identical from the Natural-Cure point of view. The procedure, whether the fever is measles, scarlet fever, rheumatic fever, typhoid, or any other form of fever, should be as follows, results being in all cases equally excellent if the treatment is carefully and faithfully carried out.

To begin with, the patient must be *fasted completely*, being given only water and orange juice. (*No milk*—nothing else at all.) According to the severity of the fever it may be necessary to carry on the fast for from a week to two or even three weeks. The signs which will tell those administering the treatment when to break the fast will be *the clearing of the tongue of the patient* and the steadiness of body temperature at 98 degrees Fahr. The clearing of the tongue is an infallible sign to go by, as it shows definitely that all toxic matter has been burned up by the fever and the tissues are quite clear again.

During the fasting period the warm-water enema or gravity douche should be used every day—sometimes twice a day in serious cases— to cleanse the bowels. Once feeding is begun, it can be used less and less frequently until the time when normal bowel action has restarted, when it can be dispensed with altogether.

During the course of the fever the best way of reducing temperature *naturally* is by means of the cold pack. This can be applied to the whole body in the case of malaria, typhoid, etc.; to the chest in the case of pneumonia; to the throat in the case of diphtheria, etc. In general it is best to apply a body (or trunk) pack several times a day in all cases, with one to the throat, too, if needed. The pack is made by wringing out a sheet or other large square piece of linen material in cold water, wrapping it right round the body and legs of the patient (twice round would be best), and then covering completely with a small blanket or similar warm material. For the throat pack the linen may be covered with flannelling. Cold or tepid sponging of the whole body of the patient is also good ; and, if the patient can stand it, a cold bath and a quick return to bed is very good too. (This can only be done in slight cases, though.) With regard to the packs, these can be applied every three hours during the day whilst temperature is high, and kept on for an hour or so. The body should be well sponged with tepid water after removing the pack. In cases where reaction to the body pack is poor, hot-water bottles may be applied to the feet, and also against the sides of the body.

The foregoing simple procedure is all that is required to cure—really cure—any fever, the patient being in far better health thereafter than for many years before, because of the thorough internal cleansing he will have received. AND NO COMPLICATIONS WHATSOEVER WILL RESULT. They cannot, because no suppressive measures have been employed to cause such complications. Of course there will be anxious times for those undertaking the carrying out of the treatment—it would be folly to deny this (in some cases there may be a crisis to pass through before the smooth waters of recovery are entered) ; but if the treatment is carried out as directed, and *no feeding allowed or drugs or sera given*, then a complete and perfect cure MUST result.

Unfortunately, many people are not quite sure of themselves when carrying out treatment of this sort, and if any untoward happening arises they are apt to get panicky and send for a doctor. This is the worst thing possible, for the doctor will at once insist upon the patient being fed, and will proceed to administer his drugs and sera. As no doubt the patient has already been fasted for a few days, the entrance of beef-tea or milk into his system, plus the drugs and other paraphernalia of orthodox medication, will at once cause matters to take a turn for the worse. (I have known of this happening in several cases.) The result is that the case often ends fatally ; this, however, is blamed on the fasting and in no way on to the medical treatment employed, and the relatives responsible for initiating the fast are thus led to believe that it is due to their " faddism " and foolishness that this tragic end has been brought about.

This point is stressed expressly because, as has just been said, the author has known of the foregoing happening several times during the course of his experience. The great thing is for those administering the treatment to keep their heads and just carry on with the simple methods advocated. If any crises occur, they will pass off quite favourably because nothing is being done to interfere with their natural (and therefore successful) termination in any way. And as the whole fever process is a normal move towards the future health and self-regeneration of the patient, no crisis, however alarming on the surface, can do other than help on the healing process. Indeed, these crises are only special manifestations of the self-cleansing process already taking place, and are extra-special efforts on the part of the natural forces of the body to get rid of morbid deposits in special organs or structures. That is why interference with their progress— by means of drugs and unwise feeding—will tend to react so adversely upon the luckless sufferer. His whole organism is wrought up to the highest pitch during the crisis, and the intervention of outside agents just brings matters to a sudden climax, with the result that death sometimes results.

From the foregoing considerations it is always best to bring in a Naturopath, *where at all possible*, to supervise the carrying out of the treatment ; but, as already said, if people will only have enough faith in the efficacy of the methods employed—and they have proved themselves over and over again in thousands of cases the world over— then anyone with sufficient confidence in themselves can supervise the treatment in any given case. A complete cure MUST ensue if the treatment is carried out properly.

As regards feeding after the fever, this must be very carefully done. There should be no undue hurry to get the patient on to a full diet again. He should be placed on the *exclusive fresh fruit diet* outlined in the Appendix for the first few days, having nothing but grapes and oranges or other fresh, ripe, pulpy, juicy fruit for the first two days (the juice only the first day, the juice and pulp the next), and the more solid fruits after. After, say, three or four days on the all-fruit diet, milk may be added to the dietary (fresh and unboiled, or slightly warmed ; never hot) for a further two or three days, taking up to two pints daily, or a little more, and then the *full weekly dietary* outlined in the Appendix can be gradually adopted. It goes without saying, of course, that this scheme of dietary should be adhered to strictly thereafter, if the patient wishes to consolidate the beneficial effects upon his system of the successful treatment of the fever, and if he wishes to avoid any trouble in the direction of further disease in later life. So-called " nourishing " foods such as broths, beef-tea, etc., should NOT be given at all during convalescence. They are the worst possible foods to give one who is just recovering from the effects of disease, as they contain more toxic material in their constitution than any other known kind of food. They consist almost exclusively of water and the waste and morbid products of the animal system. As *real* food their value is nil.

With regard to the use of fruit juices during the fasting period, any fresh fruit juice may be used instead of orange juice, such as diluted lemon juice, grape-fruit juice, etc., or vegetable juices ; but if none of these is procurable in any given case, just water alone will do quite well. The only thing is that the fruit or vegetable juices help on the cleansing process more rapidly because of the body-cleansing elements they contain.

ALPHABETICAL LIST OF FEVERS, WITH SPECIAL REMARKS

Chicken-pox.—See general remarks on fevers in the preceding pages *re* general treatment ; see also Section 1 (*The Treatment of Children's Ailments*), page 109, where the disease is dealt with in detail.

Diphtheria.—See general remarks on fevers in the preceding pages *re* general treatment ; see also Section 1 (*The Treatment of Children's Ailments*), page 110, where the disease is dealt with in detail.

Enteric Fever.—See *Typhoid* (page 421).

Influenza.—Influenza is being included in the present section because it is an acute disease exactly similar in every way to a fever, its typical symptoms, as with all acute diseases, being high temperature, prostration, pain in limbs, nausea, etc., etc. No disease receives more attention at the present time than influenza, and if one listens to the medical view upon the matter as reported in the popular Press it would seem that what we have to do to rid the world of " this dreaded scourge " is to furnish huge sums of money for research work so that scientists can find the germ of influenza, and thus enable the medical profession to deal with it successfully. It does not seem to occur to those who either make or print or read these remarks that the germs of tuberculosis, diphtheria, typhoid, pneumonia, and many others are well known to the bacteriologist, without in the least preventing the continual occurrence of these diseases !

No amount of research work to discover the germ of influenza is going to prevent or stamp out influenza. Although the disease is what is known as a germ disease, it is *not primarily due to the action of germs*, as people believe, but depends for its development in the first place upon a toxic and run-down condition of the system of the person concerned, as a result of wrong feeding habits and general wrong living. As already pointed out in the general remarks on fevers at the beginning of the present section, *no disease germ can take lodgment and become active in the system of one who is perfectly clean and wholesome within*. This remark holds equally good of influenza as of all other germ diseases. It is the bodily condition of the sufferer which we have to look to every time, and not the germ. Germs are merely superficial agents in the matter.

When people have been living for years in the conventional way, eating the wrong food and having insufficient exercise, wearing unhygienic clothing, sitting always in stuffy rooms or equally stuffy cinemas or theatres, keeping late hours, etc., etc., their systems are *bound* to get clogged with waste material and morbid deposits, and it is because of *this* that they fall such ready victims to the dreaded "flu." Especially is this so if they are in the habit of loading their system with purgative drugs, etc., or have been the victims of much previous suppressive drug treatment.

As with all acute diseases, influenza originates through a lowering of the vitality of the individual concerned (worry, overwork, and excesses of all kinds being the most potent factors concerned in bringing about the lowering of vitality in question) ; and it has only to make a start in one person here and there for more and more people to "catch" it from them, because all these people are in an equally low vital state themselves, with their systems also choked up with waste matter. That is how an epidemic starts. It only needs a few to make a beginning for more and more to go down with it, because, as just explained, the vast majority of people in civilised countries live in more or less exactly the same way—within limits— and are thus equally ready for the development of the disease within their systems.

It is generally noticed that an epidemic starts during or just after the winter, when vitality is low (especially after the Christmas "gorging" bout !), or after a great crisis, such as the Great War, when physical and nervous tension is relaxed, the reason being that the natural forces of the body take the opportunity thus afforded of indulging in a little bout of much-needed internal " spring-cleaning " (which is all that influenza really is !).

We have said that, like all acute diseases, influenza is a natural attempt at self-cleansing, and it follows therefore that if rightly treated, nothing but good can ensue so far as the future health and well-being of the sufferer are concerned. It is because the origin of influenza is not rightly understood in medical and scientific circles, and because the disease is not rightly treated, that so much ill-health and suffering follow in its train and so many deaths occur.

There are very few common diseases which bring so many complica-tions in their train as influenza when treated along orthodox medical lines, and this is entirely due to the suppressive nature of the treatment employed and the crass feeding which is allowed. That is why pneumonia so often develops after " flu," kidney trouble, heart trouble, ear and chest trouble, etc. All are due to the wrong methods of treatment employed, which have checked the natural cleansing process taking place and forced toxic matter deeper and deeper into the system again, where, plus the drugs administered by the doctor, they take lodgment in this or that vital organ or structure, to the detriment of the organ or structure concerned and of the whole general health of the sufferer.

It is because of the ease with which the disease is passed on from one to another, and the equal ease with which complications may arise during treatment (often leading to death), that influenza has filled the public mind with such dread. But if the matter were only seen in its true light, there would not be the slightest need for all this fear and dread. It is just that ignorance is being allowed to lead ignorance in the matter that all the trouble has arisen. Let natural methods of cure be generally adopted during the next influenza epidemic, and not only would there be no deaths or dreaded complica-tions to fill the papers with scare headlines, but every person treated would be in far better health after recovery than before, because his system would have received a thorough internal cleansing—a cleansing which it very much needed, be it noted. Let these same individuals live thereafter along Natural-Cure lines, as regards diet, etc., and the statistics for disease in this country would show a remarkable decrease in every direction within a very short time. And all this without one penny having been spent on research work, public health services, and the like ! Just think of the saving that this would mean to the

413

country as regards sick-pay, insurance benefit, doctors' bills, etc. and of the all-round improvement in national efficiency that would ensue, as a consequence of the greatly improved health of the population as a whole !

But there you are, people *will not see* these things in their true light (especially our leaders of medical thought and opinion !), and so more and more money is asked for every year for research work to discover and " stamp out " the " dreaded germ " of influenza, whilst thousands upon thousands of deaths continue to result annually from the disease—*as it is supposed*, but really through the totally unwise manner in which treatment is carried out.

Treatment.—As regards treatment for influenza, this is exactly the same as for any other acute disease ; and the general procedure for fevers given in the preceding pages can be followed out in every case of influenza with nothing but the best results. Of course, whereas in a fever the initial fasting period may last from a week to two or three, in influenza the fast may only have to be carried on for from two or three up to five or seven days, according to the severity of the case. When all temperature has subsided and convalescence is assured (the tongue need not necessarily clear fully in these cases, because the fast is not intended to be conducted to a finish as with a fever), then a day or two on the *all-fruit diet*, followed by a further day on fruit and milk, can be undertaken, after which the *full weekly dietary* outlined in the Appendix can be gradually embarked upon. The more closely this scheme of dietary is adhered to thereafter, the less likely is it that future attacks of " flu " will occur. IN NO CIRCUM-STANCES SHOULD ANY DRUGS BE TAKEN.

NOTE.—It is quite possible for one living on a healthy dietary for even a year or two to develop influenza, but that is only because his system has still plenty of toxic matter in it and is in need of cleansing. If the disease is treated along correct lines, this excess toxic material is removed, and it only means that the future health of the individual has been further enhanced. Thus, looked at in the right light, all the things that people dread most, such as fevers, colds, influenza, etc., are really blessings in disguise—*if rightly treated* ; because they simply remove toxic matter from the system of the individual con-cerned and thus pave the way for better and better health—always provided, that is, that sensible methods of living are adhered to thereafter.

When people find themselves getting influenza year after year (or sometimes twice a year), it is not obscure germs that must be blamed for this, but THEMSELVES. It only shows in what a deplorable state their body is, and how weak is their vitality. Such people are badly in need of a thorough course of health-building treatment along the lines consistently laid down in the present book.

Malaria.—Malaria is the fever most common to tropical and subtropical regions, and it is generally assumed that Medical Science has a sure cure and preventive for the disease in quinine. The malaria parasite is introduced into the human system through the bite of a certain mosquito, and it is claimed that quinine has the power to destroy the poisons set up by the parasite. To those who look upon all disease in the usual superficial way, that is quite sufficient ; but to those who look below the surface in these matters and seek for first causes, things are not quite so simple as they seem.

To begin with, no one whose blood-stream is in a really clean condition can " catch " malaria, no matter how many times he may be bitten every day by the malaria mosquito. As with all other infectious diseases, it is to the bodily condition of the individual concerned we must look every time, whether the disease is malaria or any other fever. It is quite true that the malaria mosquito introduces the parasite into the human system, but unless that system is in such a toxic state that the parasite can develop there, not the slightest trace of malaria will there be.

Because of their habitually superficial view of all disease, our medical scientists and research workers lose sight completely of this fundamental fact; and because they have in quinine, mepacrine, etc., drugs which definitely have a direct effect upon the malaria parasite, they consider that the malaria problem has been quite solved so far as they are concerned. From their point of view all you have to do in malarial regions is to take quinine every day to *prevent* malaria; but if the disease should develop " in spite of these precautions," then take more and yet more quinine until the disease has been removed. The fact that quinine is *not* a sure preventive for malaria, and that even when the disease has been " cured " by its administration it always tends to return, never seems to affect in the slightest this implicit medical belief in the unrivalled value of quinine in the treatment of malaria.

If malaria could be really cured by quinine, *why is it that everyone so treated is liable to recurrent attacks of the disease for ever after?* Surely that is hardly what one would expect from a form of treatment which is universally hailed as a *specific cure* for a disease ? It is only when we view the matter from the Natural-Cure angle, however, that we begin to see things in their true light. Quinine is a most deadly and destructive drug, and as used in the treatment for malaria it *suppresses* the action of the fever, but at the cost of the malarial poisons being retained in the system for ever after. That is why the recurrent attacks occur. Medical Science cannot explain this phenomenon, but Natural Cure can, quite simply and easily.

Not only are the malarial poisons retained in the system as a result of treatment by quinine, but the body of the patient is also filled with large quantities of quinine too. And it is because of *this* that the ear trouble, the eye trouble, and all the other complications connected with the medical treatment of malaria arise. (Quinine has a most destructive effect upon the ear structures, and often upon the eye structures too, causing deafness and blindness in extreme cases, but *always interfering* with hearing to a certain extent.) The liver and spleen are permanently enlarged as a result of medical treatment for malaria, and this entirely because the system—through the medium of the two important organs in question—has been trying its best to cope with the drug, at the cost of permanent impairment of the health of the two organs themselves. It can truly be said that *no one* who has been treated for malaria by means of quinine is ever really healthy again. Such an individual is *always* liable to be suffering from one complaint or another.

So much, then, for the much-vaunted quinine treatment for malaria. The disease owes its origin *not* simply and solely to the introduction of the germ into the human system by the malaria mosquito (the germ is merely the superficial causative factor) ; it owes its origin far more to the wrong habits of living of the individual concerned, which have led to his system being clogged with accumulated systemic refuse and morbid material. *It is on this soil that the malaria germ breeds.* When one thinks of the way in which civilised people live in the tropics —*especially white people*—then the main cause for the presence of malaria will become at once apparent. Meat meals two or even three times a day in a sweltering climate, a preponderance of tinned and other denatured foods, plenty of whisky and other alcoholic liquors, and a daily quota of deadly quinine, and there you have the cause of the trouble in a nutshell.

It is a noteworthy fact that native races living on the natural foods of the district are usually quite immune from the disease ; it is white settlers and those living upon the conventional *civilised* dietary who " catch " malaria. If it is the germ which is the prime agent in the matter all the time, why is it some escape so completely from the disease whilst being exposed equally with others to attack from the malaria mosquito ?

Treatment.—The typical symptoms of malaria are well marked : chill, fever, and sweat occurring every day, every second day, or every third day. The most common form of malaria is the *tertian*, appearing every two days. The chill is preceded by nausea and vomiting, headache, backache, and general discomfort. The entire body shakes, the teeth chatter, the pulse is rapid and irregular, the temperature is high though the skin is cold, and the kidneys are very active. The chill lasts for from ten minutes to an hour or longer, and is then followed by intense heat, headache, rapid pulse, redness of the skin (with or without eruption), and possibly by delirium and unconsciousness, which may last for from two to six hours. Then comes a period of profuse sweating with fall of temperature, weakness, feeble pulse, and possibly restful sleep. This experience is repeated every two days whilst the fever lasts. Symptoms in forms of malarial fever other than the tertian form just described are very similar.

As pointed out in the preceding pages, the disease is an *acute disease,* and if treated rightly can lead to nothing but the definite enhancement of the health of the individual concerned. *And there will be no recurring attacks !* It is only when the disease is suppressively treated by means of quinine, and the malarial poisons retained in the system for ever after, that the disease keeps on recurring for short spells every now and then—a conclusive sign that the malaria has most definitely *not* been cured, but is latent in the system all the time !

As regards the proper treatment to adopt in malaria, this is exactly as given in the preceding pages for the general treatment for all fevers ; and if this general plan of procedure is carried out, nothing but the most beneficial and lasting results can accrue. ON NO ACCOUNT SHOULD QUININE OR ANY OTHER DRUGS BE GIVEN.

SPECIAL NOTE.—The taking of quinine to " prevent " malaria is a mistaken procedure, because the only means of preventing the disease (in the true sense of the word) is to live in such a way that no soil for the development of the germ is present within the system. To secure this immunity, *what is required is a dietary suitable for a hot climate*—that is, one in which juicy fruits and vegetables predominate largely, and in which meat and other flesh foods are conspicuous by their more or less total absence. The taking of alcoholic liquors also largely paves the way for the development of malaria through the lowering of the tone of the system that takes place.

If one wishes to avoid malaria in malarial regions, therefore, the correct thing to do is NOT to take quinine, but to live wisely and cleanly. If one should fall victim to an attack (even when living in such wise), then it will be sure to be mild, and if treated as directed will soon pass completely, leaving the individual concerned in better health than before, because the fasting treatment employed will have given the system a thorough internal cleansing.

As pointed out in the section dealing with diseases of the ears, nose, mouth, and throat, many cases of ear trouble are due *directly* to the taking of daily doses of quinine in tropical climates for the supposed prevention of malaria ; whilst long-standing aural troubles are always intensified by the habitual taking of the drug.

Measles (also German Measles).—See general remarks on fevers in the preceding pages *re* general treatment ; see also Section 1 (*The Treatment of Children's Ailments*), page 112, where the disease is dealt with in detail

Meningitis.—See general remarks on fevers in the preceding pages *re* general treatment ; see also Section 1 (*The Treatment of Children's Ailments*), page 120, where the disease is dealt with in detail.

Pneumonia.—The treatment for pneumonia is no different from that for any other fever, and should be exactly along the lines indicated in the general plan given in the preceding pages. In this case, though, chest packs will be more helpful than full body packs, or else the two can be alternated with good effect.

The general symptoms of pneumonia are as follows : The disease usually begins with chill, high fever, severe headache, and soreness and aching of the whole body. There is a cough, with evidence of pain in the lungs, whilst breathing is much faster than usual, and there is often duskiness of the skin. The patient coughs and expectorates to release the mucus and other toxic material which is fast accumulating in the air-cells of the lungs. As pointed out more than once in the present book, pneumonia often results from the suppressive medical treatment of former disease, *especially* influenza.

Pneumonia in children is dealt with in detail in Section I (*The Treatment of Children's Ailments*), page 106.

Rheumatic Fever.—See general remarks on fevers in the preceding pages *re* general treatment ; see also Section I (*The Treatment of Children's Ailments*), page 113, where the disease is dealt with in detail.

Scarlet Fever.—See general remarks on fevers in the preceding pages *re* general treatment ; see also Section I (*The Treatment of Children's Ailments*), page 114, where the disease is dealt with in detail.

Smallpox.—It is generally considered that in vaccination the medical profession has a sure preventive of smallpox ; but when once the origin of fevers in the human system is understood, the futility of measures such as vaccination for the prevention of disease is at once made obvious.

Smallpox is a virulent type of fever, and it flourishes where conditions of living are very unclean both *without* as well as *within* the system. *It is because of the vastly improved methods of sanitation and general living in most civilised countries to-day* that smallpox is growing so scarce in these same countries, and not at all because of the practice of vaccination. It is a noteworthy fact that those countries which still insist upon compulsory vaccination at regular intervals, such as Japan, have more smallpox than those countries in which the practice is no longer strictly enforced, such as Germany and England ; and it is the contention of the Nature-Cure School of Thought that vaccination ITSELF serves to keep the tendency to smallpox alive in those civilised countries still liable to the disease, by passing the virus on in the blood-stream of one generation to the next, and that if the practice were discontinued altogether, there would be far less smallpox in the world than even now.

Cholera is another type of fever which was just as prevalent in civilised countries a century ago as smallpox, and this fever has died out even more completely than smallpox, simply because of the better methods of sanitation to-day. The medical profession ascribes to vaccination the reason for the decline in smallpox, but why should cholera—*a fever of almost identical origin*—be almost wiped out in

419

civilised countries without any forms of preventive treatment what-soever, except better methods of sanitation and general living ?

As a matter of fact, the practice of vaccination not only serves to perpetuate the possibility of smallpox in countries where it would otherwise have died out altogether by now, but it serves to introduce into the system of the one vaccinated morbid products which intensify any disease-tendency already present ; and many a person who has been vaccinated has been found to develop this or that serious disease after vaccination without being able to account for the cause of it, and even death has been known to occur as a direct result of the practice of vaccination. In any case, how can the morbid and diseased products of human beings or animals serve to protect the human organism from disease ? Surely it must be obvious to any sensible individual that such a practice only adds still more poisonous matter to a system already burdened with hereditary and acquired poisons ? The result *must* be an adding to the disease-bill of the nation, rather than a subtraction from it.

It is true that smallpox itself is far less prevalent in this and other civilised countries than it was a century ago, but what about the " newer " diseases such as influenza, neurasthenia, diabetes, cancer, etc., which have arisen to take its place ? Surely no one can say the world is less free from disease to-day than a hundred years ago ? There is more disease now than then. And the practice of vaccination has played its part in bringing about this increase of disease—especially chronic disease—in the countries in which it has been practised upon an unsuspecting population, who were led to believe that through its agency they would be warding off disease instead of courting it.

In many countries vaccination is now no longer strictly enforced. Great Britain no longer has compulsory vaccination but there is still a great deal of pressure on young mothers by doctors and welfare clinic personnel, which should be firmly resisted.

As regards the treatment for smallpox, this should be exactly the same as for any other fever, as outlined in the present section. The surest preventive against smallpox is cleanliness INSIDE as well as OUTSIDE the body.

Typhoid Fever.—Typhoid (or enteric) fever is very frequently met with in these days, and consists primarily in inflammation of certain small glands in the small and large intestines, from which inflammation a great variety of symptoms proceed, giving rise to the characteristic features of the disease. Typhoid fever is supposed to be due to a germ known as *Eberth's bacillus*, which is taken into the body through the medium of food, water, etc. As already pointed out in the general remarks *re* fevers at the beginning of the present section, it is not the germ *as such* which is of importance in the development of a fever, and this is equally true of typhoid as of all other fevers.

Typhoid fever can only develop in a system where there is a great accumulation of toxic waste and other putrefactive material in the intestines, for it is upon this that the germ flourishes. *Without such a soil it is harmless.* If one's intestines are full of such morbid matter (as a result of constant constipation following on general wrong living), then typhoid can readily develop there, *especially* if much meat or other flesh food is habitually eaten ; because it is the nature of such food to decompose and putrefy readily within the intestines and so bring a large quantity of bacterial and other toxic material in its train. More especially is this so in a hot country or during a hot spell, for in these cases decomposition and putrefaction take place with greater rapidity than at other times. This accounts for the greater prevalence of typhoid fever in a country like America, where much meat and other flesh food is eaten, in a hot climate, than in a country such as, say, England, where the temperature is less sultry.

Typhoid may sometimes take two or three weeks to develop, and is therefore often very baffling to the physician to diagnose at first. It begins with a tired feeling, loss of appetite, intense headache (especially in the forehead), nausea, and frequent diarrhœa The tongue is coated, and the back and body and bones ache unmercifully. Often there is bleeding from the nose, and frequently chills, followed by sweating, which may lead to the erroneous diagnosis of malaria.

Many precious days are often lost by medical practitioners in waiting to see if the disease *really is* typhoid, and many a case has been lost —or great harm done to it—in this " waiting " period. From the Natural-Cure point of view it does not matter in the least if the disease is pneumonia, or typhoid, or what not. If there is fever, the patient is *at once* fasted, and so the cure is in progress and the patient well on the way to recovery before the orthodox medical practitioner has made up his mind what the disease is !

Treatment.—It has already been said that fasting is often employed by the medical profession for the treatment of typhoid fever, with —as one would expect—excellent results. But this is not so always. Many hospitals insist on feeding their typhoid patients with milk or other " suitable " food, with the result that all sorts of complications ensue. The only correct treatment for typhoid—one from which no ill after-effects *of any kind* need be expected—is that of fasting ; and the general plan of treatment for all fevers given in the preceding pages can be carried out with nothing but the very best results in any case of typhoid fever.

If such treatment is employed, the individual so treated will start off afresh with intestines thoroughly cleansed of putrefactive material (as a result of the fever and its proper treatment) ; and if sensible feeding habits and ways of living are adopted thereafter, the said individual will have literally a new lease of life given him. His general health-level will be 100 per cent. higher than before. *And all because of the fever, mark you* (and its right treatment, of course).

Typhus Fever (Yellow Fever, Cholera, etc.).—These, the most virulent types of fever, are just as amenable to natural treatment as any of the less serious forms. Their origin is due to filthy conditions both outside and INSIDE the body. It is customary in these days to ascribe these fevers to bad external conditions of living, and entirely to ignore the internal condition of the sufferer as a factor in the matter, yet that is the most important factor of all. The fact that cholera and typhus are so rare these days, because of better methods of sanitation, etc., shows how readily Nature will respond to any effort made to keep her laws regarding cleanliness and health.

NOTE RE ANTI-TOXIN TREATMENT OF FEVERS.—Anti-toxin treatment for fevers has been hailed as one of the greatest medical and scientific blessings of our age. It is said that many thousands of individuals who would most assuredly have died otherwise have had their lives saved through its aid. When disease statistics are looked at, there is no denying that the mortality rate for certain fevers has subsided to a certain extent since the introduction of anti-toxin treatment, but, on the other hand, there are many instances on record where such treatment has most definitely brought about the death of the patient.

It can be stated quite definitely and finally that treatment aimed solely at destroying the germs of fevers—which is what anti-toxin treatment is—can never really cure the fever. It may succeed in destroying the germs, but in that case all it has done is to put an end to the self-cleansing work (with the germs as superficial agents) which was going on within the system of the individual concerned as a result of the fever. In other words, *the disease has been suppressed*, in exactly the same manner in which drug treatment operates. Thus, although a fever may be checked (" cured ") by anti-toxin treatment, the morbid material which was at the root of the trouble is still left in the system after the treatment, plus the sera of the doctor, etc. So the way for future disease—especially chronic disease—is readily paved.

No treatment which does not aim at the removal of the toxic material underlying all fevers, and which it is the express object of the fever to burn up, can be curative in any real sense of the word.

MISCELLANEOUS

Abscesses—Bunions—Corns—Headaches — Obesity — Rupture — Thinness -
Warts—Worms—Wryneck (Torticollis).

IN the present, and last, section of the practical portion of the present book, all the various disease-conditions which do not fit readily into any of the other sections are being dealt with together; so that the fact that such things as corns and bunions are here found side by side with disorders such as thinness and obesity must not be taken to mean that these latter conditions are not deemed of greater consequence than the former. It just happens that the author can find no other place in which to deal with them.

Abscesses.—Abscesses are accumulations of morbid material (pus), and can be found in both the internal and external structures of the body. When an abscess is present it is a sure sign that the person in question is in a high state of toxicity—as a result of wrong feeding habits, former suppressive medical treatment, etc.—and the only correct procedure to adopt in these cases is that which will get down to this underlying toxicity and remove it, thus paving the way for the natural dispersal of the abscess itself. If an abscess is treated in the ordinary way by lancing, fomentations, etc., such treatment is merely external; it does not affect in the least the underlying toxicity of the system which has brought on the abscess in the first place. Consequently, even if the abscess is removed by such treatment, the system of the individual concerned will still be just as toxic as before, and so the appearance of further abscesses at any time has been in no wise prevented.

Treatment.—The correct treatment for abscesses must therefore be twofold: it must be both *external* and *internal*; and the procedure given for *Boils* in Section 2 (page 130) can be applied with excellent results in all cases of external abscesses, gum-boils, etc. Not only will the abscess be removed by such treatment, but the whole system of the individual concerned will have had a thorough internal cleansing, and so the appearance of future abscesses will have been effectively prevented.

It may be necessary in certain extreme cases to have the abscess lanced; but even so, the scheme of treatment here advocated should be carried out, as only in this way can the system be thoroughly cleansed of morbid material and the way to future health paved.

In the case of abscess on the liver or lungs or other vital organ, these conditions will require personal naturopathic treatment. In such cases the abscess has formed as a result of the former suppressive treatment of disease in a highly toxic system, or—as with the case of abscess on the liver—as a result of the reabsorption of poisons from the intestines following on habitual constipation (the poisons in question being brought to the liver and stored up there by the portal vein).

Bunions.—Bunions form as a result of badly fitting shoes or boots. If shoes or boots are too narrow or too short, the big toe-joint is forced inwards, and a bunion gradually forms, as a result of the inflammation and enlargement of the joint following on the constant pressure and irritation supplied by the ill-fitting footwear. When once a bunion has appeared, the only sensible thing to do is to have properly fitting shoes or boots which will give the feet—and especially the toes—all the free room they want for movement. Surgical treatment for the removal of bunions has been found of value in certain cases, but on the other hand, patients have had the joint straightened only to find that walking from then on, is a most awkward and painful procedure, worse in many ways than before the operation. For relieving pain from bunions, the Epsom-salts foot-bath is most useful ($\frac{1}{4}$ lb. of salts to a bowlful of hot water). Osteopathic foot treatment is also beneficial.

Corns.—Corns form as a result of pressure on the toes and skin surfaces of the feet, through incorrect footwear, the toes being often malformed, to begin with, from the same cause. Chiropodial treatment can do much to keep the corns in check ; but if one wishes to get rid of them entirely, the only thing to do is to wear shoes or boots which exert no pressure at all on the foot surfaces, especially on the toes. The modern craze for high-heeled shoes amongst women is the cause of an enormous amount of foot trouble, for the high heel pushes the toes forward into the front of the shoe, where, owing to its narrowness, the toes are crammed together mercilessly and exposed to all the inconveniences to which it is possible for them to be subjected. Can we wonder that corns and bunions result from such treatment ?

For relieving aching and troublesome feet there is nothing better than the Epsom-salts foot-bath. For this $\frac{1}{4}$ lb. of Epsom salts is dissolved in a bowlful of hot water. The feet should be bathed for from five to ten minutes night and morning, if possible.

Headaches.—Headaches may be due to a variety of causes. Eye-strain is a frequent cause of headaches; whilst liver disturbance, stomach derangements, constipation, and kidney trouble can all give rise to the condition. Nervous disorders, strain, overwork, etc., can also be the cause of headaches, as can a variety of other factors. Where headaches are very severe and persistent, tumour of the brain may be present.

It will be obvious from the foregoing that the one really effective way to deal with a headache is to seek out its cause and *remove* this. For only in this way can further headaches be prevented. To take drugs to deaden the pain of a headache—drugs such as aspirin, etc.—may succeed in giving relief for the time being, but it only means that headaches will continue to appear with increasing rapidity thereafter, because not only has the cause of the trouble not been removed, but the deleterious elements contained in the drug will have definitely intensified the systemic factors lying at the root of the trouble. Such a way of dealing with headaches is extremely foolish and short-sighted, if nothing more. For instance, if one suffers from habitual constipation and is plagued with continual headaches as a result thereof, why not try to get rid of the constipation instead of taking drugs merely to relieve the headache? By doing the former, you get rid of both the headaches and their cause once and for all, besides building up the health of the system as a whole; by foolishly doing the latter, both the headaches and their underlying cause are perpetuated indefinitely, and intensified.

Treatment.—Where headaches are definitely due to eye-strain,
Treatment.—Where headaches are definitely due to eye-strain, the methods advocated in *Better Sight Without Glasses* should be put into operation as soon as possible. The results secured will prove of the greatest benefit to the health of the individual concerned, in every way, specially eye health. Where the cause of the headaches is stomach or liver or kidney or bowel trouble, etc., treatment should be for this underlying condition as outlined in the various sections of the practical portion of the present book. ONLY IN THIS WAY CAN THE CAUSE OF THE HEADACHES BE OVERCOME, AND THE HEADACHES PERMANENTLY REMOVED.

For the relief of a headache when present, never resort to the use of drugs ; the best thing to do is to lie down and place cold compresses over the forehead. Often, especially when the headache is due to digestive causes or bowel congestion, a warm-water enema will relieve matters considerably in a short time. Where the headache is due to nerve strain, overwork, etc., obviously complete rest for a period will be required to overcome the condition. To take drugs to deaden the pain and then carry on is the worst thing possible. This can only lead to further and further trouble of the same kind, with serious consequences to the health of the whole nervous system in time (a complete breakdown, for instance). For such " nervous " headaches are merely a sign of a debilitated and overworked nervous system— a nervous system requiring rest and recuperation. Gentle massage to the forehead is often beneficial in relieving headaches.

Obesity.—Obesity is a disease. It is a condition in which there is fatty degeneration of the tissues of the body, its main causes being wrong feeding habits, lack of exercise, and general slackness of living. In abnormal cases there is a general deterioration of the functions of the various glands and organs of the body.

As a general rule, no disease-condition is more easy to cure than obesity, providing the right methods of procedure are adopted to start with. All that is required is proper dieting, together with the encouragement of suitable exercise to tone up the body and increase the power of the eliminative organs. If this is done, not only will the obesity be overcome, but the individual in question will find himself (or herself) in far better health than before, because of the great health-building value inherent in the treatment.

Unfortunately it so happens that there is a great "slimming" craze at the present time amongst the more ardent female followers of Dame Fashion who happen to be burdened with a little extra flesh, and a variety of freak forms of reducing (or overcoming obesity) have come into vogue as a consequence, with the inevitable result that every method of reducing—the natural method included—is regarded as a freak one, and equally as dubious as the rest. People have adopted this and that form of diet—usually on the advice of a " beauty specialist " (or similar guide to female grace and beauty) who understands nothing whatever about the essential points of the diet question—and, not knowing in the least what they were doing, have brought disaster upon themselves, with the result that all forms of dieting have been assumed to be equally worthless and fraught with danger to the health of those misguided enough to undertake them.

Such a point of view is very short-sighted indeed, but understand-able enough in the circumstances, especially when we have the medical profession frowning upon dieting in general and advocating amongst their patients the use of such things as thyroid tablets instead. In the section on *Diseases of the Glands* (Section 6, p. 200) it was pointed out how foolish and harmful it is to resort to such methods of reducing, and many and many a woman has brought herself to serious illness simply through undertaking a course of such treatment.

The fact that so many of their patients are adversely affected in health by thyroid treatment does not seem to affect the prevalence of its use in medical circles in the slightest, however, and, with the medical sanction thus afforded to the drug treatment for obesity, more and more patent preparations are appearing on the market pur-porting to " cure " obesity in the shortest possible time, " without any risk to the person undertaking the treatment, and without their having to give up one iota of their favourite dishes, cakes, etc. ! " (SLIM WHILE YOU FEED !).

No wonder the public is confused about what to do in the circum-stances, and that it generally does the wrong thing !

Treatment.—If people undertake systems of dieting devised by those who have no genuine understanding of the subject, with unfortunate results, surely that is no indication that *all* forms of dieting are un-sound ? *A suitably planned course of dietetic treatment is the only scientific way of dealing with the question of obesity* (in conjunction with suitable exercise and other measures for promoting and increasing elimination). Let not the over-weighted individual have the slightest fear of following out a scheme of reducing treatment along the following lines ; it will pave the way for vastly improved health and energy, as well as reduce weight towards normality in a *natural* manner.

To begin with, a period on the *all-fruit diet* outlined in the Appendix should be undertaken. This should be for from five to seven, ten, or fourteen days, according to how the patient feels. The longer this initial all-fruit period can be carried on with, the better will it be in every way. Then the *full weekly dietary* outlined in the Appendix can be begun. This dietary should be adhered to as strictly as possible from then on.

According to the needs of the case, further short periods on the all-fruit diet, say two or three consecutive days at a time, should be undertaken at monthly intervals.

During the first few days of the treatment, and after if necessary the bowels should be cleansed nightly with a warm-water enema or gravity douche; whilst if constipation is habitual, the rules for its eradication given in Section 9 (page 275) should be put into operation. The daily dry friction and sponge (or sitz-bath) detailed in the Appendix should be gone through every morning in conjunction with the physical and other exercises also given therein. A hot Epsom-salts bath should be taken twice weekly if at all possible. (These baths will be very helpful.)

The patient should make a regular habit of having a walk for from two to four miles *every* day, if possible twice a day. The more walking that can be done, the better will it be. These days of motor-cars are very bad for the obese, as they encourage the minimum of walking and lead to general slackness and indolence. All exercise is good, *in moderation*.

The drinking of much fluid should be discouraged; only drink when thirsty, and then only between meals, never at meal-time. If the reducing is to be successful, the great bulk of the daily dietary *must* be made up of fruits and salads—the natural cleansing foods; whilst the following foods should be most carefully avoided: white bread; white-flour products in general, especially rich cakes, pastry, puddings and pies, macaroni, etc.; sugar, jams, and all preserves; cream; much butter or oily or fatty food; boiled, mashed, or fried potatoes; fat or rich meats or other flesh foods. Tea, if taken at all, should be very weak, whilst coffee should be cut out entirely, as also should alcohol. No condiments, pickles, sauces, etc., should be used.

If the foregoing simple home treatment is carried out, every obese person can increase his or her general health-level from 100 to 400 per cent. in a very few months. It is just a matter of determination and perseverance, that is all. And surely the reward in store is more than worth the effort entailed?

ON NO ACCOUNT SHOULD ANY DRUGS OR TABLETS OF ANY KIND BE TAKEN.

Rupture (Hernia).—When a person is ruptured it is generally supposed that all that can be done is either to have the rupture removed by operation or else to wear a truss. These measures relieve the situation certainly, but leave the individual concerned in a perpetually weakened condition thereafter, so far as his bodily efficiency is concerned.

Very few people indeed realise that rupture (hernia) *is really curable* in a great many cases, if only the right method of procedure is adopted ; but this is undoubtedly the case. The cause of rupture is generally supposed to be strain ; but without a weakened condition of the internal muscles of the abdomen, strain itself would not cause a rupture. It is only when the muscles in question have become progressively weakened through lack of exercise, general slackness of living, distension of the abdomen through unwise feeding or drinking habits, etc., that a sudden severe strain may bring on a rupture.

In his book *Self-Treatment for Hernia,* Mr. Harry Clements, N.D., D.O., the well-known Naturopath, makes this point very clear, and shows that by undertaking suitably planned exercises to tone up these weakened muscles of the abdomen, the tear in the muscle-walls can be naturally repaired and the protruding portion of the intestines brought back to its natural position again in many cases, thus completely curing the rupture. Not only will the rupture be cured by this treatment, but, what is of great importance, the possibility of further ruptures taking place will be effectively removed, because the abdominal muscles will have been so strengthened by the treatment that, apart from some exceptional occurrence, the muscles will be able to withstand successfully any more than ordinary strain exerted upon them.

Every ruptured person is advised to read what Mr. Clements has to say about the matter and to follow out detailed instructions for the natural treatment that he gives. Some people who have worn trusses for many years have been able to discard them after carrying out the régime.

Thinness.—Thinness is a condition due to an inability on the part of the system to assimilate food properly and so build up or replenish worn-out tissue. It is generally supposed that when a person is thin, all we have to do is to " feed him up " and everything will be all right again. But as the food already being eaten is not being assimilated, the extra food is not assimilated either, so that the person in question finds his system becoming more and more congested with unused food materials, and often becomes *thinner* as a result of this fattening process, instead of the reverse.

In practically every case of thinness the intestinal tract is so clogged with catarrhal matter and other toxic deposits (as a result of former wrong feeding habits, chronic constipation, previous disease, etc.), that the glands which assimilate food into the system after its digestion in the stomach and intestines are unable to carry out their work. Obviously the only thing to do in these cases is to undertake treatment which will cleanse the intestines of their toxic accumulation and so make better assimilation possible. Thus it comes about that a fast is often one of the best ways of curing thinness, strange as it may seem. For once the assimilative process is working properly, food is readily dealt with by the system and proper use made of it. The ordinary thin person *never* makes full use of any food eaten—most of it is just wasted.

When we remember that it is not so much what we eat that matters, as how much of it we are able to assimilate, perhaps if I say that many people will be able to overcome thinness *merely by cutting down the number of meals they have daily*, it may not appear so absurd a statement when looked into fully as it does at first glance. People eat far too much food as a general rule—especially many thin people, who imagine that by so doing they are going to put on much-needed weight ; and merely by reducing the quantity of food eaten every day to, say, half, the thin individual will often find himself putting on weight simply because he is not overloading his system with food materials as heretofore, but giving his assimilative organs an opportunity really to deal with the food eaten and make good use of it.

From the foregoing the folly of trying to get thin people fat by cramming them with food will be at once apparent. The point is that in their present state it does not matter what you give them, it will never be utilised properly by the system. On the other hand, let them so take themselves in hand that the assimilative process is got into proper working order again, then very little food will be sufficient to go a long way with them. It is not a question of bulk at all.

Treatment.—If the thin person has been able to assimilate the gist of what has just been said—even if the assimilation of food presents

431

a difficulty at the moment !—he will understand the necessity for a thorough cleansing of his system as the first step in overcoming his trouble. He should therefore carry on as follows : Go on to an exclusive *fresh fruit diet* (as outlined in the Appendix) for from five to seven or ten days—the longer the better. Then the *fruit and milk diet* (also given in the Appendix) should be adopted for a further period, beginning with two pints of milk a day and increasing (in the manner stated) up to five, six, or more pints daily. (Milk is the finest food for increasing weight once the system is ready for it—as after a fast or the fruit diet—but not when crammed into the system on top of a lot of other food.)

If the fruit and milk diet is agreeing well, it can be continued with for from two to four weeks or longer with every benefit ; then the *full weekly dietary* outlined in the Appendix can be begun. The diet sheet should be adhered to as strictly as possible thereafter. For the first three months after commencing the diet, from a pint to a pint and a half of milk may be added to the dietary daily, with the fruit and salad meals.

During the first few days of the treatment the bowels should be cleansed nightly with a warm-water enema or gravity douche ; whilst if constipation is habitual, the rules for its eradication outlined in Section 9 (page 275) should be put into operation forthwith. The dry friction and sponge (or sitz-bath), and the breathing and other exercises given in the Appendix, should be gone through regularly every morning. A hot Epsom-salts bath should be taken twice weekly for the first month or so, and once weekly thereafter.

Every effort should be made to tone up and increase the power of the system, and fresh air and outdoor exercise form two essentials of the treatment which must never be neglected. The habit of breathing deeply when out in the open air should be cultivated, as the more oxygen that can be taken into the lungs, the better will the assimilative processes of the body work.

The body must not be clogged up with useless food products, and white bread, white-flour products such as cakes, pastry, puddings, pies, etc., boiled or mashed potatoes, sugar, jams, confectionery, and all such sugary and starchy foods should especially be avoided. These are the worst possible foods where the clogging of the tissues with toxic waste materials is concerned. Fruits, salads, milk, eggs, wholemeal bread, butter, cheese, and nuts are the foods most suitable. Avoid strong tea and coffee ; take no condiments, pickles, sauces, etc.

Avoid all preparations for increasing weight, and all "fattening" foods such as cod-liver oil, malt extracts, etc.

Warts.—Warts are often disfiguring things, and it is very difficult indeed to say exactly how they are formed. It would seem that constitutional factors are at the root of the matter in these cases, leading to some defect in the proper development of the skin surface in certain areas.

As regards treatment for warts, there, natural treatment has very little to offer, unfortunately. A course of systematic cleansing treatment—such as for *Boils* in Section 2 (page 130)—may be of value in certain cases, but it is impossible to guarantee anything in the way of results. The only thing is that such treatment must increase the general health of the individual concerned, if nothing more. It would seem that burning by chemicals or electrical treatment must be accepted as the best methods known at the moment, however much such forms of treatment depart from the standards of Natural Cure.

Worms.—There are various kinds of worms which appear as parasites within the human system, the most common being the *thread-worm*, *the round-worm*, and *the tape-worm*. The eggs of these parasites are introduced into the system through the medium of food or water (especially of under-cooked or badly-cooked meat), and the pig is the animal from which most of the trouble with regard to round-worms and tape-worms arises.

The question of thread-worms was discussed in full in the section on *Children's Ailments* (Section 1, page 122), and it was there pointed out that before the parasite could develop there must be a ready soil for its growth in the shape of toxic accumulations in the intestines of the individual concerned. It was further emphasised that the only form of treatment which is really effective in dealing with such a condition is that aiming at removing this toxic filth on which the worms breed, and so effectively preventing their further growth within the system. (For the treatment of thread-worms the reader is referred to the section in question).

As regards round-worms, the conditions making for the development of the parasite in the human system are similar in essence to those referred to just now with regard to thread-worms, and the same treatment can be adopted with equally good results in this case too

With regard to tape-worms, conditions here demand that the individual concerned should undertake a fairly prolonged fast in order to get rid of the parasite. Such fasting treatment is always best carried out in a Natural-Cure home or under the personal supervision of a Naturopath.

On no account should drugs be taken for the extermination of worms ; such drugs are always harmful to the system, and in any case they do not remove the soil of toxic matter upon which the parasites breed. Only natural treatment can do this.

Wryneck (Torticollis).—This is a condition which can be helped very much by manipulative treatment at the hands of a competent Osteopath or Naturopath. Exercises for the neck and head are also very good. Those given in *Better Sight Without Glasses* will be very useful.

PART III

APPENDICES

APPENDIX A

THE FEEDING OF CHILDREN

THE advice re the feeding of children that follows in this section is taken from the book *How to Feed Children from Infancy Onwards* by Mr. Stanley Lief, founder of *Health for All* magazine, with his kind permission. As this small book on child feeding referred to is now out of print, the present section can be taken as a sort of precis of the contents of that book, for the help of readers of the present volume anxious to rear their children on right lines.

Proceeding with our precis of Mr. Lief's book on child feeding, therefore, we commence as follows:—

FEEDING DURING THE FIRST YEAR OF LIFE

We have already stressed that *wrong feeding* in infancy is the chief factor concerned in the development of all children's ailments, and the main points to bear in mind are the following :

(1) All children when born should be breast-fed where at all possible. They should be given four feeds a day at four-hourly intervals, and *no night feeds*. If the child should wake at night only water should be given.

(2) If, for any reason, it is impossible to breast-feed the child, then it should be fed on goat's milk or cow's milk—the former preferably —diluted with water, and with milk sugar added (in accordance with the table to be given hereafter). *No artificially prepared, patent, or tinned-milk foods are to be given*—just goat's or cow's milk, with added water and milk sugar.

(3) Where a mother can partly feed her child, she should give it two feeds of her own and two bottle-feeds, or one of her own and three bottle-feeds.

(4) Where children are entirely breast-fed, they need nothing other than the milk they are receiving from their mother ; children bottle-fed should receive some orange juice daily, in addition to the bottle-feeds. Breast-fed babies may be given orange juice if desired, but it is not essential to them.

(5) Weaning can take place after nine months with breast-fed babies ; but whether breast-fed or bottle-fed, no baby should receive anything but milk (and orange juice) for the first year of its existence. NOTHING ELSE AT ALL SHOULD BE GIVEN. No starchy foods or anything else. It is the giving of starchy foods such as bread, oatmeal, etc., to young babies at weaning which leads to the early development of such child ailments as coughs, colds, measles, whooping-cough, etc., etc., especially so as the starchy foods used are always in the refined state, and with other demineralised foods such as white sugar added to the dietary.

(6) At the age of one year a baby should be receiving about a quart of full milk with fruit juices daily. (*Milk should never be boiled* ; it should be just warmed to a temperature of about 80 degrees Fahr.)

The following table is merely a general idea of what should be given. Some babies will need more, some will need less. It is the baby's *own* inclinations which must be studied, rather than set rules. Never force a baby to take food if it does not want to, and never overfeed. If a baby shows no inclination for food on a certain day, then give it just so much as it wishes for and no more. Never adopt the mentality which says the baby *must* have so much food every day whether it wants it or not. On the other hand, if a baby shows signs that it is not satisfied with the quantity of its food, and wants more at a feed, then give it as much as it wants. Let the child's hunger (or lack of it) be the guide all the time.

Daily Amounts for Bottle-fed Babies

Child's Age.	Milk.	Boiled or Distilled Water.	Milk Sugar.	Orange Juice.
	Ounces.	Ounces.	Teaspoonfuls.	
2-6 days	2½-3	7½	1	—
7-10 days	3½-4	10	2	—
11-15 ,,	4½-5	12	2½	½ teaspoonful
16-30 ,,	6	15	4	½-1 ,,
1 month	6-7	12	5	1 ,,
2 months	9-10	14	6	2 teaspoonfuls
3 ,,	12-14	15	7	3-4 ,,
6 ,,	18-22	10-12	8	2 tablespoonfuls
8 ,,	24-26	8-9	8	2½ ,,
9 ,,	28	7-8	8	3-4 ,,
10 ,,	30	5-6	8	3-4 ,,
12 ,,	32	—	8	3-4 ,,

The above amounts represent the total of the four feeds to be given in one day.

After weaning, other fruit juices and vegetable juices may be given as well as orange juice.

FEEDING OF CHILDREN FROM ONE TO TWO YEARS

When children reach the age of one year, most parents assume that they can be given bread, eggs, milk puddings, and even meat to eat. Such feeding is the very basis from which the vast amount of child disease of to-day springs ! A balanced scheme of daily feeding for a child from *one year to eighteen months* is :

Breakfast.—All the milk the child desires.

Second Meal.—All the milk the child desires, including fruit juice. (The juice may be put into the milk or given separately.)

Third Meal.—All the milk the child desires.

In addition to orange juice, prune or raisin juice may be given, also vegetable juices if desired. A piece of raw carrot or raw apple can be given to chew, and a little fruit or vegetable pulp may be added to the dietary after the fifteenth month. A crust of wholemeal bread may be given occasionally (for chewing purposes) after that time too; but the eating of bread should be left till later on, as starchy foods are not properly digested by the infant system until the age of two years, when all the first set of teeth have appeared and thorough mastication is possible.

Remember that milk should never be boiled, but be only just warmed (about 80 degrees Fahr.).

Up to the eighteenth month (or even longer) it is best to feed the child out of a bottle, as this ensures proper ensalivation.

From eighteen to twenty-four months the diet should be :

First Meal.—All the milk the child desires.

Second Meal.—From four to six ounces of fruit juice or vegetable juice.

Third Meal.—All the milk the child desires.

More fruit and vegetable pulp can be added to the dietary during this time, and more raw fruit or vegetables to chew on (and eat). A wholemeal crust or wholemeal hard biscuit can be given more frequently, too, during this time. *Give no sugar at all, or sweets.* The child will get all the sugar its system requires—and in the best form—from the fruit juices, fruit, etc. *Sweets are the most pernicious things possible to give children !*

FEEDING OF CHILDREN FROM TWO TO THREE YEARS

At two years of age the child can be allowed to eat starchy foods, because by that time it will be able to masticate and deal with them properly ; but parents should see that all bread and other cereals are thoroughly masticated in the mouth before being swallowed. *This is most important !*

A balanced diet for a child from two to three years of age is as follows:

First Meal.—Orange or other fresh fruit, one kind of sweet fruit (raisins, figs, dates, or prunes), and milk.

Second Meal.—A whole-wheat product such as " Shredded Wheat," " Force," " Granose," or wholemeal toast, and milk.

Third Meal.—Steamed vegetables with toast, milk; *or* as the morning meal.

If the child should be thirsty between meals, give only water to drink. Nothing in the way of tea, coffee, etc.

FEEDING OF CHILDREN FROM THREE TO FIVE YEARS

Most people believe that meat is an essential in the child dietary (some going so far as to introduce it at the age of one or so !) ; but this is quite wrong. Until a child is five years of age it is not in a position to deal with flesh foods adequately. The thyroid gland, which plays such an important part in the metabolism of animal protein foods—of which meat is one—is not in full working order until the end of the fifth year of life. There is not the slightest need to give meat even after the fifth year, but parents who wish to do so may, in accordance with the child menus (from five onwards) to be given hereafter.

A Balanced Diet for Children from Three to Five Years

First Day

Breakfast.—An apple. Stewed prunes (as many as the child wants). A glass of milk.

Noon Meal.—Medium-sized baked potato with a little butter. String beans or other vegetable. Cottage cheese.

Evening Meal.—Wholemeal toast, butter. Lettuce and watercress Glass of milk.

Second Day.

Breakfast.—" Shredded Wheat " eaten dry. A banana (very ripe). Glass of milk.

Noon Meal.—Vegetable salad. Wholemeal bread and butter. Soaked prunes.

Evening Meal.—Figs. An orange. Glass of milk.

Third Day

Breakfast.—Apples, raw, baked, or stewed (as many as the child desires). Glass of milk.

Noon Meal.—Baked potato with butter. One steamed green vegetable. Glass of milk.

Evening Meal.—" Force " or " Shredded Wheat." Some dates. Glass of milk.

Fourth Day *

Breakfast.—Wholemeal toast, butter. Glass of milk.

Noon Meal.—Two steamed vegetables. Cottage cheese. Baked apple.

Evening Meal.—Fresh fruit (such as an apple, pear, orange, grapes). Sweet fruit (raisins, figs, prunes). Milk.

It must be pointed out again that milk *should not be boiled*, but may be warmed if desired. It should be unpasteurised if possible. Do not force the child to eat ; let its own hunger be the guide all the time. If the child does not feel hungry for any particular meal, let it miss the meal altogether. When it is *really* hungry, a child will eat anything placed before it. Never cajole therefore, but simply let the child have its way. Its own instincts are always a better guide in these matters than our own ideas or theories, let us repeat

No doubt many parents will note with surprise that not only is meat or fish or other flesh food excluded from the foregoing scheme of diet, but even eggs also. The fact is that eggs are too highly-concentrated a form of protein food to be suitable for young children. Lest such parents will not believe that a child can be adequately nourished without the presence of eggs (or egg custard, etc.) in the dietary, they can be assured that the whole scheme of child and infant feeding here outlined is not just the result of mere theoretical reasoning into the food question, but the actual outcome of many years of *practical* experience in the realm of dieteties. Children brought up and fed in the manner herein indicated will prove far fitter and healthier *in every way* than children brought up in the conventional manner on the demineralised, devitalised, and high-protein foods of our present era.

Parents assume that the " children's ailments " of to-day are something inevitable. *So they are—if children are fed as they are to-day !* But such ailments would be far from inevitable if a scheme of child feeding were universally adopted such as is herein outlined for the benefit of readers of this book.

Further points to be stressed are : no sugar is to be given to children ; no sweets or confectionery *of any kind* , no condiments, sauces, seasonings, etc. ; no tea or coffee. *Sweets are the most pernicious*

* After the fourth day's menus return to those for the first day and continue in that way.

things it is possible to give children, it must again be pointed out. The less any child sees of them, the better will its health inevitably be.*

FEEDING CHILDREN FROM FIVE YEARS ONWARDS

After the child has passed its fifth year it may adopt a scheme of feeding more in line with that of its elders ; and a balanced weekly dietary for children from the age of five onwards is here being given as a guide to all parents as to how such children should be fed for sound health and fitness, and *not* for disease.

CHILD'S WEEKLY DIET-SHEET

First Day

Breakfast.—One apple, one orange, four or five dates, glass of milk.

Lunch.—Poached egg, steamed spinach (or other green vegetable), baked potato in skin. *Dessert* : baked apple.

Evening Meal.—Wholemeal bread and butter, with lettuce, tomatoes, watercress, or celery, etc. A few stewed prunes to follow if desired.

Second Day

Breakfast.—" Shredded Wheat " or " Force," with raisins and milk.

Lunch.—A selection of fresh fruits (apples, pears, grapes, or oranges), a sweet fruit (dates, figs, or prunes), and milk.

Evening Meal.—Wholemeal bread (or " Ryvita ") and butter, with lettuce, tomatoes, watercress, celery, etc. Milk.

Third Day

Breakfast.—Two apples, one banana, milk.

Lunch.—A little chicken or lamb, with one steamed green vegetable steamed carrots or turnips. *Dessert* : stewed fruit.

Evening Meal.—Wholemeal bread and butter, with lettuce, tomatoes, watercress, celery, etc. One or two figs or a few dates.

Fourth Day

Breakfast.—Grapes, prunes, milk.

Lunch.—Poached egg, one steamed green vegetable, potato baked in skin. Apple or pear.

Evening Meal.—Wholemeal bread (or " Ryvita ") and butter, with lettuce, watercress, tomatoes, etc. *Ripe* banana.

* The child will get all the sugar its system needs from fresh and dried fruits. This is sugar in its *best* form.

Fifth Day

Breakfast.—" Shredded Wheat " or " Force," with raisins and milk.

Lunch.—A selection of fresh fruits (apples, pears, grapes, or oranges), a sweet fruit (dates, figs, or prunes), and milk.

Evening Meal.—Wholemeal bread and butter, with lettuce, tomatoes, watercress, celery, etc. Milk.

Sixth Day

Breakfast.—Half grape-fruit, apple, three or four figs, milk.

Lunch.—Steamed fish, one steamed green vegetable, steamed carrots or turnips. *Dessert* : baked apple.

Evening Meal.—Wholemeal bread (or " Ryvita ") and butter, with lettuce, watercress, tomatoes, celery, etc. *Ripe* banana.

Seventh Day

Breakfast.—One apple, one orange, one pear, glass of milk.

Lunch.—Nut cutlet or grated or cottage cheese, with one steamed green vegetable, potato baked in skin. *Dessert* : stewed prunes.

Evening Meal.—Wholemeal bread and butter, with lettuce, tomatoes, watercress, etc. ; a few nuts and raisins.

SOME NOTES ON THE FOREGOING DIET-CHART.—Milk should always be either cold or just warmed, never boiled.† For stewing fruit, always use either honey or Demerara sugar, *never* white sugar. Never give stewed rhubarb. When giving a cereal in the morning it is best to let the child eat it quite crisp or else with just a little milk on it. Do not let it get soft and mushy before eating, for that will prevent proper ensalivation of the food, which is so essential to its thorough mastication. The rest of the milk can be taken afterwards.

Allow no eating between meals. Do not give tea or coffee, and do not allow drinking with meals, except in the case of milk (which is a food really and not a drink). Water can be taken between meals *as thirst dictates.* (It will be found that on the foregoing diet a child will not be nearly so thirsty as on a conventional diet.) Some orange juice in water (or alone) can be given first thing in the morning, and

† It should also be *unpasteurised* if possible. Milk that has been pasteurised has had much of its food-value impaired.

a hot lemon drink (with honey) at night. See that the child masticates all its food properly ; do not allow any " bolting " of food. If a child does not feel hungry, do not press it to eat, but allow it to miss a meal. It will eat soon enough when in need of food.

Give no white sugar or jams, marmalade, etc. Keep the child away from ice-cream, pastries, puddings, and pies. Do not give even milk puddings ; these are too " mushy " to be a satisfactory food for children —or for anyone for that matter—and being made with refined cereals are very defective from the health point of view. Sweets and confectionery of all kinds should be " taboo " ; such things work more havoc in the child system than anything else in the food line that the ingenuity of man has devised.

In the case of children who are quite healthy and are following the foregoing diet-chart, these may be given a piece of home-made wholemeal fruit cake *occasionally* (as a special treat), with the evening meal, or a wholemeal scone and honey, or a piece of good chocolate. But the above must not be allowed children who are suffering from some ailment and are following the diet-chart for the purpose of cure. The former may also have a little cream or egg-and-milk custard two or three times weekly.

THE SHORT FAST RÉGIME

When undertaking a short fast, the procedure should be as follows. When you rise in the morning, you should take no food. All you may have is the juice of an orange (in a glass of warm water if preferred) every two hours from 8 a.m. to 8 p.m. NOTHING ELSE WHATEVER may be taken, otherwise you might just as well continue with your ordinary food, as the value of the fast will be lost entirely. If orange juice disagrees, take water only or vegetable juices.

EACH DAY WHILE FASTING you should see that the bowels are cleansed of the effete and poisonous matter thrown off by the self-cleansing process now being set up by the body. This is MOST IMPORTANT, for, if omitted, the body will reabsorb the poisons, and your fast will have been more or less in vain. A gravity douche is the best appliance to use.

SYMPTOMS WHICH MAY ARISE DURING FASTING, BUT NEED CAUSE
NO ALARM

Slight Fever. If this makes itself felt, a little warm water may be drunk.

Dizziness, headache, faintness, insomnia, palpitation. If any of these symptoms appear, they will pass off as the fast progresses, and undue importance need not be attached to any of them.

Coated tongue and bad taste. Both these are very common symptoms, and are indications that the work of cleansing the tissues of accumulated toxins is progressing.

DIET AFTER THE FAST

When you break your fast after three or four days, you should take *milk* (fresh, unboiled) *only* for a whole day, sipping slowly a half-pint at two-hourly intervals during the day. The next day you should have the following food at five-hourly intervals :

Breakfast.—Juice of two oranges, grapes, and an apple (well masticated).

Midday.—Salad of lettuce, watercress, tomatoes, mustard and cress, grated raw carrot (dress with olive oil and lemon juice). Wholemeal toast (cold) and butter. A pear or an apple.

Evening Meal.—*Steamed* cabbage (or brussels sprouts, spring greens, savoy, etc.) and carrots, with stewed prunes, figs, or raisins as a second course.

After these two days you should take food in accordance with the suggestions contained in the treatment for your case in the practical section of the present book (*Part II*). If you have been advised to go on a *fruit diet* after the fast, the day on milk and day on special diet should be omitted.

SPECIAL NOTE.—To break an *extended fast*, the reader is referred to the treatment of *fevers* in Section 13 (page 408).

THE ALL-FRUIT DIET

When on the all-fruit diet you should have three meals a day of *fresh, juicy fruits,* such as apples, pears, grapes, grape-fruit, oranges, pineapple, peaches, melon (or any other juicy fruit in season), *but no bananas or dried, stewed, or tinned fruit,* AND NO OTHER FOODSTUFF WHATEVER.

For drinks, lemon water unsweetened or water either hot or cold may be taken—nothing else.

If any food—such as bread—is taken with the fruit meals, the whole value of the treatment will be lost.*

* If losing much weight on the all-fruit diet, those already underweight may add a glass of milk to each fruit meal.

SPECIAL NOTE.—*See that all fruit is quite ripe before eating ; unripe or sour fruit is no good at all.*

THE FRUIT AND MILK DIET

For the fruit and milk diet the meals are exactly the same as for the *all-fruit diet*, but with milk added to each fruit meal. You begin with two pints the first day, and increase by half a pint daily up to four, five, or even six pints a day, according to how the milk agrees (or else in accordance with the special recommendations made in the treatment for your case). The milk should be *fresh* and *unboiled*, but may be slightly warmed if desired. It should be sipped *very slowly*, and may be taken between meals as well as at meal-time as required. *It should be unpasteurised if possible.*

THE RESTRICTED DIET

The following diet, when the *restricted diet* is indicated in the treatment for your case, should be followed out for a period up to fourteen days :

Morning.—Oranges, or orange and lemon juice, or grape-fruit. (Never use sugar for grape-fruit.)

Midday.—Salad (raw), composed of any of the vegetables in season, attractively prepared. Dressing should consist of olive oil and lemon juice—*never vinegar*. *Dessert* : raisins, prunes (soaked), figs, or dates.

Evening.—Raw salad, *or* one or two vegetables steamed in their own juices, such as spinach, cabbage, carrots, turnips, cauliflower, etc. Finish the evening meal with a few nuts or some sweet fruit such as apples, pears, plums, or cherries.

NOTE.—If bread or potatoes or other starchy food is taken, the effect of the diet will be lost. Nothing should be added to the above list if good results are desired. No drinks other than water should be taken.

With regard to quantity, let your hunger be your guide.

THE FULL MILK DIET*

When you begin on the full milk diet you have a glass of milk every two hours from 8 a.m. to 8 p.m. the first day, a glass every

*Where milk is scarce the best substitute is "Slippery Elm Food," a drink of which, unmalted, can be taken with fresh or dried milk and water every two hours during the day.

hour and a half the next, and a glass every hour the third day. Then the quantity of milk can be gradually increased until you are taking a glass every half-hour from 8 a.m. to 8 p.m., if such a quantity can be tolerated fairly comfortably. The milk should be *fresh* and *unboiled*, but may be slightly warmed in cold weather if desired. It should be sipped *very slowly* (through a straw is best). It is not desirable to have the milk too creamy ; some of the top cream should be skimmed off when the milk taken daily exceeds four pints. *Milk should be unpasteurised if possible.*

If constipation is very pronounced when on the full milk diet, up to a dozen dates or prunes may be eaten during the day to help on bowel action. In any case, drinks of fruit juices may be taken at intervals during the day, between the milk drinks.

When coming off the milk diet on to ordinary diet, the procedure should be as follows :

Have milk as usual up to 3 p.m., then have nothing up to 7 p.m., when a salad meal should be taken. Do the same the next day, and on the third day you may go straight on with the next diet as prescribed for you in the treatment for your case.

A WEEK'S MENUS FOR ADULTS*
First Day
Breakfast.—Juice of two oranges, grapes, and an apple.

Lunch.—Salad of lettuce, watercress, tomato, grated carrot and beetroot. Wholemeal toast (cold) and butter. A few raisins or dates.

Evening Meal.—Poached egg on steamed spinach, steamed carrots and celery. Baked apple.

Second Day
Breakfast.—Soaked raisins, an orange. Glass of milk.

Lunch.—Raw vegetable salad made from as many salad vegetables as desired. Cottage cheese. Wholemeal bread and butter.

Evening Meal.—Steamed fish, any two steamed vegetables. Soaked dried fruit.

Third Day
Breakfast.—Fresh fruit salad. Glass of milk.

* The simplified dietary outlined at the end of this section can be followed by those unable to follow out the detailed weekly diet plan here given.

Lunch.—Lettuce, celery, banana, and date salad. Wholemeal bread and butter.

Evening Meal.—Lamb or mutton chop, or nut cutlets, with steamed cabbage, marrow, onion, or leeks. Stewed fruit.

Fourth Day

Breakfast.—One raw juicy fruit in season, one sweet dried fruit.

Lunch.—Poached egg on spinach, baked potato in jacket, steamed greens. Baked apple.

Evening Meal.—Purée of vegetables. Salad of as many salad vegetables as desired, with wholemeal bread and butter.

Fifth Day

Breakfast.—An apple, a few soaked prunes, a glass of milk.

Lunch.—Salad of lettuce, cabbage, tomatoes, and grated carrot, with chopped dates and seedless raisins. Wholemeal toast (cold) and butter. A pear or some grapes.

Evening Meal.—Buttered cauliflower, steamed carrots, baked potato in skin. Grated nuts, or grated cheese. Baked apple.

Sixth Day

Breakfast.—Half a grape-fruit, grapes, an apple.

Lunch.—Raw vegetable salad, cottage cheese, wholemeal bread and butter. A few raisins, dates, or figs.

Evening Meal.—Chicken, two or three steamed vegetables. Fruit.

Seventh Day

Breakfast.—An orange, a few dates, a glass of milk.

Lunch.—Lettuce, cabbage, celery, and grated beetroot salad Wholemeal toast (cold) and butter. Ripe mashed banana.

Evening Meal.—Nut cutlets (or poached egg), steamed onions, marrow, leeks, turnips, or carrots. Fresh fruit salad.

NOTES ON THE FOREGOING DIET-CHART.—The midday and evening meals on any day may be reversed as desired, but it is not permissible to take the lunch for one day and the evening meal for another. Any vegetable mentioned on the diet-chart which is not in season may be substituted by any other suitable which is in season. Where chicken is mentioned, those who cannot afford it may have rabbit or lamb in its place.

All salads should have a dressing of either olive oil or lemon juice, or both. If both should happen to disagree, have nothing at all on the salad. Never use manufactured " salad creams," salad dressings, seasonings, sauces, etc. *Use no vinegar either*. Such things are very bad indeed, and completely spoil the value of a salad.*

Fruit should always be as *ripe* as possible ; no sour, unripe fruit should ever be eaten.

Milk, where mentioned, should always be fresh and unboiled, but may be slightly warmed in cold weather if desired. Those under thirty (and those underweight) may have a glass of milk *every morning* with the fruit breakfast, if desired ; those over fifty (and those over-weight) should have nothing but *fresh fruit* for breakfast (no dried fruit or milk at all), unless they are doing hard manual work. If milk disagrees in any particular case, it should be left out entirely from the dietary.†

In the colder months a little vegetable soup—made by simmering fresh vegetables—may be taken occasionally before either the midday or evening meal. Never use potatoes, beans, peas, or lentils for this, and always cut the vegetables up very fine. It is advisable to take the soup from a quarter to half an hour before the meal, as liquid taken with meals tends to weaken the digestive juices.

Those who would like to have no cooked food at all—and they will derive great advantage by so doing—may substitute salad for cooked vegetables where mentioned on the chart, and either egg or cheese or nuts for meat, fish, etc.

Vegetarians should substitute either egg or cheese or nuts for flesh foods where mentioned on the diet chart.

Where stewed fruit is mentioned, this should always be stewed with either honey or Demerara sugar—never white sugar. Never use rhubarb or sour unripe fruit for stewing purposes—always use *ripe* fruit.

Those who are following the diet chart for purposes of cure should add nothing whatsoever to it ; those, however, who are merely following the diet chart with the intention of increasing all-round general fitness, may add a little cream or egg-and-milk custard to the

* For winter salads, cabbage, sprouts, carrots, beetroot, turnip, etc., may be used. All ingredients should be finely shredded or grated.
† Those doing hard manual work may have dried fruit with the breakfast meal *every* morning, if desired; also milk.

dessert course of the midday or evening meal three or four times weekly, if desired.

The following is a simplified dietary that can be taken if for any reason the full weekly diet plan outlined in this section cannot be followed.

Breakfast.—Fresh fruit as obtainable, or grated raw carrot or other raw salad-stuff ; with prunes or other dried fruit if wished, or ALL-BRAN or other bran product. Milk to drink, or *Bourn-vita* or *Ovaltine*.

Midday.—Steamed or casseroled vegetables, as obtainable, potatoes always in skins when taken ; with either a poached or scrambled egg or grated cheese or fish or meat or a vegetarian savoury. *Dessert* : stewed fruit or a baked apple ; or jelly or junket.

Evening.—Good-sized raw salad, of any suitable ingredients obtainable ; with wholewheat bread or crispbread and butter or margarine. Prunes or other dried fruit as dessert ; or as for midday.

Those suffering from gastric or duodenal ulcer or colitis, may find it best to substitute *Turog* or *Daren* bread for full wholewheat bread at first, having this toasted and eaten cold. These patients may also find it advisable to have all cooked vegetables sieved at first. All patients may have a vegetable drink at night flavoured with *Marmite* or *Yeastrel*, with advantage. (To make this, cut up vegetables finely, cover with water, bring to the boil, then simmer for an hour or so, and strain. Then add *Marmite* or *Yeastrel* as wished.)

WHEN AND WHAT TO DRINK

Drinking with meals should always be avoided, as it has a harmful effect upon the digestive processes because of the dilution of the gastric juices which takes place.

Always drink at least *half an hour* before a meal or about *three hours* after.

A glass of hot water or fruit juices diluted with water, on rising or before retiring, will be found very helpful in cleansing the body of waste matter and toxins, and would be especially beneficial in conjunction with the natural treatment you are now undergoing.

The best drinks are *water* (either hot or cold) and fruit *juices* (with or without water).

Milk is *not* a drink, but a food, and is best taken in conjunction with fruit.

Strong tea and *coffee* should be carefully avoided, as both these drinks have a bad effect upon the digestive and nervous system, also on the kidneys and heart. A cup of *weak* China tea, *without sugar*, may be taken during the afternoon, however, by those who desire it. This will do no harm at all. No food should be taken with the drink, though.

For sweetening a drink of hot water and lemon juice, the best thing is honey.

The desire for excessive drinking should always be regarded as a sign of disturbance of function—of a diseased condition.

Never drink because you think you ought to, but when you really want to do so. On a diet such as is being prescribed for you, very little drinking will be found necessary, as most of the food is already in a diluted condition, for all natural, uncooked foods contain a large percentage of water in their composition.

CONSTIPATION AND ITS CURE

When we realise that constipation is due to a relaxed condition of the muscular structure of the colon and intestines, brought about by a diet of refined and unnatural foods or inattention to the body's demands, we know that the only logical way in which the disorder may be overcome is by restoring power to the essential muscles.

The condition of the eliminatory musculature in the constipated person is exactly similar to that which is seen, say, in the arm of a person who, because it has been broken, has had it in a sling for some weeks. The muscles of the arm will be found to have relaxed to such an extent that its owner will be unable to make it perform its normal functions. He must exercise it gradually, and in time normality will be regained.

Therefore, in order to restore natural tone to the eliminatory musculature, it is quite apparent that we must exercise it. The best way in which this process may be carried out is by the following régime, once you have adopted a diet which provides sufficient bulk after digestion to stimulate the muscles of elimination to action.

As all muscular structure is kept in tone by actual use and is built up by exercise, you must exercise the muscles of elimination twice each day in the effort to build them up to normal. In no circumstances should purgatives or such-like aids to enforce bowel action be used.

To SUCCEED YOU MUST REGARD THE FOLLOWING AS A MOST IMPORTANT RITE : On two occasions every day, say at 9 a.m. and 7 p.m., you should attend stool, and make an effort to evacuate the bowels, whether the impulse to do so is present or not. On each occasion you should try to obtain a natural movement, *but without undue strain*. The idea is to *coax* the bowels into action by means of *gentle pressure*, rather than to use undue force. In this way you will be exercising the muscles and gradually building them up to normal activity and usefulness.

Let it be understood that results will not follow immediately. It will all depend upon the degree of relaxation of the muscles how long it will be before satisfactory results ensue. However, the attempts will be quite successful in time, in every case, if persevered with ; and when once the bowels have been made to move naturally, it will be found that they will respond with increasing frequency as the regular efforts are pursued. Ultimately, two habitual daily movements will be obtained.

It must be emphasised that the diet must be kept right, and the daily regular efforts never relaxed, except for the most compelling reasons. In this way only lies success.

As instructed in the various treatments, the enema or gravity douche should be used to cleanse the bowels until they begin to function normally of their own accord, as a result of the instructions given above. As necessary, the enema or douche should be used *nightly* up to the end of the first week of treatment, and *every other night* thereafter as required.

THE USE OF THE ENEMA OR GRAVITY DOUCHE

The procedure for the use of the enema or gravity douche is as follows :

Fill the container with water at about body heat—98 degrees Fahr., that is (this can be tested by means of a small thermometer if desired). Next, well grease the nozzle with either vaseline or olive oil. Then place the container on a suitable hook from four to six feet from the ground, and lie on your back on the floor (on a sheet or cloth). Insert the enema into the rectum and gradually allow the water to run into the bowel.* When all the water has entered the nozzle can be removed, and it will be found that the water stays, in quite of its own accord. Keep the water in for a few minutes, then turn on your left side, then on your face, next on your right side, then on your face again, and finally on to your hands and knees. Now let the water out altogether into a receptacle placed handy for the occasion, and it will be found that either the waste matter will come away with the water or a desire to empty the bowels will be felt shortly afterwards.

This is an absolutely harmless method of cleansing the system and occupies not more than five minutes.†

The enema or douche should be used *every night* for the *first week* of the treatment if necessary, and *every other night thereafter* in those cases where a natural movement of the bowels is not yet being obtained. Once natural bowel action begins, it should be dispensed with altogether, unless there is any future tendency towards constipation, when it should be used again.

THE MORNING DRY FRICTION

Dry friction baths are a very superior means of exciting to increased activity all the functional processes lying at or near the surface of the body. Proper activity of the pores of the skin is essential to the enjoyment of a high grade of health. If such a bath is taken regularly, one is assured of the possession of a healthy skin, as the pores are then certain to be active.

This bath can be taken with a rough dry towel or with a moderately soft bristle brush (the latter is better). If a brush is going to be used, the best way to test the bristles to see whether they are suitable for this purpose is to rub the brush over the back of the hand, and if the sensation is not unpleasant, it can be depended upon for satisfactory use on the body—i.e., after one has become accustomed to the friction. Naturally the skin will be a little tender at first, but it will gradually become toughened. If a brush is used, the procedure should be as follows :

* See that the water is ready to run freely before inserting into the rectum.
† For *babies,* a small bulb enema containing *one to two ounces* of water should be used. For *children,* from *one to two pints* of water should be used for the enema. For *adults,* from *three to four pints* of water should be used.

452

Take the brush in one hand and begin with the face, neck, and chest. Then brush one arm, beginning at the wrist and brushing towards the shoulders. Now stoop down and brush one foot, then the ankle and leg. Then do the other foot and leg, and next the hips and central portion of the body. Continue brushing each part until the skin is pink. Use the brush quickly back and forward on every part of the body. The whole process does not take very long—about a minute or so.

If a towel is used it should be fairly rough, and the same process gone through as above explained.

THE COLD SITZ-BATH

This bath is a very valuable aid in building vitality and increasing the general functional vigour. It is especially recommended for heightening the strength of the organs lying in the region of the hips. It increases the circulation in these parts very greatly, hardens and strengthens the tissues, and is an important adjunct to the building of nervous vigour and sexual strength. It has a decidedly invigorating effect upon the whole sexual organism, and it greatly assists in influencing the regular movement of the bowels.

Bath-tubs made especially for taking a sitz-bath are difficult to obtain nowadays, but an ordinary bath or hip-bath can be used just as well. The procedure is as follows:

Fill an ordinary bath-tub with cold water to a depth of four inches or so, and sit in it so that the feet, the seat, and the sexual organs are for the most part in the water. Only the seat and feet should touch the bottom of the tub, while the knees are always above the water.

The knees are now spread apart and the water is vigorously dashed over the abdomen with the hollow of the hand. The throwing of the water is followed by a brisk rubbing of the abdomen with both hands. After this process has been carried on for a while, all the parts immersed in the water (except the sexual organs themselves) should be rubbed vigorously with the open hand. Then get out and dry with a rough towel. When you become stronger, the rubbing-dry process should be carried out with the hands. This is in itself a good exercise and improves the condition of the skin

The whole of the foregoing process should take from two to three minutes at first, but its duration should be gradually increased as you become more accustomed to it. If you feel warm after the sitz-bath, you can usually be sure you have not overdone it.

SPECIAL NOTE.—During the colder months it is advisable in certain cases to add a little warm water to the sitz-bath so as to just take the chill off. But as a general rule, the colder you can stand it, the better.

THE COLD SPONGE

An alternative to the morning sitz-bath is the cold sponge, which should be taken as follows :

Wring out a towel in cold water, and rub the whole body in the manner described for the *Friction Bath* (page 452). If, during the process of rubbing, the towel becomes too dry, it should be wrung out again.

SPECIAL NOTE.—Elderly people taking the morning sponge (and those with weak hearts) may have the water tepid.

THE EPSOM-SALTS BATH

In all disease-conditions acid waste products are always present in the tissues, and by helping to neutralise these, the Epsom-salts bath provides one of the simplest home remedies—in conjunction with the rest of the treatment you are undergoing—for alleviating this excessively acid condition. It is especially effective in cases of rheumatism, sciatica, neuritis, lumbago, catarrh, colds, or other catarrhal or uric-acid affections.

It is prepared as follows : Dissolve from two to three lb. of *commercial* Epsom salts in an ordinary bath of hot water. Remain immersed in the bath for from ten to twenty minutes.

This bath should be taken just before retiring to bed, and care should be exercised not to get chilled afterwards.

Wherever Epsom-salts baths are indicated in the treatment for any special disease, at least one ordinary hot cleansing bath should be taken as well every week. Never use soap with the Epsom-salts bath, as this interferes with its beneficial effects.

Commercial Epsom salts for the bath can be obtained fairly cheaply through most chemists, including the multiple stores such as Boots. They are usually sold in 7 lb. bags costing a few shillings.

SPECIAL NOTE.—People with weak hearts should be careful about taking Epsom-salts baths. Anyone who cannot stand a hot bath well should not take these baths at all. It is best to take the baths as hot as possible, but with those in a weak state or with elderly people, it is wiser to have the bath not too hot—just comfortably so. If a full bath is not possible, an Epsom-salts hip-bath may be taken instead. Use 1½ lb. of salts for the hip-bath.

THE HOT AND COLD SITZ-BATH

The hot and cold sitz-bath is especially valuable for all disease-conditions connected with the kidneys, bladder, and sex organs generally. It is also of great value in troubles affecting the intestines. especially the large intestine (or colon), such as colitis, dysentery, etc, The best time to take the hot and cold sitz-bath is at night, just before retiring.

The arrangements are as follows: Place a large bowl or hip-bath beside the ordinary bath, the former containing from four to five inches of cold water, the latter the same depth of hot. Get into the hot bath, sit in it for a few minutes, then get out immediately and sit in the cold one. Remain in that for just one minute, then get back into the hot sitz again, and repeat two or three times in all.

SPECIAL NOTE.—In very cold weather the cold sitz may be slightly warmed, if desired; but the colder you can stand it, the better will its effects be.

WET PACKS

Wet packs are a simple yet very effective means of reducing fevers and inflammations of all kinds.

The procedure is as follows : Wring out some linen material in cold water, wrap two or three times round the affected part, and cover with some flannelling. Secure in place. The packs are put on at night as a general rule, and removed in the morning.

In the case of fevers the packs can be put on several times during the day, for an hour or so. For a pack for the alleviation of a fever (or other serious inflammatory condition), it is best to use a trunk or whole body pack, and for this purpose a sheet should be wrung out in cold water and wound round the trunk or whole body two or three times, then covered with a blanket or blankets. Where reaction to the trunk or full body pack is poor, hot-water bottles may be applied to the feet and also to the sides of the body, or hot bricks wrapped in flannel may be used.

REMEDIAL EXERCISES

The following system of exercises forms an excellent set of all-round exercises for men and women who have not too much time at their disposal in the morning. The full time taken by the exercises is just eight minutes, and those undertaking them will be amply rewarded in greatly increased strength and fitness for the time spent in carrying them out. *After* the exercises, the morning dry friction and sitz-bath or sponge should be taken.

The movements represented in the exercises have been specially selected because of their great organ-squeezing, body-twisting, and spine-stretching qualities. It does not matter so much whether you build up your biceps, but it *is* important that you keep the muscular walls of the stomach and abdominal region firm and the spinal tissues well stretched. To keep the muscles of the trunk of the body firm and vigorous means to keep internally fit. A system of exercises such as the following, therefore, practised each day, in conjunction with a general scheme of health-building treatment as advocated for your case, will greatly enhance your possibilities of achieving that return to a condition of really sound health which I know you so earnestly desire.

To the man or woman who is not accustomed to the performance of exercises it may seem, at first, that the system here given is rather strenuous. However, the poorer your muscular condition is, the more rapid will be the response and improvement. If you find the whole system too difficult at first, begin with half the number of exercises, and as you become accustomed to them add the remainder gradually. (*The exercises are reproduced on pages* 458-9).

Each exercise should take just one minute to perform.

BREATHING EXERCISES

The following breathing exercises are intended especially to develop greater lung capacity and to assist in forming the habit of breathing deeply and properly at all times. Their value in improving the health of those undertaking them cannot be overestimated, as it is upon the oxygen we breathe into the lungs that the whole work of metabolism ultimately depends. The more deeply and properly we breathe, the better is the oxygen supply, the better is the body able to carry on its work, and the better is our health as a direct consequence.

The different exercises about to be enumerated should be repeated from six to ten times each, according to the endurance and the amount of time at disposal.

Exercises.—(1) Jerk the shoulders forward in several separate movements, inhaling more deeply at each forward jerk. Exhale slowly bringing the shoulders back to the original position.

Reverse the exercise, jerking the shoulders backwards in similar manner while inhaling. Alternate the movement, forcing the shoulders forward, then backward.

(2) Stand erect, arms at side. Inhale, raising the arms forward and upward until the palms touch above the head, at the same time rising on the toes as high as possible. Exhale, lowering the toes, bringing the hands downwards in a wide circle until the arms touch the thighs.

(3) Stand erect, hands on hips. Inhale slowly and deeply, raising the shoulders as high as possible, then with a jerk drop them as low as possible, letting the breath escape slowly.

(4) Stand erect, hands at shoulders. Inhale, raising elbows sideways ; exhale, bringing elbows down so as to strike the sides vigorously.

(5) Inhale deeply, then exhale slowly, at the same time clapping the chest with the palms of the hands, covering the entire surface.

(6) To stimulate the action of the diaphragm : Lie flat on floor or mattress, the head unsupported. Relax the muscles all over the body, then inhale deeply, using the diaphragm only, raising the wall of the abdomen just below the ribs without elevating either the chest or the lower abdomen. Take about four seconds to inhale, then exhale in twice that length of time, contracting the abdomen below the ribs.

(7) As often as possible during the day, especially when in the open or when walking, fill your lungs to the fullest extent as many times as possible. A correct full breath should be taken in the following manner :

EXERCISE 1

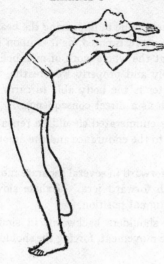

1. From an upright position, feet apart, bend body as far back as possible, as shown in the illustration, inhaling. Return to original position, exhaling, thus completing the exercise. Repeat 8 to 15 times.

EXERCISE 2

EXERCISE 3

2. From an upright position, with feet together, arms overhead, bend body down, touching the floor near the toes, keeping the knees firm, exhaling. Return to original position, inhaling, thus completing the exercise. Repeat 10 to 16 times.

3. From an upright position, heels together, arms bent, lower body to position shown in illustration, exhaling. Raise body to original position, inhaling, thus completing the exercise. Repeat 8 to 12 times.

4. Lie face down, flat on the floor, hands clasped in the small of the back. Raise upper body, stretching arms to position shown in illustration, inhaling. Return to original position, exhaling. Repeat both movements 6 to 12 times each.

EXERCISE 4

458

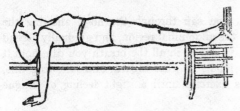

5. From a position shown in illustration, lower the centre of the body until the hips touch the floor. Return to original position, thus completing the exercise. Repeat 6 to 12 times. Breathe normally.

6. From an upright position, with arms hanging at the side, feet apart, bend body down to the right, stretching the right arm well downwards, and bringing the left arm up, as shown in the illustration; then bend to the left, stretching the left arm down and bringing the right arm up. Repeat on each side 10 to 16 times. Breathe normally.

EXERCISE 6

EXERCISE 7

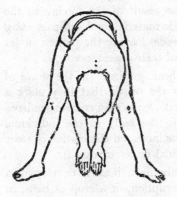

EXERCISE 8

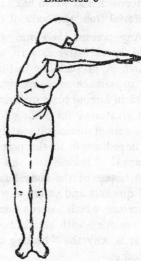

7. From an upright position, with feet well apart and arms overhead, bend the body down with a swing, touching the floor with the palms of the hands turned to the front, as shown in the illustration, exhaling. Raise body to original position, inhaling. Repeat each movement, alternately, 8 to 16 times.

8. From an upright position, with heels together, arms held shoulder-high in front, twist the body to the left as far as possible, without moving the feet, as shown in the illustration. Then twist the body to right, bringing the arms to the right. Repeat in each direction 10 to 20 times.

Draw in all the breath you can through the nose, allowing the expansion to commence in the abdominal region, and gradually ascend to the chest. After you have drawn in all the breath you can, hold it for a moment, and try to inhale another breath, and following this, exhale fully. Repeat this exercise until a slight feeling of fatigue ensues.

COMPLICATIONS WHICH MAY ARISE DURING TREATMENT

It frequently happens that when a course of natural treatment is undertaken, the patient suddenly finds himself developing a heavy cold, or a skin eruption appears, or there is an outbreak of boils, etc. Such manifestations are all signs of the cleansing and healing work taking place within the organism, as a result of the treatment, and should give rise to no alarm on the part of the patient. Such outbreaks or disturbances are merely the result of the forcing to the surface of the body of deep-seated toxic material, and will pass away in due course, as the treatment proceeds, leaving the patient in far better health as a direct consequence of their appearance.

Such disturbances are known as " healing crises " in the world of Naturopathy, and are called such for the reason that they mark a temporary crisis in the process of cure taking place—a crisis engendered by the healing forces at work within the body of the individual concerned, and which has as its aim the increased elimination of toxic material from the body of the individual under treatment.

Any person, therefore, who suddenly finds himself developing a cold, or excessive catarrh, or a skin eruption, or a crop of boils, or diarrhœa, or such-like disturbances, under treatment, should *welcome* its appearance as a sure sign that the treatment is doing its allotted work in forcing toxic material out of his system, and should not blame the treatment for adding further troubles to those he already has. The cure of disease ultimately depends, *in every case*, upon the removal of impediments to the proper functioning of the organism, and the removal of toxic waste and other deleterious material from the cells and tissues of the body has been shown in the present book to be the quickest and surest way of bringing this about. Any movement, therefore, which hastens this eliminative and cleansing process should be regarded with satisfaction by the patient undergoing treatment. That is why the " healing crisis " is so much to be welcomed when it comes.

It must be pointed out that not every patient under treatment will develop a " healing crisis," yet others will develop two or even three. It all depends upon the constitutional make-up of the individual concerned, and cannot be forecasted in any way. The great thing is to *be prepared* for such crises to appear during treatment, and to accept them in their true light. The information given in the various sections of the practical portion of the present book will make it quite easy for any patient to cope successfully with any occurrence of this nature which may arise during treatment.

In the natural treatment of fevers " healing crises " often occur, and it is because these sometimes appear so serious to those tending the patient, giving the appearance that the patient is growing very much worse, that it is always best to have a Naturopath in attendance in all such cases. But even here, without personal naturopathic advice, if those responsible for the carrying out of the treatment will keep their heads, and realise that what is taking place is only a special recuperative effort on the part of the healing forces at work within the body of the patient, and, when past, will mean that a decisive step towards final recovery has taken place, then such crises can be readily weathered in every case. The thing is just to keep calm and carry on with the treatment, and do whatever common sense dictates for the immediate relief of the patient. In most cases nothing at all will be required to be done, except to keep the patient as comfortable as possible. The crisis will pass off as *naturally* as it has come.

It is worth mentioning here that cases are on record where a fever was in process of being fasted, and, a healing crisis having developed, those undertaking the treatment, not having a Naturopath nearby to consult, have grown panicky and sent for a doctor. The result has been that the doctor has at once proceeded to inoculate the patient with some serum or other, and insisted upon the patient being fed in accordance with his own views regarding the treatment of fevers, and this, coming on top of the previous fasting treatment, has resulted in the death of the patient. Of course it was the fasting which was blamed for the death of the patient, not the doctor's treatment at all !

The tragedy is that if, in these cases, those responsible for the administration of the treatment had only kept their heads when the crisis appeared, and carried on as before, the patient would have got over it quite all right, and would soon have been convalescent.

A particular case that can be cited is one of a boy of twelve who developed diphtheria. His parents decided to treat him themselves, without the aid of a doctor, along Natural Cure lines. The boy was fasted for several days and was getting on splendidly, when suddenly he began to bleed profusely at the mouth and nose. The parents grew alarmed at this (although, if they had only known, this was a very good thing indeed, a real " healing crisis "), and sent hurriedly for a doctor. When the doctor arrived he proceeded at once to inject anti-diphtheria serum and told the parents to begin feeding the boy. The result was that within forty-eight hours the boy was dead. The blame, of course, was laid at the door of the fasting ; not on the medical treatment superimposed upon it !

SOME RULES FOR GENERAL LIVING FOR THOSE UNDERTAKING TREATMENT

Many persons undertaking a scheme of home treatment for a particular ailment, as outlined in the present book, will find various difficulties of one kind or another arising. Not everyone's environment is exactly alike, and all that can be done is to give a general scheme of treatment which each individual must adapt as best he can to his own particular circumstances. But there are some general rules of living to which *all* can subscribe, once treatment is begun, and which are outlined below. If adhered to, they will make the process of cure far easier and surer than would otherwise be the case.

(1) The first thing is to enter upon the treatment with the feeling that you are going to do your *utmost* to make a success of it. Remember that *health must be earned*, and in achieving it you will be more than amply rewarded for all the efforts you have made.

(2) Try to be as cheerful as you can all the time. A cheery and optimistic outlook is an inestimable asset to have along with you in your fight to regain health. Remember that the mental factor is of the utmost importance where the production or the eradication of disease is concerned, and the *right mental attitude* is therefore a fundamental necessity if you wish to gain the fullest advantage from the treatment you are now undergoing. Remember that depression, fear, anxiety, and such-like emotions are due to a lowered state of the system and of the nerves especially, and realise that by substituting their opposites—hope, courage, determination, etc.—you are effectually neutralising their effects upon you and paving the way for their ultimate elimination from your mental consciousness.

Instead of thoughts like " I shall never get well," " Everything is going wrong with me," " The whole world seems against me," etc., etc., you must keep in your mind thoughts such as " Now I am *going* to get well," " I *know* I am going to get well because the treatment I am undertaking is *bound* to help me to secure health," " My troubles are due to my *own* folly and ignorance and will be rectified by my *own* efforts now I have been shown the right way," etc.

(3) Remember that *the worry habit* does more to sap vitality and initiative than any other single factor, and remember also that the way to overcome it is by *right thinking* and *right action* along the lines consistently laid down in the present book.

In essence worry is due to a depleted nervous system and lowered nervous tone, and the more you strive to build up your health along the lines here laid down, the more surely will you be paving the way for the eradication of the worry habit. As your health improves and nerve power is increased and the nervous condition built up, so *inevitably* must worry cease to occupy a dominant position in your mental consciousness. *That is a thought worth pondering upon frequently by everyone.*

(4) In all that has here been said, the importance of the mental factor in the curative treatment of disease has been stressed and the use of beneficial mental self-suggestion encouraged. A good thing for all those undergoing treatment is to make a regular habit each night, before falling off to sleep, *of visualising themselves as they would like themselves to be.* " Picture to yourself what you would be like full of radiant health and vitality," and keep that picture in your mind when you fall asleep. Such self-suggestion is in the highest degree beneficial.

Another good thing is to start the day by affirming to yourself your determination to get well in spite of all obstacles, and to repeat several times with emphasis : " *Now to begin again on my new treatment which is doing me so much good and is going to make me really well in time.*"

Daily self-suggestion of this nature can do far more good from the curative point of view than most people would imagine.

(5) Turning from the mental to the physical, the patient must always see to it that he has as much fresh air and outdoor exercise as his environment and physical condition will allow. Never over-exert

yourself in taking exercise, but remember that a good walk, of a few miles each day, is an excellent thing for you, if you are able to undertake it. All forms of exercise are good, providing they are not too strenuous ; but taking everything into consideration, walking is the best exercise, and the cheapest and simplest too.

(6) Always see that your bedroom is well ventilated at night ; it does no good at all to sleep in a stuffy atmosphere. Also wear the minimum of underclothing. The best kind to wear is the cellular mesh-type, such as " Aertex " and " Lahmann." If you must wear extra garments, because of the cold, let them be *external* garments, not garments next the skin.

(7) Keep to the three-meals-a-day plan outlined for you in your treatment, and have no " snacks " of any kind in between. Never eat when you are overtired or overwrought in any way. Food at such times will do you more harm than good. Never come to a meal in a hurry, and try to have a short rest after a meal. Do not rush away immediately after eating to catch a train or to do some strenuous work. Always masticate your food thoroughly, and *enjoy* each mouthful. If, for any reason, you do not feel hungry for a meal, then miss it, and wait for the next. It is never good to force oneself to eat because it is meal-time. Above all, *never overeat*. It is always best to undereat rather than to overeat ; but in general, let your own hunger decide.

(8) Keep faith in yourself and in the treatment you are undertaking. *Remember*, it has set the feet of many thousands of others on to the path to health again, after being cast aside as incurable by the medical profession, and it can do the same for you if you will only carry on with patience, perseverance, and determination.

Read this whole section through several times a week.

APPENDIX B

FIRST-AID SECTION*

Apoplectic stroke—Artificial respiration—Asphyxiation—Bites—Bruises—Bumps—Contusions—Burns and scalds—Choking—Cuts and wounds—Ears, foreign bodies in—Exhaustion—Eye injuries—Fainting (insensibility)—Fits—Fractures — Freezing — Hæmorrhages—Heat exhaustion — Hiccough—Nose bleeding—Nose, foreign bodies in—Poisoning—Seasickness—Shock—Snake bites—Sprains, strains, and dislocations—Sunburns—Sunstroke—Toothache.

A FIRST-AID SECTION has been included in the present book so as to make it as complete and comprehensive as possible. When faced with an accident, an injury, etc., many adherents of Natural-Cure methods do not quite know what to do for the best, and hesitate to adopt orthodox measures, believing that they might be suppressive in some way. This is particularly true of the orthodox treatment for cuts, wounds, etc., the antiseptic drugs used on these occasions really *interfering with* rather than helping the healing process. It is hoped, therefore, that the present section will supply a long-felt want in the homes of the many thousands of followers of Natural-Cure methods of living.

Apoplectic Stroke.—The treatment for apoplexy, or paralytic stroke, has been given in full in Section 4 (page 162) ; here we propose to give the necessary first-aid treatment for dealing with a stroke when it occurs, and so helping the patient as much as possible in the initial stages of the case.

When a stroke occurs, the patient should be laid quite flat, with the head and shoulders slightly raised. Then the fleshy parts of the body and the extremities should be briskly rubbed for a few minutes. Wet packs applied to the body and the extremities will help to draw the blood away from the head, as also will a hot mustard bath applied to the feet. (Wet packs are described in detail in the Appendix, Part A.) A warm-water enema should be given as soon as possible to clear the bowel—this is a most helpful procedure indeed.

If it is necessary to carry the patient some distance, he should not be transported in a vehicle, but carried on a stretcher.

Artificial Respiration.—In many kinds of accidents, such as drowning, strangulation, asphyxiation by poisonous gases, and in serious cases of fainting and stupor, it may be necessary to resort

---

* The author wishes to acknowledge his indebtedness to the late Dr. Henry Lindlahr's book, *The Practice of Natural Therapeutics*, for much of the information contained in the present section.

to artificial respiration in order to restore normal breathing. Here are one or two of the simpler methods of artificial respiration :

(a) Quickly remove the clothing from the upper part of the body, lay the patient prone upon his stomach, and place a small wad made of clothing or any other suitable material at hand under the forehead in order to elevate the nose and mouth sufficiently to allow free breathing.

Kneel athwart the legs of the patient and place the spread hands on both sides of the small of the back ; exert steady but gentle pressure, thus compressing the lower ribs and chest. The pressure is gradually released, allowing the lungs to fill with air. This alternating compression and relaxation is then steadily continued at the same rate as the normal rate of breathing, which is about fifteen breaths to the minute in an adult and a little more in children. With adults, therefore, each complete movement should take up about four seconds, including expiration and inspiration, and about three seconds with children.

(b) The same method may be applied with the patient lying on his back. Make a roll of clothing and place it under the small of the back so that the head lies lower than the chest. Then kneel astride of the hips, place both hands, fingers spread as far as possible, on the lower ribs below the nipples of the breast, and count slowly *one, two, three, four*. While counting one and two, compress the lower chest gently but firmly and relax the pressure while counting three and four. Continue this alternating compression and relaxation until normal breathing commences (providing life is not extinct). A sudden trembling and heaving of the chest and flushing of the face will indicate when natural breathing commences.

While compressing the chest, the operator should at the same time apply strong vibration. This is accomplished by vibrating the hands loosely and vigorously from the wrist joint. The slow, uniform counting corresponds to the tempo of regular normal breathing.

(c) Another, more commonly applied, method of respiration is the following : The patient lies upon his back and a small roll of clothing or other soft material is placed under the small of the back in order to raise the chest and to facilitate expiration. The operator then stoops over the patient, and, grasping the patient's arms just above the wrist, first moves them above and back of the head, and then brings the arms down, in an outward circular movement, to the sides of the body, doubling them at the elbows and pressing the forearms on to the chest.

Inspiration is induced by the arm-raising movement, and expiration by the downward movement. The alternate movements must be continued at the rate of fifteen *complete* movements to the minute for adults and twenty to the minute for children.

The method described under (*a*) is the best to use in cases of drowning as it prevents the falling back of the tongue into the throat and facilitates the escape of water from the mouth. Another way of aiding the release of water from the lungs is to place both hands under the patient's stomach, as he lies upon his face, and, compressing the internal organs, raise him for a few inches at short intervals, partially doubling the body upon itself.

Asphyxiation.—Asphyxiation or suffocation is a condition of un-consciousness and insensibility resulting from suspended respiration. It is caused by a deficiency of oxygen in the system and an excess of carbon dioxide. It may be produced in several ways, viz. by strangulation, smothering, choking, drowning, etc.

The treatment consists, first, in artificial respiration—just previously described—and, secondly, in restoring the circulation of the blood and nerve currents. The latter part of the treatment is carried out by means of cold rubs and massage. For the cold rubbing a cloth can be dipped in plain cold water or else in water in which some common salt or some Epsom salts have been placed ($\frac{1}{4}$ lb. to a large bowlful). The fleshy parts of the body and the extremities should be rubbed vigorously with the cloth and then given a good massaging.

Some cases of asphyxiation may require long and persistent effort to revive them. Cases have been known where a person has been brought round after three or even four hours of continuous effort.

While rescuing a person from a room filled with smoke or poisonous gases, a wet handkerchief or other suitable piece of wet cloth should be tied over the mouth and nostrils. Breathing should be restrained as much as possible, and the windows of the room should be opened at once, or broken if necessary.

Bites.—Bites by snakes, dogs, or cats, or by persons in a maniacal condition, should be sucked out immediately if they can be reached, either by the victim himself or by a friend. The mouth of the one performing the operation must not contain any wounds or abrasions, and the mouth should be thoroughly rinsed with water after each withdrawal of blood, if at all possible. The wound, if necessary, should be widened by an incision and cleansed with dilute lemon juice. Immediately after this, there should be applied a wet bandage or a wet pack.

To prevent any possible infection from a bite, a fast for a day or two (or longer if deemed necessary) should be undertaken, followed by a further period on the *all-fruit diet*, after which normal diet can be begun if the patient feels quite all right. It must be emphasised that FASTING is the surest method of preventing any poisoning from bites or stings of any kind.

In cases of snake-bite it is very unwise to administer whisky or stimulating drugs. These only make the condition worse, not better, in the end. Very few people die as a direct result of snake-bite ; on the other hand, very many have died as a result of the hasty administration of large doses of whisky after a bite. The worst results occur with people who are not usually in the habit of taking alcohol, the large quantity of whisky given tending seriously to complicate the effect upon the system of the snake poison and the shock from the bite, death often ensuing as a result.

Bruises, Bumps, and Contusions.—The best treatment for these are wet packs or clay packs. (See Appendix, Part A, for details of how wet packs are applied. A reference to *Clay Packs* will be found at the end of Section 2, page 140). Raw beefsteak applied to bruises acts in a similar manner to wet packs.

Burns and Scalds.—When the clothing is afire, one should not run about excitedly, as this will only fan the flames to greater intensity. The best thing to do is to throw oneself prone on the ground and extinguish the flames by rolling over and over. Rugs or blankets may be used by the victim of the accident, or by those who are trying to save him, for the purpose of smothering the flames. Rolling on the floor prevents the inhalation of smoke and flames, and also the burning of the face and hair.

While removing the clothing from one who has been badly burned or scalded, do not tear the clothing off where it is stuck to the flesh, but cut around these places.

The best treatment for burns and scalds consists in applying a mixture of ordinary baking soda (bicarbonate of soda) and olive oil. This treatment for burns and scalds is as effective as it is simple. The alkaline sodium neutralises the poisonous acids which form in the sores, and the oil keeps the flesh in a softened condition and prevents caking and cracking.

In cases of very extensive burns or scalds, immersion of the whole body in a bath of water at body temperature or just over (100 degrees Fahr.) is often very beneficial. The patient may have to be kept in the water for days, until such time as the flesh can be exposed to the air without any undue suffering.

Burning of the eyes and face by strong acids, slaked lime, etc., is best treated by the immediate application of olive oil and baking-soda mixture.

Choking.—Infants and young children frequently choke through swallowing small playthings or other foreign objects. Adults may choke through getting fish bones stuck in their throats or through attempting to swallow a large piece of meat, etc.

If the patient is a child, place him face downwards over your lap and slap him vigorously between the shoulders. If this does not remove the obstruction, then compress the nostrils, which forces him to open the mouth and throat widely, and insert the fingers of the other hand very quickly into the mouth and try to grasp the obstructing object. If this is not possible, tickle the palate with a feather or a finger or a handkerchief rolled to a point. This will induce coughing or hawking, which may dislodge the obstruction.

An adult may throw himself over a chair or table with the head hanging downwards, while another slaps him vigorously between the shoulders, or, if necessary, performs the operations mentioned in the previous paragraph.

Cuts and Wounds.—Cuts and wounds should be thoroughly cleansed with warm or cold water, and then treated with dilute lemon juice. It is a very great mistake to pour iodine into a wound or cut. This really makes the process of healing far more difficult than would otherwise be the case, and many cases of septic poisoning of wounds or cuts can be directly traced to this action. Air, light, and water are the best remedies for cuts or wounds.

It is wrong to close cuts with adhesive plaster, because this prevents elimination and shuts off air and light. In large wounds, however,

16*

the edges may be kept together by means of narrow strips of plaster —just sufficient to keep the lips together for healing and to allow drainage. When bleeding has stopped, the cut or wound should be covered with porous gauze, in order to let the light and air in.

If the wound should prove painful or become inflamed, frequent bathing in *cold* running water is the best remedy for this. USE NO ANTISEPTICS OR MEDICAL PREPARATIONS OF ANY KIND.

Ears, Foreign Bodies in.—Insects in the ear may be killed by the injection of alcohol or oil, and then removed by syringing or by means of a wire loop. In cases where peas or small beans have got into the ears of children, do not use water, as this will make them swell. Use a wire loop, or attach a strip of adhesive plaster to the foreign object and pull it out that way.

When trying to remove objects from the ear, pull the outer ear up and back. This straightens the canal and makes the removal of the object in question much easier. The wire loop is the best thing to use as a general rule for the removal of foreign substances from the ear.

Foreign bodies in the nose may be removed in similar manner to those in the ears.

Exhaustion.—See *Heat Exhaustion* (page 474).

Eye Injuries.—For black eye caused by injury, blows, etc., the best treatment is the immediate application of cold water and cold-water bandages.

For burns in the eyes, see treatment for *Burns and Scalds* (page 468).

For the removal of grit or other foreign bodies in the eye, the best thing is to pull the lid of the affected eye outward, and bend it backwards over a toothpick, a match, or other suitable piece of wood. This exposes the inner surface, and the object can then be removed with a piece of cotton material if embedded in the lid, or with a toothpick or sharp instrument if embedded in the cornea. Cold compresses and cold eye-baths are the best way of treating inflammation.

Fainting (Insensibility).—Find out first whether the unconscious one is alive and breathing. Hold a mirror, a piece of glass, bright piece of metal, or a feather before the mouth and nose. If the patient is still breathing, the bright surface of the mirror will be dimmed by the breath or the feather will move.

Another method of determining whether life is extinct is to raise the eyelid and touch the white of the eye. If life is not extinct, the eyelid will twitch.

Observe the odour of the breath. This will indicate such poisons as alcohol, chloroform, ether, etc. If the tongue has been bitten it indicates epilepsy. If the eyes are sensitive to touch and light, there is no brain injury. Unequal contraction of the pupils indicates brain trouble. Pupils contracted to pin-points indicate opium poisoning. Slow, weak breathing indicates collapse or shock. Snoring or stertorous breathing and slow, weak pulse indicates brain trouble (stroke). Rapid pulse points to sunstroke. A hot skin and rapid pulse indicate sunstroke or high fever. Cold skin and weak pulse may be the result of fainting, freezing, or of acute alcoholism.

If the patient is still breathing, place him in a comfortable position, the head somewhat lower than the rest of the body. Open or cut the clothing wherever it constricts the body, and expose the patient to a draught of fresh air. If in the open, fan the air over his face. In order to stimulate heart action, apply alternate hot and cold compresses to the chest ; sprinkle or dash cold water over the face and neck ; also apply hot and cold fomentations to the spine. Give the extremities a good rubbing with the hands. If breathing is very slow and faint, apply artificial respiration, as described earlier in the present section (page 465) ; also dash cold water on the neck and on the soles of the feet.

Other additional measures which are very valuable in many cases are : salt-water rubs, made by wringing out a cloth in salt water and rubbing the fleshy parts of the body and the extremities therewith, and the administration of a warm-water enema. DO NOT TRY TO ADMINISTER WATER OR STIMULANTS WHILST THE PATIENT IS UNCONSCIOUS—THAT WOULD ONLY CHOKE HIM.

When the patient revives give sips of fresh water or water mixed with acid fruit juices. *Do not give whisky, brandy, or other alcoholic stimulants*. The reaction produced after the first stimulating effect of such drinks often proves fatal in serious cases.

Fits.—As opposed to fainting, which may be due to a variety of causes, fits are due to epilepsy in every case. When a fit occurs, nothing must be done to try to check or suppress it ; this would be very injurious. The fit must be allowed to run its course. All that can be done during an attack is as follows : Place the patient in as comfortable a position as possible and elevate the head slightly. If the fit occurs in the house, expose the patient to a draught of fresh air. Pull the lower jaw forward so that the lower row of teeth projects over the upper. This will keep the windpipe open and prevent choking and suffocation. Push a piece of cork or a rolled handkerchief between the teeth in order to prevent biting of the tongue. Do not attempt to open the clenched hands ; that serves no useful purpose at all.

See also full scheme of home treatment for *Epilepsy* in Section 5 (page 184).

Fractures.—In the case of a fracture a doctor should be sent for at once. In the meantime excessive bleeding may be stopped as described under *Hæmorrhages* below.

Freezing.—Frozen limbs, ears, nose, or other fleshy parts of the body should be rubbed vigorously with ice-water or snow. Great care, however, must be taken not to break the frozen parts ; they are brittle, and may break easily.

If a person has become unconscious through freezing, he must be taken into a cold room and treated with cold rubs by means of either ice-water or snow until the circulation in the various parts is restored. As before stated, great care must be taken not to break the frozen parts.

If breathing and heart action are very low or imperceptible, artificial respiration should be resorted to, but with due precaution. When normal breathing commences, place the patient in a cold bed and heat the room very gradually. When the body becomes warm, rub with warm flannels, but the frozen parts must still be treated with cold applications and snow rubs.

Warm the body from within by giving hot lemon water sweetened with honey or brown sugar. Black coffee with lemon juice will stimulate heart action and circulation. DO NOT GIVE ALCOHOL IN ANY FORM. The benumbing after-effects of strong stimulants such as these will induce numbness and sleep when wakefulness is necessary to resist the freezing.

Hæmorrhages.—(*a*) *Hæmorrhages from the mouth.* — When the blood is of a dark colour and looks as if it were mixed with coffee-grounds or food materials, it comes from the stomach and the hæmorrhage is caused by cancer. If the blood is mixed with food materials but is of a bright red colour, the hæmorrhage is caused by an ulcer in the stomach.

For first-aid treatment the patient should be placed in a recumbent position and given small quantities of cold water and lemon juice to sip at frequent intervals. A trunk or body pack will draw the blood away from the stomach and relieve congestion. (For details of how a pack is made, see Appendix A.)

(b) *Hæmorrhage from the Lungs.*—When the blood is bright red and foamy and free from food materials, it comes from the lungs and is caused through breakdown of the lung tissue. It is not necessarily fatal. Under the natural treatment of lung diseases, hæmorrhages frequently occur during the crisis periods, and are then a form of elimination. In many such cases recovery from tuberculosis has been preceded by copious hæmorrhages. It is best to rest in bed after a hæmorrhage (in order to give the disrupted tissue a chance to heal), and to fast.

(c) *Hæmorrhages from Cuts and Wounds.*—If the blood is bright red and comes in spurts, it is an indication that some important artery has been severed, and a ligature should be applied without delay *above* the wound. (In the head, neck, etc., it should be *below* the wound.) If on the trunk of the body, pressure should be made just above or below the wound, between it and the heart. Any solid object, a piece of wood, rock, or anything convenient, held in position firmly by a bandage or belt will serve the purpose.

If the blood is dark in colour and flows smoothly, then some vein has been opened, and the ligature should be applied just *below* the wound (except in the head and neck, when it should be *above* the wound). Any strap, rope, or handkerchief may be used for this purpose ; and the ligature may be applied more tightly by inserting a stick, pipe, or similar object below the knot and twisting it.

Do not try to remove any clots of blood ; they are Nature's provision for stopping the hæmorrhage. Hæmorrhages from large arteries may be stopped temporarily by compressing the blood-vessel with the fingers. Cold water is very effective for stopping hæmorrhages. If possible, it should be allowed to run over the area around the wound in a constant stream. This inhibits the circulation and favours the clotting of blood. Care must be taken *not to run the water directly on the wound itself, however*, as this might prevent the forming of clots. In order to accomplish this, it is as well to place some protecting object directly over the wound, and allow the water to play freely over and around this. Water mixed with lemon juice applied directly to the wound acts as a natural antiseptic and astringent, thus favouring clotting. Clay or mud packs must *never* be applied to open cuts or wounds. (See also treatment for *Cuts and Wounds*, page 469).

Heat Exhaustion.—Heat exhaustion is usually the result of injudicious diet in summer, excessive clothing, and of working in close, hot, badly ventilated rooms. The principal symptoms are faintness or syncope, a cold and damp skin, and a rapid and feeble pulse. When death results, it is due to heart failure ; but most cases recover. It is not fatal as often as sunstroke.

As regards first-aid treatment, the patient should be removed to a cool place and given a brisk rubbing with a cloth wrung out in cold water. If heart action is feeble, a hot lemon drink will stimulate this. The head should be frequently laved with cold water. Cold packs to the body will be very beneficial in many cases. (See Appendix A, for details of how wet packs are applied.*) If the body temperature is subnormal and death seems imminent, the legs should be wrapped in woollen blankets saturated with hot water. (Care must be taken not to scald the flesh.) Around the wet blanket wrap several layers of dry sheeting or a dry blanket in order to retain the heat. The patient should take at intervals small quantities of hot lemon and water.

Hiccough.—This is a spasm of the diaphragm, caused by nervous irritation of some kind. It may be due to digestive disturbances or to irritation caused by systemic or drug poisons. In chronic form we find it usually associated with mercurial, phosphorus, strychnine, and other drug poisoning.

Ordinary hiccough requires little or no special attention. If it persists, one of the best remedies is to sip water until one or two of the spasms have been missed. Anything that will break the regularity of the spasm will stop it. Out of this fact grew the old-

---

* If reaction to the packs is poor, hot-water bottles can be placed around the body, in addition.

fashioned notion of " frightening the hiccough " by sudden motion or exclamation.

In its most serious forms, that due to drug poisoning, hiccough needs full naturopathic treatment for its overcoming. Manipulative treatment is very beneficial in these cases, but a full scheme of natural treatment is required.

Nose Bleeding.—The best thing to do in these cases is to lie down and sniff cold water mixed with lemon juice. The lemon juice has an astringent effect and thus helps materially in stopping the bleeding. Avoid vigorous blowing of the nose. If the bleeding continues, cold compresses applied to the neck, at the base of the brain, will be beneficial. Do not attempt to catch the blood yourself, if the bleeding is copious ; just lie quite still and let someone else catch the blood in a basin or cloth. This is the best way to facilitate clotting of the blood. See also *Nose Bleeding*, Section 4 (page 170).

Nose, Foreign Bodies in.—See *Ears, Foreign Bodies in* (page 470).

Poisoning.—The first thing to do in all cases of poisoning is to empty the stomach. This may be accomplished by swallowing large quantities of warm water (containing the appropriate antidote, if such be known), and by tickling the palate with a finger or a feather, thus causing copious vomiting. The washing of the stomach must be repeated several times. If mouth and throat are not burned, a rubber tube may be pushed down the throat into the stomach, and, by means of a funnel, warm water may be poured down the tube until it overflows. The end of the tube outside is then suddenly lowered below the level of the stomach and water siphoned out of it. This process may be facilitated by the patient lying prone on his face during the draining of the stomach.

In emergency cases, mustard, common salt, or powdered alum may be given as emetics in the proportion of one teaspoonful of either to a glass of water. A lukewarm solution of soap in water is a simple and efficacious emetic. If no emetics are available, cold water should be taken copiously, and vomiting induced by tickling the throat.

After washing out the stomach (as described in the first paragraph), white of egg, milk, or sugared water should be given freely. They are soothing to the inflamed membranes and give the stomach something to work on. The bowels should be washed out repeatedly with warm-water enemas, in order to eliminate the poison from the intestines. (A little common salt may be added to the enema water if desired.) When the patient is strong enough, hot baths and wet packs will stimulate elimination of the poison through the skin. (See Appendix A for details of how packs are applied.)

In corrosive sublimate or other forms of mercurial poisonings, retained rectal enemas of milk or white of egg beaten up in warm water will help to neutralise the destructive action of the metallic poison.

In all cases, fasting, with dilute fruit juices, should be enforced until the system has eliminated the poison and the injured membranes of the internal tracts have been repaired. Where the latter have been severely burned, fruit juices may cause burning pain unless they are very much diluted with water. In the mild dilute form they will antidote the destructive effects of the poisons.

So-called antidotes are effective only when administered immediately. The general rule is : against acid poisons administer water mixed with baking soda or fresh lime ; against alkaline poisons use dilute vinegar. Milk and white of egg can be used in either case, as they dilute the poison and give it something to work on besides the tissues of the body.

Narcotic poisons like opium, morphine, belladonna, digitalis, poisonous mushrooms, ptomaines, alcohol, strychnine, etc., cause loss of consciousness, stertorous breathing, redness of the face, cramps, and delirium. If the victim of poisoning is unconscious, artificial respiration must be resorted to, and the neck, chest, and other parts of the body sprinkled with cold water. (See earlier part of the present section for details as to how *artificial respiration* is carried out, page 465.) A brisk, cold, salt-water rub is very efficacious in reviving the vital activities. As a stimulant, small doses of black coffee can be given

Arsenic, phosphorus, Paris green, vitriol, carbolic acid, hydrochloric acid, and lye do not as a rule cause unconsciousness, but give rise to violent pains in the œsophagus, stomach, and abdomen, followed by choking and vomiting. Some of these poisons burn the lips, mouth, œsophagus, and stomach ; such burns may be treated with a solution of baking soda or powdered chalk. The treatment otherwise is the same as given for alkaline and acid poisoning. IN ALL CASES OF SERIOUS POISONING A DOCTOR SHOULD BE CALLED IN AS SOON AS POSSIBLE.

Ptomaine poisoning results from eating putrefying or decayed meats, fish, cheese, ice-cream, or other animal food products. The usual symptoms are collapse, subnormal temperature, and pain in the digestive tract. Nature generally tries to remedy the trouble by vomiting and diarrhœa, and both these forms of natural elimination should be encouraged by the swallowing of large quantities of warm water, and by the administration of warm-water enemas.

The treatment for ptomaine poisoning is very much the same as for other forms of poisoning, and after the stomach and intestines have been cleansed as thoroughly as possible by the measures described in the previous paragraph, the patient should drink copious quantities of fresh water mixed with acid fruit juices. This is much better than the taking of poisonous antiseptics.

While temperature is subnormal, trunk or full body packs will be beneficial ; these may be supplemented by hot-water bottles placed over the packs if reaction is poor. (See Appendix A, for details of wet packs.) If the subnormal condition is followed by inflammation and fever, the treatment should be as for fevers as given in Section 13 (page 408). In any case the patient must fast, on water and fruit juices, until the digestive system is quite normal again. (See also *Ptomaine Poisoning*, Section 9, page 300.)

External poisoning, by means of plants such as the poison ivy, etc., should never be treated by suppressive drugs, but should be treated by the usual natural methods for inducing elimination through the skin and other organs of depuration. If possible, the sufferer should be thoroughly washed or scrubbed all over as soon as the presence of the poison on the skin has been detected. This will greatly lessen its harmful effects. If soap and water are not procurable for this, water only, or even sand or tufts of grass can be used for the purpose.

This thorough cleansing of the body should be followed by the administration of full body packs, repeated at frequent intervals, and by frequent cold ablutions. The packs and cold ablutions are the best means of allaying the intolerable itching and burning. (For details as to how packs are applied, see Appendix A.) General systemic treatment (as for a fever) should also be instituted, by means of fasting, the use of the enema, etc., as detailed in Section 13 (page 408). Fasting, and a raw food diet to follow, are especially beneficial in these cases.

Here are some antidotes for acute poisoning :

By *lead* : magnesia, soda, or chalk water.

By *phosphorous* : thick liquid gum, white of egg, flour, bread, magnesia and cold water, for the purpose of enveloping and isolating the poisoning. Do not give milk or liquids containing alcohol or oily matter.

By *caustic acids, such as sulphuric, muriatic, carbolic, or nitric acid* : large quantities of soap, chalk, salt, lime water, or milk.

By *copper and verdigris* (frequently contracted through foods or drinks prepared in copper vessels or by drinks from soda-water fountains when the copper has become exposed through the wearing away of the zinc lining) : dilute white of egg, milk, water mixed with honey or sugar.

By *iodine* : starch or flour paste.

By *nitrate of silver* : strong salt-water solution, white of egg.

By *oxalic acid* : chalk or lime water.

By *strychnine* : meat burned to a cinder, decoction of acorn coffee, tan or gall-apple.

By *arsenic* : warm milk, sweetened water.

Seasickness.—Although so unpleasant to endure, seasickness can never be really harmful in its effects. Indeed, many people are far better in health after a bout of seasickness, owing to the thorough cleansing their digestive system will have received as a result thereof. The main cause of the trouble is an interference with the centre of equilibrium, which is situated in close proximity to the left ear, this in turn affecting the entire nervous organism, and especially the nerves supplying the digestive system, thus causing intense nausea and vomiting.

As regards a cure for seasickness, it may be said right away that *there is none* ; but the following directions have in many cases either prevented or greatly alleviated its symptoms :

Before embarking on a sea voyage it is best to have a fast for a day or two, using the enema to cleanse the bowels, and to live as closely as possible to a raw food diet when on board. This may be rather difficult in some cases, but the more the diet approximates to a fruit and salad diet, the better will it be. The heavy, rich, greasy foods served with such over-abundance on board ships undoubtedly have much to do with the bringing on of the gastric disturbance. Much of the invigorating effects of a sea voyage are lost by the crass over-eating which takes place on such occasions, so that the adoption of a more or less simple raw food diet will add much to the health-giving effects of the trip in every way, besides doing a great deal to obviate the possibility of seasickness.

Apart from dietetic measures, another most important point *is to relax oneself as much as possible when on board.* Many people involuntarily tense themselves against the rolling of the ship, and in this way bring on seasickness. If these people would make up their minds to RELAX as completely as possible, and let their bodies go with the movement of the ship, it is surprising what a difference that will make as regards liability to seasickness. (The same thing applies to train-sickness. If the sufferer will only *let himself go* with the vibration and movement of the train instead of tensing himself against it, he will find train-sickness soon becoming a thing of the past, in the great majority of cases.)

Shock.—Shock is characterised by collapse and frequently by loss of consciousness. It may result from excessive loss of blood or physical injury, or by emotional factors such as sudden fright, grief, anxiety, or anger. In many cases of death due to injury it is the shock occasioned at the time which is the real cause of the death rather than the injury itself.

Treatment for shock should be the same as for *Fainting* given earlier in the present section (page 470). If there is hæmorrhage, this should be treated in accordance with the instructions given under that heading. Where the trouble is due to emotional factors, cool behaviour and reassuring suggestions are necessary to dispel fear, allay anxiety, etc.

Snake Bites.—See *Bites* (page 467).

Sprains, Strains, and Dislocations.—Sprains and dislocations of joints must be attended to as quickly as possible by a doctor. (An Osteopath or Chiropractor would be better if such services are readily procurable.) Until medical treatment is forthcoming, cold compresses and cold packs will relieve and reduce inflammation. (See Appendix A, for details of packs and their application.)

If swelling or pain makes it impossible to remove parts of the clothing or shoes and stockings, these should be cut away with a sharp knife. It is not advisable to apply hot applications of any kind. Rest of the injured member is essential after the adjustment has been made.

Sunburns.—Many people, who have no idea of how to sunbathe, expose their bodies for too long a time to the sun's rays, and as a consequence get their skin burned, sometimes rather badly. The best treatment for such a condition is the application of a mixture of baking soda and olive oil. Cold compresses will also help in these cases in relieving pain.

Sunstroke.—Sunstroke is caused through exposure to the direct rays of the sun in a heated atmosphere. Loss of consciousness is caused through the sun's rays acting directly upon the brain and the cardiac and respiratory centres in the medulla.

The characteristic features of sunstroke are suddenness of onset, loss of consciousness, pallor, feeble pulse, and rapid failure of the heart and respiration. The condition may be a very serious one, and often terminates fatally, especially if treated along orthodox lines. Those addicted to the free use of alcohol are most likely to fall victims to sunstroke.

The patient should be quickly undressed and cold water poured all over his body, also over the head. This should be followed be brisk salt-water rubs. A cloth is wrung out in cold water in which common salt or Epsom salts has been placed ($\frac{1}{4}$ lb. to a bowlful), and the body briskly rubbed all over with it. In place of salt-water rubs the patient may be wrapped in a wet sheet, which must be kept wet by pouring cold water over it from time to time.

If collapse has taken place and vitality is very low, the patient must be put to bed and well covered with blankets, so as to produce a warm reaction.

Toothache.—Toothache is surely one of the most excruciating tortures ever suffered by man. There are two general types of toothache : the acute inflammatory, accompanied by heat and swelling ; and the cold neuritic or neuralgic. As regards alleviative treatment for these two types of toothache, this should be as follows.

The acute inflammatory toothache is best treated by retaining cold or cool water in the mouth until it warms up, when it should be spit out and replaced. At the same time cooling compresses or packs should be applied to the cheek on the affected side. (See

Appendix A, for details of how packs are made and applied.)   Gentle massage of the lower head and neck will bring relief in some cases, and manipulative treatment is very beneficial too.

In the neuritic type of toothache there is no heat or swelling, but intense pain, and hot applications sometimes give more relief here than cold.   A remedy worth trying if the former treatment fails to give relief, is partly to fill a muslin bag with hot salt—as hot as it can be borne—and apply to the affected cheek, holding the bag in place with a bandage.

If toothache persists, a dentist should be seen as soon as possible. Never use pain-killers to deaden the pain of toothache or drugs of any kind.   A general all-round scheme of health-building treatment, along Natural-Cure lines, is most beneficial in cases where toothache is of frequent occurrence, as it is a toxic condition of the system which is at the root of the trouble in such conditions, and systemic cleansing treatment is the surest method of getting rid of the trouble in a permanent way.   In all cases where toothache is present, the patient should be fasted while the symptoms are severe.

INDEX

INDEX

INDEX

INDEX